RAMBLES IN VEDĀNTA

RAMBLES IN VEDĀNTA

B.R. Rajam Iyer

MOTILAL BANARSIDASS PUBLISHERS
PRIVATE LIMITED • DELHI

Fourth Reprint: Delhi, **2015**
First Edition: Kolkata, *1946*

ISBN: 978-81-208-0912-3 (Cloth)
ISBN: 978-81-208-0913-0 (Paper)

MOTILAL BANARSIDASS

41 U.A., Bungalow Road, Jawahar Nagar, Delhi 110 007
8 Mahalaxmi Chamber, 22 Bhulabhai Desai Road, Mumbai 400 026
203 Royapettah High Road, Mylapore, Chennai 600 004
236, 9th Main III Block, Jayanagar, Bangalore 560 011
8 Camac Street, Kolkata 700 017
Ashok Rajpath, Patna 800 004
Chowk, Varanasi 221 001

Printed in India

by RP Jain at NAB Printing Unit,
A-44, Naraina Industrial Area, Phase I, New Delhi–110028
and published by JP Jain for Motilal Banarsidass Publishers (P) Ltd,
41 U.A. Bungalow Road, Jawahar Nagar, Delhi-110007

ब्रह्मविदाप्नोति परम्

He who knows the supreme attains the Highest

Tait. Upa., II, i, I.

DEDICATED TO

ALL SEEKERS AFTER TRUTH

AS A GUIDE IN THE FIRST STEP TOWARDS
THE PRACTICAL REALISATION OF THE VEDANTIC IDEAL
AND IN LOVING MEMORY OF THE GIFTED EDITOR
OF THE 'PRABUDDHA BHARATA' (1896-98)

FOREWORD

When I was asked to write a Foreword to the late lamented Sreeman B. R. Rajam Iyer's "RAMBLES IN VEDĀNTA", my first reaction was to decline the offer with a polite plea that I may be excused from this great task; for, it occurred to me that a Foreword to the book which was verily a commentary on Vedanta was akin to a commentary on the Viswaroopa of the Lord Himself.

Even a cursory glance at the contents and the range, richness and variety of the subjects included should make one feel that Rajam Iyer has delved deep into the fountain of Vedanta and spent years in understanding their intricacies, and mastering their mysteries. This range and richness is not merely confined to the subject matter; it equally holds true of the richness of linguistic and literary flourish. If there are closely reasoned out essays on subjects of great controversy, there are pleasant tales that drive home the Vedantic truth in the manner in which the great sage Veda Vyasa did through his Mahabharata and the Puranas.

Then there is the Imitation of Vyasa; one is reminded of Thomas A. Kempis's Imitation of Christ. With such wealth both in respect of content and form, the book would stand on its own without a Foreword and as the Publishers in their first edition have said: "Good wine needs no bush". Certainly Rajam Iyer's RAMBLES IN VEDANTA needs no Foreword.

It is indeed a sturdy, untiring soul that has rambled through the inexhaustible fields of Vedanta. While rambling through these fields, Rajam Iyer's eyes have been peering carefully through these and have sought out the essence from the externals. Every one of Vedanta's doctrines—the theory of Karma, renunciation, asceticism and a host of others have through the ages suffered from distortions at the hands of those advocates who, though well-intentioned, have somehow missed the total perspective and made a *religion* of the *parts* that fascinated them most. These have also suffered from misrepresentations by ill-informed foreigners who having no access to the originals had to rely on unauthorised English translations of them attempted by half-baked scholars. But in the learned volume before us, such distortions have been corrected, and again and again, we find the author placing every doctrine, view and way of life in its proper setting and perspective, thus absolving these of charges that are only too common, charges such as the pessimistic tone of Indian philosophy, its negative and ascetic ideals as they are made out even by Albert Schewetzer, a sound scholar, known for his catholicity.

The head and the heart are equally developed and Vedanta makes man not only a fit recipient of *Moksha* or final absorption in the Infinite, but also a wise man in this world able to transact its business unperturbed and unaffected like the lotus leaf on which dew drops settle and fall off. It enables man to free himself from that whirligig of *Karma* that shunts him from one birth to another even when he is engaged in *karma*; for, it reveals to him the cardinal secret of participation in *Karma* while avoiding its effects. In short, it takes man on to the state of the Jivanmukta who takes everything in the stride, sorrow and joy, heat and cold, life and death.

Rajam Iyer lived for just 26 years (1872-1898). In such a short span of life, he became a profound scholar in English literature and at the same time mastered the Vedantic lore. He was thus a harmonious blend of the East and the West—an integrated personality.

In 1896, at the young age of 24, Rajam Iyer, inspired by the "cyclonic monk" Swami Vivekananda, started the renowned journal *Prabuddha Bharata* (Awakened India) devoted to religion and philosophy and was its editor till his death in 1898.

One who reads through these rambles in Vedanta will not fail to see vividly the personality of Rajam Iyer, the mellowed one, a Jivanmukta who, having freed himself, felt in all compassion, that he should share with others that knowledge and Vedantic technology by which such a blessed state could be achieved here and now.

For the past over three decades and more, I have known many devout souls devouring Rajam Iyer's book *Rambles in Vedanta* and earnestly recommending its reading to their friends. This is a great tribute to a man who was not "rich" in money or high up in social life, but was certainly "rich" in ethical and spiritual values and high in the world of the "voluntary poor". As Longfellow has said, such great men leave behind their foot-prints on the sands of time, and Rajam Iyer has certainly done so and generations to come will profit by his writing.

Appropriately the book ends with a chapter on Satsanga and the need for aid in man's sojourn through life. I leave the reader here that he may have the Satsang of the author and the aid that he offers him in every page and line of the book.

S. Ramakrishnan
Editor, "Bhavan's Journal", and
Joint Director and Executive Secretary,
Bharatiya Vidya Bhavan.

Bombay,
August 6, 1973.

PREFACE

EVERYONE who takes up this volume will naturally ask at the very outset—"Who was this Rajam Aiyar whose rambles in the region of the Vedanta are herein reproduced?"—and he has not to wait long for an answer. Rajam Aiyar was no administrator who sunk his soul in state-craft, no lawyer who loved and lived for money, no pedant whose glory was to preach, no fame-hunting patriot, no title-thirsting millionaire, no reformer of the world, no *Bairagi* with a beard, no *Swami* who offered salvation to souls—no, he was none of these. He was a simple sincere seeker after Truth, a humble individual who first saw the light of the world in 1872, in a remote corner of Madura—*Bhaktula Gunta* (now "Batlagundai"), once the site of a holy lake near which *Bhaktas* gathered and sang the praises of the Almighty; a diligent student who, after passing through a brilliant course of English education and graduating in 1889, turned to poetry and philosophy and yearned to realise the Truth of Existence : a restless soul that thirsted for the knowledge of the Infinite and found the highest peace and bliss in devotion and meditation, in the study of the Upanishads and the Gita, in rambles and recreations in the Vedanta, which he recorded from time to time in the *Prabuddha Bharata*, and in that sweet communion with the Atman, latterly vouchsafed to him, which made him truly realise that this life is but a preparation for a higher one and enabled him, at the early age of twenty-six, to face

Death without fear or frown, and to pass away from his mortal coil, calmly and cheerfully.

The variety of the *Pabulum* presented in this volume will be found pleasant and delicious both by the young and the advanced. While every morsel it contains is nutritious and easy of assimilation, not a few delicacies will be discovered which are exquisitely spiced and flavoured with stories and illustrations from the Puranas. The aim which runs through all—from the short fancy of Suka's advent to the long life-tale of Vasudeva— is the realisation of the Self, the knowledge of the Atman, the elaboration and impression of the sublime Truth taught by all religions, by the Vedas and the Puranas, by the hoary sages of antiquity, by the Lord Sri Krishna, and reiterated by the Lord Jesus Christ in those hallowed words which will live for ever—"What shall it profit a man, if he shall gain the whole world and lose his own soul?"

Who can read through the history of "Nanda, the Pariah saint," without feeling elevated and ennobled in thought and spirit? Who can listen to the discourse on "Bhakti", yet forget the prayer which Prahlada, the ideal Bhakta, addressed to the Lord—"The only blessing I crave from Thee is not to forget Thee, even if I be born a worm or a reptile?" Who that contemplates the "Glory of Suicide" can fail to despise this Bastille of the senses and long for the emancipation without rope or knife, fire or poison—the effacement of the lower self, which alone can lead unto *Kaivalya*, the silent happy union with the Infinite? And who that peruses the notes on "Nataraja" and "Seshasayana" can continue to scoff at symbols or miss to realise that they are but aids to imagination and embody grand and lofty laws of the Life Eternal, which are sealed book to the Christian Missionary whose bigotry does not permit him to look beneath the surface behind the form, and alas, to many a modern Hindu—the hybrid product of the East and the West—whose God is his brain and whose universe ends with his senses?

"The world knows nothing of its greatest men," said a poet. Too truly, it often knows only of those who trumpet their own fame, whose memorials are raised, whose monuments are erected, whose names are carved on stone and marble, whose biographies are manufactured! but ah, what memorial, what monument, what biography is needed to proclaim the greatness of this inspired lad of six-and-twenty summers, whose musings and meditations are no mean bequest to posterity?

MADRAS
August, 1905.

————————

CONTENTS

INTRODUCTION

PROSPECTUS

In the wonderful disposition of Providence, it has been designed that Truths revealed, perhaps for the first time to the sages of our country and treasured up by them in a monumental form, should cross oceans and mountains and spread among nations utterly foreign to us both in their past and their present lives. The Kantian revolution in Western philosophy, the outpourings of the Upanishad-intoxicated Schopenhaur, the abstruse metaphysics of the Post-Kantians, the revival of Sanskrit study, the theosophic movement, the conversion and activity of Mrs. Besant, the remarkable lectures of Max Muller, the Great Parliament of Religions and the timely appearance of Swami Vivekananda, have all been unswervingly tending to the dissemination of those great Truths ; Kripananda, Abhayananda, Yogananda and a whole host of converts to Vedantism are springing up everywhere. Science itself has become a willing tool in the hands of our ancient philosophy. The word 'Vedanta' is nearly as familiar on the shores of Lake Michigan as on the banks of the Ganges.

In the midst of such revivalistic stirring noise and fervour abroad, it is painful to notice that materialism—such is the result of the one-sided Western education given in our schools and colleges—should in one form or another still have a considerable sway in our own country. With a view to remedy this sad state of affairs, as far as it may be in our humble means, it has been arranged to start a journal devoted to our religion and philosophy called the *Prabuddha Bharata* (Awakened India). It will be a sort of supplement to the *Brahmavadin* and seek to do for students, young men and others, what *Brahmavadin* is already doing so successfully for the more advanced classes. It will with that view endeavour to present the sacred Truths of Hindu religion and the sublime and beautiful ideal of the Vedanta in as *simple, homely, and interesting* a manner as possible, and amongst others, will contain Puranic and classical episodes illustrative of those great truths and high ideals, philosophical tales, novels of modern type, short articles on philosophical subjects, written in a *simple popular style free from technicalities* and the lives and teachings of great sages and Bhaktas irrespective of caste, creed or nationality, who are and ever will be the beacon lights of humanity.

OURSELVES

THE ready response with which our prospectus has been favoured on all sides, the eagerness with which our movement has been welcomed, and the support that has been generously promised to us in several quarters, all show that the time is ripe for similar undertakings, that there is a real demand in the country for spiritual nourishment—for the refreshment of the soul. But a few years ago, the *Prabuddha Bharata* or the *Brahmavadin* would have been utterly impossible. The promise of many a Western "ism" had to be tried, and the problem of life had itself been forgotten for a while in the noise and novelty of the steam-engine and the electric tram ; but, unfortunately, steam-engines and electric trams do not clear up the mystery ; they only thicken it. This was found out, and a cry, like that of the hungry lion, arose for religion and things of the soul. Science eagerly offered its latest discoveries but all its evolution theories and heredity doctrines did not go deep enough. Agnosticism offered its philosophy of indifference but no amount of that kind of opium-eating could cure the fever of the heart. The Christian missionary offered his creed but as a creed it would not suit ; India had grown too big for that coat.

Just then it was found, and here is the wonder of Providential disposition, that the eyes of the Western world were themselves turned towards India, turned, not as of old for the gold and silver she could give, but for the more lasting treasures contained in her ancient

sacred literature. Christian missionaries, in their eagerness to vilify the Hindu, had opened an ancient magic
chest, the very smell of whose contents caused them to
faint. Oriental scholars, the Livingstones of Eastern
literature, had unwittingly invoked a deity, which it
was not in their power to appease. As philologists are
succeeded by philosophers, Colebrookes and Caldwells
give birth to Schopenhaurs and Deussens. The white
man and his fair lady stray into the Indian woods and
there come across the Hindu sage under the banyan tree.
The hoary tree, the cool shade, the refreshing stream,
and above all, the hoarier, cooler and the more refreshing
philosophy that falls from his lips enchant them. The
discovery is published ; pilgrims multiply. A Sanyasin
from our midst carries the altar fire across the seas.
The spirit of the Upanishads makes a progress in distant
lands. The procession develops into a festival. Its
noise reaches Indian shores and behold ! Our motherland
is awakening.

We all remember the story of Sleeping Beauty—
how she was shut up by enchantment in a castle where
she slept a hundred years, how during that time an
impenetrable wood sprang up around her, and how at
last she was disenchanted by a fair young prince and
married him. India may be likened to that Sleeping
Beauty : she has slept very long indeed and thick
forests of confusing creeds—social, political and religious—have grown up around her. The enchantment
that sent her to sleep was Providence itself, the most
mysterious of all kinds of magic. When she began to
sleep, the fair young prince (the modern civilised world)
now wooing her was not on the scene. At present,

however, the lover's suit is progressing, the thick forests are clearing away, and the marriage of the East and the West, which promises to come off in no distant date, will be one of the grandest, the most romantic and the most fruitful marriages known to history.

The awakening we speak of, of which there is an abundance of symptoms on every side will, however, not be like that of an eagle which rises from sleep with renewed vigour and strength to roam and to fight, but that of a nightingale melting the hearers' hearts with its soft sweet melodies. Already the message of our Motherland has gone to nations burning with social and political fever, and soothed them. *To serve in the spreading of that message, and help in clearing away the haze that naturally prevails in our newly awakened country, after so long a sleep will be the ambition of the journal* we have been enabled to bring into life today. The task we have set to ourselves is lighter than it would otherwise be, as there are journals like the *Brahmavadin* already working in the field with wonderful results. Ours is only a humble attempt in the direction of these journals and *simplicity and fervour will be our chief aim.* We have a great faith in the system of teaching principles by means of stories and indeed, as Swami Vivekananda wrote in his letter to us : "There is a great, great chance, much more than you dream of, for those wonderful stories scattered all over the Sanskrit literature to be rewritten and made popular." For these stories are not like the unhealthy, sensational, fifth-rate French novels of the day, the cobwebs spun by idle brains, but the natural flowers of great minds that could, from a Himalayan-like philosophic attitude, take a sweeping

and sympathetic survey of the human race. That is
why they bear the stamp of immortality on them.
Centuries rolled away before the Ramayana and Mahabharata appeared, and centuries have yet to roll on
before another of their kind can be made. They are not
older than the mountains, but they will live longer than
the mountains, and have more influence. One special
feature of these stories is that *they have a different
meaning for every stage of human growth*, and the ordinary
man as well as the philosopher enjoys them, though
each understands them in his own way. The reason for
that is, that these stories were composed by men, far
advanced in the ladder of human progress, some of whom
indeed, were on the top-most rung. *Extracts and adap-
tations from these great books will be a chief feature of our
journal.*

It is not, however, intended to fill the whole journal
with stories only. Every issue will contain a number of
articles on serious subjects ; but care will be taken to make
them simple and interesting, and the technicalities of
metaphysics will be scrupulously avoided. We shall
endeavour to act up, as far as we can, to the advice which
Swami Vivekananda has kindly given us with regard
to the conduct of the journal :—"Avoid all attempts
to make the journal scholarly : it will slowly make its
way all over the world, I am sure. Use the simplest
language possible and you will succeed. The main feature should be the teaching of *Principles* through stories.
Do not make it metaphysical at all . . . Go on
bravely. Do not expect success in a day or a year.
Always hold on to the highest. Be steady . . .
Be obedient and eternally faithful to the cause of Truth,

humanity and your country and you will move the world. Remember it is the person—the life, which is the secret of power, nothing else . . ."—and he has generously undertaken to contribute to the journal as often as he can.

Though an organ of Hindu religion, the 'Prabuddha Bharata' will have no quarrel with any other religion : for, really speaking, all religions are simply different phases of the same Truth, different methods of approaching God. "I am in all religions as the string in a pearl garland," says the Lord. What humanity is to man, what existence is to living beings, that, Vedantism is to religions : it is their common essence, their inner unity, and as such, it can possibly have no quarrel with any of them—the whole has no quarrel with the part. On the other hand, it approves of the existing differences, and even welcomes their multiplication, so that no man might be left godless for want of a religion suited to his nature.

This Vedantic ideal of religious unity, or rather, of religious variety implies, not merely the spiritual growth of the individual from stage to stage, but also the growth of society by the due co-ordination of creeds. The Prabuddha Bharata will deal with both the aspects of the ideal. The individuals make up the society, and the advancement of the former necessarily results in that of the latter. At the same time, society acts upon the individual, and conditions him. As the two are thus found to act and re-act on each other, it is necessary that, side by side with the ideal of individual perfection, that of social perfection should also be presented. The ideal society, according to the Vedanta, is not a millen-

nium on earth, nor a reign of angels, where there will be nothing but thorough equality of men, and peace, and joy—the Vedanta indulges in no such chimeras—but one, where religious toleration, neighbourly charity, and kindness even to animals form the leading features, where the fleeting concerns of life are subordinated to the eternal, *where man strives not to externalise, but to internalise himself more and more,* and the whole social organism moves, as it were, with a sure instinct towards God. This ideal will be steadily presented in these pages, but no attempt will be made to restore old institutions which have had their day, any more than to restore to life a dead tree. *Our object will be to present the ideal,* which, fortunately, never gets too old, *leaving everyone to seek his own path of realisation.* The policy of breaking away from society and that of allowing it to grow of itself have, both of them, their uses and are equally welcome. But it is our firm conviction, that any real social advancement towards the ideal can only be effected by the example and teachings of men, who are intimately acquainted with the foundations of our society, or for that matter, any society whatsoever, who, by means of their own perfection, can understand the successive stages of human evolution as fully and as naturally as the old man understands the child, the boy and the adult, who know that, whether we will or no, the progress of the society as well as of the individual is always Godward, and know also that the means has always to be consistently subordinated to the end. Society is no toy and its architects *cannot* be ordinary men. The truest social reform has, at all times, come only from men, who strove to *be* good, rather than to *do* good, men from whose personal goodness sprang social advancement, as naturally, as noiselessly and as beautifully as the smell from the full-blown rose.

Having thus far stated, at some length, the objects and methods of the present journal, we leave it to our readers to judge for themselves how far they are right and deserve encouragement. The movement would not have sprung into existence but for the active support of some really great men. "To work we have the right" and the fruits are cheerfully resigned to Him who guides all and Himself wants no guide.

RETROSPECT

THE present number concludes the first volume of the *Prabuddha Bharata*, and it is now time enough to ask what we have learnt from it. Thus questioning ourselves, we find we have learnt many things. Indeed, even its short history is remarkably full of lessons, and one of the most important which we, *i.e.*, those who are connected with it, have learnt and which we shall do well to carry with us to the very end of our lives is this—sincerity of purpose and purity of heart work wonders even in this "iron age". We had no grand ambitions when we started the journal such as bettering the world and so on. All that we wanted was to improve ourselves, and we had a conviction that what is good for us may at the same time be useful to some others. Nor had we any such motives as fame, position, money, etc. The idea of starting the journal struck us providentially, as it were, and whatever may be its fate in the future, we should be eternally grateful to God for having allowed us to enter into the work with singularly pure hearts. We were at the time perfectly free from both Rajasic self-confidence and Tamasic ambition. In such a happy state which we shall ever remember with pleasure, we sought and obtained permission from where such permission should be obtained and "commenced operations". What success has attended us is due entirely to the blessings we received and the purity of our hearts. And that success has been of no small measure. On every side we were "crammed" as it were, with sympathy, and everywhere, men—for whom we cannot be sufficiently thankful—identified themselves with the cause quite unsolicitedly and worked for its success. So that at the very starting we had 1,500 subscribers and every month the number has been steadily increasing and now it stands at about 4,500. Our journal thus happens to be the most widely circulated monthly in all India. Besides such patronage from the public at large we were unsolicitedly favoured with expressions of encouragement and appreciation by several eminent personages whose words are always entitled to our respect.

*   *   *   *

All that we can say is, that we shall work with zeal and sincerity, no matter what the result might be. "To work alone we have the right but not to the fruit thereof." *To work without motives and without caring for results*— this is our ideal, and may He who is both inside and outside us, who without eyes sees everything, and without ears hears everything and whom the Vedas proclaim to be our Self, enable us to work without self-conceit and false ambitions ; may He allow us the privilege of being pure in heart and good in all we do and say ; and may we work—so long as we have to work—without forgetting that all work in this world is subjective more than objective and helps ourselves rather than others.

B. R. RAJAM IYER : A SKETCH

MR. RAJAM IYER was born in 1872 at Batlagundai, a village in the Madura district. Nothing that is of interest is known of his early life, except that he was a shy boy and never used to join in the ordinary boyish games and amusements. After passing his F. A. examination at Madura, he came to Madras in 1887 and joined the Christian College from which he graduated in 1889. During the next three years, when he was attending the Law College at Madras, he devoted considerable attention to English poets and novelists, and in course of time he acquired a marvellous insight into the genius and art of English poetry, which is undoubtedly the grandest and most elevating portion of English literature. Endowed by nature with an imagination which was at once lofty, subtle and wild, and a keen sensibility, he revelled by turns in Shakespeare, Byron, Keats, Shelley, Wordsworth and George Elliot. He seemed to have been most profoundly influenced by these masters, especially Shelley and Wordsworth, and to have permanently imbibed a genuine passion for Truth, power and beauty, of which their poetry contains a purest and truest expression in such a vast variety—a passion which very soon developed into the philosophic yearning for realising the Truth, the Atman itself. He did not confine himself to the English poets. He acquired a like insight into the beauties of the poetry of Thayumanavar, the great Tamil saint, and of the great Tamil poet Kamban, whom Mr. Rajam Iyer considered as the greatest poet of the

world. Some idea of Mr. Rajam Iyer's appreciation of
the leading English poets may be formed from the
following pithy summing up by him of their respective
merits—"Byron is an ocean-spirit so grand and powerful,
Keats is a moon-spirit so sweet and sensuous, Shelley is
an angel fluttering in the mid-air between earth and
heaven, Wordsworth a spirit of the lonely star standing
aloof, self-luminous and witnessing all things with un-
ruffled peace and ease ; Tennyson is a sweet bard." Mr.
Rajam Iyer's abilities first attracted the attention of the
public in 1892 when he published in the pages of *The
Christian College Magazine* his excellent criticism on
Kachikalambakam, a Tamil poem by the late professor
Ranganadha Mudaliyar, which is but an imitation of a
species of medieval and most artificial poetry. About
the same time, he began to publish as a serial in the pages
of *Viveka Chintamani*, his famous Tamil novel *Kamalambal*, which the late P. Sundaram Pillai considered "would
do great credit to any first-class magazine in Europe."
In the author's own words, the novel records "the innermost experience of a restless soul which struggled much,
and, after a long course of suffering, has at last found a
fountain all undefiled and pure to slake its thirst of
ages." The novel also aims at popularising Kamban,
the great Tamil poet, by bringing into currency the rich
expressions with which he has gifted the Tamil language.
This being the main object of the novel, it is also a
faithful portrait of Hindu life and manners and is
replete with sentiments breathing the subtle and imaginative poetry of Shelley and Wordsworth. Already,
Mr. Rajam Iyer had apparently come under the
influence of Vedanta philosophy of which the conclu-

sions are largely adopted in his novel. Even English
poetry was no longer sufficient for his growing imagination.
For, in his own words : "Poetry gives both pleasure and
pain ; it has to record both the greatness of the universe
and the littleness of man.   Then again it cannot fall in
love with the sultry day, the dirty tank, the barren
desert and things of that kind of which there is no lack
on earth.   At the best therefore poetry is but a resting
place on the wayside, *a Mantapa* on the road to the
temple.   A higher happiness than what poetry can give
is the birthright of man.   It is his prerogative to be
eternally and changelessly happy, to rejoice as much
at a sultry weather as at a moonlit night, to regard with
equal composure the wanton wickedness of men and their
benevolent self-sacrifice, not merely to weep with joy
at a Cumbrian sunset and fly into space with a singing
sky-lark's flight but to 'mingle in the universe and feeling
what he can never express, but cannot all conceal,'
become himself the sun, the setting, the splendour, the
sky-lark, the singing and the sky and all the rest in the
glorious universe. Man is destined to conquer the
heavens, the stars, the mountains, and the rivers, along
with his body, his mind, and his senses, and even in this
life, to dissolve himself into boundless space, and feel all
within himself the roaring sea, the high mountain, the
shining stars, and the noisy cataract.   In this sense, he
is the Lord of the creation—its exultant and all-pervading
Lord, the Parabrahman of the Vedas, and at this stage
he is above all anger, all meanness and all wickedness.
The rage of the intellect and the storm of the senses are
all over, and in the mind of the highest emancipated man,

there is an eternal moony splendour, boundless beatitude that is above all expression."

In 1894 he seriously set his heart upon realising this infinite happiness to which the whole creation is moving consciously or unconsciously. For two years he went about from place to place in the hope of finding some one who could cure the fever of his heart, otherwise preferring to remain alone and obscure and seeking the privacy of his own glorious light. About the close of 1895 in Madras, where he always preferred to live because, as he said, he could lose himself in that wilderness of houses and be obscure, and in the busiest part of the town, he found some one who could put him in the way of acquiring that peace and happiness for which his soul was panting for sometime past. From this time up to his death, he addressed himself to his supreme duty with a single-mindedness, devotion and self-sacrifice which may be called truly heroic. Nothing could ruffle the sweet serenity and the even temper of his mind, and in the moment of the greatest physical agony, which he experienced during the attack of intestinal obstruction in 1896, and when face to face with death now, he never fretted, faltered, or feared. He sought the company of no one except that of his Guru, and preferred to hide himself in the light of his own thought or rather *Existence*, for even thought and speech he felt as a burden. He was either meditating, reading devotional or philosophical works, or writing for the *Prabuddha Bharata* ; and towards the close of his short life he devoted nearly the whole of his time to meditation, so much so that he found the editing of the journal a burden. To all who went to him, he was exceedingly

kind and courteous, and to the few who knew him intimately, he was a source of great strength, illumination
and blessedness. Generally, he was sparing in speech,
and it may be said he uttered a single speech and a
thousand silences. He was most remarkable for his
absolutely unoffending nature and cheerful calmness
under trials.

During the two years the *Awakened India* was in
existence, Mr. Rajam Iyer was its sole editor. It is not
for us to speak of the merits of the journal under his
editorship. But we may say that he brought to his work
a real and intimate knowledge of the subject. He had
himself realised, in no small measure, the Truth he was
expounding and always spoke from the innermost experience of his soul, and herein consisted the rare value
of his writings. His one aim was throughout to present
the Vedanta in its purest and simplest form without
losing sight of its essentially human and poetic interest
and to remove, so far as it lay in his power, the several
misconceptions and mysticisms which have gathered
round it. To this end he assiduously studied the
Upanishads, the Gita and the works of Sankara. During
these two years, he was not merely writing all the leaders,
but, under several *nom-de-plumes*, almost all the articles
appearing in each issue, of which his stirring account of
Nanda—the pariah saint—is the most typical.

In our view Mr. Rajam Iyer was a most beautiful
and genuine flower of English education considered in
its moral and spiritual aspect, not the less so because
it bloomed and blushed unseen. A poetic soul, nursed
and fed by the greatest masters of English poetry he
gradually outgrew their influence, only to come under

the influence of the highest poetry of the Upanishads
and of the Atman itself. As must have been observed,
the transition from poetry to philosophy was so gradual
and imperceptible. Mr. Rajam Iyer used to remark
that true poetry and true philosophy are identical and
the end of both is the same. Surely God must be the
reward of a whole-hearted devotion to what is grand
and beautiful.

While Mr. Rajam Iyer's life thus illustrates on the
one hand the possible power of poetry as a means for
salvation, it illustrates on the other that God is His own
law and reveals Himself under any conditions and that
he certainly refuses to be bound by the orthodox conditions. A young man, yet in his twenties, without
actual experience of life, becoming an aspirant after
salvation is what would not appeal to an orthodox
imagination. A real Vedantin and yet a devoted
husband, an untiring though a silent worker, with a sympathy, in its universality, with antipathy itself, Mr.
Rajam Iyer was a most practical and convincing protest
against all the superstition and idle apprehensions
currently entertained of Vedanta, whose end, he was
always holding, is the highest culture. All men are
bound, and are working, and that with a view to be happy.
They differ only in the sort of happiness which they
obtain and in the manner of obtaining it. The happiness we generally obtain is more or less impermanent :
while ourselves trying to be happy, we inflict harm on
others. Now the Vedantin, too, works for happiness,
but works with the immediate object of realising an
absolutely permanent happiness without causing the least
injury to others. Now the chief value and peculiarity

of Mr. Rajam Iyer's life consist in that he so early felt and recognised the value of such happiness and of an ideal so purely transcendental and impersonal, under conditions apparently out of the way of and hostile to such recognition and, succeeded in realising his own Self—the One without a second.

G. S. K.

Before closing we may remove a misapprehension which seems to have crept into some quarters. It was remarked that "Mr. Rajam Iyer died a martyr to his philosophy." If this means an insinuation that any *Yoga* practice followed by him, led to his ill-health and untimely death, we hasten to assure Mr. Rajam Iyer's friends and admirers that the *Nishta* or contemplation by which he realised the Atman was none of the common breath-stopping or tip-of-the-nose watching kind. He lived a glorious and happy life, and died a natural and peaceful death. We who were with him till his last moments were struck with his serene and calm bearing to the last ; and we could not wish to live more wisely or die more calmly.

P. S.

IN MEMORIAM

B. Ṙ. RAJAM IYER

DEAR departed soul! Can sincere love
From here below add to thy bliss above?
Can all my tears repay those happy hours
Spent with thy charming book in shady bowers?
Can praise from lips untaught in flattery's lore
Enchant thee just to live a little more?
Vain hope! Yet as grief demands, for thee shall fly,
Wherever thou art, this tribute small—a sigh.

    While yet a boy I met thy book; it soon
Took me to fields of bliss till then unknown.
Though many a realm of fiction I had seen,
Nowhere so quite at home as here I'd been.
For those were sweets by foreign flavour marred,
But this was by a mother's hand prepared,
Thy genius has a fragrance over it shed
Which will in ever increasing circle spread.
I loved it once to love it evermore,
For of natural charms it has an ever-fresh store.
The Tamil Muse that slept so long spell-bound,
Now by thy magic touch awoke and found
Her voice, and learnt her sweet dreams forth to pour—
Alas! Ere she had done thou wert no more!
Thy trumpet first awakened India's soul
To her new surroundings and her final goal.
When all the world was growing loud and red,

Over words and books and forms of faith long dead ;
When men were doubting what their creed should be,
Thy religion was love and charity,
Innate in thee as sweetness in the rose,
Both preached and practised to thy friends and foes.

Far from the circle of friends couldst thou have
                                        guessed
There was a hand desirous to be pressed
Against thine own ? Or of a boyish heart
Hoping some day in thy love to earn a part ?
With thee how soon this vain world I should learn
To forget, its petty hopes and fears to spurn.
To shut conversation's door against noise and care,
In all thy harmless funs to have a share ;
Or talk of things that claim our best concern,
Eternal Truth that does all things govern
Infinite Love too great to be scrutinised—
Dreams that must melt away in mere verse
And leave me all alone my griefs to nurse !

Too early snatched away ! Hadst thou a glimpse
Of thy own fate, when thou didst write :[1] "It seems
Ah, these were dreams too good to be realised !
The world was not for *our* pleasure made ;
For why should dry leaves live and blossoms fade" ?
Yes ; why, when all thy work was not yet done,
Shouldst thou leave life, its joys but just begun ?
How much more should thy country be in debt
To thee, hadst thou but lived a short time yet ;
To thee that thy short life couldst make so fine

[1] Said in his novel "Kamalambal or The Fatal Rumour."

And use so well! How many hearts like mine
Would be reclaimed from gloom and bless thy art
That shows in serious cares a humorous part!
Ah, gentle soul! Thy heart it much did grieve
To see the misery thou couldst never relieve!
It sought and led the way to its native Light
Where there's no sin to weep, no wrong to right.

But men like thee come not here every day,
Their visits are rare as those that angels pay;
And while they stay and work the world sleeps on,
And only wakes long after they are gone.
And from their footsteps vainly tries to trace
How much they did and suffered in life's race.
Men eat the fruit and then ask how it came—
Who put the seed being gone, they honour his *name*

But ah! Of what avail my wailing now?
Mysterious Providence would have it so.
A free gift, thou wert sent us here unasked;
A free gift, thou must elsewhere too be tasked.
Thou art recalled from here to a better place
Only to serve thy Lord in worthier ways.
There's justice even in chance, there's not a dust
Blown by the wind but to a purpose just;
While we like little children cry and gasp
To catch the thing too big for our little grasp.

What though the flower be dead, the fragrance
                                    lives
What though thy form be gone thy spirit survives
In thy immortal book, to charm and lure

Our souls to worlds of exalted thoughts and pure.
Thine are the charms that mind to mind endear,
Thine are the happiest hours we have had here.
Remembrance still thy name in its sacred pages
Shall hold embalmed with love ; and coming ages
Shall shed a pious tear ere closing thy book
And cast on it one longing, lingering look !

A Dreamer

FAREWELL

WE regret very much to intimate to our subscribers that we are forced to stop the journal with this issue, as we find the loss sustained in the premature death of our editor, Mr. B. R. Rajam Iyer, irreparable. Except the few "Contributions" and the "Extracts," all the articles were written by him, some under the following pseudonyms : "T. C. Natarajan", "M. Ranganadha Sastri", "A Recluse",and"Nobody-Knows-Who". And if the articles were pleasing and edifying in a high degree, it was because the writer had himself some realisation of the Truth, and his views were developed under the teaching of a great sage, the "Mauni" whose "Meditation" appeared in the journal.

Even before he came in contact with the sage, the writer had a most marked religious bent, as shown by the leader[1] of this issue, which was the article which first attracted our attention to him. On reading the article in the *Brahmavadin* in 1895 we felt the hand of a great man and longed to find him. And when we sought him out, we found him an unpolished diamond. He had himself been in search of a master for over two years, and we most opportunely fell in with him and took him to the sage, whom he accepted as his Guru after some preliminary discussion. He soon received the necessary polish and his thoughts found vent in the *Prabuddha Bharata*. To praise his articles would look like self-

[1] *See* 'Man—His Littleness and Greatness'.

praise, but those who have enjoyed and profited by them need no such words from us. Suffice it to say that the sage above referred to remarked of the articles that they were "*Arulvakku*"—inspired words.

To those who would read between the lines, it must have been evident that the *Prabuddha Bharata* presented a peculiar interpretation of the Vedanta, and in this sense the journal had a marked individuality or personality, that of its editor, or of the sage, his Guru. It is our belief that the extraordinary popularity of the journal all over the length and breadth of India and even abroad was due not so much to the Vedanta merely as such promulgated by the journal as to the peculiarly beautiful and non-mystical interpretation which the journal presented. And as there is none to our knowledge who can rightly fill the place of the saint-editor whom we have lost, we are unable to continue the journal as other journals or magazines might under similar circumstances have been continued.

The journal was not started with the object of making money, but that of preaching the Truth, Truth broad and open as day-light and free from the hundred superstitions, mysticisms and misconceptions which adhere to it. Although, through the kindness of our subscribers, the journal was a thorough success as a business concern, yet in the interests of Truth it is our most painful duty to bring the journal to a close in spite of the sore disappointment which we are aware this message will cause to our many subscribers, to whom we take this opportunity of bidding a sad farewell.

I

IDEALS OF VEDANTA

RAMBLES IN VEDANTA

MODERN CIVILISATION AND THE VEDANTA

A CERTAIN country gentleman living in one of the re
mote out-of-the-way villages of the South, once happened
to pay a visit to Madras and there, in a bad hour, purchased a time-piece and took it home. His old grand-
mother, aged 90 winters, had never heard of such a thing
before, and therefore, from the very first viewed it with
suspicion, which its constant 'tick-tick' did not very much
tend to set at rest. A few days after the introduction of
this novelty, a child died in the house and the old woman
got exceedingly angry with the time-piece, for she attri-
buted the misfortune to it. If anybody fell ill in the
house, it was on account of that wicked 'tick-ticking'
time-piece ; if any sorrowful news was heard, it was on
account of that wicked 'tick-ticking' time-piece. She
worried her grandson, day and night, to remove it out of
the house or give it away to some enemy, but he unfortunately liked it as much as she feared it, and would not
part with it. The result was that on a certain dark
night, the blind old woman broke open her grandson's
room, took out the time-piece and striking it several
times, threw it into the house of her neighbour, an enemy
who was only too glad to find it there, the next morning.
Such was the strength of her superstition.

Superstitions, however, do not seem peculiar to age or sex, and a new superstition is now getting into vogue that just as the time-piece in the story killed the child and brought misfortunes into the family, the study of the Vedanta and the spreading of Vedantic ideas would destroy all civilisation and material advancement and render life not worth living. The Vedanta, however, is incapable of any such crime ; it has too strong a faith in the providential government of the world, to think that anything there, be it science, arts, industry or religion, came into it by mistake. Its only aim is to better, as far as it can, the individual and the society.

To enter into the subject, there are two important faculties in man, *viz.*, the heart and the intellect. Each of these, the Vedanta says, must be developed but not the one at the expense of the other. They are placed together that each may help and guide the other, like a pair of horses drawing a carriage. The business of the heart is to feel and to love, but it often makes mistakes ; then reason comes to its help and corrects it. For example, the old man in his death-bed weeps for the children born and yet unborn he is leaving behind, but reason tells him that he is trusting to broken reeds ; that children, friends, relatives, wealth and lands follow him not beyond his grave, and that he has to make his journey all alone. Similarly, it is the business of reason to discriminate, to argue and to judge, and left to itself, it also makes mistakes, which the heart corrects. "Stay," says the alchemist to his weeping wife, in Balzaac's novel, "stay, I have decomposed tears, tears contain a little phosphate of lime, some chloride of soda, some mucus and some water." To him weeping meant only that much. This is reason left to itself, and here the heart says : "Learned idiot, look behind, it is the heart that weeps." So then, the heart and the intellect are capable of correcting each other, and they can, not only correct, but also develop each other.

The perfect man is a beautiful combination of the head and the heart, and he has no quarrel with either, for, he knows the place and sphere of each. Individuals make up the society and, roughly speaking, it is their heart-portion that reveals itself in religion and the head-portion that takes shape as civilisation. As in the individual the heart and the head mutually correct and develop each other, so in society also, religion and material advancement, faith and science, ought to be the companion and guide of each other. It will be a mistake to cry down civilisation and hold up blind irrational religion, as the be-all and end-all of existence ; and it will be equally absurd to extol the latter and cry down the former. The end of existence is not blind irrational religion, nor is it barren intellectual science ; it is the harmonious blending of the head and the heart, of love and light, of faith and knowledge ; it is religion culminating in philosophy, and science developed into wisdom. Perfect knowledge is all love ; perfect love is all knowledge.

The Vedantin, therefore, has no quarrel with science and civilisation, any more than he has with faith and religion. What he says is, that science should get spiritualised and religion get rationalised, and that each should know its place, and that there should be no conflict between the two, any more than between the eyes and ears of a man. They should mutually help each other and develop each other. This happy union has, however, seldom been arrived at. Many an ancient civilisation has fallen down owing to its one-sided development—as often happens in the individual. How many examples do we see of men developing into fanatics, just because reason does not come in time to aid the emotion and lead it onward and how many, of men, who are intellectual giants, but are incapable of love or sympathy. Similarly, with regard to society, we see great political empires falling down, side by side with spiritual movements, and the same history that records the downfall of Egyptian, Alexandrian, Grecian and Roman civilisations, mournfully records the extinction of Paganism, the collapse of the Papal Empire, the cessation of religious epidemics, like that of the holy dance of the middle ages, the failure of the Franciscan reform and the futility of Portestantism and a multitude of other movements. The secret of the failure in both cases is that the head and heart of the society did not properly complement each other in time, as was required.

The great modern civilisation is not more infallible than the ancient ones, for it is even more materialistic than its predecessors. It glories over its fancied conquest of nature, is proud of its few real victories, and has a little too much of self-assertion. It forgets too often, that it has not even pierced through the outer veil of Nature and that Nature has been blessed like Draupadi, the excellent wife of the Pandavas, with an inexhaustible number of vestures, one beneath another and more wonderful. To disrobe her is an impossible affair. The deeper you go the more dazzled you become ; sheath after sheath might be plucked away but sheath after sheath yet remains. Modern civilisation is somewhat too conceited to think of this, and it must become a failure, unless it listens to the cry of the unsatisfied heart which fortunately is making itself heard. Luckily for the modern world and perhaps for the first time in modern human history, 'the still small vioce' of the heart is heard just at the right hour and there is a prospect,—nay, a near probability—of the intellect and the heart meeting together and aiding and developing each other. Science is getting gradually spiritualised and religion is beginning to be established on rational scientific basis ; the old and prolonged conflict between them is slowly dying away ; they are now mutually correcting and developing each other, and out of their union may possibly spring up the ideal society of the Vedanta.

To leave the future to itself and return to the point, the Vedanta has no quarrel with science or civilisation. It says : "Indulge as much as you can in the revelries of science, conquer worlds, build empires, 'rift the earth, flash the lightnings, roll the waters, weigh the sun,' nay, even make new planets and launch them into space, but always remember, that these are not the end of existence, but that the heart must be satisfied as well as the intellect. The voice of the heart should be listened to, and the instincts of love, mercy, charity and religion should not be disregarded." The danger in modern civilisation is, that man has a tendency to externalise himself more and more and to fancy, that eating, drinking and going after creature-comforts are the sole aim of life. He creates for himself artificial wants and unnatural hunger, and sickens himself with unhealthy selfishness

3

or pestilential discontent. As Swami Vivekananda when addressing an American audience said : "It is one of the evils of your Western civilisation, that you are after intellectual education alone and there is no safe-guard with it. There is one mistake made ; you give this education but you take no care of the heart. It only makes men ten times more selfish and that will be your destruction."

That modern civilisation is lacking in some of the noble elements of humanity has been pointed out by many of the leading writers of the age :

"Your average Englishman," says Carlyle, "does not greatly care whether there be a God or not, provided the price of stock does not fall. If you want to awaken his real beliefs, you must descend into his stomach, purse, and the adjacent regions."

"The ruling goddess of England," mournfully observes Ruskin, "may well be described as the 'Goddess of Getting On' or 'Britannia of the Market'. It is long since you built a great cathedral, but your railroad mounds are vaster than the walls of Babylon, your railroad stations vaster than the temple of Ephesus and innumerable ; your chimneys are more mighty and costly than cathedral spires ; your harbour piers, your warehouses, your exchanges all these are built to your great 'Goddess of Getting On'. She formed and will continue to form your whole nature as long as you worship her."

Swami Vivekananda says in his usual vigorous style "Intellect has been cultured ; result, hundreds of sciences have been discovered, and their effect has been that the few have made slaves of the many—that is all the good that has been done. Artificial wants have been created ; and every poor man, whether he has money or not, desires to have those wants satisfied and when he cannot, he struggles and dies in the struggle. This is the result. Through the intellect is not the way to solve the problem of misery but through the heart. If all this vast amount of effort had been spent in making men purer, gentler, more forbearing, this world would have a thousand-fold more happiness than it has to-day."

The following lines from Tennyson aptly describe the effects of modern civilisation.

> Science moves, but slowly, creeping on from point to point,
> Slowly comes a hungry people, as lion creeping nigher.
> Glares at one that nods and winks behind a slowly dying fire
>   *   *   *   *
> Knowledge comes but wisdom lingers and I linger on the shore,
> And the individual withers, and the world is more and more ;

Yes knowledge comes but wisdom lingers. There was an emperor whose name was Mahabali. He had conquered the whole world, all the Devas, Asuras and men, and yet was not satisfied in his heart. He asked his minister if there were no more kingdoms to conquer and was told that there was one other kingdom and that was his own self. "What shall it profit a man if he shall gain the whole world and lose his own soul" said the Blessed Lord Jesus. And this conquest of self is the most difficult thing. It requires a perfect harmony between the head and the heart, perfect knowledge and universal love. "Oh Lord ! that art all knowledge, light and bliss and that dwellest in my heart, it is easier to tame the wild elephant and make it obey our bidding, to bind the mouths of the tiger and the bear, to ride on the back of the lord of beasts—the lion—, to play with the poisonous cobra, to convert the different metals into gold and live thereby, to roam in the world unseen, to make the gods our slaves, to enjoy eternal youth, to pass into another body, to walk on water, to stand on fire and develop powers incomparable—all these easier far than to subdue the mind and remain in blissful rest," sang a great Tamil sage.

It is this conquest of mind, this realisation of the great Self or God—the little man losing himself in universal love and wisdom, and becoming himself 'the Lord of the universe, the Brahman who is greater than the universe, the Great One, the Infinite, who is concealed within all beings according to their bodies, the only pervader of the universe,'—which is the highest ideal of humanity, the noblest and the truest civilisation. The education of the heart, the cultivation of love, and the total annihilation of selfishness, are the necessary means to the attainment of this high and blissful civilisation, and without the cultivation of the heart, without the help of rational religion completing itself in philosophy, without knowledge or science developing into wisdom through the sacred and saving influence of the heart, all the railways in the world, all the manufactories and steam ships that have been built or are to be built, can never make man a trifle better in himself than he is.

The attitude of the Vedanta towards modern civilisation is exactly the same as that towards marriage. Those to whom marriage is a necessity let them marry by all means ; but the object should not be sensual

enjoyment, but the increase of good and the propagation
of the race (this is the meaning of the Mantra pronounced
in the Hindu marriage ceremony). Marriage must be
looked upon simply as a preparation for a higher life,
in order that real renunciation might become possible.
Some do not feel marriage a necessity, and they need
not marry. Renunciation, *i.e.*, mental renunciation, is
the common ideal for both of them. Similarly, to those
that feel curious to know about the outer world, the
Vedanta says : 'Better fifty years of Europe than a cycle
of Cathay,' for, to such, the modern civilisation is an
invaluable help as it destroys *Tamas*, (laziness and
ignorance) and readily makes them 'the heirs of ages.'
Some, however, are free from the above curiosity and are
all the more eager to know themselves. The ideal for
both is the same, the knowledge of the Self or wisdom.
Our lower civilisation is but a preparation for the higher.
Besides, just as it is the same for the sage, whether he
is with his family or alone, married or unmarried, it is
the same for him, whether he is in the midst of society
or alone. He might live in the forest like Suka or rule
kingdoms like Janaka. The latter fought battles,
improved commerce, agriculture and industry and is
reported to have been one of the justest kings of
the world, and withal one of the greatest of Indian
Vedantists.

To conclude, modern civilisation is rather one-sided,
but has in it the possibilities of growing perfect. Its
chief defects are its present materialistic tendency of
regarding the enjoyment of creature-comforts of life as
an end in itself, and the want of a proper ideal. This

civilisation is simply a preparation for the higher and
the truer one and the aim of the Vedanta is, not to destroy,
but to improve and elevate it, by correcting its tendency
and furnishing it with an ideal.

SUKA AND THE STEAM ENGINE
OR
THE WORLD'S PROGRESS

LET us fancy, and fancying has been our work ever
since the world began, that the great Rishi Suka comes back
to our midst to have a look at the nineteenth century
civilisation. Doubtless, there would be much which he
could not make out, much which he, in his good old days,
would not have even dreamt of. Especially, if he goes to
England or America, he will see things which, if he were
an ordinary man, might boundlessly excite his curiosity
and interest. The busy steamships ploughing the main,
the busier traffic of nations, the huge workshops and
manufactories which form a leading feature of the modern-
day world, electric trains, telegraphs, telephones, talking
machines and other vast and wonderful inventions and
contrivances of the age—What will Suka think of these?
Supposing he is led to one of the great industrial exhibi-
tions of the day, will he not get stupefied with wonder?
The answer is: 'Not likely' All the machines and
manufactories of the world and all the wonderful inventions of the age will hardly succeed in eliciting from him
a word of surprise, and if an enthusiastic Locksley speak
to him of the fairy tales of science, and spread before
him the vision of the wonders that would be—'heavens
filling with commerce, argosies of magic sails—pilots of

the purple twilight dropping down with costly bales' and 'the parliament of man and the federation of the world,' he might smile and say : 'What if these be ? These are no wonders ; you are but children.' Even if all the stars in heaven were made by the sheer might of man to shine in the day, and he were enabled to cross from Mars to Venus and from Venus to Mercury as easily as from one room of a house to another—nay, even if he were enabled to make a million new stars and launch them all into space, it is not likely that the philosophic calmness of our Suka would be disturbed with curiosity or wonder. Ask him if the world has not become better than it was in old days, and he would laugh and say : 'What do you take the world to be? It is the Supreme Self, the Atman, changeless and eternal, shining through a vast variety of conditions (*Upadhis*) created by Maya (energy). Maya is constant and so your world neither grows nor decays. But this Maya, these *Upadhis*, and this world are only the dreams of the ignorant. To the wise all that is, is God.'

What could Suka mean ? The Upanishads say :

He who dwelling in the earth is within the earth, whom the earth does not know, whose body is the earth, who within rules the earth is thy soul, the Inner Ruler, immortal.

He who dwelling in the waters is within the waters, whom the waters do not know, whose body are the waters, who within rules the waters is thy soul, the Inner Ruler, immortal.

He who dwelling in the fire is within the fire, whom the fire does not know, whose body is the fire, who within rules the fire is thy soul, the Inner Ruler, immortal.

It is one and the same Self that is in the earth, in the waters, in the fire, in the man, in the stone and in

the animal, but it is in them under extremely different
conditions. Man is different from the animal as such,
the animal is different from the stone as such, the wind
is different from fire as such, but as pure *Existence*,
man, animal, stone, wind, fire, are all one. All things
that are, have *ipso facto* this element of Existence, and
this Existence is not a mere dead one, for the whole
world is instinct and bristling with life. The stone that
lies as dead is not really so ; it has a life and a consciousness peculiar to itself. It is this underlying
existence, this ultimate, inner life and consciousness
pervading all through the universe which is called the
Self. Under certain conditions, (*Upadhis* as they are
called in Sanskrit) it appears as a man, under others as
a stone, under others as a beast, under others as a star,
and so on. As Swami Vivekananda says : 'As a man
you are separate from the woman, as a human being
you are one with the woman. As a man you are separate
from the animal, but as a living being, the man, the
woman, the animal, the plant, are all one : and as
existence, you are one with the whole universe. That
existence is God, the ultimate unity in this universe ;
in Him we are all one.' This common unity manifests
itself in an infinite variety of conditions, and forms
what is called the universe. All the endless differences
which we see are differences only of conditions, of
circumstances. Indeed, the world is nothing but a
mass of conditions superimposed upon the Self, and
creation means nothing more than the superimposition
of these conditions, or, to speak from a different standpoint, the manifestation of these conditions.

Now, as the totality of these conditions makes up
what is seen as the world, the energy or power (Sakti or
Maya) through which they become manifest is the sum-
total of the energy in the universe. This sum-total,
science assures us, is a constant quantity. Western
science has conclusively established that the quantity of
energy in the world is constant, *i.e.*, it cannot be less one
day, and greater another, less in B. C., and greater in
A. D. As our philosophers put it in their usual poetic
way, the wife of the Lord—Parvati, Lakshmi, Sakti or
Kali as she is called,—is, though she has given birth to
children innumerable and worlds innumerable, yet a
blooming girl. What follows? The Self or God is
beyond growth and decay ; so also is Sree, *i.e.*, the energy
which creates the diverse conditions through which
that Self shines. It is obvious therefore that the
world, which is the combination of the Self and Sree
Prakriti and Purusha—is incapable of progress and
decay. It cannot be better one day and worse another.
All that is possible is only change. The energy in it
may be latent at one time and manifest at another. The
energy in the seed, for instance, is latent, that of the
tree is manifest ; and when the tree springs forth from
the seed and grows, the energy in the world does not
increase, no new thing is brought into it : there is simply
a change of conditions. The world as a whole neither
improves nor declines. What were once seed, earth,
water, and air, now combine together and form a tree ;
and similarly when the tree is pulled down and cut up
into chairs and tables, what really happens is simply a
change of conditions. What was before of the form of
a tree and called such, is now changed in form and is

called a table or a chair as the case may be. There is change only in name and form. Or, to put the same thing in another way, the new thing is in essence the same as the old, but posterior in time, is different in size and shape, *i.e.*, in space, and has a few more links in the chain of causation—in other words, is different from the former in space, time and causality. So again in the building of a pyramid, in the construction of a steam engine, in the demolition of an ancient castle, in the falling down of an ancient empire, all that really happens is but a change of conditions, a change in name and form, a change in time, space and causality—neither improvement nor decay so far as the totality of the world is concerned.

That there is nothing new under the sun is a piece of profound philosophy. Only it does not go far enough. There is nothing new under the sun and beyond the sun. Continents became oceans, oceans became continents, mountains became seas, and seas became mountains, mammoths died and man sprang—did the world improve or decline? It did neither. All that really happened was only a change of conditions, a change in name and form, a change in time, space and causality. So again in the organisation of large joint stock companies, in the building of huge manufactories, in the vast and wonderful mechanical contrivances of the age, 'in the steamship, the railway and the thoughts that shake mankind'—in short, in all that goes by the name of modern civilisation, there has been only change and not improvement, so far as the totality of the world is concerned : the world as a whole has neither got better nor worse. All our civilisation is nothing, really speaking, but a change in name and form, a change in time, space and causality.

But is this change at least absolutely real? There might not have been any improvement, but has there been at least a real change? 'No' is the reply from the East and the West alike. Time, space and causality, says Kant, are merely forms of the mind. 'The name and form of the pot are not in the clay but in your mind' says Sankara. They are not where the mind is not manifest. The mind then, is a kind of spectacles: when you look through them, the world appears bound down and diversified with the conditions of time, space and causality—these innumerable names and forms, just as to the jaundiced eye everything appears yellow. It is given to man, and here is his highest privilege, to leave behind this differentiating mind—to remove at will the spectacles-like mechanism, so to speak, which creates this world of names and forms, and soar into the regions of pure unconditioned consciousness. In that blissful state of halcyon rest and calmness, the waves of names and forms die, and there is neither caste nor creed neither steamship nor railway, neither animal nor man, neither mountain nor sea, neither male nor female, neither death nor life, neither heaven nor hell. All these immense worlds, all our glorious civilisation and all the innumerable differences that attract and repel us by turns, all vanish; and what remains is the pure unconditioned, eternal and blissful Self, the Atman or God.

It is said that there is a kind of magic oil known in Malabar and that when a lamp is fed with it, the whole area illumined by its light at once appears covered with a multitude of ugly snakes crawling and creeping over one another. The dreadful vision continues until all the oil is consumed, and no one that sees it can, unless he knows the secret, ever take it for a vision. The mind may be likened to that magic oil. It has been steadily presenting to us a vision which we, not knowing the secret, have been mistaking for an eternal reality and got hopelessly terrified at. To him that knows the secret, there is no fear.

All this world, this infinitely differentiated world together with the improvements, as they are called, which have been introduced into it, is found to be a phantasmagoria presented by the magic lantern of the mind, a mere hallucination, and flies away like a dream after waking, when the great, profound and blissful secret of the Self is known and realised. A certain Brahmin performed a great sacrifice in honour of Indra, and the latter, pleased with him, asked him what he wanted. The avaricious Brahmin at once asked for the Kalpaka tree—the most favourite treasure of Indra,— and the request was granted. The tree had one most remarkable property, and that was, that whatever its possessor thought in his mind actually came to pass. The Brahmin thought that it would be well for him to have wealth, and at once there came an abundance of gold and silver : he was greatly pleased and then thought it would be well to have kingdoms, and at once there came more kingdoms than he could rule : then he thought of women, and at once there was a brilliant host of them. All these things happened so rapidly that the poor Brahmin thought they might all of them, including the tree, be a mere dream and pass away, and so it was at once : the tree, the wealth, the kingdoms and the women, all of them vanished as suddenly as they came. The mind is such a Kalpaka tree. It presents to us just such a vision as we want (or wanted before) ; the world is beautiful and pleasant, or ugly and miserable, and we are happy or unhappy just as the mind chooses. It is a very wonderful Kalpaka tree, this mind, and when we question its reality, and the reality of the things it gives us, the whole vision passes away and we find we have been dreaming.

Absolutely speaking, then, all our civilisation, the triumphs of science, politics and philosophy, the glories of agriculture, industry and commerce, are all dreams from which we are all of us bound to awake some time or other—a conclusion not perhaps palatable to some, but truth is truth 'for all that'.

"WHAT IS VEDANTA?"

A CHRISTIAN missionary remarks : "What is Vedanta?"
One man gives one answer and another a different one.
It seems to me to be a name to conjure with and no
more. Vedanta is usually regarded as pure pantheism ;
but the modern use of the term is different. "What do
the promoters of 'Awakened India' mean by it?"

From the above remarks, it is seen what an amount
of confusion exists in regard to the proper definition
and scope of the philosophy which goes by the name of
'Vedanta'. This confusion is not confined to our Christian
brethren alone, but it also extends to some of the highly
intelligent and learned Sanskrit scholars, Eastern and
Western alike.

These scholars are learned in the sense that they
have devoted their whole life-time in trying to have only
an intellectual grasp of the subject, but never had any
practical experience or realisation in life of the great
truths taught in it. Truly, it may be said : "Thou hast
hid these things from the wise and the prudent and hast
revealed them unto babes." While these scholars thus
differ from one another in the understanding of the
subject, it is pleasant to see that there is no material
difference among the teachings of the great teachers of
humanity, who having realised those truths in practical
life each in his own way, have given expression to the
same truths but in a manner suited to the condition of
the people among whom they lived. Mere learning is one

thing and practical realisation is another. Those only who have striven to learn these truths from practical teachers—who are still to be found in fair numbers in this pre-eminently religious country—have not failed to see clearly for themselves the sublimity of the Vedantic teachings.

Roughly speaking, the students of the Vedanta may be said to be of three kinds. First, those who undertake the study of the Vedanta with a view to realise for themselves the "grand truth," the "unity" underlying the incessantly changing and unreal phenomena of this world, and thus get liberation or salvation. They seek for themselves a practical guide or *Guru*, and devote their whole life to attaining that realisation by constantly listening to the teachings of the *Guru* (*Sravana*), by pondering over the truths heard (*Manana*) and finally by striving to realise those truths by means of constant meditation according to the methods taught by the *Guru* (*Nididhyasana*). Such sincere persons are called "*Mumukshus*," and they will sooner or later get at the truth ; and it is for them alone that Vedantic works really exist. Among such *Mumukshus* there never has been any material difference in opinion as regards the teachings of the Vedanta ; whereas, among those who have tried to learn it from books, there ever has been a disagreement even on some fundamental point or another connected with the subject. It is the same with respect to Christianity or any other religion. For instance, where men have tried to learn religion from books and scholars as in Protestant countries, the only result has been the creation of innumerable sects ; on the other hand, where religion is acquired from practical teachers and saints as in Roman Catholic countries, there has been unity. That is why among the Roman Catholics the lay people are not allowed to read their scriptures, and that is why in Vedantic works very great stress has been laid on *Sravana* or hearing a Guru's teachings rather than on the reading of those works.

The second class of students are those who undertake the study for making a livelihood, or for earning "name and fame," or as an intellectual recreation. It is to this class that the generality of Vedantic scholars belong. They have tried to get only an intellectual grasp of the subject, and their knowledge though vast is more or less misty. They generally lose themselves in vain disputations or learned discourses, and very rarely get at the truth. We may well say with the great Tamil poet, philosopher and saint, Thayumanavar : "Blessed are the ignorant. For, what shall we say of our plight, who are learned and yet know not the truth? Learning is so mighty that if any one were to lay great stress on the importance of *Gnana* or knowledge (for salvation), we can establish, on the contrary, that *Karma* (rituals) alone is all-important, and *vice versa*. Again, if a great Sanskrit scholar comes (for discussion), we silence him with any amount of quotations from Tamil literature, and similarly if one clever in Tamil literature were to come, we shut him up by citing a few stanzas in Sanskrit. But, can this learning, oh Lord! which enables us to confound and silence all, can this learning lead us to salvation?"

Lastly, come those that study the Vedanta with the mere idea of criticising its teachings. They only

4

look at the apparent superficial discrepancies that are
met with at the outset, and condemn the whole system.
From them the truths of the Vedanta will ever remain
hidden ; for, they only see in it what they wish to see,
and hence make no progress in understanding the deeper
truths. It is only such persons that criticise the Vedanta
so freely ; and, generally speaking, the greater the ignorance of the subject, the louder and more incisive is
the criticism. To this class of students belong some of
our Christian brethren, a specimen of whose criticisms
on that gem of books, the Bhagavad-Gita,—one of the
authoritative works on the Vedanta—can be had at any
Christian Tract Depot. That is why the Vedanta is a
stumbling block to many of our Christian missionaries
and our Social Reform friends. Therefore, the only
way they can understand the Vedanta is to approach
it with a sympathetic attitude, find out the best practical
examples of its votaries—who are fortunately not very
rare—and learn from them the truth, getting the doubts
that may arise cleared by free discussion. The necessity
for such a teacher and guide will be obvious when one
considers, how, in spite of the simplicity and lucidity
of the language of these Vedantic works, there is such
a misconception of the ideas expressed. Take, for
instance, the idea of *Renunciation* of this world as the
surest way to salvation. A literal understanding of the
principle has evoked many a criticism, and led many to
doubt the soundness of the principle. Many are the
homes that have been rendered desolate by this blunder
about *renunciation*. But from the very early times the
great teachers of humanity have warned mankind against
this physical renunciation. (Vide *Pitfalls in the Vedanta*).

As Swami Vivekananda says : "The Vedanta teaches that the world should be renounced but not on that account abandoned. To live in the world and not be of it is the true test of renunciation." With the above remarks as to the course one has to pursue in trying to understand the truths of any religion, we may pass on to the consideration of the question, "What is Vedanta?"

The Vedanta is the philosophy contained in the Upanishads, the Brahma Sutras and the Bhagavad-Gita. These three are called the 'Prasthanatrayas' or the three legs on which that philosophy rests. It is known as the Vedanta, because it claims to be the end of the Vedas.

The Vedas used in the broadest sense mean knowledge ; and knowledge is infinite and eternal, and no limit can be set to it in this eternally mysterious and infinite world. So are the Vedas infinite and eternal. They comprise all that has hitherto been known, as well as all that may hereafter become known. In a restricted sense, the term is used to denote spiritual knowledge, as in spiritual knowledge all other knowledge is fulfilled ; and hence also it is applied to the Hindu scriptures, which contain the essence of all knowledge. All the inspired outpourings of sages; ancient and modern, all the Bibles, Zendavastas, Dhammapadas and Koran yet given to humanity, as well as all the arts and sciences are included in the term Vedas ; and the Christs, Buddhas and Sankaras of the future can speak nothing but the Vedas. As has been observed by Swami Vivekananda : "The Vedas are without beginning and without end. It may sound ludicrous how a book can be without beginning or end. But by the Vedas no

books are meant. They mean the accumulated treasury
of spiritual laws discovered by different persons in
different times. Just as the law of gravitation existed
before its discovery and would exist if all humanity
forgot it, so it is with the laws that govern the spiritual
world ; the moral, ethical and spiritual relation between
soul and soul, and between individual spirits and the
Father of all spirits, were there before their discovery,
and will remain even if we forgot them." In other
words, it is the accumulated experience of ages handed
down to posterity in all climes and all ages. That these
experiences differ according to surrounding circumstances too varied and too numerous to mention, ought
to be conceded by every thinking person ; and the Vedas
include all these varied experiences or knowledge. And
Vedanta means the end of knowledge.

Here perhaps it may be asked : "If the Vedas denote
the unlimited fund of knowledge, as it is said to be, is
it not rather surprising that a certain philosophy should
claim to be the end of this seemingly endless Vedas ?"
The contradiction however is only apparent. All
knowledge is of two kinds : the one concerns itself with
the outward properties or attributes of things as perceived by the senses and the intellect, i.e., the knowledge
of the Phenomenon ; and the other deals with the inner
nature, the underlying reality or the essence of things—
the Noumenon. The former will ever remain imperfect,
as, in proportion to the advances made in various sciences
which have been dealing with the knowledge of this
phenomenal aspect of this world, the unknown has not
only been receding further and further but has also been
growing bigger and bigger. We analyse water, and

find it is made up of oxygen and hydrogen; but what is oxygen and what is hydrogen who can say? Where there was one thing unknown before, there are two things now; and the mystery of nature has got thickened instead of being solved.

> "Veil after veil will lift—but there must be
> Veil upon veil behind."

The man of science is as wise to-day as he was centuries ago as regards the great problems of life and existence. Science examines the world with a frantic eagerness but does not get at the bottom; it furiously knocks itself against a barrier beyond which it cannot go.

If, however, instead of looking at the phenomenal aspect of things, we proceed to examine their inner nature—the noumenon, we find that all the differences in the world are differences of "time, space and causality," or of "names and forms," (*Nama* and *Rupa*); and that these "names and forms," or "time, space and causality" are, deeply considered, but forms of the mind, *i.e.*, appearances or pictures projected by the mind; and that where the mind is subdued and at rest, the inner unity, the ultimate substratum of this phenomenal universe reveals itself. This common unity, this under-lying essence is God, timeless, spaceless, and causeless; and the world from this stand-point is nothing but God manifesting Himself in different names and forms. There is not an atom outside Him. "In Him the world lives, moves and has its being." "He is the wise man who sees everything in God and God in everything."

This is objected to on the ground that it is pantheism. We say it is not. For, pantheism is defined as "the

doctrine that the universe taken or conceived of as a
whole is God, or the doctrine that there is no God but
the combined forces and laws which are manifested in
the existing universe." It is plain that the Vedanta
never denies the existence of God ; for, it emphatically
asserts that there is but One Existence, which is God.
Nor does it say that the combined forces and laws which
are manifested in the existing universe go to make up
the conception God. Then what does the Vedanta
mean, when it says that we should see God in everything ?
It means that if we calmly analyse this phenomenal
world, we see that all the differences in the world are
resolvable into differences of *name* and *form* only, or, as
it has been termed in Europe, differences of "time,
space and causality." If from any object we take away
the *name* and *form*, what remains is the inner essence
or reality. "It is the Atman beyond all," as Swami
Vivekananda eloquently puts it, "the Infinite, beyond
the known, beyond the knowable ; in and through That
we see this universe. It is the only reality. It is this
table ; It is the audience before me ; It is the wall ;
It is everything, *minus* the *name* and *form*. Take the
form off the table, take away the name ; what remains
is that It................It is the name and form that
make the difference. It is the name, the form, the
body, which are material, and they make all this difference.
If you take off these two differences of name and form,
the whole universe is one. There are no two, no three,
but one everywhere. Out of this one Infinite Existence
all these are manifested through name and form." The
same idea is expressed even more lucidly when he says :
"There is but One unit Existence, and that One is appear-

ing as manifold. This Self, or Soul, or Substance, is all that exists in the universe. That Self, or Substance, or Soul is, in the language of non-dualism, the *Brahman*, appearing to be manifold by the interposition of name and form. Look at the waves in the sea. Not one wave is different from the sea, but what makes the wave apparently differ? Name and form; the form of the wave, and the name which we give to it, 'wave.' That is what makes it differ from the sea. When name and form go, it is the same sea. Who can make any difference between the wave and the sea? So this whole universe is that One unit Existence; name and form have created all these various differences." So long as one's attention is fixed on the outer attributes of matter, upon the changes brought about by name and form, one cannot see the inner essence. But the moment one's attention is turned from this heterogeneous world of names and forms to the inner essence, one sees and ought to see God in everything; for God is the inner essence of all existing things. We must remember that the Vedanta does not say, for instance, that the tree we see before us is God. So long, of course, as we look upon the tree as tree, it is nothing more than a tree; but when we dive deep, leaving the name and form behind and try to realise the inner essence of the tree, we see nothing but God. And that is what the Vedanta means when it asks us to see God in everything. The difference between the Vedanta and pantheism may be thus summed up. According to pantheism, God is the sum or totality of phenomena; while, according to the Vedanta, God is the underlying essence of phenomena—

which are but the result of name and form superimposed upon the essence.

Therefore, of the two kinds of knowledge,—of the phenomena and the noumenon—that which finds the world, the whole existence in its essence to be God is *wisdom*—the true knowledge, which is itself the end of all other knowledge ; for, "When we know Him all the world is known." Though the knowledge of the outer phenomenal world is ever on the increase, and though this knowledge may be a great help in attaining to the true knowledge, yet all men have, at some time or other, to find out that such knowledge can never become perfect, and, that to reach the truth that can satisfy the heart, they have to pass beyond appearances, beyond names and forms. In other words, knowledge can have rest only in wisdom (*Gnana*) ; and a person is said to have attained the end of knowledge, when he has attained the realisation of his own Self, or found the end of all knowledge in *wisdom*.

Few men, however, perceive this ; and fewer still have the requisite courage to overcome the mind which presents this terrible dream-vision of an infinitely differentiated world. They are therefore content to carry on their traffic in the phenomenal world. Unable to seek wisdom, they pursue knowledge. Though the majority no doubt are ever seeking knowledge, yet there are a few who have found its end in wisdom.

Thus we see that the Vedanta is really the end of knowledge—wisdom, as it professes to be ; for its greatest triumph is that it dives beneath the vision of names and forms, and reveals the inner essence of the universe as

God, thereby unfolding at one stretch the full meaning of the universe. It is therefore snpreme knowledge or wisdom, and richly deserves the name.

A FIRST PRINCIPLE

FROM MARUTHAIVIRAN[1] TO MAHAVISHNU

IN the previous article, we had occasion to determine the province of the philosophy of the Vedanta. In its practical application, it consists in the purging out of the grosser elements in man, in the complete subjugation and voluntary surrender of the lower human nature, "in working out the brute and working in the God," in the attainment of that "peace which passeth all understanding." To enjoy that peace for the space of even a second is equal to the benefit, says Yoga Vasishta, of a *Rajasuya* sacrifice ; to live ten minutes in the enjoyment of that beatitude of the nuptials with God confers the benefit, says the same enlightened authority, of an *Asvamedha* sacrifice.

The difficulty of attaining that state of peace—"Om Santi, Santi, Santi," all peace, peace, peace—is so great that Thayumanavar[2] says : "It would be easier to fly in the air, to wander unseen, to walk on fire, to play with the lion and the cobra, and to do ever so many other wonderful things " ; the ascent on flying machines and balloons is nothing when compared to the difficulty of entering into the inner bower of the human mind, which

1 A terrible deity worshipped by the low classes, •especially at Madura (South India).

2 Reader, be not tired of this name as that poor peasant was of the name of Aristides in Grecian History, for he is the man who has made philosophy most poetical in the South.

58

is an abode of bliss and peace sweetly combined like sugar with honey—retreating there into that bower and standing four-square to all the storms that might blow around, and to the battery that might go on pulling down the rampart walls of the body, the social organism and the state, and utterly unmindful of the war that might be going on in the outer world. To so retreat like the snail, to draw one's out-going energies within 'like the tortoise that draws its limbs within in times of danger'—Gita, II, 58—is a rare privilege attained by the grace of God, by the blessings of the Guru, and by constant practice. The Tuscan artist that viewed at evening from the top of Fesole or in Waldarno 'the spotted globe of the Moon' is nothing before the man who is able to draw himself within himself. Indeed, the toil and turmoil of the modern-day life, the noise and din of the work-a-day world, which seems to progress terribly with the progress of the suns, as indicated by that melancholy and fortunately false expression, "struggle for existence," is pitiable and terrible to think of. There is really no struggle for existence : all this apparent elbowing and pushing is a result of the false idea we have about ourselves, of the end in view we have set before ourselves, viz., to struggle and survive. We are struggling not for existence ; for, as a great poetess has said : "We are bound to live as far as the impetus that sent us here lasts, for the God that made us is not dead." We are all of us struggling, not to survive, but to live freely and happily, steering consciously or unconsciously towards that peace of mind "which passeth all under-standing," and which is the crown of the constant practice of knowledge and virtue. Alas ! How difficult it is for the man of the world, the man · of the. Gujili,[1] to enjoy peace of mind for even one minute! How that long desired repose eludes our grasp like fairy gold! While wealth comes and goes, while youth leaves us stranded on the shore, while old age threatens us with its fallen jaw and a fearful prospect when that peace is most needed. You cannot see people in London, and you should not see, for, says Washington Irving, they are literally in the market, and with them time is money. We poor men have time to gather the fallen leaves, but hardly time to burn them in winter and have a little fireside. "I had been for six months in Italy," says Ruskin, "never for a single moment quit of liability to interruption of thought by day or night whenever I was awake. In the streets of every city there are entirely monstrous and inhuman noises in perpetual recurrence —the violent rattle of carriages driven habitually in brutal and senseless haste, creaking and thundering under loads too great for their cattle, urged on by perpetual roars and shouts; the bellowing and howling of obscene wretches far into the night, clashing with the Church-bells in the morning dashed into wreckless discord from twenty towers at once, as if naughty devils to defy and destroy the quiet of God's sky and mock the loss of His harmony; filthy, stridulous shrieks and squeaks reaching for miles around into the quiet air from the rail road stations at every gate; and the vociferation and legs and frantic noise of a passing populace whose every word was in mean passion or in unclean jest." How pathetic in the same strain is

---

[1] The Madras market where stolen and other miscellaneous articles find a sale.

the complaint of Schopenhauer against the dust in the
road and the reckless noise in the streets under the
friction of elbowing! The thoughtful man wants repose;
and many a time and oft has retired into the forest or
hid himself in the cave, to have a single hour under the
calm sky, to roam "retired like noon-tide dew"—leaving
the noisy world to itself—near the running brooks
"murmuring a music sweeter than their own," and to
try with all a Guru's grace to retreat more within himself
without either eyes or ears, himself his world and his
own God. How many a Bharata has descended from
his throne in the midst of regal enjoyment for the quiet
air of heaven and the quieter retreat into the inner
world! To conquer this kingdom behind the curtain, to
gain this dominion of the Self is the final aim, the
summum bonum of life.

This, however, being very difficult of attainment,
it is necessary that there should be steps leading to this
sanctum sanctorum. I cannot ask my innocent old
grand-mother or my busy domestic wife to retreat all at
once into her internal Self; that requires a warrior's
strength and more than a warrior's courage. What
do you think stands between them and their empire,
reader? Remember Nanda's tale elsewhere told, and
its moral. There are Viran, Irulan, Katteri, Verian,
Nondi, Chamundi, and a whole host of aboriginal deities
with big bellies and difficult appetites. Nay, not merely
they. Go to the same story again; we are slaves;
Nanda, Ananda, this sportive *Atman* playing within
its prison like a calf leaping to the length of its tether,
is a Pariah slave. He has his master to obey and kinsmen to fear: and how many masters have we? How

many passions mocking us at every turn, opening loose
our coat, though we are trying to button and close it
up to the chin, and robbing us every moment of our
master's cap! Our belly is a great monitor, the agricultural god that we have to feed. We make all sorts
of noise and keep up this world of strife; and ourselves
die in the midst of the fray, sweating and bleeding
desperately—our place taken by another whose way is
exactly similar: such being the case, how difficult it
is for us to attain without a ladder to the peace of
Heaven!

Have you ever contemplated, serious reader, upon
the diversity that exists around you, the infinity that
confronts you on every side, the multitude of lives
visible and invisible that live in the water, that float
in the air, that enter into your nostrils, that flow in
your veins, that people the starry heavens—what an
infinite multitude, what a desperate diversity, so that
Sri Krishna himself said: "*Nanthosti mama divyanam
vibhutinam Parantapa*"—There is no end to my wealth
phenomenal, O my friend Arjuna! You or I cannot
describe it. Why! Comparing that multitude to an
ocean, the ocean is a speck in that infinity, but we are
obliged to talk by our own play-things: take that
infinity as an ocean, take a wave, take its crowning
froth, take the top thereof, nay, take therein a particular atom; in that atom is folded up this whole mass
of humanity. Consider that mass at present and look
into the vast variety that exists there. We do not
know if the bear differs from the man, more than one
man from another. From an Iago, who could not
endure the happiness or virtue of others, to a Buddha,

whose heart was melting with abundant flow of love to
all mankind and whose only object was the advancement of human virtue; from Dame Darkmans, the
cynical philosopher who wished everything to be turned
to dust and ashes, to Francis de Assissi, to whom the
nightingale was a sister and the lark a brother; from
the raging pestilential witch that wanted every marriage
to be turned into a funeral and regarded more the funeral
cakes than the marriage *Bhuri* (gift), to a Sankara,
whose love to the world was spontaneous like the light
of the moon, who could approach the leper cast off by
the village and, finding in him the qualities for discipleship, confer upon him the highest good, the blessing
of divine instruction; from a daring and intriguing
Lady Macbeth to a gentle philanthropic Miss Florence
Nightingale; from the cunning courtfool with motley
gear pandering to his belly like a pig to Sri Krishna,
who could change a hero's melancholy into philosophical
solace and purge the illusion of self by the vision of the
Brahmin going round the fire—what an infinite variety
of characters, which Shakespeares, Scotts, Kalidasas
and Kambans cannot sufficiently do justice to; what
permutation and combination of a few apparently
simple qualities rendered complex for the artist and
philosopher. Oh God! How rich is Thy wealth; how
abundant the variety of Thy manifestation; what a
field for working out past *Karma* (the result of past
action); and with all that, what singular unity! So
that if any religion were possible for all, a common underlying net work of principles becomes also possible, and
a vast complex religion may safely be built upon the
rock of that foundation impregnable for all time.

Religion is an essential factor of human progress, a necessary element in society. "Man has structural relation," says Kant, "with three things, God, world and soul." He cannot escape these. They hunt him wherever he may be. He may hide himself in soft-pillowed leather cushions, he may shelter himself under the laughing lips of women, or he may ascend mountain-like peacock thrones; but wherever he may be, as the sky always is above him and envelops him, so does this problem of life and death. It haunts him like a night-mare and presses for solution. A solution he must give even from the lap of his lady-love, even from the Sandwich islands, even from the solitudes of the forest, even on mountain-like peacock thrones.

Agnosticism is only a passage in human progress. It marks the transition stage where superstitious early faith is about to be changed to philosophical religion. Nature gives sound blows; and the child diet of a Mellin's Food of an unscientific belief ceases to satisfy. But progress is not destruction but building up. So through this process of Agnosticism which is nothing but the destruction of unquestioning faith, religion will get scientifically erected up into philosophy. Doubt is the interval between the morning breakfast and the late dinner. The newly built High Court[1] tower has to be tested by artificial battery or natural storm, and then alone may the judges safely hold their sittings there. Similarly, when the dear child is dying before one's face and prayers avail not, when the beautiful wife is suddenly transformed into an ugly leper, when the

[1] At Madras.

Huzur Sheristadar finds himself suddenly dismissed for no apparent cause, when the world appears inimical, sinful and unjust, when a Kuchela struggles for livelihood with a battalion of naked children and a half-clad wife, and while Ravana enjoys a mountain-like golden palace and controls the spheres—and physical science seems to account for creation and destruction by its laws of matter and energy—doubt arises. It might often culminate in despair and suicide. But killing is no ending. Only the curtain falls, the scene changes, and the hero appears dressed up in a new fashion—that is all. You may doubt the existence of God and live in it for some time. But you, who cannot long doubt whether your young Amy returns your love in spring time or not, can you long doubt if you have a soul to save? No! Huxley did not die a sceptic. Indeed, scepticism cannot be a religion; and though "honest doubt is better than half the creeds," it is not itself one. Young Amy's hair is turned to grey in spite of the doctor's drugs. Youthful Locksley's blood is down once again. God again comes for a share in his heart. Young Amy, young no more, is too shrivelled to occupy that cavity. Nature administers good whipping; many an evil comes and goes; there is a knock against the knavish pate, a curse against the day that brought him down, when Amy takes to a gilded fool. Adversity is yet a toad having a precious gem in its head, and that gem is philosophy. Social science was studied in youth and other sciences in manhood, but these are not enough. Some day the warrant comes and the knock is heard at the door. "*Duk kring karane*" (grammar) does not save. Another science has to be sought after. God

5

is its teacher and God is its reward. Is not religion
necessary now? Thank God there is a belly here, the
God Ganesh, that nature has a whip and death comes
for a share of your heart. "Blessed are they that mourn,
for they shall be comforted." "Blessed are the poor
in spirit for theirs is the Kingdom of Heaven."

Religion thus being a necessity, and shades of human
character being too infinite for even a Shakespeare or
a Raphael, it necessarily follows that there must be
different grades for different men, crutches of different
lengths for men of different heights, different rungs in the
ladder of spiritual progress all connected and held
together by a firm philosophy which stands as their
common basis and supports them for all eternity.
When young, we thought that as the propositions of
Euclid are one and the same for all mankind—though
some knock their heads in vain against the deductions—
so, if there should be a religion, it should be common
to all mankind. The difference is that geometry is not a
matter of human aptitudes, there are no tendencies in
it, it is all exact like the laws of astronomy or physical
science. The law of gravitation is the same for the
Yogi and the ordinary man. Moonlight is innocent of
the distinction of rich and poor. But one kind of wife
will not suit all the world : one man wants her to be
black, another wants her to be noisy and quarrelsome,
a third desires her to be effeminate and modest, a fourth
requires her to wear stockings all day long and talk
nothing but English. A mother does not suit the fancy
of all her children. Likewise, religion is a matter of
mind ; there is no exactness in it except in its final
philosophy. Even in the roads there is considerable

difference, and that is why a Guru is so seriously insisted upon.

Some over-wise men think that their intellect is their Guru, or that the impersonal God is their Guru. But when they enter into the awful solitude of the narrow way, when they climb the steep ascent swimming against the gravitation of the earth, when the loneliness of the path, its pitfalls and dangers and snares and sphinx-questions begin to be suspected, then the necessity for a Guru will be apparent. The warrior requires a charioteer. Until then the over-wise man is half a fool wishing to "rush in where angels fear to tread."

So then, different grades of religion, or rather different religions cemented together by one common philosophy and recognising their bond of unity being necessary, it becomes next clear that these various grades differ in their tendencies, each however leading to its next higher. It may be asked, how is this possible ? How can one religion be connected with another and where is the possibility of a common philosophy ? And if such a philosophy be possible, what are its fundamentals ? To take a simile—we are not to travel far, our India is rich enough in illustrations—the Northern Hindi·speaking Bania is in some respects a different man from the Malayalam-talking Nambudri ; but between these races of North and South, the rich Parsis of the Western coast and the poor fishermen of the Coromandel, there is still a common bond through political affinity, homage to the same philosophy and homage to a common sacred literature ; the Ganges is the common propei y of the whole race, the Himalayas are the pride of all the country ; Rameswaram has its

devotees from the snowy hills to the Southern çape.
Thayumanavar chants the Upanishads in Tamil ;
Sankara preaches them in Sanskrit ; Buddha takes his
transmigration theory from the Vedas ; and even the
Fire-worship of the Parsis is nothing unknown to ancient
Rishis. The fisherman who suddenly loses his child
comforts himself with the same doctrine of *Karma* as
the *Sanyasin* of Benares. The Congress is a common
institution of modern days. The Muhammadan Akbar
rendered the Srutis into Arabic ; and the Indian
Mastan is not far different from the retired Yogi. So
then, India, peopled as it is with a vast variety of races,
has yet a nation with common sympathies and common
interests.

Similarly, the dread Maruthaiviran, who killed with
his legendary axe one thousand persons in the course of
a single night (the English soldier is requested to laugh
in his sleeve), has a close kinship with the Jesus of
Nazareth, the Allah of the Koran, the Krishna of the
Gita and the Vishnu of the milky sea.

1. They are all of them gods.

2. They are all worshipped.

3. Man has hopes in the possibility of being saved
by them.

4. All the worshippers want to be saved from the
misery of the world. Only, one thinks that he alone
will be saved, and that even for that he will have to
wait till the Judgment Day ; another thinks that he
could be saved only by a multitude of black-eyed girls ;
a third thinks that without the honour of moustaches,
sharp steel axes and high-heeled shoes, there can be no
God ; another thinks that unless a virgin could bring

forth a child, there would be no salvation for any one
on earth ; another thinks that unless his God could love
ten thousand and three women and be in all their houses
at the same time, there could be no *Moksha* ; another
yet thinks that unless his God sleeps, the world could
not get on for one moment. By the way the true
Vedantin has an odd humour in him like the man in the
story who cried *Bebbebe* to everyone that came to him.
He can enjoy as a spectator the big drama of the
world, he not being the stage king or an imitation
fool. To every thing in common he has a nod of assent.
Maruthaiviran must have high-heeled shoes, he says,
for

Yatha pasyati chakshubhyam tat tadatmeti bhavayet....
The high-heeled shoes, the whiskered figure that walks
upon them are both God, he says. And if Mahavishnu
sleeps on the milky sea, he says, it has a splendid inner
meaning (for which see Part II). Krishna, he adds, is
bound to be imprisoned in all lovers' hearts alike, and
so on.

But it is difficult to be so impartial. The Muhammadan wants his Houris and Houris alone. The
Vaishnavite wants his God to wear *Pulvis Alba* alone.
It is all the story of the blind men that saw the elephant.
A child thinks that sugar is the sweetest thing in the
world, another the mango, a third a silk cloth, a fourth
the car festival, and so on. All want something sweet.
They are all agreed on that one thing. It is the same
with these men. They all want to be saved but each
wants his own Heaven.

5. All want somehow to leave this wicked world

soon. Some say that Satan came and disturbed it. Others say we reap what we sowed.

6. All believe in their own immortality. All the world may die, but John Bull and Virasami have faith in their own eternity.

7. All believe that sin is bad and that virtue alone is good, though it is difficult for most men to do as they feel.

8. All agree in thinking, though our fishermen are not distinctly conscious of it, that the evils of the world are due to selfishness, and that, if the self be destroyed, the root of the misery is cut down.

9. All, superstitiously or otherwise, fall at the feet of men who have cast off their little selves and risen as pillars to Heaven.

10. No man finds it possible to live long without a religion, though he represents his God with a big turban, or with a silvery beard, or as laughing on the peacock, or dancing with a flute, or sleeping on the milky sea, or contemplating on the silver mountains, or mourning on the cross, or lisping in His virgin mother's arms. All these are true to the Vedantin to whom nothing in this God-ruled world is out of placé. Only, some men are looking at the sun from the wells that they have sunk, others from the pits in which they are hiding themselves, others with yellow-coloured eyes, others yet from up-stair houses, others through windows and glass panes, others from balloons and flying machines, a few with telescopes on Fesole heights, and a few others with flowers mixed with water at the birthplace of the Ganges on the never-dying Himalayas, uttering there the *Mantra* of *mantras*, the *Gayatri* (the Indian prayer).

How there are different stages and how through all of them there runs a unity of Godhead as a string in a pearl garland, to use Sri Krishna's phrase, is a subject which we reserve for a future occasion.

————————

HINDUISM AND RELIGIOUS EVOLUTION

ALL religions, however different they may be in the rituals they insist on, the doctrines they preach, and the promises they hold forth to humanity, have among them a large number of common elements, which, as we have seen, constitute their essence, and which, on that account, render their comparison with one another possible. A river has little in common with a mountain, and cannot therefore be compared with it. But one river and another can well be compared. Likewise, religions, on account of their common essence, admit of comparison with one another. Indeed, they merely relate to different stages of human evolution, and have each its place and value in the spiritual economy of the world. We shall not, however, enter here into any offensive comparison of particular religions, but shall content ourselves with indicating the general principles of religious evolution and determining in their light the place of Hinduism. Speaking from the evolutionary standpoint, we shall see that Hinduism is one of the most comprehensive and most highly evolved religions, and that it is, on that account, the religion of that highest of philosophies—the Vedanta.

Religions may roughly be classified into four groups ; one, inculcating fear ; another, teaching love, but love for earthly rewards or heavenly enjoyment ; the third, teaching love pure and simple, without any bargaining ; and the fourth, insisting on Knowledge or Wisdom as an end in itself. It is not, however, for one moment suggested that these groups stand out separately marked out in actual life. The element of fear predominates in some religions, love in some, and knowledge in others. In the majority of religions all these elements are simultaneously present, though combined in different proportions.

The second of the four groups—that which relates to bargaining love—is the one which commonly prevails as religion. The love in the second and the third may, each in its way, be divided into love for the human race or the brother, and love towards God or the Father. In Buddhism, love for the neighbour seems more insisted upon than love towards God. In Christianity on the other hand, we have an equipoise, as it were ; man and God each claiming an equal share of the human heart, though, in practice, their claims are not perhaps often as well heeded as desirable. In popular Hinduism too, there is a similar equipoise ; but, we are talking without any prejudice whatever, the balance is a little more firmly adjusted, though our religion is far from being perfect. The innumerable *Chattrams* in the land ; the numberless towers that newly rise with joy toward heaven every year—by the way, Ruskin asks : 'How many cathedrals have you built, O Englishmen, since St. Paul's ? Is there any ratio between them and your manufactories ?'[1]—the habit of feeding crows and other birds before dinner ; the veneration paid to the cow and other animals ; and a very strong faith in private first-hand and unquestioning, though often indiscriminate, charity, prevailing in our land—supported as it is with

---

[1] These are not his very words.

the wholesome superstition that God, who came down on earth to enslave a Brahmin, and convert, with a mango, a pious *Vaisya* woman into a saint,[1] might be among the beggars in human form—and the long lists of saints, *Bhaktas*, philosophers and *Rishis*, beginning from time immemorial and happily not yet ended : all these eloquently testify to the fact that the love to man, to lower animals, and to God, preached by the great men of old, is not wholly dead in the Hindu heart.

The first of the four groups in the classification above given, namely, the religion of fear, is the beginning of all religion. The awe-inspiring miracle of thunder and lightning ; the rich and pompous heraldry of the heavens ; the stars, the eyes of heaven 'glistening from above with immortal pity for the lot of man ;' the awful solitude of the midnight hour which turns even atheists into God-fearing men ; the noisy cataract that makes a dreadful music at bed time ; the lonely ocean that rolls on wave after wave, symbolising the purposeless struggle on earth, and, as a melancholy Jacques would have said, weeping in a voice worthy of the Himalayas, as if its sorrowful roar would represent the noise of the huge market of the world ; the traditions of Hells burning like furnaces and spreading 'a fiery deluge fed with ever-burning sulphur unconsumed ;' the stories of accursed souls flitting across the air and even knocking at the doors of houses at midnight, in the shape of legless ghosts ; the conception that there is a dark whiskered Yama (Death) sitting on a throne and adjudging, or a Chitragupta writing accounts of our actions, or a God on high

[1] The reference is to the lives of two Saivite saints, Sundara and Karaikkalammai.

holding the scales in his hand ready for judgment; the selfishness, the pomp, the vanity, and the wickedness, of the world: all drive poor man, even in our 'present leaden age,' to seek refuge in God; and often, when the hand is about to take the sword for murder, the vicious nerve that prompted the deed trembles with fear. This fear is the beginning of all knowledge. The river runs its silent course heedless of man; fire burns with a vigour which comes, he cannot say whence; the earthquake shakes cities; volcanoes destroy the work of ages: man fears and trembles. There is a God everywhere, he says; *Riks* he sings, one to Fire, one to Water, one to Air, in Azteç or Sanskrit as the case may be; a fetich is put up, a hymn is sung: religion begins, knowledge commences. The poor fisherman, who eats from hand to mouth, has built a new boat, and is about to launch it into the black waters: he burns camphor as incense; and a corresponding bottle of liquor is offered as sacrifice to Varuna, the God of the Sea. Here is fetichism, if you please; but that is religion or the germs of it, its protoplasm. This is the first part of Hinduism—the first rung of the ladder.

This same fear, however, leads to love. No man can long be content with a terrible bearded God sitting with an axe in His hand, 'beside a river of nectar, careless of mankind.' We want a Father, a merciful Father, who would look after our interests, hear our prayers, and redress our grievances. We want him to be loving, not to be always Maruthaiviran, but to be Minakshi, or Kamakshi, or Rama, or Krishna, and have a fair face, at least, for those that do good. And as love and sympathy are the best means of approaching our neighbour, so sympathy and love alone can reveal to us God, 'the work of whose fingers is the heavens, the moon and the stars, which He has ordained all for man.'

Love is at first selfish and low ; and man, seeking refuge from fear, begins with praying humbly for his own safety and 'for the subjection of his foes.' He says : "Lord, how long shall the wicked triumph ! By the blast of God they perish and by the breath of His nostrils are they consumed !" But it is soon found out that the motive of vengeance is a bad *Karma* (action), that 'curses come home like chickens to roost'. We had been to Chidambaram, where we saw a woman, who had bathed in a tank and had offended the municipal gods by washing her cloths in the water, sincerely pray ing to her Kambattadimurugan (an image carved on a pillar) that the guards of the tank should be severely chastised, if it be true that God resided within the pillar. A very good religion that, comfortable and human ; Renan said : "If you want a God, it must be human." But when a glimpse of the virtuous God is once obtained, His martyrdom on the cross, His holy and eternal sacrifice of Himself, or His silent and beneficent con- templation under the Bo-tree, tears start from men's eyes, the heart that brooded vengeance is softened for ever, and the tongue that wanted the punishment of the enemy now prays for pardon, and in the midst of burning fire the martyr cries aloft to Heaven : "O Lord, let not this sin be laid to the account of my persecutors, it is not their fault."

Incense goes up to heaven, not merely for the subjection of foes, but also for the granting of boons. "The poor, the sickly, the pious, and the wise seek for me," said Sri Krishna (Gita, VII, 16). At least one half of the seekers really bargain with God. The young student who wishes to pass his examination, breaks cocoanuts in the temple. A dying peasant in England said to his Bible-woman, "At your request I believe in Christ, and he, as a gentleman, will, I have no doubt, keep his word, and grant me Heaven." This kind of 'milking the gods,' however, ceases when a glimpse of God is obtained. The child Dhruva, when he saw God and his glory, cared not to ask for a seat on his father's lap, the first object of his penance. Bartering with God is the religion of the majority of the Hindu mother, when she hangs her little cradle, that that God, who blessed her with a child, might sleep there in the night ; and of the ancient sage like Hebrew who prayed for the crushing of his foes, as well as the Christian who carried the palm tree to Palestine and the Muhammadan who prays day and night with beads for the possession of the damsels in Heaven. This is the second part of Hinduism.

The third part is pure love, the result of having felt however dimly, the sweetness of the Lord conceived either as an old man with a silvery beard, or a young girl beautifully decorated with diamonds, or in any other manner. It may here be remarked that idolatry is the prevalent religion of the human race. Our eyes are naturally turned outside, and it requires an effort to turn our vision inward. "Until you get hold of the highest absolute God in his formless form," says a great sage, "you cannot afford to throw overboard religions and their conceptions of God." "In the Word (the Vedas), in the Word's end (the Vedanta), in the Srutis

of that Vedanta, in the ever-stainless *Chitakas*, in the
hearts of those who have inquired and of the lovers,
resides, my dear God," says Pattanattuppillai (a great
Tamil philosopher), "and not in stone and copper, as
the ignorant suppose." But the same Pattanattuppillai
sings of the raised foot, the bent hand, and the third
eye of Nataraja. No contradiction. The religion of the
majority is essentially idolatrous; and even to such a
refined philosopher as Pillai, the image has its value.[1]
Indeed, idolatry has not been more severely condemned
in any other country than in India; and it may be
added that the abstracted space of earth, water, air, or
sky, or worse, the utter nothingness that does duty for
God in the mind of the iconoclastic Protestant, is really
a more mischievous form of idolatry than that of our
country. God is not space, anything more than He is
gold, or silver. The conception of God varies according
to the mental aptitudes of the worshippers. "In whatever way men worship me, even so I appear unto them."
(Gita, IV. 11). Love, especially the unreflecting and
pure love we are now speaking of, though idolatrous
in its early stage, is elevating; and the picture of Radha,
the amorous Radha, adorned with golden bangles and
jewels, her face speaking the divinest grief, waiting with
flowers in her hands on the Jumna sands, waiting for
the silk-clad dancing Krishna with his favourite flute,
and knowing not the hours as they passed on, is beautiful
enough and inspiring, even when taken literally.

To take another example of high and disinterested
love : there was once a great man, now a saint, who

---

[1] For its meaning, See Part II, Symbology—Nataraja.

meditated on Sri Krishna as his pet child, mentally bought for him a golden cradle, sang midnight lyrics over that fancy cradle, and wept in woman's dress that Devaki sent forth her golden child, born flute in hand, over the dark Jumna floods which parted when the prisoner father carried him over to Yasoda's palace. To take another instance : there was a flower girl, a Brahmin by birth, who declined all her suitors and insisted on marrying Vengadava (God Vishnu) of the Northern hills ; such was the intensity of her love that she dreamt that Lord Madhava entered her chamber and married her with great pomp, and waking found her dream realised—not concretely of course ; and unto this day the idol at Srivilliputur, her native place, enters the house of her descendants once a year, resides there for a day like a veritable son-in-law, and returns home with a rich dowry of pumpkins red and white, plantain leaves, and big copper and bronze vessels. This is Hinduism of a type, let nobody dare despise it.

Higher or lower comes a royal saint, who is willing to lose all his kingdoms, if only for the bliss of being born in the Tirupati hills as a fish in a pond which pious *Bhaktas* might feed on, or as a stone at the temple gate which devotees might walk over and crush down ; he would die to be the necklace of Vishnu, or his conch, or bow. Such love as the following lines,

> It is the miller's daughter,
> And she is grown so dear, so dear
> That I would be the jewel
> That trembles in her ear :
> For hid in ringlets day and night,
> I'd touch her neck so warm and white.

so beautifully picture, is possible towards a much higher and a more beautiful Being than the miller's daughter. One devotee looked upon God as his most intimate friend, and played with Him, and even blamed Him in the familiarity of his love. Another regarded Him as his father, and would do nothing else than obey His will and do His bidding. Narada says : "Attachment through glory, attachment through duty, attachment through worship, attachment as a servant, attachment as a friend, attachment as beloved, attachment as self-sacrifice, attachment by identification, attachment by misery in separation, as in the case of lovers, thus the one love takes eleven modes." (Sutra 82).

However various the forms, in essence love is one and the same ; and to the lover, the world ordained by God whether as father, mother, friend, or child, is divine. The heart, that truly loves sees Him and Him alone in all the world. The crow is God, its croaking is God, the evening sun is God, the parrots as they play on the peepul-tree are God, the bees that hum on the river side are God, the leper that suffers is God, the whole world is transformed into the Lord by the alchemy of love. Henceforth there is left in the heart only the milk of human kindness, love to the neighbour and love to God. It is of this love that Narada says : "Love cannot be made to fulfil desires, for its nature is renunciation." (Sutra 7). Again it is said : "Love is surrendering all actions to God and feeling the greatest misery in forgetting Him."

When the celestial heights of love above described are reached, higher peaks become visible and have to be climbed. The epithets, father, mother, lover, child, and others, applied to God, do not satisfy. In all these there *is* a veil of partition between God and man, however thin, which the lover can no longer endure. He must become one with his love ; he must become Love itself. The definition of love, in this its highest sense, is, "it is the unbroken feeling of the Universal self in one's own self." Here and here alone does the Personal become the Impersonal ; here and not before does idolatry truly cease ; here it is that Love is Light, and Light is Love.

Thus does love lead to Wisdom, the highest grade in the classification we started with. Wisdom or merging into God is a very rare privilege, before attaining which the whole ocean of *Maya* has to be traversed, the curtain of ignorance to be torn to pieces, the Isis behind the veil to be realised. The *Gnani* alone, of all men, knows God as He *is*—"the perfect infinite spirit who is like the sun after darkness, than whom nothing is greater, nothing more subtle and nothing older." (Sweta. Up., III. 8—9). The very ground on which such a wise man sits is sacred ; his foot-prints are worth all the spheres that roll in the heavens ; his service to humanity is more than the service of the Himalayas or the sky, it is the service of God himself. "The preservation of one human soul from perdition," says the Talmud, "is equal to such a meritorious work as if one had preserved the whole world with all its beautiful creations." And how many souls does not a *Gnani* save by the silent magic of his sanctity. To save even one man for ever from the miseries of the phenomenal world is much more valuable than building a multitude of hospitals for the sick or *Chattrams* for the poor, for disease and hunger constantly recur and can never be fully removed. The whole

6

universe is within the *Gnani's* heart, the whole but without the disturbance of name and form, all glory, all silence, eternal, and peaceful. "To attain to this state of blessedness," says a sage, "I would pant like a calf for its missing mother, and would cry 'O Father, O Lord, O my beloved Lord, come, come and embrace me and make me yours'."

We have now traversed over the whole area of Hinduism, though in a brief and superficial manner. Hinduism is satisfying ; it has the elements of fear towards God and love, and what is more, it is true light, it is realisation. One step leads to another ; a connected ladder it is, a veritable Jacob's ladder from earth to heaven. It is universal and extremely well adapted to all the stages of human evolution ; and that is why it is so tolerant and so receptive. Had Christ been born in India, he would have found a place in the list of the *Avatars*. Mary of Catholicism has in the South almost become Mariammal. And Miran of Nagore (Tanjore Dt : South India), is already the common property of both the Hindus and the Muhammadans. The fisherman that prays to the Ocean God for the safety of himself and his new boat, with liquor bottle and camphor, has religious kinship with the *Rishi* who prays on the banks of the Sindhu (the Indus) saying : "O God, grant light unto me, illumine my mind as the sun, Thy viceroy, illumines the world"—the same *Mantra* that ages ago our ancient fathers uttered on the monarch of mountains, the same that the Brahmin is taught to repeat to-day, the prayer that asks not for bread, or money, or for a night's shelter, or for the subjection of foes, but for the abounding Light of Heaven which shines all inside, for the 'impulses of a deeper birth' that come is solitude. Hinduism is realisation from beginning to end, it is philosophy applied ; and of the genuine cultured Hindu it may well be said :

> In common things that round us lie,
> Some random truths he can impart ;
> The harvest of a quiet eye,
> That broods and sleeps in his own heart.

Here, in this privilege of feeling and realising God conceived as He might be, according to various mental aptitudes, either as a fetich, or father, or *Atman*, is Hinduism, the religion of the Vedanta.

THE UNIVERSALITY OF THE VEDANTA

WE have seen that religion is a constitutional necessity with man, that it is not possible for him to pull on for a long time in this world of strife without conscious relationship with God. We have also seen that one common religion will not suit all mankind, and that, with increasing knowledge of man's growth and tendencies, all dreams of a universal religion appear more and more chimerical. Religions have to differ according to different stages of human evolution ; but these, different religions may, as has been already hinted, be well cemented together into a compact whole by the power of a liberal and comprehensive philosophy.

Hinduism is really a very peculiar religion : it is, as we have seen, one of the most highly evolved of all religions, and, at the same time, the most conglomerate perhaps. It has eaten up almost all the great religions, and has assimilated with itself their best parts. It was said of Vali, the great monkey-chief of the Ramayana, that he had the peculiar power of drawing to himself half the strength of his foes, and thereby defeating them. A similar thing may well be said of Hinduism. Great and noble religions came in contact with it ; but it has devoured them all, as the magic rod of Moses did the serpents of the Egyptian sorcerers. Says Monier Williams : "It may with truth be asserted that no description of Hinduism can be exhaustive which does not touch on almost every religious and philosophical idea that the world has ever known. Starting from the Veda,

Hinduism has ended in embracing something from all religions; and in presenting phases suited to all minds. It is all-tolerant, all-compliant, all-comprehensive, all-absorbing. It has its spiritual and its material aspect, its esoteric and exoteric, its subjective and objective, its rational and irrational, its pure and its impure. It may be compared to a huge polygon, or irregular multilateral figure. It has one side for the practical, another for the severely moral, another for the devotional and imaginative, another for the sensuous and sensual, and another for the philosophical and speculative. Those who rest in ceremonial observances find it all-sufficient ; those who deny the efficacy of works, and make faith the one requisite, need not wander from its pale ; those who are addicted to sensual objects may have their tastes gratified ; those who delight in meditating on the nature of God and man, the relation of matter and spirit, the mystery of separate existence, and the origin of evil, may here indulge their love of speculation." It has been growing for centuries, nay ages, and is still a compact organism, though huge, with an infinite capacity to expand. In spite of its numerous imperfections, its officious, and too often mischievous, interference with society, and its lazy conservatism, it has,—at least in theory, often also in practice—the unity of Godhead of Christianity, Muhammadanism, and other monotheistic religions, all the ethical perfection of Buddhism, all the liberty of thought of Agnosticism, all or all that is practicable in the charity of Socialism, and all the love and respect for humanity which Positivism has ; nay more, for in its eyes humanity itself is Divinity. Really a huge structure is this Hinduism ; and to the superficial observer it is simply incoherent and mad ; but when one looks into it closely, one discovers that there is 'a method in its madness,' and that its heart-beats are surprisingly rhythmic and sound.

But whence this health ? And what gives to it its compactness, receptivity, and many-sidedness ? What kind of spirit is it that pervades through this monster fabric of a religion enlivening it from top to bottom ? Is it the spirit of nationality or the bond of a common language, which unites together its various parts ? No, it is the spirit of the philosophy on which it rests. Hinduism really is not one religion, it is a number of religions, a galaxy of spiritual lights knit together, 'like a swarm of fire-flies tangled in a silver braid,' by an immortal and all-embracing philosophy. It is a veritable Parliament of Religions, where different creeds have met together, in fraternal kinship and republican equality, under the guidance and support of a liberal and paternal philosophy. This philosophy is, our readers need not be told, the Vedanta, which can as we shall see, knit together not merely the different members of Hinduism, but all the religions of the world.

The Vedanta is essentially çatholic, because it re-cognises more than any other philosophy the grand and universal law of evolution, 'which none can stay nor stem.' Man is its study, man who develops from the brute into God. It takes hold of him from his earliest starting-point and unfolds to him his fullest possibilities. The most primitive and barbarous section of mankind is not too low for its notice, and the highest possible realisation of Divinity is the end which it promises to all alike. Its range is therefore the widest possible ;

and as every man has his religion, however grotesque, primitive, and barbarous, all the religions of the world, from the lowest fetichism to the highest *Brahmagnana*, came within its pale. The religion of fear, the religion of love, and the religion of light, all fall within its scope. Its mission is to take up man just where he is, and lead him onward, inspiring him with hope and filling him with such light as his mind could grasp. "Order and progress" is its watchword. The snake-worshipper who thinks that the serpent is the only God, is told that the serpent is God ; but, as that God must be omnipresent and all-wise, he is gradually led on to believe that the serpent is only one of the many symbols by which He may be worshipped. One step further : the symbol is forgotten, or obtains an esoteric meaning, acceptable even to the philosopher, and the thing symbolised becomes all in all. Similarly again, if a man begins with taking a fancy for adorning his God with skulls and beads, he is told that his fancy representation signifies the highest, the mightiest, and the most beneficent Being, and that the skulls and the beads have an inner and beautiful signification ; and thus gradually God gets better of the idol.

The above is exactly the process by which it was possible for Pariahs like Nanda, Tiruppan and others, to grow into saints. The fullest possibilities are presented to every one, irrespective of his particular caste and creed ; and that is how in the grand religious republic of the Vedanta, Brahmins often get degraded into fetich-worshippers, and men of the lowest castes come up as saints and sages and command the worship of all the country. The Brahmin saint, Sundara, sang : "I am the slave of the slaves, of the potter Tirunila,[1] shepherd Anaya, the hunter Kannappa, the oil-monger Kaliya, and the *Chandala* Nanda ;" and the majority of the Vaishnavite saints, whose praises are chanted forth every day by Brahmin lips at Srirangam, come from castes the members of which were worshippers of demoniac gods or hideous images ; and even to-day, how easily has it been possible for many a low caste Hindu to shake off his clan worship and rise to higher regions of spiritual realisation. In the United States, every man, no matter what his profession, has the liberty to hope that he might one day be the President of the United States, provided he has the capacity and good fortune required. An exactly similar freedom prevails in India in the religious sphere, however hard may be the caste restrictions ; and it is open for barbers and washermen to push on towards the realisation of *Atmagnana* if only they have the mental capacity for it. The process by which such an evolution becomes possible is extremely mild and natural, and is worthy of conscious imitation, especially by foreign missionaries. The Vedanta does not convert, but makes the man grow for himself, by simply presenting the living and grand ideal. The examples of perfected men exercise a silent influence upon the whole community, and instil into every man, irrespective of caste or profession, the hope of himself becoming one. The result is, from the Pariah to the Brahmin, every one aspires in his own humble way for religious realisation through one or other of the four ancient great methods, *Karma, Bhakti, Yoga,* and

[1] Saivite saints.

Gnana, according to his mental aptitude and capacity. The spirit is throughout the same, however different may be its manifestations, and throughout there is an eager and hopeful looking forward towards the ideal of liberation (*Moksha*).

A peculiarity of the Vedanta, which undoubtedly contributes to its universality, is that it has a strong faith in the Providential government of the universe, in the omniscience of the immanent Power that resides in the world ; consequently, it never hastily condemns anything, but draws attention to the good that may be in it. It has an unshakable faith in slow and natural growth, and seeks to correct, not by force, but by the silent magic of grand and powerful ideals. To take an example : flesh-eating is a prevalent vice among mankind ; the Vedanta preaches kindness and love towards lower animals, and strongly condemns flesh-eating ; and many sects have accordingly totally abstained from this relic of barbarism ; but it must take a long time for all mankind to become vegetarian in its diet. And till then, the Vedanta says to the flesh-eating Sudra, "friend, if you are so fond of meat let the animals you kill be an offering to your God before becoming your food." The advantage is, a new idea is brought in, which will have its own wholesome effect, until the example of the higher castes could prevail against this barbarous custom. Even the Indian robber differs in some peculiar respects from his brethren of other countries : he never starts out on his holy pilgrimage without solemnly praying to his gods ; and a portion of his plunder invariably goes to the deity. One day or other, the robber realises that his profession is not exactly the best that could be thought of, and that he will have to suffer for his sins, not only here but also hereafter. The God-idea 'then grows upon him and induces him to retire from the field, a sadder but a wiser man. The great Vaishnavite saint, Tirumangai Alwar, was in his *Purvasrama* (before he became a *Bhakta*) a robber. He had a genius for robbing and was a veteran in the trade; he had a large following and was deservedly notorious. On a certain dark midnight, he was within the walls of the great temple of Srirangam, robbing the sleeping God Ranganatha. Silk umbrellas, silver utensils, golden thrones, diamond necklaces were all helped out of the temple; but a gold ring on Ranganatha's toe remained tempting the infatuated robber. He tried his utmost to force it out, but it would not come, and he was determined not to leave it. His teeth were employed to bite it out, and while thus struggling, he felt or fancied he felt blood oozing out of the toe, and lo! there stood Ranganatha before him in all His glory. The robber drew back, and at once broke out in a glorious hymn to Narayana, one of the very best in Tamil literature. The spoils of his night's adventure were all returned; and the robber who would dacoit Ranganatha became a *Bhakta*, and built His temple—the one which still stands. The Divine Thief (*Taskaranampati*) got the better of the human thief.

This is how the Vedanta works: whatever was, was necessary, it says; and sympathy is the secret of its success. It condemns no man as accursed, gives up none as hopeless, but embraces all mankind within its fold, trusting to the silent work of time, the unfaltering law of *Karma*, and the power of living ideals, for the growth of both the individual and the society. This will explain how Hinduism is a multitude of creeds, closely knit together, and how its perplexing variety has a substratum of unity, which permeates it through and through as its *Prana* or vital principle.

The Vedanta is not only broad and liberal, but also strong enough to be the backbone of all the religions in the world. There is nothing in it, which is not deeply and firmly rooted in the nature of things ; and its theories are such as no logic, however penetrating and rigorous, could dislodge. Its truths stand the severest test, and can be verified by the best of proofs—direct, personal experience. It shrinks from no question and is the only philosophy that completely solves the problem of life. It postulates nothing and insists upon nothing which cannot be verified. Religion is often said to be a matter of faith ; true it is, but this license is at times extended to philosophy also. If both religion and philosophy be alike relegated to the domain of faith, then both must perish. Philosophy is the rational sanction of religion ; religion as vulgarly understood is philosophy made popular ; and in its highest sense, *viz.*, realisation, it is philosophy lived out, applied. Religion and philosophy must always go together, and any divorcement of the one from the other is extremely mischievous, and often proves fatal to both. Christianity as taught by Christ is one of the noblest religions in the world ; but as it was rested on no philosophical backbone, it is gradually losing its power ; and if it survives from the shocks of recent scientific researches, it can be only by being consciously rested on rational sanction. Such rational sanction is being rapidly discovered ; for the truths which Christ taught have in them the stamp of immortality, but the unphilosophical church, which erected itself on them, hid their light under a bushel of rituals and theories about creation, birth-place of man, and other subjects which—however much sanctified by the name of religion—geology, physical science, and history could have no patience for. The Vedanta on the other hand never lays any stress on any non-essential doctrine which scientific researches can displace. It never mistakes the purpose of religion, and takes care not to intrude on the province of science and history. Even its theory of creation, beautifully and consistently elaborated as it is, it lays no stress on ; and it says, an enquiry into the successive steps into which this material universe grew, belongs to science, and not to philosophy ; it is enough for its purpose that the world, evolved in whatever order, is only phenomenal and can be nothing but a manifestation of the universal consciousness or God. To the real Vedantin who seeks to realise God in this world and with his own body, a hereafter is perfectly immaterial. He does not trouble himself about what lives he led in previous incarnations, as dog, horse, serpent, etc., nor about the dark- or light-filled *Lokas* he may pass through after leaving the body. It is enough that in the course of a single hour his mind is, by transmigrating from one thing to another, under-going a series of births and deaths, and that he could, by alchemising that mind into the universal conscious-ness, put an end to the ever-recurring misery of birth and death, and become God Himself. The stronghold of the Vedanta could never be shaken. It is the one school of religious philosophy which never threatens with a 'believe, or you will be ruined'; but invites the most elaborate and searching enquiry. It shrinks from no questions, and outdoes all other systems in the rigor of its logic, the boldness of its intuition, and the final results of its search.

It is the one philosophy which dares to call man God Himself, not merely the son of God or His servant. Universal Brotherhood is too low an expression to denote its abounding love, it speaks of universal selfhood. 'He who sees the universe in himself and himself in the universe,' say the Upanishads repeatedly 'is the sage,' the perfected man.

Thus, we have seen that the national philosophy of India on which her religion is based, is broad enough to comprise within its sphere all the religions of the world, and strong enough to make them enduring and useful. Whether they will or no, consciously or unconsciously, all these religions are based upon the eternal verities of the Vedanta, for its range is nothing less than the range of the whole human race. It is conscious of its strength, and has entire sympathy with the diversity of religious creeds; nay, it welcomes even a vaster variety, because it is eager that no man in this world should suffer for want of a religion suited to his nature; and whatever 'isms' may spring up in the unknown future, must fall necessarily within the boundless fold of the Vedanta. In its broad economy, every religion is accommodated in the proper place, and is made to lead on to higher religions with nobler ideals.

The sooner religions recognise their place and their kinship with the Vedanta, the better it will be for them and their growth will be sooner ensured. But for the support of such a philosophy which makes all the world akin, Hinduism would have ceased to be a religion long, long ago, and would have become a barren fossil to be dug out of oblivion by laborious antiquaries. It is exactly the want of such an enduring and liberal philosophy that has made Christianity shake to its foundations before the onslaught of modern science. It is the want of such a bold and all-embracing philosophy, that has robbed Buddhism of its pristine nobility and love, and split it into a number of lazy and ceremonious churches, and supplemented the pure *Hinayana*—Buddha's little vessel of salvation—with the half mythical *Mahayana*,—the large vessel of salvation. It is the want of such a generous and sympathetic philosophy, that has made Muhammadanism a by-word for religious intolerance and fanaticism. One peculiarity of the Vedanta is, as we have already indicated, that it never interferes with forms. It concerns itself solely with the life of religions. The Christian need not renounce his Christianity, the Buddhist need not give up his ancient faith, the Muhammadan may stick to his Mecca and the Koran; and yet all these may *consciously* follow the Vedanta, and seek with fervour to realise its highest promises. Nay, their love to their respective Prophets and Bibles will become more dignified, more enlightened, and more sincere; and religious animosity will subside and the world move on to its great end with less friction.

A GREAT SUPERSTITION

It is a superstition to suppose that superstitions are confined exclusively to the uneducated masses. The educated have their own superstitions which, by the very fact of their being more subtle than those of ordinary men, are more dangerous and detrimental to progress. To fear certain evil because one's left eye throbs, or expect guests in the house because the crow caws in the court-yard, or the fire hisses in the oven, is no doubt supersti-tious, for obviously the optical nerves, the crow and the kitchen fire have no right to be ranked as prophets, but it is none the less a superstition to think that the Vedanta is nothing but mysticism and robs man of everything natural and interesting by making him a living corpse absolutely dead to the world. Exceedingly strange notions prevail in our own country about the final state of self-realisation, and it is not unusual to see all sorts of strange and fearful stories, based on mere hearsay reports, put into currency by men who come out as teachers and who might be expected to know better. It is no wonder, then, that Western writers who take their ideas from Eastern exponents, should look upon the end promised by the Vedanta as extremely un-natural, mystic and dreadful. It is freely ventilated in some quarters that the object of the Vedanta is, by means of certain methods of self-torture and auto-mesmerism, to enable man to live on earth as long as he pleases, to see strange visions, to subsist without food, to lie buried underground like a worm or lie on the sea sand or hill side, proof to wind and weather like a piece of rock and as insensible to human emotions and the woes of suffering humanity—a consummation sufficiently unattractive even to intelligent Eastern minds and positively dreadful to the European mind, accustomed to a practical view of life. M. Renan, when on a visit to Egypt, was shown on the banks of the Nile a human body which, he was told, had been lying there on the scorching sands already for about twenty years, without showing any sign of growth or decay, and belonged to a mystic in trance condition. The great French critic did not even pause to inquire into the truth of the story, but exclaimed with vehemence that the world was not one whit better for the misguided mystic's trances and that, so far as he himself was concerned he did not care whether the body before him had life in it or was a mere carcass about to rot and bleach on the burning shore. We do not say that Renan's attitude was wholly proper or that every other cultured spectator would have taken the same view and passed by with equal indifference, for curiosity at least might have prevailed and induced some inquiry into the matter, nor have we any interest in denying the possibility of such physical states, but what we do say is, that the attempt of the Vedanta is not to turn man into a stone or a worm, powerless either for good or for evil, a living carcass, not more beneficial than an embalmed mummy, though may be more interesting. And nowhere in the Upanishads, in the Gita, or the Brahmasutras which together constitute the tripod on which that philosophy rests, is such a carcass state glorified or pointed out as the goal of human aspirations. The question is directly

put by Arjuna to his divine cousin in the Gita what the
marks of the man are who is steady in wisdom, how he
speaks and how he moves, and the Lord in His reply
does not say he will be motionless like a mountain-snake
or buried underground like an earth- orm, but that he
will be free from desires and move about in the world
unaffected and always intent on the Supreme. In that
most beautiful of the Upanishads, the Kataka, young
Nachiketas is told by his divine preceptor : 'When all
the desires cease which were cherished in his heart, then
the mortal becomes immortal, then he obtains here
Brahman. When all the bonds of the heart are broken
in this life, then the mortal becomes immortal; this
alone is the instruction (of all the Vedas)'. In describing
the state of freedom, Yama does not tell his pupil that
the body becomes stiff like a rock and insensible to wind
and weather. In the Brihadaranyakopanishad the
active king Janaka and the giant debater Yajnavalkya
are the most prominent sages. Again, in the Chhandogya
Upanishad there is no mention of immortality to the
body either in the elaborate teachings of Sage Uddhalaka
to his beloved son Swetaketu, or in the interesting conversation between Narada and Sanatkumara. Besides,
the episode in the same Upanishad, Indra the king of
the gods and Virochana the king of the Asuras, repairing
to Prajapati for instruction, is specially meant to show
that wisdom consists in discriminating the *Atman* from
the *non-atman*, and not confounding the one with the
other as the Asura chief foolishly did. The Man-
dukyopanishad distinctly points out the *Atman* as
being different from all physical states; and in the
words of the Varahopanishad, just as striking at an

7

anthill will not destroy the serpent within, so no amount of bodily torture can kill the mind within. मन एव मनुष्याणां कारणं बन्धमोक्षयो: Mind is the cause of man's bondage and liberation, says the Amritabindupanishad, and what is required, is not to make the body hard like steel or preserve it by means of herbs and drugs, for wisdom is not proportionate to the number of years one lives on earth, but to purify the mind, to enable it to realise its true infinite nature and thereby rid it of all desires and other passions. The Vedanta will certainly be mysticism, if it seek to make a man live without food, enable him to preserve his life as long as he pleases or get stiff like a corpse, dead entirely to the world though an obscure spark of life may yet linger in the system. The Vedanta will be mysticism, if it seek to enable man to work wonderful feats just as flying in the air, leaving the body at will and wandering in space unobstructed like a ghost or entering into the bodies of others and possessing them like spirits and doing similar things of an unnatural character. The Vedanta will certainly be mysticism, if it seek to make a man read the thoughts of others, or lay him in an eternal trance, where he would be more dead than alive both with reference to himself and others. It does none of these. It is neither black art nor magic, neither Rosicrucianism nor spiritism nor demonology and has an utter disregard for phenomena of all kinds. It says : यद्दृश्यं तन्नश्यं whatever is seen perishes and seeks that which is imperishable, that by whose light everything else is seen, that which is the background of all appearance, that speaking with reference to which, naught else really exists. It says : 'You may fly in the air like a bird but that will not help you. For, whether you are down on earth or up a thousand miles above it, still the vain, impure traitorous mind, the conjurer of all conjurers, is with you and you are still a poor little creature, vain of your feat of jugglery, a 'tiny-trumpeting gnat' in the boundless empire of space above and below, though so big in your own microscopic vision. You may control your breath and remain motionless for hours, nay years till dust covers you, but do not even stones do the same? You may remain a thousand feet below the ground, and cities, rail roads and temples might have risen upon you; but your fossil-like existence, discoverable only by geological enterprise, does not mean salvation, for, at that rate, the tiny worms and insects which every stratum of earth exhibits on excavation, should be better sages than you. You may live without food, but that is nothing, for dyspepsia does not mean *Brahma--Jnana*. What is really required of man is that he should know what the real 'I' means and realise its boundless glory, in which, suns and spheres, constellations and milky-ways are like drops which nature's mighty heart drives through thinnest veins. A very feeble echo of such realisation which nevertheless serves to show that such realisation is nothing 'uncanny', mystic or fanciful, is uttered by the poet when he says:

The All-embracing, All-sustaining One,
Say, doth He not embrace, sustain, include
Thee? Me? Himself? Bends not the sky above?
And earth, on which we are, is it not firm?

*   *   *   *

And does not All—that is,
Seen and unseen, mysterious All—

Around thee and within,
Untiring agency,
Press on the heart and mind ?
Fill thy whole heart with it—and when thou art
Lost in the consciousness of happiness—
Then call it what thou wilt,
Happiness ! Heart ! Love ! God !
I have no name for it !

A similar experience is described by Tennyson from
a slightly different standpoint in the following lines :

For more than once when I
Sat all alone, revolving in myself
The word that is the symbol of myself,
The mortal limit of the self was loosed,
And passed into the nameless, as a cloud
Melts into heaven, I touched my limbs—the limbs
Were strange, not mine—and yet no shade of doubt,
But utter clearness, and thro' loss of self
The gain of such large life as matched with ours
Were sun to spark—unshadowable in words,
Themselves but shadows of a shadow world.

If these experiences of Goethe and Tennyson which
after all are mere unguided, intuitional and chance
glimpses of the truth, be mysticisms, then we take no
objection to Vedanta also being called by that name.
Certainly why should not the Vedanta be mysticism,
when love, poetry and happiness are so—happiness of
which the great sage of Geneva said : "To be happy,
to possess eternal life, to be in God, to be saved, all
these are the same. All alike mean the solution of the
problem, the aim of existence. Happiness has no
limit because God has neither bottom nor bounds and
because happiness is nothing but the conquest of God
through love." Finiteness, narrowness of vision, littleness of understanding brought about by our constantly

taking things to be just what they seem without pausing
to inquire how they arise and where they rest, have
become so much the habit with us that we raise an
uproar and cry halt when the least endeavour is made
to overthrow the limits of finiteness and realise the
infinite. The prisoner of Chillon who fell in love with
the chains which bound him, is a typical representation
of man who so dearly cherishes his littleness and loves
his finiteness, which after all is but a habitual fancy.
The utmost which our limited vision could bear without
getting dizzy is the poet's flight into the boundless world
of space with the joyous skylark which 'soaring sings
and singing soars' or with the west wind which drives
away loose clouds like decayed leaves claiming kinship
with earth, air and ocean, a noble brotherhood, a spirit
all disembodied and immortal though apparently bound
in mortal coils. But in the very course of such flight
the mind turns inward, where time and space are as
zero and its finiteness vanishes for the moment, an experience beautifully recorded as follows :

He looked—

Ocean and earth, the solid frame of earth
And ocean's liquid mass, beneath him lay
In gladness and deep joy. The clouds were touched,
And in their silent faces did he read
Unutterable love. Sound needed none,
Nor any voice of joy ; his spirit drank
The spectacle : sensation, soul and form
All melted into him ; they swallowed up
His animal being ; in them did he live,
And by them did he live ; they were his life.
In such access of mind, in such high hour
Of visitation from the living God,
Thought was not, in enjoyment it expired.
No thanks he breathed, he proffered no request

Rapt into still communion that transcends
The imperfect offices of prayer and praise,
His mind was a thanksgiving to the power
That made him ; it was blessedness and love !

The Vedanta teaches nothing unnatural, forced,
false or fanciful. It only tries to make permanent and
develop to their fullest capacity the blissful experiences
which almost every pure mind has, when the bonds of
mortality are suspended for a moment and the soul
enjoys its dominion of boundlessness. Such experiences
often surprise men when the mind is rapt in spontaneous
communion with nature or loses itself in some contemplation of transcendental interest. The Vedanta says
that 'the home, sweet home' is there inside, where the
apparently finite becomes infinite or rather realises its
infiniteness and proves by rigorous logic as beautiful
as unassailable, that nature with its thousandfold pro-
duction and destruction, which drive us with their
variety into the delusion of finiteness, is but 'the reflex
of our inward force, the phantasy of our dream,' and
leads us step by step under the practical guidance of
the Acharya without whose divine help no real progress
is possible, to the unfailing recognition of our infiniteness.
This realisation then, instead of being a sort of mysticism
or self-hypnotisation induced by artificial methods, an
unnatural end attained by unnatural means, is the
highest conceivable poetry, true and natural as attested
by the occasional experiences of all especially of poets
who lived in the enjoyment of an ampler ether and a
diviner air and instead of being something to be afraid
of and avoided as weakening is a most desirable state,
and is called *Samadhi* or *Samyaksthiti*, the proper state,

the state of equilibrium. What is there more poetic
than the realisation of the identity of the soul and
Brahman referred to in the following passage of the
Kathopanishad :

य एष सुप्तेषु जागर्ति कामंकामं पुरुषो निर्मिमाणः ।
तदेव शुक्रं तद्ब्रह्म तदेवामृतमुच्यते ।
तस्मिँल्लोकाः श्रिताः सर्वे तदु तात्येति कश्चन ॥ एतद्वै तत् ॥
अग्निर्यथैको भुवनं प्रविष्टो रूपं रूपं प्रतिरूपो बभूव ।
एकस्तथा सर्वभूतान्तरात्मा रूपं रूपं प्रतिरूपो बहिश्च ॥
सूर्यो यथा सर्वलोकस्य चक्षुर्न लिप्यते चाक्षुषैर्बाह्यदोषैः ।
एकस्तथा सर्वभूतान्तरात्मा न लिप्यते लोकदुःखेन बाह्यः ॥

That soul which is ever awake even in sleep, sending
forth the variety of ideas, is said to be all pure *Brahman*,
all immortality ;—all the worlds are held in (as it were,
in suspension), there is nothing which transcends it.
It is this. As the *one* fire pervading the universe
appears in so many forms in the variety of objects, so
the inner self of all, ever one, appears to take on so many
forms, but is ever beyond them. As the sun who en-
lightens everything has nothing whatever to do with
the numerous ills the eye may perceive, so the inner
self of all, ever one, has no connection whatever with
the joys and sorrows of the world, being ever beyond
them.

Realising the glory of the inner soul the sage
exclaims : 'I am not the body, how could there be
death, hunger and thirst for me ? I am not the senses,
how could there be *Samsara* for me ? I am not the vital

airs, how could there be motion and rest for me? I am not *Ahamkara*, how could there be grief and joy for me? I am all pure and unconditioned and eternal and blissful Brahman.' This grossly misunderstood leads to blind mysticism and leads to unnatural attempts to live without eating, to preserve the body, remain senseless, corpselike and so on. Rightly understood, it means the body, the senses, the intellect, etc., of the wise man do perform their functions, while he stands unmoved amidst their action like a mere witness, and in the words of 'Srimad Bhagavata', the perfected man inasmuch as he has found his self, recks not whether his body, brought about and carried off by chance, stands or falls even like the drunkard, senseless with intoxication, recks not whether the cloth he wears remains or falls away.

There is one other aspect of the subject under discussion, which is worthy of careful consideration, namely, the relation of the wise man to the world whether his individuality perishes like a bubble and gets erased out of existence on account of self-realisation. And upon this we shall discourse at some length on some future occasion.

KARMA YOGA

To remove our ignorance, to open our eyes now blind-folded by Maya, and lead us back to the fountain of bliss, our own Inner Self, is the purpose of all the scriptures of the world, and has been the one endeavour of the great sages who, by their lives and teachings, blessed our sad planet. The lives of these latter were all voluntarily dedicated to the service of suffering humanity, and all of them have uniformly striven to draw us nearer and nearer the centre of our being. With this glorious and unselfish end in view, they have clearly marked out for us the road to salvation, and also indicated the milestones in that road, the successive stages through which the spirit progresses towards its goal. Especially in our country, the idea of there being a something beyond this world of change and suffering, this penal colony as it has been styled, is presented to us at every turn in life, in marriage, in our daily obser-vances, in funeral ceremonies. *Sraddhas*, nay, even eating for the satisfaction of our hunger, the Vara-hopanishad says, should be looked upon as a sort of worship of the Atman within.

Indeed, in few countries has the evolution of the soul been traced from its earliest starting point to its final destination so fully as in ours ; and nowhere else has the path for liberation been indicated with so much clearness. That path has in our books been divided into four sections, the first of which is called Karma Yoga, the second Bhakti Yoga, the third Raj Yoga, and the fourth and the last Gnana Yoga. Yoga means the path or method whereby the soul attains its union with the Supreme. These four Yogas are sometimes also called four feet. Of these, Karma Yoga is the first from the bottom; it is the first rung in the ladder to Heaven; for it is farthest from the ideal, *viz.*, the cessation of all sense of duality and consequently of all action. Karma Yoga, rightly practised, leads to Bhakti Yoga; which in its turn leads on to Raja Yoga; which last gradually brings us *Gnana* or wisdom, the realisation of one-ness with the Brahman who alone really exists. A sense of difference is the very life of action, for all action implies a doer, a deed different from the doer and an object or instrument of action different from both; but says the Sruti: 'Those who believe in duality are not masters of their own selves and go to perishable regions, while he who realises the reverse becomes his own king.' There is duality in Bhakti Yoga also, *i.e.*, in the earlier stages, but *Bhakti* lessens the restlessness of the mind and proportionately destroys the illusion of manifoldness, for the *Bhakta* sees only the Lord of his love in all the universe. Bhakti Yoga is thus higher than Karma Yoga while Raja Yoga is superior to even the former, for it is a conscious effort at union with the Deity which, during its fulfilment, forms what is called Gnana Yoga. The course of evolution thus begins with Karma Yoga and ends with Gnana Yoga. That this is so, not merely stands to reason, but is also the opinion of the scriptures, as may be seen from verses 8 to 11 of Chap. XII of the Bhagavad-Gita.

It is not however for a moment asserted that Karma ceases as soon as Bhakti begins, and Bhakti as soon as

Yoga, and that Karma, Bhakti and Yoga are all absent in the *Gnani*. For, as we have already seen that the *Gnani* is the best Karma Yogin and that thoroughly motiveless action is possible only in' the case of the *Gnani*. So in the case of Bhakti also, the highest or Para Bhakti[1] is very nearly equal to wisdom, so much so that Sankara has defined Bhakti in his Vivekachintamani as meditation on one's own Self. Again the words *Yogi* and *Gnani* are indiscriminately used for each other in several passages of the Upanishads and the Gita. Karma, Bhakti, Yoga and Gnana do not therefore mutually exclude each other. On the other hand, every Yoga is a fulfilment of the preceding one. Bhakti is the fulfilment of Karma, Yoga of Bhakti and Karma, and Gnana of all the preceding three. What is meant then by saying that these four Yogas are distinct divisions of the trunk road to release is only that Karma or action is predominant in Karma Yoga, Bhakti in Bhakti Yoga, and so on. Every Yoga is named after the element which is predominant in it.

The question may be asked, why these four Yogas? The reply is, because the Vedanta philosophy is universal and covers the whole ground of human evolution. One method will not suit all men. 'Some men have mystic tendencies; they must realise God by means of inner searching, by examining into the nature of mind in all its working. Others are of emotional tendencies and must adopt devotional methods; they must concretise their ideals in a Personal God. Others are philosophers

[1] *Vide* article on Para Bhakti.

pure and simple ; to them the idea of dependence upon a Being outside of themselves does not appeal, and reason and sheer force of will alone can help them. Lastly, there are men who require activity in order to make progress and for them is the science of Karma Yoga.'

Although the germs of Karma Yoga are contained in the Upanishads, and although it is a natural inference from the lessons which they inculcate, yet we owe it to the genius of Sri Krishna that action which is a necessity of our nature has been shown, if performed properly, to go a great way towards liberating us from the thraldom of Maya. The Bhagavad-Gita is *the* book on Karma Yoga, and no where else do we find the path of action indicated with so much of clearness and beauty. Indeed it was Sri Krishna who elevated action to the dignity of a Yoga.

The Karma Yoga of the Gita should not however be confounded with what is known as Karma Marga, as opposed to Gnana Marga, which is sometimes styled Dhuma Marga, the smoke-filled path, by which performers of sacrifices and other rituals enjoined in the Karma Kanda of the Vedas, the Purva Mimamsa and the Smritis based upon them, attain to celestial regions such as the world of gods, the world of the forefathers, and so on. The Karma Yoga of the Vedanta means the path whereby one progresses towards liberation by the proper performance of the work that comes to hand. Karma in the latter has a much broader sense than in the former. In its broadest sense in which it is often used in the Gita, it applies to any kind of activity either of body, mind or the sense, as Sankara says in his com-

mentary on verse IV, 18. More specifically, it means
duty or work in which one engages. In the term Karma
Marga, on the other hand, it denotes Vedic sacrifices
and rituals by which one secures the right for entering
higher and higher worlds of enjoyment after death.
The Karma Yoga of the Gita brings about purity of
mind, and through it wisdom; Karma of the Karma
Kanda is Kamya, *i.e.*, for the gratification of desires,
while Karma in the Gita is Nishkamya, *i.e.,* free from
desire and motiveless.

'O Arjuna,' says Sri Krishna, 'Kamya Karma is
much lower than Nishkamya Karma; therefore take
thou to the latter which leads to wisdom. Those who
desire for fruit feel miserable' (*Gita*, II. 49). Action,
as we have already seen, can never give us liberation.
'Perfection,' says Swami Vivekananda, 'can never be
attained by work. We may work through all eternity,
but there will be no way out of this maze; you may
work on and on and on, but there will be no end.'
'Wise men,' says the Naradaparivrajakopanishad, 'escape death by knowing the Brahman. There is no
other road to salvation.' That even Vedic sacrifices are
no better than other Karma in procuring us our salvation is clearly expressed in the following verses of the
Mundaka Upanishad :

'Perishable and transient are verily the eighteen
supporters of the sacrifice on whom, it is said, the inferior work (Kamya Karma) depends. The fools who
consider this work as the highest, undergo again even
decay and death. In the midst of ignorance, fools
fancying themselves wise and learned, go round and
round, oppressed by misery, as blind people led by the

blind. Living in various ways in ignorance, youths
imagine, we have obtained our end. Because the performers of work from attachment are not wise, therefore suffering unhappiness, they lose heaven, when the
fruit of their works has become nought. Fancying
oblations and pious gifts to be the highest, fools do not
know anything good. Having enjoyed the fruit of
their works on the high place of heaven which they gained
by their actions, they enter again this world or one that
is lower' (I, II, 7-11). Then the Upanishad proceeds
to say, 'Let the Brahmana, after he has examined the
worlds gained by works, renounce the world, reflecting
that there is nothing that is not created, all being the
effect of work. For the purpose of knowing that
(which is not created), he approaches, sacred wood in
his hand, a teacher who knows the Vedas, and who is
solely devoted to Brahman.'

To go to the teacher, and that with the senses
subdued and mind at rest, as required in the next verse
of the above Upanishad, is however not possible for
most men. Many there are who, though aware of the
insufficiency of work, are yet, too active and *Rajasic* in
their character and are by the principles in their nature,
bound 'to be up and doing,' like Arjuna to whom Krishna
said : 'O son of Kunti, thou that are bound by past
Karma and the duties of thy order art going to fight
even against thy will, as one compelled to do so' (*Gita*,
XVIII, 60). It is for such men that Karma Yoga is
meant. It will raise them a step nearer the ideal which
they are unable to approach by any other means. 'In
this world,' says Sri Krishna, 'there is nothing so purifying as *Gnana* ; but the Karma Yogi realises for him-

self that *Atma Gnana* in course of time' (*Gita*, IV, 38).
Karma Yoga then stands midway between Karma
Marga and Gnana Marga. Karma of the Karma Marga
not only does not liberate man but binds him more and
more, for it creates newer and newer desires, while the
practice of Karma Yoga kills out desire, and secures
emancipation from the thraldom of Maya. Says the
Gita : "The Karma Yogi attains the release which
comes of wisdom by leaving off desire for the fruits of
action, while he who being prompted by desire is attached to them becomes bound." (V—12).

Two elements are indispensably required in Karma
Yoga—non-attachment or indifference to the fruits of
action, and dedication of the work to God. Krishna
says to Arjuna : 'O Dhananjaya, do thy duty with thy
mind fixed upon the Lord, leaving off all attachment
and without caring for the fruits of thy action. Equanimity of mind whatever may be the consequences of
one's action—this is what is called Karma Yoga, (*Gita*,
II, 48). Both these elements are necessary and great
is the virtue of action performed with utter indifference
to results and dedicated to the Lord. "That which is
done as Nishkamya Karma will never be vain : there
can be no harm caused by it. Even a small portion of
the virtue of such Karma will enable man to overcome
much fear." (*Gita*, II, 40). Karma Yoga then though
the first of the four Yogas is productive of wonderful
results. Indeed, when two such elements combine as
non-attachment and a feeling of worship, what doubt is
there that the result will be glorious ?

In the first place, non-attachment brings about
freedom from grief and fear ; attachment is the first

child of Maya and nearly all the misery of the world is directly due to it. To be non-attached is to be fearless. Bhartrihari says : "Everything in the world is fraught with fear. It is non-attachment that makes one fearless." A man who works unattached is above grief and fear. Secondly, as the Karma Yogi dedicates his work to God, he approaches nearer and nearer the centre of his being, his inner Self. The God-idea gradually grows upon him, until he realises that he, as a member of the phenomenal world, is simply an instrument in the hands of God, that it is God that speaks through the universe. A steady practice of Karma Yoga will enable a man to say with Thayumanavar : 'Everything is thy property, O God ; everything is Thy doing ; Thou pervadest the whole universe' ; and he will realise the meaning of the celebrated verses of the Brihadaranyaka Upanishad, which describe the glory of the Antaryamin, the 'Inner Ruler, Immortal,' such as, 'He who dwelling in the mind is within the mind, whom the mind does not know, whose body is the mind, who from within rules the mind, is thy Soul, the Inner Ruler, Immortal.' (*Bri. Upa.*, III, vii). It has been well said : 'Prudent men abandoning the fruits of action attain wisdom and obtaining release from the bonds of life reach that state which is free from grief.' (*Gita*, II, 51).

It is in the nature of all Karma to destroy *Tamas*, laziness and the like, but Nishkamya Karma gradually kills out *Rajas* also for, as non-attachment and worship form its elements, it is the best antidote for pride and selfishness. True *Satvic* humility characterises such Karma, and it is only this Karma which can be properly said to involve self-sacrifice. For, however glorious may be the work which one might perform, if he does it with a sense of self-consciousness and pride or with motives such as fame, there is no sacrifice of self but propitiation, and it is much inferior to ordinary Nishkamya Karma, not to speak of such a memorable act as that of Emperor Civi who cut off flesh from his own thigh to save a pigeon, or that of the Rishi Dadhichi who gladly gave his backbone to Indra who asked for it. 'Ordinary Karma is much lower,' says Krishna, 'than that which is Nishkamya' (*Gita*, II, 49).

The great Bhishmacharya of the Mahabharata was a wonderful example of a Karma-Yogi. The story of his resigning his throne and taking the Brahmacharya vow for the sake of his father and step-brother is too well-known to need mention here. Before the great war, he took hold of every possible opportunity to advise Duryodhana to make peace with the Pandavas. He told him, times without number, that his cause was unjust and would not succeed, and that not even gods could resist the Pandavas in battle. That obstinate and evil-minded prince heeded not his words however, and often charged him with being partial to the Pandavas. The battle of Kurukshetra was the result, and though Bhishma had, till the very eve of battle, pleaded for the Pandavas, yet when duty called him, he fought better than all the rest together, causing immense havoc among the Pandava army. Yet he had no enmity against the Pandavas or attachment to the Kauravas ; fighting as he did was in his eyes a duty, and being called upon to perform it, he did so as a true Karma-Yogi without attachment and without caring for the results. Even his death was, as it were, due

8

to his sense of duty. He died because the situation required it, because he thought he was bound to die. How he gladly brought about his own death will, though well-known, bear repetition here. In a war council held in the Pandava camp Yudhishtira proposed to consult Bhishma himself as to how they may obtain victory over the Kauravas. Bhishma had told him, 'I will give thee counsel, but fight I shall never for thee, since I shall have to fight for Duryodhana's sake.' Dharmaputra's proposal was approved, and accordingly Krishna and Pandavas went to the grand old man and asked him : 'Tell us, O grandsire, the means by which we may vanquish thee in battle, by which sovereignty may be ours ; and, by which our army may not have to undergo such destruction as you are now causing. The great Bhishma replied : 'As long as I am alive, victory cannot be yours. Truly do I say this unto you. After however I am vanquished in fight, you may have victory in the battle. If therefore you desire victory in the battle, smite me down without delay. I give you permission, ye sons of Pandu, -strike me as you please. After I am slain all the rest will be slain. Therefore do as I bid.' Then he frankly told them that he would be killed by Arjuna fighting against him placing Sikhandin in the front. Really a remarkable incident is this ! Our poor world has not seen many such heroes as Bhishma who would lay down their lives purely out of a sense of duty. Because he had promised to give counsel to the Pandavas, he gladly told them, when they asked him, how he himself might be killed !

Though such 'man-mountains' are not met with in modern days, our ancient literature abounds in instances of heroic self-sacrifice. For were not Rama, Lakshmana, Bharata, Janaka, Sita, Krishna, Buddha and others mighty Karma-Yogis? One thing common to these heroes is spirituality. By spirituality is not here meant any adherence to doctrines, to narrow theological dogmas and beliefs, but a strong faith in something beyond this world of selfishness and hate, a contempt for earthly life and prosperity and an incapacity for meanness. The world was nothing in their eyes, and they lived wedded, as it were, to eternity. It is this spirituality which was the secret of their heroism. They were great Karma-Yogis because they had strength of character and an unshakeable faith in the Supreme—not like the little worms that we are, crawling on earth with no better ambition than to hoard up its dust and no better occupation than to steal, fight and kill. The sage of Chelsea is perfectly right when he says: "The question between man and man always is, will you kill me or shall I kill you?" Mean and petty scrambling for the propitiation of our false self as if there is nothing higher than that—this is our lot. But those great men of old moved in a world much higher than ours; they loved each other even when fighting and readily sacrificed themselves for the sake of duty. All this they did because they never lost sight of the 'Star above the storm.'

Without this element of spirituality, Karma-Yoga is impossible. 'To work for work's sake, without motives,' is all very well in words, but when one begins to follow it in practice then the difficulty will be present. That is why in almost every verse of the Gita which speaks of Karma-Yoga, both the elements—non-attachment and the sense of worship—are combined. Indeed the first is almost impossible without the second, for the mind is unable to leave off desire unless it recognises the existence of something better than the things it desires. Absolute non-attachment is an impossible condition. The mind can leave hold of lower things only if it is sufficiently attracted by higher things. Service of man and worship of God should therefore go hand in hand until they become one and identical. It has been wisely observed : 'Service on the physical plane is good ; service on the mental or psychic plane is better : the altruistic effort involved in both requires the impulse of the higher worship as a goad.' The absence of this impulse robs the Karma-Yoga of Buddhism (not the Buddhism of modern days) of half its worth and makes it nearly impracticable. Besides, it is an immense advantage that we are, as in our system, reminded of God at every turn in the course of our evolution.

Not merely is Nishkamya Karma of advantage to the individual, but even as work, it will be much better than that which is done with motives. That work is the best which contains in it the least quantity of personal equation. He is the best actor, for example, who, for the time being, identifies himself with the part he is playing. The greatest works of art were executed by men who forgot themselves in the work. He is the best musician who loses his little self while singing. All high work is impersonal and spiritual, being free from the considerations of self and the hankering after results.

Nishkamya Karma is therefore the best Karma. It very much helps the individual's growth and at the same time brings about the greatest results. But he who attempts to practise Karma-Yoga because it is so beneficial, is not a Karma Yogi, for he works with motive. 'Honesty is the best policy, but he who acts on that principle is not an honest man' is the saying. In the same way, Nishkamya Karma is the best Karma and brings about most marvellous results ; but he who attempts to do such Karma *because* it is so, is not a Karma-Yogi and cuts the ground under his own feet.

BHAKTI

In the whole course of a soul's journey, beginning from the very beginning of time and never resting until it fully knows and realises itself as the one thing existing in all the universe—*Ekamevadwitiyam Brahma*—the one God without a second—few events are more momentous and epoch-making in their nature than the springing up of strong and genuine *Bhakti* or love and devotion towards God. This *Bhakti* transforms the whole human nature ; when one obtains it, verily one is "born again"—born not from the mother's womb into the "false life" of sin and sorrow, but born into the truer and larger life which all of us are destined to enter into some day or other. Sincere love towards God makes man a *Dwija* or twiceborn much more really than any ceremony can do. Once a man obtains, by his *Punya* or the virtue of his good actions during a long course of lives, this blessing of true devotion to the Supreme, life obtains for him a larger meaning and the world gets transfigured by his love into Heaven. He is no longer the man he was before ; communion with the Source of all love, purifies his nature and elevates him to the rank of a Godman. Everything that he sees, everything that he hears and feels, becomes filled with a new and ethereal poetry, all for his enjoyment, and he is rocked gently and sweetly in the cradle of love by a motherly Providence till he loses himself in a blissful union with the Divine, the ineffable glory which the most poetic Upanishads vainly struggle to render in the language of words.

The real *Bhakta* is one in several thousands of men.
Even in so spiritual a country as ours, the number of
Bhaktas, excluding of course the *soi-disant*, the fanatical,
the superstitious, and the sectarian, may be counted
on one's fingers. When we see what *Bhakti* really
means, the cause for its being so rare a thing will become apparent. *Bhakti* is love which the wise have for
God, and which is as intense and unremitting as the
love which the non-discriminating have for the fleeting
objects of the senses. Its nature is extreme devotion
(*Premarupa*). "Love is immortal," says Narada, "obtaining which man becomes perfect, becomes immortal,
becomes satisfied ; obtaining which he desires nothing,
grieves not, hates not, does not delight in sensuous
objects, makes no efforts for selfish ends ; knowing
which, he becomes intoxicated with joy, transfixed and
rejoices in the Self. It cannot be made to fulfil desires,
for its nature is renunciation." The *Bhakta* is happy
only in unremitting communion with God, and finds
the greatest misery in forgetting Him. "The days on
which I failed to sing of Him are days on which I did not
really live," says a great sage. "The only blessing I
crave from Thee," said Prahlada, the ideal lover, "is
not to forget Thee, even if I be born as a worm or reptile."
The longing for God which the real *Bhakta* has, is well
illustrated in the Upanishads. "Choose sons and
grandsons," said Yama to Nachiketas, "who may live a
hundred years, choose herds of cattle, choose elephants
and gold and horses, choose the wide-expanded earth,
and live thyself as many years as thou listest......
I will make thee enjoyer of all desires, all those desires
that are difficult to gain in the world of mortals, all

those desires ask thou according to thy pleasure—these
fair ones of heaven with their cars, with their musical
instruments and the like, as they are not to be gained
by men. Be attended by them, I will give them to
thee." Unlike most of us whom infinitely lesser and
vainer things are enough to intoxicate and madden,
Nachiketas had only one reply—"The boon which I
have to choose, is what I said, *viz.*, the knowledge of
the *Atman*" (*Kath. Upa.*, I, 23—27). Here is an
example of the real *Bhakta*. The glory of such rare
flowers of humanity may be realised when we remember
what Sri Krishna says again and again concerning them—
"I am in my lover and he is in Me" (*Gita*, IX, 29). "I
bear all the burden of my lovers' concerns" (*Ibid.*, IX. 22).
"Those who preferring only Me leave all works for Me,
and, free from the worship of others (Cupid, Mammon,
Mars, and others of the brotherhood), contemplate and
serve Me alone,—I presently raise up from the ocean of
this region on mortality" (*Ibid.*, XII, 6, 17). "Place thy
heart on Me, O Arjuna, and discover Me by thy understanding, and thou shalt without doubt hereafter enter
into Me" (*Ibid.*, XII, 8).

Bhakti is the most natural and at least in the earlier
stages the best means for drawing the mind away from
sensuous objects and enabling it to realise God. We
are miserably steeped in ignorance, and suffer every
moment to be led astray by those 'traitors in the camp,'
our passion-filled senses and our mad monkey-like mind,
which roves about in a silly and purposeless fashion,
without any rest either at day or night. It is really
melancholy to reflect upon the villainous and nomadic
ramblings of the human mind, and more especially,

upon our miserable inability to check its wicked and
truant disposition. Says Sankara : "The five creatures,
the doer, the elephant, the butterfly, the fish and the
bee come to grief in gratifying a single sense, *viz.*, sound,
touch, sight, taste and smell, respectively. Then what
to say of man who has all the five senses to please?"
"Man is a pendulum betwixt a tear and a smile," said
Byron, but this but feebly expresses our situation.
The motions of a pendulum are measured, and what a
poor simile is that for the reckless and unruly adventurer
within us. The same mind, however, which is our
worst enemy when left to itself, is our most precious
helpmate when tutored and regulated. 'The mind is
the cause for both the bondage and emancipation of
man' (*Amir. Bin. Upa.* also *Gita*, VI, 5, 6). "O Mind !
Why wanderest thou so wickedly?" said Thayumanavar,
addressing his mind, "a thousand times have I advised
thee to cease rambling and seek Him whom no amount
of disputation, no amount of *Hata-yoga* practices, nor
even a knowledge of the Vedas could discover ; check
thy rambles or I shall kill thee." Again, when by the
proper subjugation of the mind and the blessings of the
Guru he had realised the Truth, he exclaimed : "My
mind, who hast made me know thy real nature and
realise my real divinity, thou hast proved my best
friend, my real teacher, and my life's best saviour." The
use of *Bhakti* consists in bribing the mind to give up
its low and blind attachment to the objects of the senses
for the sake of the Father of love and the Source of all
things. It is the easiest, the most natural and, at the
same time, the best means for inducing the mind to turn
away from appearances and find its final refuge and

abiding place in the Fountain of all wisdom, in the ineffable glory of the great boundless *Satchidananda*, the Creator, the Preserver and the Destroyer of this real-seeming world, the one Supreme Being, who yet is unchanged, unchangeable, and eternal.

Man runs headlong in his pursuit after pleasure, and when, in the course of his pandering to the senses, nature administers some sound blows, he finds, in the language of the Upanishads, that what is good is different from what is pleasant, and cries for help from the Father that is in Heaven. Here are the earliest germs of *Bhakti*. The feeling of dependence slowly matures into love, and, in the words of Sri Krishna, "after many lives, man learns that all that exists is Vasudeva and worships Me ; very rare is such a good man." (*Gita*, VII, 19). To see God, and Him alone, in all the diverse phenomena of the universe, to rejoice in the wealth of His infinite manifestation and revel in the realisation of the truth that, behind the illusion of the universe, the Brahman alone really is and that "It is not of a gross body, It is not subtle, not long, not wide, not red, not viscid, not shadow, not darkness, not air, not ether, not adhesive, not taste, not smell, not eye, not ear, not speech, not mind, not light, not life, not entrance, not measure, not within, not without". (*Brih. Aran. Upa.*, VII, iii, 8). What a privilege this realisation, and now blessed the love which deserves it ! Truly says Narada : "Inexpressible is the nature of love, like the taste of a dumb man, devoid of the three qualities, without desires, ever increasing, continuous, having the nature of subtle perception. Having obtained love, the *Bhakta* sees that alone, hears that alone, speaks that alone, and thinks that alone. Worshippers who have this one object in life are the greatest. With choking voice and hairs standing on end, and with tears talking to each other of love, they purify their families in the world. They are the source of holiness in holy places. They make *any* work good work, and scriptures Holy Scriptures. They are full of divinity. Their forefathers rejoice. The gods dance with joy. This earth finds protectors. Among them no distinction is to be made of caste, learning, beauty, birth, wealth, occupation, etc., because they are His." "In their hearts," to quote the words of a great Muslim mystic, "there is the great ocean of divine love, the world present and the world to come are but as figures reflected in it ; and as it rises and falls, how can they remain ? He who plunges in that sea and is lost in it, finds perfect peace."

"The vast majority of men," says Swami Vivekananda, "are atheists. I am glad that, in modern times, another set of atheists has come up in the Western world, the materialists, because they are sincere atheists ; they are better than these religious atheists, who are insincere, talk about religion, and fight about it, and yet never want it, never try to realise it, never try to understand it. Remember those words of Christ : 'Ask and ye shall receive, seek and ye shall find, knock and it shall be opened unto you.'......A disciple went to his master and said to him : 'Sir, I want religion.' The master looked at the young man, and did not speak ; only smiled. The young man came every day, and insisted that he wanted religion. But the old man knew better than the young man. One day, when it was very hot, he asked the young man to go to the river with him, and take a plunge. The young man plunged

in, and the old man after him, and held the young man
down under the water by his force. When the young
man had struggled for a good while, he let him go, and,
when the young man came up, asked him what he
wanted most while he was under the water. 'A breath
of air,' the disciple answered. 'Do you want God that
way? If you do you will get Him in a moment.' Until
you have that thirst, that desire, you cannot get religion, however you struggle with your intellect, or your
books, or your forms. Until that thirst is awakened
in you, you are no better than any atheist, only that
the atheist is sincere, and you are not."

This 'thirst for God' is what is called *Bhakti*. It is
not, however, always accompanied by *Gnana* or wisdom,
which alone can bring about salvation. All *Gnanis*,
i.e., wise men who have realised God are *Bhaktas*, but
all *Bhaktas* are not necessarily *Gnanis*. The reason is,
it is possible to love God without fully knowing His
real *Swarupa* or form. Indeed it is impossible to climb
up all at once to the absolute Brahman. Just as a
man has to sit before lying down, so the natural way to
the Abstract God lies through the worship of outward
and mental images formed of Him. "In whatever
form a man worships Me, even so I appear unto him,"
said Sri Krishna (*Gita*, IV, 11). The real *Bhakta*, though
he might begin with idol worship, gradually finds in the
image before him the symbol of omnipresence, divine
grace, boundless power and eternal life. "O God Siva,"
sings a Saivite saint addressing the *Sivalingam* in a
particular shrine, "who hast Thy dwelling in Tiru-
perundurai, Thou who hast blest me, and Whom,
forgetful of all else, I contemplate as the Sun of

Wisdom, shining in my mind after dispelling the darkness therein, I examine atom after atom, and there is not one particle of matter which is outside Thee but Thou are not aught that is visible, and yet naught exist, without Thee. Ah! How could one know Thee as Thou art." To the real *Bhakta* the images in the temple are all so many different forms of God; and when in due course he attains wisdom, those images obtain for him a fuller meaning and speak to him of the indescribable abstract God whom he has realised. Thus sings Pattanattu Pillai, the great Dravidian sage : "O God Siva, Thy wearing the moon on Thy head is to show that Thou are the Lord of Wisdom ; Thy holding the *Trisula* is to show that Thou art Thyself the Trinity ; Thy riding on the bull is to show that Thou art the God of goodness ;......though boundless be Thy glory, Thou art as small as my heart could hold ; though formless be Thy form, all the universe is Thy manifestation ; though Thou canst not be made by the hand of man, Thou willingly takest any form Thy lover gives Thee ; though Thou art in truth alone without a second, Thou art the Lord of so many souls ; though Thou art everywhere, Thou livest not with the wicked."

Worshipping God through images and symbols, or as Iswara, the Lord of the Universe (*Saguna*), instead of as the absolute, changeless and unmanifest *Brahman* (*Nirguna*), is, of course, not the highest form of worship, but even of this the majority of men in the world are not really capable. *Nirguna* worship is much more difficult than *Saguna*. "Those whose minds are attached to My invisible nature have the greater labour to encounter," said Krishna (*Gita*, XII, 5). *Saguna* worship is therefore called *Apara-bhakti* or the lower form of devotion. It is of course an illusion, because it mistakes physical or mental images for the formless God. There are, however, two kinds of illusions known in the *Vedanta* as *Samvadi-bhrama* and *Visamvadi-bhrama*. The following is an example of the latter. Suppose a light is kept in a closed room and casts its rays through the key-hole, and a man mistaking the rays for a gem, runs up to the key-hole, the gem is not to be found either in the key-hole or in the room; the illusion in this case is called *Visamvadi-bhrama*, because it did not lead the man to the thing sought for. If, instead of the light, there had been a real gem casting its rays through the key-hole, the man attracted by them might have easily discovered the gem, though not in the key-hole yet inside the room ; the illusion in this case is called *Samvadi-bhrama*, as it somehow leads to the wished-for-object. The *Saguna* worship or *Apara-bhakti* is in its nature *Samvadi-bhrama*, because it finally leads to the realisation of the *Nirguna Brahman*. On the other hand our endless pursuit after sense objects is *Visamvadi-bhrama*, as it leads us more and more away from the happiness and peace of mind which we seek. One illusion cures another and in this homœopathic treatment, the mind which is attracted and repulsed by turns by the illusory, fleeting things of the world is gradually induced to seek refuge and consolation in the highest of illusions, Iswara, the Lord of the world, the reflection, so to speak, in the mirror of *Maya* of pure, *Chaitanya*, the absolute, attributeless *Brahman*, who alone really is.

This *Bhakti* is of three kinds—*Bahya* or external,

Ananya or the exceptionless, and *Ekanta* or the solitary. The passionate adoration of the Deity when the *Bhakta* flies to him for refuge from the miseries of existence, voiced forth in language like the following—'My father Isa's feet are cool like the music of a faultless *Vina*, or the gentle light of the evening moon, or like zephyr which sweetly blows from the South'—and indeed, all worship of God as a being outside us and worthy of adoration, is *Bahya-bhakti*. *Ananya-bhakti* is generally defined as the worship of one particular Deity in preference to all others. In a truer sense, however, it means the worship of all deities, without exception, as so many forms of a particular Deity chosen for worship (*Ishta Devata*), as when Nammalwar, the great Vaishnavite saint, sings : "Him who is himself all, Him who is the source of all animate and inanimate existences, Him the ancient one who is Himself (*i.e.*, Vishnu) and Siva and Brahma in manifestation, Him who is sweeter than honey, milk and suger-cane and nectar, the One who dwells in my body, mind and life, Him I felt and realised." In the same way, Appar, the Saivite Saint, sings : "He who is like honey and milk and who is the living Light, He, the Great One, who is Himself Vishnu and Brahma, and pervades the roaring sea and mountain chains, has his dwelling in Chidambaram ; and the days on which I failed to sing of Him are days on which I really had no life." Seeing all other deities in one's *Ishta Devata* is *Ananya-bhakti*. Whatever the chosen deity, the *Bhaktas* really worship only the same God. To quote from Nammalwar, "Worship, O ye men, Brahma, Vishnu, or Siva. Study them, know them, and sing of them again and again. Whatever ye worship, ye worship the same Being." "As all rain falling from the skies finds its way into the ocean, the prayers addressed to all deities go to the one Adorable Being" is a part of the Brahmin's daily prayer. "Even those who worship other gods through ignorance, worship only Me, though in the wrong way," says Sri Krishna (*Gita*, IX). *Ekanta-bhakti* consists in being absorbed in the contemplation of the manifold qualities of God (*Anantagunakaiyana*), His infinite mercy, His omnipotence, His mother-like tenderness to *Bhaktas*, His omniscience, His purity, and His faultless glory. "The endless one who has *mixed with* me," says Nammalwar, "no words can express. Say ye then how could I express the unspeakable." Again, "He who is of the colour of the clouds, who wears a bright crown and has four arms, who holds the bright *Chakra*, the *Sanka* and the *Gada*. He lives *within* me." Such mixing, such indwelling, such ineffably blissful absorption is *Ekanta Bhakti*, the highest form of *Saguna* worship.

How *Apara* or the lower *Bhakti* leads to *Para* or supreme *Bhakti*, and how the *Saguna* God develops in the mind of the *Bhakta* into the *Nirguna Brahman*, will be considered on a future occasion.

PARA BHAKTI OR WISDOM

WE have seen what *Apara-bhakti* or *Saguna* worship is. It is but a step and a very necessary one towards the highest form of worship,—absorption into the deity— in which alone can the mind find its final resting place. "God," says the Yoga Vasishta, "is neither Vishnu alone, nor Siva alone nor any embodied being, for all bodies are merely compounds of the five elements; nor is God the mind; but He is the *Gnana*, the Self, beginningless and endless. Can He be the little things, body, mind and the like? As *Brahmagnana* is illimitable, actionless and without either beginning or end, such *Gnana* alone is true and fit to be attained. But in the case of the ignorant devoid of wisdom, worship of forms alone is ordained to be the best. Just as wayfarers, when they are unable to travel a long distance are told that their destination is but a call distant in order not to let their spirits droop, so persons devoid of wisdom are told to worship diverse forms at first though the wise say that they will not reach the Self merely through the worship of these various forms (*Saguna* worship)."

> Strong limbs may dare the rugged road which storms,
> Soaring and perilous, the mountain's breast ;
> The weak must wind from slower ledge to ledge,
> With many a place of rest.

This will explain how Kabirdas, one of the greatest of modern saints though by birth a Muhammadan and a worshipper of the abstract formless Alla, was initiated into the details of *Saguna* worship by God Himself as

129

9

the story goes. Of course when one stops with *Vacha-kainkarya*, *i.e.*, merely talking about religion, it matters not whether God is *Saguna*, with form or *Nirguna*, without form but, when he enters into practical realisation, it is very essential that the conception one has, should not be too far above his mental aptitude and capacity.

Though we have to begin with this *Saguna* worship, we should not end there, nay, cannot end there; for some day or other it will not fail to strike us that the visible object or mental conception which we worship as God cannot be the eternal and changeless reality behind the Universe, and that the understanding within us, which conceives of the deity must be greater than the conception itself. The real God must, we shall sooner or later discover, be really inconceivable by our minds. The insufficiency of *Saguna* worship will thus become apparent, and the worshipper will gradually proceed to understand and realise the Inconceivable beyond. In addition to this insufficiency, there is what may be regarded a danger in *Saguna* worship which, however harmless in the earlier stages, will unless guarded against, prove a great barrier in the way of Self-realisation. The danger to which we refer is the tendency which there is in that worship to externalise the mind and fire the emotional side of man. "Religion in Christian countries at least," says a great writer "has been made for too much a thing of sentiment. It has its use no doubt in prompting the initial effort, but when the path is chosen, it would seem that single-heartedness of aim and firm determination were the dominant qualities required."

The ecstatic dance of *Bhaktas*, their alternate weepings and rejoicings, their spasmodic trances and visions are all essentially emotional in their nature, and as action and reaction are equal and opposite in the psychic as much as in the physical plane, this excess of emotion is necessarily followed by a corresponding dejection and weariness and often seriously impairs both the mind and the body. "To us," says the writer above referred to, "whose aim is passionless tranquillity which no emotion can shake, must not the control of the feeling of pleasure be as important as that of pain? The *Bhakta* often loses the control of his mind and suffers himself to be passively dragged along as best as it chooses and the result naturally is feverish excitement or irksome dejection." Even so cautious and temperate a devotee as Thomas-a-Kempis, was a victim to such shifting states of mind and the note of melancholy resignation is more prominent in his 'Imitation' than that of uniform, sustained, cheerful and healthy fervour which is the characteristic of the Upanishads. "It is a good council," he says, "that when thou hast conceived the spirit of fervour, thou shouldst meditate how it will be with thee when that light shall leave thee; and again, "My son! Thou must not depend too much on this affection which may be quickly changed into the contrary." This 'conceiving the spirit of fervour' is avowedly a matter of chance. How different is this confession from the following passage from the Upanishads! "In my illumined heart the Sun of Wisdom doth ever shine; He never riseth nor doth He set ever" (Maitreya Upa., II). Unlike the *Bhakta*, the *Gnani* is free from excitement and dejection and as has been very wisely observed : "his attitude towards humanity will also find a parallel in his attitude towards divinity ; for, the passionate adoration will have been left behind and will have given place to the carelessness of the divine serenity." "Let the wise," says the Upanishad : "sink his senses in the mind, sink his mind in reason, sink the reason in the great soul and that in the Brahman" (Kath. Upa., I, iii, 13).

In spite of the weakness to which we have referred, *Apara-bhakti* is an excellent preparation for the attainment of *Gnana*. It really corresponds so far as its results are concerned, to what is called *Sadhana-Chatushtaya*, the four great qualities for Vedantic discipleship, for it brings about an intense desire for emancipation, *Mumukshutvam*, humility, patience and like virtues, a disregard as strong as genuine for earthly and heavenly rewards and *Viveka*, *i.e.*, discrimination of the real from the non-real, of the essential from the non-essential. The lower form of *Bhakti* then is an excellent discipline and entitles one to the favour of the *Guru*. And when the real *Guru*, the adorable one, as the Upanishads style him, is sought and found, the fever of the heart ceases, the *Bhakta's* abnormal excitement having fulfilled its mission, gets gradually sobered down and the highest instruction which the teacher gives to the disciple is : "As fire gets gradually extinguished when the fuel is exhausted, so the *Chitta* or mind gets tranquilised by its out-goings being checked......In the calm and tranquil mind one finds inexhaustible bliss" (Maitreya Upa., II). Here, at this stage, begins *Para* or Supreme *Bhakti*. The *Saguna* God gives way before the *Sadhana* or the secret method for attaining to the *Nirguna* into which the disciple is initiated by the teacher and the love and devotion which were hitherto employed in the worship of the former are now transferred to the finding out, and the meditation of, what is called *Anirvachaniya Jyotis*, the Indescribable Light of the Self within. Here is *Para-Bhakti*. "The contemplation of one's own real Self is *Bhakti*," says Sankara. In the same way, Sandilya says : "Love is the unbroken feeling of the Universal Self in one's own Self." Here will be seen the full force of the following *Sutras* of Narada : "Love is immortal, attaining which man becomes perfect, becomes immortal, becomes satisfied, and obtaining which he desires nothing, grieves not, hates not, does not delight in sensuous objects, makes no effort for selfish ends (how could he ?), knowing which he becomes intoxicated with joy, becomes transfixed and *rejoices in the Self.*"

This *Bhakti* is deservedly termed *Para* or supreme, because it is not merely emotional and spasmodic and it does not depend on any external, fleeting and mutable objects. Even the highest *Saguna Bhakta* is one man when he is in the temple, and another when he is outside. These *Bhaktas* depend by the very nature of their *Bhakti* on external environments, external purity and external rituals and they generally attach importance to time and place. The *Para-bhakta*, on the other hand, requires none of these external helps. The God whom he worships is within himself, unchangeable, eternal and blissful. *Deho devalayah proktassajivah kevalas Sivah*......The body is called the temple and the Jiva in it is verily Siva (the Brahman), (Maitreya Upa., Ch. IV : also Skandopanishad) and the method taught by the teacher for reaching that God is in the disciple's own mind. To the *Para-bhakta* what is there external to God by which to worship Him? Says Thayumanavar: "I cannot worship Thee O God! in any embodied form, for I see Thyself in the very flowers (required for worship) and seeing Thee there how could I pluck the dew-filled gems: nor can I raise my hands for worshipping Thee. I feel ashamed to do so as Thou (the worshipful one) art within me all the while." In the same way the Upanishad says: 'In the light-filled ethereal cavity of the heart, the Sun of the Atman does always shine. He neither rises nor sets and thus (there being neither morning nor evening) how could we make our morning and evening prayers (*Sandhya*)?'

In *Apara-bhakti* or *Saguna* worship the Diety is invoked (from the heart as the idea is; *Avahana*), to a particular seat (*Asana*), His feet are then washed and the water is drunk. He is then bathed, dressed and after that, He is decorated with sacred thread, and sandal, and worshipped with flowers, rice and *Dhupa* (incense), *Dipa* (light), then some offering is made to Him, after that the worshipper goes round the Deity, falls at His feet and utters prayers. Lastly the Deity is taken up from the seat, restored in idea to the heart of the worshipper. This may appear to foreigners as somewhat strange but it embodies and concretely represents a very grand and beautiful truth—that God lives really in the heart, and worshipping Him as external to us, be it as here in the shape of an inspiring image, or as the Father in Heaven, or in any other dualistic way, is really the objectification through our senses of the inconceivable Inner Self. In *Para-bhakti*

there is no such objectification and so says Sankara:
"How could He be invoked from one place to another
who is everywhere? How give a seat to Him who is
Himself the seat of all?......how bathe Him who is
eternally pure?......how go round Him who is
infinite?......how bow to Him who alone really is—the
one without a second?......how take Him back (into
the heart) who is already inside, outside and everywhere? Pure *Puja*, the supreme worship therefore is
the feeling at all times and in all places of the oneness
with Him and the realisation of the truth 'I am He,
I am not the body nor the senses nor the mind nor the
intellect nor the will nor *Ahankara* (the false individuality),
nor am I the earth, nor water, nor fire, nor air, nor ether,
nor smell, nor taste, nor sight, nor touch, nor sound.
I am He, the eternal witness, the only one, the true,
the Blissful Brahman'." In the same way the Yoga
Vasishta says: "The annihilation of all *Bhavanas* or
mental conceptions constitutes the pure worship (*Puja*).
The avoidance of the identification of I with the body
which is concretised Karma, is the supreme *Aradhana*.
Sincere worshippers of the Self should ever regard all
forms and places as no other than Brahman and worship
them as such. Enjoying with a sweet mind and a non-
dual conception, whatever objects one comes by and
not longing for things inaccessible is *Gnana-archana, i.e.,*
the sprinkling of flowers in the worship of the Atman."
In a beautiful passage peculiarly sweet, we are told,
to those engaged in active realisation, the Mandala
Brahmanopanishad says: 'The cessation from all
action is the true *Avahana* (the real invocation to God),
true *Gnana* or wisdom is the seat of the God of Self, a

pure and blissful mind is the water by which that
Diety's feet (the Turiyapada) are washed, complete
mental tranquillity is the water-offering, the uninter-
rupted feeling within the mind of light and bliss welling
up as from a fountain of nectar is the *Snana* (bathing)
of the Deity. Seeing the Atman alone in all that one
sees, and the knower knowing himself, form respectively
sandal and sacred rice (*Akshata*) in the worship. Serene
contentment forms the flower, the fire in the *Chidakas*
is the *Dhupa*. The sun in that *Chidakas* is the *Dipa*
and union with the nectar-filled, moon-like light is the
food offering. Steadiness is the real *Pradakshina* (going
round the Deity). The feeling of 'I am the Atman' is
the *Namaskara*, the bowing at the feet of the Deity ;
and the highest praise is silence (*Mauna*).

Para-bhakti is called *Sakshat Sadhana* or the direct
and immediate means for attaining salvation while
Apara-bhakti is called *Parampara Sadhana* or the indirect means. The one is like rice ready for eating,
while the other is like paddy. Religion in its highest or
rather its truest sense, namely, realisation, begins with
Para-bhakti. Then, when the adorable *Guru* initiates
the eager disciple into the great mystery, Raja Guhya
as the Gita puts it, and utters the memorial words 'That
art Thou,' then and not before does religion begin.
Apara-bhakti, religious studies and all other things only
clear the ground and prepare it for receiving the seed of
wisdom. *Tatwamasi*—'That art Thou' is the beginning
of religion, and *Ahambrahmasmi*—'I am Brahma' is the
end ; and *Para-bhakti* is the means whereby religion so
well begun reaches its completion, whereby the mask
of imperfect and struggling humanity is finally thrown

off and the soul within stands revealed ,and realised in its fullest glory as the One blissful Existence, the great *Satchidananda*, whose ineffable glory, the mighty Self-intoxicated sages of old, vainly struggle to render in the language of words.

Para-bhakti is the highest flower of the human mind, the most beautiful that it can put forth, and its fruit is nothing less than waking once for all from the nightmare of life and realising that blissful existence, after realising which, as the Gita says, nothing further will have to be known. Truth, absolute Truth is the reward ; and the highest Truth is the highest freedom, the highest bliss and the highest life. He who by divine grace conceives the celestial fire and lives the life of the *Parabhakta* even in the dream state as the *Srutis* say, be his caste, country and religion what they may, commands the worship of the gods.

————

FREE WILL versus FATALISM

A VERY interesting controversy has been going on in the Western world for several centuries as to whether and how far man is the free agent of his actions. The question has been discussed from a variety of standpoints and by a host of competent writers, but is yet an open one and must ever remain so, unless studied in the light of the Vedanta as we now propose to do. The empire of the Vedanta is getting wider and wider day by day. The time has come not merely for the old religions of the world which are at present outside the pale of the Vedanta to reconsider their basis and adjust themselves to its high and inspired rationalism, but also for all philosophical questions to be opened afresh and discussed in the light of its conclusions. Such of the latter as seemed closed for ever, urgently call for a fresh discussion, while those which are still open, like the one which forms the subject of this article, invoke the help of the Vedanta for their solution. That there is no hard nut which the Vedanta cannot crack in the domain of religion or philosophy, may be judged from the solution it gives of the problem which we have now taken up.

The Western philosophers who have written upon the subject are divisible into two classes, one party chiefly consisting of moral and religious teachers, and the other, of men of science. The opinion of the latter, which may be denominated as the scientific view, is that the will of man is as much bound by the law of causality as the rest of the phenomena of the universe, and is therefore not free ; while the other party holds that 'whatever may be the claims of determinism in the province of physical science, man's actions are not determined, for he is endowed with free will.' This opinion is generally considered as the moral or religious view and forms the backbone of Christian theology or rather mythology, according to which man's fall from Paradise was due to his own fault and not to the decree of God, due to the abuse of his own will which was free and not to 'the least impulse or shadow of fate'. God is made to say :

> For man will hearken to his (Satan's) glozing lies
> And easily transgress the sole command,
> Sole pledge of his obedience ; so will fall
> He and his faithless progeny. Whose fault ?
> Whose but his own ? Ingrate, he had of me
> All he could have ; I made him just and right,
> Sufficient to have stood though free to fall.

The biblical story of man's fall and redemption evidently concedes freedom of will to man. And indeed without this freedom, ethics would be impossible, and religion absurd. For unless a man be the free agent of his actions, how could he be made to account for them ? There is no responsibility where there is no freedom ; and neither reward nor punishment could with any justice be meted out to a man for having done a thing not of free choice but out of compulsion. If man were not free, not merely earthly justice but even divine justice would be unjust. Heaven, Hell and Judgment would all be vain mockery, virtue would be no virtue, and vice no vice ; piety, love, mercy as well as power, strength, intellect would all lose their merit, and man being chained to a fate which he could not over-power, would be no better than a piece of wood or stone. Fatalism, if it were to be admitted wholesale, would evidently cut at the root of both ethics and religion.

But all this, it is said, does not establish the doctrine of free will. If fatalism be true, it must be accepted even at the cost of ethics and religion. If man be a puppet in the hands of a mysterious something, which we shall agree to call fate, let us freely say so and correct our ethics and religion to suit the truth, instead of sac-rificing the latter for their sake. At any rate, with what justice could we venture to claim immunity for man from the great law of causality which is as uni-versal, as unbending and governs all the rest of the world ? Indeed few truths have been established with greater certainty than that every effect must have a cause adequate to produce it, and this applies as much in the department of human activity as outside it. Therefore man's actions are the result of sufficient causes, such as education, temperament, ancestry, en-vironment, and the like and being thus determined, they are not free. Materialists even go farther and re-gard the mind and its attributes, its higher qualities not excepted, as having emanated from matter and standing therefore in the relation of an effect to the outer or objective world. But this as it may, there is no doubt that man, 'being a part of the great cosmic whole, has to conform to its laws and is shaped by its events. And having of necessity to conform, he is not free either by organism or by environment.'

The limitations set upon the freedom of the human will are, according to the fatalists, twofold. The first is that which is generally called fate, and hampers the movements of man in the outer world ; and the second is a constitutional limitation which determines his mental activity and very subtly intermingles, in the relation of a cause to its effect, with even the most imperceptible and minute workings of his will. Thus bound both inside and outside, man plays his part, or rather is made to play his part in the universe, which though vast is a compact organism instinct with energy, if not with purpose.

Now let us examine the nature of these limitations and the extent of their sway upon the will of man. In the first place, it is a fact of everyday experience that the course of life does not run uniformly, that now we are thwarted with failures and mishaps, and then flattered with success, and that at every step in our journey on earth, we are attended by a mysterious something which either hampers us by its presence, or surprises us with its favours. Two men of equal talent and equal facilities engage in the same trade at the same time, but independently. In a few years' time, one occupies the front ranks of society while the other wanders perhaps, with an empty purse and a broken heart. Gold too often, 'glitters on the forehead of the fool,' while the wise man has nothing but his wisdom to live upon. Again, one period of a man's life, is not like another. Napoleon was at one time the terror of Europe and at another a prisoner in the hands of Hudson Lowe. These are events of daily occurrence, but not the less instructive on that score ; and, when we look into them, we feel bound to admit the active play of an undefinable something which somehow intermingles with and moulds the fabric of experience. The existence of such a factor is distinctly recognised by the unsophisticated throughout the world, and differently christened at different times as fate, luck, fortune, and so on, according to the part it plays. Ever since the world began, the complaint has been that merit and fortune do not go hand in hand, and the disparity between both has been a puzzle both to religion and philosophy. Mythology conveniently saddled the responsibility for such apparent injustice on Clotho and sisters of the abyss of Demogorgen who 'with unwearied fingers drew out the threads of life.' The advent of Christianity was fatal to the fates themselves; they have perished distaff, knife and all. But Fate remains, the terrible bugbear, and he has not yet been brought to book.

Meanwhile unscientific fatalism which pretends to bridge up the chasm between merit and fortune, is a sort of vulgar compromise, and evades the question instead of answering it. To name a thing is not to explain it; so to attribute the apparent injustice in the world to the operation of fate is no solution of the difficulty, for the question remains, 'How sprang this fate into existence? Who made it and what regulates it?' If it be replied that God is the author of fate, the position becomes worse, for what makes God partial, since the destiny of no two persons is alike? It is true that 'there is a power which shapes our ends, rough-hew them how we will'; but to identify that power with God lands us in a serious difficulty, and is utterly irreconcilable with our notions of a moral government of the universe. It might perhaps be asserted that fate is an expression of the Divine will and is simply another

name for the play of Providence, inasmuch as our trials
and successes prove, when observed closely, to be for our
own good. The order in which they happen, the moral
effects which they create, the lessons, which they teach,
the experience they bring, the wonderful fitness, that
strikes the observer, of the events to the person, and the
maternal care which seems to attend the happening
of every event, making life with its variety of experiences
a course of extremely judicious meditation, as it were, to
the soul—all these distinctly point to a design and prove
to a certainty that these trials and successes cannot be
the work of blind caprice. We seem every moment to be
advancing towards perfection, 'moving with a sure
instinct towards God,' and therefore fate which shapes
our ends appears to be simply another name for the will
of God. This may be so and the educative value of fate
is readily admitted, but since very little of ethical progress is achieved in the course of a single life and as, if
man were measured by the deeds performed in that short
span of earthly existence, the spirits of more than
nine-tenths of the human race should be sought for in
hell, fate loses its value and the purpose which we at-
tributed to it is vain. Hence, however valuable may
be the philosophy of Parnell's *Hermit* as a source of
consolation, it is hardly reconcilable with our experience
of men, for man learns far too little in the course of a
single life and very few die as good men. A brief life of
a few years which is all that Christianity gives man (and
how many die in infancy), is too short an educational
course, and we confess our inability to appreciate the
justice with which God, according to the Christian
faith, sends to hell beings to whom He did not give a

sufficient opportunity to learn and become better. Nor
could we understand the grand purpose which some
ascribe to fate seeing that, according to their own admission, the service it renders is in most cases hardly
worth naming.

Thus we see that the popular and religious, or as
we might as well call it, the unscientific conception of
fate is hardly satisfying ; but scientific determinism
too would not appear to be much better. We are ready
to admit with science that fate cannot be an accident
in a world which is throughout governed by the law of
causation, and that its workings, however whimsical
and unregulated they might appear, can be no infringe-
ments of natural law. Fate, we agree, simply represents
a causal series lying outside man which interferes with
man's actions and limits his freedom. But the question
remains why one man's fate is different from that of
others. It may be said that each personality attracts
to itself conditions similar to its nature from the outer
world which control it and constitute its fate. Well
and good ; but how to account for the play of fate
before personality sprang into existence ? The very
conditions of one's birth are determined by fate, and
it would be absurd to speak of one having attracted to
himself the fate by which he was brought into life. It
would be like saying : 'I was present during my father's
marriage with my mother.' The attraction theory
then does not apply in the case at least of ante-natal
fate. Again how to account for the difference between
what are known as good time and bad time in a man's
life. It is within the experience of almost every one
that certain periods in life are particularly full of

mishaps, failures and disappointments, but within a few years the wheel of fortune gets turned, the sky clears and life becomes unusually bright and enjoyable. The attracting personality is in both cases the same, but yet the workings of fate so widely differ. The theory of attraction therefore falls to the ground. It does not explain ante-natal fate, nor does it sufficiently account for the workings of later destiny. Scientific determinism is thus hardly more satisfactory than popular fatalism, so far as the first limitation set on the freedom of the human will is concerned. Though it gives us a theoretical proof that Dame Fortune cannot be blind as the poets wrongly assert, it has to confess its ignorance of her ways and the principle that guides her in the distribution of her favours and frowns.

The fact is, fate has not been understood in the West. There has been a desperate attempt to make it appear reasonable and bind it by some law, but the authors of the attempt could hardly be congratulated on their success. The reason is, they confine their attention entirely to the present as it appears, and totally ignore both the past and the future which are hidden from view. To solve the riddles of the universe solely on the evidence of the senses is as impossible as crossing the Ganges on the back of a mud horse. We have to admit other proofs than *Pratyaksha Pramana* or direct perception and materialistic science which mistaking the apparent to be the entire reality, refuses to look beyond into the hidden half of the universe, can never hope to become a philosophy, though it might excite our wonder now and then with its geological and astronomical feats. This has been understood in our country

10

and the best or rather the only explanation of fate is furnished to us by the Vedanta which begins with mistrusting the apparent.

Its doctrine of Karma clears all our present doubts. Fate according to it is no self-created tyrant, nor a blind old woman often crossing us in our path, but on the other hand, a result of our own deeds, a ruler whom we ourselves raised to the throne and honoured with crown and sceptre. We bound ourselves by ourselves and, this self-created bondage is what is called fate. According to the Vedanta, we alone are responsible for our slavery, neither the high God nor the objective world. The essence of the doctrine of Karma is : 'that which we sow we reap' ; and this sowing and reaping we do, not merely in the present life but have been doing ever since the world began. We have passed through innumerable lives and this present life is but a day in eternity. Western science and Western theology however antagonistic to each other in other respects are yet one in forgetting alike both yesterday and to-morrow in the toil and worry of to-day. Now, however, there is a slow awakening to the consciousness that the present could not have suddenly sprung into existence and that it should be bounded on one side by an infinite past and on the other by an infinite future. Reincarnation is a scientific truth and the doctrine of Karma which is based upon it is a great gain to philosophy.

According to this doctrine, every little act we do is a causal agency and generates results in proportion to its inherent energy, and there not being a single moment in our lives in which we do not act—action here means the activity of either body, mind or the senses—the

Karmic results we generate in the course of a single life are incalculable. Of this vast hoard created in one life, man enjoys only a fraction in the course of that life; for it is impossible for him to enjoy the whole, as only few of his actions bear fruit before his death and as he is performing Karma (action) even in the last moments of his life. The unspent Karmic results are not lost; they get stored up, part in his soul in the form of character and tendencies and part in the outer world, and present themselves in coming lives as fate. Karma (the result of actions—Karma is used in two senses, in some places for action, and in others for the result of actions) is of three kinds. That which gave birth to and determines the conditions of the present life is called *Prarabdha*. The store of past Karma yet unspent is called *Sanchita*, while the Karma generated by the actions of the present life which will become available in a future life is called *Agami*.

Here then is a most rational explanation of fate; it is nothing but unspent Karmic result, and our sudden disappointments and successes in life are thus not a result of blind chance, but of our own work in the past. There is a world's difference between the Eastern and Western conceptions of fate. In the West, it is looked upon as something outside man for whose workings he is not responsible; in the East, it is regarded as one's own making in the past. In the West, as arbitrary; in the East, as rational and regulated. In the West it has been the despair of both religion and philosophy; in the East it has been explained and accounted for.

Free will is a necessary corollary from the Vedantic

explanation of fate. What man made he can unmake and the solemn assurance is :

> You are not bound ! the Soul of Things is Sweet,
> The Heart of Being is celestial rest ;
> Stronger than woe is will ; that which was Good,
> Doth pass to Better—Best.

This is not however the last word of the Vedanta in the matter, and the more important part of the discussion has to be reserved, for want of space, for a future occasion. The second, limitation on the freedom of man's will, which is the stronghold of determinism will then be examined, and the final opinion of the Vedanta on this interesting controversy will be given as well as the authorities bearing out that opinion.

KARMA AND FREEDOM

By a strange perversion of things, the doctrine of Karma has come to be identified with fatalism in the narrow sense of the word, though there are no two things which are so diametrically opposed to each other. Free dom is the very essence of Karma ; and, since it is a thing done, it can be undone by the doer. The Hindus are not fatalists, but know the difference between fate and free will.

Says the great law-giver Manu :—

> Thou canst not gather what thou does not sow ;
> As thou dost plant the tree, so will it grow. (IX, 40.)

> Success in every enterprise depends,
> *On Destiny and man combined,* the acts
> Of Destiny are out of man's control
> *Think not on Destiny but act thyself.* (VII, 205.)

> Whatever the act a man commits, whate'er
> His state of mind, of that the recompense
> Must he receive in corresponding body. (XII, 81.)

> Let all men ponder with attentive mind
> The passage of the soul through divers forms,
> Of Brahma, gods and men, beasts, plants and stones
> According to their good or evil acts,
> And so apply their minds to virtue only.   (XII, 22, 42, 86.)

Here in a nutshell is the whole theory of Karma. The precept is, 'Think not on Destiny but act thyself.' Karma thus, instead of being identical with fatalism, is diametrically opposed to it.   It is an incentive to action, for it does not mystify fate and frighten man, but gives a most rational and scientific explanation of it and assures him that, though the present of which he himself was the author is irrevocable, he may at least better his future. The doctrine of Karma is thus at once an incentive to action and a source of consolation. Whatever in the present is unchangeable is the result of past Karma, and there is no use of complaining about it or of pettishly accusing God. That which is bad now might be made to pass into good in the future, and that which is good to better and best, for 'stronger than woe is will'. Fatalism cuts at the root of ethics, while Karma furnishes the strongest basis for it, for it says, 'By injuring others you injure yourself.' Fatalism destroys faith, while Karma is the best safeguard for it, for it says : 'It is not God that is to blame but yourself.' This is why scepticism which is making a havoc in other countries is conspicuous in ours by its absence. Fatalism means irrevocable bondage, while Karma presupposes freedom of the will. Says the Amritabindu Upanishad :

मन एव मनुष्याणां कारणं बन्धमोक्षयो: ॥

Mind (or will) is the cause of man's bondage and freedom. Sri Krishna says :

उद्धरेदात्मनाऽऽत्मानं नात्मानमवसादयेत् ।
आत्मैव ह्यात्मनो बंधुरात्मैव रिपुरात्मनः ॥
बन्धुरात्माऽऽत्मनस्तस्य येनात्मैवात्मना जितः ।
अनात्मनस्तु शत्रुत्वे वर्तेतात्मैव शत्रुवत् ॥

'Man should raise himself by himself (mind) : he should not ruin himself for he (his mind) is his own friend as well as his own enemy. The mind is the friend of him who by himself, has conquered it, but to him who has not restrained himself, the mind becomes an enemy' (*Gita*, VI. 5-6). In the face of these and number-less other statements of the same kind in our books, it is really surprising that the doctrine of Karma and fatalism should have been confounded with each other by a set of ingenious critics who are honestly struggling to enlighten us on the dark points in our Sastras. Indeed, unless freedom of will be granted, all the scriptures in the world including the Gospels of Christ and our own Vedas, containing injunctions such as :

उत्तिष्ठत जाग्रत प्राप्य वरान्निबोधत ।

'Awake, arise, seek the great ones and obtain wisdom' (*Kath. Up.*, III, 14) might without a sigh be consigned to the bottom of the sea.

Here the determinist comes forward and says : 'We grant that you have to use your discretion and choose between alternatives every moment of your life, but is is not your very choice *determined* by your heredity, temperament, education, environment, and the like, so that you could never have acted differently from how you really acted? It being so, how do you claim that your will is free?' Here is the second of the two limitations imposed according to the fatalist on the liberty of the human will, and this we described at the outset as a constitutional limitation which determines man's mental activity and very subtly intermingles in the relation of a cause to its effect, with even the most imperceptible and minute workings of his will. This is the last arrow in the determinist's quiver, the *Brahmastra* to which he resorts as a final refuge, and we have to reckon with it. It would not do to say, as a recent writer does, "If any fact is clear, it is the conscious choice, whereby I decide to follow this course in preference to that; for although every fact in my experience, every trait of character and every circumstance may be such as apparently to determine my conduct for all future time, it is not until I say, 'I am ready' that the chosen career of self-sacrifice and service, or whatever the choice may be, becomes a living fact." This is a position which is easily overthrown by the determinist, who says that not merely our final choice but even our waverings, our willingness or otherwise to act, and, indeed, all the minutest workings of our will are *determined*, and are as rigidly bound by necessity and as completely obey the law of causation as the phenomena of the material universe. 'You say you are ready,' says he, 'because you cannot but say so.' The microcosm is as much governed by law as the macrocosm, and to place the actions of man on the same footing with the workings of Nature would seem to be scientifically unimpeachable and be the only position thoroughly consistent with the principle of unity which has been discovered to exist in the world. Accordingly Dr. Paul Carus, in his thoughtful and pre-eminently suggestive book, 'Fundamental Problems', compares a man who acts of his free will to a magnet pointing to the North according to its own inherent quality. He says: 'Those who maintain that free will and determinism are irreconcilable contradictions, start from the apparently slight but important error that *compulsion* and *necessity* are identical. They think that what happens from necessity proceeds from compulsion somehow. They overlook the fact that there is a necessity imposed from without as well as a necessity operating from within, the former acts by compulsion, from outward mechanical pressure as it were, while the latter works spontaneously, though necessarily in accordance with the character of the man, constituting his free will. For instance, a man delivers to a highwayman his valuables because he is compelled to do so by threats or even blows : he suffers violence ; his action is not free. But if a man, seeing one of his wretched fellow-beings suffering from hunger and cold through extreme poverty, and overpowered by compassion, gives away all he has about him, this man does not act under compulsion. He acts from free will, but, being such as he is, he so acts of necessity, in accordance with his character.' He adds that if a magnet placed without outward pressure on a pivot be endowed with sentiment and gifted with the power of speech, it would say, 'I am free, and of my free will I point towards the North.'

Dr. Paul Carus admits determinism but very ingeniously points out that determinism and free will are simply different aspects of the same thing. "Free will and determinism," he says, "do not exclude each other. Free will is the postulate of morals, determinism is the postulate of science. The actions of a free will are not irregular or without law : they are rigidly determined by the character of the man that acts."

The doctor is perfectly right when he says that determinism does not exclude free will, but in our opinion, he concedes a little too much to the determinist by agreeing to place the workings of the human will on the same footing with the phenomena of the outer world. We grant that the law of causation is a universal law, that it is the 'internal harmony and the logical order of the world,' and that the actions of man are as much subject to that law as the occurrences in the physical universe, but here the parallel between them is at an end. The magnet points to the North and cannot but do so, when no pressure is put upon it; it knows no alternatives and has to make no decision; a man on the other hand acts in a particular way even when he might have acted otherwise, and he does so because the decision rests with him. At every step he has to choose between alternatives, and his act is determined no doubt in the sense that it is an effect proceeding from proper causes, but one of the causes is his will, which is by its nature free. We do not for a moment assert that this will is free to the fullest extent and can do whatever it pleases, but it is free under certain limitations. The situations in which it finds itself placed and the alternatives which present themselves before it are determined, but not its choice between those alternatives.

Our meaning will become clearer if we examine once again into the doctrine of Karma. According to this Vedantic doctrine, the only bondage which man is subject to, is the result of his own actions (*Karma Bandha*). The doer is by nature free, for Karma implies a free doer, but every act he does produces a twofold result which clings to him, first, a tangible result, and secondly, a tendency good or bad. Past Karma influences the present life, therefore, in two ways; first, in the shape of a man's character or tendencies, and secondly, as external fate. The self-conscious man, Jiva is by nature free, for otherwise the doctrine of Karma would be meaningless, but he having by his own act imposed upon his freedom this twofold limitation, all that is left to him is only a power to choose between the alternatives which fate brings before him, and in choosing between them he may either follow his tendencies generated by past Karma or struggle against them. Both the situation and his tendencies are determined, but within this twofold limitation there is a narrow scope for free choice. The faculty of choosing is what we call will, or, in Vedantic language, *Chitta*. But for this free *Chitta*, neither progress nor retrogression would be possible. The will is by its own nature free, and asserts itself every moment of our lives, and every little act that we do is a result of three conjoint forces— our free will, our character, and our fate. The simile of the magnet would imply that man is merely a bundle of tendencies, and indeed the doctor says explicitly that it is man's character that *constitutes his free will,* which is putting the cart before the horse. He is his tendencies, his character *plus* his will which is free by birthright. According to the nature of his Karma and the character generated by it, this will obtains a wider or narrower field for its play and, though character thus determines to some extent its activity, it does not create it, but on the other hand is created by it. The argument therefore that the minutest workings of human will are determined, and that consequently it is not free, falls to the ground. Man's will is free and much freer than the blind force which manifests in the physical universe.

Here the determinist will ask : 'What right have you to place man on an exceptional footing ? Do you not offend against the all-pervading principle of unity that governs the world ?' We answer that the unity underlying the constitution of the world leaves abundant scope for manifoldness, for it is essentially unity in diversity, and embraces an infinite variety of stages in manifestation, and that it is not we that place man on a higher pedestal, but he is so placed by Nature herself by the very fact of self-consciousness or egoism which in Vedantic parlance is called *Ahankara*. As Ferrier has so rightly observed : 'Man alone has the capacity to look into himself, and consciousness or ego is his distinguishing feature........The lower animals, though endowed with reason as in building nests, etc., *do not know* that they exist. Man alone lives this double life— to exist and to be conscious of existence, to be rational and to know that he is so. Animals are wanting in consciousness or self-reference, because conscience, morality, responsibility, etc., based on it are absent in them.'

This consciousness, or rather self-consciousness, gives man a much greater scope than the magnet. It gives him a larger tether and, what is more, always keeps telling him that he is free. As Swami Vivekananda says : 'This curious fact you cannot relinquish, your actions, your very lives will be lost without it, this idea of freedom, that we are free. Every moment we are proved by nature to be slaves, and not free, yet simultaneously rises the other idea, still I am free. Every step we are knocked down as it were by Maya and shown that we are bound, and yet the same moment, together with this blow, together with this feeling that we are bound, comes the other feeling that we are free. Something inside tells us that we are free.' The idea of freedom is involved in self-consciousness. Had Dr. Paul Carus used the word *'self-consciousness'* instead of *'sentiment'* in the sentence, "Were the magnet endowed with *sentiment* and gifted with speech, it would say 'I am free and of my free will I point toward the North'," he would have been in our opinion correct. The idea 'I am free' is co-ordinate with self-consciousness, and refuses to die so long as egoism lasts ; hence it is ranked with the latter by the Vedanta as one of the essential principles (*Tatwas*) in the soul, the *Jivatman*. It has been well observed : 'We are placed in charge of ourselves by the fact of self-consciousness.' When man by bad Karma descends to the lower rungs in the ladder of life and becomes, say, a plant or stone, self-consciousness disappears, and with its disappearance the will degenerates into blind force, devoid of the power of conscious choice between alternatives which constitutes what in man is free will.

The doctrine of free will is, however, only the exoteric doctrine of the Vedanta. For free will depends on self-consciousness or *Ahankara*, false individuality, the destruction of which is the one lesson of the Upanishads. The individual soul, *Jivatman*, is really a figment of nescience (Maya) and when it realises its falsity and loses itself like a river in the sea, into the one Reality (एकमेवाद्वितीयंब्रह्म), in other words when the truth of such sayings as : 'O Swetaketu, that art thou', 'the self is all this', and the like is realised, the individual will disappears and with it its freedom and its bondage.

This oneness (*Adwaitam*), this *Bhuma* (the Infinite), where one sees nothing else, hears nothing else, understands nothing else (*Ch. Up.*, VIII, xxiv, 1), is beyond the reach of sight or speech or thought न तत्र चक्षुर्गच्छति न वाग्गच्छति नो मन: (*Ken. Up.*, I, 3), and could hardly be described in terms of Will or Force, for all these more or less involve the idea of duality, and are expression more nearly allied to the phenomenal world than to the Noumenon. Again, even in the phenomenal plane, the world, as we see it, is nothing but an extension of the Brahman, as there can be nothing outside the Infinite, and all the actions in it are therefore really the actions of God. So says Thayumanavar: 'Everything is Thy property, O God; everything is Thy doing; Thou pervadest the whole universe.' In another place he says: 'There is nothing which is my doing, as the state of "I" is impossible without "Thee". So says the Upanishad, 'He who dwelling in the mind is within the mind, whom the mind does not know, whose body is the mind, who from within rules the mind, is thy Soul, the Inner Ruler immortal' (*Bri. Up.*, III, VII). The esoteric doctrine, so to speak, of the Vedanta is therefore neither that of free will nor that of fatalism. It is that whatever is done is really the doing of the *Antaryamin*, 'the Inner Ruler immortal,' and that not an atom can move except at His bidding, for there is nothing outside Him. The realisation and the consistent following out of this truth in practical life are not however so easy as might appear, for there is our *Ahankara*, egoism, always asserting itself, and pretending to be the sovereign lord of the universe. But when this egoism is subdued and the will which fancied itself to be free is surrendered, miraculous are the results which follow, a truth so beautifully presented in the 'Draupadi Vastrapaharanam' scene in the Mahabharata. To be able to say at all times and in all the situations of life : 'O God, Thy will be done' is really a privilege, and it will gradually deliver man from the thraldom of Maya.

> Our wills are ours, we know not how :
> Our wills are ours, to make them Thine,—

these lines of Tennyson represent correctly the first two phases of thought, and the third and the last in that in which the ours and Thine both alike disappear, and which is glorified by the great Yajnavalkya, who says to his wife :

तद्वा एतदक्षरं गार्ग्यदृष्टंद्रष्टृश्रुतं श्रोत्रमतं मन्त्रविज्ञातं विज्ञातृ नान्यदतोस्ति द्रष्टृ नान्यदतोस्ति श्रोतृ नान्यदतोस्ति मन्तृ नान्यदतोस्ति विज्ञातृ तस्मिन् खल्वक्षरे गार्ग्याकाश ओतश्च प्रोतश्चेति ॥

'Oh Gargi! This immutable One is the unseen Seer, the unheard Hearer, the unthought Thinker, the un-known Knower ; there is no seer beside This, no hearer beside This, no thinker, no knower beside This. In this immutable One, Oh dear Gargi ! is interwoven the *Akasa* (the last essence of all existence).'

'Be thou only my instrument,' said the Lord to **Arjuna** (*Gita*, XI, 33).

————

MAN HIS LITTLENESS AND HIS GREATNESS

FAMILIARITY, it has been said, is our worst enemy. There are ever so many things in this world, which because we see them daily, we have ceased to be curious about. 'How few of us look at the sky,' Ruskin asks. Indeed, very few really see it, for it has been our companion from the earliest moments of our lives, and has by its assuring constancy lulled to rest the spirit of questioning. The child stares with surprise at a stranger, but never so at its own mother. To Miranda, the desert-bred maiden, Fernandez, though quite as much man as her own father, is full of curiosity and interest. For the same reason, we look more wistfully at a new spinning-wheel than at the sky with all its serried phalanx of stars. If, however, the same sky with its gilded heraldry, had not been when we were born and were to surprise us with a sudden arrival, our wonder and curiosity would reach a poetic height, and the lowest of the little men of earth would lift up his hands with awe and reverence and pour forth in the simplicity and fulness of his fear a hymn of praise with almost Vedic vigour. But now look at our dulness. The sky is hourly, minutely phenomenal. No two moments of its life are alike : clouds pass and repass ; the sun rises and sets with epic pomp, the moon shines out with lyric sweetness ; there is a ceaseless rising and falling of the curtains above, and the scenes there are being endlessly shifted ; but the majority of us are perfectly dull to such charms, though we know absolutely nothing about them.

But why talk of the sky : we are hardly concerned
with it ; how far it is going to meddle with our day's
work, the meteorological chart shows us, and that is
quite enough for all our practical purposes ; let us go
to things nearer home ; let us take man himself, the
one object in creation with which we are most closely
concerned. Very few men can rid themselves of human
associations ; in work and out of work we are always
with men. 'Society, love and friendship' is the silent
cry even of our spare moments. But what do we know
of man ? Nothing. He comes and goes, we do not
know where. One man is a poet and another a warrior,
we hardly know why. Man breathes while he lives, but
at the moment of death breath fails : no human physiology can tell us satisfactorily enough what it is that
lies breathless, and what that which was breathing,
why we came, and where we go, if the life we lived ends
with death, and whether we are matter, or spirit, or
soul, or mind, or the senses, or everything, or nothing.
The great and profound mystery that encircles us all
around baffles our feeble attempt to unravel it, and it
was in the fulness of this sense of the darkness around
that Goethe cried out : 'We are eternally in contact with
problems. Man is an obscure being : he knows little
of the world and of himself least of all.' In the same
way Rousseau has said : 'We have no measure for this
huge machine—the world. We cannot calculate its relations ; we know neither its primary laws nor its final
causes. We do not know ourselves ; we know neither
our nature nor our active principle.' These are great
sayings—the sayings of men who have at least shaken
off the dulness of familiarity. To feel the mystery, to

11

understand the problem, to recognise the feebleness of our understanding is itself a privilege in the world, where man too often falls a victim to the sense of familiarity, and, being hardly able to raise himself above his little concerns that rise in successive surprise, resembles the fisherman swimmer on the sea who, while battling with its wavelet for the sake of prey, feels not the majesty of its voice or the glory of its storm.

We of to-day are, however, the heirs of ages and great men—god-like men have been before us ; and in the light of the visions they have had, and the truths they have bequeathed to the world, we shall proceed to chalk out however vaguely the range of the curious self-reflecting animal called 'man',

इन्द्रियाणि पराप्याहु रिन्द्रियेभ्यः परम्मनः ।
मनसस्तु परा बुद्धियों बुद्धेः परतस्तु सः ॥

i.e., the senses are higher than the body, the mind is higher than the senses, the intellect is higher than the mind ; the soul or the *Atman* is higher than all these.

Man has been called 'the roof of creation' ; but he can hardly be so called if we take his body alone into account. Though he is 'express and admirable', as Shakespeare puts it, in form and moving, animals there are which are stronger, more beautiful, more majestic and better than he is in the qualities of the body. Huxley considers the horse the best built animal in creation. There is a majesty about the tusked Indian Elephant to which the best gladiator can lay no claim. The bearing of a lion is more royal than that of a born king. The gait of a well-bred bull of Southern India would shame that of a warrior. The peacock's spreading its feathers is a splendid festival. Not even Nurjehan had the soft complexion of a parrot. The skylark, the 'pilgrim of the sky', is much more privileged than man chained down to earth. The cobra that spreads its hood at the sound of sweet music is almost divine, while the Garuda bird that hymns across the sky is certainly so. Man, then, is no more favoured than other animals in creation, in point of physique, and is indeed a more dirty animal than many a wild beast. Schopenhauer considers the faces of most men common-place. Pattanathu Pillaiyar, the great Dravidian philosopher, says : 'I have survived the shafts of women's eyes : My lord has made me one with Him. So whether I live or die it matters not, my happiness is all the same. Still it is disgusting to bear company with this body.' The pride of man is not therefore his body. The dignity he has and the majesty of his 'heaven-erect' face are primarily due to the grandeur of the spirit that beams forth from within.

Passing on from the body of man to his senses and mind there too we find he has little reason for pride. So far as the activity of the senses is concerned, he is almost inferior to animals. Schopenhauer goes to the length of putting him down as decidedly lower than most animals. There are men that make the tiger and the bear good and virtuous. The tiger and the bear have enemies marked out instinctively. The tiger does not interfere with the crow, the bear kills not cats. Man on the other hand has no such discrimination with respect to his quarrels. 'All sheep and oxen, yea, and,

beasts of the field, the fowls of the air, and the fish of
the sea and whatsoever passeth through the paths of the
seas'—all are his possible enemies. From the innocent
ant upwards to man himself, there is not one animal
which he hesitates to injure for his purposes. In the
storm of the senses the most sacred of social relations
are set at nought. One word, *Dayada*, meaning a cog-
nate, has become a synonym for foe. Schopenhauer,
says : 'Do we desire to know what men morally considered are worth as a whole and in general ? We have
only to consider their fate as a whole. That is want,
wretchedness, affliction, misery and death. If men
were not as a whole worthless, their fate would not be
so sad.' And then when we take the question of criminal
responsibility into account, when we remember that
man has few instincts of enmity to obey and has a will
free to use and abuse, we hardly know where to place
him in the list of living animals. The ant and the spider
have taught many a man. The parliament of the bees
would shame the assembly at the Westminister Hall.
The gentleness of the cow is proverbial. Serpents with
their ear for music and their taste for flowers and smells
would shame a poet. Man's boundless selfishness, his
vanity, his cruelty, his arrogance and wantonness are
purely devilish and Hamlet might well ask : 'Who
would bear the oppressor's wrong, the proud man's
contumely, the pangs of despised love, the law's delay,
the insolence of office and the spurns that patient merit
of the unworthy takes ?' Indeed a great French writer
has remarked that he is not worth living who has not
in the midst of men even once seriously thought of
suicide, 'Blow, blow, thou winter wind, thou art not so

unkind as man's ingratitude,' has in it a philosophy that must be appreciated. Pascal said that half the evils of the world would vanish if only people will learn to be quiet, but that man cannot; and as the Gita says, he is doing *Karma* and sowing the seeds of sinful life every moment of his existence. The rage of the lion, the rancour of the elephant, the ferocity of the tiger, the venom of the serpent, the low cunning of the fox, the ugly instincts of the boar, the vileness of the rat have all their counterpart in the mind of man. Nay, he often overdoes these so-called lower animals and is weaving a constant and ever thickening web of hatred and desire as naturally as a spider weaves its cobweb.

Now passing on to man's intellect, we observe he leaves many animals far behind. Indeed the intellect is a saving element in him. Newton losing himself in his mathematical calculations leaves the earth far behind. Archimedes running naked from the river with a grand discovery in his head is a demigod in human form. Galileo, 'the Tuscan artist viewing the moon through optic glass' from the top of Fesole is a veritable mountain spirit. But, alas! How few are our heroes, how few when compared with the vast and never ending wilderness of men. Every man has intellect, but, mixed up with his senses, it is no more a sanctuary to shelter him, but a whirlwind to toss him to and fro, on the already stormy sea of this sensuous world. Intellect, the precious gift of man, in most cases prostituted, and, in professions like that of the lawyer and the merchant, proves often a curse to the society and to the individual. It may be that it is given to us 'to fill the heavens with commerce,' 'to rift the hills, roll the waters, flash the lightnings, and weigh the sun.' As Renan says, the world has a destination, and to its end it goes with a sure instinct. So forward, forward let us range, that the great world may spin for ever down the ringing grooves of change, and as we go let us sing a triumphant anthem to the deity of knowledge—the goddess Saraswati.

But in the highest height of knowledge where are we ? What we once knew to be water we now know to be oxygen plus hydrogen ; but what is hydrogen and what is oxygen—who can tell ? What we once knew to be an element we now know to be a compound, but what further can we say ? In biology, in geology, in physiology, in astronomy, in physics, in chemistry, and in fact in every one of the various branches of human knowledge there is an imperial edict : 'Thus far shalt thou and no further' thundered forth in solemn majesty ; and as we go farther and farther, the mystery thickens instead of dissolving, so that at last after an untiring, earnest and almost frantic pursuit after the phantom of knowledge, the verdict has come forth from the lips of no less an apostle than Kant that ontology is unknowable. It is, however, an old conclusion given out in all humility by Socrates in Europe and Sankara in India. Newton's metaphor, that he was but playing on the shore of the roaring sea of knowledge, was no mock humility. I take a drop of water, I call it water and cast it away. Turner takes it and draws it on a piece of paper. Tyndall takes it, weighs it, examines it by the microscope, and wonder of wonders—innumerable creatures are found living in it, all full of life, full of consciousness, and full of activity and carrying out their mission on earth with as much earnestness and freedom as man. Poor Tyndall is struck dumb with awe and wonder, lets fall the little drop and swoons away in meditation. As for knowing that drop of water, neither you, nor I, nor Turner, nor Tyndall can do it, it is impossible and absolutely so—a melancholy conclusion no doubt, but inevitable.

In point of intellect, then, though we are far superior to other animals, with the ever ringing 'I know nothing,' we have no special reason to be proud—much less to glorify ourselves as the lords of creation. We hardly know what beings beside ourselves live, what powers they have, what worlds hang out on space. We do not know the air we breathe, the earth we stand on, the stars that shine above—'those innumerable pitiless, passionless eyes in the heavens which burn and brand his nothingness into man.' But we know that the universe is boundless, that there are millions and millions of worlds like ours, that the whole creation is unutterably grand, and that we ourselves with the littleness of our body, the lowness of our senses, with the feebleness of our understanding and with our wickedness, vanity, and ignorance are unspeakably insignificant. We are atoms, poor insignificant atoms in this mighty, measureless and glorious universe. In the old superstition man was the centre of the world, but

He is now but a cloud and a smoke who once was a pillar of fire
The guess of a worm in the dark and the shadow of its desire.

There is one faculty, however, in man which goes a little way in making up for this extreme littleness. It is the faculty of imagination : it is a magic possession as precious as the fabled jewel in the head of a toad. It is a priceless faculty with which we can measure the universe. Of it the poet has said—

> Whatever God did say
> Is all thy plain and smooth uninterrupted way:
> Nay even beyond His works thy voyages are known.

Poetry, I mean the highest imaginative poetry, like that of Shelley and Wordsworth is its most fragrant flower. True, we cannot understand the universe, but we can enjoy it. As Wordsworth so beautifully puts it 'The poet is content to enjoy the things which others might (or might not) understand.' Shelley really measures the sky when he sings—

> Palace-roof of cloudless heights,
> Paradise of golden lights !
> Deep, immeasureable vast
> Which art now and which wert then !
> *   *   *
> Presence-chamber, temple, home
> *   *   *
> Even thy name is as a good,
> *   *   *
> Generations as they pass
> Worship thee with bended knees.

Nay, not content with this, he is able to go farther and say,

> What is heaven ? a globe of dew, etc.

Here is poetry of the most splendid kind, a tacit but rapturous recognition of the power of the human mind, which tramples under foot the low cares of life, and

soars aloft like the sky-lark into the domain of boundless space, becoming for that time that boundless space
itself. No fetters can here bind the man, nothing can
check his heavenward flight; and no one here at least
can say : 'Thus far shalt thou.' Sing Forth, O spirit,
till your dirty bonds break asunder, for thou art on the
road to salvation, very near the radiant throne of the
Almighty who rejoices in thy flight and welcomes thee
with open arms. Here man is grand, nay, boundlessly
so.

Even this is not the height of man's glory, for poetry,
gives both pleasure and pain : it has to record both the
greatness of the universe and the littleness of man.
Then, again, it cannot fall in love with the sultry day,
the dirty tank, the barren desert and things of that
kind, of which there is no lack on earth. At the best,
therefore, poetry is but a resting place on the wayside,
a *Mantapa* on the road to the Temple.

A higher happiness than what poetry can give is the
birthright of man. It is his prerogative to be eternally
and changelessly happy, to rejoice as much at sultry
weather as at a moonlit night, to regard with equal composure the wanton wickedness of men and their benevolent self-sacrifice, not merely to weep with joy at a
Cumbrian sunset, and fly into space with a singing sky-
lark's flight, but to 'mingle in the universe and, feeling
what he can never express but cannot all conceal,' become himself the sun, the setting, the splendour, the
sky-lark, the singing and the sky and all the rest in the
glorious universe. Man is destined to conquer the
heavens, the stars, the mountains, and the rivers, along
with his body, his mind, and his senses, and even in

this life, to dissolve himself into boundless space, and
feel all within himself the roaring sea, the high mountain,
the shining stars and the noisy, cataract. In this sense,
He is the Lord, the Parabrahman of the Vedas, and at
this stage he is above all anger, all meanness, and all
wickedness. The rage of intellect and the storm of the
senses are all over, and in the mind of the highest emancipated man, there is an eternal moony splendour,
boundless beatitude that is above all expression. Now
he can sing with the author of the Maitreya Upanishad—

अहमस्मि परश्चास्मि ब्रह्मास्मि प्रथवोस्म्यहम् ।
सर्वलोकगुरुश्चास्मि सर्वलोकोस्मि सोस्म्यहम् ॥

i.e., I am myself, I am others, I am *Brahman*, I am
the author of creation. I am the *Guru* to the whole
world, and I am the whole world, and I am He, for he
is himself the *Atman*, the birthless, changeless, deathless *Atman* whom swords cannot kill, fire cannot burn,
water cannot moisten and wind cannot wither. This
then is the height of human glory, which man, senseless
man, is bartering away every moment for the low
pleasures of life—this his birthright which, blinded by
passion, he sells away for 'a mess of potage'!

Most of us do not know ourselves : we do not realise
our resources ; we do not think about the treasures
that lie concealed within the four walls of our little frame.
The Vedanta philosophy, like Manackal Nambi in the
story of Alavandar, invites us to take hold of our priceless birthright and be eternally happy. This the grand
promise of the Upanishad which, not few have found,

is kept to the very letter. Having thus known the potentiality of man, the greatness to which he is heir, the psalm shall no longer be :

'O Lord, our Lord, how excellent is Thy name in all the earth, who hast set Thy glory above the heavens, when I consider the heavens the work of Thy fingers, etc.,' but :

'O man ! O man ! How excellent is Thy name in all the earth, who hast set Thy glory above the heavens— who art Thyself the heavens, the sun, the moon, and the stars, and the God that made them all'—*Aum Tat Sat.*

FAITH

FAITH is a necessity of life. Life is impossible without
it. And the very first thing we do is to believe.
"Thought may shake or strengthen faith : it cannot
produce it. Is its origin in the will ? No ; good-will
may favour it, ill-will may hinder it, but no one believes by will, and faith is not a duty :—it is an instinct,
for it precedes all outward instruction." As Count
Tolstoi says : "If a man lives, he believes in something.
If he did not believe that there is something to live
for, he would not live. If he does not see and understand the unreality of the finite, he believes in the finite.
If he sees that unreality, he must believe in the infinite.
Without faith there is no life."

Man is what he believes. For instance, if he believes that the world is created for him and that his
lower self is the God at whose feet he should throw
flowers, then he becomes a narrow-minded withered-up
little thing, incapable of any great and truly useful
achievement. If on the other hand, he believes himself to be one with the mighty all-conscious Soul of the
Universe, and sees all things in himself and himself in
all things, he becomes God and leaves behind either in
the visible world of action and strife, or, in the invisible
one of thought and spirit, a legacy which will last for
evermore, gathering additional strength in every age,
creating numberless Christs, Buddhas and Sankaras,
and maintaining the world much more really than the
blind physical forces which seem to do so. A man's

faith thus determines what he is and fixes his place in the Universe.

It should however be clearly recognised that the value of any particular belief is in proportion to its being correct. Faith should at no time be allowed to oppose itself to truth ; for all delusions are injurious and hinder the progress of the spirit. It is true that reason does not create faith, but whatever the faith be, it must stand to reason. It is the sanction of reason which raises faith from a mere instinct to the rank of inspiration. All the great men known to fame and these yet greater, who were beyond its reach, were inspired men, men having tremendous faith which was at the same time reason-proof. The teachings of these men, which form the scriptures of the world, stand on unshakeable, eternal verities revealed to them by their sterling faith which had passed through the crucible of reason and become brighter and purer for it. The noble truths of Buddha, the Sermon on the Mount, the Bhagavad-Gita and the sublime philosophy of the Upanishads, all stand on the unshakeable Maha Meru of Truth round which the sun, moon and stars have travelled for centuries and will travel for ages without making one syllable of them old and useless for all their incessant rotations. Faith in its highest or rather its real sense is truth and instead of being opposed to reason is built upon it. There is no greater enemy to the world than narrow unenlightened faith. As Amiele observes : "That which is a mere prejudice of childhood, which has never known doubt, which ignores science, which cannot respect or understand or tolerate different convictions—such a faith is a stupidity and a hatred,

the mother of all fanaticism........To draw the poison-
fangs of faith in ourselves, we must subordinate it to
the love of truth. The supreme worship of the true is
the only means of purification for all religions, all confessions, all sects. Faith should only be allowed the
second place, for faith has a judge in truth. When
she exalts herself to the position of supreme judge, the
world is enslaved ; Christianity, from the fourth to the
seventeenth century, is the proof of it." Faith should
only be allowed the second place ; yes, by itself and
when unenlightened. But when it weds itself to truth
and gets enlightened, it works wonders, it rules the
world and sustains it : it 'makes man whole.'

Mere intellect can do little : at best it can only knock
against the Unknowable, and, like Duscasana, the brother
of Duryodhana who, attempting to strip the chaste
queen Draupadi naked, was confounded with fear and
surprise at the successive layers of cloths which seemed
to grow, by Sri Krishna's grace, over her body, each cloth
more brilliant and costly than the preceding one ; dry,
unaided, uninspired reason lifts off veil after veil from
Nature's body only to find that there is 'veil upon veil
behind'. Reason can write learned books on politics,
invent newer and newer engines of destruction, fight battles
and conquer nations, argue most metaphysically, frame
theories after theories, analyse, dissect and decompose
everything in the outer world ; it can 'rift the hills, and
roll the waters, flash the lightnings and weigh the sun,'
but it cannot step one inch beyond the relative and the
phenomenal, and much less can it afford any answer to
the great and fundamental problems of life ; and like the
spectre at Macbeth's table, the ghost of the murdered

soul grins and groans by turns at the revel of reason.
'The intellect,' says Swami Vivekananda, 'is only the
street cleaner, cleansing the path for us, a secondary
worker.' This is why the sage of Konigsberg said :
'The sphere of faith transcends the sphere of reason.'
'Human reason,' says Thomas-a-Kempis, 'is weak and
may be deceived, but true faith cannot be deceived.'
'Faith is the evidence of things not seen.'

This faith is not, as we have already indicated,
merely the 'believe in Christ and you will be saved' of
the Christian missionary, but faith founded on reason.
Blind belief has its uses, but it will, if not in this life at
least in some future one, melt away like the 'paradise
which lies about us in our infancy' when the fruit of
the tree of knowledge is tasted, that is, when awakened
reason asserts itself and the problem of evil presses for
solution. At a particular stage in human evolution
the question of 'to be or not to be' assumes a serious
aspect, and

> The slings and arrows of outrageous fortune,
>
>   *   *   *
>
> The oppressor's wrong, the proud man's contumely,
> The pangs of despised love, the law's delay,
> The insolence of office and the spurns
> That patient merit of the unworthy takes

all tempt man to make 'his quietus with a bare bodkin'
and the blind faith in a fatherly and merciful God flies
away like darkness before light. Here begins the real
search after God. The following is the experience of
a great man who passed through this stage. "I said to
myself," says Count Tolstoi, 'It is well, there is no God,
there is none that has a reality apart from my own
imaginings, none as real as my own life—there is none

such. Nothing, no miracles can prove there is, for miracles exist in my own unreasonable imagination.

"And then I asked myself : 'But my conception of the God whom I seek, whence comes it ?' And again life flashed joyously through my veins. All around me seemed to revive, to have a new meaning. My joy, though, did not last long, for reason continued to work.

"The conception of God is not God. Conception is what goes on within myself ; the conception of God is an idea which I am able to rouse in my mind or not as I choose : it is not what I seek, something without which life could not be." Then again all seemed to die around and within me and again I wished to kill myself.

"After this, I began to retrace the process which had gone on within myself, the hundred times repeated discouragement and revival. I remembered that I had lived only when I believed in God. As it was before, so it was now : I had only to know God, and I lived : I had only to forget Him, not to believe in Him, and I died..........I should long ago have killed myself if I had not had a dim hope of finding Him..........A voice seemed to cry within me ; 'This is He, He without whom there is no life. To know God and to live are one. God is life.'

"Live to seek God, and life will not be without Him. And stronger than ever rose up life within and around me, and the light that then shone never left me again."

Pretty nearly the same experience is described by the poet in the following words :

> If e'er when faith had fallen asleep,
> I heard a voice 'Believe no more,
> And heard an ever-breaking shore,
> That tumbled in the Godless deep :

A warmth within the heart would melt
The freezing reason's colder part,
And, like a man in wrath, the heart
Stood up and answered 'I have felt.'

Here is the resurrection of faith, but it is yet in the clouds, owing most probably to the unspiritual character of modern Christendom. 'Where all are blind, the one-eyed man is king' is the saying and final realisation of Count Tolstoi is looked upon by him as a sufficient recompense for the mental agitation he suffered, only because he is in modern Europe where spirituality is at a low ebb. Had he been in India, he would have pushed on the search farther and would never have rested till he saw God face to face, and the stage through which he passed is just the stage in which, in the blessed *Gnana Bhumi* (land of wisdom) of ours, the great *Guru* (Parama Acharya) appears and with a love which looks for no reward and purer in its nature than the love of father, mother, husband and wife and altogether divine, gives his protecting hand to the despairing soul and takes it one by successive steps through the straight old path of the seers, to its final destination. Ah, in what words can the divine *Guru* be praised ; where is the language which could give words to express the greatness and the wisdom of the *Guru* ! The disciple sings

॥ ओं ॥
सवाकारं सर्वमसर्व ं सर्वनिषेधावधिभूत ं यत् ।
सत्यं शाश्वतमेकमनन्तं शुद्धं बुद्धं तत्त्वमसि त्वं ॥
नित्यानन्दाखण्डरसं कं निष्कळमक्रियमस्तविकारं ।
प्रत्यगभिन्नं परमव्यक्तं शुद्धं बुद्धं तत्त्वमसि त्वं ॥

प्रत्यस्तमिताशेषविशेषं व्योमेवान्तर्बहिरपि पूर्णं ।
ब्रह्मानन्दं परमाद्वैतं शुद्धं बुद्धं तत्त्वमसि त्वं ।
ज्ञातृज्ञानज्ञेयविहीनं ज्ञातुरभिन्नं ज्ञानमखण्डं
ज्ञेयाज्ञेयत्वादिविमुक्तं शुद्धं बुद्धं तत्त्वमसि त्वं ॥
अन्तःप्राज्ञत्वादिविकल्पैररनृष्ठप्रत्यग्रूपं भद्दशिमात्रं ।
गगनाभं सत्तामात्रं समरसमेकं शुद्धं बुद्धं तत्त्वमसि त्वं ॥

but is not satisfied. There is only one language which could express it all and that is the language of faith, implicit faith. This faith is not blind. It is most rational, for the *Guru* first convinces the disciple, satisfies his intellect and then storms and captures his heart. The teacher wants not mere *Sraddha*, faith, but also *Viveka*, discrimination, and both are reckoned in the Vedanta as necessary qualifications for the student and the highest experience which the *Guru* reveals is supported not merely by the Srutis, but also *stands to reason and is confirmed by realisation*. Faith in the *Guru* is not then a blind belief; intellect and reason are not to be smothered and crushed, but fed and satisfied; until they lie in perfect confidence and repose without wanting to assert themselves. The *Guru* says not merely 'Believe and you will be saved' but 'Believe only if it stands to reason, and if it so stands, then have firm faith in it; for mere intellectual assent avails nothing.' The heart cannot ignore the head, for then intellect will some day or other prove a 'traitor in the camp' and have its revenge, but both the head and the heart must be satisfied, though it is the latter that finally receives inspiration. Faith in the *Guru* then is not mere belief. This faith is even superior to devotion, for there is no difference in it between the teacher and the taught, as there is between the devotee and the object of his devotion. The disciple worships and loves the *Guru* as his own Self and the *Guru* also loves the disciple as he loves himself. There is no duality in this faith ; it is all bliss and no two souls meet together in closer union than those of the *Guru* and the disciple. They understand each other as no others do ; they love each other with no human love ; they are both one in reality—they are one God not two. The *Advaitam* (non-duality) between the *Guru* and disciple is first realised and immediately after the *Ekameva* (the only one) of the universe. The nature of this faith is total self-surrender and the literal carrying out of the *Guru's* instructions, and its ultimate expression is *Mauna* ; for it has been said : 'The man of faith obtains wisdom.'

This faith in one's *Guru*, in the Christ, or in other words in one's Self (the higher Self) asks no favours, for what could he who has such faith, ask for, being above desire and seeing nothing outside himself. But exactly for this reason every event in his life is a genuine miracle and divine in its nature, for says Sri Krishna : "I bear the burden of the concerns in the life of those who are constantly employed in worshipping Me" (*Gita*, IX, 22).

Swami Vivekananda rightly says : "As certain religions of the world say a man who does not believe in a personal God outside of himself is an atheist, so says the Vedanta, a man who does not believe in himself is an atheist. Not believing in the glory of your own soul is what the Vedanta calls atheism." This however should be properly understood. To say : 'I can do anything and everything' just as Napoleon is reported to have said : 'Thou shalt have none other gods but me' is *Asuric* (worthy of *Asuras*) and utterly incompatible with the *Satwic* humility which is the characteristic of the sage. The 'I' should not refer to the lower ego which should be killed, but to the higher Self the only reality. We shall make our meaning clearer by an example. A ship in which Julius Cæsar was a passenger, was overtaken by a storm and the captain feared for the safety of the crew when Cæsar said : 'Fear not, man. Dost thou not know who is in the ship ? ' This is an example of *Rajas* pure and simple, of faith in oneself, in one's lower ego which is a cause of bondage and misery. On a very similar occasion the Christian Saint Ignatius said : 'The winds and the seas obey our Lord' and betrayed not the least apprehension or fear, but he was a little troubled in mind that he had not served God as he ought to have done. There was more of *Satwa* in this, but by far the best example of faith is that of the Indian sage whom Alexander threatened to kill and who replied : "Me you can never kill. I am He, the eternal and infinite. Me swords cannot pierce, fire cannot burn, water cannot moisten nor winds wither. How could I be slain ?" To be always filled with the idea of one's being the Atman is real faith and this is the *Karma-phalatyagam* (abandonment of the fruits of one's action) of the Gita, the *Sahaja-sthithi* (the free, natural state of Self-realisation), of the Vedanta and its immediate results are fearlessness and peace of mind. Come what may and go what may, it always remains unshaken, for it is permanently wedded to eternity.

WORK AND SAINTSHIP

"By works the votary doth rise to Saint,
And Saintship is ceasing from all works."
Bhagavad Gita.

OUR ignorance is simply appalling. Verily has it been described as an unfathomable ocean of darkness. 'Who made this utter darkness my home,' cries Thayumanavar, 'and reduced my knowledge to lightning-like flashes?' When the divinity within us reveals itself in such occasional flashes we realise the slavery we are in, the depths of ignorance in which we are sunk, but the moment their glare vanishes, we forget our position and fall in love, like the prisoner in the story, with the very chains that bind us. 'Aho!' exclaims the sage, pitying the lot of man who, forgetting his real Self which is infinite, fancies the fleeting world to be all-in-all, 'look at the wonderful work of ignorance; it has magnified an atom into a mountain and reduced a mountain to an atom.' We have lost all sense of proportion, or rather, an adequate sense of proportion is impossible to us so long as we are what we are—the victims of illusion. No wonder then, that truth is not always welcome to us and that in our ignorance we often glorify our very bondage.

One such example of our worshipping our own fetters is doubtless the false importance we attach to active work, active benevolence and the like, and the preference we often give to them over calm meditation and silent worship. The sage who buries himself in Self-realisation is generally regarded as a mere lumber and active work is proclaimed as the be-all and end-all of existence. 'Get leave to work,' says the poetess, and adds '*it is the highest you get at all*.' To seek for Truth with the utmost singleness of purpose and the most unflinching courage, to kill at all 'sense of separateness,' and become the transcendental Reality that lies behind the universe, by a course of a most intense and the most absorbing meditation—all this is nothing, and 'getting leave to work' is the highest that one can get! Referring to this deification of action, a great English writer justly observes : 'What is bred in the bone comes out in the flesh. Like the sportsman, who, by the most curious perversion of logic and glorying in his very shame, defends the brutality of slaughter or the cruelty of hunting an animal to death on the ground, forsooth, that the courage of the human animal is thereby fed and increased (as if true courage required to be kept up by such means !), so the man, who has been brought up to Western ways of thinking, not only fails to realise the very first axiom of true thought, but with the perverted idea of his race glories in his very shame, for he exalts action above meditation.' When we come to know what is really meant by action, and what place it occupies in our evolution, we will have no hesitation in fully endorsing the above remarks, and proclaiming that not getting leave *to* work, but getting leave *from* work is the ideal to which one should aspire with all his heart.

For, what is action ? Action is a necessity of our nature. By the very nature of things it has been forced upon us. We have not to get leave to work ; we are bound to work There is not a single moment in which we really are not working. Here working or action is of course not confined merely to physical or external activity. The corresponding Sanskrit word *Karma* has been thus defined by Sankara :—*Karma* is the activity or restlessness of the body, mind or the senses. In this its largest sense, 'there is never a single moment,' says the Gita 'when man does not do Karma ; for all men who are not masters of themselves are compelled by the principles in their nature to do Karma.' (III. 5). Until we transcend nature and become masters over ourselves, we are always working and bound to work ; and all compulsion is slavery though we may not realise our position.

Nor is this all. The necessity to which we are subject is itself a child of ignorance. For whence came the necessity to work thus incessantly ? The only satisfactory reply to this question is furnished by the Vedanta. Few systems of philosophy go deep enough to supply an answer and the theories of Divine Will, Fatalism and the like offered by others, are hardly satisfying. The truth is, as the Vedanta says, we are ignorant of the fact that all that exists is one infinite undefinable ocean of *Pragnana* (consciousness) and there is no duality anywhere. 'Verily,' says the Chandogya Upanishad, 'that immensity (*Pragnana*) extends from below, it extends from above, it extends from behind, it extends from before, it extends from the South, it extends from the North—of a truth it is all this.' (VII, xxv, 1). Our sense of separateness is then mere ignorance. And 'where there is, as it were, duality,' says the Brihadaranyaka Upanishad (IV, v. 15), 'there sees another, another thing, there smells another, another

thing, tastes another, another thing, there speaks
another, another thing, there hears another, another
thing, there minds another, another thing, there touches
another, another thing, there knows another, another
thing.' In other words there arises the necessity to
do Karma. The genesis of Karma is more fully given
elsewhere in the same Upanishad as follows. The root
of Karma is desire and the root of desire is *Sankalpa*
which may be figuratively described as the out-breathing
of the Atman through Maya. The earliest beginning
of manifestation is *Sankalpa*. In other words, as soon
as the Unmanifest began to manifest itself, duality
sprang and then naturally desire, and through it Karma,
and through it of course plurality, *i.e.*, the world.
Karma then is due to desire, which itself is the off-spring
of duality, which again originated through *Avidya* or
ignorance.

According to the Vedanta then, we alone are
responsible for our misery; it does not make the
lightest attempt to throw the blame on any one else.
That we are incessantly compelled to work is our own
fault. Ignorance is the cause of bondage. This explanation of the Vedanta is the best conceivable; for
no fate outside us can reasonably be held responsible
for our slavery; and to attribute our suffering to the
Will of Providence is against all pious and enlightened
conceptions of God. We suffer, because we fancy ourselves separate from Him, the only Reality. We are
really infinite, but think ourselves to be finite; we are
really eternal, but through our ignorance fancy ourselves mortal; and the moment we cut up by our misguided imagination the indivisible One into parts,

selfishness, desire, passions, Karma and slavery follow.
We are restless then, because we are ignorant ; we
incessantly work like slaves, because we do not know
who in reality we are. All this is not mere theory ;
for it could easily be seen that as soon as we realise our
infinity, our eternality, our oneness with all that is,
all Karma must in reality cease ; no more could there
be any compulsion to work ; for as the Brihadaranyaka
Upanishad says : 'How does one, to whom all has become his own Self, see anything, how smell anything,
how taste anything, how speak anything, how hear
anything, how mind anything, how touch anything, how
know anything ?' According to the Vedanta then, or,
as we might as well say, as a matter of fact, the necessity under which we labour—that of having to perform
Karma and thus sowing the seed for successive rounds
of births and deaths is due to our ignorance. We fancy,
through *Avidya*, that we are separate from the Brahman
and that the world exists apart from us. As soon as
this idea of separateness comes, the mind, the senses,
and the body, all become active and the result naturally
is Karma. And any action however noble, however
benevolent and however praiseworthy according to
our false standards, is necessarily the result of ignorance
and therefore cannot be absolutely good. 'However we
may try,' says Swami Vivekananda, 'there cannot be
any action which is perfectly pure or any which is perfectly impure, taking purity or impurity in the sense of
injury or non-injury. We cannot breathe or live
without injuring others and every bit of food we eat is
fallen from another's mouth : our very lives are crowd-
ing out some other lives. It may be men or animals or

small microbes, but some one we have to crowd out. That being the case, it naturally follows that perfection can never be attained by work. We may work through all eternity, but there will be no way out of this maze : you may work on and on and on but there will be no end.'

It clearly follows from what we have said that getting leave to work cannot be the highest we can get. We are bound to be incessantly active and every act which we do, however good it may appear to us, is necessarily the combined result of ignorance and compulsion and besides, is a mixture of good and evil. We work not as masters but as slaves, not wisely but in ignorance and our work can never be absolutely good. The Gita says : 'Every work hath blame as every flame is wrapped in smoke.' Such being the nature of action, can that be our ideal ? Certainly not, unless ignorance, slavery and evil could satisfy our wants. Deification of action then practically means worshipping our fetters or, to use the words of the writer above quoted, 'glorying in our shame.' Action or restlessness is not the ideal. Our deepest and the most persistent impulses all point just the other way and they deserve to be respected. They are really the voice of the Deity within us, and it is through them and not against them that we can possibly work out our salvation, and they all un-mistakably point towards rest or repose, towards know-ledge, towards freedom and towards truth. Happiness, truth, freedom, goodness, these are the ideals or rather, *the* ideal for, they are really but different aspects of the same ideal. There is not a single moment in our lives or for that matter, in the life of any sentient being, in which the struggle to reach the ideal, the groping through in the dark after freedom, truth, and happiness is really absent. Even things which we are wont to call inanimate struggle for them. Indeed all change, all restlessness, all activity is for repose and freedom. Like all the rest of the universe, we also work then, not for the sake of work but for the sake of rest. There is only one man who works for work's sake and that is the *Gnani* (wise man) for whom nothing more has to be gained, and who ever working does not really work (*Gita*, III, 27), but for us who are always consciously or subconsciously seeking happiness and rest, action is the means and actionlessness the end. So the Gita says :

> By works the votary doth rise to saint,
> And saintship is ceasing from all works.

We work in order that we may be freed from work. The highest then is not to get leave to work, but to get leave from work.

The only possible way to escape the necessity to work, to transcend nature which has enslaved us is to clear up our ignorance which is the mother of all our misery. 'The natural cows are not cows,' says the Narada Parivrajaka Upanishad, 'but they are the real cows who think that they are different from the Brahman. Wise men escape death by knowing the Brahman. There is no other road to salvation.' 'If in this world,' says the Kena Upanishad, 'a person *knows* the Self, then *the true end* (*of all human aspiration*) is gained ; and great is the loss of him who does not thus

know' (II, 5). That ignorance is the cause of our
slavery and knowledge of our real nature alone can
free us from it is very well put in the following Sruti.
'Those who believe in duality are not masters of their
own selves and go to perishable regions, while he who
realises the reverse becomes his own king.' 'I am
immoveableI never become old. I am immortal. I am
without the distinctions of mine and another's. Wisdom
is the essence of my nature. I am verily the ocean of
the bliss of *Moksha* (freedom)' says the sage, in the
Atmabodha Upanishad. *Moksha* is defined as freedom
from the bondage of attachment which arises through
ignorance (Sarvasaropanishad). To the sage who 'breaks
the bond of ignorance by knowing the supreme immortal Brahman dwelling in the heart' (Mund. Upa., II,
I. 10) the necessity for doing Karma ceases, 'for he is
his own king' and has transcended nature. He is free,
he is blissful, he enjoys supreme rest and he is himself
the Truth, for Truth means 'the Absolute and the only
Existence (the Brahman) of which the Vedas speak'
(Sar. Upa.). In him all the ideals meet. 'He is the
adorable one,' say the Upanishads, 'All beings pray
to him who knows the Brahman.' To such a man, there
is nothing more to be done. 'The man who rejoices in
his Self, is satisfied and happy in his Self, has no more
Karma to perform. To him no benefit could arise by
doing Karma here, nor does any loss accrue by not
doing; and there is not in all things which have been
created, any object on which he has to depend' (*Gita*,
III, 17, 18). 'My ignorance has fled,' says the sage,
'I cannot say where. My little self which was doing
Karma is dead and I have nothing more to do as a

necessity' (Atma. Upa.). 'To the Yogin, who is glad-
dened with the nectar of wisdom, and whose duties
have all been performed, there is nothing to be done.
If there be' it is added, 'he is not a real knower.' 'Let
men sorry or ignorant,' says the Tripti Dipa, 'make
themselves busy from desire of a son and the like ; but
I do not ; for I have nothing to wish for, being full of
joy. Let them who wish to go to other worlds perform
Karma ; but how should I, who am all the worlds in
myself perform Karma, what am I to perform and for
what purpose ? ......I shall, though my deed is done,
live for the good of the world in the path prescribed in
the Sastras.'

To transcend nature, to destroy ignorance and attain
perfect surcease of work, and be, what in truth we unconsciously are, the true, the omniscient, the infinite and
the blissful Brahman, 'beyond the gaining whereof' as
Sankara says : 'there remains nothing to be gained,
beyond the bliss whereof there remains no possibility
of bliss, beyond the sight whereof there remains nothing
to be seen, beyond becoming which, there remains
nothing to be become, beyond knowing which there remains nothing to be known,' and which has been described as 'the highest end, the best riches, the supremest
world, the greatest joy'—this is the ideal. To check
the ignorant wanderings of the restless mind and know
that changeless illimitable *Pragnana* in our real nature
and thus escape Karma, in a word to do nothing is the
best thing to do.

It is not, however, for a moment asserted that action
is useless and that great souls, who in the past have
shed their life-blood in the cause of righteousness and

justice, or for their country's sake, did a foolish thing. Action has its place and a very necessary one in our growth. As the Gita says : 'By works the votary doth rise to Saint.' One beautiful contrivance in the Government of the Universe is that our very fetters help us, in course of time, in obtaining our freedom and thus, it is given to us so to work that we will have to work no longer as bondsmen. Freedom from work or saintship is the end which, whether we will or no, and consciously or unconsciously, we are struggling to attain every moment of our lives.

It need not be feared, however, that to become a saint is to become dead to the world. How sages serve the world and how work leads to saintship are subjects which we shall consider on a future occasion.

SAGES AND THEIR REAL USEFULNESS

APART from our inability even to comprehend it, union with Godhead, absolute identity with the Brahman, which numberless sages have realised, both in our country and elsewhere, is distinctly our destination and the highest that will surely fall to our lot at the end of our often wearisome pilgrimage in the world. To regard as the ideal anything lower than this, such as 'getting leave to work' and the like, is really to limit our vision and hinder our growth. 'Better aim at a lion and miss it, than hunt a jackal and catch it' is the proverb.

We have seen what the true ideal is, but in these days, the philosophy of the shopkeeper is so much in the upper hand that it is not enough that a thing is true, it must at the same time be useful. Utility is the guardian angel of the society, the tutelary goddess at its gate, and even Truth has to bend her knees before her and beg for admission. This surely is not a good feature. Is it not enough for a man's being honoured that he has found out and reached the Truth? Should it also be proved that he is of some use to this dream-world? Homer, we may be sure, never troubled himself about this question of practical utility or to use a familiar phrase 'earthly use' when he composed his 'Iliad'. A bag of rice is of more 'earthly use' than the statue of Venus; is that the standard? If so, to trade in liquors is certainly more profitable than reading the Upanishads, and to convert our temples into factories and workshops may be a useful reform. Utility! It is the merchant's metaphysics, and when any nation trusts to it for guidance, we may be sure its decline is close at hand.

Even according to the utilitarian standard however, the idle sage is of greater value to the society than many an active reformer. In the first place, that a nation is capable of producing a sage is the surest sign of its vitality. It is not every country that can produce sages. A sage is no journeyman's work of Nature. 'Of thousands of mortals, one strives for wisdom, and of thousands of those that so strive, one knows Me according to my true nature,' says Sri Krishna (*Gita* VII, 3). The sage then is the ripest, the sweetest fruit of the tree of the universe, and woe to the man who speaks lightly of him. It has been very wisely observed : "When the 'self', as we understand it, is annihilated— when the soul has been able to endure the transcendent vision of itself as Deity—wnen difference no longer exists, and the one is merged in the all, the storehouse of spiritual energy is thereby replenished, and all humanity receives an impulse that raise them a step nearer the divine union also—nay, further, the divine impulse after passing through man descends to vivify the lower creation. The whole universe is thrilled by it !" To develop ourselves to the utmost is therefore the highest service that we can ever do to the universe. 'The sympathetic relief of physical suffering is well ; the teaching by which man's mental horizon is widened, and man's moral nature is elevated, is better. They both form but worthy preludes to the higher goal. But best of all is to *become* the spiritual pabulum by which humanity lives.'

A sage, a genuine sage, not the Birmingham article we so often meet with in these degenerate days, but a man of sterling worth and wisdom, like Vasishta, Vyasa, Suka, Valmiki and others,—is one of those rare phenomena, in the occurrence of which the whole universe becomes filled with joy. That the gods danced in the sky and filled the earth with showers of flowers, that the winds blew sweet odours, and the trees put forth flowers, even out of season, when the great Ramas, Buddhas, Christs and Krishnas were born, are not mere poetic fancies; they all embody the truth, though in a figurative way, that the universe becomes thrilled with joy at the birth of its greatest saviours. One atom can never move without dragging all the rest of the world along with it, and no man can ever become a sage therefore, without proportionately raising the whole world. The highest service that we can ever do to the world is, therefore, to become sages.

India was at its best, at the time of its greatest sages. The world has yet to see another court like that of Janaka, the royal sage of Videha. Some of the most prosperous and best governed kingdoms of the world flourished in the times of Vyasa, and Valmiki, Ikshvaku, Raghu, Dasaratha, Rama, Bali, Dharmaputra, Sibi, Mandhata, Parikshit, these and many other kings of undying renown were contemporaries of our *Rishis*. The Vedas abound in astronomical allusions and there were few sciences unknown to the seers of the Upanishads which have been discovered by modern nations. Even the art of war seemed to have attained a wonderful degree of perfection in those remote days. It is foreign to our present purpose to enter into the history of an-

13

cient India, but what is claimed is, that the palmiest days of our poor country were in those remote ages when the Upanishads were first composed, and when the country was saturated with the spirit of those mighty utterances, and filled with sages who lived as the personal embodiment of the truths contained in them.

A sage is, indeed, the surest guarantee for a nation's life and strength. A nation may lie dormant and apparently dead, but the noose of Yama will never fall upon it so long as there is left in it one sage, one perfected man alive. Whatever may be the present condition of our country, however helpless and impotent it may appear, there can be no cause for despair until its sage-producing capacity has not wholly gone from it. So, this is the test for a nation's greatness—has it produced any sage, any great adorable character? If it has not, its prosperity will be short-lived like the wealth of a thief. Many a great empire has tumbled down without leaving any trace behind and without the possibility of ever reviving, solely for want of spiritual strength, for want of inspiring traditions and ever enduring spiritual ideals; and the curious phenomenon is that while so many nations have come and gone, India the oldest of them all, stands in the midst of their sad wreck which history unfolds to view, still young and vigorous though so old, with seemingly endless capacity for producing, if need be, newer and newer sets of saints, sages, warriors, kings and poets and blessed with a strange sort of virginity like the daughter of Yayati in Mahabharata, who, the moment a child was born to her, could become a virgin again and thus bring forth any number of children without losing her youth. And the only explanation for this wonderful phenomenon is that it owns the *Amritakalasa* (the fountain of life)—the Upanishads, and that its soil has been, times without number, blest by the footprints of the mighty lords of creation who—such was the strength of their self-realisation—could destroy, as it were, by one glance the countless multitudes of worlds above and below, saying : 'Discard shall we, as a vessel of filth, the whole macrocosm and the microcosm' (Adhyatma Upa.). What we here speak is history reliable and exceedingly instructive. And in the light of this great fact, the highest service which a true son of India can do to it is, not to reform it after the model of infant nations not yet past even *Balarishta*, the ills of infancy, nor to try to revive old institutions, old sacrifices and old rituals, thereby forcing the country backward by thousands of years, but to develop oneself to the utmost and become a grand sage of the old *Rishi-type*. This is the highest service imaginable at this juncture ; if this were not possible, the next best is to prepare the country for the appearance of such sages by cleansing it of the innumerable shams and superstitions that now linger in and corrupt it. And when the sages come, not as now, here and there rarely, but in large numbers, the whole country will fully awake like the serpent-bound army of Rama at the sight of Garuda and then will be seen revived in tenfold grandeur the glories of ancient India.

When the sages come, with them will come reformers, workers, saints, poets and others, for, all these are really the servants of those sages. They merely render into deeds the thoughts of these latter.

As Swami Vivekananda rightly says: "Even the Buddhas and the Christs are but second-rate men; the greatest men of the world have passed away unknown. These highest ones silently collect ideas and the others, Buddhas and Christs, go from place to place preaching and working. The highest men are calm, silent and unknown. They are the men who really know the power of thought. They are sure that even if they go into a cave and close up the door, simply think five thoughts and pass away, these five thoughts will live through eternity. They will penetrate through the mountains and cross oceans and travel through the world and will enter into some brain and raise up some man, who will give expression to these five thoughts." Such is the power of the idle sage.

Another way in which the sage does good to the world is by the silent power of his example. In our haste to do, we often forget the value of example. Indeed, it would be no exaggeration to say that character is formed more by the silent influence of examples which steals on one than by the training which one actually receives.

The skies that speak not, the silent hills, the seas, 'vast, voiceful and mysterious,' the silent influence of surroundings, and in fact all nature which suggests more than speaks, these do more for us than the books we read and the words we hear. The voice of silence is more valuable than the voice of speech. What is said, teaches less than what is left unsaid, and the highest teaching so beautifully symbolises in the Chinmudra scene under the banyan tree, is silence (*Mauna*). The world really owes its best to men who were content to be, rather than ambitious to do. The reforms of men like Ramanuja, have created results which are just the reverse of what their large hearts aspired to bring about, while the hold of the seers of the Upanishads on the world is ever on the increase. Let us not however be misunderstood. Every country owes much to its active workers, but the best in every country is due to those mighty men who lived more than worked, who worshipped more than served.

Then again, work here is always subjective rather than objective, for, as has been well said, the world is like a dog's curly tail and can never be thoroughly mended. In helping others, therefore, we really help ourselves and the converse cannot but be true, for we cannot help ourselves without at the same time helping others. In the earlier stages of individual evolution, for instance in Karma-Yoga, the truth of this is self-evident, but it is no less true in the later stages, Bhakti-Yoga, Raja-Yoga and Gnana-Yoga. What is really good for us, must necessarily be good for the universe, for the part is not opposed to the whole. Each of us has a well-defined and necessary place in the economy of the universe ; we are members of it and when we grow, the world also grows with us. The world may be likened to a big tree putting forth leaves, flowers and fruits. Just as no single fruit can ripen without the whole tree ripening in proportion, so our advancement necessarily means the advancement of the whole universe. Therefore *being* necessarily means *doing* and the highest life is the highest service.

It has been very wisely observed that 'the state in which the rulers are most reluctant to govern is best and most quietly governed, and the state in which they are most willing is the worst.' This beautiful observation of Plato involves a precious truth which may well be extended to other departments of activity than governing a state. For instance, it may be said that the teacher who is most anxious to teach, often teaches little, while he who has no idea of teaching, often teaches best. The Upanishads, for example, came from men who were not in the least ambitious of assuming the role of teachers and from whose minds the distinctions of teacher and the taught had been completely wiped out. These ancient seers, who have given to the world the richest legacy it has and at whose feet numberless generations of men of all creeds and countries have sat and will sit till the very end of the world, never communicate a single truth, however simple, as if they were authors of it. Suka learnt it from Vyasa, Vyasa learnt it from Narada, Narada learnt it from Prajapati, Prajapati learnt it from Vishnu and so on *ad infinitum*. Now-a-days every man passes for an original writer, if he could steal a few sentences from others, and the more one steals without acknowledgment, the more is one original, and all of us are teachers and philosophers! This is the difference between real teaching and teaching. So in doing also, those who are anxious, do little, while those who have no ambition for active service, turn out to be our greatest benefactors. Unconscious work, *i.e.*, work for which the author takes no credit is always the best, just as the Upanishads which are *Apaurusheya* (impersonal). Therefore did Jesus say : 'Let not your left hand know what your right hand giveth.' To fancy that 'every flower enjoys the smell it gives' is an unholy sentiment and has its inspiration from our own littleness which will never allow us to do a good thing without getting vain of it—a littleness so common that the poet says : 'Pride is the last infirmity of noble minds' and for which the 'absolute and final' cure is to know that what work is done is done by *Prakriti* (Nature) and that the Atman, which alone really is and which we ourselves are, is eternal, infinite and actionless.

Though the sage is under no compulsion to do Karma, it does not follow that he never does Karma. Says Sri Krishna : 'I myself Arjuna, have not in the three regions of the universe anything which is necessary for me to perform, nor anything to obtain, which has not been obtained ; and yet I live in the performance of moral duties. If I were not vigilantly attentive to those duties, all men would presently follow my example.' (*Gita*, III, 22 and 23). In the same way the *Gnani* also, though he has nothing to gain by the performance of Karma, still works for the benefit of the world. Indeed, he lives solely for the good of the world and his whole life is a voluntary dedication to the service of the suffering humanity. But for such sacred and unselfish dedication, where should we have been? All the world's scriptures, those eternal books without which the world of man would have been no better than a forest infested with wild beasts, are, to use a Vedic expression, the breath of sages. And in India, our everything we owe to these sages, not merely the scriptures but even the sciences including that of war. The very rivers and mountains of our land, though partly a gift of nature, came to us through our sages who have invested them, each in proportion to their natural importance, with a wealth of tradition and a halo of glory and made them so different from the rivers and mountains of other countries.

One most noteworthy feature with regard to these sages is that whatever they do, bears on it the impress of truth and eternity, and is most far-reaching and permanent in its results. Take for instance the Upanishads, the authors—who they were God alone knows—say again and again with regard to their conclusions, 'This is truth'; 'this has been established'; 'this has been declared'; 'we have heard it told' and so on. And these conclusions have stood the test of ages and are more unshakeable than the Himalayas. Age after age their empire widens and they seem to have been permanently tied up with the world. Contrast with them the conclusions of modern philosophers, philologists, ethnologists and even scientists. In these days the longest life for a theory seems to be ten years, and the rage for theorising is such, that, to cite an example, within the last few years the imaginary home of the Aryan, has been made to travel from one end of the world to another.

To turn to lesser works, the Ramayana and the Mahabharata, for example. They are the wonders of the world. As colossal as the pyramids but far more educative and humanising, they were the preservers of India during the dark ages—the long night of ignorance in which the Vedas were practically non-existent for the people at large, and but for them our national virtues would have been totally lost and ourselves should have ceased to exist as a nation long ago. For centuries they served as our natural Bibles, but unlike the other Bibles they both amuse and elevate. And even from a literary point of view they excite our wonder, for, the world has yet to see poets who could give us Sita, Savitri, Draupadi, Rukmini, Rama, Dharmaputra, Bhima, Arjuna, Bhishma, and a host of other immortals and above all that Lord of immortals, Krishna, even to understand whom is a feat not yet accomplished by the best intellects of our time. Let us next glance at the work of our sages as law givers. Whatever might be the evils in our society at the present day, is it not a wonder that they are so few considering the sufferings we as a nation have gone through for scores of centuries? The mighty law-givers of old have permanently moulded the character of our society and, through their superhuman strength and foresight it is, that we as a nation have survived the number-less onslaughts made on us by every passer-by for scores of centuries. Bad times these were, but our sages have carried us safe through them, and henceforth, there is no fear. How could a nation die which has not conquest and tyranny but renunciation and divinity for its ideals? And in what words could those mighty sages of old be praised—who, in a world where struggle for existence and the survival of the fittest, or, in other words, selfish-ness and hatred, would seem to be the order of things, had the foresight and wisdom to choose renunciation and divinity as the ideals for our nation and had the boldness to launch it in a race with other nations all of which are now dead, having given place to newer and newer ones, while ours still survives in health and vigour?

The secret for the success of sages in their under-taking is that they do nothing for themselves, and even doing, they do not do. "He who beholds inaction in action and action in inaction is wise amongst mankind," says the Gita (IV, 18). 'Inaction in action' means doing but with the knowledge that the real self or the Atman is not the doer. The sage never thinks that *he* does a thing, for the 'he' no longer exists for him. He is one with the Atman which is always actionless, and in his eyes, really there is nothing done and much less does he care for the fruits of his actions. When finishing his Sutras, Narada says :—"So says Narada without caring what others might think of him."

This is the spirit in which sages do their duties. As they are really free from all selfishness and egotism it is really God that speaks and acts through them. 'That such and such is the truth was declared unto the *Rishis* by the Invisible voice,' says the author of the Sarvasaropanishad. Through them, God shines in the world. God manifests himself through all, but our selfishness and egoism suppress that manifestation as dark clouds hide the sun, but these being absent in the sage, he is God himself and whatever he does is really the work of God. 'I regard the sage as Myself,' says Sri Krishna (*Gita*, VII, 18).

———

IS THE WORLD REAL OR FALSE?

I

THE unparalleled 'boldness, depth and subtlety of speculation' of the Vedanta are nowhere more prominent and striking than in its discussion of the important question of the reality or unreality of the universe. This great question has been one of the main subjects of inquiry in all systems of philosophy, and all great thinkers have, with more or less boldness, ventured to aim a dart at and pierce through 'this solid-seeming world,' but most often they have been duped into unquestioning satisfaction by the Proteus-like Maya, the mother of all forms and the tutelary goddess of the universe, merely changing her dress and face and appearing as though she had been slain by the poisoned shafts of those philosophers and had given place to a more decent-looking and worthy successor. In reality, however, no black stone had got transformed into a fair Ahalya and the philosophers who would try the criminal world had themselves been tried and found unfit to hold the trial.

A signal instance of what we are saying is to be found in modern Western philosophy. As successors of the giant doubter Descartes, there arose on British soil two great inquirers, one of whom questioned the existence of the innate ideas of man, the inner world, and the other questioned that of the outer world. But on account of a fatal error, both of them missed the point, and their successors to this day are fighting over the utterly profitless (from a metaphysical point of view) and deceptive question of the relative superiority of mind and matter. On one extreme stand the materialists who, like a man trying to stand on his own shoulders, struggle hard to prove that mind evolved out of matter and are vexed to find that the phantom they arduously seek ever eludes their grasp. The other extreme is occupied by the idealists, who on *a priori* grounds seek to establish that ideas alone exist and not the outer world, a veritable wild-goose chase, as Sankara proves—whose arguments directed against the Indian counterpart of Berkeleyan idealism, the Vignanavada of the Buddhists are, by the way, the best refutation of all forms of Western idealism as well. He rightly observes that in every act of perception we are conscious of some external thing corresponding to the idea, that the existence of the outward thing apart from consciousness has to be accepted on the ground of the nature of consciousness itself, as when perceiving a post and the like we are conscious not merely of the perception, but of a post and the like as objects of our perceptions, that thing and idea are therefore distinct and that ideas being of a fleeting and non-luminous nature require for their very perception the changeless substratum of the ulterior intelligent Self.

Between these two extremes of materialism and idealism stand the so-called realists who would well let alone both mind and matter and quietly acquiesce in the existing state of things making only a few minor adjustments, such as giving the credit of secondary qualities like colour, etc., to the mind and leaving the rest like shape, size, etc., to matter itself. We may also deal unto them as they do unto the world and let them alone recording their quiet harmless and submissive disposition and the equity of the partition they make between the 'Dayadis' mind and matter. All the great philosophers of Britain belonged to one or other of the five schools of philosophy, Nihilism, Materialism, Natural Realism, Constructive Idealism and Pure Idealism, but we need not trouble ourselves here with any of them, for, though they started on an examination of the universe, the question soon became for them whether matter alone existed or ideas alone, whether matter was perceivable in itself, *i.e.*, immediately, or whether it was simply a permanent possibility of sensation. Strangely enough, they were deluded into the notion that a correct cosmology could be obtained by an examination of matter from the standpoint of the mind and settling account between these two anti-thetical factors which they respectively called Non-Ego and Ego, while what ought to have been done was to look at both mind and matter from a higher stand-point. Though they vaguely saw that both these cosmical factors together made up the phenomenal world, they divorced cosmology from ontology with the result that while the latter became either impossible or grotesque (as, for instance, when idealists began to theorise about the Divine mind, and so on), the former got dwindled into the theoretical psychology much less certain in its theories and less valuable in practice than physiology and other sciences. On account of this divorce they lost the only vantage ground from which a survey could be made of both mind and matter ; in other words the whole phenomenal world, and consequently their cosmology is neither physics nor meta-physics. Rightly says Mr. Ferrier : "The contest between matter and mind is silly and frivolous to the extreme." It reminds us of the old quarrel between the belly and the members.

The war between mind and matter is known to the Vedanta, for, it always classes what is ordinarily termed mind along with matter as forming part of the inferior *Prakriti* of the Self. Accordingly says Sri Krishna : "The great elements, *Ahankara*, *Buddhi* and also the *Abyakta*, the ten senses and the one (the *Manas* which is composed of thoughts) and the five objects of sense ;

"Desire, hatred, pleasure, pain, the aggregate, intelligence, firmness (and all other qualities of the inner sense or mind)—the *Kshetra* has been thus briefly described with its modifications" (xiii, 5, 6).

All these things together constitute the body, so to speak, of the Self and are regarded as matter (*Kshetra*), because, as Sankara says : 'They are knowable.' The terms 'ego' and 'non-ego' do not therefore mean in the Vedanta mind and matter as in Western philosophy, but relate to the far more natural and scientific distinction of the Knower and the thing known. This distinction is most important and is the real beginning of metaphysics. As Mr. Ferrier very well points out "Our apprehension of perception of matter is the whole subject of metaphysics. The old psychologists put a division between perception and matter which is impossible." Elsewhere he says : "Both mind and matter change. Does the observer also change ? No. There cannot be a new observer for every new thing observed. If there were, no observation, no knowledge, no consciousness could ever take place." The very same thing, namely, that ideas (perception of matter) require an ulterior permanent observer to apprehend them—which forms the real subject of metaphysics—is said by Sankara in a much more defined and elaborate manner.

He says : "By maintaining the idea to be illuminated by itself, you will make yourself guilty of an absurdity no less than if you said that fire burns itself. Possibly you will rejoin that if the idea is to be apprehended by something different from it, that something also must be apprehended by something different and so on *ad infinitum*. And moreover you will perhaps object that as each cognition is of an essentially illuminating nature like a lamp, the assumption of a further cognition is uncalled for, for, as they are both equally illuminating, the one cannot give light to the other. But both these objections are unfounded. As the idea only is apprehended and as there is consequently no necessity to assume something to apprehend the Self which witnesses the idea (is conscious of the idea), there results no *regressus ad infinitum*. And the witnessing Self and the idea are of an essentially different nature and may therefore stand to each other in the relation of knowing subject and object known...... Moreover if you maintain that the idea lamp manifests itself without standing in need of a further principle to illuminate it, you maintain thereby that ideas exist which are not apprehended by any of the means of knowledge and which are without a Knowing Being ; which is no better than to assert that a thousand lamps burning inside some impenetrable mass of rocks manifest themselves (without any one to see them). And if you should maintain that thereby we admit your doctrine since it follows from what you have said that the idea itself implies consciousness, we reply that, as observation shows, the lamp in order to become manifest requires some other intellectual agent furnished with instruments, such as the eye and that therefore the idea also, as equally being a thing to be illuminated, becomes manifest only through an ulterior intelligent principle, and if you finally object that we, when advancing the witnessing Self as self-proved, merely express in other words the Bauddha tenet that the idea is self-manifested, we refute you by remarking that your ideas have the attribute of originating, passing away, being manifold and so on (while our Self is one and permanent). We thus have proved that an idea like a lamp requires an ulterior intelligent principle to render it manifest." (*Com. Ved. Sut.*, II, 2, 28).

The recognition of this ulterior principle, which at the same time is permanent and intelligent is the starting point of all real philosophy and is the only way to escape out of the paradoxes into which Western psychologists have been led. Mr. Mill, who, perhaps more deeply than any other philosopher, examined into the nature of the mind, defines it as a permanent possibility of feeling and at the same time, finds that he is unable to explain the phenomena of remembrance, expectation and the like on that definition and his confession of this inability is one of the best indirect proofs for our theory of the Atman. He says: "A remembrance of a sensation, even if not referred to any particular date, involves, the suggestion and belief that a sensation of which it is a copy or representation actually existed in the past, and an expectation involves a belief more or less positive that a sensation or other feeling to which it directly refers will exist in future. Nor can the phenomena involved in these two states of consciousness be adequately expressed without saying that the belief they include is that I myself formerly had or that I myself and no other shall hereafter have the sensations remembered or expected. (Compare with this what Sankara says : "That remembrance can take place only if it belongs to the same person who previously made the perception, for we observe that what one man has experienced is not remembered by another man. How indeed could there arise the conscious state expressed in this sentence 'I saw that thing and now I see this thing' if the seeing person were not in both cases the same?......We admit that sometimes, with regard to an external thing, a doubt may arise whether it is that or is merely similar to that. For, mistake may be made concerning what lies outside our minds, but the conscious subject never has any doubt whether it is itself or only similar to itself. It rather is distinctly conscious that it is one and the same subject, which yesterday had a certain sensation and to-day remembers that sensation"). "The fact believed is" (Mr. Mill continues), "that the sensations did actually form or will hereafter form, part of the self-same series of states, or thread of consciousness, of which the remembrance or expectation of those sensations is the part now present. If therefore we speak of the Mind as a series of feelings, we are obliged to complete the statement by calling it a series of feelings which is aware of itself as past and future ; and we are reduced to the alternative of believing that the mind or ego is *some-*

*thing different from any series of feelings or possibilities
of them*, or, of accepting the *paradox* that something,
which *ex hypothesi* is but a series of feelings, can be
aware of itself as a series of feelings" (in other words
that ideas are self-luminous, the impossibility of which,
we have already seen, has been demonstrated by
Sankara). The only conclusion is that the Ego is something *different* from all series of feelings or possibilities
of feelings, which according to Mr. Mill's definition
constitute the mind. This is exactly what our great
philosopher says : "Unless there exists one continuous
principle equally connected with the past, the present
and the future, in other words, an absolutely unchangeable Self which cognises everything, we are
unable to account for remembrance, recognition and so
on, which are subject to mental impressions dependent
on place, time and cause." (*Com.* on *Sut.*, II, 2, 31).

No proper analysis of the mind is possible without
leading us to the conclusion above indicated. The
existence of an unchangeable permanent and intelligent
Self which is conscious of all series of feelings, possibility of feeling, and states of mind and at the same
time, as Mr. Mill is forced to admit, *different* from them,
i.e., not identical with them, is an indubitable fact.
It is present in all individuals and abides unchangingly
in infancy, youth and old age. It is the witness of all
states of consciousness and is the substratum of all
series of feelings and sensations however rudimentary
these may be, and, 'there being nothing in the world
which has not some kind of sensation however slight,
it pervades the whole universe. Besides, being beyond
mind, it is above time, space and causality which, both

in Indian philosophy and according to Kant, are only forms of thought. Therefore it clearly follows that the Self or Atman is eternal, infinite and changeless. From this it could easily be seen there could exist nothing outside this Atman, for the *real* existence of any such thing would contradict what we have proved, namely, that it is eternal, changeless and infinite. Nor could there exist anything in it, as that would mean that It is not unchangeable.

* There are many other ways of arriving at this conclusion. To take only one; after what we have said, it will be easily seen that the world is nothing but a combination of three things—matter and mind both of which form the *Kshetra* and the Self, *i.e.*, the knower which is called *Kshetrajna*. This is exactly what the Gitacharya says : "Whatever is born, the unmoving or the moving, know Thou, O best of the Bharatas, that to be from the union of *Kshetrajna*" (XIII, 26). Upon this verse Sankara observes : "Now, of what sort is this union of *Kshetra* and *Kshetrajna* meant to be ? The union cannot be of the nature of any particular relation through union of part as between a rope and a vessel, inasmuch as *Kshetrajna* is like *Akasa* without parts. Nor can it be of the nature of *Samavaya* or inseparable inherence, inasmuch as it cannot be admitted that *Kshetra* and *Kshetrajna* are related to each other as cause and effect (each being opposed in its nature to the other).

"We answer thus : The union between *Kshetra* and *Kshetrajna*, between the object and the subject—each being opposed in its nature to the other,—is of the nature of mutual *Adhyasa* ; *i.e.*, it consists in confounding the one with the other as well as their attributes without discriminating between the nature of *Kshetra* and that of *Kshetrajna* just as a rope and a mother-of-pearl are respectively confounded with a snake and silver for which they are mistaken in the absence of discrimination. The union of *Kshetra* and *Kshetrajna* which is of the nature of *Adhyasa*—which consists in confounding one with the other (as for instance, when a man says, 'I am stout,' 'I come,' 'I am happy,' and so on)—is a sort of illusion (*Mithyajnana.*)" The world being a result of this *Adhyasa* is only apparently real 'like the elephants and palaces projected by a juggler's art, or like a thing seen in a dream or like a *Gandharvanagara*' (as imaginary city in the sky).

This position, though unassailable, has nevertheless been much misunderstood naturally enough, owing to the difference of standpoints from which the question has been viewed, and therefore requires considerable explanation. We are however obliged to stop here for the present for want of space, but shall resume it on a future occasion, when the opinion of Srutis, to which we have made almost no reference to-day, will also be expounded at length.

IS THE WORLD REAL OR FALSE?

II

This so solid-seeming world after all, is but an air image over Me, the only reality ; and nature with its thousandfold productions and destruction, but the reflex of our inward force, the phantasy of our dream.—Carlyle.

A CAREFUL analysis of the universe leads us, as we have seen, to the conclusion that there is, as a substratum behind the various and constantly shifting states of matter and mind, a permanent and changeless Self which appears to unite with them and be a witness to all their modifications. We say 'appears to unite' for we have also seen that this union is only *Adhyasa* (erroneous superimposition) and consists in confounding the one with the other. Says Sankara : "It is a matter not requiring any proof that the object and the subject (*i.e.*, the *Kshetra* and the Self or *Kshetrajna*) whose respective spheres are the notion of the Thou (the non-ego) and the Ego and which are opposed to each other as much as darkness and light are, cannot be identified. All the less can their respective attributes be identified. Hence it follows that it is wrong to superimpose upon the subject whose Self is intelligence and which has for its sphere the notion of the Ego—the object whose sphere is the notion of non-ego and the attributes of the object, and *vice versa* to superimpose the subject on the object. In spite of this, it is on the part of man a natural (beginningless) procedure which has its cause in wrong knowledge (*Avidya*) not to distinguish the two entities

213

and their respective attributes although they are absolutely distinct, but to superimpose upon each the characteristic nature and the attributes of the other and thus coupling the Real and the Unreal to make use of expressions such as *'that am I'*, *'that is mine'*." But for this mutual superimposition which is due to *Avidya*, there will be no such thing as the world ; for, as the Lord has said, whatever is born, the moving or the unmoving, is from the union of *Kshetra* and *Kshetrajna*. The Self does not really unite with the Non-self and the duality of the knower and the things known into which the world gets reduced is itself a result of *Adhyasa*. As Sankara says : "The existence of a knowing personality depends upon the erroneous notion that the body, the senses and so on are identical with or belong to the Self of the knowing person. For without the employment of the senses, perception and the means of right knowledge cannot operate. And without a basis (the individual soul), the senses cannot act. Nor does anybody act by means of a body on which the nature of the Self is not superimposed. Nor can, in the absence of all that, the Self which in its own nature is free from all contact becomes a knowing agent." (*Com. Ved. Sut.* Introduction).

Elsewhere he says : "The Immutable Consciousness (the Self) is spoken of by *a figure of speech* as the cogniser just as in virtue of its heat, fire is said by a figure to do the act of heating. It has been taught in the Gita by the Lord that the Self has in itself no concern with action or with its accessories or with its results. They are imputed to the Self by *Avidya* and are therefore said to belong to the Self only by a figure" (Com. on the

Bhagavad-Gita, XII, 2). The Self by itself is thus neither perceiver nor actor nor enjoyer, but by its being confounded with *Kshetra* or Non-self, it appears in the form of a finite individual soul acting, perceiving and enjoying and is variously called *Jiva, Chetana Prakriti, Kshetrajna* (on account of its contact with *Kshetra*), *Purusha* and so on. 'Extrapersonal attributes are superimposed on the Self, if a man considers himself sound and entire or the contrary as long as his wife, children and so on are sound and entire or not. Attributes of the body are superimposed on the Self if a man thinks of himself (his Self), as stout, lean, fat, fair, as standing, walking or jumping. Attributes of the sense-organs if he thinks I am mute or deaf or one-eyed or blind. Attributes of the internal organ when he considers himself subject to desire, intention, doubt, determination, and so on. Thus the producer of the notion of Ego, (that is, the internal organ) is superimposed on the interior Self which in reality is the witness of all the modifications of the internal organ and *vice versa* the interior Self (which is the witness of everything) is superimposed on the internal organ, the senses and so on. In this way there goes on the natural beginning and endless superimposition which appears in the form of wrong conception, the cause of individual souls appearing as agents, and enjoyers and is observed by every one.'

This wrong conception of the eternal and boundless Self being something which is changing and finite, this sesne of separateness which is due to *Avidya* is really the basis of the phenomenal world. Though the Self does not change, it appears to do so and is mistaken to be actor, perceiver and enjoyer, that is, is one word, Jiva and just as when a person is dreaming, the objects seen in his dream appear to him to be real, similarly so long as one fancies himself to be a Jiva *apart from the Self*, the world which is its play-field and which is composed of the ninefold *Samsara* of actor, action, acting, knower, knowledge, thing known, enjoyer, enjoyment and the thing enjoyed, is real to him. Narada said to Pururava : "If here be I (the individual soul, the Jiva) then there is Thou (things cognised by the Jiva) and the 'I' and the 'Thou' together make up the world. But the moment the 'I' is found to be false, the world vanishes." So also does Sankara say : "And if the doctrine of the individual soul has to be set aside then the opinion of the entire phenomenal world—*which is based on the individual soul*—having an independent existence is likewise to be set aside."

Here the intelligent reader will not fail to ask : "Well, let the Jiva which acts, enjoys and perceives be, if you please, a fictitious entity with reference to the Self from which it fancies itself to be separate and let also the world which springs from its identification with Non-self be false. But does not this presuppose that there are two things Self and Non-self equally real and distinct though only appearing to unite in the shape of the phenomenal universe ? How could one say then, as our Sastras declare that the Self alone is real ? A very pertinent question to be sure and there are many ways in which one might proceed to answer it. But the best method perhaps is the one suggested by the Gita. The Lord says : "Earth, water, fire, air, ether, *Manas* (*Ahankara*), *Buddhi* (*Mahat*) and *Ahankara* (*Avyakta* combined with *Avidya*)—thus My *Prakriti* is divided eightfold. This is the inferior (*Prakriti*) : but as distinct from this know My superior *Prakriti*, the very life, O mighty armed, by which this universe is upheld" (*Gita*, VII, 4, 5). In commenting upon these verses Sankara rightly points out that earth, etc., are not gross substances but the rudimental elements, Tanmatras as they are called, which are nothing but the objects of the senses. Thus earth here means odour which appeals to the nose, water, taste which appeals to the tongue, and so on. In this grand classification then, the Lord has divided the universe into two factors the Jiva (the superior *Prakriti*) the perceiver, actor and enjoyer and things which correspond to its activity. These together constitute the *Prakriti* or manifested Nature of the Lord or Self. Both depend on the Self and owe their existence to It, and of the one, *i.e.*, the Jiva, we know that it is a fictitious entity the result of a wrong sense of separateness, but what is the relation between it and the other the *Achetana Prakriti* or *Kshetra* ? These two as Mr. Ferrier rightly points out are identical. He says : "To think of light without allowing the thought of seeing to enter into the thinking of it is impossible. We begin and end in thinking of *the seeing* of light. So with regard to all coloured objects such as trees, houses, etc., they can be thought of only by our thinking of our seeing of them......Similarly with regard to sound and hearing. So every objective is found to have a subjective clinging to it and *forming one with it*. The faculty and the object are inseparably united." This is exactly what the Sruti says : "Now we will explain how in the same knowledge (*Pragna* or Self) all beings are also absorbed.

Speech verily milked one portion thereof : its object the name was placed outside as a rudimentary element : the vital air verily milked a portion thereof ; its object the smell was placed outside as a rudimentary element........the mind verily milked one portion thereof : its object, thoughts and desires were placed outside as a rudimentary element"—(Kaushitaki Up., III).

On the above section Sankara observes : "The organs of sense cannot exist without *Pragna* nor the objects of sense be obtained without the organ, therefore—on the principle, when one thing cannot exist without another, that thing is said to be identical with the other—just as the cloth being never perceived without the threads is identical with them, or the false perception of silver being never found without the mother-of-pearl (the basis of the illusion) the false silver is not different from it, so the objects of sense being never found without the organs are identical with them and the organs being never found without *Pragna* are identical with *Pragna*." This is in other words means that the *Achetana Prakriti* or *Kshetra* does not exist independently of the *Chetana*, but is only another aspect of it and the latter in its turn is not independent of the Self. Thus the non-self (the last form of which is the rudimental element of *Akas*) gets merged in the Jiva which as Sankara points out 'enters within the whole universe and thus sustains it' ; and the Jiva in its turn gets merged when it knows itself into the all-absorbing Self. It is thus the Jiva which, so to speak, projects the non-self, for it becomes what it perceives, and when there arises the slightest differentiation in the shape of a Jiva, the footing being lost, the natural result is rolling down and down and the creation of an infinitely variegated universe.

It is in this sense that the world is compared to a dream. Just as the horses, chariots and palaces which one sees in his dream are perfectly real to him so long as the dream lasts, in the same way so long as one fancies oneself to be actor, perceiver and enjoyer, that is, in one word *Samsari*, so long it does not enter one's mind that the world of effects with its means and objects of right knowledge and its results of actions is untrue, but when he wakes from this dream of his being something finite and limited then for him all phenomena cease. So says the Sruti : "Where there is *as it were* duality, there sees another another thing, there smells another another thing, there tastes another another thing, there speaks another another thing, there hears another another thing, there minds another another thing, there touches another another thing, there knows another another thing, but how does one to whom all has become mere Self, see anything, how smell anything, how taste anything, how speak anything, how hear anything, how mind anything, how touch anything, how know anything?" (*Bri. Up.*, IV, 5, 15).

When, by the grace of the Acharya, one realises that the individual soul or Jiva is not different from the Self, but only appears to be so, he gets, above all delusion and grief and above the death to which according to the Upanishads he passes who herein sees diversity. It is through such realisation that the *Rishis* have declared for the good of us all : "All this is born of Me (that is, the Self), all this exists in Me and all this gets absorbed in Me : I am all this wonderful world."—(Kaivalyopanishad). "Verily I extend from below, I extend from above, I extend from behind, I extend from before, I extend from the South, I extend from the North, of a truth, I am all this : verily the Self extends from below, the Self extends from above, the Self extends from behind, the Self extends from before, the Self extends from the South, the Self extends from the North, of a truth, the Self is all this" (*Chh. Up.*, VII, 25). When this boundless light of the Self is reached, then and then alone can the truth of the unreality of the universe be fully understood. The opinion of the Srutis which are nothing but the statements of men who realised the Self, to whom the Self was not a mere logical theory, nor a metaphysical unknowable but the only reality, is unmistakable on the subject. The Tejobindopanishad says : "If there be anything outside Me, it is surely unreal like a mirage. The world may be said to exist if one could be frightened by the words of the son of a barren woman. The world may be said to exist if an elephant could be killed by the horns of a hare. The world may be said to exist if one's thirst could be quenched by drinking of the mirage." Says the Mahopanishad : "O Nitaka, a wild elephant is tied up in a hole in a corner of a mustard seed, a mosquito is fighting with a herd of lions in the cavity of an atom, an infant bee has devoured Mount Mahameru, seated on a lotus seed ; think of the world whose nature is illusion as being only as real as the above" (*i.e.*, if the above things be true then it is also true that the world exists).

Surprisingly bold as these words appear, there is no use of quarrelling or finding fault with them, for their authors speak from a standpoint about which we are utterly in the dark. Verily what is daylight to them is dark midnight to us. They attained a place where they merged their illusory finiteness into that all-absorbing and all-felicitous immensity, that transcendental *Bhuma* "where they saw nothing else, heard nothing else and knew nothing else." That was their home, sweet home and that is our home too, but we are far, far away from it wandering in ignorance among the deceiving variety of phenomena. In the words of the Sukarahasyopanishad we are sleeping the sleep of ignorance and dreaming the dream of I and Mine (Jiva and the world), because we mistake the non-self for the Self but, as a man who remembers in his dream that he is dreaming, is very near waking, so for those who are firmly convinced even by intellectual inquiry that the Self alone is real and that the confounding of it with the Non-self is the cause of this dream of the world, the waking may not be far off and the trumpet tongue of the teacher uttering the memorable words 'That art thou' may rouse them ere long from their slumber and make them open their eyes to the right, in the cool bliss of which, they will forget their past sleep and dream and even the gracious voice that woke them up.

In the meanwhile, to' call the world unreal while being in it and of it would be an Irish bull, and the soldier who cried that he was dead should be considered much saner than a man who without giving up his little personality and selfish ways, without having approached the Teacher and realised the Self, calls the world a dream, a delusion. In this connection it may not be out of place to remind certain Christian critics of the Vedanta that its sublime truths are not meant for mere theoretical comprehension and intellectual criticism, but for practical realisation after a steady course of service and training. Somehow we have now the *Bhava* (notion) of our being finite little selves, and the manifold world diversified according to the tendencies that spring up and develop in every one of us is only a modification (*Vikara*) of this *Bhava*—this erroneous sense of separateness. As the individual souls proceed in the slippery road of *Avidya*, these tendencies increase in strength and number and as the result, more and more diversified does the world get for them. Now in order to check this suicidal career of creating newer and newer foes and dragging a heavier and more and more lengthening chain at every step, the one thing most needed is a proper inquiry into the nature of the Self and the final cure for the multiplying misery of life in the phenomenal world is to know that one is 'not this', 'not this'—body, the senses and so on—but That, that which has no name by which to be called; and the richest legacy which a most loving father gave to his most beloved son Svetaketu, was a simple sentence of three words "Thou art that".

It should not be understood for a moment that the non-existence of the world is limited to certain states. What the Vedanta says on the other hand is, that the world is not merely unreal in certain states of consciousness, but that it is really non-existent. Just as when a rope is mistaken for a serpent the latter does not exist there and never did and there was only the rope all the while, in the same way the Self alone exists and the world is with reference to it an illusion. Instead of the Self being a result of the experience of a certain state of consciousness it is the world that depends upon and is limited to such states. The Self exists before we realise it and after we realise it. It exists at all times and when we realise it, we find that that is the only reality.

That this is the opinion of the Srutis also is clearly pointed out by Sankara in his commentary on the Vedanta Sutra (II, 1, 14). He says : "Nor can it be said that this non-existence of the phenomenal world is declared (by Scripture) to be limited to certain states ; for the passage 'Thou art that' shows that the general fact of Brahman being the Self of all is not limited by any particular state. Moreover scripture, showing by the instance of the thief (*Kh.*, VI, 16) that the false-minded is bound while the true-minded is released, declares thereby that the unity is the one true existence while manifoldness is evolved out of wrong knowledge. For if both were true how could the man who acquiesces in the reality of the phenomenal world be called false-minded ? Another scriptural passage 'From death to death goes he who perceives therein any diversity' (*Brih. Up.*, IV, 4, 19), declares the same, by blaming those who perceive any distinction. Moreover, on the doctrine, which we are at present impugning, release cannot result from knowledge, because the doctrine does not acknowledge that some kind of wrong knowledge, to be removed by perfect knowledge, is the cause of the phenomenal world. For how can the cognition of unity remove the cognition of manifoldness if both are true ?"

Though thus the Self be the only reality and the universe an illusion based upon it, we differ with regard to our attitude towards them not only between one another, but every one with reference to himself. Before inquiry we believed things to be what they seemed and had not an intellectual recognition of a per-manent substratum behind the impermanent phenomena. After enquiry we are able to acquiesce at least in theory that the world is not absolutely real. At the same time, speaking from the intellectual plane, it is not absolutely unreal, for, its existence is our indubitable experience and it is at this stage that the Srutis designate Maya as different from both *Sat* the real and *Asat* the unreal, as *Anirvachaniya*, that is, as something which is inexpressible. The world appears as one vast *Mahendrajala*, magical illusion, ordained by the Almighty Self. So far we can go intellectually. There is however a stage in which even this appearance vanishes and where the world is not felt any more than a dream in the waking state. It is here that Maya really ends and it is with reference to this state that the Sarvasaropanishad says that though Maya is beginningless yet she has end. This is the state of *Samadhi*, but realisation does not mean this particular state alone, but includes as well what is called the *Sahajasthiti* or natural state being that in which the sage whose mind is filled with peace moves about as the Gita says : 'without attachment, without selfishness, without vanity and rests, happily in the nine-gated city of the body having renounced all actions by thought and therefore neither acting nor causing the act.' In this state the world appears, but the seer knows that it is utterly unreal and as a mirage appears to be water even after one has known that it is not water, so even after one has realised that what exists is only the Atman, the world will appear to be real, but it is an illusion which can no longer deceive him. To reach this glorious state of freedom from all delusion, one has to practise *Samadhi* for a long time under the instruction of a gracious teacher, and merely to say that the world is unreal will not enable one to reach the reality any more than a man in the dark reach the light by merely crying 'darkness, darkness.' The reality has first to be seen and then only will the unreal become unreal to us.

We have discussed at some length one of the most important problems of philosophy though we cannot pretend to have done anything like justice to it. The conclusion to which our analysis and discussion led us, though there is only one way of realising it—initiation from the Acharya and steady practice of *Samadhi*—is intellectually provable in many ways and instead of approaching the question from psychology as we did, one may proceed ontologically or cosmologically and will, we are sure, reach the same conclusion provided one does not get nervous and stop in the middle.

THE WAR

WAR is the first law of nature. If there is one thing which can be said to be *the* characteristic of the whole universe, it is war. There is war in the waters, on the earth, up in the heavens, war everywhere. "Thou hast killed all and all have killed thee," said the Tamilian sage Pattanattu Pillai. When Prince Siddharta was taken by his father to 'see the pleasance of the spring,' he beheld the beauties of the season and rejoiced to see nature in its gayest attire like a Circassian beauty decorated for her marriage.

> But, looking deep, he saw,
> The thorns which grew upon this rose of life ;
> How the swart peasant sweated for his wage,
> Toiling for leave to live ; and how he urged
> The great-eyed oxen through the flaming hours,
> Goading their velvet flanks : then marked he, too,
> How lizard fed on ant, and snake on him,
> And kite on both ; and how the fish-hawk robbed
> The fish-tiger of that which it had seized ;
> The shrike chasing the bulbul, which did hunt
> The jewelled butterflies ; till everywhere
> Each slew a slayer and in turn was slain,
> Life living upon death. So the fair show
> Veiled one vast, savage grim conspiracy
> Of mutual murder, from the worm to man
> Who himself kills his fellow ;

and sighing said : "Is this that happy earth they brought me forth to see ? Go aside a space and let me muse on what you show."

Now, why is this struggle ? It may be that it is all for good and that lasting peace may be the result of this incessant war. But why should good come through

226

evil and peace through war? This question has been asked in all countries, but most of the religions of the world have sought to explain it away through the aid of a mythological machinery of wars in heaven, Satans, Beelzebubs and Ahrimans. Modern philosophies have as a rule shirked the question and sought to remedy the evil by means of utilitarian ethics, hedonistic calculus and so on. But they have not done even as much service as those unscientific and childish religions which substitute mythology for philosophy, and their cures are mere temporary make-shifts, a truce for the time being with the demon of war, rather than real remedies; for they have not even diagnosed the evil properly and much less ascertained its cause.

What is this struggle for? These philosophies have nearly all of them assumed that it is for existence, which is far from the truth. Indeed if bare existence can satisfy the creatures of the world, nearly all the misery of life would vanish and the advice of Jesus, "Take no thought for your life, what ye shall eat or what ye shall drink; nor yet for your body, what ye shall put on. Is not the life more than meat, and the body more than raiment? Behold the fowls of the air; for they sow not, neither do they reap, nor gather into barns: yet your heavenly Father feedeth them. Are ye not much better than they? Consider the lilies of the field, how they grow; they toil not, neither do they spin. And yet I say unto you, That even Solomon in all his glory was not arrayed like one of these. Wherefore if God so clothe the grass of the field which to-day is and to-morrow is cast into the oven, shall He not much more clothe you, O ye of little faith? Therefore take

no thought saying, what shall we eat? or what shall
we drink? or wherewithal shall we be clothed?" will
instead of being an ideal to aspire to, at once become
a realised fact; all struggle will cease and with it all
misery. Struggle for existence is an expression which
when examined loses its meaning, for since it is an observed fact that existence itself is struggle, it would mean
that one struggles to exist and exists to struggle, in
other words, one struggles to struggle. The fact is few
care for mere existence. The will to live has its genesis
not in the desire to live for living's sake but in the desire
for the happiness which life is imagined to give. Existence
is in itself too watery a thing to suit the tastes of the
many and, if that were its own end, there would be
room enough in the world for double the number of
lives it now has.

The recent tragedy at Moscow at the time of the
coronation of the present emperor of which most of
our readers have probably heard was a miniature allegorical representation of the terrible drama of life.
There was enough of cakes for all present and if they
had waited patiently, every one would have got a decent
share; but all of them rushed one before the other to
get the cakes and the result was they fell upon and trampled one another in the hurry; several thousands of
lives were lost and the day of rejoicing became one of
lamentation throughout the country. What happened
in Russia was only a sharp, clearly cut, high-relief representation of what happens every day in the world.
No creature is content with bare existence, content
with what comes to it in the natural course of life, but
all run after pleasures and in the race kill one another

and lose even what they would have obtained otherwise. The struggle in the world therefore is not for existence. It is for happiness. Truly says the Sruti : "Who would have moved or who would have lived if happiness did not pervade all space ? "

The modern theory of struggle for existence is thus not altogether correct, and consequently the methods, based on that theory for the alleviating of struggle and wickedness and lessening the friction of life, by the generous and sympathetic philosophers of the West avail very little. The best and the most accurate diagnosis of the case is made by the Vedanta which says that creatures struggle not for existence, but for happiness. In their own nature they are blissful, for the *Swarupa* of the Atman or the Self of all is *Ananda* or bliss, but through the force of the ineffable Maya, they forget themselves and look for the happiness of which they are themselves the fountain and storehouse in things outside, and the result is dependence and misery. All creatures instinctively struggle for happiness, because their native home is bliss, but on account of *Avidya* or ignorance they seek for it in the wrong place, in the outer world in which they live and move so long as the delusion of its being blissful continues. Sooner or later in the course of evolution it is found out that happiness is within and not without and then begins the conscious attempt to return to the blissful source from which beings started in the race of life. As the famous verse of the Taittiriya Upanishad beautifully puts it : 'Happiness is Brahman ; from happiness even are verily born these beings ; by happiness when born they live ; happiness they approach, (happiness) they enter' (III, vi). "To come back to the point from which we have been projected," says Swami Vivekananda, "is the great struggle of life. Whether people know it or not, it does not matter; but whatever you see in this universe of motion, of struggle, in plants, in minerals or anything, is a tendency to come back to the centre and be at rest. As it were there was a tremendous equilibrium and that has been destroyed, and all parts, and atoms and molecules are struggling to find the equilibrium again, and in the struggle they are combining and forming and re-forming all this wonderful panorama of nature, all to get back to the equilibrium again. So all social struggles, wars and fight, human struggles, and competitions in plant life, animal life and everywhere else are but expressions of that eternal struggle to get back this equilibrium."

The term happiness which we have so often used should not be confounded with pleasure. It is simply another name for the equilibrium to which Swami Vivekananda refers, another name for God. Says Amiel "To be happy, to possess eternal life, to be in God, to be saved—all these are the same. All alike mean the solution of the problem, the aim of existence . . . Happiness has no limits because God has neither bottom nor bounds, and because happiness is nothing but the conquest of God through love." Everything in this universe consciously or unconsciously seeks for this happiness; but where it is unconsciously sought for as in the majority of cases, the search is, through *Avidya*, carried on in the outer world, and the result is pleasure and pain by turns—the *Dwandwas* as they are called.

There are however here and there at every time some

blessed souls who are anxious to rise above these *Dwandwas*
or pair of opposites, who do not like to be befooled by
Maya and consciously seek for happiness in the truest sense
of the word—'the conquest of God through love.' The
struggle in which they engage whose aim is nothing less
than to annihilate the whole of the sense-world, to make
it unreal, *Mitya* and to obtain the Reality behind it is
worth all the battles ever fought on the earth put together
and deserves to be styled The War *par excellence*. All
the great Indian epics, the Ramayana, the Mahabharata,
the Skandapurana are only allegories of this great war
against the world of Maya. Arjuna (the human soul)
is asked to fight against the children of Dritarashtra—
the offspring of *Moha*, and in the great fight, Krishna
the Atman stands by the side of the struggling soul and
urges it on to fight. Said the Lord : "Do thou arise,
and obtain glory. After conquering the enemies, enjoy
the unrivalled dominion (*Swarajyam*). By Myself have
they already been slain ; be thou an apparent cause,
O Savyasachi." The very same advice is given in that
wonderful book 'Light on the Path' :—"Stand aside
in the coming battle ; and though thou fightest, be not
thou the warrior. Look for the warrior and let him
fight in thee. Take his orders for the battle and obey
them. Obey him, not as though he were a general,
but as though he were thyself, and his spoken words
were the utterance of thy secret desires ; for he is thyself, yet infinitely wiser and stronger than thyself.......
Then it will be impossible for thee to strike one blow
amiss. But if thou look not for him, if thou pass him
by, then there is no safeguard for thee. Thy brain
will reel, thy heart grow uncertain, and in the dust of

the battlefield, thy sight and senses will fail, and thou
wilt not know thy friends from thy enemies." (II, 1-4).
The warrior here is the *Guru*, Sri Krishna in human
form, without whose grace and love the war could not
be fought with success, nay, could not even properly
commence. The method of fighting the great war of
which we are speaking is beautifully described in the
following passage of the Maitrayani Upanishad :—

One should first cross over the sense-objects, the
senses and the body composed of the elements (*i.e.*,
cease all identification with these) and then, with the
bow of courage which is furnished with the string of
renunciation, should aim the dart of non-attachment
at the first watchman in the gate leading to Brahman
and kill him. This watchman whose name is egoism
has *Avidya* or false knowledge as his turban. Avarice
and envy are his ear-rings. Sloth, sleepiness and sin
are his club-sticks. He, the master, who is attached
to these, wields the bow of lust furnished with the string
of anger, hurts all creatures with the dart of desire.
Having slain him, one should cross the limits of *Hridaya-
akasa* (*Chit-akasa*), on the boat called *Aum* and when
the light of Brahman begins to be perceived enter into
the *Brahmasala* (the hall of Brahman) slowly and
cautiously like a man getting into a mine for obtaining
the minerals in it. He should enter into the *Brahma
Kosa* (the last sheath, *Anandamaya*)—which is hidden
behind by four other sheaths—by the secret method
into which he was been initiated by the Acharya.
Beyond this lies the Atman who is holy, pure, indestructible, calm, beyond the vital airs and the mind,
eternal, undecaying, firm, immortal, birthless and free

and who rests in his own glory. Beholding the Atman who thus rests in his own glory, one looks (as a mere witness) upon the wheel of mortal life as the revolving wheel of a car (which can be stopped at will).

The hard nature of the struggle is admitted by all who know about it. Arjuna says: "For the *Manas* is verily restless, O Krishna, turbulent, strong and tough. Therefore I deem the control (of it), quite as difficult as to control the wind (VI, 34). In this connection, the story of Mahabali in the Yoga Vasishta is very instructive. The king, feeling very much the same grief as that of Alexander the Great, at having no more kingdoms to conquer, asked his minister to find out some new occupation for him. The minister replied: "True it is that you have conquered all the world, but there is a kingdom which is larger and more wealthy than those you have conquered. Until you conquer that, you can hardly regard yourself as a hero." The king to whom the map of the world was very familiar asked in surprise where that kingdom lay and who its king and said that he would start immediately to subdue it. The wise minister replied: "The sovereign of that empire is a very mild and inoffensive person easy to be captured, but his minister is a very cunning, intriguing diplomatist and it is impossible to kill him by any means and unless he be subdued, no one can even approach the kingdom." The king said: "Is it so? I should be all the more eager to capture that kingdom, my name is not Mahabali if I do not conquer it. Tell me at once where it is and prepare yourself at once to start with me." The minister coolly replied: "That kingdom is within yourself." The king was struck dumb with surprise, and at last said : "You speak the truth. The Atman, the inner ruler immortal could not even be approached unless his minister—mind—is subdued. But ah ! the difficulty of it. Still what is the good of gaining the whole world and losing one's soul !'' From that day forward, the story adds, the king devoted himself to Brahmanishta.

The apt simile of Sri Sankara in which he compares the mind to a maddened monkey drunk and bitten by a scorpion is well-known. As a great sage once beautifully observed, one might more easily dig a pit and bury his shade under it than kill the mind. The mind can never be slain, for in its nature it is eternal. It has however to be subdued. And the only way for it is pointed out by the Lord who says : "Doubtless, O mighty armed, the *Manas* is hard to control and restless ; but by practice, O son of Kunti, and by indifference it may be controlled (VI, 35). Little by little let him gain tranquillity by means of *Buddhi* held in firmness ; having made the *Manas* abide in the Self, let him not think of anything'' (VI, 25).

Upon the latter verse Sankara observes : "He should make the *Manas* abide in the Self, *bearing in mind that the Self is all and that nothing else exists. This is the grand secret* of *Yoga* (VI, 25). But what is that sort of practice that is to be commenced and how to make the *Manas* abide in the Self? The only means for doing this is to approach a *Guru* who is wise, well-versed in the scriptures, sinless, free from desire, knowing the nature of Brahman, who has attained rest in spirit, like flame extinguished by the fuel being consumed, whose kindness is not actuated by personal considerations, and who is anxious to befriend those that seek for help and addressing him when he is not otherwise engaged, "Salutation, O Lord, full of compassion, O friend of those who bend before thee, sprinkle on me thy grace, O Lord, heated as I am by the forest fire of birth and rebirth, gratify my ear with ambrosial words as they flew from thee mingled with the essence of thy Self-experience, and the bliss afforded by *Brahmajnana* sacred and cooling. Happy are they who come into thy sight even for a moment, for (they become) fit recipients and are accepted as pupils," practise as he bids and slowly and steadily proceed in the path of liberation guarded as by an angel by his grace obtained through obedience and respectful demeanour.

THE VEDANTA AND THE EMPEROR OF
EMPERORS

SPEAKING with reference to a particular empire, there is nothing so absolutely seditious in its character, so directly tending to create mutiny against the powers that be, and, what is still worse, so fully conscious of its power to overthrow their government there in the long run, whatever be its strength, as the Vedanta. It is decidedly ultra-radical, and in spite of its cloak of peace and the apparently saintly resignation, with which its professed adherents accommodate themselves to the course of events and submit to all kinds of compromises, it is ever secretly and steadily plotting to undermine the very foundations of the government in that empire, and, in its eagerness to overthrow, cares not whether what it tries to subvert, be good or bad. It cares not whether the sovereign, ruling there, be young or old, whether his ministers, viceroys and deputies are many or few, whether his dominions extend far and wide or only cover a limited area. There is no surer or more dangerous enemy to constituted authority in that empire, than the Vedanta, and woe to the government in it which, mistaking its scope and aim and deceived by its peaceful and venerable appearance, harbours it in its dominions or even suffers its existence there. Numberless kingdoms, especially in this country, all belonging to that empire, have crumbled to dust without the slightest chance of reviving, even in future *Yugas*, hundreds of thrones in it have been burnt to ashes, their antiquity, their gorgeousness, pomp and splendour notwithstanding and the kings who sat on them with 'pride in their port and defiance in their eye,' the terrible Sultans of their kingdoms, and surnamed 'the great,' 'the conqueror,' 'the tiger,' 'the lion,' and so on, have been hurled down and banished into the primeval void, their sceptres broken, and their huge royal household scattered to the winds—all, because they injudiciously gave shelter and bread to the dangerous Vedanta. What they did was a grave political blunder, for which they have dearly paid, and their example must serve as a terrible warning to all sensible governments in the empire, which have the slightest regard for their safety. The French revolution did not work greater havoc among the monarchies of the West,—for, the mischief it did, has much of it been repaired and time will heal the few remaining sores—than the traitorous philosophy which is so actively advocated in these days.

The whole Vedantic literature is criminal in character ; every word of it is a covert sedition against the emperor ; its best part, the Upanishads are so many war songs and the Gita plainly and boldly commands its readers to fight against him, fight without scruples and without regard to consequences, while the Ramayana, the Mahabharata and the like are so many powerful suggestions in the same direction. They are the histories of terrible fights and wholesale massacres which took place in that empire, presented in a classical and permanent form, that they may serve as perennial fountains of mischief and mutiny and excite every successive generation to rebellion against its sovereign, feasting their ears and stirring their hearts with accounts of ancient battles. War against the ruling government there, is their only theme, and no government in that empire, therefore, if it really wishes to live, should tolerate their study. It is true, that all these books talk so much about the glory of peace and take care to crown all their important discourses with the words 'Santih, Santih, Santih' but the peace they talk of, is peace after the overthrow of the empire, after all authority there, is put down for good.

The very method of their warfare is remarkable and perfectly in keeping with their character. At first they do not openly declare war, but like some clever lawyers who begin with apparently irrelevant and remote questions and cunningly drive their victims to an uncomfortable corner from which they could not escape, these books appear, at the commencement, to be as if they are most innocent and to have nothing to do with the complex politics of that empire and end with working out a complete political revolution. The lessons which they teach seem, in the beginning, to be very favourable to good government, so that the sovereign himself gladly embraces them and remodels his government in their light with great self-complacency, little suspecting that his course is suicidal and will end in his being throttled to death, in a close hand-to-hand wrestle, in his own palace. 'Give room to sit down and I shall make room to lie down,' is the saying, which receives nowhere a better illustration than in the practical conduct of the Vedanta ; and to encourage it, is like catching the Tartar, and can end only in the downfall of the government of that emperor, with all his retinues, parliaments and armies. And what is even more audacious is, that, immediately after the victory, the Vedanta issues a grand public proclamation that there never really was either king, government, subjects or slavery and that all was a mere illusion. Can audacity go farther?

Here it may be asked, if the Vedanta be really so dangerous and so inimical to the ruling authority, how does it happen that it has survived numberless monarchs from the time of Janaka, nay very much earlier. Had no one the good sense to peep behind the masque, and discover and punish the traitor? If even a single kingdom had been overthrown through the mischievous plotting of the Vedanta, would not have all the other kingdoms—and there have been thousands of them—made common cause against that traitorous philosophy and nipped it in the very bud? Besides, there is not the slightest allusion in our books to its alleged political power; and what is even more wonderful is, that many of our ancient kings were themselves professed adherents of that philosophy, and according to some theorists, it owes its very origin to the royal *Rishis* of old India.

Our reply is, the government to which we refer and to whose well-being the Vedanta is so much opposed, is not a mere mushroom government, enduring for the brief space of a few centuries or tens of centuries at the most, but one of infinite standing, and, indeed, as old as the world itself. The emperor of that kingdom wields infinitely greater power over his dominions, than any so-called sovereign does over his petty estates and the Vedanta, having to reckon with such a mighty emperor, hardly minds other monarchs, who are such only by a figure of speech. King Janaka once ordered a Brahmin to be expelled from the country for some serious offence but when the latter asked him what the extent of his dominions was, he reflected for a moment and said, "Nothing really belongs to me; there were so many emperors who, each in his turn called the earth *his*; they have all gone, but the earth remains as ever. Therefore I have no empire which I can properly call mine; nothing belongs to me, not the men, nor the lands, nor even my family; nothing being thus my dominion, you may stay wherever you please." King Janaka spoke the truth, and all the so-called sovereigns of the world are in the same predicament. The Vedanta does not trouble itself with such fictitious emperors and empires. But there is a vast empire, where government is much more real and where, not an atom can move except at the direct bidding and under the eye of the mighty and omniscient Emperor, who is little less than God, at least, within the limits of that dominion; and it is against such a giant Emperor that the Vedanta directs its subtle manœuvres. Where is such a kingdom? Our maps have no record of such an empire anywhere, and history has not a word to say about it, it may be asked; nevertheless, no empire is more extensive, more powerful or more real, and where it is, what it is and what its extent, will all become plain, if we but mention the name of the world-renowned sovereign of that grand empire. Not to keep the reader's mind any longer in suspense, we hasten to say that his name is *Ahankara* (egoism) or as people fearing to mention his full name say "I"—a very expressive symbol, which, besides being his name, denotes at the same time his rank which is number 1, he being the very *first person* in all the worlds.

This Emperor of emperors, this mighty and all-dreaded monarch, at whose bidding the earth rotates upon its axis, and stars wander in space, sits 'high on a throne of royal state', the name of which, the wise say, is *Avidya* (ignorance) and holds in his hand the terrible sceptre of passion. He wears on his head a huge turban which some call Vanity. Avarice and Envy are his resplendent ear-rings. Sloth, Sleepiness and Sin are his mighty club sticks. He holds in his hand the tremendous bow of lust, which is furnished with the string of Anger, and by which he hurts all creatures piercing them with the dart of Desire. Intellect is his wife, though not a legal one, as it is well-known, in some quarters. With her, and more often without her, he rides the magnificent car of the Body, which is drawn with more than lightning speed by ten wonderful horses, the Senses of action and perception, followed by a vast and splendid retinue of *Vasanas* or mental impressions. In such regal state, he constantly travels in all the ten directions, creating, conquering and destroying as he goes. From the bottom of the world to its very top, extends his empire, which for convenience sake, is divided into as many kingdoms as there are created things, all personally governed by Him. Everything in that empire, even the tiniest creatures, which the most powerful microscopes cannot discover, even they feel his mighty presence, and at his command, fight, kill, marry and enjoy. It is at his bidding that the thief steals, the murderer slays, the lawyer pleads and plunders, the trader carries on his commerce, the statesman plots and the lover gets mad. It is at his bidding, that ants feed on insects, the lizards feed on ants, snakes feed on lizards, kites feed on snakes and man feeds on all.

16

It is at his bidding, in short, that all the worlds perform
their wonted task and reveal such an infinite variety
of scenes, so full of bustle and war and mirth and woe.
Says the great sage Thayumanavar : "The moment
Ahankara or egoism springs up in men, the world-Maya
gets diversified, and who can describe the greatness of
the ocean of misery which springs from it ?—flesh,
body, organs, inside, outside, all-pervading ether, air,
fire, water, earth, hills, deserts, shows innumerable,
things invisible, forgetfulness, remembrance, griefs and
joys—the never-ending waves of the ocean of Maya—their
cause Karma, their cures, numberless religions with
numberless founders, God, disciples, methods numberless, with authorities for all the practices, and logic—one
might more easily count the minute sands in the sea."
Such is the power of *Ahankara*. He is at the bottom
of the world, the mighty Atlas on whose shoulders it
rests, and but for whom it could be nowhere.

It is against such a mighty emperor and not against
any self-sufficient individual, who, putting on a crown
on his head, fancies he is the sovereign of the world,
that the Vedanta carries on a persistent war. It commences operations in a very simple way, at first throwing
out only a suggestion or two and that in a well-chosen
hour, in a thoroughly courtier-like fashion. To take
an example : a man, let us say, loses his son of whom
he was very fond. His grief is inconsolable, the world
loses all charm for him and life becomes insupportable.
Just then the Vedanta makes its appearance with a
very sad countenance and instead of boldly and directly
impeaching the sovereign *Ahankara*, the cause of all
this mischief, timidly suggests : 'This is the result of

bad Karma, you ought to have done some great injury to some one in your last birth and that is why you suffer in this.' With this consolation, which, it may be observed *en passent*, is in perfect accordance with truth, unlike those administered by other religions, which, under the circumstances, would say some such thing as : 'Your son is in heaven with God and you will reach him as soon as you die'—is coupled a valuable hint to the effect that one can attain greater happiness, at least, in the next birth, only by doing good acts in the present one. The sad event thus offers a good opportunity to the man for becoming better, and he does some good things, say, builds a *Chattram* or endows a temple and is glad for having done so, which means that the emperor *Ahankara* is delighted at his own goodness and unsuspectingly thanks the Vedanta for having made him happy and thus gives it a surer footing. The mind gets somewhat purified, and the study of Vedantic literature is begun. The books are first looked upon as so many interesting stories, a second perusal results in finding in them a half truth here and a half truth there, some grains of wisdom amidst much chaff. There is a subtle and almost unrecognised inducement to read them a third time, and now it seems that even the chaff has some concealed meaning or at any rate sets off the rest to advantage, and the whole appears grand and poetic. If nothing else, one could at least pass off for a scholar, poet and philosopher by studying them. Pride, however, is the forerunner of destruction, and, ere long, it is discovered that fame avails little in the practical struggle in the world, and that even good acts meet with a bad return.

The lessons, till now in the lips, now go down deep into heart, that the only means to be happy is, to do good without caring for the results.

Here begins the practice of Karma Yoga, the dignity and power of which are hardly known to the scriptures of other religions. The grand precept : 'Do thy duty without caring for the result, thou hast right only to the action but not to the fruits thereof,' aims a strong blow upon the foolish emperor *Ahankara*. Even a stronger blow is dealt to it, when the next step is taken, when the practice of Bhakti Yoga commences. And the once mighty emperor so shelved away into the lumber room and a powerful regent appointed in his place, for the true *Bhakta* dedicates whatever he does to God. 'Whatsoever thou dost, whatever thou eatest, whatsoever thou offerest, whatsoever thou givest, what-soever thou dost of austerity, O ! Kaunteya, do thou as an offering unto me.' This is the advice to the *Bhakta*, and he who is able to follow it, no longer does anything, as his own act. But, even here, the victory over *Ahankara* is not complete, for there still continues the false knowledge of one being the aggregate of the body, the senses and so on, and, though at times the misery of mortal life is forgotten in the ecstasy of love, it asserts itself often, and the emperor, not being slain, takes every opportunity to thrust himself into the court and make his presence felt. Fortunately this is not the acme of individual progress, there is a step still higher, which forms the theme of the best part of Vedantic literature and which consists in the lover losing himself in the ocean of God, or, more accurately speaking, realising his oneness with God, whom he was hitherto

worshipping as something different from him far off
somewhere above the clouds, but whom he now re-
cognises to be his own inmost Self, an experience referred
to by Bhagavan Sri Sankaracharya, in the following
verses :

न मे द्वेषरागौ न मे लोभमोहौ मदो नैव मे नैव मात्सर्यभाव: ।
न धर्मो न चार्थो न कामो न मोक्ष श्चिदानन्दरूप: शिवोऽहं शिवोऽहम् ॥
न मे मृत्युशङ्का न मे जातिभेद: पिता नैव मे नैव माता न जन्म ।
नबन्धुर्नमित्रं गुरुर्नैवशिष्य श्चिदानन्दरूप: शिवोऽहं शिवोऽहम् ॥

"Neither love nor hate, neither ambition nor illusion,
neither pride nor the least tinge of jealousy, nor good,
spiritual or temporal, nor desire, nor liberation ; —I
am none of these, I am all bliss, the bliss of unconditioned
consciousness."

"Death I fear not, caste I respect not, father, mother,
nay even birth, I know not, relatives, friends I recognise not, teacher and pupil I own not ;—I am all bliss,
the bliss of unconditioned consciousness."

The realisation of this unconditioned bliss can only
be obtained through the practice of Gnana Yoga which
is nothing but an open war against *Ahankara*. When
matters gradually reach such a crisis as to necessitate
war, the Vedanta thrown off its masque and plays its
part openly. It distinctly says that the emperor
himself is the cause of all the sufferings in the kingdom,
that he should be slain at any cost and that conquest
of him is sure, he owing his very existence to a fraud.
It boldly proclaims that the real I is *Satya Gnana Ananta
Ananda*, eternal, pure and unconditioned, the Light of

lights where this variety of names and forms has no existence and that therefore *Ahankara* whom people dignify with the appellation 'I', is a mere usurper, a villainous upstart and pretender and that the sooner he is extinguished, the better would it be for all. 'Awake, arise, seek the great ones and get understanding' (Ka. Up., III, 14). 'Great is the loss of him who realises not the Self in this life' (Ka. Up., II, 5) says the Vedanta, and adds, "The body itself is called by the wise, the temple, and the Jiva in it is itself the unconditioned Siva" (Maitreya Up.). 'Thou art that which transcends all names and forms, and which alone is real.' Can sedition go farther? But the Vedanta does not stop here. It creates mutiny, finds out the commander, the *Guru* and reveals the truth and when that is realised, *Ahankara* with all his armies and kingdoms, disappears like a dream after waking, his kingdom, the world, is found to be a mere illusion, and his wife, Intellect, is permanently wedded to the Lord, who alone is real, and loses herself in the embrace with Him, like a river in the sea. Here the sage proclaims : "There is no dissolution, creation, none in bondage, no pupilage, none desirous of liberation, none liberated, this is the absolute truth" (Sri Gaudapada's Karika, II, 32). Now the war is at an end, and what remains is Peace Absolute.

Om, Santih, Santih, Santih.

THE GLORY OF SUICIDE

THE play of Hamlet is almost unanimously regarded as the very best of Shakespeare's dramas, and indeed, as one of the best productions of human genius in the West. Its greatness—it is also agreed—is due not merely to its artistic excellence, the daring with which the poet creates critical and difficult situations and the wonderful ease with which he handles them, the richness of the imagery and language in which he reveals to intoxication or the profundity and minuteness of his observations on men and nature—qualities in respect to which several others of his plays have a claim to be ranked equal with, if not even superior to it—but chiefly to the unique greatness of its hero. Wonderfully rich as the creative faculty of Shakespeare was, so much so that his plays form a new world in themselves, a beautiful Visvamitra Srishti, in our opinion. 'Hamlet the prince of Denmark' is by far the best of his children. Other dramas reveal to us Shakespeare the poet, lending the gorgeous colours of his fancy and imagination to the varied scenes of life and vivifying them with his faculty divine, but the terrible tragedy of Hamlet reveals to us Shakespeare the philosopher, 'whom man does not delight nor woman neither,' to whom 'this brave overhanging firmament, this majestical roof fretted with golden fire, appears no other thing than a foul and pestilential congregation of vapours' and all the uses of the world are 'weary, stale, flat and unprofitable,' while its few pleasures are merely as the perfume and suppliance of a minute, and who, when called upon to act seriously puts to himself the question, which is better, 'to be or not to be', 'whether it is nobler in the mind to suffer the slings and arrows of outrageous fortune or to take arms against a sea of troubles and by opposing end them'. Here in this a play all dalliance with Nature is set aside, even its love scenes are melancholy unlike those of Romeo and Juliet, the Tempest, As You Like it, Othello and others, and have a tragic end ; and that end too is not heightened by the heroism of human passion as in Romeo and Juliet not rendered ghastly and terrible by jealousy kindled by malice as in Othello, but is sorrowful because the gentle emotion of love was blasted by a rigorous and searching philosophy, so cynical as to reveal in such '*fine* revolutions' as a fair lady's head becoming chapless, eyeless and lipless and knocked about with the sexton's spade. This cynical seriousness is not itself philosophy but is the beginning of it. It is true to life though it comes very late in the course of evolution, and the play of Hamlet is great exactly because it portrays to us the struggles and despair of a highly evolved and introspective soul, which, being no longer able to abide contented in the life of the senses, looks straight into the meaning of the world, but finding there only a gaping void instead of the solid kernel, burns with an inextinguishable agony of despair.

This desperate discontentment with the world and its uses which the great dramatist has so graphically depicted, is not, as some critics fancy, the result of morbid temperament brought about by the accidents of training, environments and so forth and therefore curable by more congenial surroundings or what are called the healthy influences of home, society and so on. It is not an accident caused by accidents but an inevitable stage in the progress of the soul. The fault is not in the temperament of the individual, however unhealthy, inconvenient and dangerous that may be, but in the nature of the sense-world itself. Such pessimistic dissatisfaction with the phenomenal world simply indicates that the imprisoned soul within has gathered strength enough to assert itself. It is the voice of Prometheus refusing to be bound, the beginning of a grand internal revolution in which the bastile of the senses is sought to be reduced to dust. It marks the vigorous awakening of the inner man who was hitherto lying passive and confined in his prison cell.

"He is not worth living," said a great French philosopher, "who has not even once seriously thought of committing suicide." Indeed it is impossible for thoughtful men to be satisfied with this deceptive world where everything promises so fair and proves so bad. We are on all sides surrounded by an infinite network of deception, everything we love leads us into snares and pitfalls and like the moth which, attracted by light rushes into it and dies, so every moment we run after pleasures and plot our own destruction. Byron rightly said :

> Oh pleasure, you're indeed a pleasant thing
> Although one must be damned for you no doubt.

We are so selfish, narrow-minded, jealous, wicked, and vain, that it seems one might search with a torch in one's hand in broad daylight as did the Grecian philosopher of old for a good and honest man. The littleness of the so-called great men is something appalling. The wicked, the cunning and the unscrupulous, roll in wealth and luxury, while good, simple, truthful and innocent men, lead a life of starvation and misery. Duryodhana, the personification of evil, enjoyed more of worldly prosperity than did poor Dharmaputra to whom every one appeared good and virtuous and who, on account of his unpractical humility and truthfulness, suffered hardships for which there was no adequate recompense so far at least as his earthly life was concerned. Sita, the incarnation *par excellence* of chastity and other womanly virtues, underwent woeful trials in a foreign country and in the hands of a frightful demon and even after her redemption from captivity enjoyed little happiness and, suddenly exiled by her husband, had a gloomy and pitiable end. Seriously considered, the world with its apparently arbitrary and unjust dispensations, the petty struggles with which it abounds and its numberless scenes of woe which would prove either that it is an anarchy, or, if governed at all, is governed by a heartless and gigantic Nero, appears to be a monstrous error as incorrigible as ugly, and moves along dancing like a rudderless ship in a stormy sea. "Absurdity," says a great thinker, "is interwoven with life. Real beings are animated contradictions, absurdities brought into action. By far the greater number of human beings can only conceive action or practise it under the form of war— a war of competition at home, a bloody war of nations abroad and finally war with the Self." "The question between man and man always is," says Carlyle, "will you kill me or shall I kill you?" 'Life lives upon death' and the fair shadow of the world 'veils one vast grim conspiracy of mutual murder from the worm to man who himself kills his fellow.'

Our life, as the Devas said to prince Siddhartha, is a moan, a sigh, a sob, a storm, a strife.

How truly does the poet say

> We look before and after
> And pine for what is not ;
> Our sincerest laughter
> With some pain is wrought ;
> Our sweetest songs are those that tell of saddest thoughts

and how pathetic and natural is his invocation to Misery

> Clasp me till our hearts be grown
> Like two lovers into one,
> Till this dreadful transport may
> Like a vapour fade away
> In the sleep that lasts always

and his cry, "I fall upon the thorns of life, I bleed ; the heavy weight of hours has chained down and bowed one too like thee (the west wind)."

It is all well to plead 'duty of happiness' and preach that life is a glorious inheritance, but most often this philosophy is post-prandial and derives its inspiration from well-filled belly rolling on a sofa and protected on both sides by soft and shining leather cushions, and therefore it cannot always hold good. With the problem of life unsolved ; with evil and misery, the twin demons of life staring us in our face at every step ; with a mind always bent on deceiving, extremely wanton, restless and unsteady and raising a constant barrier between ourselves and truth ; with dirty, little and many-holed body which we fancy to be 'express and admirable in form and moving' and to be all in all, as though there were neither sun, moon nor stars above us nor anything below; with an intellectual vision whose range does not exceed much over six feet above the earth; and living in a world which seems to be at times a monstrous anarchy and at others a strange penal colony filled with apparently impenetrable mazes and enigmas—to fancy that we are the roof of creation, the pillar of the universe and the image of our Maker and be happy with our mortal lot, is, to say the least of it, thoughtless and childish. Like reeds planted in the middle of a rushing torrent and waving helplessly in response to every passing gale and wavelet, man trembles at every petty occurrence and is ever a sorry 'pendulum betwixt a tear and a smile.' Being in this state, to proclaim the glory of life, is like a child rushing to a snake which is advancing to bite him. How many thoughtful men have not exclaimed: "Would that I have never been born!" Man enters the world weeping, a significant fact which reveals the nature of the whole mortal life, as the very first utterances of Shakespeare's heroes at once reveal their respective characters in their entirety.

We have with us a picture called 'Pantheon Universe' in which are grouped together in the mansion of fame all the great heroes of the Western world from Adam downward. One striking feature of almost all the faces there is a settled expression of melancholy. Here and there a foppish king or a shallow *Lokayata* (Materialist) peeps out with a smile as though, pea-cock thrones and microscopes have solved the whole problem of life. But the greater majority seem to be pondering with

eyes almost glistening with tears on the sphynx questions
around us and appear struck with the littleness of man,
his slavery to passions, his weakness and vanity.
Truly does Faust exclaim :—

> I curse whate'er entices
> And snares the soul with visions vain ;
> With dazzling cheats and dear devices
> Confines it in this cave of pain !
> Cursed be, at once, the high ambition
> Wherewith the mind itself deludes !
> Cursed be the glare of apparition
> That on the finer sense intrudes !
> Cursed be the lying dream's impression
> Of name, and fame, and laurelled brow !
> Cursed, all that flatters as possession.
> As wife and child, as knave and plough !
> Cursed Mammon be, when he with treasures
> To restless action spurs our fate !
> Cursed when, for soft, indulgent leisures,
> He lays for us the pillows straight !
> Cursed be the vine's transcendent nectar,—
> The highest favour Love lets fall !
> Cursed, lso, Hope !—cursed Faith, the spectre !
> And cursed be Patience most of all !

Such being the real state of earthly life, which only
shallow optimism or childish thoughtlessness can prevent
us from realising, the best thing for a thoughtful and
wise man to do is, to put an end to himself. Of all
animals, man alone has the power voluntarily to kill
himself once for all ; and it is on this account, that to
be born as man is regarded as a great privilege and indeed considered as even superior to becoming gods. There
is a nice little story in the Aitareya Upanishad of the Rig
Veda, that the *Devas* when asked to enter into a cow's
body and next a horse's body, declined saying : 'This is
not sufficient unto us,' but when asked to become men

they gladly did so. *The one ground and in our opinion the only one on which man has the right to be placed above other animals, nay, all the rest of animate creation, is his power to commit self-murder.* In point of physical frame, the senses, mind and even in point of intellect, he is outdone by several other creatures and the gods of the celestial regions above decidedly excel him in all these. But there is one privilege which is given to him and him alone in all creation and to enjoy which all other creatures have in course of time to assume the human form and that is his power to annihilate himself.

If so, it may be said the solution of the problem of life is very easy, for it requires only a piece of cord and nail. We say yes, it is very easy and does not require even so much as that. It is in the words of a sacred book easier than closing one's eyes or plucking a full-blown flower. And we would add it is even easier, for it does not require the slightest physical exertion, not even a muscle has to be moved. Though so easy, it is yet a complete solution for all the enigmas with which we are surrounded, for all the great problems which have exercised philosophers from the very beginning of the world. Suicide without the aid of a rope or a knife or poison and without falling into the sea or a river or breaking one's neck! Very strange indeed, yet such a thing exists. The method for it is a very secret one handed down through a long line of *dead* men from eternity. *To deserve it and obtain it and effectually use it, these are the only difficulties in the way*, but when these are overcome, we become dead, dead once for all. Evil, sin, suffering, all these at once disappear, for the annihilation is complete. After committing suicide in the aforesaid strange way, we need not be afraid of grief and joy, even in the 'shadow land' where spirits are said to dwell without food and clothes, and heaven, hell and future life will all lose their meaning for us. No God can henceforth punish us; there will be no judgment on us above or below, and no Karma can trouble us, for we become dead, wholly dead.

But how to commit such a secure and promising suicide? Howsoever we may die, the spiritualists tell us, only the curtain drops and the scene changes, and by some mysterious machinery we are wafted into another world where the history of pleasure and pain repeats itself in another form. Pious theologians go even farther and threaten that the certain reward of suicide is a 'dungeon horrible on all sides round' flaming as one great furnace and revealing by its 'visible darkness sights of woe, regions of sorrow, doleful shades, where peace and rest can never dwell, and hope never comes that comes to all and where flows a fiery deluge fed with ever burning sulphur unconsumed,' and things of that kind. Not a very fine prospect to be sure! But the authors of our books, the great sages who gave us religion are more generous and promise as a certain result of *honest* suicide, 'the highest wealth, the best riches, the greatest joy,' beyond gaining which they say, 'there remains nothing to gain, beyond the bliss of which there remains no possibility of bliss, beyond seeing which there remains nothing to see, beyond knowing which there remains nothing to be known.' The sage, having committed suicide, exclaims: "The mind attaining peace, I do not find even a trace of the universe in the free depths of myself, in the indescribable ocean of the bliss of self-realisation. Has it set, is it broken, is it shattered to pieces, is it dissolved, is it pounded to dust, is it swallowed up, is it gone to decay?' We must admit however that there is a difference between the suicide which the theologians condemn and that which the Upanishads extol. The one is killing the body which is to coin a new word 'body-cide', while the *other is the killing the self which is the real suicide, and which consists in killing out the false sense of our being separate from 'Ekamevadwaitam,' the One only without a second, whose glory the Vedas declare.* On account of *Avidya,* ineffable ignorance, we fancy ourselves to be finite little selves separate from Brahman, and it is this selfhood which is, as we have repeatedly seen, the cause of all suffering, sin and evil and of all phenomena in the universe. When we kill out the self, all bonds dissolve themselves into nothing, all phenomena are realised to be illusory and vanish and we reach a place from which there is no return into the deceiving sense-world. The real suicide and the only one which wise men ought to have recourse to, is therefore killing the self which is the source of all mischief and not the body which, by *Avidya,* is mistaken for the self. *The only way of committing this suicide is by the practice of Yoga under the safe guidance of a living dead man, a Jivan-mukta as he is called, one who has succeeded in killing himself.* No amount of poison, nor swords, nor fire can effect this suicide which is purely a mental process and requires no *physical* exertion.

Ah, who can describe the glory of this suicide! Where is the language which can venture to translate the Untranslatable, to express the Inexpressible from which 'words as well as the mind turn back without being able to comprehend It.' The moment the lower self which thinks itself to be finite, enveloped in ignorance, sinful or virtuous, enjoying or suffering in a huge world which seems to be *there* already and oppresses it on all sides with limitations, the moment this self is killed, Brahman the eternal infinite immoveable, causeless, perfect, pure, imperceivable, calm, free and blissful Brahman, the up-lifted thunderbolt through fear of whom fire burns, sun shines, wind blows, clouds pour out rain and Death stalks upon the earth, the unconditioned *Bhuma* where the sun does not shine, nor the moon, nor the stars and much less this earthly fire, which yet is not darkness but the glorious Light of lights and to obtain a glimpse of whose cool moony effulgence is to get mad after Him and long for Him as no Romeo did for his Juliet, this Brahman stands revealed. Having seen this, men forget their mortal nature and becoming sages break out in a language which we the worms of earth can hardly comprehend. Every word they speak is an Upanishad in itself, their very faces shine with a strange and unearthly brightness and they exclaim : "Discard shall we the whole microcosm and macrocosm, the bodies that crawl below and the worlds that hang out above as vessels of filth"—an idea which the poet catching a glimpse of the infinite within has echoed forth as follows in a moment of divine inspiration :

> What is heaven ? what are ye
> Who its brief expanse inherit ?
> What are suns and spheres. .
>
> . . . , ...
> . . . .
>
> Drops which Nature's mighty heart
> Drives through thinnest veins. Depart ! etc.

Now listen to what a great suicide says :

मय्येव सकलं ज्ञातं मयि सर्वं प्रतिष्ठितं ।
मयि सर्वं लयं याति तद्ब्रह्माद्वयमस्म्यहं ।
अणोरणीयानहमेक तद्वन्महानहं विश्वमिदं विचित्रं ।
पुरातनोऽहं पुरुषोऽहमीशो हिरण्मयोऽहं शिवरूपमस्मि ।
नपुण्यपापो मम नास्ति नाशो नजन्म देहेन्द्रियबुद्धिरस्ति ।
न भूमिरापो मम वह्निरस्ति न चानिलोमेऽस्ति नचांबरं च ।

Everything is born of Me, everything rests in Me,
everything gets absorbed in Me. I am that Non-dual
Brahman. I am more subtle than an atom and at the
same time very great. I am all this wonderful world.
I am the Ancient, I am the *Purusha*, I am Iswara. I
am All-light and All-bliss.

*   *   *   *

Virtue and sin do not belong to Me. Destruction
there is none for Me. Birth, body, senses and the intellect do not belong to Me. I am above earth, water,
fire, air, and *Akas*.—Kaivalyopanishad.

What is there higher than this ?

II
ELEMENTS OF THE VEDANTA

THE OBJECT OF VEDANTA

IT was a very 'beauteous evening calm and free' like the heart of a saint. Nature seemed to be wrapt up in herself in blissful meditation—like a sage in Samadhi. The birds had gone to their nests ; the cattle were safe in their sheds, and after the day's toil, man was either saying his prayers, or enjoying the repose that reigned throughout. The nightingale alone was pouring forth a flood of the softest melody which accorded very well with the sublime stillness of the hour. The song of any other bird would have appeared silly at that time. The gentle, unobtrusive smell of the flowers of the evening enhanced its sweetness, while the gentle stream of the infant moon-light of the time lent to it an ineffable charm. The Jumna was flowing on at its usual majestic pace, and on its silver sands, now become classical by the wealth of associations, and on that splendid moon-lit evening, entered Krishna accompanied by the Gopis, and Radha, Janaki and Savitri. The favourite flute was soon on his lips, and the tune he sang at that silent hour,—ah ! who can describe it—was to the galaxy that surrounded him a veritable magic spell. This harmony was not however to last long, for shortly after, Krishna noticed a calf lying dead at a few yards' distance from them, and when approached, it was found to be his most favourite one. The sorrow for the loss was general, but after musing for a while, Krishna said : 'No matter : it can be restored to life. There is one way for it and only one, and that is, that every one of you should speak out what she most sincerely desires at this hour, what thoughts the moonlight, the river and this evening hour put into her mind. This, if honestly and frankly said would bring back the calf to life. Such is the power of 'truth'.

This was agreed to, and the ladies began one after another to speak out their hearts. One Gopi said : 'I should most like to undisturbedly enjoy the music of thy magic flute, O my Krishna ! That I value above all others.' Another said : 'I wish to swim with thee in this delightful moonlight in this Jumna which flows on like melted silver.' A third said : 'I have always been longing, and the desire is now intensified, O Krishna, for as much independence as man has, longing to set at naught all social superstitions about women's modesty, weakness and so forth, all of which merely mean women's slavery, to wear male attire, and walk about with a stick in hand and shoes and turban just wherever I please. Women's life, as it is, is simply a curse.' A fourth said : 'I should like to be a *Rishi* saying his prayers on the Himalayas and performing ablutions on evenings like these at the very birth place of the Ganges.' Another said : 'I wish to go about helping the poor, looking after the sick and the wounded and carry consolation and peace to desolate homes. What selfish enjoyment could be desired in this world so full of misery ?' 'I should like to be a great orator,' said another, 'delivering, on evenings like these, eloquent speeches on the reform of society, advancement of civilisation and so on, and be talked about everywhere.' 'These do not please me', said another, 'I should like to be the very harmony that reigns in this hour, the inner calm that pervades the world this splendid evening.'

The turn passed on—one wanted wealth, another jewels, another beauty, and so on—till it came to Savitri and she said : 'My only wish, at all times, is to have you my Krishna, incomprehensible cunning Krishna, all for myself.' Then followed Radha saying : 'Beautiful as our bodies are, I wish that we should cast them off and be the very Love that binds us both. I wish to be all Love and nothing else. There is nothing sweeter or more beautiful.' Last came Janaki's turn and she said : 'My Lord, what a curious drama you have caused in so short a time ! All my sisters here have spoken the truth, but what pleased one did not please the rest, and that is because the things desired have no intrinsic virtue of their own. One thing however is common among all here, namely, a desire for happiness and that too for that kind of happiness, knowing which the mind does not wish to know further and where it permanently abides. It is this stability, this fullness of knowledge and this happiness that all seek alike, but they seek for them exactly where they are not. The large catalogue of things now desired by them itself shows that it is not in the power of any external thing to give what they seek. I have learnt this, and knowing this, sit calm : and in the *myself* or rather the self that alone remains (for the *my* is a changing external thing) are all the three— permanence, bliss and knowledge. All I desire is, that I should desire nothing and be the self alone.' No sooner were these words spoken, than the calf, which had already begun to show signs of life, rose up and danced with joy before the lovely group.

Janaki's words in the above story are pregnant with wisdom. To understand them aright, we shall study

the story a little more closely. Gopi Lakshmi wants
jewels : she thinks that they would make her happy.
Here, evidently the desire is not, for jewels as such, but
for the happiness which she expects them to give. Gopi
Sarasvati thinks about Lakshmi's request within herself
'Jewels I have known, they please it is true, but only
for a while. A more lasting pleasure is that of learning ;
nobody can rob me of that ; so I want learning. It
will make me perfectly happy.' Had Lakshmi already
known about the happiness which jewels give, doubtless, she would have asked for something else. It is
therefore plain that the mind seeks not for mere happiness, but for happiness with a new element of permanence
added to it, and it tries one thing after another and
says : 'this won't do : this won't do.' Had the happiness from jewels been stable and all-sufficient, the mind
would have rested there, and there would have been no
longing to know about learning and the happiness that
it could give. In other words the knowledge of jewels is
not all-sufficient, because the happiness from it is not
all-sufficient and stable. Where there is perfect happiness
there the mind does not seek to know further, for desire
means insufficiency—want. Therefore perfect bliss is
identical with all-knowledge (i.e., the absence of necessity to know further), and no bliss can be perfect unless
it be all-knowing as well as permanent. So perfect
happiness means all-permanence, all-knowledge and
all-bliss. The mind is constantly seeking for perfect
happiness, i.e., for the above indivisible triad. Life is
nothing but a chain of experiences and under the prompting of the inner impulse to seek this triad, we try one
thing after another, wealth, learning, beauty, fame, etc.,

and after ages and ages of experience come to know what Janaki said—that no external thing can ever give what we seek.

The result is, the mind gives up the futile search and ceases to do its only function—that of projecting itself into the external world, and searching for and collecting experience. But the cessation of this function does not mean total annihilation of life. There is an ultimate substratum of consciousness behind the mind, as is daily seen in sound dreamless slumber where the mind is at rest. This consciousness is always present, it is permanent. Does it want to know anything outside itself, or does it want anything at all? No, for the mind by which it communicated with the outer world, has already given up its work as useless. When I go to office, I wear my coat and turban. Suppose I resign my office work as not worth my while; then I lay aside the turban and coat and remain free. Similarly when the search after external things is found not worth the while, the mind is laid aside and the consciousness behind it lives by itself : it does not want to know anything outside, nor does it want anything at all, and it always is. In other words it is all permanence, knowledge and bliss. It is this threefold compound which is called 'the Self'.

The mind, in all its longings after external things, is, as we have seen, really seeking the above indivisible compound—the Self—only in the wrong place, as the beetle in the story of Sir Walter Raleigh's escape from prison, that went seeking after butter smeared on its own head. Therefore does the Upanishad say : 'Behold, not indeed for the husband's sake the husband is dear, but for the sake of the Self is dear, the husband.

Behold, not indeed for the wife's sake the wife is dear, but for the sake of the Self is dear, the wife.'

The Self is not myself, or thyself for, the 'mine' and 'thine' belong to the mind which, as we have seen, must cease before the Self is realised. In the light of the Self, the differences of I and You are not. The aim of the Vedanta is to point out where the Self is and how it can be reached. Whether we will or no, we or rather all living creatures are really seeking the Self in all their doings and the Vedanta only helps us in shaping our efforts in the right direction.

HAPPINESS

To be happy, to possess eternal life, to be in God, to be saved—all these are the same. All alike mean the solution of the problem, the aim of existence . . . Happiness has no limits because God has neither bottom nor bounds, and because happiness is nothing but the conquest of God through love.

THE beautiful scene on the Jumna described in the last chapter did not close with the resuscitation of the calf. Janaki's words raised new topics and gave an altogether new turn to the general conversation of the conferers. The first to speak after the calf arose was Gopi Maitreyi.

She said: 'Krishna, sister Janaki's words have created a doubt in me. She stated that happiness is the end which all alike seek. Is not that a low and unworthy aim in a world where misery stares us in the face all around? Had not rather charity and love be set up as the ideal? *You* only are worthy to clear my doubt; so enlighten me, O Krishna.'

'Maitreyi, my love,' said Krishna, 'A certain child was weeping, it could not say, it did not itself exactly know what it wanted. It wanted something and cried. It was offered a doll; it turned it over and over for a while, but soon cast it away. Then a fruit was offered to it; it ate a little bit of it and then threw it away in anger. Then a picture was tried, then a book, then a toy, but the child did not get composed until it had what it sought. Like that child, you do not know what you really want and try one thing after another, but your mind can never rest unless it obtains what it really seeks—permanent and all-knowing bliss. You cannot help seeking this eternal bliss, the great Self, any more than a stone thrown up can help falling towards the earth. Everything in the universe is constantly gravitating towards it consciously or unconsciously. All other things will please for a time and then will be thrown away. How many things have you not yourself tried within these few years and thrown away? Do you not remember, that once on these very sands, you desired me to get your jewels made like the wild flowers of the forest and put into them their smell too? I complied with your request, but in a few months you got tired of them. Now you want to exercise charity and love and help the world—a much nobler and a more unselfish desire than your former one. But in both, the end sought for is happiness, for desire means want, insufficiency of happiness; and you will feel miserable unless you are allowed to help the world. Like the child I spoke of, you have not yet understood what you seek. The thief who steals, the ruffian who murders, the soldier who falls without a murmur on the field of battle, the patriot who loves his country more than his home, the lover that is busy weaving love songs—all alike seek happiness only, but in extremely different things. The end is the same, the means differ, some being good, some bad, others indifferent. But you may be sure of this that no external thing can ever give you what you seek. True and permanent happiness is only possible, when the hunt after external things is given up as futile and the mind subsides.'

Maitreyi was satisfied with the reply, but Gopi Gargi asked: 'Is it not selfish, O Krishna, to seek this happiness which you yourself call the self?'

"No, my dear," replied Krishna, "The happiness I speak of is all-happiness, all-knowledge, all-permanence; it is infinite. Do you think that that infinite bliss is immured in what you call 'yourself' and 'myself'? The ocean is more easily swallowed up by one of its droplets, the universe is more readily devoured by an atom, than the great, boundless, unconditioned and eternal bliss called the Self is crammed up within your little frame. 'Yourself' and 'myself' denote little, exclusive, differentiated and narrow things; for what is 'yourself' is not 'myself', and what is 'myself' is not 'yourself' You call your mind and body 'yourself'; but all notions of your being a body, an external thing, and all the wild-goose-chase of your mind must cease before the happiness of the Self can be realised. So long as you think yourself as apart from others, you are little and this infinite happiness cannot be realised. Give up your little self and the great Self stands revealed. Selfishness is the worst enemy to this high realisation. It limits one's vision, makes one little, reduces one to a worm and how then could the infinite Self be perceived? The higher you rise out of the *Patala* (dark, nether world) of your little self the nearer you are to the heaven of the Supreme Self. Charity and love to others will gradually lift you out of that *Patala*. So train yourself that you may love others better than you. Sink your little self in the great ocean of love, wear it away to nothingness by constant exercise of charity and, when by this holy exercise the little self is rubbed away, the great Self stands realised. Love is a precious balm, a sovereign cure for the wound of selfishness. It polishes your heart, baptises your understanding and purifies your whole nature. It transforms the beast into the man and the man into God. Nothing is dearer to God than love. When all yourself is lost, when you become all love, then the highest enjoyment is at hand. Happiness therefore is identical with all love."

'Oh, I have made a wonderful discovery, O Krishna,' cried Seetha.

'If so, let us have it,' said Krishna, 'and see how wonderful it is.'

'My discovery is,' replied Seetha, 'that happiness is not merely all-love, it is also all-knowledge, for where there is the least thing yet to be known, the mind gets into unrest and happiness becomes imperfect.'

'You are right my dear, you are right; ah!. what a grand discovery and who else could have made it!' exclaimed Krishna.

'Is not this happiness then identical with pleasure?' asked the serious Savitri.

'They are as fire and water, as light and darkness. The one is all-knowledge, the other is all ignorance. A certain poor man begged for bread all day long, but did not get enough. So he grieved within himself and was going home, when suddenly on his way, he perceived a bright thing shining like silver; he was rejoiced at its very sight and eagerly took it in his hand, but to his misfortune, he found it was not silver but mother-o'-pearl. The poor man's grief knew no bounds, he cursed his fate and went home more sorrowful than before. Man's lot on earth is exactly similar; he wants happiness, firmly believes that a certain thing could give it, longs for it, gets it and is pleased; but his pleasure is closely followed by pain, for he soon finds he was deceived, that the thing he got does not give him the happiness he looked for in it; so another thing is tried, then another and so on. Pleasure then is counterfeit for happiness—the illusion of happiness in a thing which cannot give it, like that of silver in mother-o'-pearl. It is deceptive and fleeting and is bounded on one side by want, and on the other by pain. Never confound happiness with pleasure. Pleasure tickles the mind and passes away, happiness is permanent and beyond the mind—the mind must subside before it can be realised; pleasure is deceptive, happiness is true; pleasure is the child of ignorance and illusion, happiness is all-knowledge; pleasure is selfish and feeds selfishness; happiness is all-love and involves the killing of the self; pleasure is derived from external things and is dependent on them; happiness is beyond external things, beyond the body and the mind and is independent. Dear Savithri, the two things should never be confounded.'

"Ah! what a splendid evening we have spent and how much have you taught us, O Krishna!" exclaimed the sweet Radha, "All things in the universe are consciously or unconsciously seeking happiness, but in the majority of cases, it is sought for in external things: and want, pleasure and pain are the result. The mind which carries on the trade with the external world must 'close its shop,' before happiness can be realised. Happiness therefore is beyond the external world, beyond the body, beyond the mind, beyond the intellect, beyond all sensation, beyond what is known as 'yourself' and 'myself', is permanent, eternal, infinite, all-knowing, all-loving, all-truthful, all-independent, and is the great Self the Atman—nay, it is you, my sweet, precious,

loving and artful Krishna." 'I see,' ejaculated Krishna,
'I see, you have all become philosophers ; henceforth I
cannot control you, so I go,' and accordingly he put his
flute to his lips and singing : 'so I go, so—I—go, the
merry shepherd goes,' began to walk forth, and the
beautiful Gopis one and all of them went merrily running
after him followed by the calf which knew not how to
walk but danced and jumped.

———————

A STRANGE VISION

WE have seen in the two previous chapters that all of us, consciously or unconsciously, are every moment of our lives in hot pursuit after happiness, which however acts with us the will-o'-the-wisp. There is an Indian play in which a boy is blindfolded and led by another : the former enquires how far a particular place is from where they stand, and the latter replies : "Only a little distance off" ; the boy walks a little farther, and then puts the same question ; again walks a little, and repeats the question ; but every time the question is put, the same reply is invariably given ; and after wandering a long while in this playful fashion, the eyes are unfolded, and the boys return to where they started from. Our search for happiness in the external world is like this childish play : what we seek is always just a little way off. We therefore concluded that the mind must die ; or, in other words, cease its functions, before happiness, which seems to be not outside but within ourselves, is realised. But what do we mean by saying that the mind must die ?

One morning, a few years ago, I was reading a favourite book of mine, when I came upon the words : 'what profits a man to speak, when his mind is not yet dead ?' I could not make out the passage : "the death of the mind—what does it mean ?" I said to myself : "and how could those speak whose minds are dead ?" My curiosity was roused. I respected the author of the book so much that I could not call the passage absurd ; at the same time, I could not help thinking so. The words themselves, owing perhaps to the difficulty of their sense, had a strange fascination for me, and kept ringing in my ears all the day. In the evening, I was present at a post-mortem examination, and I was closely observing the process of dissecting the human body. The words of the sage I referred to, occurred to me at that time, and suddenly a desire rose in me to see the inner man dissected and laid bare to view as easily as the outer frame. I had not of course the materials for such an internal dissection, and so I had to go to bed with my desire unsatisfied. At about 4 in the morning, a strange vision appeared to me in my dream. A *Sanyasin* of rather a majestic stature, in a very venerable appearance, with his long hair matted and folded up, round above round, like the coils of a serpent, with sacred ashes shining in his bright forehead, with a beard which lent to him a rare *Rishi*-like aspect, and clad in orange-coloured robes, appeared before me. I and a friend of mine, who were talking together, immediately rose and prostrated ourselves before the great *Yogin*. He commanded us to rise, and gave sacred ashes first to me and then, muttering a few words by way perhaps of incantation, to my friend, and lo ! my friend fell down at once, and my own eyes began to whirl ; a few seconds more, I felt that my vision had become clearer in some mysterious manner, and that I was able to see into the inner reality of things : everything around me seemed ready to unfold the secrets of its nature. When I looked at my friend, I saw, to my great surprise, that his body melted away like dews before the sun, leaving behind a vast effulgence, which became clearer every second, and finally stood divided into five big luminaries, arranged one above another but still connected together. The lowest was a tremendously big mass of light of the size of the moon, and equally bright, but of a beautiful red colour. It was constantly rolling and changing within itself, and often projecting itself this side and that like fire burning. Above it, and connected with it by a stream of orange light, was a circle of effulgence, much bigger in dimensions, perhaps as big as the sun; it was of a bright yellow colour. It was a little steadier and the sight of it was really charming; above it, and of nearly the same dimensions, was a huge blue light even steadier; above it still was a vast expanse of violet, which seemed to be constantly changing and running in occasional streams, towards the three lights below, now towards the one and now to the other. In spite of its brilliancy, it was rather terrible to look at; and constant changes within its body made it even ugly. It was very busy, and had constant transactions with the other spheres. It was really a relief when my eyes crossed over this ugly ocean of violet to a vast abundance of billliant, spotless, white, spreading itself like an ocean of milk as far as eyes can reach, which was above all the other spheres. While the latter spheres were constantly changing within themselves, it was in a perfectly halcyon state of repose, without even a ripple to disturb its even tranquillity. It was the purest of the group and had in it a beauty, a perfection, a calmness, and a serenity which no words can describe. It was the most splendid thing that I have ever seen in my life, and my eyes were riveted to it. I stood spell-bound before it, and was about to lose all my consciousness in the silent music of its splendour when lo! the great *Yogin* who sat by me, gently struck me with a golden wand and directed me to look at the lesser lights. The series of the tremendously big and wonderful globes of lights before me, was really a strange vision. They covered altogether an immeasurable area on all sides and even my newly acquired vision was not enough to gauge their vast proportions, especially when I strove to have a view of the biggest and topmost light, I had to strain my eyes considerably, and even then, I could have only a glimpse of that ocean of whiteness.

The strange magician before me touched the lowest light with his golden wand and said : "By the power I have from the Lord of Light, I bid thee speak, stop thy mad monkey-like restlessness for a moment, and tell me who thou art and what thy name ? " At once that luminous vision bowed to the *Yogin* and replied : "Master, all honour to thy sovereign feet, I am thy humble servant *Manas* (that faculty which communicates with the outer world through the senses). I am still doing what my master bade me do ; my work is to wander forth and gather all I can from whatever opens out to my view, the senses are the doors by which I sally out ; not a moment's rest have I. By the power thou gavest me, and with the help of those above me, I create, sustain and destroy all the world of plants, animals, stars and men, and carry on thy eternal sport." "Very well," replied the magician, "On with thy work until I bid thee cease." At once the red light began to be restless as ever. The magic wand was then directed to the golden light above, which was imperiously commanded to unfold its secrets at once. "My Lord," it said, stopping for a while its work, and bowing, "My Master, thy humble servant worships thy golden feet, my name is, as you choose to christen me, Intellect or Reason, people call me thy brightest image on earth. My work is to look into the harvest which the wandering *Manas* hourly brings, and select the good from the bad. When last we dissolve in thee, I shew my neighbouring spheres who and where thou art. Without me, they may not know thee." The golden wand next went up to the third circle of light, which said : "My Lord ! accept my worship, thy humble servant sketches forth into action what Reason wishes to see done ; myself and he are co-labourers ; and whatever he says, I try to do ; desire and deed belong to me, and I am called Will."

The conjurer then raised his wand towards the violet mass, and bade it speak. It was more haughty in disposition, and cared not even to bow before him : "My name is Ego, the lower self," it said, "or *Ahankara*, as I am deservedly called. All the lower spheres are mine by birth-right. I am their lord and sovereign, and know no superior. As with all kings, uneasy lies my head that wears a crown. I am in constant worry ; and my moods hourly vary : such is the fate of all sovereigns. I created myself and cannot die ; but who are you ? I command thee stand and unfold." "Yes," replied the conjurer with a smile, and, raising himself up to his full height, coolly gave a severe blow to the impertinent Ego that would command. The walls of my room, in which, strangely enough, all these lights seemed shut up, resounded to the noise of the blow. Poor Ego lost all colour and died away in a second's time, and with it, wonderfully enough, all the other spheres. Red, yellow, blue and violet, all died away at once ; and what remained—a boundless ocean of brilliant white, the same as the topmost one, but apparently enlarged, if infinity could be enlarged, by the addition of the four great lights that died ; a vast effulgence, in the light of which suns, moons, stars were as nothing ; a soft calmness which no words can describe ; a beauty un-heard of in the highest poetry of any land ; a spotless radiance, before which my eyes quailed, and to which I myself was drawn as if by an invisible magnet. The conjurer of *yogic* pomp and mysterious powers, who sat by my side, sprang up as soon as he saw the unseeable brightness before us, and crying : "I am thou and thou art I," dissolved in that ocean of light and disappeared once and for ever. I stood like one enchanted for a few seconds, and felt a strange sensation of blessedness creeping over me, which gradually absorbed me, and, drawing me into the magic ocean of bliss, made me feel like a rain-drop lost in an ocean.

I do not know how long I remained in that state of unconscious and ineffable bliss ; when I woke, it was 7 in the morning. The inquisitive rays of the sun had advanced far into the room ; and my children—five of them they were—were sitting upon me, and making desperate attempts to rouse me to a sense of the world in which they were. I woke up much against my will, and would fain have resumed my fairy slumber, but that was not to be. I felt extremely happy, and the remembrance of the blessedness of my strange sleep did not quit me the whole of the morning. I was all kindness and joy that whole day and the wonderful vision I enjoyed on that memorable night, is as vivid to me now as if I had seen it but an hour ago.

I thought over the details of my vision, or rather, dream, as indeed it must have been. The doubt about the death of the mind which had previously troubled me was now solved. I found that *Manas*, Intellect and Will were all of the same essence as God or *Atman* into which the *Sanyasin* and myself were both dissolved. They appeared distinct through *Ahankara* ; and when that was destroyed by the magician's wand, they returned to their original common essence. Analysing further, and reflecting upon the statements, so to speak, of the several parties, I found that *Manas*, Reason, Will and *Ahankara* were all one in nature, and different only in the functions they performed ; for *Manas* is nothing but knowledge, perception, or consciousness of the outerworld. Reason is nothing but the knowledge, perception, or consciousness of the mind refined still further ; for the mind gathers impressions from the outerworld, and reason selects among them what is good and bad. The mind perceives the outerworld, reason in its turn perceives the mind. In other words the mind is knowledge acquired through the senses, and reason is the knowledge of that knowledge. In the same way, Will is knowledge applied, it is perception directed upon reason, and applied. *Ahankara* is the sum total of these perceptions, the knowledge of the mind, the reason and the will. All these are constantly changing, and *Ahankara* is therefore so unsteady in its moods. It is nothing but the individual personality of man, the human consciousness which separates 'you' from 'me'—the sum total of the various states of mind, grief and joy, pleasure and pain, and other pairs of opposites, as they are called. It identifies itself at one time with

the body, as when we say : "I am strong or weak";
another time, with the mind, as when we say : "I am
glad or I am sorry, etc." ; and when we say : "I wish
or I do," it is one with the will.

The white light above the sphere of *Ahankara* is the
knowledge which witnesses all its varying moods; it
is necessarily changeless, for, otherwise, there can be no
connected consciousness of the varying states of the
mind. It is that faculty in us which perceives the
individual personality, and is called *Sakshi* or Witness,
the higher Ego. In every moment of our lives, the
inner man or knowledge, as we might now call it, or
Pragnana is performing five functions simultaneously :
the first is gathering impressions from outside; the
second is that of sorting them ; the third that of acting
upon them ; the fourth that of expressing itself as "I
see and think and do" ; and the last, that of simply
witnessing these various functions. It is knowledge
itself pure and simple. What is termed Mind, *i.e.*,
from *Ahankara* down to *Manas*, is also knowledge, but
distorted into distinct appearances through the false
medium of the *Ahankara* or the lower self. The example
of a prism will best illustrate this. As the prism dis-
perses one light into several colours, so does this *Ahankara*
or the assertive personality of man disperse knowledge—
which alone really is, and which is One without a
second—into the several appearances of the *Manas*, intellect, etc. When *Ahankara* is killed, *i.e.*, when man
comes to know that his *individual consciousness is not
really different from Consciousness or Pragna as a whole,
but only appears so*, the *Manas*, the intellect and the
will lose their false individuality, and what remains is

knowledge undispersed and concentrated. It is this knowledge or consciousness which really is called God or *Atman*. The death of the mind therefore means nothing more than that it knows and realises that it is not really different from universal consciousness or *Pragna*, but only appears to be so, in other words, it 'enters into the Kingdom of God by being born again'.

GNANA OR WISDOM

In the course of the three preceding chapters we have established some very important conclusions, *viz.* :

1. Wherever there is life, there is a longing for happiness—which has at the same time to be permanent and all knowing—a seeking, constant and unremitting, though blind, for the great Sat-Chit-Ananda, the Self within.

2. No external thing, however, can ever give the bliss so unceasingly sought.

3. To obtain this happiness then, the mind which traffics with the outer world must die.

4. The death of the mind means nothing else but the clearing up of its ignorance about itself and realising that it is not, as it believed so long, really different from the Atman or *Pragnana*, the ever blissful Self within.

It clearly follows from the above simple truths that the mind being *Pragnana* is itself the seat of all bliss and that like a millionaire going about begging for a few pies not knowing what he is worth, this really blissful mind wanders about seeking for happiness not knowing its own nature (*Swarupa*). When the mind or rather the inner man, the Jiva realises its identity with the Atman or *Pragnana*, in other words its own real nature and then alone, the happiness which it so unremittingly seeks will be obtained, and it will cease to wander, for as the Atmopanishad puts it 'the wealthy man will not seek poverty.' The above truths have been put in a thousand different ways in our books, but all roads lead to Rome. We are miserable, we want to be happy, but we persistently seek for happiness in the wrong place, just exactly where it could not be found. The only solution possible for the vast mass of misery is to find out where real and permanent happiness is and to obtain it. We must strike at the very root. Temples, *Chattrams*, asylums, hospitals and work-houses can never completely solve the problem. They are merely temporary expedients, make-shifts for the moment. This remedy is 'neither absolute nor final' as Kapila has so well put it. The only solution, the only cure for the ills of life is the removal of ignorance. In some mysterious manner of which we shall speak later on, the mind fell into the error of regarding itself as something different from the Atman or *Pragnana* which alone really exists. Here came the fatal mistake, the primary cause of innumerable rounds of births and deaths, of selfishness, quarrel, hatred and other passions. This primary ignorance, this false sense of separateness which has made us the narrow-minded selfish little things we are, is called in Vedantic Texts *Maya* or *Avidya*.

Creation with its accompaniments, misery, transformation and death, began just at the point where the mind thought, ignorantly of course, that it was separate from the Atman. So *Avidya* or *Maya* is described as the cause of the world. 'The root of *non-atmaic* things is *Maya*—her nature is ignorance. She is what is called *Mulaprakriti*, she is the *Gunas* in their separate states, she is *Avidya*. In these diverse ways she it is, that lies spread out as the universe' (Sarvasaropanishad). Through *Maya* or ignorance, the One became two, and when it became two, it also necessarily became many. The process of extension through which the unmanifest became manifest is thus allegorically described by the Brihadaranyaka Upanishad :

"Prajapati, the first born embodied soul did not feel delight. Therefore nobody, when alone, feels delight. He was desirous of a second. He was in the same state as husband and wife are when in mutual embrace. He divided this twofold. Hence were husband and wife produced......He approached her ; hence men were born. She verily reflected : how can he approach me, whom he has produced from himself ? Alas I will conceal myself. Thus she became a cow, the other a bull. He approached her. Hence kine were born. The one became a mare, and the other a stallion, the one a female ass, the other a male ass. He approached her. Hence the one-hoofed kind was born. The one became a female goat, the other a male goat, the one became an ewe, the other a ram. He approached her. Hence goats and sheep were born. In this manner he created every living pair whatsoever down to the ants.

"He knew : I am verily the creation : for I created this all. Hence the name of creation. Verily he who thus knows (that is that his Atman is the world) becomes in this creation like Prajapati." I, iv, 3, 4, 5.

We cannot afford to pause here to consider in detail the meaning of the allegory but its general import is plain. It describes how one became many as soon as it became two through the force of space, time and causality, how misery sprang with division and how that misery is curable only through the knowledge of the identity of the one and the many. That *Avidya* which creates two out of one creates the many also is described in the following words by the great Tamil sage Thayumanavar : "When the sense of 'I' takes possession of any, the world,—Maya, spreads out in wonderful diversity ; and who could describe the ocean of misery that springs out of this? Flesh, body, organs, inside, outside, all-pervading ether, air, fire, water, earth, mountains and deserts, vast successions of visible and invisible things rising like mountain chains, forgetfulness recollections, waves of grief and joy or the ocean of delusion, actions that breed them, religions with various prophets as their founders to cure sins, gods, *Bhaktas*, Sastras and methods and disputations to support them. Ah ! One might more easily count the sands on the seashore than tell this battalion of evils springing all from one primary cause of this false sense of separateness."

The cure for our misery and the only cure that is absolute and final is then the removal of *Avidya* or ignorance. If that be removed its child *Ahankara* the false sense of "I" will die, and in the language of the Adhyatma Upanishad, the Self will shine of its own accord, freed from *Ahankara*, like the moon freed from an eclipse. *Gnana* or wisdom then is the panacea for the ills of life. 'Awake, arise ! Seek out the great ones and get understanding !' says the Upanishad (Kath. Upa., III, 14). 'He who obtains wisdom in this life obtains immortality. Great is the loss of him who does not obtain it in his lifetime. Those heroes who behold the soul in all they see have this world and live in immortality' (Ken. Upa., II, 5). Nothing but knowledge of the Atman can give us salvation. Says Thayumanavar, 'Though one lives the life of a *Bhakta*, goes on pilgrimage round the whole world and bathes in the sea and in the rivers, though one does penance checking hunger and

thirst in the midst of fire, though one satisfies his hunger
with fallen leaves, water and air and keeps a vow of
absolute silence, though one lives in inaccessible mountain caves, though one cleanses his veins and arteries
through Yogic powers, though one controls his breath
and drinks the nectar from the moon in trance, though
one makes his little body live for *Kalpas*, though one
might do all these, can salvation be attained, O blissful
Guru! except by wisdom?' In the same way the
Mundaka Upanishad says: 'In the midst of ignorance,
fools fancying themselves wise and learned, go round
and round (*i.e.*, from birth to birth), oppressed by misery,
as blind people led by the blind. Fancying oblations
and pious gifts to lead to the highest, fools do not know
anything good. Having enjoyed on the high place of
heaven which they gained by their actions, they enter
this world or one that is lower. Those again who with
subdued senses, with *knowledge* and the practice of the
duties of a *Sanyasin* (*i.e.*, one that knows the supreme)
in the forest follow austerity and faith, go freed from
sin through the sun (by the northern path or *Gnanamarga*)
to where abides the Immortal spirit of inexhaustible
nature.' That nothing but *Gnana* or wisdom can bring
about salvation is repeatedly emphasised in the Upanishads and Sankara has elaborately proved that
Gnana, not *Karma*, can directly secure slavation. In
this connection the following discussion (freely rendered)
between the *Guru* and the disciple from that wonderful
Tamil book 'The Kaivalyam' will be found interesting:

Disciple: Will not good acts themselves reveal the
Brahman?

Where is the necessity then for Vedantic inquiry?

Guru : If you want, my son! to find out the real man beneath a mask, what will be the good of your running and leaping and jumping and standing on your head and dancing upon a high pole, instead of watching his movements and observing his actions and nature? In the same way the Self cannot be known by merely the study of the Sastras, or by the performance of sacrifices and penances or by *Mantras* or by ceremonies or by feeding the poor.

Disciple : A dirty glass, O holy father! can only be cleaned by washing it with one's hands and not by mere intellect ; in the same way should not the ignorant mind be cleaned by Karmas rather than by inquiry and wisdom?

Guru : My son, in the case of the glass the impurity is real (but in the case of the mind the impurity is false for it only falsely thinks itself separate from the soul). In the case of a pebble on the other hand darkness or impurity can only be unreal, merely a shadow. In the former case physical means like washing, etc., are required, in the latter, the mind alone will do to know that pebble is really pure. In the same way ignorance of the mind as to its own nature can only be removed by *Gnana* or wisdom.

But what is *Gnana* ? Says the Niralambopanishad : '*Gnana* consists in knowing that nothing in the phenomenal world exists apart from *Chaitanya* or the Brahman who is both the seer and the seen, who pervades all things and is equal in them all and who really is not of diverse forms like pot, cloth, etc., and realising the Self through subduing the senses, serving the *Guru* and hearing and meditating on the Atman and by

practising the *Sadhana* (means) taught by the *Guru* for
realisation.' This is perhaps the best and the most complete
definition that has been given of *Gnana*. According to
this definition, *Gnana* involves first a clear intellectual
grasp of the nature of the self through the most searching
inquiry, and secondly, the realising for oneself the truth
through the grace of the *Guru*. Of course we can here
confine ourselves only to the intellectual part of the subject
leaving the second part which consists in practical realisation to those who care for it. Analysing the first portion
of the definition we see that three important statements
are involved in it. (1) The seer and the seen are both
of the *Pragnana* or *Chaitanya*. (2) This *Pragnana* pervades
all and at the same time has no limitations of name and
form. (3) Even things that are different are really nothing
but *Pragnana*, in other words the differences that exist
are only illusory.

It may probably be asked here, is not this definition
of *Gnana* too wide? Is it not enough to say that *Gnana*
consists in knowing intellectually and then realising
through experience that the mind or rather the Jiva is
not different but indentical with the Atman? Is it also
necessary to say as the definition does that the seer, the
seen and *Pragnana* are all of them one, in other words,
the Jiva, the world, and the Atman are all in reality
one? The prime cause of our misery is ignorance of
the fact that Jiva and the Atman are identical. To
cure this, is it not enough to prove the identity of the
two, is it also necessary to establish the identity as the
definition involves, of the three, the Jiva, the Atman
and the world? We reply, yes. In the first place the
happiness we seek or the Self within, we have already

seen (Chap. II), must be eternal and infinite as well as permanent and all-knowing. Therefore it follows that there can be nothing outside this Self. To say that the world is not the Atman is inconsistent with the conclusion that the Atman is infinite. To further strengthen our position, let us approach the question from another starting point.

We have already established (Chap. III) that the Jiva, the inner man whom we have been loosely calling 'mind' is not essentially different from the Atman, and that it is miserable, because it is ignorant of its real nature. Of course, *Manas*, intellect, will, *Ahankara*, and the *Sakshi* or the witness, all perform different functions, but it is an axiom that difference of functions does not mean difference in nature or essence. One man may at one and the same time be the husband of his wife, the son of his father, the master over his servants and the servant of his master, similarly *Pragnana* is at one and the same time *Manas* (intellect), *Ahankara* (will), and *Sakshi* (the witness). But what is gained by proving that the mind is really *Pragnana* if its different functions are all real and have to be performed? The capacity of a husband is different from the capacity of a servant and it will be ridiculous to confound the two though they both belong to the same man. So what good is there in proving that the Jiva is really the Atman and therefore all blissful, if it has to perform different functions and wander and make itself miserable? I may be really and in law a millionaire but so long as I am kept out of it by an irresistible power and compelled to be poor, what can I do but beg and be miserable and of what use is my

19

wealth to me? Similarly, if the Jiva be compelled to perform its five functions which necessarily disperse its glory and make it miserable, what use is it to prove that it is in its nature happy? Its Happiness is then like a treasure guarded by a blood-thirsty demon. True; but is it really compelled to perform the different functions? Can it not avoid them? The reply is naturally how can it, so long as there is the world from which it cannot but take impressions, analyse them, act upon them and eat there from the sweet and bitter fruits of life? A man cannot help being a husband, servant and master, so long as there are wives, masters and servants outside him. Similarly, so long as there is a world external to the Jiva and with such vast difference as we behold in it, how can it escape being attracted and repulsed and distracted by it? As Swami Vivekananda says: 'this moment we are whipped, and when we begin to weep, nature gives us a dollar, again we are whipped and when we weep nature gives us a piece of ginger bread and we begin to laugh again.' This is how the world deals with us; and what good will it be for us to know that our real nature is all happiness if we cannot escape being played upon by the world in this fashion? The only possible way of effecting the desired escape is to know that the world is nothing outside our real nature. Flying away to forests, burying ourselves in caves or closing up our eyes and ears cannot save us from the world. The forests and the caves are themselves in the world and the shutting up our senses can be no remedy for there is nothing to prevent us from dreaming. The only possible way of escaping from the world is by knowing that it is not the ugly thing it seems, the methodless madness it appears, the tyrant which it seems to be over us but that it also is *in reality* the *Pragnana* and therefore identical with our own *real* nature. 'He who sees himself (*i.e.*, the real he, the Atman) in all creation and all creation in himself does not go to disgusting states, but becomes liberated. When a man beholds all beings as his own Self, in that state in which all beings have become to the wise man his own Self, then to such a one who beholds all alike, where is delusion, where is grief?' (Isa. Upa., 5, 6). As the Brihadaranyaka Upanishad picturesquely puts it, 'Prajapati was afraid, therefore man when alone is afraid. He then looked round : since nothing but myself exists, of whom should I be afraid? Hence his fear departed : for whom should he fear, since fear arises from another.' There is no way of escaping nature's tricks unless we examine and ascertain that the world is nothing outside our mind. It has its existence only there. When there is another, naturally there is fear, we become subject to attraction and repulsion; we at; once get liable to be played upon. It follows then, that to establish the identity of the Jiva and the Atman will be of no avail unless it includes also the identity of the world with them. Here will be seen the wisdom of the definition which says that *Gnana* consists in finding out by reason and practical realisation that the seer, the seen and the *Chaitanya* or *Pragnana* are all one. Until the realisation of this grand unity comes, there can be no escape from the world and no cessation of the functions which distract the mind and prevent it from being happy. Here in this connection, let us read a chapter from the Upanishads.

The question is put : "Whom do we worship as the Atman? What is His nature?" and the answer is "He is that by which one sees form, by which one hears sound, by which one apprehends smells, by which one expresses speech, by which one distinguishes what is of good and what is not of good taste.

"The heart and the mind, self-consciousness, pride of dominion, discrimination, good sense, knowledge of the Sastras, understanding, perception, thinking, the power of endurance, sensibility, independence of mind, recollection, determination, perseverance, the will to live, desire, submission, are all names of knowledge (that is, they are all different aspects and functions of the same *Pragnana*).

"This Atman is Brahma, this is Indra, this is Prajapati, this, all the gods and the five great elements. Earth, Air, Ether, Water and Fire, this, all those which are made up of fractions of those elements, this is the cause of all what is born from eggs, what is born from the womb, what is born from the heat, what is born from the sprouts, horses, cows, men, elephants. Whatsoever has life—what moves on foot, what moves by wing and all that is immovable—all this is brought to existence by knowledge *Pragna-Netram* ; is founded on knowledge. The world is brought into existence by knowledge ; knowledge is the foundation, Brahma is knowledge (*Pragnana*). He, Vamadeva, having by that knowledge departed from this world and in the world of Heaven obtained all desires, became immortal" (Aitareya Upa., Ch. iii, Sec. 5).

According to this Uapnishad, not merely the inner man whom we have been calling the mind and who more correctly should be styled the Jiva is the **Atman**, but the whole Universe. The whole world is brought into existence by knowledge, says the Upanishad. 'Knowledge is the foundation, Brahma is knowledge.' The word 'knowledge' by the way is apt to be misleading. The word in the text is *Pragnana*, for which unfortunately there is no proper English equivalent. Knowledge and consciousness denote functions more than the substance, and generally involve three things, the knower, the known and the act of knowing. *Pragnana* on the other hand is no function. It is the thing-in-itself of which knowledge, consciousness, etc., are functions, we shall therefore adhere to the word *Pragnana* in future. The above passage from an Upanishad of the Rig-Veda tells us in the simplest and the most direct form possible that all that exists including you, me, animals, plants and stones are all modifications of the same *Pragnana*, 'sparks from the same furnace' as another Upanishad puts it. They are waves, bubbles and froth of one vast ocean of consciousness, and as such are different only in name and form. If we succeed in proving this bold assertion of the Upanishads, the theory of the Vedanta would be complete. The full truth, however of the grand unity of which the seers speak, could only be grasped by actual realisation—*Sakshatkara Anubhava*. The *Rishis* spoke what they knew; now we have to begin at the other end; we have to know what they spoke. What were truth to them are theories to us. We shall first intellectually examine and understand them, and then proceed, such of us as are allowed, to seek for ourselves independently to realise in its full glory the grand unity of which the Self-intoxicated seers so rejoicingly speak.

THE ATMAN

BEFORE compelling the stupendous and 'real-seeming world' before us to take off its mask and unfold itself to us, it may be well to consider in some detail the nature of *Pragnana* with which we have to prove its identity. We have already seen that it is the real Self within us as distinguished from the false Self or personality and that its nature is Sat-Chit-Ananda. We have also seen that it is really changeless, being the *Sakshi* or witness to our changing moods and that *Ahankara* (our personality), will, intellect and *Manas* are not different from it in essence but only in functions.

Let us see what this means. All change is necessarily in space and time ; change is inconceivable unless in space and time and whatever is changeless therefore transcends space and time, in other words, is infinite and eternal. *Pragnana* being changeless is therefore infinite and eternal ; besides, being changeless, it cannot be an effect, for every change is an effect due to some cause. This *Pragnana* is our real Self and so we called it the Atman. We are in reality infinite and eternal ; and our regarding ourselves as finite and mortal is therefore a result of ignorance, *Maya* or *Avidya* as it is called. We shall examine into the nature of this *Maya* later on, but it is a fact that all of us are really infinite and eternal ; we are all *Pragnana* and *Pragnana* being changeless and therefore indivisible, th re is no real finiteness anywhere. There can be no plurality of infinite existence ; *Pragnana* therefore exists alone without a second and all appearances of finiteness are

294

necessarily unreal. They are mere illusion. The infinite *Pragnana* appears as a multitude of finite things like a single sun appearing as many in different vessels of water—says the Vedanta. It clearly follows therefore that our *Manas*, intellect, will and *Ahankara* are all illusory modifications of the Atman and all that exists, all these innumerable worlds, these suns and stars and moons are only apparently different from the Infinite *Pragnana*—our own Atman. So says the Sruti : 'Verily I extend from below, I extend from above, I extend from behind, I extend from before, I extend from the South, I extend from the North—of a truth I am all this....Verily the Soul extends from below, the Soul extends from above, the Soul extends from behind, the Soul extends from before, the Soul extends from the South, the Soul extends from the North—of a truth the Soul is all this' (*Chandogya Upa.*, VII, xxv).

The conclusion appears a very bold one to be sure ; but the logic of the argument is rigorous and irresistible. We are obliged to admit a changeless factor within us as the necessary background for all our changing moods ; and that factor by the very fact of its being changeless is infinite, eternal and indivisible. Our *Manas*, intellect, will and *Ahankara* are, we are bound to admit, not different from it in essence but only in functions ; and these functions, the inner man or Jiva performs, because it fancies itself and the world outside to be different from *Pragnana* through ignorance. In truth there can be nothing outside the infinite *Pragnana* ; nor could there be anything inside it, for being changeless it is indivisible. Things may be different, says the Vedanta, which by the way is un-

surpassed in its analysis of the subjects it treats of, in
three and only three ways,—different in kind like a tree
and a hill, or of the same kind but separately existing
like one mango tree and another, or different as part
and whole like a tree and its stem. The infinite and
indivisible Atman cannot admit of anything outside
and different from it in kind, for in that case it cannot
be infinite, nor could there be a similar thing outside it,
for, then there will be two infinities which is impossible
nor could there be any part of it for it is indivisible.
Therefore the Atman exists alone without a second.
The Atman is 'without distinctions' (Mandukya Upa.,
7). There is nought beside the Atman, say the Upanishads repeatedly and it being infinite and indivisible,
all finiteness is mere appearance. One thing never becomes many but can appear as many is an axiom. 'All
this is born of Me (*i.e.*, the real Self), all this exists in Me
and all this gets absorbed in Me......I am all the
wonderful world' (Kaivalya Upa). 'He is the Self of
all. He is all. There is nothing outside Him. The
changeless Atman is one without a second. There is
nothing so real as He. He it Sat, He is Chit, He is
Ananda ; this Atman is one without duality' (Narhsimha
Up.). 'There is no world outside the Atman. There is
no bliss outside the Atman. There is no refuge outside
the Atman. All the world is (made of) the Atman.
There is nothing outside the Atman anywhere. There
is not a rush outside the Atman. There is not even a
husk outside the Atman. All the world is in reality the
Atman (Thejobindu Upa., VI). Since diversity in the
universe must necessarily be unreal, the same Upanishad
adds : 'If there be anything outside Me, it is surely

unreal like a mirage. The world may be said to exist if one could be frightened by the words of the son of a barren woman. The world may be said to exist if an elephant could be killed by the horns of a hare. The world may be said to exist if one's thirst could be quenched by drinking of a mirage.' 'Thou art all. Thou art all. Thou art all.... There is nought outside Thee. It has been established that all that is seen is unreal' (Maha. Nara Upa., I).

The universe then has no real existence apart from the Atman and all differences are necessarily mere appearances. This is a logical conclusion which we are bound to accept, though its truth can be found out only by Self-realisation—by realising that we are infinite and eternal. We shall deal with this subject more fully later on, when we examine the nature of the universe itself ; we came across this point in our inquiry into the nature of the *Pragnana*.

We have said that the nature of the Atman is Sat-Chit-Ananda, Existence absolute, Knowledge absolute and Bliss absolute. It cannot but be these, for unless it be absolute existence, its infinite nature is impossible. It is knowledge, for its very nature is *Pragnana* (intelligence, or consciousness) ; and absolute, because there is nothing outside it : and we have seen it is Bliss itself. Sat, Chit and Ananda, however, are not qualities of the Atman ; they are its nature (*Swarupa*). They are merely different aspects of the Atman and whatever is Sat is necessarily Chit and Ananda and *vice versa*. If they were qualities, they might exist separately at least in idea from the Atman, but the Atman can be nothing unless it be Existence, *Pragnana* and Bliss ; it is impossible to separate them even in idea from it. These therefore are not attributes but different names, as it were, of the same thing according to the aspects from which it is viewed, like the names Buddha, Siddharta and Gautama which denote, one and the same person. It is impossible to predicate any qualities of this absolute Existence-Knowledge-Bliss for they would limit the illimitable and imply duality and all that we could say of it could only be different names of it due to the different aspects from which we read it, as for instance, Ancient, Immoveable, Self-creative, Unborn, Unknowable, Pure, Bodiless, Immortal, and so on.

From what we have hitherto said, the Brahman or God cannot be different from the Atman. The soul of the Universe must be identical with the real Soul within us ; otherwise there would be two infinites. But let us proceed to discuss the nature of the Brahman separately.

THE SELF IN US

WE proposed in the last chapter to proceed to discuss the nature of Brahman; but, on second thought, it appears desirable to add a few more words to what has already been said with regard to the changelessness of the Atman. Those who have followed our treatment of the subject with patience would remember our analysis of the mind or the inner man. Every act of the mind, we said, involves five different functions—those of *Manas*, Intellect, Will, *Ahankara* and *Sakshi* or witness. The last of these, we observed, should be changeless, being the necessary background of the constantly varying states of mind.

The question has been asked, both in our country and elsewhere, if this witness should necessarily be changeless. A particular school of Buddhistic philosophers, known by the name of *Kshanika Vignana Vadins* assert for instance that the 'I' in us is not a changeless entity, but simply a series of cognitions or ideas referring to the ego, called in their philosophy Alaya-Vignana. There is another series, they say, consisting of ideas referring to external object such as colour and the like, and this series is called by them Pravritti-Vignana. Both the series are said to exist side by side with each other and the first is said to be the cause of the second. According to this school then, not merely are our ideas changing but also the knower, the 'I'.

This position has been ably refuted by that eminent champion of Vedic Monism, the great Sankaracharya in his Sutra Bashya. In commenting upon Vedanta

Sutra, II, 2, 25, Sankara says : "And on account of
remembrance the philosopher who maintains that all
things are momentary only would have to extend that
doctrine to the perceiving person (*Upalabdhri*) also ;
that is however not possible on account of the remembrance which is consequent on the original perception. That remembrance can take place only if it
belongs to the same person who previously made the
perception. For we observe that what one man has
experienced is not remembered by another man. How
indeed could there arise the conscious state expressed
in the sentences : 'I saw that thing and now I see this
thing,' if the seeing person were not in both cases the
same ? That the consciousness of recognition takes
place only in the case of the observing and the remembering subject being one and the same, is a matter
known to every one ; for if there were in the two cases
different subjects the state of consciousness arising in
the mind of the remembering person would be : 'I remember another person made the observation,' but
no such state of consciousness does arise. When, on
the other hand, such a state of consciousness does arise,
then everybody knows that the person who made the
original observation and the person who remembers are
different persons and then the state of consciousness is
expressed as follows : 'I remember, that that other
person saw that and that.' In the case under discussion,
however, the Vainasika himself—whose state of consciousness is 'I saw that and that'—knows, that there is
one thinking subject only to which the original perception as well as the remembrance belongs, and does
not think of denying that the past perception belonged

to himself, not any more than he denies that fire is hot and gives light..We admit that sometimes with regard to an external thing a doubt may arise whether it is that or is merely similar to that. For mistake may be made concerning what lies outside our minds, but the conscious subject never has any doubt whether it is itself or only similar to itself. It rather is distinctly conscious that it is one and the same subject, which yesterday had a certain sensation and to-day remembers that sensation."

Referring to the question of impermanent self, Vyasa says in Sutra, II, 2, 31 : "And on account of the momentariness of the Alaya-Vignana, it cannot be the abode of mental impressions." In his comment on this Sutra, Sankara observes : "Unless there exists one continuous principle equally connected with the past, the present and the future, in other words as absolutely unchangeable self which cognises everything, we are unable to account for remembrance, recognition, and so on, which are subject to mental impressions dependent on place, time and cause."

Another argument for proving the existence of a changeless, witnessing self is that ideas are not self-illuminating and require something else to apprehend them. "By maintaining the idea to be illuminated by itself, you make yourself," says Sankara, "guilty of an absurdity no less than if you said that fire burns itself." He adds : "If you maintain that the idea, lamp-like, manifests itself without standing in need of a further principle to illuminate it, you maintain thereby that ideas exist which are not apprehended by any of the means of knowledge and which are without a knowing being, which is no better than to assert that a thousand lamps burning inside some impenetrable mass of rocks manifest themselves. And if you should maintain that we admit your doctrine, since it follows from what we have said that the idea itself implies consciousness, we reply that, as observation shows, the lamp in order to become manifest requires some other intellectual agent furnished with instruments, such as the eye, and that therefore the idea also as equally being a thing to be illuminated becomes manifest only through an ulterior intelligent principle. And if you finally object that we, when advancing the witnessing self as self-proved, merely express in other words the Buddha tenet that the idea is self-manifested, we refute you by remarking that your ideas have the attributes of originating, passing away, being manifold and so on, while our self is one and permanent."

We have thus seen that the real 'I' in us is a changeless factor. The existence of such a changeless entity is inferable from our fleeting mental states and cognitions, though its best proof is the realisation of the *Maha Vakya* (a great saying) 'I am Brahman'. This much however we can understand with the help of our feeble reason, that that entity being changeless is infinite and eternal also, for the fact of its transcending space and time is involved in the very idea of changelessness. Change is possible only in space and time and everything in space and time undergoes, as we see, constant change. The Atman being chnageless is therefore infinite and eternal, and from this it necessarily follows, as we have already seen, that *Manas*, Intellect, Will and *Ahankara* are all of them mere illusory modifi-

cations of that Atman and that all that exists, all these
innumerable worlds, these suns and moons and stars
are only apparently different from the infinite Atman
whose nature is *Pragnana*. 'Where one sees nothing
else, hears nothing else, understands nothing else, that
is the Infinite,' says the Chandogya Upanishad (VIII,
xxiv, 1). 'Whoever sees variety in Him proceeds from
death to death' (*Bri. Upa.*, IV. iv. 19). 'The Atman
is *Adwaitam*, *i.e.*, without (the three) distinctions,'
says the Mandukya Upanishad. 'He is without parts,
without action, tranquil,' says Swetaswetara.

That the Atman is attributeless and undefinable is
well expressed in the following Sruti : This Self is not
this, nor aught else. It is unseizable, for it cannot be
seized. It is not scattered, for it cannot be scattered.
It is without contact, for it comes not in contact. It
is without colour, it is not subject to pain or destruction'
(IV, v, 15). 'Where does that Infinity abide, my Lord,'
asked Narada of Sanatkumara. The sage replied : 'It
abideth in its own glory or (if you enquire where is that
glory I say) it doth not abide in its glory' (*Ch. Upa.*,
VII, xxiv, 1).

The realisation of the unity expressed in such statements as 'Verily the Self is all this' is the one purpose
for which the Upanishads were revealed to mankind.
'He who is aware of this, *i.e.*, the Self extending from
above, below and everywhere,' says Sanatkumara,
'seeing the Self thus, thinking it thus, and knowing it
thus, becomes one whose entire devotion is to the Self,
whose recreation is in the Self, whose felicity is the Self,
he becomes self-resplendent. He is able to accomplish
whatever he desires in all the regions of the universe.

Those who believe otherwise having others for their masters go to perishable regions. For them nothing is accomplished in any of the regions of the universe.'

'Such is the glory of the Atman who is to be heard and thought upon and known.'

———

III

THOUGHTS ON THE BHAGAVAD-GITA

INTRODUCTION

OF all the great treasures bequeathed to us by our fore-fathers, there is none, excepting, of course, the Upanishads, so priceless as the Gita. It is a veritable song celestial and in its universality rivals God Himself. There is not one system of ethics, religion, or philosophy that does not silently take a corner in that wonderful little book which is, as it were, the Pantheon of the world. The most apparent contradictions find there a common meeting place and in the boundless diversity of its elements, there is a harmony as sweet and inspiring as that of the rainbow. The several members of the human body do not more willingly work together, the different strings of a well-tuned violin do not more beautifully harmonise, than the great and apparently contradictory systems of the Sankhya, Yoga, Karma, and Bhakti in that celestial song of the Lord, and in the words of the great prayer *"Akasat pathitham thoyam,* etc.," it may well be said that all the rivers of the great religions of the world joyously empty themselves in the ocean of the Gita. Here is what an English writer has to say about it—"It is the work of the highest spiritual genius, the most deliberate and careful constructive skill, the most earnest desire of spiritual unity, and a spirit is moving through its speculative depths that could not be found within the limits of any creed— the spirit of universal religion."

One great feature of the Gita is, that it is not too high for even the infant inquirer, nor too low for the highest philosopher. It provides with a singularity of breadth, for every stage of human evolution and has something to teach every man that makes him better and purer.

Another feature is that it is infinitely rich in its suggestiveness. One reads it a hundred times and even then one cannot say that one has done with it : and the reason for it is that the Gita is not a treatise on philosophy nor a handbook of theories, but a conversation—a conversation, not however, between one man and another, nor one which took place several thousands of years ago which grandmotherly history has preserved for us, but a daily, nay hourly, minutely conversation between every man and God. As there is poetry in every one of our doings—reading, weeping, laughing, etc., so there is philosophy too, for philosophy is but the higher form of poetry, and we are conversing with God, in the sense of the Gita, every moment of our lives. This is why the Gita is so perennial in its suggestions. It appeals to you in every phase of your life, in every mood of your mind, and as you are infinite in your inside, so is the Gita. You are living ever in its presence and there is a verse for every one of us there, in that book of life. Living as we do, as much under it as under the sky, let us know where we are and learn to regulate *all* our actions in its abounding light and live more and more consciously in its presence. It is with this purpose that, that little book has been prescribed, among a host of others, for constant reading (*Parayana*).

THE TWO QUESTIONS AT THE OUTSET

BEFORE entering into the subject of the Gita, it may be well to consider the circumstances under which it was born. As it is well known, it was delivered by Sree Krishna to Arjuna on the occasion of one of the greatest battles of the world. Here, two very interesting questions naturally present themselves—(i) why it was delivered to Arjuna in preference to others, and (2) why the particular hour of battle, so apparently unfitted for calm thinking was chosen.

Taking the first question, it seems exceedingly strange at first sight, that Krishna should have chosen Arjuna for his disciple, while there were better men available in the Pandava camp itself. There was, for instance, Yudhishtira the very incarnation of virtue. Literature has no better example to present, of human goodness than this Dharmaputra who was in truth the hero as a good man (goodness demands more courage and heroism than wickedness) and whose whole life was one continued proof of the greatness of goodness.

Once Krishna, with a view to point out the contrast between Dharmaputra and Duryodhana, sent the former on the mission of finding out a handful of wicked men, and the latter on that of discovering a few really good and faultless men. Duryodhana conducted his search with great zeal, for he had been assured that a sacrifice jointly performed by them would totally destroy the Pandavas; but not one good man was available to him in all the world. Dharmaputra's search was equally vain, for, not even robbers, murderers, parricides and

309

matricides, were in his opinion wicked, but only ignorant at the worst. To this royal sage endowed with
angel's eyes, everything appeared celestial. Certainly
Krishna could not have obtained in all the world a
worthier disciple than this incarnation of purity, virtue
and goodness. And then, there was Sahadeva, who, by
his practical asceticism and firm morality, richly deserved a divine teacher like Krishna. His inmost conviction, as he sincerely expressed it on the occasion,
when the gooseberry fruit incautiously plucked by Arjuna
had to rejoin the tree, was, that truth was his mother,
wisdom his father, virtue his brother, mercy his friend,
humility his wife and patience his child. It would
therefore appear, that Sahadeva or Dharmaputra better
deserved the privilege of instruction from Krishna than
the warlike and worldly-minded Arjuna. The latter had
practised none of the austerities they had trained themselves in, and had more even than Bhimasena, gone after
worldly pleasures. He was indeed a polished gentleman (gentlemen were possible even in those days) with
a sweet disposition, pleasant manners, refined tastes and
genteel accomplishments. He could evidently sing and
dance, and ladies (and a decent lot they were) fell madly
in love with him. He was certainly the most beautiful
of the five brothers, and with his proud whiskers, broad
chest, long extended arms, well proportioned limbs
and royal mien, and with the *Gandiva* (his bow) in his
hand was really a standard of male beauty and physical perfection and a veritable 'glass of fashion and
mould of frame' in his days. The story goes, that
Iswara himself longed to see his beautiful back, and
hence arose the idyllic Himalayan scene immortally

wedded to Bharavi's verse. The celestial damsel Urvasi conceived a mad passion for him, while he was unsuspectingly sleeping in one of Indra's groves ; but to be a gentleman, to be loved by celestial damsels, to be able to sing and dance, however valuable they may be in the harem, are not counted among the qualifications for Vedantic discipleship.

But we find that somehow, from the very beginning, Krishna was more attached to Arjuna and had more to do with him than with his brothers. The first important occasion on which we hear of Krishna in connection with the Pandavas, was that of Draupadi's *Swayamvara* ; and it was under his prompting, that Arjuna competed for the hand of the royal maiden. He contrived to marry him his sister, undertook to drive his chariot for him, and on the eve of the Bharata war, publicly declared : 'Thou art mine and I am thine, while all that is mine is thine also. O Partha, thou art from me, and I am from thee, O bull of the Bharata race ! no one can understand the difference between us.' This attachment however was not a matter of mere accident or personal predilection and Bhishma once had occasion to say that Arjuna and Krishna were Nara and Narayana, and were repeatedly born when destructive wars were necessary, that they existed only for the destruction of the *Asuras* and the establishment of virtue. They came into the world of men with a special purpose, and in the great war through which the first part of that special purpose was accomplished, Arjuna was the instrument and Krishna the inspirer. The second, the more positive and the more enduring part—the recrowning of dethroned virtue was accomplished by the deliverance of the Gita and in that likewise, Arjuna and Krishna complemented each other. Krishna was born for the whole human race and in the universal and divinely beautiful idyll of his life and work, there is no chapter greater, more sacred, and more fraught with consequences to humanity than that of the Gita. For teaching that Gita he could not have found a more convenient disciple than Arjuna who was, as it were, the universal *type* of man as such, Nara, man not fallen into beastliness nor evolved into divinity. By teaching him he taught it to the whole mass of humanity and that is how it is so truly universal and provides for every one from the humblest beginner in religion to the loftiest philosopher. A discourse with advanced men like Dharmaputra or Sahadeva would not have started with the rudiments of philosophy, and therefore would not be equally universal.

Arjuna then was chosen not because he was an *Adikari* (one qualified), but because he was not. To go into the question a little more fully, there are four qualifications required of every seeker after wisdom. The first is discrimination of the real from the non-real, the permanent from the perishing, of God from the world. The second is indifference to the fruits of one's action here and hereafter. Attachment is the fetter that binds us. Few of us do a thing for itself; we are always going after results and making ourselves slaves to them. This slavery must be got over before wisdom can be realised. The next requisite is a group of six qualities— Sama, Dama, Uparati, Titiksha, Samadhana, and Sraddha. Of these Sama is 'not allowing the mind to externalise.' Dama is 'checking its internal activity.'

Titiksha is 'non-resistance, forbearance.' Uparati is 'not thinking of the senses or sense objects.' Samadhana is the serene concentration of the mind and Sraddha is faith in the truth of religion and in the teacher. The last qualification is an intense desire for emancipation or *Moksha*.

Had Arjuna all these qualifications, when Krishna taught him ? The answer is he was lacking even in the first—a clear and strong discrimination of the real from the unreal, for he was immoderately grieved at the prospect of his friends and relatives being slain in the battle, and then, what is even more significant, he prayed Krishna not for final salvation (*Moksha*), but for the solution of his immediate problem. With any other companion than Krishna, that solution would have rested on comparatively low and common considerations, such as worldly prosperity, social justice, Arjuna's valour, *Veeraswargam* (the heaven of the brave that die in battle) and would in all probability have involved few serious transmundane issues. Arjuna might have been appeased and the battle might have been fought all the same but the battle-field of Kurukshetra would not mean to us anything more than the plains of Thaneswar. Indeed Arjuna's grief was essentially mundane, there were in it the fear of sin and hell, the fear of misery even if success be theirs and that of social disorder and family extinction, on which point all the Pandavas, Bhima included, were very sensitive, but it disclosed no longing for *Moksha* without which, in the field of Vedanta, no one is counted as an *Adhikari* for *Gnana* (wisdom). It was Krishna's genius that gave to this purely mundane grief of Arjuna an unequalled philosophical dignity, and raised his narrow and individual problem into a universal, world-wide one ; and all praise and glory to that great ideal teacher, who took hold of a favourable opportunity in friend's life, to give forth to the world his great message of consolation, peace and love, and all honour to the few memorable tears which Arjuna shed on the battle-field. Never before or after, was human grief assuaged with such heavenly balm, and never before or after, was it assuaged in such a permanent way. Of all men, Arjuna had the privilege of such heavenly consolation, not because he was eminently good and virtuous like Yudhishtira, nor because he was wise and contented like Sahadeva, but because he was Nara—the typical man, the standard representative of the world of men—the man, by teaching whom all humanity was taught and not merely the advanced or philosophic portion of it.

All that has hitherto been said is however superficial, and to the philosopher, who by a sort of divine prerogative perceives the inner truth of things, will appear as a child's prattle. The question has to be asked and answered, who was Krishna and who was Arjuna ? 'I am the lord of the Universe without birth or beginning, (X, 3, etc.) says Krishna and he is, as Sree Santananda Saraswati remarked, the best authority on Himself. He is 'The great Atman residing in the hearts of all beings, the cause of beginning, existence and end of the universe (X, 18), the Innermost Unity, the Supreme underlying Essence in the sun, moon, stars, men, animals, in short in all the world—not one that came and went or was born and died, but the Eternal Teacher, the Lord of the world, the Paramatman. And Arjuna is Nara, the typical human mind, the refined mechanism in man which reasons and distinguishes, which knows what is good and evil, which discriminates right from wrong, and which can, when properly guided, reflect back the great Self. 'Nature sleeps in the plant, dreams in the animal and wakes in men' and this waking is the result of the refined *Upadhi* (vehicle) of the Self in man—the human mind. Krishna is particularly attached to Arjuna and is constantly with him, *i.e.*, the Self or Atman is always with the mind and it is through its presence and power that the mind moves. Krishna marries his sister to him, induces him to compete for Draupadi's hand, helps him in his hunt after pleasure, leads him into the battle-field, drives his chariot and enables him to win in the end. All this has now a new meaning. By and through the Atman the mind is brought into contact with Nature, and gathers experience. The Atman is with the mind in weal and woe, indeed causes both weal and woe, leads it into the struggle of life, guides it through struggle and finally enables it, by killing both its good and bad *Vrittis* (Duryodhana and his brothers as well as the allies of the Pandavas), to gain the victory. Krishna is the constant companion, friend, guide and teacher of Arjuna. The Self never leaves the mind, is with it in weal and woe. Krishna is the Paramatman and Arjuna the human mind in which the knowledge and conquest of Nature is completed, and consequently the Self is reflected back on itself—in other words knows itself, and the Gita is nothing but the conversation between Krishna and Arjuna in the sad and awful hour of battle, *i.e.*, between the Atman and the mind when the latter is repelled by the outer world, is vexed and grieved and forced to seek refuge in TRUTH—in the Atman. But we are entering into the second of the two questions we proposed to ourselves at the outest.

If Krishna wanted to teach Arjuna, why should he have chosen for it the awful and anxious hour of battle? The tumult of the field, the beating of drums, the flying of colours, the blowing of trumpets, all rousing the sleeping brute in man, combined with the braggart shouts of infuriated combatants, the tramping of horses and the rattling of chariots—these obviously were anything but fitted for calm philosophical reasoning. Strangely enough however, this hour of the battle seems to have been peculiarly precious to Krishna. He had long waited for it. He had known Arjuna for a very long time, he had been with him in society and in the forest, with others and alone. If leisure had been a consideration, no better days could have been found than those they spent together in the Kandava forest; but Krishna knew that the time was not then come; he waited for an opportunity when the heroic heart of his companion would lose confidence in itself, when its rage of valour would subside, and fear, which alone is the beginning of all true knowledge, would invade that impregnable fort. The whole of Arjuna's previous life was but a preparation for that one moment, in which, with tears in his eyes, he cried out : 'Save me, O Krishna, from this confusion. Thou art my teacher, O teach me what to do.' Krishna had busily ripened him for it : he had stood by him in weal and woe and obtained for him every gratification he desired. When he wanted to marry Subadra he contrived to bring them together, when he wanted to marry the daughter of the Pandyan King, it was Krishna that equipped him forth as a snake-charmer and procured him admission into the royal harem. In the Kandava forest the future author of the Gita initiated his companion into the mysteries of conjugal love. In these and similar ways, he had lulled to rest by due gratification the feverish desire for pleasure, and the days the Pandavas spent in the 'black forest' in the company of great *Rishis*, hearing from them many tales of great moral worth, had softened all of them, Bhima included, most of all Arjuna, so that it was not in a sudden fit of grief, but in the due course of evolution, that he exclaimed : 'Seeing these my kinsmen arrayed, O Krishna, eager to fight, my limbs fail and my mouth is parched, my body quivers and my hair stands on end, *Gandiva* (his bow) slips from my hand, and my skin burns all over, I am not able to stand and my mind is whirling' (1. 28-30) and sank down on his seat.

Sweet are the uses of grief : it softens the heart, and ripens the understanding ; it has a mellowing effect like the dews of December, and often has it been the instrument of salvation. In all Vedantic treatises, the student is made to weep before the *Guru*, before he is saved. Sorrow has often made saints of men, and in the intensity of grief, the sensory organs of mortals have been made alive to sights and sounds far above those of the earth. In the *Periya Purana*, the child *Tirugnanasambandha* is represented as having been rewarded for his weeping with Parvati's milk ; and in life, the weeping child it is, that first receives the caresses of the mother. The first of the four truths that Buddha discovered under the Bo-tree was that the world

is filled with misery; and the first right thing in
Buddhism is the recognition of the sorrows of life and
grief for them. Sorrow is the sweet unction to the
heart, and as the Lord said : 'Blessed are those that
mourn for they shall be comforted.'

'Knock and it shall be opened,' is the precept; but
no one so happily knocked as Arjuna, and like Saul
who went in search of asses and found a kingdom, he
pressed for a solution of his immediate problem and,
for the intensity of his grief and the earnestness of his
demand was rewarded with a solution not merely of
that problem, but also of the great one of life. No sooner
did he get unmanned and let slip his *Gandiva*, than
there came for him an elixir from heaven which ravished
his senses and raised him far above the tumult of the
battlefield, and his own question even at so early a
stage as the 3rd chapter is no longer : 'Shall I kill my
brother or will he kill me ?' but, 'Shall I attain *Moksha*
and how ?' All that was required of Arjuna was that his
heart should lose confidence in itself, and filled with
grief and fear, seek for guidance and help. The hour of
the battle was the first hour in which the manly heart
of the warrior felt itself weak, and Krishna had
eagerly awaited the hour and ripened him for it in the
latter's interests as well as in those of the world.

Now, let us recall to mind the true meaning of
Krishna and Arjuna, and in its light see what the battle-
field of Kurukshetra means. It is no longer the narrow
field of a few areas in which a number of men gave up
their ghosts, and which the geographer and the historian
might busy themselves in discovering and explaining,
but the whole universe, boundless and eternal,—the

arena of the Atman, the theatre where that Atman dreams, and in the dream becomes the Jiva or 'the habitual self,' as it has been most poetically styled, and finds itself in course of time confronted with problems on every side. Kurukshetra is literally the field that was made, and therefore the world that is made by the mind. Similar to mistaking a spark of fire for a precious gem is the mistake which the mind first makes, that the world of senses it made is a world of pleasure. What was fancied to be a soft pillow to rest upon is gradually discovered to be a bone under the grinding wheel; the world of pleasure becomes a world of battle; and in a more special sense the Kurukshetra is the world, discovered when the mind has begun to inquire, to be a world of battle. Those who were or rather were fancied to be friends and relations before the battle are now seen ranged as enemies; the war has to be carried on with the very things we before loved so well. This battle is to be carried on with the help of some allies, *i.e.*, the bad *Vrittis* or tendencies of the mind have to be conquered with the help of the good; but in the end both the allies and the enemies are slain, for the *Nirvana* is where all the outgoings of the mind cease, where there is neither hate nor love, where the mind rests with itself in its native bliss.

To make the meaning a little clearer, the love of wine, women and wealth all of which begin with pleasing, end in hate—friends and relations become enemies. The love for these things is to be conquered by the love for higher things—learning, poetry, charity, God, and so on. These are the allies in the battle: but these are valuable not for themselves but 'for the sake of the

Self,' for 'rousing the great giant,' for rendering possible the blissful realisation of the Atman where the lower hates and loves cease,—the Atman which 'stands alone and without a second.'

To return to the point, Kurukshetra is the world which to the mind, which has begun to discriminate, is full of problems—a veritable battlefield. Atman the Jiva or the human mind with its wonderful faculty of discrimination is the hero; the body is the chariot. 'Know the Jiva as the rider, the body as the car, know the intellect as the charioteer and the mental *Vrittis* as the reins. They say, the senses are the horses and their objects are the roads' (Katha-Upa., III, 3, 4). The intellect (*Jnana Sakti*) being the brightest reflection of the Atman is the charioteer Krishna, the *Paramatman* in human body.

The great battle of Kurukshetra is not then a matter of antiquarian interest fought sometime ago, and somewhere but a daily, nay, hourly one. The sooner we enter into it with earnestness and zeal, the better will it be for us, for Krishna the Atman will reveal Himself to us in the shape of intellect or *Gnana Sakti* and guide us safely through it, and the victory of salvation is sure to be ours in the end.

Warrior, fight the battle bravely, fight it with a hero's courage. Krishna, Sri Krishna is always with the Gopis, the lovers, the *Bhaktas*. Fight on the battle, but not for bread, for money, for fame, for name or with any selfish end in view. The emancipated Negroes have a lesson to teach you. It is said of them that soon after emancipation they got so wild, that they would eat away the pumpkins of the forest and the paddy

that was given to them to sow; and the very seeds
were swallowed up, so that there were no means for a
fresh harvest of pumpkins or paddy. They could not
understand that, if they would only wait, they would
have a richer living the next year; or, at any rate, they
would not undergo the trouble and patience of sowing
and reaping. Most of us are doing just the same things;
we are bartering away our highest Self, our God, our
Heaven, our happiness of to-morrow, for the low
pleasures of to-day. If only we could wait a little and
refuse to pamper the beast within and fight on bravely,
the victory will surely be ours. By the grace of Sri
Krishna, our *Atman*, the inner Empire of peace and joy,
infinite and 'overflowing the bounds of this world,' will
certainly be ours. In that wonderful book *Light on
Path* occurs the following passage : "You can stand up-
right now, firm as a rock amid turmoil, obeying the
warrior who is thy self and thy king. Unconcerned in
the battle save to do his bidding, having no longer any
care as to the result of the battle—for one thing only
is important—that the warrior shall win; and you
know he is incapable of defeat, standing thus cool and
awakened, use the hearing you have acquired by pain
and by destruction of pain........" (Part II, Rule 8).
When we are steadily following the warrior within, and
when we have given up our clinging to our low self, then,
there need be no fear : God's grace is all ours. Remember the Sruti : 'Know the Jiva as the rider, the
body as the car, know the charioteer as intellect, and the
mental tendencies as the reins. They say, the senses
are the horses and their objects are the roads' (Katha-
Upanishad, III, 3-4). If your intellect be not stained,

in other words, if it be as it ought to be, the brightest reflection of the *Atman*—the charioteer Krishna—the car on which you are seated will go well, there will be no fear to the rider, provided you know how to hold the reins of mental tendencies. The senses, the fleet horses of yours, will run well and stand the war; and you need fear no obstacles on the road. The victory will surely be yours. If, on the other hand, your intellect be clouded with sensual and selfish considerations, or weakened by low cares, or enfeebled by vain ambition and avarice, or polluted by prejudice, then, there is a fatal defect in the charioteer (the charioteer was, in the ancient mode of warfare by personal combat, a very important personage; and hence Krishna is the charioteer, and Arjuna the warrior) and you will simply go to ruin.

THE ANTHEM TO THE ATMAN

To go into the work itself. We must remember that
the *Gita* was not written by Sri Krishna. It was a mere
conversation which lasted for a little more than three
hours—no other three hours have been so profitable to
humanity—and the tact with which the grief-stricken
Arjuna is carried, through many a winding path and
labyrinthian corridor, into the temple of Wisdom, and
there made to bow before the formless but radiant light
of its inner close, is simply inimitable. The task, however, of tracing the path to the inner recesses of the
temple is anything but easy ; and the combined but
utterly inharmonious light shed by rival commentators,
like the light of the wonderfully set mirrors of Dharmaputra's palace (Dharmaputra was the eldest of the
Pandavas) which led astray his poor blind uncle
Dritharashtra, has beguiled more vigilant men than the
writer into false steps ; so that it is no mock humility
to preface what is here written by saying that no originality is claimed, and that whatever appears in these
pages on this subject rests upon the authority of men
who have fought the battle of life and ventured into
the very midst of the temple, and are undisturbedly enjoying its sacred inner light, and upon the authority of
the inner meaning of the *Vedas* which godfathered those
men in their lonely ascent along the narrow way.

The most wonderful thing about the *Gita* is perhaps
its evolution. As the train of thought and the links
between its successive verses are at times missed, it may

not be out of place to very briefly sketch out the plan of at least its introductory chapters, before entering into its philosophy.

. The first thing that Krishna did was to sound the depth of Arjuna's grief. He ridiculed his melancholy, in a perfectly cousinly fashion, as untimely, mean, infamous, and equally inimical to his happiness here and hereafter. But finding that it was too deep for such taunts, that Arjuna had contrived to fall into a deep pit from which, however, much ridiculed by the most humorous of cousins, he could not help himself out, Krishna seriously set about his mission on earth. It was a glorious hour for humanity (let us not forget however the inner meaning), when Krishna like a veritable land-lord—really the *Kshetragna*—saw that the soil had been wetted and ploughed deeply enough for the reception of the seed in season, and sweetly curled his divine lips in smile. Ah! How soft that smile and how sweet and full of mercy and love and joy at the arrival of the appointed time!

"Arjuna," said he, now is it that you talk like a warrior and act like a coward? The wise never grieve either for the living or for the dead; for, there is really no death, and what appears to be such is simply a change of coat, and nothing else. After we leave our present bodies, we pass on to others as naturally as we advance from youth to manhood and from manhood to old age. Grief and joy are incidental to the world, and transitory; and he alone is wise and fitted for salvation, who is not affected by these pairs of opposites, heat and cold, life and death, grief and joy, honour and dishonour, etc., for these are unreal, and soil not the *Atman*, the

inner soul, which is eternal, indestructible and boundless.
The *Atman* within our bodies slayeth not, nor is slain;
It is not born, nor does It die; It is ancient and unknowable; no one can work Its destruction; It pervades
the whole world and is not slain with the body. "This
Atman is never born, gets never decayed, never dies
and never grows; and he that knows It to be such,
whom does he slay and who could slay him? Swords
pierce It not, fire burns It not, water moistens It not,
winds wither It not. Eternal, all-pervading, stable, immovable, ancient, beyond reach of thought, of word, or
of sight, and changeless as the *Atman* is, there is no cause
for you, O Arjuna, to grieve'." (II, 11—25).

"Even supposing that it is born with the body and
dies with it, you should not grieve; for sure is the death
of him that is born, and sure is the birth of him that is
dead. These our bodies and other things in the universe
are unmanifest in their origin and dissolution, and appear only in the middle (we neither know where we
come from nor where we go). 'What cause is there then
for lamentation? One looks upon the *Atman* as marvellous, another speaks of It as such, a third hears of
It as such, but none of these has fully understood It.
I assure you that, even if all our bodies were to be slain,
the *Atman* within them can never be slain; and so, you
should not grieve for any creature'." (25—30).

After this glorious—and by Arjuna perfectly unexpected—anthem to the *Atman*, which by its vigour
and eloquence, had the effect of stirring his mind, and
surprised him out of his untimely grief, Krishna descends
to the earth, and approaches Arjuna's problem from a
mundane point of view. Arjuna, we may be sure, does

not fully follow his companion in his heavenward flight. But the vigorous oration had, like a sudden shower that cleanses the air, or a sudden gust of wind that clears away the germs of disease, the effect of scattering the cloud that hung on him ; so that he was not after it in the same mood as he was in before. Surprise has a strange effect on sorrow ; and the earthly consideration which Krishna next presented, went home more easily to him than it could have done before.

As the passages referred to above have given rise to much misconception and ignorant criticism, it would be well for us to stop here a little, and consider what really Krishna meant.

THE CRISIS

WE have now arrived at one of the most interesting
questions in our consideration of the *Gita*. The issue
has risen from Arjuna to Krishna Himself, and many a
hard and insulting judgment has been upon the poor
author of the *Bhagavad-Gita* for the advice he gave to
Arjuna. The judges, as our readers might have already
surmised, are our friends, the missionaries, who, in
their own noble, refined and exemplary way, have either
cast serious doubts on the sanity of Sri Krishna, or worse
still, have sought to incriminate Him by certain sections
of the Penal Code. Unfortunately, the criminal who
has been thus wisely condemned, is not available for
punishment, and refuses to be produced *habeas corpus*
before the tribunal by which He was condemned un-
heard. Our brethren are more eager to accuse than to
understand, and judge before they hear : and, in their
eagerness to benefit the world by their sapient con-
demnation, they never stop to question the finality of
their judgments. Their moral and religious indignation
spares neither Rama nor Krishna ; and the fact of these
latter being looked upon as *Avatars* of God by a heathenish
'nigger' race, only excites their fury all the more.
"Love," says an English writer, "is one whether it be
called that of Christ, or Krishna, or any other individualised expression of Truth. As along as this cannot
be seen, there will be war of sects and religions against
each other, and sending forth of missionaries to insult
and irritate, to teach creeds—not love and truth. The

327

love of Krishna is deep in the Hindu heart, and cannot be thus slighted with impunity. Yet, under all these irritations, the Hindu has yet to be found who would retort by any insult or criticism of the founder of Christianity. To the Hindu, such criticism of the pure and noble of any race or age, is a dreadful crime, involving far-reaching retributive effects. It is a pity we do not think the same." To irritate and insult are easier than to understand. We know how Christ has been handled in the Free Thought tribunal, and how the Bible has fared under the dissecting lancet of its opponents. We, for our part, have no sympathy with scurrilous attacks and rash criticisms of holy men and books—no matter of what country—though we might not always succeed in understanding them.

So much for the narrow-minded attacks hurled against the *Gita* by some fanatical missionaries. Now let us turn to some of the moderate criticisms. Krishna advises Arjuna to fight, by telling him that there is really no death, that the *Atman* is ancient, eternal ; and kills not, nor is killed ; and that he alone is wise who is not affected by the pairs of opposites, grief and joy, honour and dishonour, etc., which soil not the *Atman*. Referring to this statement Bishop Caldwell attempts to prove its fallacy, by supposing it acted upon in common life, in the following words : "A man accused of murder neither denies his guilt nor pleads that he committed the act in self-defence, but addresses the Court in the language of Krishna : 'It is needless,' he says, 'to trouble yourselves about the inquiry any further, for it is impossible that any murder can have taken place. The soul can neither kill nor be killed. It is eternal and indestructible. When driven from one body, it passes into another. Death is inevitable, and another birth is equally inevitable. It is not the part, therefore, of *wise men* like the judges of the court, to trouble themselves about such things.' Would the judges regard this defence as conclusive? Certainly not......" Indeed, there seems to be great force in Bishop Caldwell's arguments, and his logic appears irresistible. Krishna's advice was really a bold one. Here is Arjuna, unwilling to fight against his friends and kinsmen, he is filled with pity and cries: "Having beheld O Krishna, my kindred thus standing anxious for the fight, my limbs fail me, my mouth is dried up, the hairs stand upon my body, and all my frame trembleth. Even *Gandiva*, my bow, falls from my hands, and my skin burns. I am not able to stand ; my mind, as it were, turns round also. O Kesava, I behold inauspicious omens on all sides. When I shall have destroyed my kindred, shall I any longer look for happiness? I wish not for victory, dominion, or pleasure. For what is dominion and enjoyment of life, or even life itself, when those for whom dominion, pleasure and enjoyment were to be coveted, have abandoned life and fortune, and stand here in the field ready for the battle?" Arjuna's arguments are apparently very sound, and any man other than Krishna—unless he was particularly interested in the destruction of Duryodhana and his host—would under such circumstances have simply, it would appear, advised Arjuna to cease fighting, and turn back from the battle-field.

All the great teachers of the world have uniformly preached the doctrine of non-resistance, and Krishna's advice to fight, given to a man who shrank from fighting,

is certainly very strange. It is no wonder, therefore
that the arguments employed by him have been charged
with being casuistic ; and what is worse, the highest
philosophy is invoked to compel Arjuna to do an apparently unjustifiable deed. The position which Krishna
took must be reconcilable with the teachings of other
great men of the world ; or there is only one alternative,
namely, that we must be prepared to give up the *Gita*
and disclaim all allegiance to its author. The principle
of non-resistance is really too deeply rooted in the nature
of things to be false or erroneous ; and one of the sincerest
admirers of Christ, Count Tolstoi, vehemently recommends a thorough-going application of this doctrine in
all departments of human activity ; and if his interpretation of the doctrine be correct, war itself would
appear to have been condemned by Christ. Plainly put,
the case stands thus. All the great teachers of the
world preach non-resistance. 'Whosoever shall smite
thee on thy right cheek, turn to him the other also,' is
a glorious ethical precept ; and the larger the application
it receives, the better should it be for both the individual
and the society. According to one of his commentators,
Jesus Christ, not the least of the prophets of the world,
condemns war itself. Peace, peace, peace ! is the one
cry of the *Upanishads*. In the face of such an overwhelming authority in favour of non-resistance, Krishna
advises a man who is wholly unwilling to fight, to engage
in a bloody war ; nay worse, He contradicts not merely
the other teachers of the world, but also Himself. For,
again and again, in the *Gita*, he recommends *Ahimsa*
(non-injury)—*e.g.*, XIII, 8. Is Krishna right, is the
question ; and very much depends upon the answer.

The case is very strong against Him, and we have arrived at a really critical stage of our discussion. But let us see if a satisfactory explanation could be had for the strange conduct of Krishna, or otherwise, we must be prepared to disclaim Him and His book. For 'There is no religion higher than truth'.

We have stated the case as plainly as possible, and now we shall proceed to look into it closely. What Krishna says may be briefly put as follows : "How is it that you talk like a wise man and act like a coward ? *The wise* never grieve either for the living or for the dead, for there is really no death, and what appears to be such is simply a change of coat and nothing else. The *Atman* within our bodies slayeth not nor is slain, It is not born nor does It die, It is ancient and unknowable, no one can work Its destruction. It pervades the whole world and is not slain with the body. This *Atman* is never born, gets never decayed, and never dies, and never grows ; and he that knows It to be such—whom does he slay and who could slay him ? Swords pierce It not, fire burns It not, water moistens It not, and winds wither It not. Eternal, all-pervading, stable, immovable, ancient, beyond reach of thought, of word or of sight, and changeless as the *Atman* is, there is no cause for you, O Arjuna, to grieve"—*Gita*, II, 11-25.

Mr. Caldwell attempts to prove, as we have seen already, the fallacy of this argument by supposing it acted upon in common life. His way of reasoning is perfectly right, and his conclusions are strictly logical ; only, his hypothesis is wrong. If the hypothesis is granted, everything else naturally follows ; but un-

fortunately, it is fatally erroneous, and therefore, cannot
be granted. He fancies the scene to be acted in common life, and this is wholly unwarranted by what
Krishna says at the very outset. Krishna is speaking
from the standpoint of a *wise man*, a *Brahmagnani*,
who has known and realised within himself the truth
that life and death are phenomenal and illusory, and that
the *Atman* which pervades the whole universe is eternal
and changeless. A mere intellectual grasp of the great
truth will never make a man wise ; and, at any rate, it
is not of *such wise men* that Krishna speaks. If a common murderer pleads before the court that the *Atman*
neither slays nor is slain, the best thing that the judge
could do is to sentence him to such punishment as he
deserves, applying his defence to his own case. The
judge might retort by saying, 'Friend, since, by hanging
you, your *Atman* is never killed, we have sentenced you
to be hanged. Of course the man whom you murdered
was never really murdered ; and just in the same way,
by being hanged, you will not really die.' The illustration which Mr. Caldwell took up is a capital instance of
what is familiarly known as *Gnanapashandhatwam* or
counterfeit wisdom. Setting aside the Bishop's *pseudo-
vedanta*, we shall turn to consider the words of Krishna
from the standpoint of a really wise man. The real
Gnani knows by reason and experience that he is himself the *Atman*, ancient and unknowable, the One without
a second, beside Which there is not even a rush, as the
Upanishads would put it, that the body which lives and
dies is only an appearance, and has no real existence
except on the phenomenal plane.

Not that the world is not, not that you and I and all the other infinite existences in creation are resolved by a logical quibble into a perfect zero. A very great misconception generally obtains among superficial students of the *Vedanta* that it totally denies the existence of this world; and often the question is very naturally put, 'If all this be unreal, why should it have been created?' The *Vedanta* is a subject in approaching which we must always remember the well-known line,

"Drink deep or taste not the Pierian Spring."

Being the loftiest speculation of the human intellect, it must be approached honestly and with a sincere thirst for knowledge; and the full reality of its highest conclusions can never be grasped except by earnest and thorough-going inquiry and patient practice. Shallow draughts of it will merely intoxicate the brain; and that is why even cultured intellects have, in handling it, been led into miserable pitfalls. What the *Vedanta* says about the world is that it is real, nay, that it is eternal, but its reality and eternality are only relative. The colour of the rose is perfectly real, but it is a fact all the same that it is not in the flower itself. Similarly the limitations of name and form, or space, time and causality, are not in the world itself. 'Things are not what they seem' is an eternal verity. It is as true of the whole world as it is of the rose. Our perception or rather the perception of all created things has an inherent power to distort and colour the things it comes in contact with. What exists is only a boundless, eternal and all-pervading consciousness, *Pragnanaghana*, by the side of which the world is a relative reality; just as by the side of the rose as it really is, the colour and other things

are only relatively real. We cannot say that our dreams
are unreal unless we know the waking state (*Jagra*);
and similarly we cannot call the world unreal unless
with reference to the changeless, universal *Pragnana*
which is called the *Atman*, the only Reality. The world
then is just like a dream, nay, it has been called a long
dream (*Dirghaswapna*), it is not absolutely unreal, but only
relatively so. To ordinary men who have not realised
the absolute Reality, the *Brahman* within, it is practically a complete reality, just as dream is to the man who
is dreaming. To those blessed souls who have fully
realised 'the Divinity that lies concealed,' the *Antaryamin*,
as it is called, the world does not really exist; but that
does not mean that they are totally dead even to its
appearance. To them it is an appearance which can no
longer deceive, a dream from which they have awoke,
but still vividly remember, a mirage which has been
discovered to be such.

The outward conduct, the *Vyavahara* of these wise
men is in no way different from that of others, except
that it is regulated by the loftiest ethics and by a love
which is as spontaneous as it is universal. They are
conscious actors in the drama of the world, having merged
their little narrow selves in the ocean of universal selfhood, and are the freest and the most fearless men and
the greatest benefactors that by example and precept,
bless our sad planet. They see themselves in everything and everything in themselves. 'He whose mind
is endued with devotion and looketh on all things alike,
beholdeth the Supreme Soul in all things and all things
in the Supreme Soul' (*Gita*, VI, 29). 'He that beholdeth
all things in the *Atman* and the *Atman* in all beings

despiseth naught' (*Isa.-Upa.*, 6). But this seeing themselves in all and all in themselves does not mean that they are blind to the apparent differences that exist between things, but that the internal eye has been disciplined, cultured and purified by love and wisdom. The change is all within, it is of *such wise men* and not of babblers in philosophy (*Vacha Vedantins*) or lip-philosophers, as they are called, that Krishna speaks when He says : 'The wise, etc............' The key to the life of such wise men is, *Kriyadwaitam na kartavyam, Bhavadwaitam sada kuru. Adwaita*, the knowledge that what exists is only one thing, is for inner realisation and not for outward action, for, the moment action commences, the actor enters the phenomenal plane. The motto means—act not your *Adwaita* in conduct but have it always in mind. The *Gnani* should act in life just as other men do, but all the while he should himself never forget that even his action is real only on the phenomenal plane. His narrow personality is a thing of the past, and he has become impersonal even in life—God himself ; and that is why it is said, killing he kills not ; 'He who is free from egotism and attachment—even though he should destroy the world, kills not nor is bound thereby' (*Gita*, XVIII, 17 ; see also V, 8, 9). That is why it is said that the *Gnani* does not really do *Karma* (*Gita*, III, 17). The actions which he does are not really done by him, but by the *Gunas* of the *Prakriti*, which work even after his individuality ceases, by the impetus of his past *Karma*, just as a wheel continues to roll even after the force that set it in motion ceases. It is only the ignorant man who is blinded by his *Ahankara* or egoism that thinks that the actions

really done by the *Gunas* of *Prakriti* (nature) are done
by him (*Gita*, III, 27).

Unless and until the grand truth we have been *trying
to express*, be fully grasped, Krishna's words in the 2nd
Chapter under reference cannot be understood. It is
too much to expect such a clear grasp of this truth from
unsympathetic and ill-informed foreigners like Bishop
Caldwell. Learning is not philosophy, and more than
linguistic attainments are required to interpret works
like the *Bible* and the *Gita*. The hypothesis on which
the learned Bishop bases his tirade is, as we said, fatally
vicious.

> Fearlessness, singleness of soul, the will
> Always to strive for wisdom ; opened hand
> And governed appetites ; and piety,
> And love of lonely study ; humbleness,
> Uprightness, heed to induce naught which lives,
> Truthfulness, slowness unto wrath, a mind
> Which lightly letteth go what others prize ;
> And equanimity, and charity
> Which spieth no man's faults ; and tenderness
> Towards all that suffer; a contented heart,
> Fluttered by no desires ; bearing mild,
> Modest, and grave, with manhood nobly mixed,
> With patience, fortitude, and purity ;
> An unrevengeful spirit, never given
> To rate itself too high ;—such be the signs,
> O, Indian prince ! of him whose feet are set
> On that fair path which leads to heavenly birth!"
>
> [*Gita*, XVI, 1—3].

If the above be the qualities of the man who has but
set his feet on the path, what should be those of him
who has attained the goal? A *Gnani* is nothing but a
personification of *Karuna* (mercy), *Maitri* (love), *Mudita*
(blissfulness), and *Upeksha* (the higher carelessness).

Rare, very rare, indeed, would be the circumstances
which would compel such a *Gnani* to commit the crime

of murder, and supposing that he does commit it, which would never be unless for the benefit of humanity, he would never plead the defence which Mr. Caldwell imagines him to do. He would know that the murder, the court, and its punishment whatever it be, are unreal. He would not care to plead for his own sake, nor would he grudge to undergo the penalty for the crime. All the while, however—and here is the difference between the wise man and others—he would know within himself that he being the *Atman*, never committed a crime *nor suffered the punishment*. Krishna never meant his words to be employed in the way Mr. Caldwell uses them, which is as absurd as a man committing adultery and, when arraigned, preaching to the court, the solemn precept of Jesus : 'Resist not evil'. It is a pity that the Bishop failed to notice what Krishna himself said—'The wise never grieve either for the living or for the dead' ; what He said, was said purely to hold forth to Arjuna the example of wise men, and He could never have dreamt such an abuse of His sublime philosophy as the Bishop indulges in. The truths which he revealed to Arjuna were meant to be realised and acted upon. And he who so realises and acts will never attempt to set them up in defence of any crime which, under extraordinary circumstances, he might be compelled to commit.

When properly understood, Krishna's advice to Arjuna under reference is as follows—O Arjuna, remember that life and death are illusory, that the *Atman* or God alone really exists, that It is ancient, immovable, neither slays nor is slain. If you fight your battle *with your mind fixed upon the Atman*, the one Reality, you will have no cause to grieve, for you will not be deceived by the illusion of life and death ; and secondly, even fighting, you will not really fight, for actions belong not to the *Atman*, but are the result of *Karma* and *Prakriti*.

We have seen that Mr. Caldwell's argument is after all a profane parody due to want of proper understanding. After unwarrantedly applying the teaching of Krishna to the affairs of ordinary life, the learned bishop proceeds to observe : "Here it must be remembered that Krishna does not base his exhortations to Arjuna on the justice of the war in which he was engaged. That ground might have been taken with propriety, and Arjuna was evidently persuaded of the justice of the Pandava cause. But Krishna's arguments are not based on the 'limited ideas' of justice and necessity, but upon transcendental doctrines respecting the immortality and impassability of the soul, which if they proved his point, would equally prove the most unjust war that ever was waged to be innocent." Hasty criticism is the bread and cheese of some people and the bishop seems unfortunately to be one of them ; and in his passion for condemning, he forgets that between Arjuna and Krishna there was and there could have been no question of the justice of the war. Arjuna had certainly no scruples on that point for the war was no sudden or unpremeditated affair ; and he did not ask Krishna about it. All that happened was that on seeing the wilderness of men arrayed before him in battle order, determined to fall victims to the demon of war before the close of the day, he was struck all on a sudden with overwhelming pity and Krishna told him how a wise man would behave under the circumstances.

Naturally the advice of Krishna appears to us at the first sight as strange as bold; and it cannot appear otherwise, so long as we are not wise men—so long as the idea of our being bodies does not leave us. To the sage from whose standpoint alone does Krishna speak, all that is, is *Atman* and the idea of his being eternal and infinite is as natural to him, as that of being mortal and finite is to us. The sage simply laughs within himself at the hold which ignorance has over us, blinded by which we attribute death to that which can never die. Our ideas of life and death, however much we may cherish them, are anything but real, and it is unreasonable that the sage should give them the importance we attribute to them. Death is simply a change of conditions, nay, even less, a change of dress as Krishna puts it. To Puranjana, (in *Sri Bhagavad*), who fancies himself a woman and weeps over her dead husband in the forest, the sage says: 'Awake, thou great soul; remember what thou art. Thou art sexless, who is thy husband? Thou art the only Reality; then why dost thou weep? Remember who thou art and wake up.' Similar is the advice of Krishna. We are all dreaming and in the long and confusing dream we are in, we fancy ourselves loving, hating, fighting and dying; there are, however, a few blessed souls here and there who have woke up from that dream and these are the wise men to whom Krishna refers; and to them there is neither joy nor grief, neither birth nor death. They being in an altogether different state of existence, to criticise them from our standpoint is, to say the least, an act of perversity which those who are anxious to wake from the dream of life will never commit themselves to. Dreaming as we are, it is a privilege to understand that we are dreaming, and that there are men who have woke up from the dream. It is a privilege certainly to grasp the idea that what is real to us cannot be real to them also.

Those who know say that the real spirit of the *Vedanta* can never be grasped until Krishna's advice to Arjuna and the story of Jada Bharata are understood in the proper light. Both teach the same lesson—that our love being a result of ignorance cannot be real and therefore does not deserve to be glorified. It may be useful to us; it may help us in growing, in drawing out the spirit within us but after a particular stage we shall ourselves see that it is a child of illusion, not different in its nature from mistaking a mother-o'-pearl for silver. We must love not the illusory and perishable bodies, but the deathless Spirit within. The sage alone really loves, all our love is selfishness; we love because to love is pleasing to us, and we love only those who are related to us, or are useful to us. Arjuna had no scruples of conscience when he slew the innumerable hosts of Kalakeyas and other Rakshasas; his heart never troubled him then, and now, when he sees *his* kinsmen arrayed before him in the battle order, he is struck with pity and feels unable to fight because they are *his* kinsmen. This surely is not love; it is too narrow and selfish, to deserve the name of love. The sage, on the other hand, loves all alike, in other words, loves because his nature is love. And to kill a living being is impossible for him, except when duty compels, and even when he so kills, he will never forget that really there is neither slayer nor the slain. This is the drift of Krishna's advice.

THE DOCTRINE OF NON-RESISTANCE

I.—NATURE AND APPLICATION

So far about Mr. Caldwell's criticism. Now we shall proceed to consider a question which we ourselves have raised, namely, whether Krishna's teaching is consistent with the doctrine of non-resistance which has been uniformly laid down in the scriptures of all countries, but whose real meaning has not been understood by its best advocates, and indeed, cannot be understood except in the light of the *Vedanta*. We shall see that Krishna's advice to Arjuna instead of being opposed as at first sight it appears to be, to that great doctrine, is in fact *the* correct interpretation of it—a point which, if established, will show that, whoever may be the prophet that proclaims a truth, one has to turn to the *Vedanta* for the correct interpretation of that truth. Indeed, the *Vedanta* philosophy is universal in its nature and affords the key to the scriptures of all countries alike, and, if they refuse to accept its aid they must go to the wall some day or other.

But a few years back, there occurred a circumstance which clearly shows that Christ can never be understood except with the help of the *Vedanta*. Count Tolstoi, one of the sincerest followers of Christ in these days, wrote a book called *What I Believe*, which attracted an immense amount of attention both in Europe and America, and the chief theme of which was the precept 'Resist not Evil'. And he put the following questions

341

in connection with that teaching : "Did Christ really demand from His disciples that they should carry out what He taught them in the Sermon on the Mount? And can a Christian then, or can he not, always remaining a Christian, go to law or make any use of the law or seek his own protection in the law? And can the Christian, or can he not, take part in the administration of government, using compulsion against his neighbours?" And—the most important question hanging over the heads of all of us in these days of universal military service—'can the Christian or can he not, remaining a Christian, against Christ's direct prohibition, promise obedience in future actions directly opposed to his teaching? And can he, by taking his share of service in the army prepare himself to murder men and even actually murder them?' These were the questions put and according to the Count's own conviction, Christ's commandment, 'Resist not Evil', is incompatible with government of any kind, legislation, courts of justice, war, and indeed, everything without which society in these days is impossible. He contends for a literal and thorough-going application of the Sermon on the Mount at any cost, and believes, that the moment it is done throughout the world, the Kingdom of God would come.

This position naturally provoked a good deal of discussion. Some critics said that by following Christ's commandment, the whole world and all good men would come to ruin ; some that force may be used for defending others though not for selfish purposes—a position obviously not warranted by the precept which admits of no exceptions. A few others recognised the commandment, and thought it was nearly cancelled by some other teachings in the Bible. Others, like Farrar, entered into the discussion,—but evaded risking a direct reply. Some plainly said that the doctrine of non-resistance was an immoral doctrine. According to others, 'the teaching of the Sermon on the Mount is a string of very pretty impracticable dreams, *du charmant docteur* as Renan says, fit only for the simple and half savage inhabitants of Galilee who lived 1,800 years ago and for the half savage Russian peasants—Sutaev and Bondarev—and the Russian mystic Tolstoi, but not at all consistent with a high degree of European culture.' 'Christ's teaching is of no use,' said Ingersoll, 'because it is inconsistent with our industrial age.'

This is how Christ has been understood in the West; his teachings are either immoral, or useless, or invalidated by those of others or inconsistent with the progress of the world. In must, however, be admitted that there is some sense in this almost unanimous disapproval of the doctrine of non-resistance as presented by Count Tolstoi. There is something in us which keeps telling that the commandment is in itself a grand and worthy ideal, but at the same time, it is obviously impossible that a whole society could ever follow it without at once getting wiped out of existence altogether. *The fact is, the commandment of Jesus is an individual ideal and not meant for the society at large.* Indeed, students of the *Vedanta* would readily see that the application of the doctrine to the life of a society is not merely harmful but altogether impossible, for every society is composed of men who are at different stages of spirit-progress, with infinitely different pasts, and infinitely different futures. No two men in the world are alike, for the

Karmas of no two individuals can exactly be similar, though all of us have to progress on the same lines of evolution. There is such an infinite variety of stages in the course of our progress, that it is impossible that all in the world can simultaneously do a thing or attain a state. For instance, to become a sage may be the common ideal for all men, but a whole nation cannot attain to sageship at the same time. This, however, does not take away the ideal itself ; the ideal is true, and will be true for all eternity, though a nation of sages is an unrealisable dream. In the same way, non-resistance is the ideal for all men alike, the end to which we have all of us to attain, though no society as a whole can adopt it as its practical morality.

Christ's teachings then, are not really dangerous to progress and so may be followed more boldly than they appear to be. That they were thought immoral and harmful, only shows that their proper application and nature were not well understood. The *Vedanta* assures us that they can at the best only serve as *ideals for the individual*, though the Western people to whom the doctrine of *Karma* is not sufficiently familiar, still persist in dreaming of millenniums and kingdoms of God on earth. All the controversy about the doctrine of non-resistance would have been avoided had it been recognised, as what it really is—*the ideal for the individual*. It is a pity that even the clergy did not lay any stress on the grandeur of the precept, but were content with regarding it as either impracticable or opposed to other portions of the Bible. This really is a melancholy state of affairs and shows how little Christ is appreciated. We *Hindus*, who can understand his teachings and appreciate them at their real worth, would seem to be much better Christians than those who regard the Sermon on the Mount as a string of pretty impracticable dreams; and we cannot altogether help sympathising with Count Tolstoi when he says: "Strange as it may seem, the church is, as churches have always been and cannot but be institutions not only alien in spirit to Christ's teaching, but even directly antagonistic to it. With good reason Voltaire calls the church *l' in fame*; with good reason have all, or almost all, so-called sects of Christians recognised the church as the scarlet woman foretold in the Apocalypse; with good reason is the history of the church the history of the greatest cruelties and horrors...... There is not only nothing in common between the churches as such and Christianity except the name, but they represent two principles fundamentally opposed and antagonistic to one another. One represents pride, violence, self-assertion, stagnation and death; the other meekness, patience, humility, progress and life." Our object, however, is not to condemn Christian churches and so we request the reader to take these extracts at what they may be worth.

We have now seen the nature and application of the doctrine of non-resistance and now, let us proceed to enquire into the meaning of that great commandment. The *Vedanta* rightly points it out to be *a proper ideal for the individual* and the same philosophy may be trusted to give us its correct meaning.

II.—Meaning

The commandment appears to be very simple but the moment we begin to apply it to practical life, we find ourselves beset with innumerable difficulties which compel us to question if it is a good ideal or if we have made any mistake in understanding it. In the first place, it is important to observe that mere physical non-resistance is not worth the name. For instance, A being stronger that B, strikes him, but, B does not return the blow though considerably mortified and goes away cursing A in his heart. Here there has been no actual resistance, but this certainly is not what is meant by non-resistance.

It is not, however, necessary that to exercise non-resistance, one should have the power actually to resist. If one does not bear any ill-feeling towards another who deals with him unjustly, he virtually exercises non-resistance. The real non-resisting man is he who can love his very enemies. He will be so good as to be able literally to follow the injunctions of Jesus, "whosoever shall smite thee on thy right cheek, turn to him the other also," and "if any man will sue thee at the Law and take away thy coat, let him have thy cloak also," and "whosoever shall compel thee to go a mile, go with him twain." Such goodness, such humility, such heroism is exactly what is involved in the practical obedience to the great commandment, "Resist not Evil". It is one of those high ideals which are so fascinatingly grand and which yet are so difficult to be followed. Just as external renunciation may really be no renunciation at all, just as external inaction may not be real *Nivritti*, so in the case of non-resistance also, mere abstaining from using force *may* not be non-resistance. It all depends upon the *disposition*, the *temperament*, and the *mental attitude* of the man. This is the first thing to be understood with regard to this great teaching.

To be non-resisting when the interests of the injured alone are involved, is comparatively an easy affair; but when another's right or safety is in danger, there arise very many difficulties in the literal obedience to the commandment. For example—suppose my neighbour's house is being pillaged by robbers; I observe them in the wicked act; I might not very much care if I were deprived of my own property and might take no steps against those who rob me; but how am I to act under the above-mentioned circumstances? Am I to resist the evil or close my eyes and keep quiet? To take, yet, another instance—suppose a woman is being outraged by a villain before my very eyes and she cries to me for protection. What am I to do? Shall I think: "Christ has said, 'Resist not evil', " and go away minding my own business? These are difficult questions to be sure. Count Tolstoi takes a similar instance, but, unfortunately, skips over the difficulty. He says: "I see that a man I know to be a ruffian is pursuing a young girl. I have a gun in my hand—I kill the ruffian and save the girl. But the death or the wounding of the ruffian has positively taken place, while what would have happened if this had not been, I cannot know. And what an immense mass of evil must result and, indeed, does result from allowing men to assume the right of anticipating what may happen. Ninety-nine *per cent* of the evil in the world is founded on this reasoning—from the inquisition to dynamite bombs and executions or punishments of tens of thousands of political criminals." The doctrine of non-resistance, as taught by Christ, is not—"kill not a man nor even wound him," but resist not evil." Tolstoi unfortunately takes extreme instance of killing or seriously wounding the evil doer. But resistance is possible without doing either. Would the Count have literally followed Christ, had he saved the girl by merely beating the ruffian in the supposed case, instead of killing or wounding him?

Nor do the difficulties end here. The word "resist" is very general and might well include in it, opposing evil by threats, abuse and the like. If so the very teacher, who commanded others to resist from evil, would have to be exempted from a necessity to act up to his teaching, for, he uses language towards the Pharisees which certainly does not err on the side of kindness. "Woe unto you *Scribes* and Pharisees," exclaims Jesus, "Hypocrites! Ye serpents! Ye generation of Vipers! How can ye escape damnation of hell ?"—language which though occurring again and again surprises us not a little, especially in the mouth of the very teacher who taught, "whosoever shall say to his brother *Raca*, shall be in danger of the Council, but whosoever shall say, thou fool! shall be in danger of hell fire."

The above are some of the difficulties which beset the practical application to life of the commandment of non-resistance. If its literal meaning be enforced, Jesus himself would appear to have sinned against it. Count Tolstoi, though he has written volumes upon this doctrine, does not help us in the solution of our difficulties, nor do the Christian writers appear to throw any light on them. Now let us turn to the *Vedanta* and see if it can help us. From the standpoint of a *Vedantin* or for that matter of a truly good man, there is in the world nothing which may really be regarded as evil. The story of Dharmaputra who, when sent out by Krishna to find out a handful of wicked men, returned without being able to find even one, is familiar to all. Evil and good are really different readings of the same thing. What appears to be evil for one is good for another, and what is good for one is bad for another. As Swami Vivekananda says : "Life is neither good nor evil. It is according to different states of mind in which we look at the world. The most practical man would neither call it good nor evil. Fire by itself is neither good nor evil ; when it keeps us warm, we say, how beautiful is fire ; when it burns our finger, we blame the fire ; still, it is neither good nor bad ; as we use it, it produces that feeling of good or bad, and so does this world." "Among frauds," says Sri Krishna, "I am game and of all things glorious I am the glory" (*Gita*, X, 36). "I am Myself misery, and Myself happiness," says the sage (*Maitreya-Upa.*, III). Viewed in this light, there is really neither good nor evil, even from a lower standpoint ; good and evil are but the obverse and reverse of the same coin. There is nothing that is absolutely good nor is there anything that is absolutely evil. Everything in the world has two sides, it is Janus-headed as it were. In everything, good and evil are so cunningly mixed that at no time is it possible to single out the one from the other. "The divine effort," says Emerson, "is never relaxed, the carrion in the sun will convert itself to grass and flower ; and man, though in brothels, jails or in gibbets is on his way to all that is good and true." Such being the nature of evil, the precept, 'resist not evil', practically means : *do not*

*abuse nor commit any act of violence against any man
with the idea of resisting evil ; for, there is nothing that is
really evil in the world.* We have no right to think that
any man is an evil-doer and proceed to chastise him
with that impression. "Judge not that ye be not judged."
This is exactly what Christ should have meant when he
said : "Resist not evil". It is really one of the grandest
precepts that ever was addressed to mankind. It
means that everything in the world is divine, not merely
in the sense that everything rests on divine sanction
but everything in the world is God, says the *Chandogya
Upanishad*. "All the world is God." "All this world is
Narayana," says the *Narayana Upanishad*. Says the
Yagnavalkya Upanishad, "Since God is in everything,
one should worship the horse, the *Chandala* (a man of
low caste), the cow, the ass, and other things, prostrating
before them like a tree fallen on earth." In a world
which is every inch of it a manifestation of the Deity,
where naught exists outside God, "what is there which
can be regarded as evil?" How grand therefore is the
precept : 'Resist not evil'. Christ says : "Ye have
heard that it hath been said, 'an eye for an eye and a
tooth for a tooth,' but I say unto you that ye 'resist
not evil'." It is a false idea to think that evil exists in
the world and that as if there is no God to remedy it,
the burden of resisting and overcoming it rests on our
shoulders. The sage says : "I am all that is, there is
nothing besides me. I am the witness of all the world,
nothing could happen except at my bidding. I am the
murderer and the murdered, the robber and the robbed,
the offender and the offended." Thus seeing himself
everywhere, how could he fight himself against himself.

If this be the correct interpretation of the teaching, it may be asked, how it helps us in the solution of our difficulty. If everything be ourself, true, complete non-resistance is secured : but how are we to act in the cases we supposed, as for instance, that of the girl who being outraged seeks our protection. The girl and the ruffian are both our own Self and how are we to act in the present case. The *Vedantin's* reply is : 'Do what duty bids, apart from all other considerations.' Do not go and resist the offender with the idea that he is an evil-doer or anything of that sort. You are placed in a particular position by God, and therefore do his bidding to the best of your power and leave off all other considerations. According to the *Vedanta*, the sage, the perfected man is in reality God himself and in the phenomenal plane he is the instrument of God. Whatever he does, he knows to be really the doing of God. He is free from all responsibility, for, his egoism is dead. He is no longer an individual separate from God. God speaks and does through him. He therefore does at all times what the situation he happens to be placed in requires, and there the ·matter ends. In the case supposed, since the girl solicits his protection he will readily give it and defend her to the best of his power, whether he succeeds or fails will be nothing to him nor would he care to abuse the offender by calling him a wicked man. Here is the highest non-resistance.

A classical example of non-resistance in the truest sense of the word is found in that wonderful book—the Ramayana. Even after the first day's battle when Ravana stood vanquished on the field, his head hung down for shame, Rama said : "Ravana, you have fought like a hero, but your fight is useless. This very instant, I can put an end to your life if I choose, but I shall not choose. I have given you a number of opportunities and shall yet give you one more, consider if it will not be good for you to deliver over poor Sita to me, consider well and act. If you heed my advice you will be prosperous; otherwise, I shall be *obliged* to put an end to your life." Such coolness, such kindness and love for the worst of enemies, these are the marks of non-resistance. Even in a cause where his dearest Sita was concerned, Rama fought not for selfish purposes nor with any wrath or indignation towards his enemy, but *for duty's sake*. He was placed in a situation in which he *was obliged to act* as he did, and not with the slightest idea of resisting evil.

The intelligent inquirer will, at this stage, certainly not fail to ask how this will be possible. The slightest things upset us and moral indignation the man of conscience is unable to control. The answer is, so long as there is the idea of evil, moral indignation is perfectly natural and quite in place; but, when one rises to the grand conception of the divinity of the universe, evil ceases for him and with it moral indignation. Doing what the situation requires and that not with any sense of egoism, but, doing as at the bidding of God, this will take the place of moral indignation and the like.

The sage who acts in this way with his mind firmly fixed in the truth of himself being the *Brahman*, is not responsible for what he does, for, it is not he that really acts; for him, as the *Gita* says, there is inaction (*Akarma*) even in action, even acting he does not act (IV, 17, 27). The great *Risih* Suka once felt a doubt whether it is possible to live an active life in the world and yet be a real sage. For the solution of this doubt he was directed to go to Janaka the great *Raja-Rishi*. Janaka answered Suka's question in a practical way. He ordered one of the criminals who were being tried in his court just then, to carry on his head a flat vessel filled with water without letting fall a single drop on the penalty of losing his head. He was guarded on both sides by soldiers with drawn swords who were commanded to chop off his head the moment a drop of water was spilt. His hands were tightly bound with fetters and he was to go round the court in a grand procession preceded by beautiful dancing girls, dancing in the most fantastic fashion. There were diverse kinds of musical instruments, gaily playing, athletes performing wonderful feats with the applause of the whole court, and he was followed by several bands of men all trying their best to divert his attention from the vessel on his head and make him turn round. The criminal, however, was all attentive to the vessel on his head and he saw nothing but the bands of soldiers who stood round him with drawn swords. Thus he succeeded in going round the court without spilling a drop of water. Janaka as soon as the experiment was over, looked at Suka's face and he said : "My doubt is now all cleared. Your mind is so entirely with the *Paramatman* as this man's was with the vessel on his head and though you are ruling a kingdom you have no touch with the world. O holy sage ! I adore thee as my master," and took leave. Now what Janaka did is exactly what Krishna asks Arjuna to do. Just as that royal *Rishi* was punishing criminals, making wars and ruling kingdoms, so is Arjuna

23

advised to fight with his mind, firmly fixed upon God
and leaving all other considerations. Krishna's advice
then, instead of being opposed to the teaching 'resist
not evil' is really the truest interpretation of it. *To do
what the situation requires without the limited ideas of
good and evil—this is what is meant by non-resistance* and
this is what Arjuna was advised to practise.

We have seen that Krishna's advice to Arjuna,
instead of being opposed to the doctrine of non-resistance, which has been proclaimed as an ideal in nearly
all the countries of the world, is indeed the truest interpretation of it. It was really a bold thing for a teacher
of morality, as Krishna was, to advise a man to fight
even against his will, and therefore it is no wonder that
critics like Bishop Caldwell attacked and censured the
Gita with all the vehemence of a foreign missionary.
We have done what we can to show that Krishna is
not so bad a teacher as our Christian friends in their
ignorance represent him to be and that the great *Gita*
deservedly called the '*Song Celestial*', is the best key to
the scriptures even of other countries.

The difficulties we had to contend will all vanish
and the explanations we had to offer become likewise
unnecessary if we call back to our minds the philosophical signification of Krishna and Arjuna. Krishna,
as we know represents the *Paramatman* eternally tutoring,
counselling, and guiding the human mind which is
symbolised as Arjuna. According to this allegorical or
rather philosophical interpretation of the *Gita*, an advice which was given to fight unmindful of the ties of
brother, father, teacher and friend is perfectly legitimate
and easily intelligible. Duryodhana and his host re-

present, as we said, the bad *Vrittis*, the evil propensities and thoughts of the mind, while the army of the Pandavas and their allies, all stand for those good tendencies, pure *Sankalpas* and noble thoughts which make for the liberation of the individual. In the battle both the good and the bad *Vrittis* of the mind have to perish, for *Moksha* or the seat of final release is absolute rest. "That is the highest state," says the *Maitrayani Upanishad*, "where all the *Vrittis* of the mind have perished and where there is neither sleep nor thought." "Let the wise subdue his speech by mind, subdue his mind by intellect, subdue his intellect in the great self and subdue this also in the quiet self" (*Kath.-Upa.*, III, 13). That the highest state is one of absolute rest where the mind is completely dead, as it were, is well described in the following *Sruti:* "The wise think that the Fourth which is cognisant of neither internal nor external objects nor of both, which is not a compact mass of knowledge, is neither intelligent nor unintelligent, which is invisible, not acting; incomprehensible, undefinable, incapable of proof and indescribable and which is the sole essence of I-am-ness with no trace of the conditioned world, all calm, all bliss, without duality. This is the *Atman*; it should be known" (*Mand.-Upa.*, 7).

For attaining to this state, the mind must be completely subdued and all activity has to cease; for action necessarily implies imperfection. "Where there is, as it were, duality, there sees another another thing, there smells another another thing, there tastes another another thing, there speaks another another thing, there hears another another thing, there minds another another

thing, there touches another another thing; but how
does one, to whom all has become mere soul, see anything, how smell anything, how speak anything, how
hear anything, how mind anything, how touch anything, how know anything?" (*Bri.-Upa.*, IV, iv, 15).
Saintship, says the *Gita*, is 'ceasing from all the works'.
The man therefore who aspires to realise the *Atman*, in
other words, to know himself, which has been described
as 'the highest end, the best riches, the supremest world,
the greatest joy,' should strictly follow the Upanishadic
precept above quoted—'Let the wise subdue his speech
by mind, subdue his mind by intellect, subdue his intellect in the great self and subdue that also in the quiet
self.' This holding back of the senses and the mind is
what is called *Yoga*. "The state which ensues when
the five organs of knowledge remain with the mind, and
intellect does not strive is called the highest aim. When
all the desires cease which were cherished in one's heart,
then the mortal becomes immortal; then he obtains
here (in this world) *Brahman*. When all the bonds of
the heart are broken in this life, then the mortal becomes
immortal; this alone is the instruction of all the *Vedas*"
(*Ka.-Upa.*, II, vi, 10, 14, 15). Such ambitions as
that of doing good to the world and so on, however good
and useful in their own way, are real hindrances in the
way of *Yoga* and therefore have to be subdued with effort.
All restlessness is imperfection and shows lost balance.
Therefore however good may be the ideas and aspirations that might spring in one's mind, however helpful
they may be in the earlier stages of spirit-progress, the
endeavour of one who has advanced so far as to long for
release from this world of *Maya*, should be to keep them

all down and strive with singleness of aim and intensity
of purpose to realise that which is the end of all *Karma*
and whose nature is absolute, blissful and imperturbable
rest.

GNANA—THE DIRECT MEANS TO MOKSHA

HAVING thus far dwelt upon a difficulty which will not fail to strike the intelligent reader at the very outset and vindicated Krishna from the charge of preaching a dangerous doctrine, let us resume the thread of our 'thoughts' and sketch out, as we proposed, the plan of the *Gita*. Krishna, we saw, began with giving a philosophical dignity to the problem of Arjuna, and raising it from the plane of narrow practical considerations, he viewed it from the stand-point of the perfect sage. After showing how, from the philosopher's point of view, there was no sin in Arjuna's fighting, he descends to the plane of a *Kshatriya* and urges his friend to fight and thereby do his caste duty. Then he propounds the philosophy of action and shows how action when performed without caring for its fruits and as a service to the Lord throws open by itself the doer to that exalted state of bliss, where man is free for ever from the liability to be played upon by the world. The tact with which Arjuna is made to forget the hour and lose sight of his individual problem is simply admirable, and the question even so early as in the second chapter is no longer, whether it is just or unjust to kill the Kauravas, but what are the marks of a perfected sage, how would he speak, what will he do and how would he behave? (II, 54). The remainder of the second chapter is taken up with a description of what is known as *Sankhya-Yoga*. Then the question comes, "If O Lord thou thinkest that wisdom is better than action, why doest thou counsel me to engage in a horrible deed?" The reply to this question forms the subject of the three subsequent chapters—three, four and five. How action leads to wisdom and how wisdom is surcease from all works, are elaborated in these three chapters with wonderful fullness, so much so, that though the germs of *Karma-Yoga* are found in the *Upanishads*, the credit may well be said to belong to the *Gita* more than to anything else, of having thrown open an almost new path to salvation, which, though by itself not all-sufficient, yet goes a great way towards the end. The mutual relation between the two *Yogas*, *Karma* and *Gnana* is explained in VI, 3, which says that for him who desires *Gnana-Yoga*, *Karma-Yoga* is necessary and for him who has attained the former control of mind is the chief requisite.

It is often erroneously supposed that *Karma* or action forms a distinct *Yoga* sufficient by itself to procure liberation, and when performed with non-attachment is as efficient as *Gnana*. That this is impossible has been again and again shewn in the pages of this journal both by argument and scriptural authority. All that *Nishkamya Karma* can do to the individual is to bring about *Chittasuddhi* or purity of mind and qualify him for the attainment of wisdom, which alone forms the *Sakshat-Sadana*, *i.e.*, the direct cause for liberation from the bonds of conditioned existence. This has been repeatedly stated in the *Gita* also, as for instance in the verse already quoted (IV, 38), which says : "In this world there is nothing so purifying as *Gnana* ; but the *Karma-Yogi* realises for himself that *Gnana* in course of time.

There can be no doubt however that the great author of the *Gita* gives a very high place to *Karma-Yoga*. Not merely does he prefer it to abstinence from work (*vide* verses from 4 to 7 of Chap. III, and 2 to 5 of Chap. XVIII), but he often goes so far as to say that ignorant men, and not those that are wise, speak of the *Sankhya* and the *Yoga*, *i.e.*, *Gnana-Yoga* and *Karma-Yoga* as different (V, 4). In the next verse he adds "that place which is gained by the followers of *Sankhya-Yoga* is also attained by the *Karma Yogis*. He who sees that the *Sankhya* and *Yoga* are one, *sees* indeed." But all that is meant by such verses, which would appear to contradict the one above quoted (IV, 38) is that the difference between the two *Yogas* is one of degree ; the latter is placed on the same footing with the former, only to emphasize the certainty of its securing the desired end, *viz.*, *Moksha*. But, since even the *Gnani* is urged to work for the benefit of others, and since action is declared indispensable in the case of all others, a doubt may arise whether *Gnana* alone by itself can lead to salvation, or whether it requires the help of *Karma* also to accomplish that end. It is admitted that the doing of *Karma* is better than abstaining from it and that action is a necessity of one's nature so long as he is bound by *Avidya* (ignorance) and is not master of himself, but it is asked whether *Gnana* cannot make for liberation without the help of *Karma*.

The *Gita* has indeed misled many, and, misunderstanding certain passages in it, there have not been wanting men to uphold the theory that *Gnana* by itself cannot secure emancipation and that it requires the help of *Karma* also. This view is endorsed by Bhartruhari, one of the early commentators on the *Brahma-Sutras* ; *Gnana* and *Karma* are regarded by these people as co-ordinate causes for *Moksha* and they are compared to the two wings of a bird, and it is said that, just as the latter cannot fly by the help of one wing alone, so man cannot attain liberation by the help of *Gnana* or *Karma* separately. It is also asserted not only that *Karma* should go hand in hand with *Gnana*, but that *Gnana* itself would get destroyed like an unwatered plant but for the nourishing support of *Karma*.

In answer to these erroneous views Sankara says in his commentary on the *Gita* : "*Gnana* kills out all sense of duality and confers liberation. *Karma*, on the other hand, depends upon the sense of differentiation of its requisites, action, causes (material and efficient) and its result. The ideas of 'I,' 'mine,' 'I am agent,' 'I am enjoyer,' 'I am a Brahmin,' 'I am a householder,' and the like have been superimposed upon the *Atman* from eternity through *Avidya* or ignorance. The knowledge, 'I am without *Maya*,' 'I am not agent,' 'I am actionless,' 'there is no result which has to be obtained by me,' 'there is naught outside me,' destroys the sense of differentiation, without which *Karma* is impossible, and *Avidya*, which is the prime source of that sense. Mere *Karma* cannot remove this sense of differentiation and *Avidya* just as darkness cannot remove darkness. *Gnana* on the other hand, kills out both, therefore *Gnana* and *Karma* cannot co-exist (and much less can be co-ordinate causes for *Moksha*). Hence only *Gnana* can bring about salvation" (*vide* his comment on XVIII, 66). In another place, he observes, "*Moksha* which consists in self-realisation is promised

only to the *Gnani*, there is no other road to it except
Gnana. To go by any other road will be useless like
going towards the East with a view to reach the Western
ocean (*vide* commentary on XVIII, 55). Says the author
of the *Vedanta Sara*, "Those learned men who wrote
the comments on the *Vedanta* before the time of
Sankaracharya, taught that in seeking emancipation,
it was improper to renounce religious ceremonies, but
that the desire of reward ought to be forsaken, that
works should be performed to obtain divine wisdom,
which being acquired, would lead to emancipation ;
that works were not to be rejected, but practised without being considered as a bargain, for the performance
of which a person should obtain such and such benefits ;
that therefore works, and the undivided desire of emancipation, were to be attended to ; which is illustrated
in the following comparison : Two persons being on a
journey, one of them loses his horse and the other his
carriage ; the first is in the greatest perplexity and the
other, though he can accomplish the journey on horse-
back, contemplates the fatigue with dissatisfaction.
After remaining for some time in great suspense, they
at length agree to unite what is left to each, and thus
with ease accomplish their journey. The first is he who
depends on works ; and the latter, he who depends on
wisdom. From hence it will be manifest that, to obtain emancipation, works and divine wisdom must be
united. Formerly this was the doctrine of the *Vedanta*,
but Sankaracharya in a comment on the *Bhagavad-Gita*
has by many proofs shown that this is an error ; that
works are wholly excluded, and that knowledge alone,
realising everything as *Brahma*, procures liberation."

This point may now be considered as fairly settled and indeed, the *Gita* itself when rightly read gives little room for doubt in that matter for, besides the verses which explicitly give preference to *Gnana*, the very arrangement of the work shows that *Karma* is simply a means for attaining wisdom and forms a lower rung in the ladder which leads to *Mukti* or release. At the end of almost every one of the first six chapters *Gnana* is glorified, and self-realisation is distinctly pointed out as the end to which *Karma-Yoga* is one of the means.

At the same time, it cannot be denied that Krishna lays special stress upon the fact that *Gnana*, instead of unfitting a man for the world, as it is vulgarly supposed to do, brings about the best adjustment to its ways. A *Gnani* need not be a recluse, he need not fly away from the haunts of men and live in lonely forests and mountain-caves and be dead to the world, but he is to live in the world and yet be out of it. He should perform actions though not for himself, yet, for the sake of others, for the world follows whatever example the wise men set. 'And they should not,' adds Sri Krishna, 'allow a difference of opinion to spring up in the ignorant who are desirous of performing *Karma*. On the other hand, they should themselves perform actions in the regular way and make others also do the same' (III, 26).

This is the essence of Krishna's teaching in the first few chapters; and this, he says, he first taught to Surya—the sun-god, Surya taught in his turn to Manu, Manu taught to Ikshwaku and then it descended traditionally to kings and sages. Here Arjuna properly asks, "Thou wert born recently and Surya was born long ago, how shall I comprehend this which thou sayest, "I was the first to declare it." Krishna's answer involves an important philosophical doctrine which we shall next proceed to consider.

————

AVATARS

I. ORDINARY THEORIES

Now we come to one of the most puzzling questions of Indian philosophy or rather theology—the question of *Avatars* (incarnation). In reply to Arjuna's inquiry "Thy birth was later, and prior the birth of The Sun; how should I understand that thou taughtest this *Yoga* in the beginning?" the Lord replied "Many births of Mine have passed......presiding over My own Nature, I am born by My *Maya*. Whenever there is a decay of religion, O Bharata, and there is rise of irreligion, then I manifest Myself. For the protection of the good, for the destruction of evil-doers, for the firm establishment of Religion I am born in every age........" (IV, 4—9). Now what are we to understand from the above?

The popular conception of *Avatara* is that *Iswara*, the Lord, descends from heaven and creates himself in a particular form and that therefore Rama and Krishna were not men, but really *Iswara* in human form. A great Hindu poet makes *Brahma* the Creator say in accordance with the popular theory, "O Narayana, that thou hast created Thyself as *Narasimha* is itself enough to prove that thou art self-created. If thou canst thus create Thyself at will what wonder that Thou didst create me!" This popular conception is often fancifully elaborated, and it is said that when Rama, Krishna and others were incarnated, *Vaikuntam*, the abode of Vishnu, became vacant for the time and that when these

Avatars departed from the earth Narayana went back to His Heaven. It is expressly stated both in the Ramayana and the Mahabharata that Maha Vishnu left the bodies of Rama and Krishna when they died and went to his abode, *Vaikunta*. This conception is on the very face of it unphilosophical, for the Lord being omnipresent, He cannot with any propriety be said to vacate *Vaikunta* or *Kailas* and go to some other *Loka*. Of course for the uncultured masses whose intellect is in an undeveloped and childish state, this picture will do, and indeed it is the best that could be thought of. And considering the nature of the people to whom it is addressed, the poetry in it is more than a recompense for the absence of philosophical accuracy, and inasmuch as anthropomorphism holds sway over the human mind, Rama and Krishna are very rich additions to the Hindu pantheon. Personal God is a stepping stone to the Absolute Impersonal, and is an invaluable help in the earlier stages of spiritual evolution, and, so long as the theory of God descending on earth and assuming the shape of man does not pretend to be an absolute and final philosophical truth, we have no quarrel with it.

But there is another theory put forward, namely, that whenever any incarnation takes place, the Logos 'descends to the plane of the soul and associating itself with it works in and through it on the plane of humanity for some great thing that had to be done in the world.' This theory appears to be plausible, but on closer examination, I venture to think that though it has an air of philosophical accuracy about it, it is as much open to objection as the preceding one, and is totally opposed to the teachings of our *Sastras*. In the first place, The Lord is omnipresent and therefore His descending and ascending have no meaning whatsoever. That He is omnipresent and that there is nothing outside Him is repeatedly declared in the *Gita* itself.

There is nought else higher than I. (VII, 7).

Vasudeva is the all. (VII, 19).

By Me all this world is pervaded. (IX, 4).

I am the Self, O Gudakesa, seated in the heart of all beings : I am the beginning, and the middle, and the end as well, of all beings (X, 20).

The Lord dwells in the heart of all beings (XVIII, 61).

Indeed there are numberless passages in which the omnipresence of the Lord, the Logos is distinctly expressed, and therefore the doctrine that Logos descends and unites with a soul with the object of incarnating is plainly unphilosophical.

This theory, however is due to a still more vicious doctrine that the Logos is something different from *Brahman*. According to this doctrine the Logos, though not different in essence from *Parabrahman*, is yet different from it in having an individualised existence and being one of the many centres of energy manifested by it. This is a view which is not merely not supported by our *Sastras*, but contrary to the spirit of the whole *Vedanta*. Both in *Vedantic* dualism and qualified monism, *Iswara* is the same as *Brahman* in every respect and in the *Advaita* it is simply an aspect of *Brahman*. It is *Brahman* looked at from the standpoint of the *Jiva*, the false self, which is bound by nescience ; it is *Brahman* reflected in *Maya*, so to speak, and viewed through that veil. Says Sankaracharya : "*Brahman* is apprehended under two forms ; in the first place as qualified by limiting conditions owing to the multiformity of the evolutions of name and form (in the multiformity of the created world) ; in the second place as being the opposite of this, *i.e.*, free from all limiting conditions whatever. Compare the following passages ; *Bri.-Up.*, IV, 5. 15......*Kh.-Up.*, VII, 24, I........ *Taitt. Ar.*, III, 12, 7........*Sv.-Up.*, VI, 19........ *Bri.-Up.*, III, 3, 6........*Bri.-Up.*, III, 8, 8.......All these passages, with many others, declare *Brahman* to possess a double nature, according as it is the object either of Knowledge or of Nescience....And although the *one Highest Self only*, *i.e.*, the Lord distinguished by those different qualities constitutes the object of devotion, still the fruits of devotion are distinct according as the devotion refers to different qualities" (Com. on *Ved. Sutra*, I, I, 11). Elsewhere he says "Thus the Lord depends (as Lord, *i.e.*, Logos) upon the limiting adjuncts of name and form the products of Nescience......Hence the Lord's being a Lord, his omniscience, his omnipotence, etc., all depend on the limitation due to the adjuncts whose Self is Nescience ; while in reality none of these qualities belong to the Self, whose true nature is cleared, by right knowledge from all adjuncts whatever" (Com. on *Ved., Sutra*, II, I, 14).

In the face of such unmistakable statements, the doctrine above referred to, which distinguishes the Logos from *Brahman* professes to be a correct statement of Sankara's teaching ! Indeed in his commentary on the *Gita* itself, this great champion of Indian monism again and again speaks of Sri Krishna as if He were *Parabrahman* Itself and not any particular centre of energy which is called the Logos and is supposed to reside in the bosom of *Brahman* and to sleep in the time of Cosmic *Pralaya* and keep waking at other times. In the very introduction, he says : "The *Gita 'Sastra* also expounds the nature of the Supreme Being and Reality known as *Vasudeva, the Parabrahman* which forms the subject of the discourse." This statement clearly and directly denies what the late Mr. Subba Row, the author, perhaps of the erroneous view under reference, says : "Strictly speaking, the whole of this book (*the Gita*) may be called the book of the philosophy of the Logos" as distinguished from the *Parabrahman*. How far this is from being right may be seen from what Sankara says. Commenting on verse IX, 1, he writes, "The word 'Now' is intended to lay stress on the following speciality concerning knowledge : this right knowledge alone forms the direct means of attaining *Moksha* as declared in the *Srutis* and the *Smriti*."

> Vasudeva is the All.
> All this is the Self.
> One only without a second.

Again in his comment on verse IX, 14, he expressly says : "They always praise Me, their Lord, *the very Brahman*, they worship me the self lying in the heart." Indeed as a mere cursory reference will show the words Iswara, Vasudeva, the Self, the Supreme Being are indiscriminately used as explanations for the 'I' of the Lord, though as in the XIIth chapter the distinction between worshipping the one and the same *Brahman* as absolute and in its nature or as reflected in *Maya*. This difference in worship certainly does not mean, as we have already seen, any difference between the Logos and *Brahman*, and there is not the slightest authority in Sankara's commentary for the view held by Mr. Subba Row who believed that he gave a correct statement of the teaching of that great philosopher (see page 58 of his Notes on the *Bhagavad-Gita*) and that the majority of the so-called *Vedantins* have totally misunderstood the latter.

Next let us see if at least the *Gita* lends any support to the apparently strange view which we are now discussing. Says the revered writer who probably originated this view, "It is generally believed, at any rate by a certain class of philosophers that Krishna himself is *Parabrahman*—but the words used by Krishna in speaking of *Parabrahman* and the way in which he deals with the subject clearly show that he draws a distinction between himself and *Parabrahman*......It will be noticed that when Krishna is speaking of himself he never uses the word *Parabrahman*, but places himself in the position of *Pratyagatma*, and it is from this standpoint that we constantly find him speaking. Whenever he speaks of *Pratyagatma*, he speaks of himself, and whenever he speaks of *Parabrahman* he speaks of it as being something different from himself."

A number of verses are quoted in support of this view but as to examine them all one by one will occupy needless space, I shall refer to a few only. In verse VIII, 11, the Lord undertakes to briefly declare the 'Imperishable goal' (*Padam*). This verse is cited as an authority for the position that *Brahman* is the seat for the Logos and not the Logos Itself, whereas it proves just the reverse. For in the verses immediately

following, Sri Krishna Himself says that those who at
the time of death think of Him reach the Imperishable
goal and that those who think of Him and Him alone
at all times easily reach *Him*, and reaching Him never
again become liable to rebirth (VIII, 12, 13, 14, 15 and
16). From this it is unmistakably plain that the Imperishable Goal is Sri Krishna himself, in other words,
Iswara and *Brahman* are not different. Again verse 21
of the same chapter, as Sankara points out, only describes the nature of the Imperishable Goal the means to
reach which the above quoted verses indicate, so that
the *Akshara* is nothing different from the Logos as Mr.
Subba Row believes. The word *Dhama*, in the verse
means rather *Swarupa* than abode. Again verses IX,
4, 5, 6, prove just the reverse of what Mr. Subba Row
asserts for Sri Krishna distinctly refers to *Brahman* as
his own Unmanifest *Swarupa*, *i.e.*, that aspect of Him
which is beyond *Maya*—the *Nirguna* aspect. Verses 13—17
of the XIIth chapter only prove that there are two
modes of worship, *Saguna Upasana* and *Nirguna Upasana*
and not as I have already stated that there are two
kinds of entities the Logos and *Brahman*. Verse XIV,
27, says, "I (the Logos) am the abode of *Brahman*,"
which means just the reverse of Mr. Subba Row's statement that *Brahman* is the abode of the Logos. Indeed
this verse is by both the commentators Sankara and
Sridhara explained as meaning, "I (*Iswara*) am the very
Brahman," *i.e.*, the *Saguna* aspect of It, in other words,
Its reflection, Its image, in the world of *Maya*. Lastly,
XV, 6, "That the sun illumines not nor the moon nor
fire : 'That is My Supreme abode which having
reached they return not,' simply means that the real

state of *Iswara* which is supreme, *i.e.*, beyond *Maya*, is *Brahman*."

None of the above verses which are cited as authorities by Mr. Subba Row indicate, as we have seen, any difference between *Brahman* and the Logos.

Besides, there is direct evidence in the *Gita* itself to show that both are one and the same. For instance Sri Krishna first says (XIII 2) "know me as the *Kshetragna*," and then in describing the *Kshetragna* distinctly calls It *Brahman* (XIII, 12), and verses VI, 29, 30, VIII, 18, 19, and XV, 18, 19, are some of the many passages in which Sri Krishna identifies himself with the *Supreme Brahman*. I do admit that he often speaks of Himself as *Iswara*, but this only strengthens my position ; or rather the orthodox *Vedantic* position that *Iswara* and *Brahman* are not two distinct entities, but only two aspects of the same Being, the *Ekamevadwitiyam* of the *Upanishads*. Indeed how could the *Vedanta* which does not tolerate the multiformity of even the universe find place for two distinct Gods ?

Even at the risk of digressing from our subject, I dwelt on this matter at such length as it forms the cornerstone of the whole philosophy of Mr. Subba Row and his followers, and the leading idea in his notes on the *Bhagavad-Gita*. Their theory of the Logos being thus shown to have no *Sastraic* authority, their other theory of incarnation according to which the Logos unites itself occasionally with the human soul and incarnates as an *Avatar* also falls to the ground, for the Logos is as omnipresent as the *Brahman* and therefore does not descend or ascend any more than the latter. If so, what is the correct explanation for the phenomenon of incarnation if indeed the latter be possible?

II. VEDANTIC THEORY

What, then, is the correct theory of incarnation? It is a truism that, whatever exists, exists only in and through *Brahman*, and that the whole world is nothing but a manifestation of Him through the medium of *Maya*, and as such, in a certain sense, the ant is as much an *Avatar* of God as Valmiki or Suka. Says the *Svetasvatara Upanishad*: "Thou art the woman, Thou art man, Thou art the youth and the maid, Thou art the old man trembling on his staff. . . . Thou art the black bee, the green bird with red-coloured eye, the cloud in whose womb the lightning sleeps, the seasons, and the seas."

From this, it does not, by any means, follow that man, woman, the black bee and the parrot are all one and the same. They all, doubtless, are in essence, in their inmost Self, one in reality, but, as phenomena, they are widely different from one another, and nothing could be more absurd than to treat them as equal to, or identical with one another in the *vyavaharic* (phenomenal) plane. Their bodies or forms are in *Vedantic* philosophy some of the manifold and endless *upadhis* (vehicles) through which *Brahman* manifests Itself, and differ among themselves in the degree in which they manifest Him, just as stones, glass and water differ among themselves in their capacity to reflect the sun. A sage, for instance, reveals more of divinity than does a poet, and the latter more than a miser and so on.

It is, owing to this difference, that, though in a wide sense, everything in the universe is an *Avatar* of *Isvara*, only, certain forms of individual existence have b en regarded as such, owing to some *extraordinary but by no means, supernatural qualities possessed by them.* To support my statement with proper authorities, the same Sri Krishna who said : 'I am both the seen and the unseen, *Vasudeva* is the All' says also, '*Wherever there is power or glory in an extraordinary degree know that I am there.*' It is such extraordinary manifestations of power and glory which should be regarded as *Avatars*, for, the Lord is in them in a special sense.

That this is the correct theory of incarnation is borne out even by the popular conception, for people usually say of any extraordinary individual, "Ah, he is an *Avatar*." History bears out that no man was regarded at his very birth as an *Avatar*. Even those who are now by common consent spoken of as *Avatars* of God, were not regarded as such at their very birth but only by their subsequent deeds. Notwithstanding the poetry with which *Srimat Bhagavata* has depicted the life of our dear *Jara Chora Sikhamani*, Sri Krishna, it is easy to see that he was not looked upon as God by his immediate neighbours, friends and relations at his very birth or infancy, though his later deeds, which were extraordinary, impressed most of them with love, veneration and awe. To take another example, it is evident, from the life of Sri Sankara that he was not regarded as an *Avatar* of Siva in his days as he is now, nor was Buddha considered by his contemporaries as an incarnation of Vishnu. The Rama of Valmiki is very different from the Rama of Tulsidas and others, and more a man than God. By this it should not for a moment be understood that I deny the divinity of these mighty heroes; on the other hand, I affirm that they were God Himself, though in a special sense, in the sense in which the Lord says : 'Wherever there is power or glory in an extraordinary degree, know that I am there,' in the sense in which Jesus, though a man like ourselves, spoke of himself as the "Son of God". Rama and Krishna were doubtless divine in their nature and *Avatars* of God, but in my humble opinion, only in the above sense; for, any other theory would, as we have already seen, be unphilosophical, and we are bound, on account of the excellence of their character, the purpose of their lives and the service they have done to the world, to speak of them as God. One great service which sages have done to us is, to point out their greatness and the divinity underlying it.

Now let us examine the passage in the *Gita* referring to the theory of incarnation in the light of the above explanation. Says the Blessed Lord : "Many births of mine have passed and of thine. All these I know, thou knowest not, O Parantapa." The meaning of this verse evidently is, that the *Jiva* whose power of vision is obstructed by *Avidya*, does not know its past incarnation, while the Lord, who is born without being born, in other words, appears to manifest himself in the shape of the variegated Universe, knows all his births being the All-knowing *Antaryamin* (inner ruler). It certainly does not follow from the above statement of the Lord that He is actually born like ourselves. Indeed, to avoid such a supposition, He proceeds explicitly to state in the next verse that He is really unborn : He says, "Though

I am unborn, of imperishable nature and I am the Lord
of beings, yet presiding over my own nature I am born
of *Maya.*" In commenting on this verse Sankara
properly observes: "Yet ruling over nature to which
the whole Universe is subject and by which deluded,
the world knows not *Vasudeva its own self,* the Lord is
born by his own *Maya.* He has a body and a birth but
not *in reality* like other people." Now this interpretation
has to be carefully understood. Else it would lead to
much of unphilosophical mysticism. It does not mean
that the Lord is really born and yet His body unlike
that of ours is transcendental as some have wrongly taken
it to mean. Strangely enough Sankara's interpretation
has by more than one revered writer been understood
as meaning that the Lord's *birth* is real, while His *body*
alone is unreal and transcendental, though Sankara
himself explicitly says that both the birth and *the body*
of the Lord are alike unreal, which means that His
manifestation is real, only so long as we are under the
deluding power of *Maya.* I am really surprised to find
that even some authoritative books lay down the theory
that in the case of *Avatars* like Rama and Krishna though
they actually lived, moved, and had their being in the
world of men, yet their bodies were not composed of
matter like those of ordinary men and this in spite of the
direct statement of Anandagiri in his *tika* on Sankara's
commentary on the *Mandukya Upanishad* that the
bodies of Rama, Krishna and others were made of elements and therefore gross and material. Indeed, Sankara
himself is as clear as desirable. According to him the
Lord says: "I have a body and a birth but not in
reality" for, He is imperishable and unborn, while the

Jivas so long as they are mere *Jivas*, have real births and bodies. What I mean is that the latter's births and bodies are as real as themselves and last as long as the illusion of manifestation continues. Whereas the birth and body of the Lord are not as real as Himself and are consequently illusory. For us, our births, deaths and bodies are real, for we are in a state of ignorance while for the Lord who is the ordainer of *Maya*, they are unreal.

It clearly follows from what we have seen that *Avatars* are real only in the phenomenal plane and that they are not caused by the Lord vacating His seat in Heaven and descending to us assuming transcendental bodies or possessing some advanced individual and uniting with his soul as departed spirits are believed sometimes to do but that they are extraordinary manifestations in the hour of need. This exactly is what Sri Krishna means when He says : "Whenever there is a decay of Religion, O! Bharata, and there is a rise of irreligion then I manifest myself." Just as in the life of individuals when there happens any great unbearable calamity of any other sharp and apparently irremediable crisis, there comes forth some sudden help or consolation from a quiet unsuspected corner and in a most miraculous way ; so in the life of nations terrible Social, Political, or Religious crises raise up one or few giant men who, considering the circumstances of the case and the readiness with which they create order out of chaos and their almost superhuman ability, strike their contemporaries as nothing less than heaven-born. It is these extraordinary manifestations of divine glory and grace which have been deservedly honoured with the glorious appellation of *Avatars* and have been rightly worshipped as God Himself.

I request the gentle reader to save me from the sacrilege of attempting to dethrone Sri Rama, Sri Krishna and other universally recognised *Avatars* from the high pedestal in which they have been placed by common consent. My endeavour, on the other hand, is to show that they are God himself and none but God. Certainly, if they are not God, who else is? If Rama the ideal of social and domestic virtues, the miracle of gentleness, goodness and valour, of heroism tempered with humility and prowess combined wih mildness, a lion in war and a lamb in peace, the ideal lover, who wept torrents at his separation from Sita, but the dignity of whose character was such, that he would not take her back, unless her chastity was publicly vouched for by the gods above, who wept almost to death on the lap of his apparently dead Lakshmana, but only a few days after, extinguished, by a single arrow, Ravana, the tyrant of all the worlds, the *"Suddha Brahma Paratpara Ram"* at whose very sight the universe melts away, trembling like a ghost at sunrise but who is dear to poets and *Bhaktas* in his human form, blue like the sky holding the *Kodanda* (his bow) in his hands and walking the earth like a poor ascetic, the sweet Ramamurti, whose name being the *taraka mantra*, is in the heart of every pious Hindu from the Himalayas to the Cape; if Sri Krishna the thrice blessed Lord who came into the world to act out in bright and never perishing relief, the divine drama of the universe, with all its apparent absurdities, incongruities and evils and showed that behind them all, was Himself, the *Kapata nataka Sutradhara* (the cunning

wire-puller of all this puppet-show), the incomprehensible Lord of thieves, who is Himself love and mercy,
but is yet the cause of all mischief, hatred and war, the
ideal child, whose little pranks which are in the lips of
every Hindu mother, are so many revelations of the
meaning of the world's scriptures, the ideal lover, whose
dalliance with the blessed *Gopis* and beautiful Radha,
teach more than all the *Upanishads* do, the cunning
diplomatist, whose subtle contrivances are the laws that
govern the world, the ideal warrior by whose very presence
the world struggles on to truth and justice, the teacher
of teachers, who taught all the philosophy of all the
scriptures, of all religions, of all the worlds put together
in the brief space of three hours, the bachelor with sixty
thousand wives, the humble hostage of Satyabhama
whose weight exceeded that of all the jewels of all his
wives and loves, but was just equal to that of a small
Tulsi leaf of Rukmani, the deceitful friend, who, by
just one wink of his eye, transformed Narada himself
into a poor woman with many children, the piping,
dancing, sporting Shepherd, always playful, always
cunning, and always love-making, the bright idyll of
whose life is unparalleled for the charm of its poetry, or
the variety of its incidents and the depth of its philosophy, Krishna the *Purna Avatar*—if these are not God,
who else could be? Rama and Krishna must be God, or
there is no God at all. There can be no other alternative. Truly does Lilasuka sing :

वरमिदमुपदेशमादियध्वं ।

निगमवनेषु नितान्तचारखिन्ना: ।

विचिनु तभवनेषु वल्लवीनां ।
डपनिषदर्थमुलूखले निबद्धम् ॥

Oh, ye who are weary of wandering in vain in the wilderness of the *Sastras*, search for the Meaning of the *Upanishads* (Sri Krishna) in the cottages of the shepherdesses, where It is tied down to a mortar.

We might add, or on the banks of the Ganges, where It stood embracing a boatman (Guha).

Our object in discussing the theory of incarnations, is not to prove that Rama and Krishna were men but that God neither descends nor ascends as the other theories on the subject suppose, but that He is everywhere, in the atom as much as in the planet, in the ant as much as in man. This omnipresence we may all theoretically recognise, but philosophy or at least the *Vedanta* is no theory. Its object is to enable us to practically realise what we intellectually comprehend. One great help to such realisation, is to direct our attention to the grander manifestations of divinity, which is almost a necessary preliminary to higher worship, which consists in seeing Him in everything and everything in Him. In the Christian Bible, God is represented as having first spoken through thunder and lightning. It was long after this, that the Prophet Elijah recognised Him in the beautiful calm of nature, and much later still, did the voice come forth 'the kingdom of God is within you'. Naturally we are more readily attracted by the grander manifestations of nature than by the lesser. That is why Sri Krishna speaks of his grander manifestations as He does in the tenth chapter of the *Gita* where He describes his *Vibhuti* (wealth of manifestation), 'Of the *Vedas* I am the *Sama Veda*, I am *Vasava* of the Gods, etc.,' before he explains that He is Himself the *Kshetrajna* in all *Kshetras* (XIII, 2), in other words, identical with the individual soul.

These incarnations then, being extraordinary manifestations of God's power and glory, are *pujarha*, worthy of adoration, but the best way in which a *Mumukshu* (seeker after salvation) could worship them, is to regard them as nothing less than *Brahman* and always meditate on them as such. It is specially with this purpose that the *Ramatapani*, *Ramarahasya*, *Gopalatapani*, *Krishnopanishad*, and *Kalisantharanopanishad*, have been composed by the *Rishis*. To look upon them as some Logos or some incarnation of some particular deity vacating Heaven and descending into earth, however good they may be for the many, would not altogether satisfy the longings of the genuine *Mumukshu*, and it is from this standpoint that the subject is discussed here at some length. And Sri Krishna himself, whenever He says 'I' in the *Gita*, always talks of Himself as *Brahman* or *Iswara*. And the same does Rama do in the *Sitaramanjaneya samvada* and the *Adhyatma Ramayana*—facts which confirm the interpretation of Arjuna and Krishna as the mind and the *Atman* with which we started at the outset of this discourse on the *Gita*.

GITA—A PRACTICAL SASTRA

It seems we may be endlessly discoursing on the *Gita*. It is one of those books, on every word of which volumes may be written. It is infinite like its author,

the more one reads it, the more mysterious and suggestive does it become. Numberless commentaries have
been written upon it, but it is more than doubtful if it
has become more intelligible on that account. It seems
to be like an impenetrable maze, where a number of
gates seem to open out, but only really lead into the
interior. Every verse in the book seems capable of
being interpreted in a number of ways, each contradict-
ing the rest ; and it is no wonder that it has become the
subject of so much of theorisation in these days when
thinkers do little more than theorising. For instance,
one says that the book of electric in its tendency and
attempts, though not with perfect success, to reconcile
all the six ancient schools of Indian philosophy. Another
says that, it is *Sankhya-Yoga* reconciler, another that
it is a *Yoga-Vedanta* reconciler, another that it is all
Vedanta, another that it is purely *Sankhya* and has
nothing to do with the *Vedanta*. All these thinkers
find authorities for their theories, all in the same *Gita*,
and fight with one another as if the book was meant
only for such quarrels, and its value depended entirely
upon the result. It is not always that the fight rests
between the contending parties, sacred names and dragged into discussion and it is not rare to hear that such
and such a commentator is a fool, such and such is a
genius, and so on. Nor is the author himself spared,
one calls Him a dangerous teacher, another that He
was an ill-qualified teacher who himself had not
known the truth, another that he was confused
himself and gave utterance to a half truth here and
a half truth there with a lot of contradictions and
absurdities.

I have no idea of deciding between these various theories, for, in my opinion, no amount of such theorisation and discussion upon the merits of the commentators and the author, can lead us to the truth. *The primary object of the Gita*, that for which it was proclaimed to the world *is to teach the way to obtain undisturbed peace*. It is the daily experience of everyone, that such peace and happiness are far from one who is attached to the world. *The only way* in which it could be obtained *is*, as repeatedly declared in the *Gita*, *Self-realisation*. All other things are only preliminaries to this. Wise men say that there are three great secrets included in the *Gita*, namely, that one should perform one's duties in life (*Swadharmacharana*), secondly, that one should discriminate between the self and non-self, and thirdly, that one should realise that everything that exists, gross and subtle, movable and immovable, and the visible and the invisible are nothing but *Vasudeva*. These secrets are respectively called *Guhya* (secret), *Guhyatara* (more secret), and *Guhytama* (most secret). The first is taught in the second, third, fourth, fifth and eighteenth Chapters. The second, in the second, sixth, thirteen and the succeeding Chapters. The third, in the seventh, eighth, ninth, tenth and succeeding Chapters.

These three secrets—so-called, not because they are to be jealously guarded from the ears of the common man but because they are sacred—represent the essence of the *Vedanta*, and indeed of all the Scriptures of the world. They form the cream of religion, and though they have been expressed in a few words, to understand them aright and realise them is a task which is beyond

the reach of more than ninety-nine per cent of the
human race. We are all accustomed to hear that God
is omnipresent and very often say it ourselves too. But
how few of us understand the idea contained in the word
omnipresence and how much fewer still are those who
really feel it in everyday life. This omnipresence of
God is the last and the greatest of the three secrets
referred to above and Sri Krishna expresses it in the words

सदसच्चाहमर्जुन

both the *Sat* and the *Asat* am I, O Arjuna. Though we
are accustomed to the expression that God is everywhere,
few of us pause to think in what way God is omnipresent.
There are difficulties connected with this idea of omnipresence. For instance one might ask : 'If God is
everywhere,' why do I not feel it, or argue, 'Since he is
everywhere, even my wicked thoughts are none but
His, and so on.' All this is said only to point out that
the above mentioned secrets are secrets though we are
accustomed to hear of them every day in our lives. It
is a great step in advance to know that they are secrets,
for that will lead us to enquire into their real meaning.

This enquiry can begin only with the help of the
Acharya who has realised the inner meaning and who
is in the position to put those who are anxious to know
the truth in the proper path. *Unaided effort can avail
little in that direction*, but when the master is sought
and obtained, one will be able to realise those truths for
oneself while with the body.

It is on account of these secrets one is required to
study the *Gita* under proper guidance. It is not a mere

theoretical book offering hypothetical solutions of the problems of life, but a practical one wherein the reader is asked to realise what is taught and see for himself whether it is true or not. When studied under a teacher, what appeared to be a bundle of tautologies and contradictions unfolds itself to view as a beautiful consistent whole, where idea follows idea in wonderful sequence and a grand philosophy is evolved in all its fulness, and the previously despair-filled, doubting and bewildered mind is feasted with a rich promise of boundless bliss where all things of mortality, finiteness and change will disappear, though the physical may appear to subsist as ever. It has been said that the *Gita* is a divine commentary upon the *Vedas*, but it is nearer the truth, as a great sage once remarked, *that it is divine compendium of the Srutis*. Every word in it stands for a number of texts and often a single expression epitomises a whole *Upanishad*. All this beauty can be perceived when only one studies it under a great *Acharya* who, besides teaching him the text, has initiated him into the mysteries and thereby placed him in an attitude at least to understand what is taught.

———— —— ——

IV

SYMBOLOGY

SYMBOLOGY

THE following are short notes on the various symbols of the Hindu Religion, like Sri Ranganatha, Nataraja, Dakshinamurti, and so on. The inner meaning of these symbols is often very grand and poetic and to enter into and understand it, will certainly be a privilege to those who are striving to realise for themselves the truths of philosophy; for these symbols were devised simply as helps to the imagination and many men have employed them with advantage. The meanings of these symbols differ of course according to the standpoint adopted and the highest, *viz.*, the *Vedantic* will be the one from which we shall study them.

NATARAJA

Nataraja means the Lord of the Stage. The idea is that the world is a stage, a puppet-show which presents the vision of life and activity through the power of the all-pervading *Atman* or God, the unseen Lord of the Stage. "Who will not dance when thou causest him to dance, and who will not sing when thou causest him to sing," says a poet-philosopher. But for the inner *Atman* all the world will be mere *Jada* (inert or dead).

The *Atman* of Self being the real teacher of the human mind, Nataraja is meant to represent the Teacher or *Guru*. There are two kinds of *Guru*—the apparent and the real, the seen and the unseen. The former is the teacher who instructs the disciple and takes him along the path—this is what we usually mean by the word *Guru*; but all teaching really comes from inside, not merely in the sense that the outward apparent teacher is but the instrument employed by *Atman* or God, but also in the sense that all growth is from within. The plant, for example, grows from within; the manure, water, etc., are simply helps to its growth. In the same way, the mind has to grow only from within, assimilating of course the teachings from outside. Nataraja then is the real *Guru* concretely represented. One of the functions of the *Guru* and perhaps the most important is to *be* what he teaches—to enforce his teachings by example. It is this idea that is the key-note to the Nataraja symbol.

The little drum in one of the right hands is meant to express the idea that God or *Guru* holds the cause of all the world, *i.e.*, sound (*Sabda Nishtam Jagad*—through sound the world stands) in his hand, in other words, all the world is in his hand, to be folded or unfolded at his own will. To the *Gnani* or wise man the world exists only if he chooses and not otherwise. The deer on one side is the mind, because the latter leaps and jumps from one thing to another as wildly as that animal. The *Atman* is far beyond the reach of the deer-like mind; and so the deer in the picture is placed near the legs. Nataraja wears the skin of a tiger which he himself slew. *Ahankara* or the skin of egoism is that tiger; it is beastly and ferocious and fiercely fights when attacked, but it has to be killed and Nataraja the *Guru* alone can kill it. On his head he wears the Ganges, *i.e., Chit Sakti* or wisdom which is most cool and refreshing and the moon which represents the ethereal light and blissfulness of the *Atman*. One foot is planted over and crushes the giant *Muyalaka, i.e., Maha Maya*, the endless illusion which is the cause of birth and death, while the other foot is raised upward and represents the '*turiya*' state, which is beyond and above the three states of waking, dream and dreamless sleep, and leaves behind, the mind, *Maya* and the world. The second right hand representing the idea of peace indicates the blessed calmness which is the glorious privilege of wisdom. In one of the left hands, is held *Agni* (fire), *i.e.,* the *Guru* brings in the *Jotis* of the *Atman* itself to attest the truth of his teaching. The idea is that the truth of the *Guru's* teaching can only be fully understood on practical realisation, in experience (*Anubhava*). The place of the dance, the theatre is *Thillaivanam, i.e.,* the body (of the individual as well as of the kosmos) spoken of as *vanam* or forest on account of the multitude of its components. The platform in that theatre is the cremation ground, *i.e.,* the place where all passions and the names and forms that constitute the vision of the world have been burnt away—pure consciousness devoid of attachment to anything outside and devoid of illusion.

The above are some of the leading features of the Nataraja symbol. The *Guru* teaches that *Maya*—illusion—should be crushed down, that the world should become subject to us and not we to the world, that the deer-like mind should be left behind, and *Ahankara* (egoism) be destroyed, and that man should ascend to the regions of pure, unconditioned consciousness free from passion and free from deception, and enjoy the calmness which is his birthright, the bliss, the light and the truth that form the Self. Viewed in the light of this inner meaning the image of Nataraja is no more a meaningless idol, a piece of stone or copper but a symbol of the highest teaching, an object that can inspire and elevate.

SESHASAYANAM

We have seen what Nataraja means. Philosophers as we are, even stones and copper are redolent to us with philosophy ; if we go on at this rate, all the world I dare say will get reduced to five elements just as the idol in the temple is composed of five metals ; and you will shortly leave even that idolatry, and proceed to find out the inner meaning of this grand symbol of the world, which is nothing but God, who is, as *Srutis* declare, subtler than the most subtle, greater than the greatest, firm like a tree and one without a second.

We shall now proceed to discuss the symbol as famous as that of Nataraja, *viz.*, Sri Ranganatha. Curiously enough there is simply a war of words in every land. The Muhammadan plucks out the beard of the Christian, who in his turn shoots him down, his turban and all, only because the latter says the true God is Allah, and the former Jehovah—the Father in Heaven. But those who are impartial will however

NATARAJA

SESHASAYAṆA

say, that Allah and Jehovah mean the same thing, and denote, the same Person—if person He be.

Ranganatha and Nataraja mean the very same thing, and refer to very nearly the same conception, only differently expressed. Nataraja is the lord of the stage, so also Ranganatha (*Ranga* means stage). The stage is the stage of the world, of the cosmos, or better still of the body and the senses. The one dances in Chidambaram, *i.e.*, the sphere of wisdom, the other sleeps on the milky sea.

We cannot sufficiently describe the glory of that conception, the poetry of the ocean of milk, the imagination of the mind that could have originally conceived it ; and the grandeur of the idea underlying it cannot be sufficiently done justice to here.

Our ancient fathers, however poor they might have been in ball-dresses, arm-chairs and steam-ships, have endowed us with the rich legacy of a silver rock, a gold mountain, a milky ocean, a heavenly river, a generous cow, a liberal tree, a white elephant, a heavenly father and a rich philosophy. We have, fortunately, down below, the Himalayas, the Ganges, etc., etc. In this grand group comes the milky sea.

The real inner meaning of this milky sea can only be learnt after approaching the *Guru* ; it is a practical affair, but there is no mystery in it. There is no attempt at organising any esoteric society. To give a glimpse as far as words will permit, the real milky sea is found out when the consciousness of the body is lost ; next, that of the mind ; and next, the idea of vacant space, which is a great hindrance in practical realisation. And the worlds of sun, moon and colours have all to be left

behind, then comes the real milky sea. The sweetness
of sugar can only be described as far as words will allow,
and not shown ; and no reader will get angry if I say
that sugar is sweet ; so, no reader, I trust, will get
offended with me for saying that the real milky sea is
glorious when seen ; that it is, to be as exact as words
will permit, the sweet undisturbed nectar-like calmness
that knows not the distinction of caste and creed, of
life and death, of freedom and slavery, of form and no
form, devoid of character and name, the calmness divine
and perfect that silently pervades all, and plays 'hide
and seek' with the ignorant, the serenity that is light,
that is grace, that is the ineffable, the effulgent *turiya*[1]
state which is beyond the maddened-monkey-like mind,
the highest of the high, which knows not union and
separation, or attachment, which knows not coming and
going, which is far and near, which is firm like a rock,
which fades not, which is beyond the five elements, which
is beyond even the consciousness of enjoyment, which
is neither one nor two, which is above the prating tongue
and the wandering mind, and which is an ocean of full,
undisturbed ecstasy : that is the real sea of milk. It
requires the grace of God and the blessings of the real
Guru to discover that sea. It is a treasure far beyond
the reach of the ambitious, the wicked, the avaricious
and the selfish, which is ever a secret refusing to unfold itself to the heart that falters or is false. 'Knock
and it shall be opened, seek and ye shall find.'

आदावन्ते च मध्ये च सृज्यासृज्यं यदन्वयात् ।
पुनस्तत्प्रतिसंक्रामे यच्छिष्येत तदेवसत् ॥

1 This fourth state as differentiated from the three stages of
waking, dreaming and sleeping.

नष्टे लोके द्विपरार्द्धावसाने महाभूतेष्वादिभूतं गतेषु ।
व्यक्तेऽव्यक्तं कालवेगेन याते भवानेकशिष्यते शेषसंज्ञ: ॥

The meaning of the above roughly translated is—

'From morn to eve and from eve to dewy morn'
That which envelops all the fourteen worlds,
The five elements, and ever shines in all ;
During the sleep in which all being lost,
That which remains unlost, that consciousness,
Is called the I or Self, and *Sesha* forms ;
Its inner light is Vishnu great, the Lord,
The love, the light, the sat, the bliss and strength.

Here is *Sesha* described but why the form of the huge
serpent ? The reason is that the serpent has been selected,
not the other snakes, by the common consent of
humanity, as an object of worship in all countries alike.
The outspread hood of the serpent, its fine ear for music
which men can never rival, with the fabled gem on its
head, its glossy and altogether beautiful appearance,
its faculty of hearing with the eyes, its comparative
innocence when not disturbed[1] and its real or reputed
allegiance to *mantras* and oaths—which we may call
serpent-honesty, its intelligence and aptitude, when
trained, to besmear human eyes with eye-salve, to mark
the human face with sandal, etc., gently and cautiously,
and several other fine qualities in it, might have contributed to the universal worship accorded to it. Few
countries have been free from the serpent fetichism.
Among the Scythians it was God itself ; and among the
Hindus it has been raised to the rank of an ornament

1 There are serpents domesticated in houses which live and
move about freely, but never interfere with the inmates.

to the Lord *Iswara*, symbolising the intelligent human consciousness.

Even a higher honour was in store for it ; traditions assert that there are five-headed serpents, more beautiful and harmless, and having a beautiful *Nagaratna* (a precious gem of most wonderful virtues) and wandering in the forests like the *Rishis*. There is a legend which tells us that Hyder Ali, previous to his Nawabdom, was a poor boy, found sleeping under a shady tree beautifully sheltered by a long five-hooded serpent, which had curled its body round and round, making a seat for itself to a height of about 3 ft. and fully spreading its hoods over the born emperor, with rich jewel shining brighter than diamonds and rubies, and casting its full lustre upon the beardless face of the orphan boy. Well, if five-hooded serpents are possible here, why not a thousand shining gems in the beautiful sea of milk, especially if it would serve as a grand and true symbol ? The serpent, we saw, represents the consciousness, and consciousness is above, below and everywhere—where is it and where is it not ? It is in the star above, in the stone below, in the waters that flow, in man, in animal, plant and stone. This consciousness 'sleeps in the plant, dreams in the animal and wakes in man'. The sun is the same all over the earth : the dead stone like an ignorant man receives that light, but in its dull way : the waters shine in the light, but reflect it not ; mirrors like blessed souls, not merely shine themselves, but also make others shine. This *Sesha*, then, which is everywhere manifest or unmanifest, is symbolised by that beautiful serpent. Besides, its infinite coils, all its huge beauty represent the infinity of that consciousness, its omnipresence and the eternity of that splendour. This consciousness, is the *Sesha* beyond all name and form—beyond time,[1] space and causality. (*Sesha* means what remains when all else is lost ; the undying, the infinite and eternal). It is on the milky sea necessarily ; for until the heavenly calm of the inner soul is realised, the beauty of the universal consciousness cannot be seen.

Vishnu the great God sleeps upon the smooth glossy bed of the serpent-back, it is a wonderful sleep however ; for, it is sleep without its darkness, it is the sleep, not of ignorance and dulness, but a sleep of light—a knowing sleep as it has been called. The idea is that God pervades all the universe 'the atom, the roaring sea, the mountain-chains and all,' but Himself like the sun, unstained by the war of the world. The sleeping means '*Urdhvapurnam adhahpurnam madhyapurnam*,' filling the above, the below, the middle, as the *Uttara-Gita* says ; and as the posture is a lying one without North or East or South or West, He fills the world 'from the tip of the nail to the top of the head,' as *Nakhasikhaparyantam, etc.*, of the *Brih.-Upa.*, means. No clouds can pollute Him, no sin can attach to him, no grief can enter into Him.

Tasya kartaramapi   mamviddyakartaramavyayam.

Gita, Iv, 13.

Though I am the Lord of creation, as I work without attachment, no action clings to me, said Sri Krishna. So, the great Lord of the universe is in knowing sleep, as the sun, to compare small things with great, though he inspires a multitude of actions, is yet himself free

1 This *Sesha* or *Ananta* is often represented as infinite time but the meaning of the *Smriti* quoted above goes beyond time even.

from them. But then this abstract God, the inner light
of consciousness, the *Atman*, pervades the whole universe,
and is everything, even the illusion of phenomena included; and now descending to the phenomenal
platform, the *Vyavaharika Satta*, as it is called—we find
creation is real, and the same abstract *Brahman* is our
father in Heaven, our punisher and rewarder. Ranganatha, as we have already seen, means the Lord of the
stage, and in the beautiful conception of the milky sea
is treasured up the whole range of philosophy, as "Homer
in a nutshell". From the abstract *Atman* to the personal God, the father and Creator, the whole range is
involved in it; for what are *Vishnu's* ornaments?—
the *Kaustubha* gem in his broad breast, the *Srivatsa*
mark on his forehead, he *conch-shell*, the *bow* and the
discus in his hands; the *Vaijayanti*, composed of five
precious gems, pearl, ruby, emerald, sapphire and
diamond, which adorns his breast. He has a rich store
of powerful shafts and a bright sword called *Achyuta*.
For an authoritative explanation of these symbols, we
have great pleasure in referring the reader to *Vishnu
Purana*—(Book I, Chapter 22).

The *Kaustubha* gem beautifully represents the pure
and everlasting soul of the world. The *pradhana* being
the chief principle of things, is very well placed as the
Srivatsa mark on the forehead of the Lord. Intellect
is the faculty that shelters us against the arrows in the
war of life and is therefore fittingly compared to the
mace (*Gada*). Even our egotism, the delusive habitual
self, which divides itself into the elements, the organs
of sense and all their numerous progeny, is very well
represented as *Isa's* conch-shell and bow; the former

makes noise, and creation being due to vibration—
Sabdanishtam jagat—the conch-shell represents the great
function of creation ; the bow very well represents the
organs of sense ; for, like the latter, they go in search
of things, and are the faculties of grasping like the bow.
But both the conch-shell and the bow (that is, creation
and enjoyment—the whole world is described as the
Lord's *lila* or sport) must have their basis on *Ahankara*
(egotism), the primary delusion of self. As Narada
beautifully said to Sanatkumara : "If there be *I*, then
there must be *you*. There then begins the mischief.
If there be *I* and *you*, then there must be all the world."
The *discus* (*Chakra*) symbolises the mind, which shames
the speed of the winds and the swiftness of the lightning.
The universe composed of five elements is a beautiful
ornament—the necklace *Vaijayanti*—to *Vishnu* the
Protector, for nothing better expresses His grandeur
and glory, who rules day and night, though sleeping, this
vast, infinite and apparently conglomerate household
of suns, moons and stars, and clouds and winds and
waters.

The sharp faculties of action and perception are
very well likened to the shafts which fly from the bow
of the senses and intellect. Wisdom is a veritable sword,
which fells down the grand tree of *Aswattha*, which
changes every moment (*Aswattha*, means that which is
not next moment), and is at the same time eternal,
because *Maya* or delusion is eternal, which has its roots
in that Supreme Lord Narayana who is sounding his
conch-shell of creation. The *Vedas* are the leaves of
this tree, because they shelter the tree from the sun
and other things. The intellect forms the branches

26

from the main trunk, and *Ahankara* (Egoism) the five elements and the deceitful organs of sense are its branches, and the senses are holes in it. Virtue and vice are its flowers ; and joy and grief are its fruits. It is the tree on which all souls live. (For a fuller explanation please refer to *Gita*, XV, 1, 2 and 3, and the elaborate commentaries on the same by Sankara, Ramanuja, Madhva and Sridhara ; and *Katha-Upa.*, II, 61).

As Madhva has beautifully said, this grand tree of *Samsara*, which has its branches in Heaven, Earth, and everywhere should be bravely felled down by the sword of wisdom—*Achyuta* of Narayana. This sword however is most often concealed in the scabbard of ignorance ; and we people are therefore going round the tree, instead of felling it down ; but even this ignorance is nothing but Narayana, for the *Vedas* proclaim that it is merely a sport, a *lila* of Hrishikesa.

Wilson, referring to this grand symbol in his translation of the *Vishnu Purana*, Book I, Chapter 22, which we strongly recommend our readers to see, says : "We have in the text a representation of one mode of *Dhyana* or contemplation, in which the thoughts are more readily concentrated, by being addressed to a sensible emblem, instead of an abstract truth. Thus, the *Yogin* here says to himself : 'I meditate upon the jewel on *Vishnu's* brow as the soul of the world ; and upon the gem on his breast as the first principle of things' ; and so on ; and thus, through a perceptible substance, proceeds to an imperceptible idea." Lakshmi of course represents the pomp, the luxuriance of the world, the Lord's glory or *Vibhuti*, as it is termed—the *Samsara adambara* or *Jagajjala vaibhava*, the great never-ending festival of illusory existence (*Maya* as it is called)—She sits near the feet, *i.e.*, the *Avidya pada*, *i.c.*, the sphere of ignorance, for ignorance is the mother of creation and the world.

That the *Seshasayana* symbol is no mere idolatry is further attested by the following extract from *Vishnu Purana*—Book I, Chap. XXII : "The Supreme eternal Hari is time, with its divisions of seconds, minutes, days, months, seasons, and years. He is the 'seven worlds, ...First born before all the first-born ; the supporter of all beings, himself self-sustained ; who exists in manifold forms, as gods, men, and animals, and is thence the sovereign Lord of all, eternal ; whose shape is all visible things ; who is without shape or form ; who is celebrated, in the *Vedanta*, as the four *Vedas*, inspired history, and sacred science. The *Vedas*, and their divisions ;......religious manuals and poems, etc., are the body of the mighty Vishnu......I am Hari, All that I behold is Hari. Cause and effect are from none other than Him. The man who knows these truths shall never again experience the afflictions of worldly existence."

V

THE IMITATION OF VYASA

THE IMITATION OF VYASA

[Under this title will appear such short stories, fables, anecdotes, sayings and the like, ancient and modern, as are worthy of the memory of the great Father of the *Puranas* whose genius delighted in combining instruction with amusement. No originality is claimed for any of these and the greater number are in the words of others.]

1. **Man never alone.——**

> Thou thinkest : I am single and alone,
> Perceiving not the great eternal Sage,
> Who dwells within thy breast. Whatever wrong
> Is done by thee, he sees and notes it all.
>
> *——The Mahabharata.*

> Heaven, Earth, and Sea, Sun, Moon, and Wind, and Fire
> Day, Night, the Twilights, and the Judge of Souls,
> The God of justice and the Heart itself,
> All see and note the conduct of a man.
>
> *——Ibid.*

2. **What is the nature of God.——**A certain philosopher was once asked what the nature of God was. He wanted three days to think over the question. On the fourth day the question was repeated and the sage asked for three days more. After that time the question was again asked and the sage wanted another three days and at last said in reply : "The more I think of Him, the more indescribable He becomes."

3. Tit for tat.—A Christian missionary was preaching to a crowd in India. Among other sweet things, he was telling the people that if he gave a blow to their idol with his stick, what could it do? One of his hearers sharply answered : "If I abuse your God what can he do?" "You would be punished," said the preacher, "when you die." "So my idol will punish you when you die," said the villager.

4. Love God for love's sake.—The virtuous King Yudhishtira was driven from his throne by his enemies and had to take shelter in a forest in the Himalayas with his queen ; and there, one day Draupadi asked him how it was that he should suffer so much misery and yet love God, and Yudhishtira answered : "Behold, my queen, the Himalayas how beautiful they are ; I love them. They do not give me anything, but my nature is to love the grand, the beautiful and therefore I love them. Similarly, I love the Lord. He is the source of all beauty, of all sublimity. He is the only object to be loved ; my nature is to love Him, and therefore I love. I do not pray for anything ; I do not ask for anything. Let him place me wherever He likes. I must love Him for love's sake. I cannot trade in love."

5. A story of Emerson.—One day as Theodore Parker and Ralph Waldo Emerson were walking, in concord, a man, greatly excited rushed up to them saying : "The world is very near an end." "Well my friend," said Emerson, "suppose the world is coming to an end, I suppose I can get along without it."

How few could say this with confidence, particularly in an age in which "the world is too much with us."

6. Where is God.—A certain school boy said to another : "Brother, if you tell me where God is, I shall give you a mango." The latter replied : "I shall give you two mangoes, if you tell me where God is not."

7. Transmigration.—Muhammad Sharif looking at some large blocks of stone lying about near his house, exclaimed with a sigh : "All these helpless things are only waiting to assume human form."

8. A simile.—There are three dolls—the first made of salt, the second made of cloth and the third made of stone. If these dolls be immersed in water, the first will get dissolved and lose its form : the second will absorb a large quantity of water and retain its form : while the third will be wholly impervious to the water. The first doll represents the man who merges his self in the universal and all-pervading Self becomes one with it. The second represents a true lover of God, who is full of Divine bliss and knowledge and the third represents a worldly man who will not admit even the least trace of true knowledge.

9. The Siddhis.—A Yogi went to a sage and claimed that he could fly in the air, remain underground for months together, lie on the surface of water and perform such other wonderful feats. The sage coolly replied : "Brother, birds fly in the air, worms lie concealed under the earth for years and fish live in water. What merit is there in your doing what the lower animals do. Try and imitate God, become divine in your love for others, in wisdom and humility. Above all, leave off vanity.

10. The mystery of creation.—One night three opium-smokers were standing by the side of a river.

The reflection of a light from the opposite bank was playing with the ripples in the river, and thus making the light appear to be burning in it. All of them wanted to smoke and for that purpose desired to ignite a piece of charcoal to put it upon the pipe. One man just went to the brink of the water and there held out the charcoal thinking it to have reached the light, for opium-smokers see distant things as though swimming before their eyes. But staying for a while in that position, he found that the charcoal was not ignited and went back to his companions thinking the light to have lost its heat. Then one of them rebuked him for his folly, saying that every one who had eyes could plainly see that the fire was in the river just where the water was knee-deep, and he snatched the charcoal from his hand and went into the stream where it was knee-deep, and there held out the charcoal just before him fully believing that it would soon be ignited ; but unfortunately he also had to come back concluding that the fire had grown cold in coming in contact with the water. Then the third man rebuked his two companions saying : "Well friends, strange it is that you have become so foolish. Why can you not see that the light is just in the middle of the river ?" So saying he went into the river with the charcoal in hand and proceeded until the water reached the arm-pits and there held it towards the seeming fire, till, shivering with cold, he had to return unsuccessful, just as his other companions had done. Similar is the case with our knowledge of the creation of the universe. We think ourselves to be wiser than our ancestors, simply because we know a greater number of facts than they did : but this only makes the matter more intricate. Our limited mind will always remain ignorant of the mystery of the limitless creation.

11. A Strange Teaching.—Bahva, being questioned about *Brahman* by Vashkalin said : "Learn *Brahman*, O friend" and became silent. Vashkalin waited a long time for a reply, but seeing nothing coming forth questioned Bahva a second and a third time, and at last the latter said : "I am teaching you indeed, but you do not understand. Silence (*Mauna*) is that *Brahman*."

12. Truth.—Once on a time a thousand Horse-sacrifices and Truth were weighed against each other in the balance ; and the latter weighed much heavier than the former. Truth is the highest refuge ; Truth is duty ; Truth is penance ; Truth is *Yoga* ; and Truth is the eternal *Brahman*.

13. Bargaining with God.—There was a certain great king who went to hunt in a forest, and there he happened to meet a sage. He had a little conversation with this sage and became so pleased with him that he asked him to accept a present from him. "No," says the sage, "I am perfectly satisfied with my condition : these trees give me enough fruit to eat ; these beautiful pure streams supply me with all the water I want ; I sleep in these caves. What do I care for your presents, though you be an emperor." The emperor says : "Just to purify myself, to gratify me, take some presents and come with me into the city." At last the sage consented to go with this emperor, and he was brought into the emperor's palace, wherein were gold and jewellery, and marble and most wonderful things. Wealth and power were manifest in this palace, and there that poor sage from the forest was ushered in. The emperor asked him to wait a minute while he repeated his prayer, and he went into a corner and began to pray : "Lord give me more wealth, more children, more territory." In the meanwhile the sage got up, and began to walk away. The emperor saw him going, and went after him. "Stay, Sir, you did not take my present and are going away." The sage turned round to him and said : "Beggar, I do not beg of beggars. What can you give? you have been begging yourself all the time." What is the difference between Love and Shop-keeping, if you ask God to give you this and give you that?

14. The tree of Samsara.—It grows upon *Brahman* as its root, out of the world-fiction *Maya* as its seed. It is an *Asvattha* (holy fig) tree, liable to destruction every moment, rooted above and branching below. It is watered by the cravings of migrating souls whose actions through the Law of Karma prolong the existence of the spheres of metampsychoses. Its trunk is *Buddhi*, the senses are its hollows ; the Great Elements its boughs, the sense-objects its leaves and twigs, *Dharma* and *Adharma* its blossoms and its fruits are the pleasures and pains of living things. The spheres of recompense are the nests in which gods and migrating souls dwell like birds. It rustles with the cries, the weeping, and the laughter, of the souls in pain or for the moment happy. Though so huge and eternal in its nature, it is unreal like the waters of a mirage and vanishes in the light of intuition of the one and only Truth, the Self beyond it.

15. Wanting God.—A certain old man used to go to the temple and pray for a very long time that God may be pleased to take him to His holy feet. Everyday he would stand for a number of hours after all others had left the temple and beg to be absorbed in the Deity with tears flowing from his eyes by force of habit. He fancied himself to be a very pious man and to excel even saints in his devotion. By his tarrying so long in the temple everyday (he) caused considerable inconvenience to the temple priest, who felt that his devotion was insincere and wanted to put an end to his practice. For this purpose, one day while the old man was standing begging and weeping, the priest hid himself behind the image of God and suddenly cried in a strange unearthly tone : "Come here, thou old man, I shall absorb thee. Come at once." The old man thought that it was God that was speaking and ran away frightened lest he might be swallowed up by Him. From that day forward not merely did he never stop into the temple, but was afraid to be alone even in his house, and would not sleep unless in the midst of several persons for fear that the wicked God might steal him away all at once. Ah! How many of us want God in this fashion!

16. From Heaven to Hell.—King Yayati was admitted into Heaven on account of the numerous acts of self-sacrifice and virtue which he did while on earth. There he saw the famous Kalpaka tree, *Kama Dhenu* the Divine cow, *Chintamani* the rare jewel, and diverse other wonderful things. There the divine damsels paid court to him, and Narada and other celestial *Rishis* eulogised him on his newly acquired happiness. Seeing all this the king felt conceited, thinking that he had acquired Heaven by means of his ability and merit and that were few others equal to him. This idea no sooner entered into his head than he found himself in Hell amidst a multitude of tortured souls.

17. From Hell to Heaven.—King Vidheha was being led to Heaven by the servants of Yama, the God of Death. On his way he saw innumerable souls suffering in Hell and crying for help. He was very much moved at this miserable sight and addressing his conductor said : "I shall stay here rather than go to Heaven while so many poor souls are being tortured here in this fashion. Leave me alone and go." They went and reported the matter to Yama. At once he himself came down and accosting the king said : "Thy virtues, Oh king, are innumerable, so that I myself have come down to take thee to Heaven. This is not a fit place for thee to stay in. Come up with me to Heaven." The king replied : "It is selfish to seek my happiness while so many of my brethren are suffering. If my virtues avail anything let them go to these my brethren, and let me suffer here in their place." Hardly did he speak thus, when Yama disappeared and Hell stood transformed into Heaven and all its denizens metamorphosed into Gods.

18. A Wonder.—Under a banyan tree there sit a *Guru* and four disciples ; the *Guru* is young but the disciples are very old ; the *Guru* teaches by silence and the disciples have all their doubts cleared. The scene of which Sri Sankaracharya speaks in these words is familiar to every Hindu. The *Guru* is Lord Dakshinamurti and the four disciples Sanaka, Sanandana, Sanatana, and Sanatkumara who were created to teach the *Nivritti Dharma* (Renunciation) to the world. The latter are old and the former young because ignorance (*Ajnana*) is much older than wisdom (*Jnana*). It is in illustration of this truth that child Skanda—Bala

Subrahmanya—is represented as vanquishing the Rakshasa Sura who was many millions of years old.

19. The Great Beyond.—There is no reply in *words* to the question what is in the great Beyond? nor can there be.

20. Self-Sacrifice.—After the battle of Kurukshetra, the five Pandava brothers held a great sacrifice and made very large gifts to the poor. All the people expressed their wonder at the greatness and magnificence of the sacrifice and said that such a sacrifice the world had never seen before. But, after the ceremony, there came a little mungoose; half his body was golden, and the other half was brown, and he began to roll himself on the floor of the sacrificial hall. Then he said, to those around : "You are all liars ; this is no sacrifice." "What," they exclaimed, "you say this is no sacrifice ; do you not know how money and jewels were poured out upon the poor, and every one became rich and happy ? This was the most wonderful sacrifice any man ever made." But the mungoose said : "There was once a little village, and in it there dwelt a poor Brahmin with his wife, son and son's wife. They were very poor and dined on alms gained in preaching and teaching for which men made little gifts to them. There came in that land a three years' famine, and the poor Brahmin suffered more than ever. For five days together the family starved, and on the sixth the father brought home a little barley flour, which he had been fortunate enough to find and he divided it into four parts, one for each of them. They prepared it for their meal and just as they were about to eat it a knock came at the door. The father opened it and there stood a guest. A guest being sacred and god for the time being, the poor Brahmin, said : 'Come in, sir, you are welcome,' and set before him his own portion of food ; and the latter quickly ate it up and said : 'Oh, sir, you have killed me ; I have been starving for ten days and this little bit has but increased my hunger.' Then the wife said to her husband : 'Give him my share,' but the husband said : 'Not so.' The wife however insisted, saying : 'Here is a poor man, and it is our duty as house-holders to see that he is fed, and it is my duty as a wife to give him my portion seeing that you have no more to offer him.' Then she gave him her share and he ate it up and said he was still burning with hunger. So the son said : 'Take my portion also ; it is the duty of a son to help his father to fulfil his obligations.' The guest ate that, but still remained unsatisfied. So the son's wife gave him her portion also. That was sufficient and the guest departed blessing them.

"That night those four people died of starvation. A few grains of the flour had fallen on the floor and when I rolled my body on them half of it became golden, as you see it. Since then, I have been all over the world hoping to find another sacrifice like that, but never have I found one and so the other half of my body has not been turned into gold. That is why I say this is no sacrifice."

21. Imitation and Reality.—A certain man had the peculiar power of grunting exactly like a pig, so much so that whenever he grunted where pigs were grazing, they would all turn round to see if any new member had come into their fold. This man's fame spread abroad and he began a tour to obtain money by means of his art. Wherever he went he erected a pandal and issued tickets for admission, all of which got exhausted very soon—such was the eagerness of people to hear him grunt. While he was thus making money in a village, a sage happened to pass by with his disciples, and it struck him that he could teach a good lesson to them through this incident. Accordingly he ordered a small pandal to be erected and advertised that even better grunting could be heard there than in the other pandal and that free of cost. The people were naturally very eager to hear it and they rushed in. What did the sage do? He brought a pig before them and squeezing it a little, made it grunt. Really the grunt was much better than the man's, but the people exclaimed : "Pooh, is this all? We hear this every day, but what is there in it? It is nothing wonderful" and went away. In spite of the loud tom-tom which he engaged not one would enter his pandal, while that of the man-pig was crowded to suffocation every few minutes. After all the people had left his pandal, the sage addressed his disciples and said : "Here is a splendid lesson for us. Men seldom care for reality but always go in for imitation. That is why this world exists which is a mere imitation, a reflection in the distorting mirror of *Maya*, of the great *Atman*. No external help is required to see the Self ; but very few want It and even if you eagerly advertise It, none will go to you except those who love Truth for Truth's sake. Reflect on this."

22. Going round the World.—Iswara seated with Parvati, once called to Him His two sons Ganapati and Subrahmanya, and addressing them, said : "I have a rare fruit in my possession and shall give it to that one

of you, who goes round the world and returns to me
first." Subrahmanya, eager to win the prize, started
on his peacock at once, which flew with its Divine
burden quicker than lightning, while Ganapati sat quiet—
until His brother disappeared out of sight and then
slowly rising, went round His parents and asked for the
fruit saying : "All the worlds that are, that were, and
that will be, are within you, and by going round you,
I have gone round all of them. Therefore the fruit is
mine." Parvati and Parameswara were delighted with
the reply and gave Him the precious fruit. Long after
this was over, Subrahmanya came sweating on his peacock
only to find that He had been outwitted.

The story should not be taken literally. It is the
philosophy in it which is essential.

The lesson briefly stated is, that God being known,
everything else is known and no study of the external
world, however comprehensive that may be, can ever
yield us the precious fruit of wisdom. "Knowledge of
course will come, but wisdom with its peace and bliss
will linger on the shore."

23. The Value of Books.—Once upon a time there
was a meeting of *Rishis* on Kailas. They had met for
obtaining a view of God Parameswara. While they
were waiting, a *Rishi* came in, loaded with a cart-load
of books. He had books in his hands, on his shoulders,
on his back and on his head. The books were all very
valuable, and he had a passionate love for them. At
his entrance in this strange manner, the other *Rishis*
burst out in a laugh, and when he asked them why, one
of them said : "God will never appear unto you, so long
as you are addicted to book-learning. Here is a learning

which is not in books and which indeed is the unlearning of all that you have learnt, and until you get that, you cannot see God." The *Rishi* felt the truth of the advice and threw all his books into the sea; at once, the story adds, God appeared in their midst.

24. The Great Samsari.—God Maheswara once came home very late, and Parvati, the blessed Mother, asked Him where He had been all the while. And He replied: "I had been to give food to my children, who are innumerable and fill all the worlds." Parvati asked: "Art Thou the real feeder of all the mouths in the universe, the sustainer even of the worms and the ants?" "Yes," replied the Lord and there the matter ended. Next day the blessed Mother hid an ant in a cocoanut shell and carefully concealed it in her lap; and when the Lord returned after having measured out nourishment to all creatures, asked him if He had done the day's work and if all souls had been fed without exception. The Lord replied, "yes" but Parvati triumphantly took out the cocoanut shell and said: "There is at least one creature, which your munificence has not reached." Siva however replied: "First look into the shell and then speak." She did so, but what was her surprise when she found that the little ant had in its mouth a fresh rice grain which was more than enough for its need. At once Parvati fell at the feet of the Lord, "Thou mighty Ruler of the worlds, Thou art the blessed fountain of love and mercy, Thy charity is universal and in the fulness of Thy grace, Thou neglectest not the tiniest worm that crawls the earth; and who could sing the glory of Thy grace and the motherly care Thou takest of the creatures below?"

Thus the Gitacharya has said : "I am the father ·of this world, the mother, the supporter and the grand sire, the knowable, the purifier, the syllable *Aum* and also the *Rik*, the *Sama* and the *Yajus*" (IX, 17).

25. What is there in Him?—A certain *Mumukshu* (seeker after salvation) was going to his *Guru* with offerings in his hand, when a self-styled *Yogi*, a pretentious and peevish man, came to him and said : "Your *Guru* knows nothing, you are a fool and he is a bigger fool ; he cannot work any miracles, cannot walk on water, nor fly in the air, nor lie buried in earth, as I can do. He knows nothing, why do you waste your time in going to him. He is an idiot and an impostor." The wise *Mumukshu* heard these words and calmly replied : "I go to him because he does not speak ill of others, nor. gets angry, which I consider the greatest of miracles." The *soi dissant Yogi* felt the force of the reply and went away abashed.

26. A Good Story.—Moses in his wanderings in the wilderness, came upon a shepherd, who was praying to God in the fervour of his soul and saying : "O My master, my Lord, would that I knew where I might find Thee and become Thy servant ; would that I might tie Thy shoe latchet and comb Thy hair and wash Thy robes and kiss Thy beautiful feet and sweep Thy chamber, and serve the milk of my goats to Thee for whom my heart crieth out." And the anger of Moses was kindled and he said to the shepherd : "Thou blasphemest. The most High has no body, no need of clothing nor of nourishment nor of a chamber nor of a domestic. Thou art an infidel" ; and the heart of the shepherd was darkened, for he could make to himself no image of one without a bodily form and corporeal wants, and he gave himself up to despair and ceased to serve God. Then God spake unto Moses and said : "Why hast Thou driven the servant away from me. Every man has received from me his mode of being, his way of speech. Words are nothing to Me, I regard the heart."

So said the Lord in the *Gita* : "In whatever form men worship Me, in that same form I appear unto them."

27. A Text and a Commentary.—There were five men, students of a certain sage who regarded themselves as very learned. One day they went to a village where they saw a quiet-looking man in rather humble circumstances. In the course of a conversation in which they displayed all their learning, the villager remarked : "One must truly die and the death of one's self is the real *Mukti* (salvation)." The learned *Vedantins* did not understand the remark and almost ridiculed the idea. However they stayed with him the whole day and took their night's rest in his house. That same night it so happened, that thieves entered the house and were carrying away the little property that was there. The visitors woke up by the noise and roused their host from what they thought his sleep. The latter rose, and in spite of their tumultuous exhortations to run after the thieves' and arrest them, remained unconcerned as if it were somebody else's house that was plundered. His conduct appeared to them as even more absurd than his remark during the day, and the next day, when they went to their *Guru*, they reported the whole matter to him, and he said : "Friends, his conduct in the night is the commentary on the text which he gave out in the day, namely, that the death of the self is the real

Mukti.'' So saying, he took his disciples along with him and paid his respects to the village gentleman whose philosophy was not mere theory but practice in daily life.

28. Right Learning.—Dharmaputra, while a boy, was taught along with other boys in school a primary reader which was full of moral precepts. The first two of these precepts were "Wish to do good" and "The one thing to be subdued is anger." The language was very simple and all the other boys learned the whole book by rote and recited all its contents to their teacher. But Dharmaputra could not proceed beyond the above two precepts. The teacher got angry with him and said : "Dull boy, the book is so very easy, that I am surprised to find you have not been able to go through it, while all the other boys know it by heart." Yudhisthira replied : "I have not yet fully understood even the first two precepts and they have not yet come into my practice, and so I am not able to proceed to learn the rest."

29. A Sharp Reply.—A gentleman in prosperous circumstances and with bright prospects before him, carelessly remarked : *"Vedanta,* they say, is a very grand philosophy, but somehow it does not enter into my head." A friend who sat by, sharply replied : "What has now happened to you that you should study *Vedanta."* The *Vedanta* is not meant for those who are intoxicated with the fancied pleasures of life, but for those who have realised their vanity and hollowness.

30. The Glory of Mental Worship.—A certain king had built a magnificent temple in honour of God Vishnu, and fixed a day for opening it in a grand, regal style. He had set apart a fabulous amount of money for the celebration of the *Kumbhabhishekam* ceremony and was arranging to send invitations to all the people of the neighbouring kingdom and their *Rajahs*, when God appeared to him in his dream and said : "A poor potter has built for me a temple in his heart and is going to dedicate it to me on the very day which you have fixed for the opening of your temple. Do you, therefore, choose some other day, for I cannot disoblige my great *Bhakta*." The king woke in the morning and reflecting upon his dream said to himself : "The poor potter's imaginary temple is much more sacred and dear to God than mine, of which I was so foolishly proud. Ah ! How much greater is *Bhakti* than wealth." So thinking, he went to the potter, and falling at his feet requested to be adopted as his disciple.

31. God in Everything.—Sage Kabir Das had a piece of bread and ghee ready for his dinner and was about to sit at the table, when suddenly a dog came running to the spot and taking the bread in its mouth ran away. The *Bhakta* at once ran after it with the ghee in his hand crying : "O Lord, dry bread is not good, is not palatable without ghee. Kindly deign to take this also." And he fed the dog with the bread soaked in ghee and himself went away without dinner. To him the very dog was God. Ah ! The glory of such love !

32. Where is God.—The enraged Hiranya said to his son Prahlada : "Where, O fool, is that God of whom you are so enamoured and whose meaningless names you incessantly repeat like a mad man ?" The boy sage replied : "To me, whatever I see is God, whatever I hear is God, whatever I smell is God, whatever I touch is God, whatever I taste is God, whatever I feel is He and none else, though to your dull eyes He is nowhere."

33. The Efficacy of Prayer.—Two men were travelling on the same road. One of them was a sceptic and the other a *Bhakta*. On their way they came across a ruined temple when the *Bhakta* piously went round it three times while the other contemptuously stood aside. As chance would have it, a thorn stuck into the foot of the former in the course of his pious circuit round the temple way, while the latter was rewarded for his impiety with a piece of silver coin which lay just before him on the ground. The *Bhakta* returned limping and joined his companion, who, showing his find, ridiculed him for his thankless piety. The *Bhakta* felt the irony of the thing and exclaimed : "There seems to be no God, otherwise such absurdities would not take place" ; just then a sage appeared on the spot and noticing that one was laughing while the other was almost weeping, inquired and learnt what the matter was and then addressing the sceptic said : "Your *karma* has ordained for you at this moment a rich treasure but on account of your impiety you got only a silver piece." Then turning to the *Bhakta* he said : "In this bad hour you might have been bitten by a serpent, but because of your pious act you got off so lightly." The explanation satisfied both and they went their way, the one confirmed in his *Bhakti*, the other regretting his scepticism.

34. Going to Heaven.—There was in the Tamil land a poetess of the name Auvaiyar, of whom the following story is told. Two of her friends were going to Kailas and invited her also. But she was engaged just then in the worship of Ganesa, and, saying that she could not go with them, did the *pujas* leisurely as usual. Lord Ganesa was pleased, and, as soon as the *puja* ended, lifted her in his mighty arm and placed her in Kailas long before her companions reached it. The story need not be taken literally, but it is the meaning that is important.

35. Our Religious Differences.—Four men, an Arab, a Persian, a Turk, and a Greek, agreed to club together for an evening meal; but when they had done so, they quarrelled as to what it should be. The Turk proposed Azum; the Arab, Aneb; the Persian, Anghur; while the Greek insisted on Slaphylion. While they were thus disputing, before their eyes passed a gardener's ass laden with grapes. At once every one of them sprang to his feet and pointed with eager hand to that purple load, "See Azum," said the Turk; "see Anghur," said the Persian; "what should be better, my Aneb, Aneb, it is," cried the Arab. The Greek said "this is my Slaphylion." They then brought their grapes and ate them in peace. The fight amongst them was simply one of words. Hence realise Oh, man! The sublime words of the *Rigveda*—"That which exists is one; the sages call it variously."

36. A King and a Sage.—King Vijayaranga Chokkalinga of Trichinopoly once presented the great sage Thayumanavar with a costly shawl which he specially got for the purpose from Cashmere. The sage accepted the gift and blessed the king. Of course, he did not attach that value to the shawl the king did, and one day he found a poor pariah woman all in rags and suffering from cold and gave away the shawl to her. The poor woman feared to take it, but Thayumanavar urged it

upon her most imploringly and made her accept it.
Report at once reached the king that the sage had insulted him by giving away so costly a present made with
his own hands, to a dirty pariah woman ; and he, as
might be expected, got exceedingly offended with the
sage and ordered him to be brought to him bound hand
and foot. Thayumanavar took this treatment in the
same spirit and with the same equanimity of mind as
he did the shawl and when the angry king asked him :
"Where is the shawl I gave you ?" he coolly replied :
"I gave it to mother Akhilandeswari (the divine mother
of the vast universe). She blesses you for it." The
king got at once ashamed of his conduct and begged
the sage's pardon.

To the real sage, everything he sees, everything he
hears, everything he does, is God. *Yadyatpasyati
chakshurbhyam tattadatmeti bhavayeth*—whatever he sees
with the eye is to Him God—says the *Sruti*. Who in
the king's eye was a pariah woman, was in the sage's
eye, none but Akhilandeswari.

37. Fate Inevitable.—It was mid-night. A dim oil-
lamp was giving light to a low-built hut in the village
of Subarnapur in Lower Bengal. The occupants of
the hut, a young Brahmin and his spouse, were locked
up in the fond arms of profound slumber. With a sudden
start the husband awoke and found a straw from the
thatch falling down on the floor. In the twinkling of an
eye the straw changed into a cobra-decapello, and bit
the sleeping wife, who groaned and died in consequence.
The Brahmin was very much astonished at this curious
incident. Leaving the cremation of his wife to his
relations, he followed the reptile, which in an instant

left the hut. After crawling a few yards, the snake turned into a jackal and killed a boy who had just come out of a house. The jackal then left that village and entered into another village and was transformed into a mad dog and killed two pedestrians. The Brahmin was silently following this wonderful creature and watching its movements unseen. He had resolved to see it to the very end.

Now it was morning; the great orb of the day was appearing in the eastern horizon. The hitherto sleeping nature was reviving to fresh animation. The mad dog again changed shape, and turned into a big buffalo and gored to death some more persons. This being done, it left that place and took the Grand Trunk Road, and after proceeding a few miles changed into a beauteous damsel of sixteen and sat under the cooling shade of a *Bar* tree. It so happened that two up-country Rajput brothers were returning home by this road after their long service in Upper Bengal. No sooner did the female figure met their eyes, than they were enamoured of her beauty. Both went near the charming damsel and the elder brother enquired her of her whereabouts, but ere she had answered his questions, she said she was dying with thirst and wanted a glass of water. The elder brother hastened to the nearest well with his *lota* and *duri*, and asked the younger to take care of the stranger in his absence. In a few minutes the elder returned with a *lota* of water, but was amazed to find that the girl was beating her breast, tearing her hair and crying piteously. The girl in a bewailing tone informed the elder Rajput that his brother had attempted to ravish her in his absence, that she had entreated him to desist from the attempt, that he had given no heed to her entreaty, and that her honour was saved only by his timely arrival. The elder Rajput's anger knew no bounds, he threw off the *lota*, and quick as lightning drew his sword from its sheath. Though the younger knew that his brother was labouring under a misapprehension, he could not wait to give an explanation, as none but a coward Rajput would delay in measuring his sword with his antagonist when challenged. A fight ensued. Both were expert warriors. Their swords clashed and flew fire. The fight was desperate. To kill or to die was their resolution. The duel went on for about half an hour, in the course of which both the brothers were mortally wounded ; they began to lose blood, fell down faint and expired at the damsel's feet.

The damsel, who had all this time been laughing in the sleeve, stood up and made toward a neighbouring forest ; and when she was in the midst of it, changed to an old Brahmin. The young Brahmin, who had hitherto been silently watching this wonderful creature, now came forward and asked the old Brahmin, who and what he was. The old Brahmin gave no answer and quickened his speed to avoid his pursuer.

The young Brahmin followed the old one in quick pace, and overtook him shortly. The following dialogue then passed between the two :

Young Brahmin.—I have been watching your actions from the very beginning. Pray tell me who and what you are, and why you committed so many foul deeds.

Old Brahmin.—Don't interfere with me. Begone, or remain at your peril.

Young Brahmin.—Had I not washed my hands of

my life, I would not have followed you to this lonely forest. I fear not death. Pray, let me know what I want to know, or I will kill myself in your presence, and thus you would be the cause of my death.

Old Brahmin.—I am a messenger of Yamaraja (Death) and to carry out the behest of my master I did what you saw me doing. If, in the natural course of events the commission of an act becomes impossible, we, the messengers of death, step in for the fulfilment of the same. Now depart in peace and leave me unmolested.

Young Brahmin.—One word more and I have gone. Pray, tell me, how, when, and where I shall meet my death.

Old Brahmin.—I cannot. Leave me.

Young Brahmin.—I will not, unless and until you tell me what I want to know.

Seeing further parley with the irresistible young man of no use, the messenger of Death replied thus, and vanished : "At the 50th year of your age, in the river Bhagirathi, you will be devoured by an alligator."

The young Brahmin became very much terrified on learning his sad destiny. However, to avoid it, he resolved not to return home, and he retreated to a place where even the name of the river Bhagirathi was known only to a very few. Here he lived in the house of a rich man who had no issue. During the Brahmin's stay at the rich man's house, the wife of the latter presented him a handsome boy ; this made the Brahmin's advent in the house an auspicious event, and he was all the more adored for it. Time went on and the boy grew in age. The Brahmin was engaged as tutor to the boy, and in a short time the boy grew very fond of his teacher.

It so happened that a grand *Yog* for bathing in the Bhagirathi drew near. People bathing there on this *Yog* occasion will have their sins of the past and present lives washed off. The rich man proposed to go to the Bhagirathi with his family and child, and bathe in it on the holy occasion. Every preparation was made for the journey. The rich man desired his son's tutor to accompany him, but he flatly declined to do so. When the boy came to know that his teacher was not going with them he sternly refused to go along with them; the mother would not go without the child. The rich man was in a fix. Now the teacher must go with the family, or they would lose this golden opportunity for washing off their sins. When much pressed, the tutor revealed all, and plainly told his patron why he feared to bathe in the Bhagirathi. The rich man argued that prophecies are not always fulfilled; in any case, they were perfectly on the safe side, as the bathing ghat would be fenced up with stout iron railings and the water in it dragged. The tutor reluctantly gave way. In due time the party reached the sacred bank of mother Bhagirathi. The family performed their ablutions. Now the tutor went to the river and dived, but no sooner was he under the water, than his pupil jumped down into the river, turned into a big alligator, caught the teacher's neck and disappeared, saying : "O! Brahmin, you have given me no end of trouble for my weakness in yielding to your request, but, see, a man can never avoid his destiny."

38. Silence is Golden.—Three men were once going

to Heaven together. On their way, they observed a kite carrying off a serpent; one of them, said: "Ah, what a pity, this poor serpent is thus carried off by the wicked kite"; and at once he fell down to earth. Seeing his fate, another of his companions exclaimed: "The wicked serpent well deserves its fate"; and at once, he too fell down. The third kept quiet, and safely reached Heaven.

The wise man never hastens to judge, but always does silently acquiesce in the ways of Providence.

39. The Mind, a Maddened Monkey.—"How hard it is to control the mind, well has it been compared to the maddened monkey. There was a monkey, restless by his own nature, as all monkeys are. As if that were not enough, some one made him drink freely of wine, so that he became still more restless. Then a scorpion stung him. When a man is stung by a scorpion, he jumps about for a whole day, so that the poor monkey found his condition worse than ever. To complete his misery, a demon entered into him. What language can describe the uncontrollable restlessness of that monkey? The human mind is like that monkey, incessantly active by its own nature; then it becomes drunk with the wine of desire, thus increasing its turbulence. After desire takes possession, comes the sting of the scorpion of jealousy of others whose desires meet with fulfilment; and last of all, the demon of pride takes possession of the mind, making it think itself of all-importance. How hard to control such a mind!"

40. Thirst for God.—A disciple went to his master and said: "Sir, I want religion." The master looked at the young man, and did not speak; only smiled.

The young man came every day, and insisted that he wanted religion. But the old man knew better than the young man. One day, when it was very hot, he asked the young man to go to the river with him, and take a plunge. The young man plunged in, and the old man after him and held the young man down under the water by main force. When the young man had struggled for a good while, he let him go, and, when the young man came up, asked him what he wanted most while he was under water. "A breath of air," the disciple answered. "Do you want God that way? If you do, you will get him in a moment." Until you have that thirst, that desire, you cannot get religion, however much you may struggle with your intellect or your books or your forms. Until that thirst is awakened in you, you are no better than any atheist, only that the atheist is sincere and you are not.

41. A Child and a Sage.—There was a good sage in the olden days well versed in all the scriptures. These scriptures did not at all satisfy the cravings of his mind, for, he wanted to know nothing less than the whole of God. Finding no help in the scriptures, he went away to a solitary place far from the haunts of men, and there built a hermitage to devote himself entirely to realise the full knowledge about God. This hermitage was situated a little way off from an arm of the sea and unless the sea were very stormy no dashings of waves and breakers could be seen or heard. All around was very placid and calm and peaceful. At such a quiet nook, the hermit whose desires were very few, devoted his whole day and night for the realisation of the one desire of his heart. Days and months passed, but he could

not make out any thing about God. Years after years
rolled away, the persevering and assiduous hermit was
as ignorant as before. Youth passed away and grey
hairs began to peep out from amongst his long brown
locks, and still the problem remained unsolved quite as
before. One day, he was walking on the beach with a
dejected and pensive look, thinking about his unsuccessful struggle and considering whether he might give
up the attempt or not, when, casting his eyes before
him he saw at some distance a little boy, just on the
brink of the water, busy with something. Thinking
that a certain fisherman's child had been left there by
its father who had gone perhaps to the open sea to catch
fish, but not satisfied as to why the father should bring
such a little child from home and leave it there thus
alone, he went up to it to inquire. The child was, however, quite unconscious of his approach, for it was very
busy throwing water from the sea on the sands with its
tiny hands. At such a novel sight, the curiosity of the
sage was roused to its utmost degree, and he began to
interrogate the boy as to who he was, why he was throwing water in that way, where his father had gone, and
sundry other things, to all of which the boy had no
time to answer—the little pretty creature was so engrossed in its apparently fruitless work. At last, when
the sage grew too importunate with his questions, the
child without wanting to be disturbed any more,
answered him once for all : "Sir, I have no time to talk
with you. Don't you see that I have to throw off all
the water of this ocean and thus dry it up?" "Are you
mad," ejaculated the sage, "you little creature! you
want to dry up the whole of this limitless ocean which

28

the whole human race together can never think of attempting?" "Why, sir?" answered the cherub-like pretty figure before him with a petulant look. "Is it impossible for me to dry up this finite ocean and see what is concealed in its depths, if it be possible for you to know and unravel the infinite profundity of God?" With this, the child vanished from the spot and was seen no more. But its sweet words which had found entrance into his heart, always rang in his ears and filled him with unspeakable joy. From that day forward he gave up his vain pursuit, and instead of trying to *know* God, he began to *love* Him. Afterwards he became a great devotee, and whenever he wanted and wept for the child who had thus saved him from a fruitless struggle, the child would surely appear dancing before him and talk with him so sweetly that he would cry out to the child : "Thou art my God, O my darling, I have found Thee out at last" and go into a state of ecstasy.

42. **An Old Man and Sri Krishna.**—There was once a certain old Brahmin who professed to be a great *Bhakta*, whatever he did, he used to say : "Krishna Krishna, this is Thy doing.' One day some paddy had been spread at his door for getting dried in the sun, when a cow came and ate it. The Brahmin at once took a stick in his hand and severely beat the poor cow, which consequently fell down and expired. At once, the Brahmin began to exclaim : 'Hari-Hari-Krishna-Krishna. This is Thy doing.' Just then Rukmani happened to be with Krishna and she adressing her Lord said : "O my Lord, what a sin has now fallen to your account." Krishna replied : "Fear not my dear, the sin of having

killed the cow is the Brahmin's and not mine. You will shortly see how it is so."

A few days after, the old man was giving a feast to Brahmins when Krishna, assuming the guise of a dirty old Brahmin, entered his house, spat on the ground here and there and committed diverse kinds of nuisance. The host thereupon began to rebuke him saying : "Is this the reward for my charity? Why do you come and disturb the feast which I am holding?" The disguised Krishna replied : "Who are you to rebuke me? Are you the real host?" The Brahmin got exceedingly angry and said : "Did I not tell you that I was the host? I will show you who I am" ; and so saying, he began to shove him out. At once Krishna showed his real form and said : "The merit of this feast is yours, while the sin of killing the cow is mine, I suppose. A very fair division to be sure. Let both be yours," and so saying he disappeared.

Like the Brahmin in this story, how often are we prone to take the merit of our successes and good deeds to ourselves, while ascribing our failures and evil deeds to the Lord.

43. Science, Religion, Truth.—*Science* : "Do you mean for me to believe in something I have never seen? God? Show Him or else I tell you that all this talk about a God is nonsense."

Religion : "Do you believe that there are stars?"

Science : "Certainly."

Religion : "You know it ; but strictly speaking have you ever seen a star?"

Science : "No, but the light, the vibrations."

Religion : "Then you do not *know* that the stars exist !"

Science : "Oh yes,—"

Religion : "How then? You said : 'Show me your God, and I will believe that there is One'; now I say to you, 'show me your star, or I will not believe you'."

Science : "But I can prove it !"

Religion : "So can I; God is not a mere theory but a fact. You yourself, Science, have proved that '*ex-nihilo nihil fit*'; something must come from something. This universe was evolved, not created, has always existed and shall ever continue to be. You, yourself, have declared the indestructibility of force and matter. God is eternal, omnipotent, omniscient. The First Cause is eternal, omnipotent, omniscient, for there is nothing to know outside of that, nothing with power except in that, since it includes the all. So the First Cause answers to our definition of God. This universe was projected from the First Cause and became the effect— effect and cause being the same. Science, tear the veil from your eyes! Look at that twinkling mite there in the sky, beyond that there is yet another universe, and another. Where is the limit? You stagger! Ah, mind is not all; there is something beyond it that staggers not; it *knows*, and that is the Soul. You see the stars? To-morrow you are blind, how know you then if they ever were? You weigh and measure matter; suppose your sense of touch should vanish, where now your proof that matter is? One little blow, a slight cut, an almost imperceptible jar to the brain and you know not whether aught nor naught exists. But far beyond the Mind is Soul,—Eternal,—Free! Realise but once thy God; That is the True, the Changeless, and only That."

Science : "And how to realise?"

Religion : "Gaze inward ; know thyself. Hand in hand shall we find the peace you seek, and hand in hand must we pursue our journey onward, not, as two, but as one, and our name shall be Truth !

44. The Heroism of a Missionary's Life.

"I hear that you are going away, Millie, is that so ?"

"Yes, I'm going next week, guess where ?"

"O, I can't !"

"Well, don't faint ; I'm going to......China ! and as a Missionary !"

"Millie, you are joking !"

"No, Miriam, I'm not joking at all, next week I will be bound for China and as a Missionary ! You know that has been my desire since a little girl when first I went to Sunday school. Ah ! You do not know what a pleasure, intense joy it will be to spread the doctrine of our perfect religion—Christianity !"

"But Millie, have you thought of what you are doing ? Thought not only of the voyage, your new environments, and the burst of feeling that will be set free, but of the effect on the Chinese also ? They are brought up under circumstances far different from ours, and facts and ideas that we, perhaps, never dream of as existing, literally branded into them from generations back. There they peacefully attend to their own duties hardly dreaming of such a disturbance as an American missionary. Dare you tear their ancient doctrines from their souls, dig them up by the root, tell them that they are wrong, and—"

"Miriam !"

"Yes, I mean it. Can't you understand ? See the world through the Chinaman's eyes and it will look

very different. You cannot teach a baby logic, much
less put Christian views into a follower of Confucius.
Dare you criticise their God? Does not He, the same,
watch over all his children? We understand the doctrines of Chinese as little as they do ours."

"Miriam! How you do talk; are you a Christian?"

"Yes, I am; but don't you understand me? don't
you see that if you only look on your side of the question
it will be one-sided? Indeed, you are doing a very noble
thing to give up your own dear land and live a stranger
among heathen, and more noble still it is, more heroic
that you give up all those endearing home ties that
alone make life bearable sometimes; but do you do good
to any one else? That is what you are striving to do,
I think."

"Miriam, Miriam, how you do turn things, and how
funny you see everything. Think of our glorious religion which has made us what we are—the most civilised of all nations—compare that religion with the
empty formulæ of the Chinese, and then ask me if I am
doing good to any one else. They do not realise how
glorious it is to have a Christ, and then Miriam, has
any other religion direct revelation from God?"

"Well, I don't know!"

"You don't know, Miriam!"

"No; do you?"

"Miriam!!!"

"Yes, I know you think me terrible but let me
illustrate my view of the case. Here you live in New
York and wish to reach Paris; in Asia, let us suppose,
is your friend who also is bound for Paris: you two
cannot reach your destination by the same road, you

must take different paths but in the end reach the same place. So with the Heathen and the Christian, they are on different spiritual planes and must therefore take different roads, but in the end reach the same goal. To say that the religion of Confucius is wrong is as absurd as to exclaim : 'There is no language except the English, all others are mere delusions !' But Millie, no one can deny that a Missionary's life is heroic and proves how firmly fixed are the roots of Christianity, when you are willing to live amid strangers the Christian's life of patience, peace, and purity."

"Well Miriam, time will tell ; we'll know better a few years from now."

"Yes, and when many years have passed, years of labour and heroism, pain and misunderstanding, when the lesson of tolerance shall have been learned by bitter experience, then Millie I am sure that each heart, whether Jewish or Buddhist, Christian or Pagan shall in the fulness of its love exclaim :

" 'Master, *not* one but *all* ; in every style, in every tongue thy sacred name shall echo ! ' "

45. Saved and Lost.—One of the most excellent of a number of good stories told at the Chicago Parliament of Religions was given by a Russian representative. A woman of very bad character, a thief, a cheat, and of generally evil repute, was dying, and on her death bed was frightened at the prospect of what might follow. Though she had had, during a long life of evil doing, no thought of religion or of God, yet now she began to cry loudly, and yet more loudly, to God to have mercy on her. So much did she cry that at last she attracted the attention of the Angel Gabriel, who came to see what the matter might be. "Oh Sir," said the woman, "what am I to do?" "What is the matter?" asked the angel. "Sir, all my life I have done not one good thing, and now, I am about to die. What will become of me?" "Is there not one good act of which you can remember? Think," replied the angel. After much thought the woman remembered that when she was a young woman she was almost starving, and found a carrot, which was the only food she had had for two days. As she was about to eat it, another woman, as badly off as herself, came to her, begging. Though it was contrary to her usual nature, the carrot was divided between them. This incident the dying woman apologetically related to the angel, who replied:—"Hold on to that carrot and it will save you." The woman did hold on, and presently died. As she was being drawn up to heaven by the carrot, many others who had died after leading a life as evil as her own began to cling to her, in the hope of sharing her escape. At that she got jealous and cried out: "Get off; the carrot is mine." That instant the carrot broke, and she fell back into the place of torment. Thus, though one small deed of unselfishness had been sufficient to outweigh her bad *Karma*, her selfishness undid, in a moment, the previous good.

He who has not conquered his self (selfishness) is his own enemy (*Gita*, VI, 6).

"Release and bondage," says the *Sruti*, "both depend on the two ideas, me and mine."

46. The Abode of God.—In the course of his exile, Sri Rama met Valmiki in the Chitrakuta mountains and requested him to suggest a place where himself and Sita might conveniently live for some time. The sage softly smiled and replied as follows :

"Thyself art the sole and supreme abode for all the worlds, Oh Rama, and the whole creation is Thy place of residence. As Thou sayest however, that Sita (Chit-Shakti) is also to live with Thee, hear, O foremost of the Raghus ! What is the proper place for Thee to live in. Dwell in the hearts of the calm and the even-tempered, of those who know no hatred or attachment, whoever worship Thee and are satisfied having performed their only duty in the world. Live, likewise, in the minds of men who are above all desires, above the influence of pleasure and pain and other pairs of opposites, in whom the sense of self has vanished and who dedicate all their actions to Thee. Make a home for self and Sita, Oh Rama, in those who do not get elated with joy nor afflicted with grief, who have no concern for the conventions of the world of *Samsara* and whose hearts have been steadied in Thy worship by continued exercise. You will find an excellent home in those who see Thee as being beyond the reach of the six *Vikaras* (lust, anger, avarice, etc.), and the cravings of the senses, who see Thee, as pervading all, as the One and the Infinite and as Existence and Consciousness absolute."

47. Reforming the World.—There was a poor man who wanted some money, and, somehow, he had heard, that if he could get hold of a ghost or some spirit, he could command him to bring money or anything he liked ; so he was very anxious to get hold of a ghost. He went about searching for a man, who would give him a ghost and at last he found a sage, with great powers, and besought this sage to help him. The sage asked

him what he would do with a ghost. "I want a ghost
to work for me; teach me how to get hold of one, sir,
I desire it very much"; replied the man. But the sage
said: "Don't disturb yourself, go home." The next
day the man went again to the sage and began to weep
and pray: "Give me a ghost; I must have a ghost, sir,
to help me." At last the sage was disgusted and said:
"Take this charm, repeat this magic word and a ghost
will come, and whatever you say to this ghost he will do.
But beware; they are terrible beings and must be kept
continually busy. If you fail to give him work he will
take your life." The man replied: "That is easy; I
can give him work for all his life." Then he went to a
forest, and after long repetition of the magic word, a
huge ghost appeared before him, with big teeth, and
said: "I am a ghost. I have been conquered by your
magic. But you must keep me constantly employed.
The moment you stop I will kill you." The man said:
"Build me a palace," and the ghost said, "It is done,
the palace is built." "Bring me money," said the man.
"Here is your money," said the ghost. "Cut this forest
down, and build a city in its place." "That is done,"
said the ghost; "anything more?" Now the man began
to be frightened and said: "I can give him nothing
more to do; he does everything in a trice." The ghost
said: "Give me something to do or I will eat you up."
The poor man could find no further occupation for him,
and was frightened. So he ran and ran and at last
reached the sage, and said: "Oh, sir, protect my life!"
The sage asked him what was the matter, and the man
replied: "I have nothing to give the ghost to do.
Everything I tell him to do he does in a moment, and he

threatens to eat me up if I do not give him work."
Just then the ghost arrived saying : "I'll eat you up ;
I'll eat you up," and he would have swallowed the man.
The man began to shake ; and begged the sage to save
his life. The sage said : "I will find you a way out.
Look at that dog with a curly tail. Draw your sword
quickly and cut the tail off and give it to the ghost to
straighten out." The man cut off the dog's tail and
gave it to the ghost, saying : "Straighten that out for
me." The ghost took it and slowly and carefully
straightened it out, but as soon as he let go, it instantly
curled up again. Once more he laboriously straightened
it out, only to find it again curled up as soon as he attempted to let it go. Again he patiently straightened
it out, but as soon as he let it go, it curled up again. So
he went on for days and days, until he was exhausted,
and said : "I was never in such trouble before in my
life. I am an old veteran ghost, but never before was
I in such trouble. I will make compromise with you,"
he said to the man. "You let me off and I will let you
keep all I have given you, and will promise not to harm
you." The man was much pleased and accepted the
offer gladly.

This world is that dog's curly tail, and people have
been striving to straighten it out for hundreds of years,
but when they let it go, it curls up again. How can it
be otherwise? One must first know, how to work
without attachment, then he will not be a fanatic.
When we know that this world is like a dog's curly tail
and will never straighten, we shall not become fanatics.
They can never do real work. If there were no fanaticism in the world it would make much more progress

than it does now. It is all silly nonsense to think that
fanaticism makes for the progress of mankind. It is,
instead, a retarding block, by making hatred and anger
and causing people to fight with each other, and making
them unsympathetic. Whatever we do or possess, we
think the best in the world, and those things we do not
possess are of no value. So always remember this curly
tail of the dog whenever you have a tendency to become a fanatic. You need not worry or make yourself
sleepless; the world will go on. When you have avoided
fanaticism then alone will you work well. It is the
level-headed man, the calm man, of good judgment and
cool nerves, of great sympathy and love, who does good
work. The fanatic has no sympathy.

48. What is Duty?—A certain young *Sanyasi* went
to a forest and there meditated and worshipped and
practised *Yoga* for a long time. After twelve years of
hard work and practice, he was one day sitting under
a tree, when some dry leaves fell upon his head. He
looked up and saw a crow and a crane fighting on the
top of the tree, and they made him very angry. He
said: "What! You dare throw those dry leaves upon
my head!" And as he looked upon them with anger,
a flash of fire burst from his head—the *Yogi's* power—
and burnt the birds to ashes. He was very glad; he
was almost overjoyed at this development of power; he
could burn, at a glance, the crow and the crane. After
a time he had to go into the town to beg his bread. He
came and stood at a door and said: "Mother, give me
food." A voice came from inside the house: "Wait
a little, my son." The young man thought: "You
wretched woman, dare you make me wait! You do not

know my power yet." While he was thinking thus, the
voice came again : "Boy, don't be thinking too much
of yourself. Here is neither crow nor crane." He was
astonished ; still he had to wait. At last a woman
came and he fell at her feet and said : "Mother, how
did you know that ?" She said : "My boy, I do not know
your *Yoga* or your practices. I am a common, everyday woman, but I made you wait because my husband
is ill, and I was nursing him, and that was my duty.
All my life I have struggled to do my duty. As a
daughter when I was unmarried, I did my duty ; and
now, when I am married, I still do my duty ; that is all
the *Yoga* I practise, and by doing my duty I have become illumined ; thus, I could read your thoughts and
what you had done in the forest. But if you want to
know something higher than this go to such and such
a town and to the market, and there you will find a
butcher and he will tell you something that you will
be very glad to learn." The *Sanyasi* thought : "Why
go to that town and to a butcher." (Butchers are the
lowest class in our country ; they are *Chandalas* ; they
are not touched because they are butchers ; they do
also the duty of scavengers, and so forth).

But after what he had seen, his mind was opened a
little. So he went, and when he came near the city he
found the market, and there saw, at a distance, a big,
fat butcher slashing away at animals, with big knives,
fighting and bargaining with different people. The
young man said : "Lord, help me, is this the man from
whom I am going to learn ? He is the incarnation of a
demon, if he is anything " In the meantime this man
looked up and said : "Swami, did that lady send you

here? Take a seat until I have done my business." The *Sanyasi* thought: "What comes to me here?" but he took a seat and the man went on, and after he had finished all his selling and buying, took his money and said to the *Sanyasi*: "Come here, sir; come to my home."

So they went there and the butcher gave him a seat and said: "Wait there." Then he went into the house and there were his father and mother. He washed them and fed them and did all he could to please them, and then came and took a seat before the *Sanyasi* and said: "Now, sir, you are come here to see me; what can I do for you?" Then this great *Sanyasi* asked him a few questions about soul and God, and this butcher gave him a lecture which is a very celebrated book in India, the *"Vyadha-Gita"*. It is one of the highest flights in the *Vedanta*, the highest flight of metaphysics. You have heard of the *Bhagavad-Gita*, Krishna's sermon. When you have finished that you should read the *"Vyadha-Gita"*. It is the extreme of *Vedanta* philosophy. When the butcher had finished, the *Sanyasi* was astonished. He said: "Why are you in that body, with such knowledge as yours? Why are you in a butcher's body, and doing such filthy, ugly work?" "My son," replied the *Chandala*, "No duty is ugly, and no duty is impure. My birth, circumstances and environments were there. In my boyhood I learned the trade; I am unattached, and I try to do my duty well. I try to do my duty as a householder, and I try to do all I can to make my father and mother happy. I neither know your *Yoga*, nor have become a *Sanyasi*; never went out of the world, nor into a forest, but all this has come to me through doing my duty in my position."

Let us do that duty which is ours by birth, and when we have done that, do the duty which is ours by our position. Each man is placed in some position in life, and must do the duties of that position first. There is one great danger in human nature, that man never looks at himself. He thinks he is quite as fit to be on the throne as the king. Even if he is, he must first show that he has done the duty of his own position, and when he has done that, higher duty will come to him.

49. Each is Great in his own Place.—A certain King used to inquire of all the *Sanyasins* that came to his country : "Which is the greater man—he who gives up the world and becomes a *Sanyasin*, or he who lives in the world and performs his duties as a householder?" Many wise men tried to solve this problem. Some asserted that the *Sanyasin* was the greater, upon which the King demanded that they should prove their assertion. When they could not, he ordered them to marry and become householders. Then others came and said : "The householder who performs his duties is the greater man." Of them, too, the King demanded proofs. When they could not give them he made them also settle down as householders. At last there came a young *Sanyasin* and the King put the same question to him. He answered : "Each, O King, is equally great in his place." "Prove this to me," said the King. "I will prove to you," said the *Sanyasin*, "But you must first come and live as I do for a few days, that I may be able to prove to you what I say." The King consented and followed the *Sanyasin* out of his own territory and passed through many territories, until they came to another kingdom. In the capital of that kingdom a great ceremony was going on. The King and the *Sanyasin* heard the sound of drums and music, and criers and the people were assembled in the streets in *gala* dress, and a great proclamation was being made. The King and the *Sanyasin* stood there to see what was going on. The crier was saying that the princes, the daughter of the King of that country, was going to choose a husband from among those assembled before her.

It was an old custom in India for princesses to choose husbands in this way, and each one had certain ideas of the sort of man she wanted for a husband ; some would have the handsomest man ; others would have only the most learned, others would have the richest and so on. The princess, in the most splendid array, was carried on a throne, and the announcement was made by criers that the princess so-and-so was about to choose a husband. Then all the princes of the neighbourhood put on their bravest attire and presented themselves before her. Sometimes they, too, had their own criers to enumerate their advantages, and the reasons why they hoped the princess would choose them. The princess was taken round and she looked at them and heard what they had to offer, and if she was not pleased she asked her bearer to move on, and no more notice was taken of the rejected suitors. If, however, the princess was pleased with any of them she threw a garland upon him and he became her husband.

The princess of the country to which our King and

the *Sanyasin* had come was having one of these interesting ceremonies. She was the most beautiful princess of the world, and the husband of the princess would be the ruler of the kingdom after her father's death. The idea of this princess was to marry the handsomest man, but she could not find the right one to please her. Several times these meetings had taken place, and yet the princess had not selected anyone. This meeting was the most splendid of all; more people than ever had come to it, and it was a most gorgeous scene. The princess came in on a throne, and the bearers carried her from place to place. She does not seem to care for anyone even on this occasion, and everyone has almost become disappointed that this meeting too is to be broken up without anyone being chosen as the husband of the princess. Just then comes a young man, a *Sanyasin* as handsome as if the sun had come down to the earth, and he stands in one corner of the assembly seeing what is going on. The throne with the princess comes near him, and as soon as she sees the beautiful *Sanyasin* she stops and throws the garland over him. The young *Sanyasin* seizes the garland and throws it off exclaiming : "What nonsense do you mean by that? I am a *Sanyasin*; what is marriage to me?" The King of that country thinks that perhaps this man is poor, so does not dare to marry the princess ; so he says to him : "With my daughter goes half my kingdom now, and the whole kingdom after my death," and puts the garland again on the *Sanyasin*. The young man throws it off once more saying : "What nonsense is this? I do not want to marry," and walked quickly away from the assembly.

29

Now the princess fell so much in love with this young man that she said : "I must marry this man or I shall die" ; and she went after him to bring him back. Then our other *Sanyasin*, who had brought our King there because of the controversy, said to the King— "King, let us follow this pair" ; so they walked after them, but at a good distance behind. The young *Sanyasin* who had refused to marry the princess, walked out into the country for several miles, when he came to a forest, and struck into it and the princess followed him, and the other two followed them. Now this young *Sanyasin* was well acquainted with that forest, and knew all the intricate passages in it, and suddenly he jumped into one of these and disappeared and the princess could not discover him. After trying for a long time to find him, she sat down under a tree and began to weep, for she did not know the way to get out of the forest again. Then our King and the other *Sanyasin* came up to her and said : "Do not weep, we will show you the way out of this forest, but it is too dark for us to find it now. Here is a big tree ; let us rest under it, and in the morning we will go early and show you the road to get out."

Now a little bird and his wife and three little baby birds lived on that tree in a nest. This little bird looked down and saw the three people under the tree, and said to his wife : "My dear, what shall be done ; here are some guests in the house, and it is winter, and we have no fire ?" So he flew away and got a bit of burning firewood in his beak and dropped it before the guests and they added fuel to it and made a blazing fire. But the little bird was not satisfied ; he said again to his wife :

'My dear, what shall we do, there is nothing to give these people to eat, and they are hungry and we are householders; it is our duty to feed anyone who comes to the house. I must do what I can, I will give them my body." So he plunged down into the midst of the fire and perished. The guests saw him falling and tried to save him, but he was too quick for them, and dashed into the fire and was killed. The little bird's wife saw what her husband did, and she said: "Here are three persons and only one little bird for them to eat; it is not enough; it is my duty as a wife not to let my husband's effort be in vain; let them have my body also," and she plunged down into the fire and was burned to death. Then the three baby-birds, when they saw what was done, and that there was still not enough food for the three guests, said: "Our parents have done what they could and still it is not enough; it is our duty to carry on the work of our parents; let our bodies go too,' and they all dashed down into the fire. The three people could not eat these birds, and they were amazed at what they saw. Somehow or other they passed the night without food, and in the morning the King and the *Sanyasin* showed the princess the way, and she went back to her father. Then the *Sanyasin* said to the King: "King, you have seen that each is great in his own place. If you want to live in the world, live like those birds, ready at any moment to sacrifice yourself for others. If you want to renounce the world be like that young man, to whom the most beautiful woman and a kingdom were as nothing. If you want to be a householder hold your life a sacrifice for the welfare of others; and if you choose the life of renunciation, do not even see beauty and money and power. Each is great in his own place, but the duty of the one is not the duty of the other."

50. Theodora.—Once upon a time there was a very kind and charitable woman called Theodora (God-given). She loved every one and was always striving to help the poor and needy, and to teach little children, and nurse the sick and helpless. One day she felt that all she could do was so little, and that there was so much suffering in the world and so much work to be done that all her efforts seemed of no avail, and she felt discouraged and said to herself : 'I am of no use in this great sea of human misery, all I can do is of so little avail, I shall never be able to be of much help to these poor people.' As she sat alone, mournfully thinking these sad thoughts, she fell asleep and dreamed. In her dream she found herself in a vast studio where there were hundreds and thousands of pictures. What appeared strange to her was that not one was finished, but they were all in varying stages of completion. Some stood on easels and were covered from sight by white clothes thrown over them, but the larger number stood on the floor, or were ranged around the walls in endless confusion. As Theodora stood there silent and wondering what all these covered canvases could contain, an old man—tall, stately and beautiful entered the studio. He did not seem to notice Theodora, but went at once to one of the easels and uncovering the picture standing on it, began to paint. He only gave it a few touches however and then carefully covering it over again, he went to the next easel and repeated the process. After silently watching the old man for some time, Theodora approached. him, and encouraged by his kind and benignant countenance, she ventured to ask him : "What are you doing, sir ?" The old man turned towards her with a bright smile and said in sweet and gentle tones : "I am the artist of the King of kings. All these are portraits of His children, who are made in His likeness. As they grow more and more to resemble their Father in Heaven through love and devotion to Him and through pure and holy living, I gradually paint their portraits, adding here a touch and there a touch, until the likeness is complete. Then the finished picture is taken away from here and hung in the palace of the King of kings to be with him forever more. These pictures on the easels are the most advanced, some are nearly done. Those on the floor are at a stand-still, waiting for the originals to again devote themselves to the endeavour to grow like the Father, while some are mere outlines, with not a single stroke filled in and many are blank canvases, waiting for even an outline of spiritual aspiration to be drawn upon them."

Then Theodora understood that all her struggles and all her work were but intended to make her grow more and more like the King her Father—that slowly, slowly the likeness grew, here a line, there a line, until perfection was reached. A great peace filled her heart and when she awoke it remained with her. She felt happy and encouraged to persevere with her efforts to help others, feeling sure all the while, that are likeness to the Father in Heaven was slowly growing, under the faithful hands of the great artists to the King of kings.

51. Who is the Real Chandala.—A recluse belonging to the Brahmin caste who had been for a number of

years performing severe austerities on the banks of a
sacred stream, had by degrees come to regard himself
as a most holy and pious man. His so-called piety consisted in holding himself aloof from the general public,
whom he considered as too low to associate with, and
whose touch and even near proximity he thought would
defile him. He imagined that his daily ablutions in the
holy water, his taking a solitary meal cooked by no
other hands than his own, his constant rectial of sacred
verses with closed eyes for several hours, and his living
far away from the habitations of other men had transformed him into a pure and virtuous man. He had not
a spark of love in the whole of his heart, nor an atom of
pity for the frailties and weaknesses of human nature,
nor any wish to make the slightest sacrifice in order to
help and guide erring mortals. His heart was like a
deep abyss, awfully dark and bleak—shut out from the
genial warmth of sun, or the purifying influence of air.
He resented any familiarity with him and would not
allow any one to approach his abode as if his presence
carried contagion with it. Although leading a life of
penance, he was a man of violent temper, which when
once roused, he found it difficult to control.

A washerman, who was a new arrival in the neighbourhood and quite ignorant of the residence of this
recluse, came to wash his linen in the very stream near
which the hermit was at the time muttering his prayers
with closed eyes—hidden by a clump of trees. The
Dhobi began to dash some dirty linen against a board
so close to the hermit that the sprinkle flew towards
the latter and fell on his body. Opening his eyes he
discovered that the unwelcome intruder was a *Dhobi*—a

Chandala who had dared to approach his sanctuary and there to defile him with the sprinkle of dirty washings. His rage knew no bounds. He abused and cursed the man and then in a very angry and loud tone ordered him to desist from his dirty work and instantly leave the place. The poor *Dhobi* who was lustily beating his linen did not hear the hermit, and innocently went on with his work. Finding his commands thus slighted, the hermit lost all self-control, and rising from his seat ran to the washerman and belaboured him mercilessly with his fists and legs till he felt quite tired. His victim stood speechless and astonished at this sudden and uncalled for attack. But perceiving that his assailant was a holy Brahmin, he could only mutter a feeble remonstrance and said : "My Lord, what has this slave done to incur your displeasure ?" The hermit replied angrily : "Why Sirrah, how darest thou approach my hermitage and defile me by pouring the sprinkle of dirty washings upon my holy person ?"

The *Dhobi* finding that he had been an unwitting intruder upon forbidden ground offered a humble apology and prepared to depart. The hermit now perceived that he had defiled himself by coming in contact with a *Chandala* and must cleanse himself. He accordingly went to the stream and bathed himself, thus purifying himself from the momentary defilement. The *Dhobi* also followed his example. The Recluse did not understand the meaning of this proceeding and asked why he had washed himself. The *Dhobi* said : "Sir, for the same reason that you washed yourself." The hermit was still more surprised and rejoined : "I washed myself because I touched you—a low born washerman—a *Chandala*—

and thus defiled myself. But why did you bathe? Surely the touch of a holy man like me cannot carry any defilement!"

The *Dhobi* weakly said : "My Lord, one far worse than a *Chandala* just now touched me through you. For the burst of passion which caused you to forget yourself and lay your hands on me was more accursed and unclean than a *Chandala* by birth. I came in contact with him through you and was thus defiled."

The scales fell from the eyes of the hermit on hearing this. He pondered over this answer of the *Dhobi* which taught him a lesson which his vaunted austerities and penance had hitherto failed to do, *viz.* : that he who conquers his passion is more mighty than he who subdues a kingdom, and that there is no worse *Chandala* than one's own ungoverned temper.

The hermit then compared himself—proud of his piety yet a slave to the sudden and violent gusts of temper—with the *Dhobi* who remained calm and unmoved even on receipt of the gravest provocation, and found how superior to him the latter was and which of the two had then acted the part of a real *Chandala*.

52. Ahankara or Egoism. There was once a war between the *Devas* and the *Asuras* headed by Sambara. In successive encounters, Sambara, and his hosts were defeated by the *Devas* and put to serious loss. Sambara, then created through his *Mayavic* power, three other *Asuras* named Dama, Vyala and Kata. "They were not subject to the bond of *Vasanas* (mental impressions) and were devoid of desires and egoism. They knew neither death nor life, neither pleasures nor pains, neither victory nor defeat, neither waging war nor retreating."

Being endowed with an enormous quantity of blind and brutal energy, they fought, as it were, mechanically and untrammelled by any anxiety as to the results of the contest. They committed fearful havoc in the camp of the *Devas* who all fled in despair and hid themselves in caves. After a time, the *Devas* went to Brahma, and told him what had happened and solicited his advice. Brahma, after meditating for a while, addressed the *Devas* thus:

After the lapse of a thousand years, Devendra will kill the *Asuras* in the war between himself and Sambara, who is now overpowering his enemies. Till then, we would advise you to act thus. Go to those Dama and others and give out that you intend to war with them. But only make a show of fighting and when they attack you, you better retreat as best you can. Repeat this process over and over again. In the meantime, the insidious *Ahankara* will have somehow crept into these *Asuras*. When this idea of "I" gets a firm footing in their minds, they will be in bondage like birds caught in a trap and can be easily vanquished. *Ahankara* which generally identifies itself with the world, its pains and its pleasures, generates desires, and desires are the worst foe of man.

The *Devas* followed the advice of Brahma, and how splendidly the ruse succeeded! In a long course of fighting in which the *Asuras* invariably won and their enemies were defeated, the *Asuras* became self-conscious by sheer contrast. This *Ahankara* brought with it also hopes and fears which the *Asuras* had not previously. "How can we maintain our health in best condition, how to strengthen our side, shall we win, or the *Devas*?"

Such thoughts now began to torment the *Asuras* and in course of time ate up all their strength. At length, they fled away panic-stricken in search of a safe refuge.

Sambara now saw the folly he had committed. True, he endowed his *Asuras* with strength enough to rout the *Devas* in fight. But he had omitted to arm them against a more formidable foe, the insidious *Ahankara*, to whose attacks they were liable. So, he now called into existence, other three *Asuras* named, Bhima, Bhasa, and Drudha, who were endowed with *Atmajnana*. With the enormous strength born of their knowledge of the eternal Reality and of their enjoyment of eternal Bliss, they fought quite with ease and confidence ; for they fought not to secure their own ends—for they had none—nor in hope of success or dread of defeat, but because their maker asked them to fight. God himself fought as it were from behind them, and no wonder, they were able to put the *Devas* to flight. It has, accordingly, been said : "Stand aside in the coming battle, and though thou fightest be not thou the warrior, look for the warrior and let him fight in thee......then it will be impossible for thee to strike one blow amiss. But if thou look not for him, if thou pass him by, then there is no safeguard for thee. Thy brain will reel, thy heart grow uncertain, and in the dust of the battlefield, thy sight and senses will fail, and, thou wilt not know thy friends from the enemies and thus ruin thyself" like the hosts of Ravana, who, under the influence of Mohanastra, saw Rama in each other among themselves and thus killed themselves.

The foregoing story taken from the *Yogavasishta* besides teaching how we are to war against our foes

internal as well as external, indicates also the course of
the evolution of the "apparent man". First, being a
mere unruly mass of matter and energy, he then becomes self-conscious and gets enthralled by the pains and
the pleasures of the world, and lastly, he shakes off the
world and its bondages or deals with them quite
sportively, like Krishna with his Gopis, holding on to a
higher and more permanent Reality which is of the
nature of Intelligence and Bliss. It will also be observed from the above story that the *Ahankara* in man
is far more powerful than natural forces including even
electricity, and the conquest over the former—which is
man's real mission on earth—is immensely more difficult
than victory over the latter. It might also have been
noticed that the *Asuras* created by Sambara on both the
occasions were alike powerful and desireless. The strength
in the one case, however, was merely the strength of the
perishable materials of which the *Asuras* had been built,
while, in the other, it grew out of and was maintained,
by undying *Atmajnana*. Similarly the dulness of Dama
and others who were of the nature of brutes had nothing
in common with the discriminating serenity and self-
possession of Bhima and his companions who were
Intelligence and Bliss themselves.

53. Real Faith.—Once upon a time Siva and Parvati
were travelling together in the heavens when they happened to pass over Hardwar, where the holy Ganges
debouches from the hills into the plains. It was the
time of the fair of *Kumbha* when thousands of people
had gathered there from all quarters of the *Bharatvarsha*
to have a plunge in the sacred stream and cleanse themselves of their sins. The spectacle that met the sight

of the celestial pair was quite a unique one. Men and
women of different races and creeds wearing various
costumes in the colours of the rainbow and talking
various dialects, were gathered together at "the door of
the Ganges". Seeing such a mass of humanity surging
on the banks of the Bhagirati, the consort of Siva who
was at that time having a spiritual discourse with her
Lord and was discussing the doctrine of transmigration,
exclaimed : "My dear, behold what a large concourse
of people has met at this sacred place to bathe in the
holy Ganges. The scriptures say that a single dip into
it emancipates a human being from re-birth and secures
him salvation for ever. The thousands who are assembled here to-day will thus obtain 'Moksha', and the
world will be empty of its inhabitants to that extent.
As this fair takes place every six years, millions of human
beings will thus be saved in a century. This is very
hopeful for the mass of humanity, steeped in abject
misery and sin." Siva replied : "My love, all the human
beings you see here to-day are not destined to be saved.
There is probably one person in a million who deserves
emancipation from sin." "How, my lord," rejoined
Parvati, "are then the Scriptures false when they
promise Mukti to every one who bathes in this most
holy stream ? Is this assurance a mere delusion and
fraud ?" Siva answered : "No, O ! lotus-eyed one, the
Scriptures are quite true, and I will just give you a most
convincing proof of what I said. I will transform myself into an old decrepit man affected with the loathsome
disease of leprosy, and lay myself down on the banks
of the Ganges as nearly dead. You become a beautiful
woman of blooming sixteen, and give out that I am your

husband and have come to Hardwar to wash myself of all my sins. In a short time I will die, and then you should weep and lament, and beg people to help you in cremating the body—but when they approach you, tell them that only those who are entirely sinless and perfectly pure should touch the corpse and perform its funeral rites. Let not any one come near the body who does not assure you that he is free from all sins and impurities. You will then receive a complete answer to the question you have just put to me regarding the truth or otherwise of the promise of salvation held out by the Scriptures to those who bathe in the holy Ganga'."

Siva accordingly changed himself into an old man, bent with infirmities of age with his face wrinkled, sight dimmed and the whole body covered with the sickening leprosy—a sight most repulsive to the eye. Leading him by the hand appeared a blooming maiden of sixteen, of transcendent beauty, but with a sad and careworn face. The pair sat near the "Har-Ri-Paidi", and the old man seemed suffering intensely from his malady. He lay himself down on the pavement to die. In a few minutes he breathed his last, and then the fair girl began to weep and lament piteously. Attracted by her cries, a large crowd of people gathered near her, and some began to offer her consolation. Others again charmed with her beauty stood there to gaze at her with admiration. Some few whose hearts were really touched with the miserable sight that met their eyes, came forward to assist the fair widow in removing the body to the current of the holy river. But with a sudden wave of her hand, she forbade them and exclaimed : "Do not, please,

touch the body unless you are wholly sinless and pure
in mind, body and speech. For no one must handle
the corpse who does not assure me on solemn oath that
he is free from all the sins committed in this or former
births, and that his heart is as stainless as crystal."
Hearing this, those who were eagerly pressing forward
at once drew back. The lady waited for a time to see
if any one else would advance to assist her in the removal and cremation of the corpse, but unfortunately,
learning that no one must touch the body unless he was
perfectly pure and sinless, no man dared to approach it.
The fair widow had thus to stop the whole day at the
"Har-Ri-Paidi", with the body of her husband lying
uncremated before her. She made several piteous appeals for help, and although her forlorn condition and
cries moved hundreds to compassion, yet knowing her
irrevocable vow, they stood apart quite helpless, gazing
at her with eyes dimmed with tears. The day waned
and the sun loomed over the western horizon about to
leap into the lap of "*Prachi*" (west), and still the body
lay unburnt. Of the hundreds of thousands assembled
there, not a single being considered himself fit to touch
the body. The bereaved widow was beginning to despair of cremating her husband's remains without surrendering her vow, when a man was descried hastening
towards her. Approaching her, he addressed her respectfully, and said : "Mother, will you let me assist
you in carrying the body to the edge of the river, and
there performing the last rites ?" The lady benignly
said : "My son, I have no objection to accept your kind
offer of help, if you can assure me that you are perfectly
pure and sinless. I trust you have already heard of

my vow." The man at once replied : "Lady, I am the most sinful being on the face of the earth, but a dip into the holy Ganges which I am going to have, will thoroughly cleanse me of all my sins and impurities." Suiting the action to his words, he instantly plunged into the river, and emerging from it, exclaimed : "Now, mother, I am as pure as newly fallen snow, and am so confident of my holiness, that I will without any further parlance, perform the funeral obsequies of your husband." No sooner did he utter these words than both the widow and her dead husband vanished.

Parvati rejoining her husband in his spiritual form, said : "My dear, the farce just played at your suggestion has furnished a complete answer to my question and I no longer doubt your word. Although thousands have come here to bathe in the Ganges, few have an atom of faith in her sanctity and purifying power. It seems they have come here for any purpose but of securing salvation from their sins. In the whole of this vast mass of humanity, there is only one person who has real and unswerving faith in the Ganges, and will ulti- mately be saved. I perceive that faith—the true un- wavering faith—alone is the secret of '*Mukti*', and un- less and until man has such faith, he can never obtain salvation, although in the present age every one glibly talks of it as a saleable commodity."

Needless to add that Parvati and Parameswara appeared in their real form before the man that so readily offered his help and took him along with them to Kailas.

54. Iswara and Brahman.—"*Iswara* is the sum-total of individuals, yet *he* is an individual, as the human body is a unit, of which each cell is an individual.

Samashti, or collected, equals God ; *Vyashti*, analysed, equals the *Jiva*. The existence of *Iswara*, therefore, depends on that of *Jiva*, as the body on the cell, and *vice versa*. Thus, *Jiva* and *Iswara* are co-existent beings ; when one exists, the other must. Also, because, except on our earth, in all the higher spheres, the amount of good being vastly in excess of the amount of bad, the sum-total (*Isvara*) may be said to be all-good. Omnipotence and Omniscience are obvious qualities, and need no argument to prove, from the very fact of totality. Brahman is beyond both these, and is not a state ; it is the only Unit not composed of many units ; the principle which runs through all, from a cell to God, without which nothing can exist, and whatever is real is that principle, or Brahman. When I think I am Brahman I alone exist ; so when you think so, etc. Therefore, each one is the whole of that principle."

55. Ahankara.—Once, Vyasa was walking over the field of Kurukshetra, when he found a little worm crawling away as fast as it could at the sound of his feet, fearing that it might get crushed under them. The sage smiled and said to himself : "We regard that creature as worthless and despicable, but look at its anxiety to preserve its life ! Ah, what a wonder !" And then by virtue of his *Yogic* powers, he found to his great surprise, that it was the eminent sage, Narada, who by some sinful *Karma*, had become the worm and, giving it the power of speech, he asked : "O worshipful sage Narada, how is it that, having got into this wretched worm life, you are so anxious to preserve it ?" The worm replied : "All praise be to you, O Vyasa ; by a sinful act I was reduced to this condition, but this is the fatal illusion, that even in this worm life, I think sufficiently well of myself and have enough to do with my own pleasures and pains. Though mean and despicable in your eyes, I am not so to myself and that is why I am anxious to preserve my life." Thus, while even the worm thinks so highly of itself, what wonder, that we look so big in our own eyes. Indeed, from the atom to the star, every particle in the universe rings with this egoism and it is this, that makes what is called the world. If by some magic, this egoism is purged out of the world, the unconditioned, universal Self or God alone will remain. Few of us are able to look beyond ourselves, to rise above this foolish 'I'.

56. Is Vedanta Pessimistic?—"All the criticism against the *Vedanta* philosophy can be summed up in this : that it does not conduce to sense enjoyments : and we are glad to admit that.......

"The *Vedanta* system begins with tremendous pessimism and ends with real optimism. We deny the sense optimism, but assert the real optimism of the supersensuous. Real happiness is not in the senses, but above the senses ; and it is in every man. The sort of optimism which we see in the world is what will lead to ruin through the senses.

"Abnegation has the greatest importance in our philosophy. Negation implies affirmation of the real self. *Vedanta* is pessimistic so far as it negates the world of the senses, but it is optimistic in its assertion of the real world."

57. Manki—the Brahmin Calf-breeder.—*Brahmaviths* value the moral and spiritual instruction imparted by the veteran *Vedantin*, Bhishma, to his disciple Dharma-

30

raja, very highly. It is maintained that the Santi and Anusasanika *parvas* of the Mahabharata, which are full of *Puranic* episodes illustrative of the great spiritual truths inculcated in the *Upanishads*, are the digests of the spiritual experience of Bhishma and other *Brahmavadins*, who to popularize the teaching of the *Vedanta* and render it more lucid and intelligible to the masses narrated many *Upakhyanas* (anecdotes) touching the characters and spiritual experiences of bygone saints and sages who lives are worth our study and imitation. Santi and Anusasanika *parvas* of the Mahabharata contain a great deal of practical teaching with practical illustrations. Of the eighteen chapters of the Mahabharata they are supposed to be the most important. *Santi* means peace of mind, and *anusasana* injunction or command. It is a matter of fact that Dharmaraja won the field of Kurukshetra at the risk of his peace of mind. His mind was so much ruffled that it did not regain its equilibrium before Bhishma put before him the cases of saints of olden days who obtained peace of mind by the adoption of the line of spiritual and moral conduct promulgated in the *Upanishads*. During this long course of instruction, Dharmaraja asked Bhishma : "Sire, how could one who gives himself up to avarice acquire peace of mind ?" In reply to this question Bhishma narrated the incidents of the life of Manki, the Brahmin calf-breeder.

"There was an old Brahmin by the name of Manki who desired to amass wealth, but found he was doomed to repeated disappointments. At last, with a little remnant of his property he purchased a couple of calves with a yoke for training them to agricultural labour.

One day the two calves properly tied to the yoke, were taken out for training in the fields. Shying at the sight of a camel that lay down on the road, the animals suddenly went towards it and fell upon its neck. Enraged at finding the calves fall upon its neck, the camel, endued with great speed, started up and ran at a quick pace, bearing away the two helpless creatures dangling on either side of its neck. Beholding his poor calves thus borne away by that strong camel, and seeing that, being strangled, they were on the point of death, and that any attempt on his part to save them was of no avail, Manki broke out in the following strain : If wealth be not ordained by destiny, it can never be acquired by even a clever man exerting himself with diligence and confidence and accomplishing with skill all that is necessary towards that end. I had before this endeavoured by diverse means and with devotion to earn wealth. Behold this misfortune brought about by destiny to the property I had. The desire for wealth which hitherto possessed my soul has never allowed me to enjoy peace of mind for even a minute. *The person that desires happiness should renounce attachment.* Ho, it was well said by Suka while going to the great forest from his father's abode renouncing everything, 'Of these two, *viz.*, one who obtains the fruition of all his desires and one who casts off every wish, the latter is the better.' *No one could kill desire by gratifying it.* It grows on what it feeds. One desire when satisfied gives rise to another. O Desire, thou art the root of evil. To keep myself out of thy reach I shall control my mind whence thou dost emanate. I shall thus put an end to thee. Thou shalt be destroyed with thy roots. The desire for wealth can never bring happiness. There is misery in acquiring it, and if it is lost after acquisition, that is felt as death. When acquired, one is never gratified with its measure, but yearns for more, and becomes greedy. I am now awakened. Do thou, O Desire, leave me. Let that desire which has taken refuge in this my body, this compound of the five elements, go whithersoever it chooses. Ye all that are not of the Soul, I have no joy in you, for ye follow the lead of Desire and Cupidity. Abandoning all of you, I shall take refuge in God. Beholding all creatures in myself and devoting my reason to *yoga*, my life to receiving instructions from the wise, and my soul to Brahman, I shall happily rove through the world without attachment of any kind, so that thou mayest not be able to plunge me again into such sorrows. I cast thee off with other passions from my heart. I shall forgive those that slander or speak ill of me. I shall not injure even when injured. With my heart contented and my senses all at ease, I shall live by what I may get. Freedom from attachment, emancipation from desire, contentment, tranquillity, truth, self-restraint, forgiveness, and universal compassion are the qualities which will henceforth distinguish me. Having cast off Desire, great is my happiness now. Like a person plunging in the hot season into a cool lake, I shall soon enter into *Brahma*. The pleasure which results from the gratification of Desire, or that other purer felicity which one enjoys in Heaven, does not come up to even a sixteenth part of the happiness which comes from the abandoning of desire. Entering into the immortal city of *Brahman*, *i.e. Jivanmukta* state, which is attained through wisdom, I shall spend my days happily like a king, my heart free from desire of any kind, and my soul enjoying its identity with the universal *Brahman*."

"With these serious remarks, Manki dismissed Desire and did not associate with her any longer," 'continued Bhishma. "He was happy with the thought that he had up-rooted desire from his mind, which attained such a state of tranquillity as he had not known before. Follow, therefore, in the footsteps of Manki, Dharmaraja, un-alloyed happiness and perfect peace of mind will be vouchsafed unto you."

Renunciation has been a trait of character peculiar to the Hindus, and it is this principle of renunciation that has guided our people through countless ages. The present civilisation brings us face to face with men who denounce the principles that have conduced to the spiritual welfare of our land of 'Philosophy and Re-ligion'. Man works according to the ideal before him. A man whose ideal of life is, like that of our ancient *Rishis*, to unravel the mystery of life and death, hates material surroundings and pleasures of the senses. On the other hand, a man whose faculties of observation do not go beyond this transitory life, satisfies himself with material environments. A lover of emancipation (*Moksha*) controls his mind and senses, as did Manki of old ; and a lover of worldly pleasures is controlled by his mind and senses. This is the difference between a wise man and others. It is therefore one of the pri-mary duties of a lover of *Mukti* (emancipation) to kill his desires, or, if it is not practicable to do so, to reduce them to a minimum inasmuch as he wishes to enjoy that peace of mind to which the greatest men of the world, sovereigns, statesmen, and warriors are alike strangers.

58. The Power of Faith.—There was a great *Acharya* or Religious Preceptor, who from time to time revealed to people the method of attaining eternal beatitude. This he did in various ways. To some he spoke at length about it; to others he gave laconic formulæ, which, if they recited and meditated upon, led them by degrees to a knowledge of the *Paramatman* and to the happiness that is the result of such knowledge. The period during which he was to instruct his disciples and others who sought enlightenment at his hands had come. Crowds of people had gathered round his *Asrama* or hermitage. Among them, there were many that had mastered the *Vedas* and *Shadangas*; many that had studied the various systems of philosophy and gained a very clear knowledge of the arts and sciences in all their branches. Many ruling princes had also come with their followers to receive instruction from the *Paramahamsa*, for *Brahmavidya* or knowledge of the *Paramatman* is dear to all—irrespective of their positions in life. The day on which the Preceptor was to begin instructing the people, actually arrived; and all appeared before him with reverential faces, and reciting stanzas from a great many poets suited to the occasion and the dignity of the *Paramahamsa*. One after another, the learned approached him and received suitable hints in the *Vedanta*. Every face that returned from the *Asrama* beamed with delight. Doubts had been destroyed like straws in a conflagration. Truth appeared before them like the distinct orb of the sun at break of day, and the way to final emancipation from the bonds

of existence seemed clear and near at hand. Large concourse of the initiated assembled in the woodlands
around the *Asrama* and, comparing notes, found the
instruction imparted to them in perfect conformity
with the tenets of the *Vedas* and the *Vedangas*. The
ruling princes also received at the hands of the *Paramahamsa* such enlightenment as placed them much above
the ordinary mortals of the world and filled them with
an internal light and peace to which they had long been
strangers. The eventful day well nigh drew to a close.
The orb of day was standing on the verge of the horizon,
to go down and leave the world to darkness. A *Chandala*
or man of the lowest order of human beings in India
appeared at some distance before the *Asrama* and prostrating himself before the *Paramahamsa* who was seated
in the *Asrama* said :—"Sire, I have long been desirous
of receiving instruction at your hands : vouchsafe to
tell me something of the *Paramatman*, that will destroy
the gloom in my mind and fill it with light and peace."
"Horror of horrors"—said the *Pandits* assembled
around—"How can a *Chandala* ask for *Brahmavidya*,
and how can the *Paramahamsa* impart it to him !" The
Paramahamsa noted the request of the *Chandala*, and
after looking at him attentively for some time, said :
"Begone !" "Well said" exclaimed the *Pandits*—"Who
knows the law better than the *Paramahamsa* ?" It was
a custom of the *Asrama* that, the next year, the people
then initiated should present themselves, and shew the
Paramashamsa the progress they made. So the next
year came, and a large concourse of people gathered
round the *Asrama*. The *Acharya* propounded a query
the answer to which would shew whether any of them

had really profited by the instruction imparted by him
the previous year. The answer was to be noted on a
piece of bark and sent up to the *Paramahamsa* with the
name of the writer. Accordingly a great many pieces
of bark went into the *Asrama*. He perused them all,
and found that there was only one among them which
contained the correct answer. It was signed :—"Begone !"
It was the piece sent up by the *Chandala*. The *Paramahamsa* declared what had actually taken place; the
learned that were assembled there were astonished at
what had happened. The *Paramahamsa* addressed them
as follows :

"You must know that faith is a powerful agent in
the enlightenment of the heart. When the *Chandala*
asked for instruction, he was told 'begone'. This he
took as his aphorism, and, meditating on it, first came
to the conclusion that he should go away from the world
and its ways, to make his path clear towards eternal
bliss. Thus, by further interpreting the same word, he
found all that was needed for the elucidation of his mind.
He believed and he knew. None of you was capable
of that degree of belief, for you have all been imbued
with ideas of your greatness as scholars. Hence it is
that the *Yogi*, 'Begone', as he signs himself, has become
a true disciple of mine." The learned, who heard this
speech, were all convinced of what the *Paramahamsa*
said, and immediately adopted a life of extreme humility
and faith. The *Yogi*, "Begone" became a preceptor
to many of them.

59. The Glory of Love.—In days of yore, there lived
a young Brahmin, named Chandrasarma with his wife
Sarada. He had been brought up in a very careless

and idle manner and by that means had contracted many vicious habits. He was surrounded by low companions and bad women; his life was a continual stream of debauchery and carnality.

At last he fell in love with a woman, named Kamala. She was beautiful, accomplished and young. She gradually gained wonderful influence over this young Brahmin and ruled him with an iron hand. He lost himself in her enticements; he left his house and remained day and night with her.

One day he went with her to a river side for recreation; but, on their way home, he was bitten by a venomous serpent and dropped down dead. Kamala, finding no signs of life in his body, ran away for fear of being charged with the murder.

Next day the corpse was seen by some and an alarm was raised. Sarada and her relatives went to the spot where his body was lying. Sarada, looking at the corpse, wildly cried and rolled on the ground with grief. Her relatives and many others tried to console her but in vain. Immediately after, a funeral pile was prepared.

When the fire began to blaze and burn high, Sarada bathed and dressed herself in pure white. She circumambulated the fire thrice, gave away all the ornaments on her body, and all the wealth belonging to her, to Brahmins and jumped into the fire pronouncing: "Hara! Hara! Gobinda, Madhava!" Such was the intensity of her love.[1]

As soon as she jumped, the great God, in the twinkling

---

[1] There is no attempt here to advocate or praise the practice of Sati. The incident is mentioned only to add force to what follows.

of an eye, took her in a *Vimana* or celestial car to Kailasa, which was the reward for her love.

In the divine world she always offered prayers to the Lord and His wife, Parvati, and was always absorbed in meditation. Parvati was pleased with her firm devotion and asked her, what everlasting blessing she wanted from Her. Sarada replied : "O Merciful Bhavani, please to condescend to show me my husband." She longed to see her husband, for she was eager to speak to him of the bliss she enjoyed in the presence of God and take him over there if possible. "Very well," replied Parvati, "Go to the hill yonder where you will find your husband."

Then, Sarada, with great joy went in an aerial car to the hill where she beheld her husband, in the shape of a devil, walking alone buried in his own thoughts and frequently uttering the words : "Kamala, Kamala." When she heard it, she burst into tears, "O my husband," exclaimed she, "I now know how much love your great heart is capable of, but neither Kamala nor I, am worthy of your great love. Oh how good it would have been if you had dedicated this immeasurable love of yours to God !"

The word went into the very depth of the ghost's (Brahmin) heart ; he stood a few seconds in mute astonishment ; then he said : "Yes, Sarada, you are right, I worked out my own ruin. Is there any remedy ? Where can I find Him ?" Sarada replied with a smile : "You ask of me, 'Where can I find Him ? But I ask you to tell me where you cannot'." But, on finding him silent, she continued : "O Chandrasarma, I will now tell you the places where the Supreme Being abides.

They, who look upon another man's wife as their own mother, and his wealth as the deadliest poison, who rejoice to see a neighbour's prosperity and are grieved for his misfortunes, their heart is His abode. He who has given up all attachment to tribe, sect, wealth, hereditary religion, worldly advancement, friends, relations, home and all, and given himself wholly to Him, in his heart is His temple wherein to abide. They who never ask for anything but simply love Him, will become absorbed in Him. He is the source of all beauty, of all sublimity. He is the only object to be loved. You must, therefore, worship Him alone and nothing else. He is to be worshipped as the one beloved dearer than everything in this and the next life. You should give up the idea of 'I' and 'Mine' and must ever try to be unselfish, and self-sacrificing. You should also realise that the soul (the life principle) which prompts you to work, is neither doer nor enjoyer but is simply a witness. If you understand and act up to the principles I have just mentioned, you will certainly enjoy that Divine Bliss which you anxiously thirst for."

Scarcely had she finished her instructions when he cried : "Quarter, O Merciful God ! Thy might is immeasurable, and immeasurable Thy Majesty ; I knew Thee not. I have reaped the fruit of my own actions ; now my Lord, succour me, for to Thee I have come for refuge."

When the merciful God heard this most piteous appeal, He took him with his wife, Sarada, to Kailasa.

60. Helping Others.—We should drown our selfishness in love, but in helping the poor and doing such things we should never fall into the danger of priding ourselves on that account. We are simply instruments, not free agents. In a certain village there was once an old woman, who lived by preparing and selling cakes. She would set about her business punctually at 4 a.m., every day. She had a cock which announced to her the break of day as punctually, so much so that in course of time she gradually got into the belief that the day would not break unless her cock raised its trumpet voice. One day it so happened that the village boys offended her : she vowed vengeance and said : "Very well, these little fellows do not know who I am. I shall remove with my cock to the next village and see how the day could break here ; let the fellows suffer an eternal night. These little fellows offend me !" She did as she vowed that very night, and the next day, when some men came to the second village from the first, she said to them : "You see, if you had appeased me, all this would have been avoided ; poor men, I pity you ; you have to suffer eternal night." They asked what the matter was and she replied : "Why, I have brought my cock over here and so the day would not have broken in your place." It is needless to add that the men had a hearty laugh at the idiotic woman's self-importance. A similar mistake we are all of us committing ; we think that, but for us such and such a thing would never happen ; we die but the world goes on all the same. We should warn ourselves against such mistakes.

61. Cause of Misery.—"Once Krishna was walking with Arjuna out of the battle-field. A Brahmin was seen going round a fire, with the idea of falling into it ; one moment more, all would have been-over. Arjuna, learned in the *Gita*, ran to rescue the poor Brahmin.

'Poor man,' said he, Krishna laughing within himself
all the while, 'why this despair, why this suicide? O
Brahmin, venerable as you are, I shall give you half of
my kingdom, go shares with you in all my wealth, only
stop from your horrible act.' The Brahmin replied :
'Who are you thus to prevent me? Your wealth, your
empires, keep all of them, and take them over with you
when you die. As for me, my only beloved son is no
more, and why should I live? Fire is ready, prevent
me not?' Arjuna dragged him away by his *Gandiva*,
fell at his feet and exclaimed : 'O Brahmin, I shall give
you anything, commit not this sin.' The Brahmin was
ready with his reply : 'Yes, yes, easily said. If your
son had died, this fire would have devoured you, I
know.' Krishna, apparently innocent Krishna, said :
'It is true ; his grief he only knows ; if your son dies
to-morrow, I too know you will do the same.' 'No, no,'
replied Arjuna emphatically : 'Even if my son dies, I
will not do it.' Krishna said, 'It is all words. The
Brahmin added : 'My grief is mine, you may talk but
let me die. I am sure if your son dies, you will also do
the same.'. 'No, no,' said Arjuna, the far-seeing Arjuna :
'I promise, I swear.' 'Give me the oath' was the
Brahmin's reply. Arjuna was true to his word, the
Gandiva was down at once ; and he leapt over it once,
twice and thrice. At once, the conjuring Krishna, the
Magician of magicians drew away the vision ; the fire
disappeared, and with it the illusory Brahmin ; the
oath alone remained. Arjuna stared at Krishna, and
Krishna stared at Arjuna in return with his black eyes
wide open (the same eyes which Ravi Varma has so
well portrayed), and complimented him for his **extreme**

unselfishness. Poor, discomfited Arjuna took back his *Gandiva* and returned to the battle-field. The evening sun set with, of course, its usual pomp; and Abhimanyu's (Arjuna's son) soul also set with it, 'to bid good morning in a fairer clime.' As soon as he heard the news, Arjuna wanted a huge fire scorching the heavens to be reared for him and his *Gandiva*. 'Yes, yes,' said Krishna, 'Remember your oath: one thing for the Brahmin, another for the Kshatriya; one word for others, another for you,—I suppose!' Arjuna was silenced. He had to choke all his grief within himself, spoke not a word, and asked for no fire. Arjuna had advised the Brahmin not to grieve; but when the turn came to him, he was not able to bear his own grief. What was the reason? The self in Arjuna had not died; it asserted itself; and the result was—one thing for the Brahmin, another for himself. The *Gita* was not sufficient to silence his self. Krishna's magic was required in addition. This low selfishness is the cause of all our misery."

62. The Story of Nachiketa.—There was a great king who had a son named Nachiketa. Prince Nachiketa did not trouble himself much about mundane matters. He had a devotional turn of mind. His instincts led him to the *Paramatman*. He was desirous of knowing all about Him. His father performed a great sacrifice, at which all the wordly effects at his command were given away to the officiating priests, the very territories of the king, including the royal domains were given away. Nachiketa asked his father in a meditative mood :—"Father, to whom do you give me?" The king replied : "I give you unto death." Nachiketa went over to the mansion of death, and lay down on the dais in front of the portal of his garden. Three days had so passed away; Yama turned up eventually, and finding the royal youth at his gate, said :—"Young man, I am sorry to see you here without food or drink for three days. The wise have said that the man, who lies at the gate of another without food or drink for a day takes away a great deal of the good that belongs to him. You have been at my gate for three days like that. I am certainly a loser to a great extent by it. Let me compensate myself by granting you three boons. Specify them as you please." Nachiketa began by saying :—"O Yama, my first boon shall be a mind free from passion and full of peace." Yama saw the direction in which the young man was moving. He replied :—"O Nachiketa, it behoves you to ask for more useful and desirable things than this. Here are fair women, excellent chariots, concerts of music, immense wealth, luxuries seldom known to men, take them and all many more like them. I shall give you long life—ay, longer life than the longest yet known on earth, with perpetual youth and vigour. Take them all, my good man and be happy." Nachiketa replied :—"O Yama, these are all sbuject to 'the taint of a to-morrow'. I want that which is eternal and which knows no beginning nor middle nor end." The young man stuck to his point. Yama endeavoured his best to get him out of it. But all his efforts were in vain. Nachiketa had his wish. The *Paramatman* was reavealed to him by Yama. The Prince returned to his father's house and lived like a *Samyamee*, or, spiritual anchorite, attending to the affairs of this world in the spirit in which one like him alone could attend to them. He used to say to every one

that asked him—"who attained pre-eminent happiness?"
—in the worlds of scripture, *"Brahmavid apnoti param"*
—*i.e.*, "He who knows the Supreme Being attains
Supreme Bliss".

63. Faith.—

Thou canst not prove the Nameless;
For nothing worthy proving can be proven,
Nor yet disproven : wherefore Thou be wise.
Cleave ever to the sunnier side of doubt,
And cling to Faith beyond the forms of faith!

64. Samadhi.—

For more than once when I
Sat all alone, revolving in myself
The word that is the symbol of myself,
The mortal limit of the self was loosed,
And passed into the nameless, as a cloud
Melts into Heaven. I touched my limbs—the limbs
Were strange, not mine—and yet no shade of doubt,
But utter clearness, and thro' loss of self
The gain of such large life as matched with ours
Were sun to spark—unshadowable in words,
Themselves but shadows of a shadow-world.

65. The Nameless!—

The All-embracing, All-sustaining One,
Say, doth He not embrace, sustain, include,
Thee? me? himself? Bends not the sky above?
.. ..
And earth, on which we are, is it not firm?
And does not All—that is,
Seen and unseen, mysterious All—
Around thee and within,
Untiring agency.

Press on thy heart and mind?
Fill thy whole heart with it—and when thou art
Lost in the consciousness of happiness—
Then call it what thou wilt,
Happiness! Heart! Love! God!
I have no name for it!

66. Gnana and Karma.—"When there is no food for the ear, a little may be given for the belly."—*Kural.*

In the course of his rambles, Jesus once went into a certain village where a woman named Martha received him into her house. And she had a sister called Mary who sat at Jesus' feet and heard his word. Martha was vexed at being left alone to attend to the supper, while her sister without minding her household duties sat listening to Jesus' preaching. So she came to him and said: "Lord, dost thou not care that my sister hath left me to serve alone? Bid her therefore that she help me." And Jesus answered and said unto her: "Martha, Martha, thou art careful and troubled about many things; but one thing alone is really needful in order to live and Mary hath chosen that good part, which shall not be taken away from her."

Referring to this story Pilgrim writes: "The story of Martha and Mary is a standing protest against our deification of action—but the churches called after the name of the great Teacher, and whose representatives have become as a rule 'mere echoes of the world's self-seeking'" have been reduced to accept the world's apologetic theory that the teachings of Christ are incapable of practical application—indeed, as the author of *Scientific Religion* points out, the present state of things in Europe has absolutely made them so.

31

But though the literal application of Christ's teaching has become an impossibility in the West, there are still spots on the earth's surface where the fever of the modern life has not yet reached, where the lust of wealth and luxury—the Gods or Demons whom the West worships—have no power to quicken the pulses in many a quiet household, whose inmates have at least inherited from their nobler ancestors a juster appreciation than is met with in the West of the ephemeral character of life, and a worshipping reverence for those who are capable of true meditation.

67. Om! Santih, Santih, Santih.—There was once a great prophet, by name Elijah, who fled away from his countrymen, as they "forsook God's covenant and threw down His altars". He took refuge in a cave and was told that God would appear to him. There came a great and strong wind, which rent the mountains and devastated the forests; Elijah thought that the Lord had come, but the Lord was not in the wind. After the wind, came the thunder and the lightning but the Lord was not in them either. Then came an earthquake; the earth belched forth fire, the rocks were torn to pieces and the mountain was rent to its foundation; Elijah looked for the Lord, but the Lord was not in the earthquake. Then followed a beautiful calm, indescribably beautiful; and Elijah knew that God was there, and so He was.

The above is a beautiful allegory. The storm, the earthquake and the other things referred to, symbolise the rage of the senses, the intellect, etc. "The mind which follows the tempestuous senses goes to ruin, like a ship tossed about in the middle of the ocean by a (tremendous) storm" (*Gita*, II, 67). God dwells in the supreme tranquillity of the mind (*Santih*). "He who is free from desire and without grief, beholds by the tranquillity of his senses the Majesty of the *Atman* or God, who is subtler than what is subtle, greater than what is great, and is seated in the heart of living beings" (*Kath. Upa.*, II, 20). "But the man whose charioteer (the intellect) is wise, and the reins of whose mind are well applied, obtains the goal of the road, the highest place of Vishnu (God)" (*Ibid.*, III, 9).

VI

PITFALLS IN THE VEDANTA

RENUNCIATION

THE path to salvation is, says the *Upanishad*, like walking on a sword; it is dangerous and difficult and requires great caution. It is like dancing on a rope hung over a vast abyss. One false step might be fatal. Hence arises the necessity for a *Guru*. A *Guru* can, however, do little, unless the student moves freely and frequently with him and gets his doubts cleared then and there.

A certain king went into a forest, and there finding a sage, fell at his feet, and asked of him the way to salvation. "Absolute renunciation" (*Sarva sanga parityagam*) replied the sage. The king asked no further questions, but thanked him and departed; and as soon as he reached his kingdom, he abdicated his throne, took the vow of a *Sanyasin*, retired into the forest, built there an *Asrama* and began to lead a lonely life. A few years passed in this way but he had not become any the wiser. So he again went to the *Guru* and asked of him the way to salvation and again the *Guru* replied *Sarva sanga parityagam*. The king thanked him and departed thinking: "True I have left wife, children, kingdom, wealth and power but I keep here an *Asrama* and live like a householder"; so he set fire to the hut and began to live in the open air. His body soon lost all vestige of royalty, became pale and emaciated; the sun and rain told heavily on his health, till at last he became a skeleton and unable even to move about. But the bliss of wisdom had not yet come to him. So he again went to his *Guru* and asked of him the way to salvation and again the

Guru said *"Sarva sanga parityagam"*. The poor king got miserably confounded. He long thought of what else he had to give up. He said : "I have no house, no money, no vessels not even a piece of cloth to wear." It struck him that he should now give up the only thing he had and that was his body. Some stories came to his mind of God having presented Himself to his devotees at the critical moment of giving up their bodies. At once, he rose up and prepared to hurl himself down from a rock. A few minutes more and all would have been over. Just then his *Guru* presented himself before him and asked him what he was about. The quondam king replied : "I am only carrying out your behest and am sure as soon as this body also is given up, I shall be saved." "Good God !" exclaimed the sage, "what a curious meaning you have put upon my words. If this body goes, another immediately comes and where then is your salvation ? I admire your perseverance, but alas ! how misdirected ! True renunciation is not the giving up of your body, but being free from attachment of any kind in your mind. You have touch with external things, only through your mind and losing that mental attachment is the only true renunciation. You heard a great truth from me, but had not the patience to ask me what exactly it meant ; you may live *in* the world but not to be *of* it—*this* is the great secret of renunciation."

Renunciation is often misunderstood. Though few people carry the error to such an extreme as in the story, many mistake it to be external ; and how many homes have been rendered desolate by the mistake ! Physical renunciation is really easier than mental and is therefore more common.

What is Real Asceticism

The river Jumna has become classical by its associations. Much larger rivers like the Amazon, the Missouri and the Mississippi dwindle into littleness by its side ; and tradition which is the crystallised poetry of national life has connected it with the name of Krishna, and thereby lent to it an extraordinary amount of sacredness and glory.

One fine evening, so the story goes, Radha and Krishna were sweetly playing together on its silver sands, when the cool breeze of the hour brought with it a rich stream of *Vedic* music. Radha, surprised at the sound, asked her lover whence it came, and Krishna replied : "My dear, it seems to come from an *Asrama* in the neighbouring woods where a *Sanyasin* lives and does penance." Radha said : "Really, these *Sanyasis* renouncing their homes, wives and children and living in the forest seem to be the holiest of men : they deserve the grace of heaven best and are sure to obtain it foremost, while a householder living in the midst of his family gets engrossed with its cares, and however pious he may be, can never attain *Moksha*." Krishna coldly replied : "may be," and began carelessly to play on his favourite flute. Radha was, however, too deeply impressed with the forest life and its poetic associations to let go the topic, and continued her praises of ascetic life. "There is something sacred," said she, "in the orange robe and the humble roof of the *Sanyasin*, and a man living in the company of tall trees and large rivers must certainly be grand himself, and God is better contemplated in the solitude of the forest than in the midst of family strife. I can conceive, my lord, of no holier men than these *Rishis* of the forest," and she added, "shall we go, my lord, to visit the holy sage who at this hour so full of calmness and repose recites the *Vedic Rik*? For, the very sight of these holy men is purifying, as the *Sastras* say." Krishna replied: "Radha, my dear, your wish is always my wish, and we shall go to the yonder *Rishi*; but to combine pleasure with devotion, we shall go to him with a funny tale. I shall disguise myself as an old hunter, but you will be the rich and beautiful princess you already are, and we shall seek in his abode a night's shelter against the beasts of prey. I shall tell him a strange story about ourselves at which you ought to take care that you do not smile."

So saying, he assumed to the infinite amusement of the lotus-eyed Radha the guise of an old hunter with wrinkled cheeks, grey hairs, hunch-back and weary feet and began to walk forth supported on the arms of the young princess.

The *Asrama* was situated in a retired corner of the forest close to the brink of a beautiful rivulet that branched off from the Jumna. It was a low but artistically shaped hut; and everything about it was neat and tidy, and bespoke of care and taste on the part of its owner. The furniture consisted of several mud vessels, household utensils, woodcutter's implements, neatly shaped wooden seats, and softly tanned tiger and deer skins; all of them arranged with considerable house-keeping skill. Outside, were a number of tall trees overhanging the hut and lending to it a picturesque temple-like appearance. There were orange robes hanging on the branches of the trees and enriching them with a saintly aspect. It was a little after sunset when the Yadava pair reached the *Asrama*, and the moon had just begun to spread her silver beams.

The monarch of the *Asrama* was a middle-aged man very fair-looking and neatly dressed in attractive orange robes which shone with a peculiar brightness in the infant moonlight. He sat on a broad stone seat outside the hut facing the east; and no sooner did Radha and Krishna behold him, than they respectfully fell at his feet. The monk blessed them, and inquired who they were and where they came. Krishna said: "O most holy one, this fair princess before you is the daughter of the king of Suvraja who came with her and a large retinue on a hunting expedition to these woods, where this morning a band of wild elephants scattered their company and set them flying in various directions. The princess got parted from her father, and when she was running across the woods without knowing where her way was, she perceived a huge tiger pursuing her as if allured by the charms of her person. She would have fallen a prey to the wild animal and her beautiful body torn to pieces by its bloody fangs, had it not happened that at that critical moment I was there and with some remnant yet left of the skill in archery for which I was quite famous in earlier days, aimed a happy dart at the animal's neck and killed it. Then I heard her tale, and taking pity on her forlorn state undertook, in spite of my age, to conduct her to her father. We wandered all the day without finding any trace of the

hunting group, and, being weary with toil and grief and
afraid of the dangers of the forest, request shelter of you
for the night in your holy abode. Your holiness is
sufficient guarantee for our safety in every way, and it
is only God that has afforded us such a secure resting
at this hour." The monk expressed sympathy for the
princess in her distress and generously offered them the
desired shelter. He showed a great hospitality towards
his guests and supplied them with such refreshments
as he had in stock, he praised the old hunter for his
courage, chivalry and kindness, was very attentive to
his comforts, and kindly gave him a drink which he
said would be greatly refreshing. The crafty hunter
thankfully accepted the drink and in half an hour pretended to have fallen asleep and loudly snored. The
princess also took her bed in a corner of the hut.
Scarcely had an hour elapsed in this way, when the
monk approached the princess and gently awoke her.
She woke and finding the *Sanyasin* on his knees by her
side wrathfully asked him what he was about. "Pardon
me, O fair one," said he, "for my impudence. Never,
never in my life have these eyes beheld beauty like
yours—so captivating, so divine. No mortal can resist
the power of thy boundless charms; and how, O my
beloved, how can I be calm while such a priceless treasure
lies so near me?" "Is this your penance, your holiness,
your renunciation, O pitiable man," exclaimed the
princess in surprise and wrath "you vile miscreant, your
Vedic learning, your holy attire, your sage-like
aspect, is it all a disguise, a sham, a pretence? Do you
know"—"Excuse me, madam," interrupted the monk,
"penance is painful, and at the best only endured, not

enjoyed ; and as for holiness and renunciation, they exist only in name, and nowhere in reality. I took to this painful lonely forest life only out of disgust, because my wife, who was beautiful, though not one-thousandth as much as you are, deserted me. God has been extremely kind to me in having thrown you, O peerless one, in my way in such happy circumstances. The moon is unendurably beautiful and waits only to be shamed by your face, and the old fool lies there snoring. The drink I have given him is a strong intoxicant and will not suffer him to rise for three more days. Now is the hour, now, O sweet angel, not royal but divine, now is the—." "Vile wretch," exclaimed Radha, and she could say no more, her utterance was choked with anger. But hardly had the above words been pronounced, when the apparently sleeping intoxicated old hunter suddenly started up in the shape of a fiercely hissing, infuriated and terrible serpent, and raised a dreadful hood towards the miscreant monk, who frightened beyond measure took to his heels. The hunter-serpent Krishna pursued him for a while, till flying with desperate swiftness he disappeared in the woods.

Radha and Krishna were soon together again, when Radha said : "How foolish I was ! I was deceived by outward appearances. Renunciation does not consist in—." But before she had finished, Krishna cried out : "Hold me, Radha, O dear, hold me. I am being dragged away, I do not know by what, hold me, hold." Radha surprised beyond measure caught his arm and held it in hers, but strange to say felt herself also dragged along with Krishna. She tried her best to keep herself firm, but to no purpose. Something, a mysterious nameless something, was dragging them on, they did not know where, at least Radha did not. She felt the electric power of the current that was sweeping them onwards, but could not know whence it came and where it took them. She implored Krishna to account for the strange phenomenon; and on being repeatedly urged by her, he said: "I myself do not know; perhaps some devotee drags us on to him by the nameless power of his love," and playfully added, "You see how hard it is to be a God." Thus conversing they were dragged on into a beautiful orchard, where to Radha's great disappointment she beheld not any bearded monk, or humble devotee absorbed in steady meditation but a gay young man reposing on a softly cushioned cot and enjoying the sweet moonlight in the midst of six young damsels who were half naked and vying with each other in pleasing him, were performing a circular dance, *rasamandala* around that august personage. "Is this your worshipper, my lord," Radha sneeringly asked; but Krishna coolly said: "We shall wait and see." Indeed, they had hardly to wait, for no sooner was their presence known, than the half-naked young damsels covered themselves in haste and fled away with shame and confusion: and the apparently gay young man sprang forth from his seat with joy, and bowing down before Radhakrishna, said: "O God, my lord, welcome art Thou, welcome. My humble heart I offer Thee as thy seat, let my tears of joy wash Thy holy feet and let my love, O Lord, be Thy acceptable feast. All my penance is a zero before Thy infinite grace. Boundless is that grace, O Lord, and unparalleled except by Thy boundless power; and

my feeble tongue longs to spend itself in extolling that
infinite power and grace, pines to die a martyr to Thy
boundless glory—glory, which, in my feeble childish
fancy, I may 'liken to a vast immeasurable unfathomable
ocean of milk.' The sun, the moon and the flood of
stars above and below are like the wavelets of that ocean,
and conflagrations and deluges are its occasional storms.
The sky, the seas and mountains and rivers, which we,
in our littleness, are wont to call great, are droplets in
that mighty measureless ocean. The law of its tides,
the music of its mighty roar and the immeasurable
wealth of its undiscovered depths, not even gods can
understand. My feeble eyes lose themselves like rain
drops in the ocean, in the beauty of Thy face and form;
and if my mind and senses quail even before Thy surface-
show, as rocket shot against the sky, if there is nothing
but Thyself to be likened to Thee, how can I know Thee,
O Lord, except by becoming Thine own self? The
Vedas say : 'Thou art all forms yet formless, all motion
yet motionless, all names yet nameless, all time and
space yet timeless and spaceless, greater than the greatest
and smaller than the smallest.' Thou appearest to me
now as a man ; but when I look into Thee, Thou risest
grander, till all the stars and suns and moons and seas
and lakes and men and beasts are seen to be the work of
Thy fingers ; and when I look closer yet, Thou art
Thyself found to be this earth and all this boundless
universe ; and when I look still farther into Thee all
these multitudes of worlds disappear, and there is found
to be nothing but eternal light, eternal love and eternal
bliss, *'Grant me, O God, to know Thee as Thyself, to
know Thee as Thou canst not be known.' "* No sooner

had the prayer crossed the lips of the gay young man
than himself and Krishna electrically rushed together
into a mutual embrace and where they were there appeared to the wonder-filled vision of Radha, a mass of
burning light, which slowly grew and devoured star
after star until the earth and all the worlds floated in
it for a while as dust in the sunbeam, and finally died a
nameless death into a spaceless column of brightness.
Neither Krishna nor the gay young man was to be seen ;
and to Radha, to whom alone was it given to see the
unseeable, there was one universal noiseless music and
ineffable, measureless joy, one bright eternal light,
before which starlight, moonlight and sunlight were as
darkness—one bliss in the enjoyment of which her
thought expired. A few hours more, and the enraptured
Radha awoke from her dream-like vision, and found
herself in her palace in the arms of her ever-beloved
Krishna. "Enchanter of enchanters," said she, "Thou
hast taught me what true renunciation is. It is not the
flying away from wife and children in body and thinking
of them in mind, not the exchanging of houses for groves
and the music of women for the song of birds. To renounce is a matter of the mind ; for physical things are
never renounced, so long as the body, the grossest physical thing, lasts. The *Samsara* to be given up is inside,
not outside ; for the fluctuations of the mind (*Chitta
chalana*), anger, lust, desire, etc., form the real *Samsara*.
*To look at you, and in your light to abandon all attach-
ment for the outer world, to be in it and at the same time
out of it, is to realise you ; and in the enjoyment of that
realisation, to forget all forms and names—this is true
Sanyasa.* The hypocritical monk left the things of the

earth in body, but kept them in his mind. The gay
young man lived in them in body, but gave them up in
mind. The one was away from God even in the solitude
of the forest, the other was with God in the very midst
of music, women and dance. That is why, O Krishna,
the former did not know you even when you went to him
and fled away from you in shame and fear, while the
latter dragged you over to him and lost himself in you
with prayer and bliss.

"Who is a *Sanyasin*? He is the real *Sanyasin*, who
leaving off all *dharmas* and the attachment of I and
mine, and taking refuge in *Brahman*, is convinced through
practical realisation of great sayings (*Mahavakya*) like
'That art thou', 'All this is *Brahman*' and 'There is here
nothing like many, that he is himself *Brahman* and
moves on in the world in undisturbed and changeless
Samadhi. He alone is worthy of worship : he is the
real *Yogi*, the real *Paramahamsa*, the real *Avadhuta*
and the real *Brahmagnani*'."

(*Niralamba-Upanishad*).

Here *Sanyasa* or renunciation is identified with the
realisation of self ; and in conformity with this, the
story may be understood in the following way :

Radha represents *Chit Sakti* or the faculty of
wisdom, and Krishna is *Swarupa* or *Atman*. The hunting (*i.e.*, running after worldly pleasures), the mad
elephants of the forest (the calamities of the world), the
tiger (fear) are all false to Radha and Krishna but taken
to be real by the monk (*rajas* or desire). Man, indeed,
daily runs after the deer (pleasure), but too often meets
with the mad elephant (desire), and is pursued by the

tiger (fear); but all the three, pleasure, pain and fear form a mere tale in the light of the *Swarupa* which like a hunter chases fear, the result of mistaking the illusion, away. Radha being the faculty of wisdom, *i.e.*, *Buddhi*, turned away from the *tamasic* illusion of the world towards Krishna or Self, can, therefore, afford to smile at the false tale of the tiger and the elephant. Though turned towards the self she is not, however, totally freed from doubt, and temptation is the result. That is why she is taken to the monk (*rajas*), though already above *tamas*, (ignorance or illusion). The nearness of the self or the approach to realisation, already made by the fact of *Buddhi* or intellect having become wisdom, saves her; and the *Swarupa* plays the serpent and threatens away desire (*Gita*, V, 59). After the overthrow of *Rajas*, *Sattwa* alone remains (*Tamas* having already been got over), and it drags on to it the *Swarupa* and the faculty of realising it, *i.e.*, Krishna and Radha. *Sattwa* is represented as a gay young man, for its nature is cheerfulness, and the soft cushioned seat is *Sukhasana* in its true sense (see *Aparoksha anubhuthi*). The six damsels are the mind and the senses, which play round the pure *Sattwa* though in vain. They are half naked and try to tempt, for if fully revealed they will rouse disgust and can never tempt. When Radha-Krishna or *Upasana Murti*, *i.e.*, self, as consciously apprehended by wisdom, approaches, they all fly away; and then *Sattwaguna* and the *Swarupa* unite together into a nameless, formless *Jyotis* which Radha or wisdom no longer consciously perceives, but swoons away in seeing. Here is the *Sanyasa* of the *Upanishads*.

When the above *Nirvikalpa Samadhi* or *Nishta* is

over, wisdom returns to a conscious life, but freed from doubt and future possibility of temptation rejoices in her light and her love to the self, in all its manifestations—hunter, serpent, Iswara and *Brahman*.

THE WORLD AN ILLUSION

In the city of M——there once lived a *Swamiar* (sage) who, because he was supposed to live on milk and plantain fruits was generally known as *Milk Swami*. He used to wander with a little bit of *Garua* cloth about his loins, and everyday there used to gather round him a large number of men to whom he preached that the world was simply an illusion, that everything was false, and so on. One day, as he was very eloquently discoursing on the unreality of the universe, it so happened that the temple elephant got mad, and breaking the chains tied round its feet, furiously rushed towards the place where the right reverend *Milk Swami* was preaching. As soon as they saw the mad animal, his disciples deserted him in the middle of his discourse and fled away. The *Swami* also, in spite of his grand illusion theory, followed them, but the elephant, as if enraged at the *Maya* doctrine which he was preaching, pursued him unmindful of every one else, and the poor man with his clean-shaven, "round" head and dirty *garua* cloth—all that he had in the world—ran for life, and blinded by fear fell into a ditch. The elephant went as far as the brink of the deep ditch, and finding that its victim had passed beyond its reach, left him to his fate and took a different course.

After the danger was long past, the devoted disciples of the Swami approached the ditch and jeeringly said to him : "You said that everything was illusion, was not then the elephant false? And knowing that, why did you fly before it and fall into the ditch?" The Swami replied : "First raise me, my friends, from this nasty ditch, and then I shall answer your question." They complied with his request and raised him from the ditch, but they all said in one voice : "We will no longer give you milk and fruits, and, instead of calling you *Milk Swami*, we will, in future, call you *Gutter Swami*, for you acted contrary to your own teaching, and jumped into the gutter to escape an unreal elephant." The Swami, finding himself safely raised to the ground coolly replied : "My foolish friends, the elephant is an illusion ; that it got mad is an illusion ; that it pursued me is an illusion, that I fell into the ditch is an illusion and that you raised me is also an illusion. Everything in the world is illusion." The disciples applauded the answer and at once ordered a large supply of milk and fruits for the Swami. One of them, however, who was more intelligent than the rest said : "Ah Swami, had you just told us all this when you were in the ditch, we would not have taken the trouble to raise you out of it," and suddenly throwing him back into the gutter asked him if it was not a mere illusion that he had been again thrown into the gutter. The poor Swami could no longer comfortably stand on his illusion theory, for darkness was setting in and he was afraid of being left all the night in the nasty pit by his *over-Vedantic* disciples. He had to admit that the gutter at least was not illusory, but how to say that that alone was real

while all the rest of the world was false? He plainly
saw that he could no longer drive a profitable trade out
of the illusion theory, and therefore withdrew it wholesale, crying at the top of his voice : "The elephant was
real, its madness was real, the ditch is real and that you
have thrown me into it a second time is also real," and
begged his ex-disciples to raise him up.

Those who assert that the world is an illusion will
have to suffer the fate of the *Milk Swami*. The fact
is, the *Vedanta* does not say that the world is a mere
illusion. On the other hand it says that it is real, nay
that it is eternal. But its reality and eternality are
only relative, for it exists and can exist only in and
through Brahman, the changeless *substance*. *When
Brahman is realised, the world no longer exists, and until
then it is a reality which no one can deny.* We can call a
dream a dream only after we awake, and similarly no
man has the right to call the world an illusion, until he
has realised the Brahman, until he has ceased to be man
and become God.

VII

SEEKERS AFTER GOD

NANDA, THE PARIAH SAINT

IT has been well remarked : "how poor a thing is man if above himself he cannot erect himself" : and this erecting of ourselves above ourselves means nothing more than drawing out and developing the divinity that lies concealed in us. Man is a compound of brutality, humanity and divinity (*Tamas, Rajas* and *Satwa*) and in proportion as the last is developed, the other two leave him. Not the least remarkable of those that succeeded in this development of divinity—this erecting of oneself above oneself—was Nanda otherwise called, as we shall see why, *Tirunalaipovar*.

Nanda was born in the *Pariah* caste, about six hundred years ago. The *pariahs* are probably the remnants of the ancient non-Aryans of the land and are, as is well-known, a despised class. They are regarded as outside the pale of the great Hindu castes—*Brahma, Kshatriya, Vaisya* and *Sudra,* and it is considered pollution for a man of the three higher castes to approach a *pariah.* They are in some places attached to land as serfs and in others live by cultivating the soil and are, for their labour, rewarded with a share of the produce just enough to maintain themselves and their families. In no case, however, have they the opportunity for growing rich or owning property. The religious generosity of the higher castes having seldom been so great as to reach this neglected factor of the community, it has been quite passively suffered to build its own society and its own pantheon, and the result is a number of gross and curious social customs and a multitude of demoniac gods.

The *parachery* (the quarters of the *pariahs*, always remote from those of the other castes) of Adhanur[1] in which Nanda was born did not, we may be sure, differ in any leading feature from those of to-day. A number of small, unventilated, single roomed, hovel-like huts with pumpkin creepers covering their tops and scattered too wildly to be classified into streets or rows, black earthenware generally kept outside the huts, broken mud walls, heaps of rotting bones and other filthy matter abounding on every side, cocks and hens that chuckled and bode their time, dogs that barked all day long, half-naked women that barked oftener and louder and troops of dirty, sun-burnt and naked children playing or quarrelling—such were the surroundings amidst which our great saint was ushered into the world. Our actions are mixed in character, partly good and partly bad and Nanda, to whom it was given, by the goodness of his previous *Karma*, to set an inspiring example to the world and grow into god, was destined, by the necessary counterpart of the same *Karma*, to be born in the midst of a barbarous community : but the beauty of Providence is such that *our very punishments are blessings in disguise*, and the apparently unfavourable conditions, under which Nanda was born, themselves proved to be, *as we shall see*, for his own good and indirectly for that of the world.

Even in his early boyhood, he was, as we may easily understand, unlike the other boys of the *parachery* : his very play consisted in making figures of God, in clay

[1] In the District of South Arcot, Madras Presidency.

i.e., as he at that age wanted Him to be—a stout, black man with bold whiskers, a huge lace turban, high-heeled native shoes, and an axe or a scythe in his hand and at the same time very trustworthy, and kind and merciful to those that sought his protection. To make such clay gods, to sing and dance around them, to carry them along in procession, to organise an infant band of *Bhaktas* (pious men) and make festivals for his gods were his chief juvenile sports. The small circular *Gopuram* (tower) of the *Saivite* temple in the Brahmin part of Adhanur had a strange fascination for his boyish imagination for there were beauty, grandeur and, as he could not approach it, mystery enough to set them forth in relief. It was this love of the grand, the beautiful and the mysterious that was remarkable in Nanda and chiefly contributed to his salvation. He would often wistfully gaze at that tower wondering at its shape, size and grandeur and busily form guesses about the treasure underneath concealed to his view, which it was meant to glorify. Often as the village god passed in procession with torchlight, music, drums and *Vedic* chant, Nanda, followed by other *pariah* boys would run forth to obtain a view, however distant of the festival and return deeply impressed with the procession and its poetic associations. He had an inborn respect for all holy things—temples, festivals, Brahmins and the *Vedas*, which his low birth tended greatly to develop.

As he grew into manhood, his imaginative fervour and piety also grew with him and deepened and he became more and more eager to contribute what he could, however humble it might be, to the service of the Lord. It is the tendency of true love to grow till it overflows the heart, and then it can no longer be shut up within, but must necessarily show itself out in action. Nanda long thought over what he could do to please the Lord : he was not rich : he was of low birth : no kind of charity readily suggested itself to him. One day while seriously thinking over the matter, it struck him, all of a sudden that he might supply temples with leather for drums. To him, there was something almost miraculous in the very suddenness of the thought and he rose up with joy and exclaimed: "the Lord has spoken to me. He has commanded me to supply His drums with leather," and he immediately set about preparing it. The Lord, indeed, does always keep conversing with us, only, we do not hear Him : and of the things we offer to him He chooses, not by their value (for He is Himself the Lord of all things) *but by the love and piety* with which they are offered. The labour of procuring leather, of wetting and tanning it and cutting it into proper sizes, henceforth became to Nanda a sacred pastime and the very smell of leather roused in his imaginative mind a group of holy associations.

He had a few friends in the *parachery* (it is a pity that their names have not been handed down to posterity) who shared his enthusiasm and sympathised with him in his labours. Every now and then he would speak to them of God's glory and grace, smear himself and them with sacred ashes, and one day, while there was no work to be done in the fields, he stole away with them (we must remember that these *pariahs* were slaves under the village landlords) to a famous temple a few miles off, called Tirupunkoor now known as Old Vaitheesveran Koil. They went round the village three times, repeatedly besmeared themselves with sacred ashes and shout-

ed forth the names of Siva. Nanda was beside himself
with pious enthusiasm and danced and wept, and after
sunset, when the temple doors were opened, sent forth
to the priest his offerings of cocoanuts, plantain fruits
and loads of leather. He and his companions stood outside the temple at a little distance from the flag staff,
and from there obtained occasional glimpses of the Image
within. Their joy, particularly that of Nanda, knew
no bounds when they beheld for the first time, though
from a distance, the mysterious *sanctum sanctorum* of
the great temple all radiant with light. The ringing of
bells, the crowds of neat looking pious devotees, the
recitation of sacred verses, the *puja*, the burning of
camphor, the worshipping with light and other imposing
rituals of the temple, and above all the *Lingam* (Image
of Siva) itself, which by its very form filled the whole
place with a peculiar solemnity and sacredness, far
exceeded his grandest expectations and impressed his
imagination much more deeply (here his low birth
was an advantage to him) than they did that of the
Brahmin worshippers inside, who were familiarised to them

There was to him there a mystery only half cleared
and a solemnity he had never known before ; he eagerly
drank in the spectacle which to him was new and
fascinating; tears flowed in torrents from his eyes and
his emotional communion with God became every moment
closer and closer, till at last he became completely absorbed in meditation and all thought expired in the enjoyment. Those that saw him were filled with wonder at
the steadiness of his devotion, his self-absorption and the
serenity that shone in his face in spite of his low caste,
and before he woke from his devotional trance a large

and admiring crowd had gathered around him. The
sensation created at the time was so great that his visit
to Tirupunkoor has made a distinct epoch in its history
and richly added to the glory of its temple, for tradition
asserts that while he was standing behind the flag-staff
and struggling to get a view of the *Lingam* inside, Siva
took pity on him and ordered Nandi (the image of a bull
placed opposite to the *Lingam* in all Saivite temples)
to move a little to one side, that His low caste devotee
might get a view of Him ; and accordingly unto this day
the huge figure of Nandi at Tirupunkoor is placed not
exactly opposite to the image of Siva but leaning to one side.

As soon as Nanda awoke from his holy trance, he
prostrated himself before the Brahmin crowd, that had
gathered about him and began with his friends to go
round the village once again. It so happened, that
while thus going round, a certain Brahmin *Pundit* was
reciting before a large audience *Chidambarapuranam*
(the story of Chidambaram)[1] from the pial of one of the
cornermost houses of the Brahmin quarters. As Nanda
passed along, he heard the Brahmin say : "Chidambaram
is the holiest place in all the world ; he that once visits
the temple there, be he a *Chandala* (outcaste), crosses
once and for ever the ocean of births and deaths" : and
then followed an eloquent description of the temple
and the inner meaning of its grand symbolism.

Indeed in point of tradition, Chidambaram is one of
the richest cities in the world. What Palestine was for
the Christians, what Mecca is to the Muhammadans,
what Sreerangam is to the Vaishnavites (the worshippers

---

[1] In the South Arcot District, Madras Presidency.

of Vishnu), that Chidambaram is to the Saivite portion
of the Hindu community. It is one of the five great
places of worship in Southern India, in each of which,
God is represented as one of the five elements. There
the representation is as *Akas* (ether), the first of the five
elements. The idea of worshipping the elements as
God is essentially *Vedic*, and is a great help in the finding
out and practical recognition of the divinity in the
universe—which latter, when examined, is seen to be
nothing but a physico-chemical compound of these
elements. In a higher sense, the *Akas* worshipped at
Chidambaram is not the ether of the scientists, but the
spaceless, timeless, unconditioned sphere of the Self.
The very name Chidambaram means the *Akas* of wisdom
and the temple there is called *the Koil*—the temple *par
excellence*. In the centre of that temple, there is a gold-
tiled *mantapam* called the *Chit Sabha*—the hall of wisdom
in which is to be seen first the image of Nataraja and
then what is known as the *Rahasya* (the secret)—
representing of course the secret of all secrets, the
characterless *Nirvana* of the Self. Of all the anthro-
pomorphic representations of the deity yet known to
man, that of Nataraja is one of the very best and the
image at Chidambaram, which is the prototype of all
similar images elsewhere, is certainly one of the most
inspiring figures that I have known. Even considered
as purely a work of art, there are few images more
faultless, more life-like and more charming. That
soft curly haid tufted like that of a *dikshitar* (a priest
of that temple), the long prominent nose, those eyes so
full of life and expression, that face in which dignity,
bliss and merc speak out and dance, the natural bend

of the arms and their ornaments, that beautiful attitude of the dancer, seeing which one fancies that the figure is really dancing, and lastly, that raised foot (*kunjidapada*) so eminently inspiring, are before me as I write, and when to the artistic appreciation of the image is joined a full understanding of its idea, its inner poetry—that from the noise of the *damaruka* (a little drum) held in one of the right hands, innumerable worlds are represented as rushing forth into life as sparks from fire, as bubbles from a spring (*Sabda Nishtam Jagat*—the world sprang out of and stands by sound or vibration) : that the other right hand expressive of the idea "be it so", represents the power which maintains those worlds under a great unerring and faultless law ; that the fire in one of the left hands, represents the mighty and mysterious power of destruction, which makes the stars, mountains and oceans "the perfume and suppliance of a minute" ; that the firmly planted right leg indicates the power of the mystery that refuses to clear up, the thick manifold veil of illusive panorama which hides the truth from us for ages together ; and that lastly, the raised foot symbolises the grace of God, which shelters and saves those that seek it, from the eternal, infinite, and terribly deceiving drama of creation, existence and destruction—it is no wonder, that men like Appar, Manikkar, Pattanathar and Thayumanavar (these are some of the great Saivite saints of the Tamil land) forgot in that Presence the petty commercial prose of our daily life, and broke forth in the highest, the most philosophical, and the most impassioned poetry, that the Tamil language has known. The idea of ecstatic dance symbolised in the beautiful image of Nataraja—the great unseen manager of the drama of the world, has been the most popular one with the *non-Vaishnavite* poets and philosophers of the South. To them, wherever an atom moves, and the world means constant motion, there, Nataraja dances. In the play of the child, the mirth of women, the war ot nations, the rolling of the stars, in earthquakes, conflagrations and deluges, in the water drop as much as in the cataract, Nataraja is dancing—eternally and blissfully dancing. To the *Vedantin*, whom nothing less than the highest will satisfy, the conception of Nataraja means the all-pervading *Atman*, through whose power, all the world presents the vision of life and activity, and the dance signifies the ecstatic condition of the soul, which has triumphed over the terrible illusion of the world and the inner enemies of anger, lust, etc.,[1] and it is under the inspiration of this great philosophical conception, that the venerable sage Thayumanavar has poured forth most of his sublime *Upanishad*-like utterances. One particular feature in the story of Chidambaram is, that Patanjali and Vyaghrapada both attained to the Presence of Nataraja—the one by his *Yoga*, the other by his *Bhakti*—a grand recognition of the truth that both *Bhakti* and *Yoga* lead, each in its own way, to the same goal. To express, even more strongly, this most important of truths—that all religions and religious methods are only different paths for approaching God—in the same temple and within a few yards of Nataraja's shrine, there is that of Sree Govinda Raja Perumal; and Chidambaram is one of the most important places of pilgrimage for the *Vaishnavites* also.

[1] For further explanation see Part IV, Nataraja.

33

Nanda paused and heard the whole story of Chidambaram from the eloquent lips of the Brahmin reciter. It acted on him like magic. The words, Chidambaram and Nataraja, obtained a strange mastery over him. He became eager to visit Chidambaram, which was not very far off, that very night, and was with great difficulty dissuaded from his object by his companions. "The temple at Chidambaram would be closed," they said, "before you reach it and besides, you are a slave to your Brahmin master, you should not forget your position so easily. We have already stayed away too long and it will be dangerous to do so longer." A lesser man in that situation might have been provoked to reply: "Is that Brahmin greater than God? I care not for him. I shall have my own way," but Nanda meekly replied: "Yes, you are right. It has pleased God to place me in the situation of a bondsman. He knows what is good for me, infinitely better than I do. To resign myself to His will, is even a higher worship than visit his temple. I shall fall at the feet of my Brahmin master, please him in all honest ways and I am sure, he will sooner or later allow me to go to Chidambaram." So saying, he returned home with his companions, but not before he had dug out with their assistance a tank, still pointed out as his, for the use of the people at Tirupunkoor. The feat was regarded as wonderful, and the idea of a few *pariahs* joining together and creating a tank, was an altogether novel one, so much so, that popular tradition attributes the work to God Ganesa, who did it in order to please his father Siva's devotee. The truth is, love works wonders and Nanda's love was of a very high order; it was not like that of some people

who go into the temple with plenty of offerings to God—
cocoanuts, plantain fruits, etc., but would not give a
pie to the beggar at the temple gate. In Nanda's eyes
all men were God's children and to serve them, was
itself a kind of worship, higher even than supplying
temple-drums with leather or making offerings to God.
After digging and completing the tank he and his
companions returned home.

Henceforth it became the one passion of Nanda's
life to visit the great temple of Nataraja. Day and
night he would pant for it. While working in the fields,
while staying at home, while laying himself down to
sleep, always his mind was with the great God dancing
as it were the unceasing dance of creation, destruction
and maintenance. Every day he would think of begging his master to let him go to Chidambaram, but day
after day passed without his venturing to do so for fear
of a refusal. He would tell his friends everyday : "I
go to Chidambaram to-morrow," but a great many
to-morrows became to-days and he had not gone : he
became a veritable "dupe of to-morrow" and his very
friends began to nickname him "one that goes to-morrow"
(Tirunalaipovar).

In the meantime, the *pariah* community of Adhanur,
among whom true *Bhakti* (devotion) was a thing
altogether unknown, observed first with curiosity and
then with alarm, the change that was coming over
Nanda. The constant repetition of the holy name of
Siva, the frequent besmearing of the body with sacred
ashes, the exercises of meditation in which he was often
engaged, and more even than these, the thorough change
that had come over the inner man, his extreme meek-

ness and humility, his constant and involuntary references to God, his inability to talk of anything but Him and His glory, his self-absorption even in the midst of work, caused real uneasiness in the minds of his ignorant kinsmen, to whom any kind of deviation from the accustomed run of life was a source of fear. He would seldom mix in the cruel and barbarous sports of his community; meat and toddy lost their sway over him. Butchery was an act of abomination in his eyes, and he discouraged it whenever he had occasion. Often while the rest of the community was engaged in quarrel or gossip, he would unconcernedly repose under some tree and meditate: he would look at the wonderful creation around him, admire the unceasing miracles of the universe—plants, rivers, mountains, trees, etc., and say: "Ah, all this deceptive phenomenal wealth is the glory of that one foot of Nataraja so firmly planted down. Beautiful as all this is, let me O God cross over to you and *see you not as you seem, but as you are.*" Then he would fix his mind on the raised foot of Nataraja and pray with eyes filled with tears to be sheltered under its blissful shade of wisdom. One day Nanda had long sat meditating in this way till his eyes were suffused with tears of joy and himself passed into a state of ecstatic trance, when a curious neighbour went near him, and finding him unconscious and his body wetted with tears, gave the alarm to the whole community that something was wrong with Nanda. The report found ready acceptance on all sides, and soon our poor friend was rudely shaken and disturbed and was at once demanded an explanation; but all that he could say was: "Knowing that there is a God, who can help worshipping Him?" which of course was not found satisfactory. The result was that a council was at once formed on the spot, and it was unanimously resolved by the wise of the community, that Nanda's malady was due to the fault of not having held feasts for their gods more frequently, and that therefore one should be celebrated the very next day.

Grand were the preparations that were made for the feast. A huge *pandal* (shed) was erected and decorated with plantain trees, cocoanuts, mango leaves and flags. Fowls and sheep were procured in abundance for sacrifice. A *Valluva* priest of oracular fame was called in, and grotesque clay figures of the mighty gods of wonderful names—*Veeran, Irulan, Katteri, Veryan, Nondi, Chamundi, Nallakarupan, Pettannan, Pavadai* and a multitude of others too numerous to be mentioned here, were made. The next morning, the whole village gathered together under the *pandal*. The clay gods were arranged in order of importance; fowls and sheep and pots of toddy were ready for the feast. Nanda was held by main force, for which however there was no need, in the centre of the assembly, and the high priest Valluvanar shook his *damarukam* (a little drum); and at once there was a wild blowing of horns and a reckless beating of "drums and timbrels loud" and, as soon as they stopped, the holy priest got inspired; god had descended unto him, and he rose making all sorts of hideous cries; about ten people held him down, perhaps to prevent his escape to heaven. Thus held down and shaking forth his *damarukam*, he delivered with appropriate gestures the following oracular utterances. "Nandan," he said, "Nandan—Nandan—Nandan is possessed with the big

long-haired devil which resides in the market tamarind
tree ; it will make him laugh and weep and run and
talk and sleep" (many people do these things without the
help of the devil) and he asked : "Does he not do all
these ? " to which there was a tumultuous reply of,
"aye, aye, how true the oracle, how right ! " Nanda said
nothing but thought within himself : "O Lord, how
wonderful is thy dance ! Here is a wonderful scene being
played in Thy endless drama !" "Kill a hundred sheep,"
continued the oracle, "and two hundred fowls and
offer them with pots of toddy to god *Karuppan* and his
brothers, and they say that Nanda will at once be cured.
The great gods are extremely angry with you for having
neglected them so long." The oracle ceased and immediately a large dancing group of middle aged *pariahs*
was arranged and they sang.

> *Pedari* great, the guardian *dev*
> Of all our fields, poor Nanda save !

Nanda added,

> None but *Nates'an* has that power,
> For he's my chosen Lord and lover.

They sang,

> O *Vira* dark with turband huge,
> Beneath thy feet we seek refuge.

Nanda said,

> No turband could you make for one
> Who filleth all these worlds alone.

They sang (admiringly),

> *Irula* fat with aspect brave,
> Thy belly is of goats the grave.

Nanda,

> Trust not ye fools ! to demons base,
> But Him who is all love and grace.

The enthusiastic dancers heard not Nanda, or at any rate heeded him not; but the dance was followed by a more serious affair—the butchering of innocent fowls and sheep. Nanda rose and vehemently protested against it, but in vain; he eloquently preached to them about the grace and glory of the Creator, invited them to throw away their wicked gods and barbarous sacrifices and exhorted them to join with him in the worship of the beautiful, eternal Nataraja, but all his words were as pearls cast before the swine; nay, worse than that, they tended to strengthen the current notions about his madness. Nanda turned away from that ignorant multitude in sorrow, and filled with pity for them, prayed to God that they might be saved. With every moment of prayer, the longing to visit Chidambaram gained new strength, till it grew irrepressible and forced him to apply to his master for leave. After considerable hesitation, the Brahmin landlord was asked; but in the meanwhile, the pious devotees of *pedari* and company, finding that their gods had no power over Nanda, had carried their appeal to the more powerful tribunal of their visible agricultural god—the said Brahmin landlord, who unlike the invisible gods vouchsafed a prompt enquiry. Nanda appeared before his master just a little after the above deputation had gone from there and made his application. The landlord was greatly enraged at the silly and impertinent request as he took it, and exclaimed: "Eh, you want to visit Chidambaram, you *pariah* fool, you want to become a Brahmin, I suppose, you rogue, you deserve to be whipped for this impertinence. You-vi-sit-Chi-dam-baram!!" Poor Nanda was thunderstruck, he felt himself undone and returned weeping without speaking a word. He went to the shade of his favourite tree, and there wept in torrents. "O God," he said to himself, "How cruel art thou! I have no right to blame the Brahmin, he of course spoke under Thy prompting, for not an atom moves save at Thy bidding. I am a poor *pariah* too low for Thy grace, Ah! how cold art thou! Thou hast no pity on this wretched, miserable forlorn creature. I have nothing to be proud of—no wealth, no beauty, no fame, no learning and as if these were not enough I am born a low caste bondsman. All this was nothing to me, so long as I had hope of Thy grace, and now I have been deprived even of that. Oh God, how then can I live!" He even meditated suicide, saying: "I shall do away with this my life and die a victim to Thy cruelty." But hope, that most wonderful of all things, again asserted itself, and after a few hours of weeping, he thought within himself: "God knows what is best for me, infinitely better than I do. I shall resign myself to His will in all things great and small. I am a rebellious spoilt child, and till I learn obedience and cheerful resignation, how can I obtain His grace? The Brahmin master might relent; and I am sure, when I am fit to enter His presence, I shall be allowed to do so." A few days after, a second application was made for leave with a similar result of refusal combined with rebuke; but the disappointment this time had a different effect on him; he consoled himself with the idea that he was not yet fitted for the holy presence, and that therefore he should strive to be more pious and god-loving and purer in heart. He redoubled his meditation that there might not be in his waking state a single moment in which God was forgotten, curtailed his hours of sleep, danced in a wild and ecstatic way both morning and evening, and at other times wept for God's grace or rejoiced over his illimitable glory. In the stream, in the bird, in the tree, in man, in short wherever he saw life, there he felt the persence of Nataraja; and under the sway of this strange fancy, often played with the stream, embraced the tree, ran after the bird and did a thousand wild things which positively confirmed his kinsmen in the idea of his lunacy. They, poor folk, tried all shorts of remedies, even bound him by fetters and tortured him, but all in vain. Even while being tortured, he would not turn away from his Nataraja to get angry with his persecutors, and if the physical suffering was unbearable he would say : "O Lord, the fault is not theirs, nothing is done but at Thy inward prompting, forgive them, if only for my humble sake." To him everything in the world was divine, and his love and tenderness to living creatures was simply boundless : he would feed the ants with sugar, would take up the worms from the roadside lest they might be scorched by sun or crushed under the feet of the passers-by, play with children and enjoy the music of the birds as if he were himself one of them.

In the meanwhile however, the harvest time had come and, his kinsmen being desperately engaged with him, work in the fields really suffered. The landlord got enraged and sent for his slaves. All of them came except Nanda, and related everything that happened. The Brahmin angrily dismissed them and sent for Nanda. Nanda came, bowed to his master and stood. The Brahmin was greatly surprised at the remarkable degree of joy, calmness and humility that shone in his

face. It clearly struck him that Nanda was no ordinary
man, and that what was misconstrued by the ignorant
pariahs as madness was nothing but an extravagance of
piety and fervour; but he did not want to encourage
him, and got really angry when the request to go to
Chidambaram was put forward; yet he was moved at
the extremely piteous, sincere and imploring way in
which it was urged and the quivering and suspense with
which his reply was awaited, as if a soul's destiny hung
upon his one word; and so he gently replied: "Nanda,
you are a really good fellow, but have fallen into wild
ways; you have not been doing your work properly of
late. This is the harvest season, the corn has to be
reaped, after all the harvest is gathered in, I shall give
you leave to go to Chidambaram. No sooner was this
said than Nanda sprang into the fields dancing and leaping like a wild deer, and a few hours later, again called
at the landlord's backyard. When the Brahmin asked
why he was wanted, Nanda repled: 'Do me the favour,
sire, to go with me into the fields,' and led the way
followed by his master; and what was the latter's wonder when he found that the whole of his vast paddy fields
had been reaped and the harvest gathered in like a mountain of gold—all the work of a single man, and that in
the space of a few hours! He could hardly believe his
eyes, and struggled to know if he was not dreaming;
what he saw was, however, no vision but a concrete and
thorough reality, and when convinced of this, he could
only say: "Nanda, you could not have done this work,
nor all your kinsmen together, what a miracle has God
worked in my fields through you. This is the reward
of your devotion—the proof to us, incredible fools, of your

greatness. Nanda, you are the greatest, holiest and purest man that I have known, God's dearest *Bhakta*, ah! what a sin have I committed by treating you as my slave,—from this moment, I am thy slave and this whole estate is yours. Bless me and recommend me to that high God who is so near and dear and kind to you."

Nanda's feat was at the same time a miracle and not a miracle—not a miracle in the superstitious sense generally attached to the word, but a miracle, a genuine miracle in that it was beyond the power and comprehension of ordinary men. Most of us are ignorant of the resources of love. Its intensity, its abundance, and its wonderful possibilities are foreign to our mediocrity and when measured by our leaden standard, appear legendary. *Love rolls the hills, leaps over the seas, annihilates the elements and shakes the universe.* What can it not do and what has it not done? It is the energy of the soul, nay it is the Soul itself, and when Nanda threw his whole soul into the work on which hung the fulfilment of his life's ambition, result was miraculous, divine. The astounded Brahmin fell at his feet; and here by the way, it may be said to the credit of our caste system, that however rigorous it may be on the social plane, it has ever been liberal on the religious one. Many of the saints worshipped in our temples are men of the lower castes, some of them being of the very lowest; and the Brahmin is as ready to-day as he was in the days of Nanda to fall at the feet of any man irrespective of caste, if any high religious merit be at least plausibly claimed. Nanda ran to his master, raised him up, repeatedly fell at his feet and with tears in his eyes said: "My lord, what a sin have you commit-

ted by bowing to your *Pariah* slave" to which the
Brahmin replied : "You are no longer either a *Pariah*
or a slave, you the holiest of men, the greatest of
Bhaktas. Go to Chidambaram, but bless me before you
go, forgive me for my treatment to you and recommend
me to God's High Grace." And saying this he took
Nanda's hands and placing them on his head implored
him to give him some parting advice. 'This is all that
your humble slave could say, my lord,' said Nanda,
'*love God as well as you love your wife, children, lands
and wealth. What more, O lord, does this uncultured
slave know ?*' The Brahmin looked up at the radiant
face of Nanda and worshipping him once again reluctantly let him go. With great many kindly expressions they parted ; but hardly had Nanda gone a
few yards, when the Brahmin ran up to him and asked :
"Nanda, dear Nanda, O my *Guru*, when may I see you
back ? when will you return ?" Nanda replied : "Now,
O my master, we part once for all. O my lord, who
really goes to Chidambaram, and comes back ? I loathe
again to enter into this mortal coil. My master, I hope
no longer to return." The Brahmin did not understand
what Nanda said, but we may perhaps do from the
sequel of the narrative.

No deer that newly escaped from the hunter's toils,
no Negro slave newly emancipated, no barren woman
just blessed with a male child, no blind man that newly
received the gift of light, was more rejoiced than Nanda
the *Pariah* who was relieved from the work which stood
between him and his God. Nay, the very gods in heaven
rejoiced to see Nanda dancing across the grassy plains
and fertile meadows as if he were a wolf springing upon

his victim, eager to spring upon that victim of victims,
Nataraja, the poorest of the poor, the poor Minakshi's[1]
mother's son-in-law, and singing:

> The drug[2] that cures my grief, the fear-not-drug,
> The drug that spreads through all the worlds alike,
> The medicine of grace, the wondrous drug
> That grows within, the drug that feasts my love;
> The drug of growing light, the drug of life
> And light and bliss, the drug that cures the ill
> Of life, the drug great and ineffable,
>
> The drug that saves the pain of death, the sweet
> Ambrosia that flows ever within.

> *Natarrja, Nataraja, Nataraja, Nataraja,*
> *Nataraja, my Lord, Nataraja, Nataraja,*
> *Nataraja, my wealth, Nataraja, Nataraja,*
> *Nataraja, Nataraja, Narthanasundara Nataraja.*

The gods are never more pleased than when they see
a good soul springing frantic, "pregnant with celestial
fire," for theirs is the world of love. The story adds,
the earth shook with joy, the grasses waved with delight
and a few rain drops of joy, fell from heaven, Nanda
sang and jumped like a veritable deer. He jumped with
delight. His eyes and ears were hardly his. He was
beside himself, intoxicated with delight. Snakes alone
can know snakes' legs. So lovers alone can know the
bliss of love. Nanda danced and wept; to him who
was able to gather up the harvest of a thousand acres

---

[1] There is a beautiful carving in stone in the temple of Madura of
Minakshi's or Parvati's mother grieving miserably for her rich
daughter having married Siva the beggar, the poorest of the poor.

[2] In these and the following verses the reader is requested to
attend more to the sense than to the metre. The original refuses to
e translated.

in a few hours, the walk from Adanur to the banks of the Colladam (the river Coleroom) was hardly a walk. The river was in full flood. The waves were rolling forth one after another for very joy as it were. There was a weird majesty about the waters as they flowed on, in some places moving without self-control like a drunkard who has lost his senses and is reeling about, in others rushing forth like a wild lion shaking his mane, in others moving and rolling like a bull with a fat hump and in others yet crawling like a mountain snake, but everywhere frantic with heavenly joy as if at the sight of the distant looming tower of Chidambaram and everywhere making a subdued harmonium or a loud organ *vedic* music of its own. Nanda looked at the river, saw the deep water yet clear, saw the living flood and claimed eternal kinship with it. Railways were not in those days, and Nanda, had he seen a train, would have exclaimed, as a friend of the writer observed, "Here is my God! carrying *all* to their respective destinations without the distinction of age, sex, position, caste or creed, and propelled on and controlled by an invisible power and making a noise (whistle) like the *Pranavam*, the great AUM, and maintaining its world inside by that noise (*Sabda nishtam jagat*—the world stands by the power of sound or vibration)." Surely there is philosophy everywhere for the eyes that would see.

Nanda saw the majestic river, danced at the abundance of Nataraja that it bore. "It danced and leapt," he said, "singing anthems to my beloved, and so I shall do" and he danced and jumped singing and singing—

Nataraja's dance is dance,
And all our dance is ignorance ;

and dancing eternal love to that eternal lover. A boat
came ; a black boatman steered it, with a sun-burnt
face, with his sweat, covered all over the body, but
bearing the traces of the white ashes it wore and smell-
ing of sweet camphor. Nanda saw him and worshipped
him, for he was Nataraja in his eyes ; and getting into
the boat for hire sang to a surprised audience about the
unfading glory of the prince of Dancers. He said :

> The drug which made me Him, the dancing drug
> That dances in wisdom's sphere, the silent drug
> The poor man's friend, the rarest drug, the drug
> Both first and last, the drug that seeks out those
> That search for it, the drug all rare to those
> That seek it not, that which my hunger soothes,
> The loneliest drug, the pure man's help, the light,
> The pride of love, the drug that drives out grief,
> The drug that cures false loves and avarice kills,
> That which Earth-hunger soothes, the drug which plays
> Hide-and-seek, the drug which is all within
> The heart that loves, that is my strength and joy.

> *Nataraja, Nataraja, Nataraja, Nataraja,*
> *Nataraja, Guru, Nataraja, Nataraja*
> *Nataraja, Jewel, Nataraja, Nataraja,*
> *Nataraja, Nataraja, Narthanasundar, Nataraja.*

The boat danced on the waters. Nanda danced on
the boat. The people in the boat danced with Nanda.
The sun-burnt boatman forgot his oar and danced with
the people. It was a dance universal, an ecstatic festival,
but a dance of ten minutes. The boat dancing this way
and that, dragged itself to the shore. Nanda leapt on
the ground—sacred it was, it was the territory of
Nataraja, put his hand into his lap searching for a few
copper coins, the fruit of his toil (pockets were not in
those days), but the boatman wept and would not take

the hire. "My master, my lord," he said, "no more a
Pariah are you, God has converted you into Himself.
I am the *Pariah* slave and cannot accept anything from
you." The great Dr. Johnson said of Burke, that if
any man stayed with him for five minutes, say, to shelter
from the rain or against the wild bull, he could discover
the orator, and so it was with Nanda. Ten minutes
were the interval for crossing the river, and within that
time the *Bhakta* was discovered and worshipped by a
band of men who became his *Bhaktas*. The boatman
left his boat. The man of business forgot it. The
tradesman neglected his trade. The ploughman threw
aside his plough. A dancing group formed itself.
They danced, danced for very joy ; danced like Nataraja
around Nanda, the centre of the group.

The tower of Chidambaram, grand, majestic, loomed
from a distance and seemed to say to Nanda :—

> O Come and dance, the joyous dance,
> O Come and dance, the Dancer's dance.
> O dance and shun all ignorance.

Nanda looked at it—the tower of Nataraja, bowed before it and worshipping it, exclaimed : "O Lord, at
whose bidding the spheres do their daily work, and the
invisible sky like Thyself keeps on in space and envelops
all, by the side of thy starry wealth and mountains and
rivers where am I ?—this poor mosquito. 'This tiny
trumpeting gnat' is not worth a drop of the mighty
ocean that roars day and night. Is not that drop more
innocent and beautiful than myself ! The white sand
that endures alike the burning sun and the falling rain
is more worthy of Thy grace than myself. Oh *Sanyasin*

of *sanyasins*! that rulest this vast household of suns, moons, stars, clouds, mountains and rivers, that I should have appeared as any thing in Thine Eyes, Ah, what a wonder! Grant, Oh God of gods, that rising from the Earth I stand firm like this tower of Thine, fixedly gazing towards heaven, turning a deaf ear and a bold front to all the winds that might blow."

A few yards more they went, the base of the tower was visible. The temple gate was in view. And Nanda sang: "Here is the gate of the *Kailas*, the gate that opens to the good alone, the gate from which no good man ever returns, that through which *Manikkar*[1] entered and sang to the echo of these high walls his divine anthems of ecstasy, the gate through which that poet of poets *Appar*[1] entered and sang his majestic *Vedas*, the gate through which *Sundarar*[1] entered and enjoyed the secret nuptials with the Prince of Lovers, the gate of that God who was feeding a prostitute's brother at the rate of one golden pie a day and finally absorbed him. My brothers and friends and kinsmen, here God is and is not. Here he is both form and no form. Here he dances and is quiet. *Here it is that the ignorant are blessed with wisdom and the wise lose their senses.* Here he is space and light. And here he is both the creator and the destroyer." And that is why *Appar* sang :—

> The Tillai Dancer, wrapt by watery fields
> Around, this helpless slave to forget and live!

Nanda continued :
> In space his dance is held, my maids,[2]
> His dance is love, his dance is love.

1 Great Tamil saints and poets.
2 *Maid*—The mind is generally addressed as *maid*.

The foot that dances so I love,
I pine with love, I die, my maids,

All (in chorus) :

Nataraja's dance is dance ; the scene
Where he dances lies all within.

Nanda :

A joyous form, a joyous form
I love his dance, my maids, I love
He dances there, my maids with love
He is my maids, a joyous form.

All :

Mahasiva, Sadasiva
The crown of kings, the help of all
Siva, Siva, Sadasiva,
Siva that dances in the hall.

Nanda :

This wretched world I scorn, my maids,
I am one with the Lord, my maids.
He passeth all my words, my maids.
How could I speak, how Oh ! my maids.

All :

The song that sings of space is song,
All other song is darksome song.
Nataraja's song is song all sweet
The song of world is song for meat.

Nanda :

Seeth he not, my maids, my mind.
Alas ! three eyes he hath, you find.
He melteth many a stony mind,
But Himself melteth not for me,
Dèceit I know not, as you see,
My maids, what fault in me you find ?

All :

> The abandon of grace, my gain,
> That gain's rich store, wealth without pain,
> Light's nectar, sweetness that doth drown,
> The gem adorning *Veda's* crown,
> The gem adorning *Veda's* crown.

Thus singing they reached the sacred precincts of Chidambaram, danced around the village, as if they were bees humming around the lotus that has not yet bared its bosom to the skies. The God within is the same God without and prompted by Him that dwells within the heart, the *Dikshitars* of Chidambaram (the holy priests of the temple, 2,999 in number, including Nataraja 3,000), who were very different from what they are to-day—everything except the sun and the moon seems to have degenerated in our country—were very learned in Sanskrit and Tamil and pious, and as remarkable for their holiness as they are now for their tufted hair in front. They saw Nanda and his associates who, though of higher caste, would not go into the town regarding themselves as lower than Nanda the *Pariah* in caste. The *Dikshitars* observed Nanda closely, and saw the light that shone on his face, the remarkable expression that marked him out as one of the chosen. They heard with delight though from a distance his holy songs.

Nanda resumed :

> He ruined me, my maids, will he
> My maids, now give me up alone ?
> The god of love with fiery eye
> He burnt, seeth He not my moan ?
> I love to see Him once, my maids,
> From my love-stricken sight he hides.

Once, once, to see his raised foot,
My evils all will fly from sight,
The foot that stretched down Yama's height
Our family God to be will suit.

All :

Rich Kalpa's shade, that shade's own sweet,
Well watered field, its harvest meet.
Beauty's form, the life within.
The dancer that doth ever shine,
The dancer that doth ever shine.
Full beamed moon, that beam's nectar,
The light of space, ether within.
The loving Lord, His joy is mine.
The dancer that doth ever shine,
The dancer that doth ever shine.
Life's light, that life's effulgent might,
Th'saving ray, that ray's firm light,
The lordly grace that rains like rain.
The dancer that doth ever shine,
The dancer that doth ever shine.
The highest path, its harvests sweet.
The blissful self, its portion meet.
The highest height, peace not yet mine.
The dancer that doth ever shine,
The dancer that doth ever shine.

They proceeded, and Nanda grew more enthusiastic as he approached the shrine. The beaming cheerfulness in his face increased in splendour. By this time, the rich autumnal *Dwadasi* (12th Lunar Day) moon, the Pride of India, of the calm skies, rising like a white lotus springing in the blue of the heavens, spread forth its love-laden music-like ambrosial rays above and below, and Nanda, the love-stricken Nanda looking up sang :—

Oh radiant, joyous, silvery moon, myself
To know, tell me a path, tell me a path.
Oh silvery moon, the lover's friend, that hath
A seat in my Lord's hair, that place for Self.
That Sea of Love to have I wish, say how.

All :

Nataraja,   etc.,   etc.,   etc.

Nanda :

> Thy nightless, dayless life, O silvery moon
> For ever to have, I die, O silvery moon.
> O radiant Silvery moon, I pine to be
> Myself, the way is hard to see for me.
> Tell me, O silvery moon, if my sweet Lord,
> Will be with me alone, Oh hard ! how hard !
> Oh hard it is, thou moon, to be with Him,
> Much too proud is He, much too proud is He.

All :

> *Nataraja,*   etc.,   etc.,   etc.

Nanda :

> To be His own self ! Oh silvery moon,
> And He be I ! Tell how, I fail, I swoon.
> A five-headed serpent,[1] thou silvery moon,
> He plays with, ever, I know not how, I own
> Oh silvery planet—He alone, the One,
> In space He dances all alas ! alone.
> Tell me, O silvery moon, O silvery moon,
> Tell me the way, the why, I swoon, I swoon.
> This world and all do form His dance they say.
> Shed forth, O moon, one ray, one single ray
> Of thine and gladden me and gladden me.
> His joyous dance is all above, above,
> My sorry dance is all below, below.

As Nanda proceeded, the love within him matured and attained to the power of the first class, or, as it is called in Sanskrit, classical love as was the case with the shepherdesses of Vraja (*Narada Sutra*, No. 21).

"One Gopi (shepherdess) as she sallied forth, beheld some of the seniors (of the family) and dared not venture, contenting herself with meditating on Krishna with closed eyes and entire devotion, by which, immediately all acts of merit were effaced by rapture, and all sin

---

[1] The soul with five senses which has life through *Iswara.*

was expiated by regret at not beholding Him ; and others again reflecting upon the cause of the world in the form of the supreme *Brahman,* obtained, by their sighing, final emancipation'' (*Vishnu Purana*).

It was the same high love to which Thayumanavar referred in untranslateable language :

> Sankara, Sankara, Sambho
> Siva Sankara, Sankara, Sambho.
> He that is first and last,
> My bliss, my love, my light,
> The speechless light how vast.
> He spoke a word, my maid.
> Unspeakable, Unspeakable.[1]
> Sankara, Sankara, Sambho
> Siva Sankara, Sankara, Sambho.

Nanda sang again :

> Dance, O dance, O my fairest daughters all,
> Till ye find out the Dancer in the hall.
> O sing and dance and Sing, O dance and sing
> By turns in circles proud, praising the king,
> Praising the King, the passionless and pure,
> Who yet Sivakami fair does e'er allure.

All :

> And lovers sweet and lovers sweet, O sing
> And dance until ye find the Dancing King,
> O Sing and dance and sing, O dance and sing.

Nanda :

> The Lord of dance and love, of dance and love
> The most powerful Lord, Vasishta's cow
> To loving hearts, the first great lover,
> The lord of boundless power, of boundless power.
> The king that dances in the hall, the poor
> Man's treasure, the light all pure, the light all pure.
> Find out my daughters all, find out the king.

1 The original is difficult to translate. Unspeakable implies the word between lovers not fit to be spoken to the public, and also it implies the word of the *Guru* rare to get and all too sacred for public ears.

All :
> O sing and dance and sing, O dance and sing
> And dance until ye find the Dancing King.

Thus did Nanda sing in ecstasy with his companions, for three days and nights.

Tradition rich in legends and folklore asserts, that all the *Dikshitars*, on one and the same remarkable night, dreamt that Nataraja appeared to them in their vision, and directed them to take into their Brahmin fold, the purest of his *Bhaktas*, Nanda the *Pariah* Saint. It was a beautiful morning, when the sun had just risen, and the *Dikshitars* had returned from their bath with sacred ashes besmeared all over their bodies and *rudrakshas*[1] hanging loosely round their necks, assembled a miscellaneous council in the *Devasabha*, their general meeting place within the temple.

Appiah Dikshitar, the eldest of the group, rose and told his wonderful dream—how Nataraja appeared before him, and related the possibility of purifying Nanda by means of a fire-bath. Kuppanna Dikshitar, his immediate successor in seniority, confirmed the dream by his own experience. Subbah Dikshitar saluted the two previous speakers, and expressed his surprise at the coincidence of his dream with those related. Nataraja Dikshitar did the same ; and all the Dikshitars simultaneously rose, and expressed the uniformity of their dreams. At once, when the wind was blowing fiercely and the sun was burning hot, arrangements were made for a sacred fire being reared.

Meanwhile Nanda had just risen from a long trance and was singing.

---

1 Wreaths of beads made from the seeds of a particular plant.

My maid, go tell my lovely Lord that I
Bow to His golden feet that dance on high.

All shouted—*Nataraja, Nataraja*, etc., etc.

Nanda attempted to resume his song, but was choked
with grief, as his long prayers had not yet borne fruit,
and he had not yet been taken to the Presence. Just
then the *Dikshitars* appeared in a body before him, and,
bowing to him, to his great surprise, related to him their
wonderful dreams, and took him over to the corner of
the South Mada Street where the fire had been prepared.
The pious devotee at once sprang into the fire joyfully
singing : "My father Isa's feet are cool like the effulgent evening moon, the faultless *Vina* (a musical
instrument), the breeze that unceasingly blows, the
spring that swells, or a tank round which bees hum and
swarm." "O pious Nanda, frantic with holy enthusiasm !
leap into the fire : fire scorcheth thee (*i.e.*, the inner
reality, thy *Atman*) not, water wetteth thee not, sword
pierceth thee not, winds wither thee not, thou art a
Brahmin, the *pariah* part of thee is burnt away. Of
thee, now, it may be said, 'Formless, yet all form ; without inside and outside ; beyond imperfection and perfection ; without mark or character ; all the *Vedas*
declare Thee to be One, higher far than the mountains,
vaster far than the horizon ; and, in the sight of the
wise enjoying the abandon of wisdom, Thou art neither
he, nor she, nor it, but beautiful simply ; no one can
know Thee.' Nanda ! purified thou art by the fire of
Wisdom, which burns away all past, present and future
Karmas."

Metaphorically all traditions are true ; and even

when taken literally, they have a meaning; for, as that wise critic Renan observes, "Faith demands the impossible, nothing less will satisfy it. To this very day, the Hindus every year walk over glowing coals, in order to attest the virginity of Draupadi, the common wife of the five sons of Kunti." Besides, we must learn to see *"how a narrative, anecdotical and fabulous in form, may be more true than the truth itself;* how the glory of a legend belongs, in a sense, to the great man whose life that legend traces, and who has been able to inspire in his humble admirers qualities, which, apart from him, they could never have invented. Often the hero creates his own legend." The legend which has so much to say about Nanda, speaks not a word about his followers. Every year the South Indian Railway train carries a multitude of people to Nataraja's shrine, but few have been invested with the halo of such a rich and beautiful legend.

Nanda passed through the crucible unhurt, nay, rose purer for the bath; what was burning and seething was now cool and refreshing; where there was imperfection, there now was perfection; where there was want, there was now happiness; where there was low *Pariah* caste, there now was *Brahmin* caste in the truest sense of the word. He was taken by the admiring *Dikshitars* from the South Mada Street through the Eastern tower gate broad like the *Vedas*, and speedily led on by the side of *Kambattadi Mantapa* (Subrahmanya's shrine) and the square tank, and across the *Devasabha*, into the common platform, midway between Sri Govindaraja Perumal and the dancing Nataraja. No damsel, richly laden with jewels and decorated for marriage with

her favourite lover, ever went with greater joy to her
nuptial bed fragrant with sandal and flowers, no humming bee ever went near the honey-filled flower "that
captive makes the surrounding winds," with greater
eagerness than did Nanda the *Pariah*, chanting forth
his extempore hymns, the *Vedas* that sprang from his
mouth, to the great Presence ; where once stood Appar,
singing his famous song meaning,

He is my Lord, He who is rare, He who lives in the bosom of the
gracious, He who resides in the temple of the *Vedas* and in the atom,
the true God yet unknown, who is sweet like honey and milk, the
abounding light of heaven, the God of gods, Brahma and Vishnu,
the great invisible spirit that pervades the rolling sea and the mountain
chains. The days on which I forgot to sing His praise are days in
which I did not live,

and similar songs ; where stood Manikkar fainting with
love and pouring forth his remarkable *Upanishads*,
where stood that sage of sages, Thayumanavar, chanting
forth his *Vedic* strains with eyes dimmed with tears ;
and where great men have left the dust of their feet to
inspire noble and pious souls that may come after them.
There now Nanda stood, and on both sides of the *Kanaka-
sabha* (the golden *mantapa*) huge ocean-voiced bells
poured forth their joyous chimes. Appiah Dikshitar
entered into the shrine, and made *puja* to God with light
(*diparadhana*) and all, in honour of the newly made
Brahmin. And not Sita freed from the demon Ajomukhi,
nor even Radha on the lonely Jumna sands, ever rushed
forth to the embrace of her beloved Lord more hastily
than did Nanda, the *Pariah Brahmin*, to the fond embrace of his idol of idols, of his dream of dreams, his
love of loves, his favourite beautiful Nataraja—Nataraja,

holding up in one hand the eternal *Atmic jyotis* to attest the truth of His silent teaching, with His right leg planted over the illusion of suffering, and His left leg raised aloft, as if in search of lovers, serving as the highest banyan tree, the richest shade that could shelter against the scorching *Samsara* (worldly existence). Nanda the *Pariah* disappeared into Nanda the *Brahmin*, and Nanda the *Brahmin*, disappeared, once and for ever, into the eternal invisible Nataraja—disappeared, swan-like singing.

> Nataraja my Lord, Nataraja my love,
> My Lord, I come, I come, my love,
> We both are only one from now ;
> Thou art I, and myself art thou.
> "In such access of mind, in such high
> Hour of visitation from the living God,
> Thought was not ; in enjoyment it expired ;
> No thanks he breathed, he proffered no request ;
> Wrapt into still communion that transcends
> The imperfect offices of prayer and praise
> His mind was a thanksgiving to the power
> That made him ; it was blessedness and love."

The admirers of Nanda, the *Dikshitars* included, were struck dumb with wonder ; and on recovering, glorified Nanda's love and Nataraja's grace in the following words :

A sacrifice he made of his warring mind, no wicked deity Thou, O Thou blessed calmness of the *turiya*[1] state, all Thy bondsman's love was as water to wash Thy holy feet. The soul that resided within him was the offering, and his life an incense at Thy holy altar—and this, not for one day, but throughout—O Thou, the honeyed juice of the *Vedas*, their nectar, their sugar, the bliss that never gluts, the kinship that silently mingles with the thievish mind, Thou God of grace that danceth an eternal dance in the beautiful assembly of the wise, the sphere of eternity, the abandon of light.

1 The fourth state as distinguished from the three states of waking dreaming and sleeping.

And all on the spot danced in a group singing,

Nataraja, Nataraja, Narthana Sundara Nataraja,
    etc.,   etc.,   etc.
Sambho Sadasiva, Mahasiva Sadasiva.
    etc.,   etc.,   etc.

O reader ! Criticise not. Remember Chaitanya and
his ecstatic rush after the moon in the water ; the mad-
man, the philosopher, and the lover are all alike, but
yet this kind of love may not be the highest. Love is
not above light, and light is not above love of the truest
type. *Love or light, it must not be transitory nor passionate outside but eternal and peaceful,* not like the volcano that bursts out in paroxysms of passion, but like
the Himalayas that stand and shake not, like the Ganges
that flows and dries not, like Nataraja himself who dances
and never tires.

We have finished Nanda's tale. But for many a
long night, let dreams of Nataraja and Nanda, the *Pariah*
Saint, to whom a beautiful chapter of possibilities was
opened, haunt us till our brains are filled with them and
think by themselves, so to speak, of the teacher that
ceases not to teach.

To the philosopher who transmutes everything into
his philosophy and lends his own eternity to even fleeting things, Nanda is not merely a slave of Adhanur, and
his life not merely a fancied legend or tradition. Nanda
is none but the *Atman*, *Ananda* or bliss which is God.
'He recognised that Happiness is Brahman ; from
Happiness, indeed, all these creatures are born ; when
born, they live through Happiness when they depart
they enter into Happiness" (*Tait. Up.*, III, 6).

In mortal coils, it is the *Jiva* playing its sports of

the world, shaping the stars, sun and moon, and forging chains of pleasure and hate. That Nanda is born in a *Parachery*, signifies that we are dealing in flesh and blood, butchers one and all. The very thought of one's body is pariahood, and requires for its *Prayaschittam* (purification) a bath in the holy waters of the *Upanishads.* Like Nanda, we are slaves, bondsmen to our agricultural god the belly, and slaves to our passions, which are our hourly kinsmen and neighbours. Like Nanda, we have a thousand wicked deities to obey, our bodily comforts, superstitions, name, fame, power, pelf, etc.

The *Parachery* is remote from the Brahmin quarters and the temple. "*Avidya* or ignorance (represented by the *Parachery*), through which sprang all this universe, is only a quarter of the *Paramatman.* The remaining three-fourths (the Brahmin quarters, etc.), are immortal and filled with light" (*Tait. Brahmameda*, 2). "I wear all this universe in a small fraction of myself," said Sri Krishna (*Gita*, X. 42). Ignorance, even in its might, is small before knowledge that burns it away. The temple is visible, though at a distance ; so there is some hope for man. To Thirupankore we have all to go—to the Sivalingam, *i.e., that which remains after deducting all phenomena, the final mark.* There, it is Nandi (Siva's bull) that obstructs the view ; Nandi is nothing but the four good tendencies of the mind, cheerfulness, calmness, patience and resignation, the four gate-keepers of heaven. It is through these that God is to be approached ; but when the presence is reached, these form a hindrance, as even the good tendencies of the mind must cease before its attaining to the state of the formless *Brahman.* By God's grace even these are

dispensed with, and the first glimpse is obtained. And
when the face of the Lord is once seen, woman is forgotten, wealth is neglected, and love to God grows on
what it feeds.

The clay gods are the idols we worship;˙ and it is
love that rules the heart, and prompts the worship.
It is Brahmin (*i.e.*, one that knows the *Atman*) that
preaches about Chidambaram and Nataraja. These we
are familiar with as the *Atman* and the sphere of Wisdom
(see Part IV) ; and it is the Brahmin's permission, *i.e.*,
the *Guru's* that is required to attain them. The *Guru*
tests the love, and love stands the test ; and now who is
great, who is small, who is *Guru*, who is disciple ? Nature
rejoices in this equality (*samarasa*). Nanda then
triumphantly goes to Chidambaram to the Presence of
the *Atman*. The tell-tale kinsmen, have all been subdued, there is a beautiful expression on the face ; the
wicked gods have long since been thrown away, *i.e.*,
the passions, the strife of the senses, and the gravitation
of the earth have all been overcome. At this stage
there are "tongues in trees, books in running brooks,
sermons in stones, and good in everything." There is
philosophy in the silent tower, in the high walls, in the
open gate, in the temple, and in Nataraja. The
Dikshitars are the gate-keepers of Heaven, the *sastraic*
support and love required for entering the Presence.
They pass Nanda through the ordeal of fire—the hair
bridge, and similar things of the *Brihadaranyaka-Upanishad*. And when Nanda rises from the fire, he is led
to the temple, and there enters into the Presence, which
the lying and the wicked never see ; he disapppers, gets
dissolved like camphor in fire, like salt in water or, as

Sri Santhananda Saraswati would say, *as an iceberg in the ocean*, disappears once and for ever, silently, like the bubble that sinks into the sea, like the wave that, after roaring loud, dies a silent death. But think not that Nanda is dead. Souls like Nanda's never die, they are immortal here and above. To-day is five or six hundred years since the poor *Pariah* slave of Adhanur lived and died, and to-day we sing his praise. In November-December, the lovely girls of the south richly dressed and beautiful like peacocks, play the merry *Kolattam* (a sort of plait-dance) singing the praise of the *Pariah* that became a *Brahmin*, and dancing the dance of the dancing God Nataraja. O reader! loving reader! let us all hasten to love, hasten to stand where Nanda stood, hasten to enter into the Presence, and lose ourselves in It silently and joyfully, a consummation in which angels rejoice, and for which gods rain showers of flowers.

Rightly understood Nanda's story is an illustration of the great teaching :

"Whosoever will save his life shall lose it: and whosoever will lose his life for my sake shall find it."

SRI ALAWANDAR THE VAISHNAVITE SAGE

FEW lives are more interesting from a biographical point of view than the one we are now writing, or afford a more striking proof of the Divine Grace which attends us all through the journey of life, though in our ignorance and perversity we do not always perceive it, and safely conducts us to our common goal. Moments there are in almost everybody's life, when the dullness of our vision, now blind to spiritual light as the eyes of an owl are to that of the day, lessens a little, and the sunshine of Divine Grace reveals itself unmistakably, and we are filled with joy and wonder and awe at the nearness we are in to the august Presence (*Sannidhana*) of the Deity. But soon *Maya* asserts herself and draws veil after veil over the divine light, until it totally disappears from view as the sun in the winter, and we are hurled back into our everyday life of salt and tamarind. It was not so, however, with Alawandar. The voice of God spoke to him, and from that moment he became a changed man. Earthly associations, earthly concerns, earthly joys and sorrows lost their hold on him, and he lived, *though on earth yet in heaven.* This heaven, however, he did not jealously keep to himself, but was anxious to share with others, and his endeavours to make it palatable to men of grosser tastes have given him a high place in the line of *Vaishnavite* teachers (*Guru parampara*). The particular school of *Vedantic* philosophy known as *Visishtadwaitam* or qulified monism which was founded by his successor, Sri Ramanuja, owes much to him, and to it, he was in a measure what Sri Gaudapada was to the *Adwaitic* school founded by his disciple Sri Sankaracharya.

Alawandar, or rather Yamunacharya, for that was his first name, was born about A.D. 1150 at Madura then the capital of the Pandyan kingdom. His father was Iswara Muni, the son of the great Nathamuni Swami. When he was only some ten years old his father died. He was put to school in the usual course, and from the very beginning discovered unusual precocity of intellect, and his teacher Bhashyacharya and his relatives rejoiced that his distinguished grandfather was reborn in him. In every class he studied in, he was the monitor, and he was often left in charge of the school. He is said to have mastered all the *Sastras* before he was twelve years old. In his twelfth year, there happened an event which all at once made him a King. It so happened one day that the teacher, Bhashyacharya, had to go out on business and so he left the school in charge of this boy-prodigy and went out. When Yamunacharya was busy teaching the classes and managing the school, there came there in search of his teacher a messenger from a celebrated *pundit* of the time who was known by the high sounding appellation of Vidwajjana Kolahala. This Kolahala was a terror of all the scholars in the kingdom, and there was not one of them who had not been challenged by him and defeated. He was under the special patronage of the Pandyan king, and had been rewarded by the latter with palanquins, umbrellas, shawls, bracelets and a considerable retinue. Puffed up with self-conceit, he had issued an edict to all who pretended to know anything of Sanskrit, ordering them to pay a certain sum of money every year by way of

35

tribute. The poor *pundits* had no other go than to obey the order, and the tribute system had been going on for a number of years. Bhashyacharya, the teacher of the boy Yamuna, was one of the tribute payers, and owing to some pecuniary difficulties his tribute had fallen into arrears, and Kolahala sent a messenger to demand it of him.

The boy Yamuna asked the messenger who he was and what the purpose of his visit. The messenger replied : "I come from him who is the lion of poets, the prince of scholars, the terror of *pundits*, him who is to all that are learned what a wolf is to sheep, what fire is to a heap of straw, what Garuda is to serpents, him whom all the world glorifies as Vidwajjana Kolahala." "That is all right," said the boy, affecting a tone of disdain, "What does your man want of our great teacher." "My man?" replied the messenger, "Yes, your master's master wants of his slave, your master, the tribute he owes." Yamuna replied : "Tell your man not to be so impertinent. Let him know how to behave towards his betters. Bhashyacharya, is not the man to pay tribute to self-conceited fools," and sent him away. Shortly after, the teacher came to the school and on learning what happened, cried in despair, "I am undone and my family is ruined. If Kolahala hears this, he will report it to the king. I shall be challenged to a debate with him, and my head will be off. Yamuna, Yamuna, you have ruined me. By your boyish conduct I am undone. I was a fool to have left the school in the care of a boy." Yamunacharya comforted him saying : "O sir, fear not. If he challenges you for a debate, I shall go for you and defeat him. Please do not get anxious on that account, I am sure I can defeat that conceited man."

In the meanwhile the court-*pundit's* messenger had reported to him all that occurred in the school, and the latter, getting exceedingly angry, obtained the king's permission to challenge Bhashyacharya, who when he received the invitation to debate, fell almost senseless on the ground. Yamunacharya comforted him, and accepted the challenge on his account, and sent word that, as it was unworthy of so great a scholar as Bhashyacharya to go in person for a debate with Kolahala, he, Yamunacharya, a student of the former, was prepared to engage in a discussion, if invited to the court with the honours due to a *pundit*, and that otherwise the debate might be held in the school and Kolahala might come over there.

This message was duly conveyed to the king and the court-*pundit*. The former, on hearing that the age of the boy was only twelve, was not for treating it as serious, but looked upon it as a piece of boyish impertinence and desired to punish him for it. The queen, who at that time happened to be by him, said, however, "Who knows what the boy may be able to accomplish? A spark of fire is enough to destroy a mountain-like heap of cotton. We do not know what serpent may be in what ant-hill. Let us not therefore be hasty. We shall examine the boy, and if he be found to have played with us, we shall then punish him. Meanwhile let him be invited to the court with due honours." The king agreed to the proposal, as it appeared reasonable, and sent a palanquin and an umbrella to the school boy—this was the way in which *pundits* were honoured in those days—and soon Yamunacharya was on his way to the court, mounted on the palanquin and honoured by the umbrella ; all the school boys followed him and a man specially appointed for the purpose went before him proclaiming in the streets, "The marvellous Yamunacharya is coming, leave the way. The lion of poets is coming, leave the way. The master of all the *Sastras—Tarka* (Logic), *Vyakarana* (Grammar) and the *Mimamsas* included, is coming, leave the way. Woe to him that dares debate with him." The boy proceeded through the street in such pompous fashion, and naturally a large crowd of men and boys followed him.

On seeing him the king laughed convulsively, and addressing his queen, said : "This boy to debate with our Kolahala ! A jackal may as well fight with an elephant ! I have never seen fun like this." The queen attentively looked at the boy and said : "My lord, you are mistaken, I am sure the boy will gain the day ; his face tells me that ; there is a brightness in it which I have not seen elsewhere. Not merely this Kolahala, but even if it be his grandfather's grandfather I am sure the boy will defeat him."

King : Yes, if a mud horse could cross a river. A calf might more easily kill a lion than this child defeat our court-*pundit*.

Queen : I am sure, it is a bad day for poor Kolahala. The victory is already the boy's. Scholarship and genius do not depend on age. If years were the standard, there is many a broken mud wall much older than us all.

King : Why do you prattle in this fashion. You will see that the boy is defeated at the very outset. If he so get defeated what will you give me ?

Queen : Yes, if he is so defeated, I will become your
slaves' slave.

King : Foolish woman ! who would venture to cross
the ocean on a mud boat ? you speak
thoughtlessly. If this boy defeats the *pundit*,
I shall give him half of my kingdom.

Meanwhile Yamunacharya waited to pay his respects to the king, and on the latter turning to him,
saluted him in the most dignified fashion, and took his
seat opposite to Kolahala. With the king's permission,
the *pundit*, addressing the boy said : "I am sorry for
your impudence, which however is excusable as you are
a child. What exactly do you want with me ?"

Yamunacharya replied : "I want you to argue with
me on any subject you like before this royal court. I
warn you out of kindness not to be self-conceited, as you
are sure to be defeated by me to-day.

P. : You to defeat me ! A dog may as well catch the
moon, silly child.

Y. : Ashtavakra was only a silly child when he defeated Bandin, who was like yourself puffed up with
conceit, and threw him into the waters. Do you know
the story, you learned man ?

P. : What an impertinent lad this ! Have you
mastered the alphabet ? Do you know how to read ? Can
you write your name without a mistake ? You to debate
with us ! A cat may more easily overpower a lion.

Y. : A little spark of fire can burn away a huge heap
of straw. A lion's whelp, though young, can kill an
elephant. A chisel, though small, can break rocks to
pieces. A drop of butter-milk curdles a potful of milk.
A little poison is enough to kill a number of men. Was

Agastya, who drank off the ocean, tall or short? Is this what you have learnt, to judge men by years? People used to say you are learned! Proceed to the business.

The *pundit* then put him several test questions in logic, grammar, etc., but, finding that he was too great a match for him, said : "You are a child. So I will no longer trouble you with intricate questions from the *Sastras*. It is unfair, like putting a palmyra fruit on the head of a swallow. So I am not for it. You had better propose questions yourself, and I shall answer them. Yamunacharya felt the advantage he had gained over his adversary, and said : "How merciful you are! How kind! You had not, however, the prudence to say this at the very outset. Had you done so, you might have saved yourself all the trouble that you took to find questions for me and the mortification you suffered from their being readily answered. No matter, however, I shall gladly do as you propose. I shall make three affirmative statements. If you succeed in denying them I will acknowledge your success and my defeat. If not, you must acknowledge your defeat. Do you agree to this condition?" The king said that the condition was a fair one, nay, advantageous to the *pundit*, and the latter also agreed. But what was his surprise when the questions came?

First question : "We say your mother, O *pundit*, is not a barren woman. Can you deny this?"

The *pundit* long thought over the matter, but found no means of refuting it. "My mother a barren woman!" he reflected, "then how was I born? To deny the statement will be to expose myself to the ridicule of all the people here. Silence would be much better than that" and so kept quiet. His jaws were fallen and he hung down his head with shame. "Why do you not reply?" asked Yamunacharya but the *pundit* did not open his mouth, and there was a general but subdued acclamation from the miscellaneous audience that had assembled there.

The second question : "I say that this king is a virtuous man ; try and deny it if you can." Poor Vidwajjana Kolahala was startled at the question. "To say that the king is a wicked man and that in his own presence ! Really this young chap has contrived a very good device for finishing my life. If I keep quiet I shall be defeated, but to reply would be much more disastrous, for the king's sword would immediately be at my neck. There is still a third question. I shall see if I can answer that at least" said he to himself and kept quiet ; the queen's face grew radiant with joy and the crowd of spectators expressed its satisfaction in no mistakable fashion.

Then came the third and last question : "I say that the queen is chaste, deny it if you can." Kolahala was thunderstruck. He saw that he was undone. He hung down his head with shame at having suffered himself to be defeated so easily by a school boy—he that had put to shame and deprived of titles, honours and all, many a renowned scholar. "What foolishness," he said to himself, "not to have known the simple thing that there are many statements which cannot be denied and to have rashly undertaken to deny anything that might be affirmed. And then such questions—who could have put them except this little mischievous chap who triumphs over my ruin ! I worked out my own ruin.

Why did I not persist that it was unworthy of me to enter into a discussion with a school boy? now the event has proved me unworthy to sit on an equal seat with him and all that I have to do is to get up, deliver over all my insignia as the court *pundit* and kiss the dust of his feet." Accordingly he rose from his seat and stood the very picture of shame in mute confession of his defeat, to the laughter and ridicule of the spectators, who had all along been wishing for such a consummation. The queen at once called Yamunacharya to her and embracing him like a mother covered him over with kisses and said: "You are really *Alawandar*," *i.e.*, one that has come to rule, and henceforth he was called 'Alawandar' by all the people.

The king pitied his ex-*pundit's* position and addressing Alawandar said: "It is true you have won the day. You are a boy-prodigy, a veritable *Avatar*. I am very much rejoiced at your success, but can you deny at least one of the three statements that you made?" The boy coolly replied "I can deny all the three" at which the king was exceedingly surprised and asked how.

Alawandar replied: "In the first place, the *pundit's* mother is a barren woman according to the well-known saying 'One tree is not a garden nor one child a child.' To have only one child, as the *pundit's* mother has, is practically equal to having no children at all, and so she is a barren woman.

"Secondly, the king is not a virtuous man for according to the *Neethivakya*—moral saying—'*Raja rashtrakritam papam*' the sins of his subjects go to him.

"Thirdly, the queen is not chaste, for like every

other Hindu woman, she is at the time of marriage first dedicated to the Gods Agni and Varuna, Indra and others."

The king was very much surprised and pleased at these replies, and at once ordered Alawandar to be proclaimed, according to his promise to the queen, king over considerable portion of his dominion and placed poor Kolahala at his disposal. Alawandar accepted the kingdom, but set Kolahala free.

Alawandar, though so young, wielded the sceptre with wonderful dignity and justice and was very much liked by his subjects. He was thus reigning for many years, and then there occurred an event which has preserved his name from that death, which has fallen to the lot of those of numberless other clever scholars and wise kings. This event was even more romantic in character and more important in its consequences, than the preceding one which made him a king and therefore deserves to be described in some detail. When Alawandar was about 35 years old, a certain old Brahmin, Rama Misra, otherwise known as Manackal Nambi sought admission to the royal presence. Seeing that he was too poor to be treated with consideration, and thinking that, if he introduced himself in the usual way, his message might not be received at its worth he contrived a curious means of approaching Alawandar. He first acquired the friendship of the head cook of the palace, and requested him to cook and serve the king a particular kind of vegetable, which he undertook to bring himself every day. This vegetable is *Satwic* in character and is very much liked by *Yogis*, being both sedative and medicinal. Nambi supplied this vegetable very regularly and it was cooked and served as regularly on the royal table. A few months elapsed in this fashion and Alawandar had got accustomed to this article of diet, when one day Nambi purposely stayed away without bringing it. Alawandar not finding it on his table, asked his cook why it had not been prepared. The cook who knew nothing of the plot laid by Nambi, simply said: "The Brahmin did not bring it to-day." "The Brahmin! Who?" asked Alawandar in surprise and, on being informed that a certain poor Brahmin was supplying it regularly, ordered that he should be brought to his presence the very next time he appeared. Nambi brought the vegetable the next day, and as he had anticipated was taken to the king.

Alawandar experienced a peculiar kind of emotion, when Nambi approached him and felt as if they had been friends for a long time and, rising from his seat, welcomed him cordially and inquired what the purpose was of his supplying that vegetable and whether he wanted any favour from him. Nambi replied; "Yes, I want a favour from your royal highness; and that is that you will be pleased to take hold of a secret treasure which your grandfather has entrusted to me to be given over to you in proper time. I have come to request you to take charge of that treasure and deliver me from the burden of the trust." Alawandar thought that the thing might be true, as his grandfather Nathamuni Swami was one of the most celebrated men of his time and particularly fond of him. He was but a child when the Swami died, and it appeared likely to him that he might have left him a great legacy stored up in some secret place to be taken hold of when sufficiently old.

Besides he was on the eve of a war with a neighbouring king and badly wanted money. So he eagerly asked Nambi where that treasure lay and how he might obtain it. Nambi replied : "I will show it to you if you go with me. It is between two rivers and within seven successive walls. A huge serpent guards it and a *Rakshasa* from the south sea comes and visits it once in twelve years. It has been laid in by a *Mantra*, and it can be recovered only by means of that secret *Mantra* and with the help of a peculiar herb of rare virtues, and not by means of mere animal sacrifices like other ordinary treasures. It is a very vast treasure and by obtaining it, you will become much richer than any other king on earth. By securing it, you can easily vanquish all your enemies, and no one can ever defeat you. It is a great legacy which your celebrated grandfather Nathamuni Swami has left to you out of love. Pray take hold of it and deliver me from my responsibility." Alawandar asked : "Is it so valuable and vast a treasure?" and said, "How good of my grandfather! and how good of you not to have appropriated it yourself, but kept the trust. I shall start immediately with my army." Nambi said : "The earlier you start, the better ; but you must come alone ; such even is your grandfather's order." "Be it so then," said Alawandar and set out with Nambi the very next day, making arrangements for the administration of his kingdom during his absence.

Nambi took Alawandar a long way from Madura, and then, when it was dinner-time, opened a copy of the *Gita* which he had with him for *parayana* (daily reading) and read out the ninth chapter in it entitled

"*Raja Vidya Raja Guhya Yoga.*" Alawandar listened
with attention to the recital, and after dinner asked
Nambi to teach him *Gita* : for in those remote days it
was a strict rule that the *Gita* should not be read except under a teacher, and the numerous translations
now in vogue, from which people find it easy to mislearn,
were not in existence then. It was sacrilegious to approach the *Upanishads*, the *Vedanta Sutras* and the
Gita without the aid of a proper instructor—an idea
which the readers of the modern-day unsympathetic and
misleading translation of those sacred books full of divine
mystery, might perhaps scoff at ; but, in the time of
Alawandar, to learn and not to mislearn was the ambition of students. So the king requested Nambi to
initiate him into the "Supreme mystery and wisdom"
of the *Gita*, which the latter readily consented to do ;
and no sooner was a regular study begun than Sri
Alawandar owing to the accumulated virtue of previous
births, felt himself transported to a new world of "an
ampler ether and a diviner air," where there was neither
the pettiness nor the struggle of ordinary mortal existence.
It flashed upon him that his "home, sweet home" was
away, far away from the prison house of the sense world ;
and when he came to the celebrated verses in the second
chapter beginning with :—

There is no existence of the unreal ; of the real there
is no cessation of existence. The truth regarding these
two is seen by the seers of the Real ;
and ending with :—

This, weapons do not cut ; This, fire does not burn ;
This water does not wet and wind withers This not.

This cannot be cut, nor burnt, nor wetted, nor dried

up. It is everlasting, all-pervading, stable, firm and eternal.

This is said to be unperceivable; unthinkable and unchangeable. Wherefore knowing It to be such, thou hadst better not grieve.

He felt as if he had suddenly recollected something long forgotten. The verses appeared familiar to him and reminded him of a thing with which he had once been very, very familiar, and he grieved because he had forgotten it so long, because he had exchanged that everlasting, all-pervading, stable, firm and eternal *Atman* in him for the fleeting, paltry things of life, and had sold the Kingdom of God for a petty principality in this low earth. He pined to realise that which is unperceivable to the senses, unthinkable by the mind and unchangeable in its essence. He at once threw off the costly robes he wore, the jewels with which he had adorned his body which he now felt to be bubble-like and unreal, fell prostrate at the feet of Nambi and beseeched to be fully instructed in the deepest mysteries of divine wisdom. He added that he did not require the treasure, however vast and valuable it might be, which his grandfather had left for him, for he was determined no more to return to his kingdom but live a beggar for the sake of discovering the everlasting treasure which lay concealed in himself. Nambi commended this earnestness and zeal, but advised him not to throw away his jewels and robes, saying: "True renunciation consists in giving up all desire, but by giving up your wealth and kingdom you do not renounce, *for you desire to be a beggar*. Be as you are in outward appearance, but be unattached in your mind. This is the secret of re-

nunciation. Also do not despise the legacy your grandfather has left for you, for he gave it out of love; but
before going to recover it, we shall, if you so desire,
stay here for some time and finish this *Gita* and then
proceed to take hold of the treasures." Alawandar
readily agreed and the whole *Gita* was gone through
leisurely.

Before it ended he became fully imbued with the
spirit of its teaching. Whatever he did, whatever he
ate, whatever he offered in sacrifice, whatever he gave
in charity and whatever austerity he engaged in, he did
all as an offering unto God and in his eyes the pain and
pleasure of others became his own, for he saw all things
in himself and himself in all things. The words of the
Lord.

"He who offers to Me with devotion a leaf, a flower,
a fruit, water—that I accept, offered as it is with devotion by the pure-minded," (IX, 26) filled his mind
with a new ambition, and he pined to realise the truth
of the Lord's promise contained in the following verses—

Fix thy *Manas* in Me only, place thy *Buddhi* in Me,
Thou shalt no doubt live in Me ever after (XII, 8).

Fix thy thought on Me, be devoted to Me, sacrifice
to Me, bow down to Me. Thou shalt reach Myself,
truly do I promise unto thee, (for) thou art dear to Me
(XVIII, 65).

After the *Gita* was completed Nambi proposed to
his disciple that he should go with him to recover the
treasure. Alawandar reluctantly consented, for wealth
in however large a quantity had now no temptation for
him, and went with his *Guru* in search of it. Nambi
led him through several Brahmin villages, crossed the

Cauvery, took him into the temple of Srirangam and, pointing to the grand image of Sri Ranganatha,[1] said : "This is the great treasure your grandfather has left you. Take firm hold of it and relieve one of the trust."

Alawandar was overwhelmed with surprise. He little knew that his grandfather had left for him the noblest and the best of legacies, found no words to praise his grace and love, and expressed his gratitude for Nambi, only by falling at his feet again and again and wetting them with tears of joy. And looking at Ranganatha he said : "O Great God, Thou hast been in my grandfather's possession, and now that he has given Thee to me Thou art mine, the God of my grandfather, the God of my family, my own God. I have found Thee at last and shall no longer leave Thee. Ah ! what a treasure has my grandfather given to me and how truly did my *Guru* Nambi speak of It as a 'very vast treasure by obtaining which you will become much richer than any other king an earth.' Ah, how vast a treasure ; It is beyond time and space, *Akhanda*, illimitable. By obtaining Thee I obtain all, for everything is contained in Thee. By knowing Thee everything else is more than known. Truly did Nambi say : 'By securing It you can easily vanquish all your enemies, and no one can ever defeat you.' All my enemies, desire, anger, lust, etc., all get overthrown at Thy very sight, and no one can ever defeat me for like the old sage Vamadeva who sang : 'I am Manu, I am Surya,' I am the Self of all. Ah, how poetically did Lord Nambi speak of Thee when he said : 'It lies between two rivers, and within seven

---

1 As to the symbology of Sri Ranganatha, see Part IV.

successive walls. A huge serpent guards it and a *Rakshasa* comes and visits it once in twelve years. Thou liest between the Cauvery and the Coleroon, and in my heart between the ever flowing streams of *Sankalpa* and *Vikalpa*. The thousand headed Adisesha guards Thee, and Vibishana comes and visits Thee once in twelve years. Truly was this Treasure before me laid in by a *Mantra*, and truly could a *Mantra* alone secure for me this possession. The sacred herb of which my blessed *Guru* spoke is the *Tulsi* of which Thou art extremely fond. O Treasure of treasures, Thou art mine, mine for ever, mine by birth-right. I shall take firm hold of Thee and shall not leave Thee." So saying he flew meteor-like towards the Sacred Image and clasping it swooned away in love. After a long while he recovered and then addressing his preceptor and saviour exclaimed : "How shall I thank you for having sought me and taken me under the shelter of your grace, and having shown me in no mistakable way that *there is no treasure on earth more lasting, more needed and more precious than God*, and *that that treasure is my birthright*. O best of *Gurus*, in what words could I extol the glory of your love which could look upon my redemption as a burden laid upon you !"

Tradition relates that Alawandar then resigned his sceptre and devoted the remainder of his life to *Bhagavannishta* or *Yogic* contemplation. He wrote a few treatises on *Chit, Achit* and *Iswara*, the triad of the *Visishtadwaitic* philosophy, which was to find its best exponent a few years after in Ramanuja. He had three unfulfilled wishes at the time of his death ; and it is said that in token of that, even after his death three fingers of his right hand remained closed, and that they resumed their natural position only when Ramanuja, who almost accidentally came to the spot where the funeral was about to take place, promised to fulfil the three wishes which were communicated to him by his disciples. The three wishes were that a *Visishtadwaitic* commentary should be written for the *Prastanatraya* (the *Upanishads*, the *Vedanta Sutras* and *Gita*), that the name of Parasara the old *Vaishnavite* commentator of the *Vedanta Sutras* should be commemorated on earth by giving it to a person worthy to bear it, and that a commentary should be written upon Nammalwar's *"Tiruvoymozhi"*, which latter was done by a disciple of Ramanuja.

36

BUDDHA

OR

THE GREAT RENUNCIATION

ON a certain fair summer morning 2,500 years ago, the
city of Kapilavastu wore a beautiful festive appearance.
The pavements in the streets were cleanly swept, "the
housewives scattered fresh red powder on their thres-
holds, strung new wreath and trimmed the *Tulsi* bush
before their doors." The tops of houses were thick-set
with flags, the towers were newly gilded, the paintings
on the walls were brightened with fresh colours. From
all the four directions huge crowds were steadily pouring
into the city ; and in a short time there was a vast ocean
of men arranged by the royal military of the capital in
theatric pomp on either side of the main streets. The
trees, towers, roofs of the houses, and walls, all bristled
with men in gay holiday attire. The whole crowd wore
a look of eager expectation and wild joy. They had
not to wait long when the cries of "*Jai! Jai!* for our
noble prince" arose near the palace gate and there came
forth a painted car drawn by two snow-white big humped
steeds. The prince, for it was he that sat in the car,
returned with both his hands the joyous greetings of his
subjects and rejoicing, said to his charioteer :

"Fair is the world, it likes me well ! And light and
kind these men that are not kings, and sweet my sisters
here who toil and tend. Drive through the gates and
let me see more of this gracious world. Ah ! how good
it is to reign in realms like these, how simple pleasure
is if these be pleased because I come abroad !"

It was evidently the first time that the prince had
a look at his capital; and he seemed to know very little
about the men that lived there and indeed about mankind in general. There was an expression of remarkable sweetness and joy in his face, softened however, by
a shade of melancholy. His big black eyes streamed
with tears of joy, but it seemed they would more willingly
weep for love. There was a royal dignity in his general
appearance but with it a humility which was nothing
less than divine. Such sweetness and love marked his
mien, that, though a prince he would, it seemed, have
leapt down from his car to raise a peasant's child that
might happen to fall down. Not far had the procession
advanced, when midway in the road crept forth an old
man bent with age and disease, with shrivelled skin,
hollow cheeks and sunken eyes, holding in one skinny
hand a worn staff, to support his quivering limbs and
crying : "Alms, alms good people, alms, alms or I die."
But such was the order of the king that ugly sights
should not appear in the streets that day. The blind,
the old, the maimed and the sickly were strictly pro-
hibited from coming out before nightfall, lest the prince
might happen to see them ; but even kings cannot shut
out fate and it had been so decreed that Prince Siddharta,
for that was his name, should catch sight of this old
miserable man whom the people around were thrusting
away from the road. But Siddharta cried : "For God's
sake don't push him so" and asked his charioteer :
"What is this thing ? it seems a man yet surely only
seems, being so bowed, so miserable, so horrible, so sad.
Are men born sometimes thus ? Does he find no food
that his bones jet forth so horribly ? What means he by

crying 'to-morrow or next day I die'?" Channa, the charioteer replied : "Why should your highness heed? he is a miserable old man on the verge of death." The prince, however, was not satisfied with this reply. "Do this miserable old age and disease and death" asked he "come to all alike, to me, to my dear Yasodhara, to Gautami, Gunga and others?"

Certainly a very strange question to ask, this! Few in the world have ever put it ; even children, somehow, reconcile themselves to sights of poverty, sickness, and death. But such was the training that Siddharta had been given by his over-careful father, that not even a mention of sickness, sorrow, pain, age or death had ever been made to him till then. On account of a prophecy which had predicted that if he would rule he would be the greatest of kings or failing that, he would wander homeless and alone for the good of the world, he was shut out from the world and was confined in a prison house of pleasure where "Love was jailor and delight its bars". Vishramvan, the place where his father anxious to see him a king of kings made him live was a magnificent group of beautiful summer and winter palaces filled with all the wealth and luxuries of Cashmere and teeming with gentle music of beautiful women, each one of whom was "glad to gladden, pleased at pleasure, proud to obey," so that, life in that fairy prison glided beguiled "like a smooth stream banked by perpetual flowers".

Here in this love's pleasure house,

> ......whether it was night or day none knew,
> For always streamed that softened light, more bright

Than sunrise, but as tender as the eve's;
And always breathèd sweet airs, more joy-giving
Than morning's, but as cool as mid-night's breath;
And night and day lutes sighed, and night and day
Delicious foods were spread, and dewy fruits,
Sherbets new chilled with snows of Himalay,
And sweetmeats made of subtle daintiness,
With sweet tree-milk in its own ivory cup.
And night and day served there a chosen band
Of nautch girls, cup-bearers, and cymballers,
Delicate, dark-browed ministers of love;
Who fanned the sleeping eyes of the happy Prince,
And when he waked, led back his thoughts to bliss
With music whispering through the blooms, and charm
Of amorous songs and dreamy dances, linked
By chime of ankle-bells and wave of arms,
And silver vina-strings; while essences
Of musk and *champak*, and the blue haze spread
From burning spices, soothed his soul again
To drowse by sweet Yasodhara.

But even Yasodhara's love and beauty, matchless as
they were and combined with such luxuries as would
shame *Deva-loka* itself, were not enough to turn the
prince's mind from the melancholy in which it was wont
to fall. *Granite walls however high are not high enough
to shut out fate.* The musing habits of the prince only
increased in the pleasure house, and the very contrivances which were meant to cheat him of his seriousness,
proved their vanity, and every day the prince grew
more and more curious to know if life was only a dull
round of pleasure and if all the world outside the fort
walls were worried with a similarly wearisome monotony.
Often in his face there was an *ennui* which even
Yasodhara "the queen of the enchanting court" could
not kiss away, a curiosity to know the outer world which
all the singings and dancings inside could not restrain.
Often would he sit àlone listening, as it were, to the
"voices of the wandering wind, which moaned for rest,

and rest could never find" and by a quick intuition would he think within himself that mortal life might be like the wind "a moan, a sigh, a sob, a storm, a strife." The problem of life—the old questions of whence, why and whither—sought him out even in those Elysian retreats and haunted him like a demon both day and night, till at last he could no longer resist the desire to see the world outside the high walls of his home.

The king, his father, afraid that the unwelcome alternative of the prophecy might come to pass, strictly forbade all noisome sights in the streets where the prince was to drive. The sight of the old man crying : "Alms ! Alms or I die" made an epoch in the prince's life, and as soon as he learnt that the lot of man was not to live in alabaster halls, in eternal youth and love, to the sound of well-tuned *vinas* and the dance of fairy-like women, that even he and his dear Yasodhara would have in their turn to bend down with age and disease, he ordered his charioteer to turn back and drive home. A deeper melancholy now settled on his face and the store of love for humanity which was already great in his heart now increased with increased knowledge. He felt an intuitive kinship with all the surrounding world and yearned to know more of their joys and griefs that he might, if possible, find a cure for the ills of life. Accordingly a second request went forth from him to the king, to let him view the city as it was and it had to be granted.

In merchant dress, and accompanied by his charioteer, the noble prince crossed the palace walls and went into the work-a-day world. They had not gone far, when a mournful voice came from the road side crying :

"Help masters, lift me to my feet, oh help." And Siddharta rushing to his help took him in his arms and placing his head gently on his lap, asked Channa what the matter was with that man. "Touch him not my master," replied the charioteer, "he has caught the plague which might pass to you also. He cannot long live with this dreadful pest." The prince's curiosity was roused. He asked : "*How* do such ills come?" "They come unobserved like the sly snake, just as chance may send" was the reply. "Then all men live in fear?" "Yes, they do, and at any moment might die." Just then there passed by their side a corpse which was being carried to the burial ground followed by a band of mourners. The prince learned what that meant, and at once his eyes were filled with tears of compassion for the lot of man, for he came to grieve and cure. The sorrows of the world were at once his, and his large heart throbbed with the anguish of the world. "Channa, lead home," he said, "it is enough, my eyes have seen enough."

Thenceforth his one aim was to find out the remedy, if remedy there be, for the woes of the world. The rubies and diamonds of the palace, the music of the *Vina*, the dance of women, all lost their charm for him, and many a time did Yasodhara catch him weeping *with no selfish grief*. She observed with anxiety the rapid change that was coming over her lord, and tried all her womanly arts to beguile him from his melancholy. The prince in return comforted her with kind words and sweet expressions of love which, however, only served to reveal the depths of the grief within.

Siddharta wept because the world was full of woe and Yasodhara wept because her lord wept ; and one

night, a moon-light night it was, while she was sleeping
sweetly pillowed on the royal bosom of her lord she
suddenly cried out with fear and turning round and
kissing her lord three times awoke him saying, "Awaken
lord, awaken and assure me that thou art here with me
and thou wilt not leave me." Siddharta woke up
surprised and asked her : "What is it with thee, O my
life. Why dost thou weep thus ? why shouldst thou
fear when I am by thy side ? what frightens thee ?"
Speaking thus, he gently threw his arms round her and
wiping her tears with his garment tried to compose her,
but the more he sought to soothe her, the greater grew
her grief and she burst out in tears saying : "My lord,
take off thy hands. Be not so kind and loving, if thou
art going to be cruel," and then suddenly raising her
face bathed in tears which seemed to lend a new beauty
to it, added : "Wilt thou really leave me, thy own poor
Yasodhara ? only say, O my love, that thou wilt not."
The prince asked her the cause of such sudden suspicion
and she replied : "Something is telling me these last so
many days that thou art thinking of leaving me and to
confirm my fear, I dreamt now—ah, what a dream !—
that a white bull came wildly coursing through the city
and a cry rose from Indra's temple, 'If ye stay him not,
the glory of the city goeth forth.' But none could stay
him and I wept aloud and locking my arms about him,
bade the gate be barred but he shook me off, trampled
the warder down and passed away. Then the four Regents
of the earth lighting from heaven swiftly swept unto our
city ; at once the golden flag of Indra on the gate
fluttered and fell, and in its place there rose amidst
showers of flowers from above a new banner all the folds

of which contained happy message for all mankind.
Then arose a fearful cry : 'the time is nigh, the time is
nigh.' I heard that dreadful cry and looking for thee,
found only an unpressed pillow and an empty robe and
not thee, my life, my love, my king, my world ; at once
my belt of pearls on my waist changed to a stinging
snake, my ankle rings and golden bangles all fell off, the
jasmines in my hair withered to dust, and this our bridal
couch sank to the ground and something rent asunder
the crimson *Purda*. Then far away I heard the white
bull low and far away the embroidered banner flap, and
once again the cry 'the time is come !' But with that
cry which still shakes my spirit, I woke, O my love,
what may such visions mean, but that I die, or worse
than any death, that thou shouldst forsake me and this
innocent little child by my side ?''
     Siddharta fully understood the meaning of those
dreams and realised within himself that the hour was
come for his glorious self-sacrifice, that he was
summoned by the power above to take up the cause of
suffering humanity. With a look full of compassion and
''soft like the last soft smile of sunset,'' he embraced his
weeping wife and said : ''Comfort thee, my dear, what need
for fear when I love thee more than I love myself. Be
sure, my love, let come what may, my love to thee will
never change. Fo a long time past my heart is burning
with passionate love for all that lives, and often hast
thou caught me musing how to save man from the thraldom of misery. Life is at best a long drawn agony, only
its pains abide, its pleasures are as birds which light
and fly ; men live and die and whirl upon the wheel and
hug and kiss its spokes of agony, its tier of tears, its nave

of nothingness. I have been yearning to know if these were
the eternal lot of man, if there is no escape from this
merciless round of misery, and if I grieve for griefs which
are not mine and burn with love for souls unknown,
how much should I not love those that share my griefs
and joys and most of all thou my dearest, gentlest, best
Yasodhara? Therefore take comfort my dear, and
whatever happens, remember that I love thee and will
always love thee well, and if sorrow falls, forget not that
there may be a way to peace on earth through our woes,
and as a proof of my unfailing love to thee, take this
my kiss."

Thus comforted, the princess went to bed, her face
still wet with tears, and locking up her lover in her
arms as if she feared that he might forsake her or be
taken away. Hardly had she slept when she sighed as
if the former vision had passed again, "the time, the
time is come."

> Whereat Siddharta turned
> And, lo! the moon shone by the Crab! the stars
> In that same silver order long foretold
> Stood ranged to say: "This is the night! —Choose thou
> The way of greatness or the way of good:
> To reign a king of kings, or wonder long,
> Crownless and homeless, that the world be helped"

—alternatives in choosing between which surely most of
us would at least have hesitated. Far different, however, was the action of the prince. No sooner did he
hear the words "the time, the time is come," than he
replied within himself, "I come, I come." The picture of
countless millions of souls struggling for escape on the
vast prison-like earth stood before his eyes in all its awful
vividness and casting a farewell look upon his weeping

Yasodhara and gently freeing himself from her lovely embrace he rose up and said within himself "Dear sleeper, thy face is still wet with tears. But the tears of the numberless struggling souls shrieking for help weigh heavier in the balance. When thou wakest, weep not at the unpressed pillow and the vacant bed, but comfort thyself that thy lover though far away from thy fond embrace still loves thee *with passionate but unselfish love*, and pray that what comfort he might be able to wring from the vast unknown for the sake of suffering humanity might be thine also along with others, nay more thine than others." Thy child may not inherit thrones and rule over kingdoms, yet, a more glorious inheritance may be his if the powers so will. "Farewell my love, farewell my child, farewell my sweet Yasodhara"; and saying thus he gently kissed her sleeping face for the last time and closing his eyes as if for fear of being wooed from his mission, stepped towards the door but thrice he opened them and came back. At last half ashamed of himself and conjuring up with all the power of his imagination the vision of suffering souls, he bade a fourth and final farewell to the innocent Yasodhara and shut noiselessly behind him the door of the apartment in which she unsuspectingly lay sleeping.

Great Siddharta, resolute Siddharta, all glory to thee!—This poor earth of ours, sorely needed help and help was never more generously given than when thou crossed the threshold of thy secret chamber where "skill had spent all lovely phantasies to lull the mind". Few have felt with thee the blow given on the neighbour's cheek as if given on their own and very few indeed have made such bold sallies into the domain of truth and brought from there such lasting treasures as thou and to few, indeed, to none else within history's ken was it given to renounce a royal couch, a vast kingdom and the loveliest of wives and that when she was in a state which would have softened the stoniest of hearts. Thy heart was the tenderest that beat, thy life the largest ever lived, for it was lived for all the world. In thee, there was not the least tinge of the lower-self. Thou wert thyself the spirit of the universe, its all-pervading life and no extravagant honour does the Hindu pay thee when he reckons thee among the *Avatars* of his God or the Buddhist when he worships thee as God himself. The other immortals of the world all seem to sink by thy side and among the pillars that have risen to heaven from age to age from our sad earth, few have risen higher than that which bears thy name. Numberless are the brave souls that dared to scoff at the Circean spell of the world and kicked away the pleasures that might have been theirs. But not even among the foremost of them, the Christs and Sankaras of the world was any whose renunciation was as glorious as that which is deservedly styled the *Mahabhinishkramana*, the Great Renunciation. In this country and elsewhere numberless souls have knocked against the prison walls of the world, but few have sought the cure for the ills of life, purely for the sake of others. Buddha was as happy as worldly circumstances could make him ; for himself he had no special cause of grief and never was that well-known saying of the English poet :

> All are men,
> Condemned alike to groan ;

> *The tender for another's pain,*
> The unfeeling for his own;

more fully illustrated than in the life of prince Siddharta.

To return to the story. The Rubicon was crossed and the beggar prince was soon on the back of his trusted steed which brought him before birth of dawn beyond his father's domains. The princely sword and belt, the last remnants of royalty were sent back to the king his father with a prayer to

> ....forget him till he come
> Ten times a Prince, with royal wisdom won
> From lonely searchings and the strife for light;
> Where, if I conquer, lo ! all earth is mine—
> Mine by chief service !—tell him—mine by love !
> Since there is hope for man only in man,
> And none hath sought for this as I will seek,
> Who cast away my world to save my world.

The beggar's yellow robe and bowl were all that he now owned—a great renunciation indeed, but a greater one was soon to follow.

True renunciation is always a matter of the mind ; it may or may not be attended with external renunciation ; very often it is, and in most cases, the latter is a great help to the former ; at least in Siddharta's case it was so.

After leaving his father's dominions, Siddharta went from place to place begging with his bowl and at nights slept on the grass, homeless and alone. He lived for a time like a *Rishi* engaged day and night in meditation. When he went out to beg, all those who saw him said : "He is a noble *Muni*, his very approach is bliss, ah, what a joy for us," and vied with one another to give him food. The majesty of his mind was ill-concealed under the poverty of his garb. His noble *rishabha*-like gait betrayed his royal birth and his eyes beamed with a fervid zeal for truth, while the beauty of his youth was transfigured by his holiness. All that beheld him gazed at him in wonder, and mothers, when they saw him go by, would bid their children fall at his feet and kiss him; and young Indian maids would silently love him and worship his majestic form often as he paced gentle and slow, "radiant with heavenly pity and lost in care for those he knew not save as fellow-lives".

On Ratnagiri, there dwelt a number of *Yogis* who practised diverse forms of self-mortification known as *Hatayoga*. Siddharta fell in with them and outdid them in the rigour of *Hatayoga* practices, and the result was as might have been expected that his health got shattered, so much so, that, when he went to bathe in river, he could not rise out of the water and had to take hold of a branch of a tree close by. He soon saw the utter futility of such physical tortures *which Vedantism has never been slow to condemn*; and leaving off the company of the gaunt and mournful *Bhikshus*, he retired with weak and faltering steps to a grove close by, where a simple shephered woman, seeing him about to swoon with weakness and hunger, kindly nourished him with fresh milk, curds and rice. The simple unquestioning faith of the woman and her pity and love, made our prince exclaim :

Thou teachest them who teach,
Wiser than wisdom in thy simple lore.
Thy way of right and duty : grow, thou flower !
With thy sweet kind in peaceful shade—the light
Of Truth's high noon is not for tender leaves

Which must spread broad in other suns, and lift
In later lives a crowned head to the sky.
Thou who hast worshipped me, I worship thee
Excellent heart! learned unknowingly,
As the dove is which flieth home by love.
In thee is seen why there is hope for man
And where we hold the wheel of life at will.

Refreshed by what he ate, he rose and went to the shade of a large *Bodhi* tree which has become immortal with him, and sat and thought under its shade. He did not stir from that shade till his inner vision was opened once for all and the light of heaven flashed in his mind in all its fulness and glory. He sat and contemplated for days and nights on the darkened mysterious problems of life, not knowing the hours as they passed along and forgetful of even meals and rest. The questions which troubled him were the old old ones, what is the meaning of life? Why all this struggle on earth? and where would it all end? This was the hour of trial. Great was the strife with him and often was he tempted. He withstood all temptations boldly and overcame selfishness, lust and desire which in a Protean variety of shapes wooed him to return to the loving embrace of his beautiful Yasodhara and to his ancestral sceptre and throne. Hard was the struggle against the army of passions that rose and waged fierce war. By intense and resolute struggle and by the force of abounding love and faith, the evil within him was overcome and the result was Siddharta got enlightened. From this moment he became a Buddha and the light of Heaven shone within him in all its *ancient* glory.

Then he arose—radiant, rejoicing, strong—
Beneath the Tree, and lifting high his voice
Spake this, in hearing of all Times and Worlds:

Long have I wandered ! Long !
Bound by the chain of desire
Through many births
Seeking thus long in vain,
Whence comes this restlessness in man ?
Whence his egotism, his anguish ?
And hard to bear is *samsara*
Found ! it is found !
Author of selfhood,
No longer shalt thou build a house for me;
Broken are the beams of sin ;
The ridge-pole of care is shattered,
Into *Nirvana* my mind has passed,
The end of craving has been reached at last.

Here was the great renunciation, true *Sanyasa* of the *Upanishads*. Renunciation does not consist in flying away from wife and children— they are not the real *Samsara* to be given up. Restlessness of the mind is the real *Samsara* (*Maitreya-Upa.*). When the mind is restless, there is *Samsara* and when it attains rest it enjoys *Moksha* (*Yoga Sika Upa.*). What is really to be given up is the restlessness of the mind, the dominion of the self and attachment. If these be given up as Buddha did under the Bo-tree, then the glory of true *Sanyasa* or renunciation is realised. Who is a *Sanyasin* ? "He is the real *Sanyasin*," says the *Niralambopanishad*, "who, leaving off all *Dharmas* and the attachments of 'I' and 'mine' and taking refuge in Brahman (or *Nirvana*), is convinced, through practical realisation of great sayings like—'That art Thou', 'All this is Brahman' and 'There is here nothing like many'—that he is himself Brahman, and moves in the world in changeless and undisturbed meditation. He alone is worthy of worship, he is the real *Yogi*, the real *Paramahamsa*, the real *Avadhuta* and the real *Brahmajnani*." He is the *Paramahamsa Parivrat* who is ever in the contemplation of the *Pranava*, the symbol of Brahma (*Paramahamsa Parivrajaka-Upa.*).

Buddha was truly one of the perfect *Sanyasins* of the world. They err who think that the *Nirvana* he promised to his followers is mere annihilation. Buddhistic *Nirvana* is not the least different from the *Vedantic Moksha*. The former emphasises the negative aspect—the annihilation of the false self (the *jiva*, the transmigrating ego), while the latter presents the positive aspect—identity with the Brahman, *Aham Brahmasmi*, Rightly has it bee⸱ said :

> If any teach *Nirvana* is to cease,
> Say unto such they lie ;

for it is nothing but the negation of our illusion and the realisation of truth. Certainly it is not the false life that the majority of us live, for

> If any teach *Nirvana* is to live
> Say unto such they err, not knowing this
> Nor what light shines beyond their broken lamps,
> Nor lifeless, timeless bliss.

The Buddhist or for that matter the *Vedantist*, "seeking nothing gains all". To him "foregoing self the universe grows I".

There was, it might be said, little that Buddha discovered for himself newly. His great doctrines, the doctrine of *Karma*, that of transmigration, that of final absorption of *Nirvana* and others were already in the *Upanishads*. *Buddha's glory consists not in having discovered new truths of metaphysics, but in having emphasised the ethical aspect of the Upanishads at a time, when*

37

exclusive attention to dry form and cumbersome rituals had all but robbed the Hindu religion of its life. Indeed, *there is nothing new under the sun* and when this is recognised it will no longer be matter for surprise that the great masters of antiquity have all taught very nearly the same solution for the problem of life. The *Upanishads* repeatedly preach *the conquest of desires, the subjection of the self.* "When all the desires cease which were cherished in his heart, then the mortal becomes immortal, then he obtains the Brahman here (in this life)" *Katha.-Upa.*, VI, 14. This is the central lesson of the *Upanishads.* And,

> Seeking nothing he gains all
> Foregoing self, the universe grows I,

is the central lesson of the Gospel of Buddha, Christ, Confucius, etc. The truth is one ; only, it is presented in diverse ways and here we see the meaning of what Sri Krishna says : "I create myself, and thus appear from age to age for the preservation of the just, the destruction of the wicked and the establishment of virtue" (*Gita*, IV. 8). Much depends, however, on the setting in which the great truths are presented. *The chief defect* in Buddha's system—no blame however, to the great master—as in several others *was, that it was not supported strongly enough by a rational and deep searching philosophy.* Every religion has to satisfy both the head and the heart and in some cases unfortunately, the necessary intellectual sanction is wanting. There is such a want in the case of Buddhism, though it is not so great as in the case of Christianity. *Another great defect was that the final end was too meagrely indicated to be properly understood* and as a consequence, Buddhism had unfortunately degenerated into something very much akin to Atheism, and reformers like Sankara found it necessary to overthrow it. If, on the other hand, the final end of man had been more distinctly chalked out and more concretely and attractively idealised as in the *Vedanta*, Buddhism would have had quite a different career. True it is, that the subjugation of mind is duly insisted upon in that noble religion, but the conquest of the mind could never fully be accomplished, unless through love of the final ideal. It is the peculiarity of the human mind that it refuses to be crushed and can be conquered only by being *bribed to love*. Indeed, it never gets annihilated but only transfigured into love. The lower self can never be abandoned except in exchange for the higher and to make such an exchange possible, it is very essential that the higher self should be attractively presented. The *Nirvana* of the Buddhists is too negative to be sufficiently enchanting, at least in the lower stages of spiritual growth and hence ensues a great difficulty in practical realisation. It is true that the *Atman* of the *Upanishads*, though a positive ideal, is in some degree an abstract and ethereal entity, but the *Vedanta* has bridged up the chasm between it and the average human mind, by means of *Sagunopasana* or worship of God with attributes, which gradually leads on to the attainment of the real, attributeless Brahman. *Buddhism as taught by Buddha, did not attach sufficient importance to God worship* ; indeed, Buddha himself, owing perhaps to the peculiar requirements of the age, discouraged enquiry into the nature of God and the origin of things.

Look not for *Brahm* and the Beginning there !
Nor him nor any light
Shall any gazer see with mortal eyes,
Or any searcher know by mortal mind ;
Veil after veil will lift—but there must be
Veil upon veil behind.
Stars sweep and question not. This is enough
That life and death and joy and woe abide.

A religion without God is however an impossibility and an authoritative "Question not" does not subdue the curiosity of man. Non-attachment is almost an impossible condition ; at the best, it only means, that the mind leaves hold of lower things for the sake of higher and, when it realises its true nature, rejects all things high and low as illusion. It is a great advantage to humanity that God, the highest of things, should be presented to man at every turn in the course of his evolution. And it is with this object that man is enjoined by the *Vedanta* to do motiveless *Karma* and dedicate it to God. "Whatever thou doest, O Arjuna, whatever thou eatest, whatever thou sacrificest, whatever thou givest, whatever thou shalt be zealous about, make each an offering unto me" (*Gita*, IX, 27). The absence of God-element is a great drawback in Buddhism and besides leaving no scope in it for *Bhakti-Yoga*, takes away very much from even *Karma-Yoga*.

Apart from these defects which time has perhaps removed, Buddha's system is one of the noblest legacies handed down from man to man. Some of the very best features of modern Hinduism owe their existence to the influence of Buddha who was in truth the last, but, one of the greatest of the interpreters of the *Upanishads* and one of the greatest of the *Yogis* that blest our earth with their examples. To few of the great religious re-

formers of the world, was it given to live such high and
noble life as Buddha lived, and if to-day we enjoy the
light of the *Upanishads*, it is as much owing to him as
to the latter reformers, Sankara and others.

Note.—**The Gospel of Buddha,** by Paul Carus (The Open Court
Publishing Company, Chicago) is a very handy volume presenting,
in the author's words, "a picture of a religious leader of the remote
past with the view of making it bear upon the living present and become a factor in the formation of the future." Few books on Buddhism
more clearly bring out the personality of Buddha, or give a more suc-
cinct account of his teachings. It follows none of the sectarian
doctrines but takes the ideal position of Buddhism. It is a mistake to
think that the religion of Buddha was a rebellion against the spirit of
the *Vedanta*. On the other hand it was really a part of the *Vedanta*,
and busied itself with overthrowing a corrupt, degenerate and lifeless
ritualism which was doing duty for the real religion of the *Vedanta*.
The glory of Buddha consists in having *emphasised the ethical aspect
of the Upanishads* at a time when bloody sacrifices, oppressive caste
restrictions, and cumbersome rituals were nearly all that were left
living in Hinduism. Buddha restored the connection between
Hinduism and its fountain-head, the *Upanishads*, which by the work
of time and other influences had been forgotten ; and thus he purified
the former. His teachings correspond, though not fully, to the *Karma-
Yoga* path of the *Vedanta*, and involves to some extent the *Raja-
Yoga* path also. *Bhakti* has in it no place, and *Gnana* obtains a feeble
and inefficient recognition. That Buddha's precepts were not in
themselves sufficient as a national religion, is further attested by the
fact of its having been found necessary to supplement them by what
is known as the *Mahayana*, the large vessel of Salvation.

It is a pity that the author does not fully grasp the *Vedantic*
doctrine of the *Atman*. He writes, "Buddhism is monistic, it claims
that man's soul does not consist of two things, of an *Atman* and of a
Manas." If Buddhism is monistic, it is because, and not in spite, of
the *Vedanta* ; and nowhere does the latter say that there are two
different things in man's soul, the *Atman* and the mind. The mind
is itself the *Atman* when freed from ignorance and the delusion of
"self". The same consciousness is *Manas* when it fancies that it is
limited and tied down to matter, and the *Atman* when this illusion
vanishes. The *Atman* is not the mysterious ego-entity supposed to
reside behind or within man's bodily and psychical activity as a distinct being, as Paul Carus represents it to be, but consciousness or
Pragna freed from error and egoism. The imperfect grasp of this
cardinal point of the *Vedanta* mars here and there the beauty of the
otherwise valuable book. It has already run four editions and has

awakened great interest in Buddhism. It is of special interest to the student of Comparative Religion, pointing out, as it does, the common ethical basis of all religions, and how it is to the glory of Buddhism that its great founder should have laid special emphasis on the one aspect of religion which always stands in the greatest danger of being forgotten or neglected.

SAINT VAYILAR

RELIGIONS have their seasons as well as years have, and as in the spring time when the whole vegetable world rejoices, flowers shoot forth, not merely from trees and plants but even from the shrubs on the wayside and fences in the garden, so in the great *Saivite* revival of Southern India in the days of the last of the Pandyans, there arose saints in multitudes from every nook and corner of the Tamil land and not merely the high and cultured classes of the community, but even the lowest castes succeeded in bringing forth *Bhaktas* like Nanda, whose names a grateful posterity remembers with reverence and love. Saint Vayilar, whose life is our present theme, was one of the children of this great revival, and though he was not of the lower castes, he was not of the first three. He belonged to an agricultural class, known as the *Vellala*, and was born in Mylapore, the native place of this journal. His life was eventless; except for the one occupation which, though it might appear dull to some, engaged him both day and night. *It was the worship of God*.

His way of worshipping was, however, peculiar. He did not find much pleasure in going to the local temple, for the worship there did not come up to his ideal; therefore he built a very grand temple of his own, the grandest perhaps ever known, with numberless towers, all of gold; high and spacious halls provided with walls of silver and pillars of gold and decorated with the costliest diamonds and rubies. The whole temple was built on a beautiful plan with five square walls one after

another, made of different metals, the outermost being
of iron and the innermost of gold. It was lit up not
with ordinary lamps but with big diamonds as bright as
the sun and of the size of mangoes. Numberless mirrors
disposed in an artistic fashion set forth the beauty of
the temple in tenfold richness. In the centre of the
temple was the *sanctum sanctorum* which rivalled the
Kailas (abode of Siva) in grandeur, and contained a
beautiful *Lingam*, the image of God, adorned with the
costliest jewels and the most fragrant flowers. On each
side of the image stood a *Kalpa* tree whose flowers spread
their divine fragrance all through the temple. It was
a very grand temple, and my tongue does poor justice
to its unrivalled beauty and splendour.

Here it may be asked : "How did he afford the
money for building so magnificent a temple, and where
did he build it ?" The answer is, he did not build it with
money but with his lively imagination which, of course,
cost him nothing except *the rarest of things, viz., love to
God* and the splendid temple was all in his mind. He
would constantly live with the God of that temple,
make *Puja* to it day and night, and forget even meals
and sleep in that occupation. He would seldom talk to
any body, for he was too busy, and he would go on
making his *Puja* without caring whether it rained or
thundered, whether it was night or day till he forgot
even the temple and God, and himself alone remained.
In course of time, the image also disappeared, and his
own soul became God. Says his biographer : "His
mind was his temple, wisdom the lamp that shone in it,
bliss the water which he poured over his God and love
the offering he made to that Deity." Tradition adds

that the glory of his silent worship gradually became
known to the world, and when he died he was canonized
on earth, and in Heaven he became one with God.

Such is the glory of mental worship. *Ah, how cheap
is Heaven and yet how dear?*

SRI TATWARAYA SWAMI

ABOUT three hundred years ago, in a place called
Veeramanagaram, the central part of the Madras
Presidency, was born the subject of our sketch as the
nephew (sister's son) of a great man with whom he was
destined to be connected in a much closer and stronger
tie than that of mere blood relationship. The latter
was senior by a few years only ; and the earthly mission
of the two being one and the same, they exhibited a
strange liking to each other from their very infancy.
Being Brahmins they were duly educated in Sanskrit
and became very learned in the Sacred Scriptures. In
addition to this, they also attained to a high degree of
scholarship in Tamil. They were strict in the obser-
vance of *Sastraic* injunctions as to external and internal
purity, conduct in life and reverence to elders and so on.
At a very early age while they were yet bachelors, both
of them took the same right view of life—there is no
permanent resting place in the world of the senses and
intellect, life is deceptive, man being preyed upon every
moment and led into pit-falls by his organs of action
and knowledge. The little pleasures which he occasionally gets are bounded on either side by pain, and
resemble the minute drops of honey in thorn flowers,
and that the only refuge from death, delusion and pain,
is to direct that vision inward and become the unconditioned and changeless One, Whose glory the
Upanishads declare, and Whom, Nature trying to
translate, heaps universe upon universe during myriads
of centuries and still does not express, her great harangue

going on from enternity, which is put to an end by the *Mauna* (silence) of mind. To get back to the centre from which all life starts, the two boy prodigies made sallies into the secret recesses of the *Srutis*, but the more they wanted to go in, the stronger became the obstacles in the way, and after years of unsuccessful moping in the dark they felt the need for the hand that would lead and *the personal light that would reveal the impersonal light within*. The world had no temptations for them, they having done all that one has to do with the world in previous incarnations; and its Sirens' songs were to them like the howlings of demons from which one would seek to fly. They did not care to marry, and were determined to be done with the false life of sin and sorrow before their breaths would stop, and they sought the truths with such one-pointedness that they were called by their neighbours and relations *Tatwaraya* and *Swarupananda* respectively. Their former names have not been handed down to us, but that is immaterial.

Tatwaraya and his uncle Swarupananda, finding the insufficiency of book-learning and being anxious to obtain a teacher, went from place to place with the eagerness with which a man "whose hair has caught fire," runs for water, but nowhere could they find a satisfactory guide. After wandering thus for a long time, they one day rested under a banyan tree in a beautiful grove, and there settled the following plan, namely, that one of them should go North and the other South, and whoever finds the teacher first and realises the Truth should become the teacher of the other This, *is the event proved*, was a wise plan. ₁was uj ꜛ ꜛ ında

went Southward; and after visiting many villages,
towns, forests, mountain-caves, river-sides and ruined
temples, besides the famous places of pilgrimage such
as Srirangam, Jambukeswaram and Paingili Vallaral,
he went to Govardhan, when all of a sudden he felt a
strange blissful sensation creeping over his body
and his hair stood on end. It was a delightful feeling
similar to what the poet describes in the following
lines :

> For more than once when I
> Sat all alone, revolving in myself
> The word that is the symbol of myself,
> The mortal limit of the Self was loosed,
> And passed into the Nameless, as a cloud
> Melts into Heaven. I touched my limbs, the limbs
> Were strange not mine—and yet no shade of doubt,
> But utter clearness; and thro' loss of Self
> The gain of such large life as matched with ours
> Were Sun to spark—unshadowable in words,
> Themselves but shadows of a shadow world.

This assertion of the Over-soul which was as blissful
as spontaneous, gave Swarupananda the hope that his
weary pilgrimage was at an end, and that the true *Guru*
he so eagerly sought was there, within the limits of that
village. The delighted wisdom-seeker went round the
village three times as a mark of honour to the holy land ;
and, entering it, inquired of the people of the village if
there was any great sage, *Mahatman*, there. They told
him that near the place was a dense reed bush, in which
lived a great man whose name was Swami Sivaprakasa,
and that he would on some evenings come out of it.
Needless to say that Swarupananda hastened to the spot
and waited outside for the appearance of the sage. One
evening the Swami came out, and the young devotee ran

to him, fell at his feet, wetted them with tears, saying : "Salutation, O Lord, full of compassion, O friend of those who prostrate themselves before Thee, hallowed be Thy holy feet. Sprinkle on me thy grace, O Lord, scorched as I am by the forest-fire of birth and rebirth, gratify my ear with ambrosial words as they flow from Thee, mingled with the essence of Thy Self-experience and the bliss afforded by *Brahmagnana*, sacred and cooling. Happy are they who come into Thy sight even for a moment, for they become fit recipients of divine wisdom and are accepted as pupils." The Swami raised him from the ground, and, looking at him, found that he was an earnest seeker. Then they conversed for a time and Swarupananda, being found to be deserving, was initiated into the mystery of *Raja-yoga*. He stayed with his teacher, hearing from him the divine mysteries of the *Vedanta*, which are too subtle and precious to find a place in books, and practising *Samadhi* in his company. After the necessary amount of practice, the Truth hermetically sealed up in the apparently simple words, "Thou art That" was unfolded to him.

In the meanwhile Tatwaraya Swami, who had wandered all over the North in quest of a teacher returned to the South with a heart laden with grief, but, seeing his uncle and hearing from him his happy history, adopted him as his teacher, and falling at his feet, sought his grace and protection. Swarupananda taught him all that he had learnt, and both remained together, spending the greater part of their time in that silent communion with God in which thought is not and expires in the enjoyment.

SRI RAMAKRISHNA PARAMAHAMSA[1]

INDIA is essentially a land of religious realisation. Throughout the community, there has been from time immemorial an anxious groping after the unknown reality beyond the phenomenal world. In one way and another, efforts have been made, some of them desperate and wild in their character, to see God face to face. All the resources of the human mind, both in its emotional and its intellectual side, have been stretched to the utmost to obtain the undisturbed and sacred bliss of Heaven—*the peace which passeth all understanding*. In India more than in any other country, Paradise has been lost and regained. The unquestioning and unsuspecting optimism of ignorance—the early Paradise of man—has necessarily to be lost, when evil, sin, and grief assert their existence, and claim a clear recognition. And pessimism, which is a necessary result of such recognition and is at present a prevalent tendency in some countries, has, at least in ours, been fortunately replaced by a final optimism, the result of *Vedantic* search and religious realisation ; and thus has Paradise been re-won.

In no other country is spirituality so marked a national character ; and if, to-day, in the midst of the most materialistic civilisations, we are able to preserve that character intact, it is due almost wholly to the influence of perfected men, who have from time to time appeared in our midst, and presented to public gaze,

[1] The following two stories being incomplete are placed at the end of this part.

both by example and precept, the great ideal of *Liberation*. From the *Vedic* times downwards, successive waves of spirituality has risen and deluged our country from the Himalayas to Cape Comorin ; and the influence of the unknown seers of the *Upanishads*, of Rama and Krishna, of Buddha, Sankara and Ramanuja, and other epoch-making characters, is still a living force in our society, and has at successive times given birth to lesser luminaries, the saints, sages and *Bhaktas* of our land. Indeed, their influence, is quite as living to-day as ever ; and we shall have no cause to complain of our present age, when we remember that it has brought forth men like Chaitanya, Thayumanavar, Dayananda Saraswati, and Ramakrishna Paramahamsa. The last of these great men will form our study for the present. In Nanda we saw a real *Bhakta* of Southern India, sprung from the lowest caste. In the Paramahamsa we shall find a genuine seeker after God of Northern India, sprung from the highest caste. Spirituality in our country is not the monopoly of any particular sect or part of the country ; and, if only to illustrate this truth, the life of Ramakrishna comes in as a fitting sequel to that of Nanda the *Pariah* Saint.

The study of Ramakrishna is of interest to us in another way also. He was a man who lived quite within the memory of many still living ; and consequently, mythology has not yet succeeded in completely burying his genuine personality within its cumbrous folds. One great advantage in his case is that we can, with the help of his disciples, and biographers, bring him back before us in imagination and study him with immense profit—how he ate and slept, and what sort of life he lived, and so on. These details are not mere biographical curiosities; they give the real clue to his character; and help us in understanding where exactly he differs from other men. We can know what is common between us and him, and what is not; and, in the light of this knowledge, struggle to develop ourselves. In him we shall find an ideal which every one of us may try to realise with advantage—a *Mahatman* not enshrouded in mystery, or concealed from mortal view, but, in the words of Max Muller, "a real *Mahatman*" whom we can understand and sympathise with.

In another way also is Ramakrishna interesting to us. Though he himself never moved in the world, or was a man of the world, and though he never professed to teach others, the influence which he exercised on Keshab Chander Sen, G. C. Ghose (the Bengali Garrick and Shakespeare), Surendranath Bose, P. C. Mozoomdar, and a large number of highly educated men, was simply extraordinary. "A score of young men who were closely attached to him have become ascetics after his death. They follow his teachings by giving up the enjoyment of wealth and carnal pleasure, living together in a *mutt*, and retiring at times to holy and solitary places all over India, even as far as the Himalayan mountains." The great apostles of the *Vedanta* in foreign countries— Swamis Vivekananda, Saradananda, Abedhananda—all come from this *mutt*; and it was the voice of Ramakrishna that thundered in the Parliament of Religions at Chicago, and is now drawing forth to the glorious philosophy of the *Upanishads* the interest and admiration of all the civilised world. If, in no long time, the merits of the *Vedanta* come to be recognised among continental thinkers, and it attains the high place which it eminently deserves among the philosophies of the world, a great part of the credit for such recognition will be the due of *the teacher who never taught, but lived his teaching*. "The state in which the rulers are most reluctant to govern," truly says Plato, "is best and most quietly governed, and the state in which they are most willing is the worst." In the same way, it may be said, the teachings of those who are most anxious to teach are often the worst, and the teachings of those who have no idea of teaching often turn out to be the wisest and the most profound. At any rate, it was so in Ramakrishna's case. He declined to be the *Guru*, in the proper sense of the word, to any one ; and, in uttering his now-famous sayings, which Max Muller regards "as the spontaneous outburst of profound wisdom, clothed in beautiful poetical language," he never once dreamt of their commanding the admiration of European and American scholars. If he was a teacher of mankind, he was unconsciously so. Writing about his wonderful influence, Mozoomdar says :

"My mind is floating in the luminous atmosphere which that wonderful man diffuses around him whenever and wherever he goes. My mind is not yet disenchanted of the mysterious and indefinable pathos which he pours into it whenever he meets me. What is there common between him and me ? I, a Europeanised, civilised, self-centred, semi-sceptical, so-called educated reasoner, and he a poor, illiterate, shrunken, unpolished, diseased, half-idolatrous friendless, Hindu devotee ? Why should I sit long hours to attend to him, I who have listened to Disraeli and Fawcett, Stanley and Max Muller, and a whole host of European scholars and divines. I who

38

and an ardent disciple and follower of Christ, a friend
and admirer of liberal-minded Christian missionaries
and preachers, a devoted adherent and worker of the
rationalistic Brahmo Samaj—why should I be spell-
bound to hear him? And it is not I only, but dozens
like me who do the same. He has been interviewed
and examined by many, crowds pour in to visit and talk
with him. Some of our clever intellectual fools have
found nothing in him, some of the contemptuous
Christian missionaries would call him an impostor,
or a self-deluded enthusiast. I have weighed their
objections well, and what I write now, I write delibe-
rately."

Ramakrishna[1] was born at the village of Sripoor
Kamerpoor in the Hooghly District in the year 1834.
He was the last of three sons, the first of whom was
named Ramkumar and second Rameswar. The
Paramahamsa was known in his childhood as *Gadadhar*,
or familiarly *Gadai*, signifying *Vishnu*—a name given
him by his father, in commemoration of a vision the
latter had, revealing to him the birth of a son who would
prove a saviour of thousands. As a boy, Ramakrishna
was somewhat lean and fair in complexion, spoke sweetly,
and was liked by everyone. A place where he was most
petted was the house of one of his friends Gangavishnu,
whose mother was exceedingly fond of him, preferring
him to her own son, and reserving the best sweetmeats
for him.

The father of Gangavishnu was a rich man, and

1 The details of Ramakrishna's life are mostly from a biography of
his in Bengali by Ramachandra Datta, B.A., one of his most devoted
Grihasta disciples.

maintained an *Atithisala*, a place where *sadhus* or religious men sojourned during their pilgrimage and obtained daily provisions free. This was a frequent resort of the boy Ramakrishna, who loved even so early to associate with *sadhus*. Those that came to the *Chattram* would decorate him with *namam*, the *Vaishnava* mark, on the forehead, relate to him religious stories, and teach him pious songs. The boy would often be fed by the *sadhus* with the food they had prepared for themselves. One day he went to the *Atithisala* wearing a new cloth, and returned home only with a *kaupin*, that is, almost naked, like a *sanyasin* and painted all over the body with *namams*. Seeing his mother, he exclaimed : "Look, I have decorated myself like a *sadhu*, I do not want any food to-day as I have already taken the *roti* (bread given by the *sadhus*)." Ramakrishna's school education was of the poorest kind. A copy of the Ramayana which he made with his own hand, and which is still preserved, shows how little he learned at school. He was sent to a *Pathasala* where *Vedic mantras* and hymns were taught but even there he did not learn anything. He had, however a good memory, and accumulated a rich store of *kirthanas*, lyrics and stories. He sang well and with a sweet voice.

Ramakrishna had his own way even from his childhood. He was greatly attached to one Dhani of the carpenter caste, a friend of his mother's. This woman took care of him from his birth and throughout his boyhood. She loved him intensely and would, forgetting the prohibitions of caste, feed him from her own hands. One day Dhani told him that she would give him *biksha* first, at his *Upanayana* (the thread-wearing ceremony) and he agreed to gratify her wish. So at the *Upanayana*, he first boldly begged *biksha* of Dhani, but his eldest brother protested against it on the ground of caste. In the end, Ramakrishna had his own way and took his first *biksha* from Dhani who became his *biksha* mother.

Ramakrishna was original even in his boyish amusements. He enacted the religious stories he had eagerly learnt ; thus he would take his companions to a lonely field, dress himself as Krishna, allot to his companions the parts of Sridham, Sudham, Kuchela and other friends of Krishna, and play the immortal *lilas* (sports) of Krishna so well-known throughout the country. At other times he would make idols and worship them. Thus passed away the first ten years of Ramakrishna's life.

When he was fifteen years old, he was married to Saradamani Devi, the daughter of one Ramachandra Mukhopadhyaya of Jayarambati, a village not far from his own. The last school that Ramakrishna attended was a free school at Jamapukur which was under the direction of his eldest brother. From there he passed on in the year 1852 to the temple of Dhakshineswar, along with his brother, who was appointed the presiding *pandit* of the place by Rani Rashmoni Dasi, who established the idols of Kali and Radha-Krishna in the temple. On the day of the consecration of the idols, there was much eclat, and many were fed. Ramakrishna fasted that whole day, and in the evening he bought in the bazaar a pice-worth of fried rice and ate it.

The temple is situated six miles north of Calcutta, the garden of the temple being on the eastern bank of the Ganges. In the northern side of the garden there

was a large Banyan tree, a hut on the southern side now
converted into a building, and on the north-east a *Bilwa*
tree. The whole place has in it a peculiar air of
solemnity, and is very well fitted to induce religious
thoughts even in visitors who are not Hindus. At this
temple Ramakrishna was first employed as *beshkari, i.e.,*
one who dresses and adorns the idols ; then in the *puja*
of Radhakrishna ; and on his brother's death, Rashmoni
Dasi appointed him for the *puja* of Kali. Ramakrishna
worshipped with extraordinary *Bhakti,* decorating the
idol with sweet-smelling flowers, or throwing *bilwa* and
jaba leaves at its feet, or singing the songs of *Sakti
upasakas* (the worshippers of the Maternal Divine
Energy) like Ramaprasad, Kamalakanta and others.
Standing before the idol with folded arms, he would cry
with tears trickling down his face : "Mother, have
compassion on me. You have been kind to Ramaprasad
and others. Why not to me ? I do not know any
Sastras ; I am not a *Pandit* ; I do not know anything,
Mother, nor do I wish to know anything. Will you not
show mercy on me, mother ? I am dying to see you. I
do not desire the *Ashtasiddhis* (the well-known eight
psychic powers, *anima, mahima,* etc.) ; I do not want
fame or name ; I long only to see you, and hear you
speak, if only one word." He uttered such prayers when
he was alone with the idol after the performance of the
daily *Archan* and *Arti,* and wept. *Bhaktas* entering the
temple at the time noticed with wonder the sincere *Bhakti*
that he had though so young. He devoted all his time
to worship and contemplation of Kali. By-and-by he
became extremely impatient and eager to see Her ; and
his heart panted after her like that of a young calf towards

its mother. All worldly pleasures ceased to interest him. And one night when he was sitting before the Goddess and was crying with his whole heart, "Mother, appear before me," he suddenly became entranced, his whole face and eyes became red, the gaze became vacant, and there was a constant flow of tears which wetted his whole body, and he had to be carried away from the temple. The whole of next day he did not open his eyes, he ate only when he was fed, and remained apparently unconscious. He was, however, frequently crying aloud, "Ma, Ma" (Mother, Mother) like a baby missing its mother.

What was the real state of his mind during this remarkable occurrence we cannot say. But from the outward signs, and judging by the opinions of *sadhus*, he was suffering from *viraha*, the pain of separation from the beloved one. He had probably seen the Mother : *this seeing the Mother should not, however, be confounded with the realisation of God, the great promise of the Vedanta.* The real God, the real Mother and Father is within ; and He is beyond the reach of the senses and the mind, by which latter is here meant that something within us which is a compound of *Rajas* and *Tamas*. We cannot *see* God, for He is not outside us, but we can *become* God. We are God unconsciously, and all that is required is *that we should know that we are God*. We sometimes fancy that God could be seen, and talk of great *Bhaktas* as enjoying visions of God ; but these visions are in reality the projection, so to speak, in the mental plane of the real God within. "Man wants help from the skies," says Swami Vivekananda, "and the help comes. We see that it comes, but it comes from

within, and he mistakes it as coming from without.
Sometimes a sick man is lying on his bed and he hears
a tap on the door, he gets up and opens the door, he
finds nobody, he goes back to his bed and again he hears
the tap, he gets up and opens the door and there is
nobody. At last he finds that it was his own heart
beating which he interpreted as knock at the door. Thus
all this vain search after the gods above, gods of the
skies, gods of the water, after it has completed the circle
comes back to the point from which it started—the human
soul—and man finds that the God for whom he was
searching in every hill and dale, for whom he was seeking in every little brook of water, in every temple, in
little churches, in worse Heavens, that God whom he
was even imagining as sitting in Heaven and ruling the
world is his *own self*."

The obtaining of visions, like the remarkable one
which Ramakrishna had, goes a great way towards the
realisation of the Deity within, and is a decided proof
of rare and genuine *Bhakti*, which, drawing the mind
away from the fleeting and illusory things of the world,
leads it onward by leaps and bounds to the reaching of
the transcendental Reality within. Even this much,—
what a rare privilege, and how few among us could boast
of having obtained a like divine vision!

For six months Ramakrishna was in the condition
of *viraha* described above, after which he gradually recovered his usual state.

After passing this stage, Ramakrishna began to
practise *Sadhanas* or religious exercises. He used to
remark that generally the fruit follows the flower but the
pumpkin is an exception. We may very well apply the

saying to himself, for, he first saw God and then performed his *Sadhanas*.

Egoism or *Ahankara*, the sense of "I," "I," in whatever one sees, or thinks or does, he considered as a thorny jungle which stands between man and God. Kill out this self, this "sense of separateness," this false individuality, the true Self or *Atman* stands at once realised —this is the eternal teaching of the *Upanishads*. Self realisation or *Brahmagnana* being the one end which Ramakrishna steadily kept before his mind, he was extremely anxious to kill out his low selfhood, his false individuality. *Thorough-going selflessness was his ideal* and to reach this, he cried every day to Kali, "Mother, destroy my *Aham* (self) and take your place there. I am the meanest of the mean, the poorest of the poor. May this idea be ever present in my mind. May I constantly feel that every being on earth, be it a *Brahmin* or a *Chandala*, or even a beast or worm or an insect is superior to me." To practically realise this he went and cleaned, it is said, the W. C. of a *Pariah*. People thought him mad or possessed, but he heeded not their gibes. He never left uttering "Ma," "Ma," Mother, Mother, and whatever he proposed to do, he first brought to Mother's notice. Sometimes he threw himself on the banks of the Ganges and cried aloud "Ma," "Ma,' in such a pathetic tone that people attracted by it, guessed he was suffering from some incurable disease, or was mad, and blessed him or prayed for him. He replied to no questions, while in this state.

Ramakrishna, as we have already said, had his own way in all things. He never once cared what others thought or said about him ; public opinion was to him

simply, to use his own simile, "the cawing of crows."
It is no wonder, the actions of such a man who dared to
set the world at naught, were somewhat strange and
looked upon by his immediate neighbours as those of
an insane person. The sympathetic reader will, however,
take a different view of the matter and instead of condemning the behaviour of the great *Bhakta*, go deeper
and wonder at the mind which was so fully and freely
dedicated to the service of the Lord and which found
the meanest things in the world entitled to the highest
love and worship. There were no longer in it, the distinctions of beautiful and ugly, *Brahmin* and *Pariah*,
high and low, or decent and the reverse. All that was,
was pure, beautiful and godly. No occupation was too
mean for him and he was the servant of all God's
creatures—a great soul surely, struggling mindless of the
world and its noisy madnesses, to get free, to become
pure and holy. To go and wash the house of a *Pariah*,
how few of us have done it or can do it! How few can
worship God that way! Cleaning the house of a *Pariah*!
*No, it was not the house of the Pariah that was cleaned,
it was the heart of the great Ramakrishna that was cleaned,
purified and made holy for the permanent residence of God.*

A word of warning here will not be altogether out
of place. The exercise which Ramakrishna did is nowhere prescribed as a condition for attaining salvation.
There are in our country some counterfeit *Mahatmas*
who roll on dunghills and cover their bodies with filth
and go about the streets with the hope of finding dupes
to admire and worship them. There is just this difference,
and it is a world-wide one, between these sages and
Ramakrishna ; *that what they do is for show and deceit,*

*while what he did was done utterly mindless of others and
solely for his own good. The test is the heart, the motive.*
If filthy occupation be the standard of spiritual greatness, the city-sweeps will enter Heaven much easier
than saints and martyrs. *No importance really lies in
external actions, though in some cases they reveal the inner
man.*

Ramakrishna found that a great obstacle in the way
of one's spiritual progress was a desire for wealth : and
in order to rid himself of it, he resorted to the following
sadhana. He would take a gold coin in one hand and
a little earth in the other and argue within himself as
follows : "O, *Manas!* They call this, money and this,
earth ; you must now examine both thoroughly. This
coin is a circular piece of gold, with the impression of
the Queen on it. It is an inert thing, with it you can
buy rice, cloth, houses, horses, elephants, etc. By
means of it you can feed many persons, go to various
holy places, you can even spend it on *sadhus* ; but you
cannot attain through it, divine bliss ; money cannot
destroy *Ahankara,* it rather increases it. It cannot
destroy desire and attachment, it breeds passion (*rajas*)
and animality (*tamas*) ; and these are incompatible with
Satchidananda, Divine bliss. You ought to avoid a
thing which while it fetches a little *Punya* or virtue
causes much *Papa* or sin, you should not even touch it."

The following was one of his favourite stories with
regard to the uses of money. A certain wealthy man
maintained an *Atithisala* (a place for feeding people) ;
a butcher was taking a cow for slaughter that way and
when it came near the *Chhatram* it lay down on earth
and would not proceed. The butcher beat the cow,

tried to drag it and used every means to make it go,
till he got quite exhausted. He then went to the
Atithisala where he was well fed. He returned with
renewed vigour and by beating and dragging, he succeeded in taking the cow to the slaughter-house, where
it was slaughtered. The greater portion of the sin of
killing the cow went to the rich man.

After thus discussing within himself about money,
he proceeded to consider the nature of the earth. "This
is also an inert substance. In this, corn is grown by
which we live, with it we build our houses, we even
make the images of our gods and goddesses with it.
Whatever is achieved by means of money is also
achieved by means of earth. Both are substances of
the same class, then why should one be preferred to the
other?" Thus reflecting he would look at both, repeatedly call the gold earth, and the earth gold, and then
shuffling the contents of each hand into the other, he
would keep on the process till he lost all sense of the
difference of the gold from the earth. Then he would
throw both earth and gold into the Ganges. The sight
of money filled him with a strange dread. He felt pain
whenever any precious metal came in contact with his
body. He avoided all talk about money; he was
tempted by many people with offers of endowments but
he stoutly declined them.

SRI JAYADEVA SWAMI

THE subject of my present sketch is one of the most remarkable men who lived in modern times, remarkable not merely for the excellent poetical works which he wrote—the most popular and the most celebrated of which is his *Gita Govinda*—but for his spotless and saintly character. The world will in the long run admit, though it does not do so now, at least the so-called civilised countries of the west, *that humility is the real heroism and goodness the real civilisation.* In those countries in particular. where there is still considerable faith in the saving power of selfish and aggressive war and in the presence of the arrant gospel of "struggle for existence and survival of the fittest," it is no wonder that mildness is looked upon with contempt and humility banished the kingdom. The so-called greatest men, leaders of thought and action, go about on their canvassing tours shamelessly blowing their own trumpets, and the contagion has caught even our country where humility has long been regarded a test of greatness, and to-day pot-bellied, buffalo-throated Pickwickian politicians strut in the streets in a jackdaw-like fashion crying themselves hoarse for advertising their greatness and begging to be called Municipal Commissioners. Whatever the present state of things, nevertheless it is an eternal truth that to be really good and humble is far more difficult than to follow the lead of the senses and fight and kill others, and it is this heroism of goodness and humility which is prominent in the character of our sage Sri Jayadeva Swami.

604

There is another great lesson which we can easily
learn from the life of Jayadeva to which it may be useful
to refer here, and it is that the Lord himself attends to
the well-being and prosperity of His devotees—a promise
which He has made in the *Gita* and that even *in the
worst trials* He shelters and protects them by the power
of His grace.

Jayadeva was born in a village called Bilvagam near
the sacred city of Jagannath. His father's name was
Narayana Sastriar, a Brahmin of a very pious and religious disposition, and his mother's name was Kamalabai.
Sastriar and his wife lived childless for a long number of
years, but very happily ; both of them were very piously
disposed and the worship of God was one of the main
occupations of their life. Indeed to Narayana Sastriar
it was the one occupation and he longed for nothing
else ; but his wife true to her sex had a secret craving
which she did not reveal even to her husband, but for
the satisfaction of which she constantly prayed God, and
that was as might have been easily guessed, to be blessed
with a beautiful and good-natured male child. She was
ashamed to be regarded by the world as a barren woman
and afraid of the hell which she thought she should have
to enter into in case she died without leaving a son—a
notion which *to all outward appearance* our *Smritis* support. One day while returning to bed, she earnestly
prayed to God for the fulfilment of her desire and slept
away without thinking of anything else ; and curiously
enough that self-same night, God Vasudeva appeared
with Lakshmi to her husband in his dream, and blessing
him and his wife said that his wife's desire would soon
be fulfilled and disappeared. Shortly after, Sastriar

woke up and calling his wife to his side reported to her his happy dream and asked her what her desire was for the satisfaction of which she had prayed to God.

This question brought out from her a confession, on hearing which, however, her husband felt extremely grieved that all their penance, austerity and devotion became useless as they had been actuated by a motive. He got angry with his wife and exclaimed : "Foolish woman, is that what you should have asked of the Lord ? You ought to have prayed not for wealth, children and other earthly possessions, but for the eternal bliss of Heaven. By your unworthy behaviour you have ruined yourself and me, for your piety was not unselfish and for its own sake." His anger was genuine and he did not speak to his wife from that moment. Poor Kamalabai regretted very much for her unworthy ambition and felt greatly grieved that she had disturbed her husband's peace of mind. She apologised to him and begged to be forgiven for her foolish conduct, but he remained completely morose and sullen and would not exchange a word with her. The result was that they fasted the whole of next day and though the meals had been cooked, the Sastriar would not eat and consequently his wife. While they thus sat grieving and fasting, there entered into their house a Brahmin who, noticing the strange appearance of the couple, inquired into the cause and managed to reconcile them both, saying that it was God's wish that they should be blessed with a worthy child, that they should not therefore grieve about it and that on the other hand they should be extremely joyful as the child which was shortly to be born of them would become a great sage, and be worshipped by a large number of people, and his fame would cover the whole land. The stranger uttered these words in such an assuring way that they regarded them as a prophecy and the speaker as God himself in human form. In accordance with this prophecy and the previous dream, a few months after, a male child was born to Kamalabai, on looking at whose beauty both the parents were transported with joy, like a blind man suddenly blessed with vision, and thankfully sang the praises of the great Lord.

We hear very little of the infancy and boyhood of Jayadeva except that he evinced very early in his life love of the highest order towards God. When he was five years old, the thread-wearing ceremony was conducted in due manner ; then the boy was educated in the right orthodox fashion in the sacred literature. When he attained age he was married to a beautiful girl of good parentage and well-developed intellect whose name was Padmavati, and who later on became one of the great heroines of our land. The next event of importance in the present biography was that the old parents of Jayadeva, Narayana Sastriar and Kamalabai entered on what is called *Vanaprasthasrama*, the third stage according to the Sastras of a Brahmin's life and left the country for the woods, there to do penance and worship undisturbed. We have no materials on which to fix the exact date of Jayadeva, but the fact of his parents entering the *Vanaprasthasrama* and some others would seem to indicate that he should have lived at least five hundred years ago ; but of this I am not certain, and the biography on which I base my sketch, is silent on the point, as might have been expected.

After the parents' departure, Jayadeva lived alone

with his wife a model domestic life. He would never eat without at least one guest and he was very lavish in feeding the poor and giving presents to Brahmins and others, and the result was that the little wealth which he had inherited from his father became exhausted in a short time ; but neither the husband nor the wife was sorry on that account, and the former readily undertook to beg in orthodox Brahmin style, and the little rice which he secured by that means, Padmavati cooked very elegantly and nicely so much so that they hardly felt the distress of proverty. Even when they were so poor they would never eat without some guest at the table. All the leisure which they had they spent in prayer and devotion. Both were of one mind and one nature, as if they were one soul in two bodies, and the whole village praised their mutual love and their devotion with one mind, towards God. Though they were young, they were respected everywhere and women, whatever their rank, tried to imitate Padmavati in her devotion to her lord and were eager to be loved by their husbands as she was by Jayadeva.

It was in this humble but happy period of his life that the poetic genius and devotional fervour of Jayadeva began to reveal themselves, and the immortal poem of his, one of the very best in Sanskrit language—his *Gita Govinda*, which has been styled, "The song of songs," was commenced. This grand poem which celebrates the glorious divine love of Radha and Krishna and of which I shall speak at length later on, begins with these beautiful words (Edwin Arnold's Translation) :

Om !

Reverence to Ganesa !

"The sky is clouded : and the wood resembles
The sky, thick-arched with black *Tamala* boughs ;
O Radha, Radha ! take this Soul, that trembles
In life's deep midnight, to Thy golden house."
So Nanda spoke—and, led by Radha's spirit,
The feet of Krishna found the road aright ;
Wherefore, in bliss which all high hearts inherit,
Together taste they Love's Divine delight.

These songs of Jayadeva soon became the favourite of the people of Bilvagam, who regarded them as next in sacredness only to the *Vedas* and sang them on all great public occasions. The fame of the *Ashtakas* was however not confined to the little village of Bilvagam, for it so happened that some of the villagers went to Jagannath to attend the great annual festival of the place, and they naturally recited several *Ashtakas* in the presence of the great God, and all that heard them were struck with their splendid music and poetry and praised them most ardently. The king of the place, who was himself a poet of no mean order, used every year to compose a number of songs in honour of the Lord and recite them during the festival and this year also he did the same but the people showed a decided preference to Jayadeva's songs by the side of which they were as water to wine, as candle light to that of the sun. The king, greatly vexed at this, lay down at night on his bed without taking any supper and cursing his fate, when a thought struck him that thirteen of his stanzas might perhaps be accepted if duly recited in the temple. The next morning he did so with the result that the people praised them and gladly sang them along with those of Jayadeva Swami.

The fame of Jayadeva thus reached far and wide, and his father-in-law who was rejoiced at his greatness paid him a visit, and after a stay of some days took with his permission his wife Padmavati for a short sojourn with her mother. A few days after Padmavati's departure to her parents' house, a rich merchant named Bhagavan Das, a native of a neighbouring village, came to Bilvagam and there meeting with Jayadeva requested him to go with him to his place and be a guest in his house for some-time. Jayadeva accordingly accompanied him, and rich and hearty was the welcome accorded to him by his friend who entertained him in his house for a number of days, and then sent him to Bilvagam in his own carriage loaded with many costly presents. Between the two villages there lay a small forset, while passing through which a band of thieves attacked Jayadeva. The helpless Brahmin gladly gave them all he had with him, his gar-ments included, but the robbers, suspecting, from the readiness with which he gave away his things, that he might have in his mind some plan by which to report the matter to the authorities and get them punished, cut off in spite of repeated appeals for mercy both his hands and feet and threw him into a ruined and waterless well.

A more miserable and helpless situation than that in which poor Jayadeva found himself it is difficult to imagine, but the great *Bhakta* bore it all patiently in the fullest confidence that what happened was not an act of the thieves but the bidding of God Himself who being the fountain of mercy would not have ordained it, had it not been for his good in some way or other. The physical pain was unendurable and he addressed many piteous appeals to heaven and attempted with some success to forget his suffering in *Yoga Samadhi*. Padma-vati returned from her father's house to Bilvagam and not finding him there got very much alarmed that he had

abandoned her and gone away as a *Sanyasi*. Her father
searched for him in all the neighbouring villages but
could not find him and so they concluded that Jayadeva
had retired to the woods or some cave to do penance.
The grief of Padmavati so young, simple and loving,
knew no bounds. Though she was a model wife she
reviewed her past career to recollect if she had done any
wrong to her husband on account of which he had
abandoned her but could not think of any. She hardly
knew what to do, her condition was miserable and
helpless. Praying and weeping became her sole occupation both day and night and all the consolations
which the good people of the neighbourhood offered her
could not comfort her much.

In the meanwhile it so happened that the king of
that province who had been out hunting came to the
very well where Jayadeva Swami was lying helpless, to
see if there was water in it to quench his thirst. But
what was his surprise when instead of water he saw a
mangled human body ! At once he ordered Jayadeva to
be lifted up and learning from him his miserable tale,
kindly arranged to take him with him. In the course of
his return to his capital he asked Jayadeva what his
name was, which the latter gave ; and as soon as the
king learnt that it was none else but the far-famed
Jayadeva, he fell at his feet and requested to be adopted
as a disciple. At once all the honours of a *Guru* were
done to Jayadeva. He was carried on a grand palanquin,
and as soon as the capital was reached, the king followed
him on foot and a magnificent procession was formed
with music, dancing and the like, and the great *Bhakta*

was installed in a stately mansion as the *Guru-in-chief* of the kingdom.

The king's love and reverence for his *Guru* grew greater and greater day by day; for, being himself already a good-natured and pious man, he was able to understand and appreciate at its proper value the fervent piety of Jayadeva and his saintly character. His one desire was to be as true a lover of God as the latter was and follow in his footsteps. He admired the patience with which Jayadeva endured his bodily suffering due to the wicked act of the thieves and envied his cheerful resignation to the will of God. He longed to adopt the *nivritti dharma,* be free like his *Guru* from all worldly concerns and dedicate his whole life to the worship of God. Accordingly one day when Jayadeva was alone in his house the king appeared without his crown and in plain clothes like an ordinary man and requested him to make him a *Sanyasi.* Jayadeva smiling said : "My son, renunciation is of the mind. One might give up wife, wealth and position and yet be not a *Sanyasi* for he might be attached to them in his mind. Therefore there is very little in external renunciation. Be thou then a *Grihastha sanyasi* just as I am *trying* to be." The king was all along under the impression that his *Guru* had "renounced the world" but when he heard the words "like me," he asked Jayadeva if he really had a wife. Then the latter told him his history and advised the king to put on his royal robes and be in all outward respects every inch a king but in his heart of hearts be far away from this world and its "lies which warp us from the Living Truth." The king felt the truth of his advice and as soon as he went home his first business was to despatch a palanquin with woman servants, costly lady dresses and a guard-of-honour to Bilvagam to fetch Padmavati.

It is needless to describe the joy of the lovely wife of Jayadeva when she heard news of her husband and her heart longed to be with him that very instant. She would not however ride in a palanquin and proceeded to walk on foot, but the faithful deputation that waited on her did not suffer her to do so and she was obliged to concede to their request. In a few hours Padmavati reached the presence of Jayadeva Swami and falling at his holy feet washed them with tears which eloquently spoke of her love and the mental pain and anxiety she suffered on account of their unfortunate separation. Jayadeva looked at her with surprise for he did not know that she had been sent for and when he saw her emaciated form which spoke volumes of her sincere love to him, a few tears crept out of his eyes even in spite of himself and he wanted to raise her from the ground, but he had no hands to do it. Pandmavati rose but looking at his mangled form which had been cruelly deprived of hands and feet, she fainted with grief and fell on the ground. Jayadeva, however, comforted her in sweet terms and gently bade her be resigned to the will of God as she had all along been. Padmavati thanked God for having been permitted to see him at least alive. Then they enquired of each other of the events that had transpired during their separation and felt as joyful as if they had just been married. The king regarded Padmavati as more than his mother and her residing in his country was like that of Lakshmi herself. So rejoiced was he at the happy event of the reunion of the pious lovers that he ordered it to be proclaimed in his country and throughout the neighbouring ones that *Bhaktas* of all creeds were welcome in his capital and that they would be sumptuously entertained by him during their stay there and loaded with presents whenever they chose to depart. From that day the streets of the city rang with the sacred names of Siva, Vishnu, Rama and Krishna and were filled with the holy songs of their pious devotees. All the *Sadhus* that came had first to visit Jayadeva Swami and then were sent by him to the king to be welcomed and entertained as they deserved.

Now the thieves who had robbed and maimed Jayadeva Swami, not satisfied with what they got by their wicked trade and thinking that it was more paying to be *Sadhus* in the king's dominions than thieves in the forest, disguised themselves as *Sanyasis* and entered the city. They were then duly conducted to the presence of Jayadeva Swami, but when they beheld the latter they were seized with fear and took to their heels. Jayadeva knew who they were and felt very sorrowful that his unfortunate presence should have stood in the way of their obtaining from the king what they wanted and so he sent men to pursue them and bring them back. The servants succeeded in doing it and as soon as the disguised *Sadhus* entered his presence he bowed to them and made a sign of worship with his lame hands and spoke to them in a most humble way addressing them as *Sadhus*, *Rishis*, Sages, *Bhaktas* and so on and sent for the king. The thieves were every moment expecting a sentence of execution, but what was their surprise when as soon as the king came he was directed by Jayadeva to prostrate himself at their feet and garland them with

flowers and treat them with every mark of respect !
Then they were removed to a palatial residence furnished
with such comfort as they had never dreamt of in their
lives and entertained as if they were members of the
royal family. They were however far from being happy,
for all the attention to them tended only to increase
their fear and they looked upon themselves as sheep
fattened for slaughter. The king perceived their strange
appearance and felt that they were not genuine *Sadhus*.
So he communicated his doubt to Jayadeva, but the
latter said : "What care we, how they look, what they
think and so on : they are our guests and wear the holy
garb of *Sanyasis*, so let us treat them as such." The
king was however not satisfied and so he again asked :
"Is sageship consistent with an inordinate desire for
wealth as I find these *Sadhus* in spite of themselves
display ?" "Why should we," replied Jayadeva, "be
anxious to judge of them ? The *Puranas* tell us that the
great sage Agastya went begging for gold in order to
marry a woman and the celebrated Yagnavalkya went
to the court of Janaka for the sake of cows and money.
So if these *Sadhus* require money you had better load
them with any amount they want and send them away."

VIII

TRUE GREATNESS

OR

VASUDEVA SASTRI

I

THE DEWAN BAHADUR AND A C.I.E.

"WHAT! Have not Ramaswamy Aiyer, Muthuswamy, Subbiah, Venkateswara Aiyer—have not all these come? You fool, why don't you go and bring them, man? I have never seen a bigger fool than you. Run out and fetch them, man," said a voice in a way which showed that it was accustomed to be obeyed. "I, I, I, I, -we-we-we-went and, a-and, a-and called them. They said, they, they, they—". "Stammer out," impatiently exclaimed the first voice again, "stammer your life out, you rascal. Run out and fetch them, I say. Then you may be stammering all day long" : and Muthu, otherwise called *Mottai* (the bald-headed) at once ran out stammering. The voice that commanded him belonged to Mr. Narayana Aiyer, the great Deputy Collector of Madura, now enriched with a prefix Dewan Bahadur and a suffix C.I.E.—for some services, "signal" as they were called, during a recent famine but more through the favour of the Government gods. You *must* certainly have heard of Dewan Bahadur S. Narayana Aiyer, C.I.E. (otherwise there is no excuse for you, and not to know him argues yourself unknown) whose name appeared so many times in print in the *Fort St. George Gazette* itself whenever he was transferred or given privilege leave, who was every year freshly immortalised in the Revenue List of the Presidency, who was more than once thanked by the very grateful Court of Wards for the able management of some estates entrusted to him, whose commonsense was vouchsafed for by the Collector, Mr. Assfoot himself, who condescended to remark that as far as he knew, his deputy was intelligent ; who was spoken of or referred to in the local newspapers at least once a month (such was the understanding), who had several times tasted the honour of a Municipal Chairmanship, and of whose other merits we can at present only say, etc., etc., etc. One thing however we could not, without greatly offending him, omit to mention, and that was, that he was known to the Secretary of State and the honourable members in the Privy Council, for, his name had been very prominently referred to in one of the Judgments of the High Court which went up to England for appeal. As soon as he heard that, that particular Judgment went up to the Privy Council for appeal, it is said but I do not profess to know this personally, that he specially thanked the Judge, who had done him the honour of a reference in his Judgment. These, however, are official matters, with which fortunately we shall have nothing more to do in the story. One or two non-official circumstances that went to make up his greatness, we must however note. In the first place he was rich. Secondly he was princely in his charities to the Brahmins and had, by public subscriptions and so forth, built many *Chattrams* and hospitals. All these made him very popular. Besides he was a man of large sympathies and noble sentiments and there was for him, as we shall see, a grand future, which many might envy.

After sending away *Mottai*, he went inside the house and there finding Vasudeva Sastry performing *puja* in his usual grand style, said : "Vasu, enough, close your shop soon ; people are waiting. To-day is not like other days : go on, finish the business soon ; look sharp."

But what was the importance of that day, that even the
Gods should be so summarily dismissed? Narayana
Aiyer was giving a feast that day to his friends in honour
of the alphabets newly affixed to his name. It was a
grand gala-day with sumptuous entertainment and
music and other festivities, and the host was really
elated with joy at the happening of so great an event in
his life and heartily spoke to his friends, of the causes
that brought it about—how his fame and ability had
attracted the notice of His Excellency the Governor,
how eagerly he was sent for, how respectful and kind
the interview was, how dexterously he managed it, how
much His Excellency was struck with the nobility of his
character, the high type of his intellect, his eloquence
and his statesmanship, and very much more in the same
strain. Indeed, it was his opinion, and his friends too
shared in it—that, if ever there was any great man, he
was one. It was difficult for him to think of himself as
anything less than a Dewan Bahadur C.I.E. When he
went to bathe, there he was a C.I.E. When eating,
again was he a C.I.E. At no moment was he anything
except a C.I.E. No other Native Deputy Collector had
that beautiful suffix. The three letters were more to
him than the three letters of the *Pranavam* of which
so much is said. And to add to this that the Governor
should have sent for him ah!—who could calmly bear
such greatness!

There was, however, one person in the household
whom the day's festivities did not seem to have pleased,
and that was strangely enough Mrs. Narayana Aiyar
herself. The Dewan Bahadur noticed the coldness in
her face; he wanted very much to be congratulated

by her—but in vain. He showed his readiness to go shares with her in the matter of his new honour, and when they were alone during the night, called her Dewan Bahadur Seetha Lakshmy (that was her name) C.I.E., to which she only replied : "I feel sleepy, let us go to bed." Narayana Aiyer, C.I.E., was exceedingly annoyed at "this cold nonsense" as he called it, but checking himself said : "I tell you this is the evil of ignorant, uneducated, illiterate wives. What! I get two rare titles Dewan Bahadur and C.I.E., and you fool, you do not know their value any more than an ass knows the smell of camphor. Tell me, who else, which other Deputy Collector, has got these titles. There's not even a Dewan Bahadur among these Deputy Collectors. And then who else had an interview with the governor? You fool, you have no education and where's the good of my telling you these. You know nothing : this is the evil of ignorant wives. We must educate our women, educate them at once." "Certainly, this very night," replied Seetha. "If getting mad over meaningless little things means education then God spare us from it. I have been watching you carefully all this day, and you have been almost beside yourself. Good God! What vanity, what self-praise, what joy at silly things and empty name! What is there in the three letters C.I.E., my dear? We may as well dub ourselves X.Y.Z., and feel mad over it ; surely man is not born for such playful nothings and if we dance to-day like a jackal that tasted honey, to-morrow we might weep like a helpless child. "Is this life?"—"I see" interrupted the mortified Dewan Bahadur, "I see, I see, it is the devil of a Vasu that has spoiled you : the wicked **Vasudeva**

Sastry as he calls himself has robbed you of your brains;
I shall break his knavish pate to-morrow and now let
the devil take care of you"; so saying he pushed her a
little and left the bedroom in no very pleasant mood.
Seetha followed him, took him by the arm, fell at his
feet, and with tears in her eyes entreated him to return;
she gently soothed his anger saying: "My dear, I have
been too rash; kindly excuse me. I was too hasty.
Do you think I am insensible to the honours showered
upon you. Are they not mine as well? They are really
more mine than yours for you have other concerns to
engage your attention, but to me you, your honours
and your fame are the only concern. What is there
more pleasing to the wife than the good reputation of
the husband. The husband is our joy, our wealth and
our God, My dear, I know you are incapable of getting
angry with me; you love me so well and our love can
never suffer......"—words which only a woman knows
how to speak and which in her mouth form a real power
*too much, even for a Dewan Bahadur and C.I.E., put
together, to resist.* With kind words, betel chewing and
sandal smearing the rest of the night passed on pleasantly
enough.

————

II

A VEDANTIC CONVERSATION

THE scene changes : you are now entering a humble, low roofed and partly dilapidated house. But take care you do not knock your head against the doorway, it is so low. The door is open and the inside of the house is anything but inviting, nevertheless, you enter and as you leave behind the pials, and cross through an isthmus-like passage, you see the building opens out into a hall, which is at once the dining room and the parlour of the house. The hall or "Sircar" as it is elegantly termed in Madras is, you find, very mean in appearance and too much at the mercy of the sun and the rain. You can find no furniture in it except one or two small planks to serve as seats. A few vessels are kept in a corner and in another there is a stone for grinding sandal, and ad-jacent to it there is an almirah containing the house-hold gods ; and, there are two rooms opening into the hall opposite to each other ; one of which is the kitchen and the other contains a large number of pots arranged over one another in which rice and other things are kept. In the centre of the hall, there is a small group sitting and talking.

One of the group—a woman said : "When I told him that one should not get mad over empty titles and think too highly of oneself, he got exceedingly angry with me. We are seldom able to look beyond ourselves."

"Very difficult Seetha, very difficult," said another, "And this difficulty is universal. Once, Vyasa was

walking over the field of Kurukshetra, when he found
a little worm crawling away as fast as it could at the
sound of his feet, fearing that it might get crushed under
them. The sage smiled and said to himself : 'We regard that creature as worthless and despicable, but look
at its anxiety to preserve its life ! ah, what a wonder !'
and then by virtue of his *yogic* powers, he found to his
great surprise, that it was the eminent sage, Narada,
who by some sinful *Karma*, had become the worm and,
giving it the power of speech, he asked : 'O worshipful
sage Narada, how is it that, having got into this wretched
worm life, you are so anxious to preserve it ?' The worm
replied : 'All praise be to you, O Vyasa ; by a sinful
act I was reduced to this condition, but this is the fatal
illusion, that even in this worm life, I think sufficiently
well of myself and have enough to do with my own
pleasure and pains. Though mean and despicable in
your eyes, I am not so to myself and that is why I am
so anxious to preserve my life.' Thus, while even the
worm thinks so highly of itself, what wonder, that we
look so big in our own eyes. Indeed, from the atom to
the star every particle in the universe rings with this
egoism and it is this that makes what is called the world.
If by some magic, this egoism is purged out of the world,
the unconditioned, universal Self or God alone will remain. Few of us are able to look beyond ourselves to
rise above this foolish 'I'."

"Aha ! how beautiful !" cried an enthusiastic girl
who was one of the group. "Is it not uncle, is it not
that our loving our husbands, rearing up children, helping
the poor are all means to get rid of this sense of I, this
little narrow selfishness ?"

40

But I must hasten to introduce the party to the reader; otherwise, according to the unwritten laws of etiquette he might refuse to interest himself in what they say. Begging his pardon for the delay, I should say, the person who first spoke is one already known to him. She was Seetha-Lakshmy, wife of the great M. R. Ry. Dewan Bahadur Narayana Aiyar Avergal, C.I.E. The enthusiastic girl that spoke last, was her daughter by name Rukmani. The one that spoke second was no other than Vasudeva Sastry the hero of our story, the gentleman, who was so respectfully referred to by the great Dewan Bahadur the previous night.

To describe him in detail, as is the fashion, he was a middle-aged man of fair complexion and well-proportioned limbs; his face was the most remarkable thing about him. There was a calmness and a serenity in it, a gentleness, a sweetness and a luxuriant cheerfulness like that of a full blown lotus flower, which an ancient *Rishi* might have envied; and in his large, beautiful eyes, there was an angelic expression of goodness, which by its silent and sweet magic could have soothed the anger of a Durvasa. The glory of these eyes, if I may say so, lay, not in occasional lightning-like flashes, but in their constant and continued revelation of the ocean of goodness, love and calmness that dwelt within. Their expression never faded, time and place had no influence on that, and they were like the unfading *Kalpaka* flowers of the *Devaloka*, and while seeing, they seemed to perceive not the external differentiated things, but by a sort of divine prerogative, the inner harmony that dwelt underneath. To look at them was like looking at milk, ever sweet and to be looked at by them—to fall within the charmed, sacred circle of their rays was a privilege which men and women alike envied. He seemed to depend for his happiness on nothing outside and he was never known to be excited either by pleasure or by pain and much less get angry. To try to provoke him was a favourite amusement among school boys. There was not the least amount of assertiveness or arrogance about him and all his motions spoke humility and love. He was a very poor man, all his income being the pittance he received from Narayana Iyer for making *puja* in his house, but he was respected more than the richest man. He was the pet of all the children in the neighbourhood, they would crawl over him, dance on his shoulders, pull him by the hair, adorn him with a saddle and ride over him or furnish him with reins and drive him like a bull. Mothers, when they were busy or had to go out, would entrust their babies to him and he would put them to sleep or sing them songs, of one or two of which, the following is a rough translation :

> Say Krishna, Rama, Govinda
> You invite me and only me,
> Call Isa, Sambo, Mah'deva
> You invite me and only me
> Of all the world I am the guard
> The Soul, the Lord, the Soul, the Lord.

The last lines of these songs would, in the original, read like an English note and excite the innocent mirth of the little children. Old Kuppipatty would never pass his house without calling him Dharmaraj. The boy Krishna would never go home, without first narrating to him all the news he had—how a white elephant was going to be brought to the temple, how he one day saw a white crow sleeping on his slate, how dogs never bark when he is asleep, how it would never rain on a Saturday, how there was a big tiger in the backyard of his house, and many more edifying things of the kind. The pensioned Tahsildar—Mr. Subrahmanya Aiyer would fain favour him with all his leisure, but for the fact that he talks *Vedanta* and *Vedanta* alone in one form or another and has no genius for gossip. Viswanatha Aiyer, the Madura Munsiff, who professed to know a great deal of *Vedanta*, would visit him at least once a day. Angi the sweeper-woman of the Madura Sub-Judge's house would say whenever she saw him : "Where is the good of wealth ? Wealth leads only to quarrel and heart-burning ; look at our Sastryar, how happy he is in the midst of adversity !" Schoolmaster Ramaswami Aiyer, who firmly believed that all the world was wicked, would say that poor Vasu was an exception, that he was dropped down here by mistake and that was why he was so poor. Vakil Sundara Iyer, who spoke nothing but lies all day long, admitted that somehow he could not tell a lie to him. Muthu Iyer, the Sub-Registrar, who was a Theosophist and had a long beard, would say that he was the best Swamyar he had seen—the holiest man he knew. Be that as it may, he is now sufficiently introduced to the reader and it is left to the latter to decide, if he would care to cultivate a closer acquaintance with him.

To return to the story. As soon as Vasudeva Sastry heard Rukmani's question, he said : "you are perfectly right my child. We should drown our selfishness in love, but in helping the poor and doing such things we should never fall into the danger of priding ourselves on that account. We are simply instruments, not free agents. In a certain village there was once an old woman, who lived by preparing and selling cakes. She would set about her business punctually at 4 a.m., every day. She had a cock which announced to her the break of day as punctually, so much so that in course of time she gradually got into the belief that the day would not break unless her cock raised its trumpet voice. One day it so happened that the village boys offended her; she vowed vengeance and said : 'Very well, these little fellows do not know who I am. I shall remove with my cock to the next village and see how the day could break here ; let the fellows suffer an eternal night. These little fellows offend me !' She did as she vowed that very night, and the next day, when some men came to the second village from the first, she said to them : 'you see, if you had appeased me, all this would have been avoided. Poor men, I pity you ; you have to suffer eternal night.' They asked what the matter was and she replied : 'Why, I have brought my cock over here and so the day would not have broken in your place.' It is needless to add that the men had a hearty laugh at the idiotic woman's self-importance. A similar mistake we are all of us committing ; we think that, but for us such and such a thing would never happen ; we die, but the world goes on all the same. We should warn ourselves against such mistakes."

"But," asked an elderly widow who sat by, "what is there in names and titles ?" "Why," said Vasudeva, "the whole world is nothing but name and form. We are all deceived with—."

Before he had finished, in rushed a woman, with a

bag in hand roaring "you be d—d. You have ventured to open the *Vedantic* shop in my own house! What wonder that I am so poor and miserable and my family has been ruined! You Rakshasis, you d—ls, let *Vedanta* fall into your houses and let all of you become as miserable as I am. I do not know when the cursed *Vedanta* will enter your families and ruin you, and make you wander in the streets for bread. You come and open your shop in my house!"

III

ANNAMMAL THE TERRIBLE

When the hawk appears in the sky, all the other birds great and small disappear into their nests at once, the whole blue sky is immediately resigned to that most terrible of birds. We had a similar scene here the other day in poor Vasudeva Sastry's house. The cultured Sita-Lakshmi, her enthusiastic daughter as well as the poor round-headed widow who had just asked a question, all disappeared, without even waiting for a formal leave, or rather taking "French leave", as the moderns have it.

Brave Vasudeva Sastry was like a jackal in a palmyra grove familiar to the rustle of its leaves, and being the less-fair-half of the great Vir—, had the courage to remain firm in his seat; but I suspect, for my nature is such, that he shook within himself at the thunder that rolled from the labial heights of the great lady who suddenly appeared—Annammal. Whatever it be, he had the philosophic calmness to keep firm to his seat and even ventured to speak.

"My dear," he said, "there was once a cat that was living in a house; the old woman of that house, in her attempt to kick down the cat, fell down herself and lost one of her eyes, striking against a wicked stick; thenceforth the cat became responsible for all the mishaps in the house, not merely for the milks spilt by herself and the butter-milk swallowed by her cunning daughter, but also for more serious things, the death of her grand-grandson, etc., etc. If she wished her daughter-in-law in one of her pleasant moods to lose her *thali* (the ornament tied round the neck of the wife as a sign of marriage by the husband), or her husband, she would invoke, not Ganesa or Iswara, but the dear white cat, which learnt that whenever there was noise in the house, it would be in its favour for it would be feasted with milk and rice that day. And, fortunately, as there was no dearth of quarrels in the house—sweet exchanges of loving words—milk and rice became the usual diet medically prescribed by the kind old lady for the white cat ; and it gradually ascended to the rank of a domestic *lar*."

The humour had an odd effect upon our gentle Annammal, and she, missing the point of comparison, thought that her lover wanted to identify her with that blind old old grandmother, and replied, raising the key of her voice a little (Vasudeva Sastry was afraid for the safety of his tottering roof), "I am neither blind nor old, you may become blind one of these days, indeed the cursed *Vedanta* has already blinded you in both eyes, otherwise you would see how ill your son-in-law is at Dindigul." This only excited the philosophic humour of our Sastry—"Socrates was only pleased with his kind wife for showering upon him and also upon his companions, pots of some unnamable things after a huge thunder accompanied with proportionate lightning," and our hero with all a hero's courage replied : "Even if I were blessed with two thousand eyes like Bhadrakali (a terror-inspiring female deity with two thousand eyes and one thousand noses), I would not be able to see from here my sick son-in-law at Dindigul." The Amazon's voice was raised a pitch higher ; and all the surrounding neighbours shook for their safety, and came out of their houses to see what the matter was.

Poor neighbours ! don't be afraid ; it is nothing but a secret conversation between our friends, Vasudeva Sastry and his dear wife. It is false and mythological, that the *Kailasa* shook, and, Parvati voluntarily embraced her husband, when Ravana took it upon his shoulders. I also was living at the time in the shape of a frog, as some of my Theosophic friends informed me, and know better. It was because Ravana told his secret to Mandodari, which his beautiful noseless sister Surpanaka had told him. A similar thing now happened, that is all. Annammal only secretly said that her son-in-law was in danger, and that it was untimely and purely *Vedantic* for Vasudeva Sastri to talk his silly talk. No exaggeration ; here I simply say what often happens to *Vedantic* husbands ; the word *Vedantic* has one sense in the *Upanishads*, another with the missionaries, a third in the kitchen. Vasudeva Sastry knew his wife's resources better ; he wanted the manifestation of her full eloquence, and in order to call it forth, dared to reply : "If your son-in-law be really dangerous, why did you happen to come away here so soon ?" This impertinence had its own effect, by an accident, or by the force of the eloquence that followed, the long hair of Annammal unfolded itself.

Shame to you Orators—Ciceros, Demostheneses, living and dead, Indian and foreign, you have spoken, spoken so many times but I never once remember having seen your hair running down in that Annammal fashion. The excited earthquake—afraid neighbours all rushed

in to take care of our hero, which sympathy only ex-
asperated the Kali more, and she gently added : "You
wretches ! you devils ! the cursed *Vedanta* has not yet
fallen upon your houses ; and this man, and that wife
of that D-e-p-u-t-y C-o-l-l-e-c-tor and that clean-shaven
widow are all talking that cursed *Vedanta* in my own
house, and that poor son-in-law of mine is *therefore* dying."
Gentlemen, now let us draw the curtain over this tremendous affair only adding that the poor Sastry was with
difficulty rescued from the jaws of his amorous wife.
It required indeed all his philosophy, and that is why
he became a philosopher, to think nothing of this grand
affair, but be laughing all the time.

Misfortunes however never come single ; and soon
after the scene, a postman came with a telegram addressed to Vasudeva Sastry. Have you ever seriously contemplated upon the postman, reader ! In the short space
of one morning, do you know how much mischief he is
able to work ? To one he brings a marriage letter, and
what partiality ! to another he brings death news. In
two hours' time, he makes some sons-in-law, and some
others widows ; some he marries to wrong wives, and
some he threatens with false suits ; others he troubles
with indifferent letters, only wasting their time and
money ; and some others he disappoints, making them
wait—"the dupes of to-morrow". But, however, he is
impartial in one thing, he exacts an unsanctioned poll-
tax from all alike, once for *Dipavali*, and another time
whenever money order comes. It was hot mid-day when
one of these liveried officers stood at the gate of our hero ;
Sastry was eating within, and his exhausted companion
was serving him with something. Our Sastry was a

kind of indifferent man and not a muscle of his face moved, when his tremendous wife who had braved all the world, came trembling from head to foot with something red in her hand, which with her two eyes she could not make out. Sastry whose humour knew no season asked her to kindly read it, she did not know what to do.

Reader! this is a religious novel, but wait, you will have enough and more of it later on, look at our *Upanishads*, how many stories they contain! so excuse me and wait. "They also serve who stand and wait."

Annammal, surnamed "the terrible", turned over and over the red thing, as if it scorched her hand, without knowing whether to read the black letters or the brass rings. Vasudeva Sastry encouraged her to read on. The poor woman, didn't know what to do, and took to her weapon; which you already know what. The post peon at the gate trembled and said nothing. The neighbours trembled once again, and the roof trembled once again; the gentleman at the gate who would never wait even at the "Awakened India Office", waited, unable to say a word; but Vasudeva Sastry was coolly going on with his meals, asking between one mouthful and another, whether the writing was in English or Tamil; his wife got still more angry, how could she say? in what schools was she educated? there were no Vizianagram Schools then. One mouthful more and the angriest wife in the world was coolly directed to go to a neighbouring house, where there was an English-knowing man. To the surprise of Annammal, the terrible, the red cover was opened and torn to pieces in her own presence, but the contents were all the more alarming.

Son / in / law / dangerously / ill / start / at / once.

We do not like to describe the emotions of that gentle lady; the post-man had to wait one hour for getting the receipt, the cool Sastry inside had to wait two hours for his butter-milk, the innocent day became *Yekadasi* (a fasting day) to Annammal. There was terrible weeping, beating of breast, tearing of hair, till all the neighbours of this street and that, rushed in once again and comforted the uncomfortable. In the evening a whistling train all smoky and crowded took the pair to Dindigul where they arrived on a moonlight night at 8 o'clock 5′ and 10″ at a big upstair house. Vasudeva Sastry carrying a big bag on his head, leisurely followed by Annammal carrying her grief, which became very loud as she climbed up the steps of the threshold of that upstair house.

THE DEATH SCENE

THE scene changes, it is 7 o'clock in the evening, the moon has spread her silver rays and is rejoicing in her own light. What shall we say of these sun, moon and stars? Somebody said they are "the passionless, pitiless eyes of Heaven," and likened them to God "who made multitudinous slaves, whom he requites for knee-worship, prayer and praise and toil and hecatombs of broken hearts with fear and self-condemned and barren hope." We know nothing of the former, but we know of the latter that our prayers are attended to, and that hearts. apparently broken are made whole by the most wonderful of magicians. This apart, the moon was like a proud pompous girl too much delighted with her own youthful beauty to attend to the sick child of her sister-in-law ; for down below, on the upstair-floor, in the open moon-light, a big varnished cot was laid on which two or three cotton matresses were spread assisted by a multitude of soft pillows, which nevertheless did not very much succeed in comforting a young man that lay there. By his side was sitting a young and beautiful girl with rare intelligence beaming in her face, but her eyes filled with divinest grief, and gently pressing his weak limbs.

"I don't know," said Krishna, for that was the young man's name, "when your heavenly father would come and help me."

Lakshmi : "It is not yet time, my dear," trembling a little as she looked into the pale face of her beloved, "it is not yet time, they will be here within one hour, my father will not stay even a single minute after having seen the melancholy telegram."

Krishna : "I am fast dying. My mind wanders, my limbs fail, my dear ! I do not know if I could see once again that divinest of faces before I die."

Lakshmi, poor Lakshmi looked one second at her lord and saw that the face of death had come upon the beautiful young man. Markandeya, even in the embrace of the *Lord of lords Siva*, lost colour when *Yama* appeared, and death had fixed his mark upon the eyes of even the *Bhakta*. In spite of the sacred ashes, in spite of the hands stretched round that strength of strength, and in spite of the flowers that had been heaped in the course of the *puja* (all this has an inner meaning), the *kalapasa*, the toils of death, had affected the bold lover, as his fearful melancholy eyes spoke out. Lakshmi noticed the dead expression of the waning moon of morn in her lover's face, and trembled from head to foot ; but checking her tears that started forth like pearls in her eyes, she said : "God that has brought us together to our mutual benefit—we have loved as no lovers ever loved, my lord !—will not desert us ; whatever might happen, I can do no higher penance" wiping her eyes which could no longer resist weeping, "than thinking of the love that you bore to me, that silently made me what I am ; your love, my lord, was my treasure, my joy, my life, my learning, my religion, and the *Vedas* that saved me. I can never forget the moments which we have spent under this cold moon, when you talked to me of God and high things relating to my soul which strengthened the training my father gave me in early youth. Remember the Lord of whom you spoke to me so much and whom you made me really love; think now of Him, my dear! as Sri Krishna, as Rama, as Nataraja or as Visveswara. Nothing is dearer to you than this one moment of life, my lord!"

Krishna: "Yes, my love; but before that, I should be with thee once again as lover and love to enjoy the roses of thy cheeks and the lotuses of thy eyes."

Lakshmi: "My lord! My lord! Nothing would give me greater pleasure than obey your bidding; but you should not, my lord! my love, let your mind wander over such silly little things now. If my cheeks were roses and eyes lotuses, would not they give me pleasure? My lord, I have enjoyed the lotus, as I enjoyed no other flowers; and the roses were as sweet to me as honey. But these poor eyes that have seen you helpless and miserable, these cheeks that have served only to grind my food when you were fasting, do they not deserve to be plucked out, my lord? What is there in these eyes, and what is there in these cheeks? Look at the blue of the sky vaster than the ocean, and as calm as the Lord of lords whom we have learned to love; look at that silvery moon shedding her flood of silent music and rich ambrosia and boundless love, and remember the Lord that made them all. Oh! how calm that moon is in spite of our selfish troubles, heedless of our low cares."

The rich and mellifluous eloquence of Lakshmi, her sweet faltering accents, her earnest emotion, her beautiful gestures as she spoke, combined with the high poetry of her speech, drove away from Krishna's mind all thoughts of the low love he had courted; and, weeping for his folly and the end of his life, when life's flame was flikering between to-be and not-to-be, said : "My dearest love, how worthy of your father ! My sweet angel, if I die to-day, my only desire is to be born in the next life as your husband or wife ; let us both, my love look once again at that blue Krishna-like sky—I through your eyes, and you through mine—and drink deep all the love, all the poetry, and all the religion of it. Look at its sad serenity, and its soft and even stillness, look once again at that silent silvery moon, and cry to Him who is beyond the skies and the moon. Pray, tell me, Lakshmi, the grand prayer your father taught you, "Come, O come, etc.,' let me hear my sweet Lakshmi."

"Yes ! My dear," said Lakshmi, and began to pray :

Come, O come, my gracious Lord,
My life's eternal guard;
Whether I live or die,
Save me, my strength, save me.
I ask not for life below,
Nor bread, nor wealth, but love ;
That I in myself might see
Thy brightness and glory.
The stars are big and bright,
But bigger still the Light
Within, and brighter far
Than all the planets are.
He is ever in me,
I am He and He is I,
Not swords can part us ever,
Nor *Maya* dare us sever.

Just as she finished praying, the terrible noise of Annammal's wailing came rolling upwards from the threshold. Lakshmi said : "My dear, our father is come" ; and, at the same time there came into the room Krishna's mother with milk in hand for her dying son. She was a bit of a fool, and would often quarrel. She

had lost her husband long since, and she had no grandson by Krishna who was her only son. At her approach,
which, to Krishna, was not altogether welcome, he
turned aside his face in disgust, and was about to abuse
her, when Lakshmi, who had by this time risen from her
seat, whispered to him, "My love! you have no quarrel
on earth, you are going to Heaven, where I shall soon
follow you." Immediately Krishna calmed himself a
little; and just then Vasudeva Sastry and his wife
ascended the stair-case, the latter growing terribly louder
and louder at every step.

Tut, silence, do you know, silly woman! where you
are going, and with whom you are going? going to a
dying son-in-law, who wants calmness more than your
weeping, and whose thoughts are more with Heaven
than with earth, and going with the calmest of men,
whose feet-dust even you are not worth. To compare
great things with small, as Suka approached Parikshit
at the hour of death, so our Sastry is going to his dying
son-in-law, as the latter yearned very much to see him.
The sick room is a holy place, where none but gentle
feet might tread. All suffering is sacred, and admits
of no mockery and no abuse. The bed on which a
human being is thrown prostrate is an altar, where the
assertive ego of the sufferer is silently submitted for
sacrifice, and where the combined incense of prayer and
pity goes up to heaven. Women, whatever their
frailties, are generally the officiating priests at the
sacrifice. Their calm self-denial, their long night vigils,
their soft soothing words, the solicitude with which they
divine the patient's wants, the strong restraint they put
upon their tears which want to roll down in torrents, the

41

patience and readiness with which they endure scenes too hard to bear even for medical men, and the silent prayer from which they never cease, convert the sick chamber into a temple, where one might kneel and worship. More philosophy is learnt and practised within its four walls than anywhere else. The spirit of man is humbled, low selfishness is forgotten, if only for the moment; and the divinity that lies concealed in us is slowly drawn out. Here, "where the stir and glare of the world is shut out and every voice is hushed," there is religion without its rituals, philosophy without its dryness, and love without its vanity. It was from the air of the sick-room and the lazaretto that Christs and Buddhas were made.

He died well, the patriarch who died with all his family round him and uttering the name of Lord Jesus. He died well, the ancient *Rishi* who by his *Guru's* grace had the last hour all for himself and crossed to the other world meditating on the Lord of the Gayatri.

Krishna! take courage, fear not, there is the high God, who is above, below, and everywhere, who is all love and all light. Remember that disease and death are of the body; that your punishment is your expiation; that you are bound to progress; that, if you die, instead of this shattered mortal coil, a new coat will come, or *no coat if you are so virtuous*. Free your mind from fear and doubt. Cheerfulness is the gateman of Heaven. And you who are round the sick bed, watch the dying man, moisten his parched lips, support his failing limbs, hasten to love, and let all your sympathy and divinity rush to the man who is already on the verge of infinity. The last words, the last looks of those whom we love are a kind of testament, they have a solemn and a sacred character; for that which is on the brink of death already participates to some extent in eternity. A dying man seems to speak to us from beyond the tomb. What he says has the effect upon us of a sentence, an oracle, an injunction. We look upon him as one endowed with second sight; serious and solemn words come naturally to the man who feels life-escaping and the grave opening. The depths of his nature are then revealèd, the divine within need no longer hide itself. Oh! be swift to love, make haste to be kind.

Vasudeva Sastry sat near his son-in-law and looked at him : tears rushed into his eyes, but he checked them with his philosophy, and clasping him in his arms, spoke some kind words which to him were like elixir.

"Fear not," he said, "only our bodies die, we can never die, we are immortal. *Let us remember our divinity.* 'Think of the God in you even in the hour of death, and you become myself,' said Sri Krishna. Try and fix your thoughts on God. Thousands die every day, do we grieve for them? It is only when death comes near us that we grieve and fear. The evil lies in our low selfishness."

"Once Krishna was walking with Arjuna out of the battle-field. A Brahmin was seen going round a fire, with the idea of falling into it; one moment more, all would have been over. Arjuna, learned in the *Gita* ran to rescue the poor Brahmin. 'Poor man,' said he, Krishna laughing within himself all the while, 'why this despair, why this suicide? O Brahmin, venerable you are, I shall give you half of my kingdom, go shares with you in all my wealth, only stop from your horrible act.' The Brahmin replied : 'Who are you thus to

prevent me? Your wealth, your empires, keep all of
them, and take them over with you when you die. As
for me, my only beloved son is no more, and why should
I live? Fire is ready, prevent me not?' Arjuna dragged
him away by his Gandiva, fell at his feet and exclaimed :
'O Brahmin, I shall give you anything, commit not this
sin.' The Brahmin was ready with his reply, 'Yes, yes
easily said. If your son had died, this fire would have
devoured you, I know.' Krishna, apparently innocent
Krishna, said : 'It is true ; his grief he only knows ;
if your son dies to-morrow, I too know you will do the
same.' 'No, no,' replied Arjuna emphatically, 'even
if my son dies, I will not do it.' Krishna said : 'It is
all words, words, words.' The Brahmin added : 'My
grief is mine, you may talk, but let me die. I am sure
if your son dies, you will also do the same.' 'No, no,'
said Arjuna, the *far-seeing* Arjuna, 'I promise, I swear.'
'Give me the oath,' was the Brahmin's reply. Arjuna
was true to his word, the Gandiva was down at once ;
and he leapt over it, once, twice and thrice. At once,
the conjuring Krishna, the magician of magicians, drew
away the vision ; the fire disappeared, and with it the
illusory Brahmin ; the oath alone remained. Arjuna
stared at Krishna, and Krishna stared at Arjuna in return with his black eyes wide open (the same eyes which
Ravi Varma has so well portrayed), and complimented
him for his extreme unselfishness. Poor, discomfited
Arjuna took back his Gandiva and returned to the battle-
field. The evening sun set with, of course, its usual
pomp ; and Abhimanyu's (Arjuna's son) soul also set
with it, 'to bid good morning in a fairer clime.' As soon
as he heard the news, Arjuna wanted a huge fire scorch-

ing the heavens to be reared for him and his Gandiva.
'Yes, yes,' said Krishna, 'Remember your oath, one
thing for the Brahmin; another for the Kshatriya;
one word for others, another for you—I suppose!'
Arjuna was silenced. He had to choke all his grief within
himself, spoke not a word, and asked for no fire. Arjuna
had advised the Brahmin not to grieve; but when the
turn came to him, he was not able to bear his own grief.
What was the reason? The self in Arjuna had not died;
it asserted itself; and the result was—one thing for
the Brahmin, another for himself. The *Gita* was not
sufficient to silence his self. Krishna's magic was required in addition. *This low selfishness is the cause of
all our misery.*" Young Krishna, while hearing the
tale from his father-in law's lips, was observing with
surprise his coolness at the prospect of his daughter's
widowhood. Sastry continued: 'Suppose a thunderbolt
falls upon my head as I speak, I won't care; for my life
is not here. I am with the Lord. He is everywhere and
all; everybody can see him except those whose hearts
are false. Ah, the peace, the coolness, the sweet calmness, the blessedness of His Presence! Ah, *who can know
it and love it not*? The coolness of the radiant moon,
the silence of the soft sky, what are they before that un-
clouded glory, the light that shakes not, the love that
quails not, the blessedness that gluts not? Oh, for one
moment of it, my dear son." As he spoke the last
words, there was a sweet angelic expression in his face,
and in his mind a soft beatitude that shone as no moon
ever did, a splendour before which the trembling lightning's light was no light at all.

One minute more, Vasudeva Sastry was nowhere.

Reader, mistake me not, his body, his flesh were all there. He was absorbed in contemplation, becoming himself Lord Vasudeva who pervades all the Universe, the infinite Spirit (*Sarvam vasudevamayam jagat*). Where was our Sastry, in the heavens, in the stars, within the moon, in the waters, in the sick-room, where was he? Was he it, or he, or she? He was all and everywhere; his form, no form; knowledge, all-knowledge; light, universal light; Self, universal Self. Have you seen how camphor melts into fire; dismiss the unburnt carbon, and what remains? Just as camphor melts into the fire, so had our Vasudeva melted into the *Parabrahman*. Five minutes passed away, ten minutes, fifteen minutes, half an hour, Sastry woke not; no one dared to speak. Even our Annammal was silent. The calmness of the hour was charming to the dying Krishna, whose limbs were steadily failing, and helped him in his contemplation.

Krishna, take courage. I see tears are starting forth from your eyes. God Yama is come; that too I see: your breath becomes intermittent; care not. Sastry wakes, he sees you, he talks to you of the playful God Krishna, he reminds you of His flute, he reminds you of the *gopis* and how they loved Him. Your breath fails, he speaks to you yet of how He appeared before them. He utters the "Om," that ocean of mystery, that sacred magic; he explains to you how it symbolises God, the *Atman* within you, and asks you to utter it. "Om" you say. "Aloud," he says. "Om" you say. "Once again," he says. "Om" you say. His calmness speaks to you even more than his eloquence, his absorption appeals to you more than even the dancing God. You look at Lakshmi for the last time; and,

weeping, look at her father, as if to say, "Take care of
her. She was my dearest love on earth," Lakshmi
sees your emotion bursts into tears, and hides her face
for fear of spoiling your future happiness. You check
yourself with a desperate effort ; and once again, of your
own accord, you say "Om". At once you start up, you
breathe your last breath, clasping Lakshmi's father
round his neck, your last friend—the kindest man that
ever lived, the strongest arm that supported.

V

AFTER KRIṢHNA'S DEATH

"HARI OM." Krishna's life on earth is finished, desperate is the weeping of the women. Even Vasudeva Sastry's eyes were dimmed with tears. Lakshmi weeps. Poor girl, you have lost your life, you cheered him up to the grave, you helped him to Heaven. God bless you. The corpse is carried to the burning ground; a melancholy procession, most melancholy, follows up to the grave. Lakshmi, poor desperate Lakshmi, seeks to follow further, but is prevented by a multitude of violent hands from falling into the fire which was rapidly consuming her dearest lover; the ocean of her grief that was hitherto choked up for the sake of her husband with a rare courage, has burst its bounds. She cries her eyes out, not for the jewels that she has to throw away, not for the hair she has to give away to the barber, but for the kindest of husbands and the best of all that loved, her richest treasure, her dearest joy.

Krishna is no more, and over his ashes we can only sing the old dirge:

> Fear no more the heat o' the sun,
> Nor the furious winter's rages;
> Thou thy worldly task hast done,
> Home art gone, and ta'en thy wages:
> * * * *
>
> Fear no more the lightning-flash,
> Nor th'all-dreaded thunder-stone;
> Fear not slander, censure rash,
> Thou hast finished joy and moan:
> All lovers young, all lovers must
> Consign to thee, and come to dust.

648

In the death of Krishna, Dindigul lost one of its best citizens; and the poor of the place, a generous supporter and friend. Krishna had large estates at his disposal and a heart much larger; and no beggar, of whatever caste, was ever turned out of his doors with a repulsive "no". Though young in years, he was the Solon of the city, and one of the prominent leaders in all its public movements. No wonder then that, on his cremation day, the whole town was in tears; and a lot of philosophy involuntarily emanated from the lips of all, young and old; and sermonising on the vanity of human life was the prevalent epidemic for the whole of the day. The dead past somehow buries its dead, and no vacancy is ever felt in the busy market of our world, any more than the death of a wave causes a breach in the bosom of the sea. The sky stinted not its usual splendour, even on that woeful day; and the sun which rose next morning looked none the gloomier for Krishna's death. Even so late as the last century, there is authority to prove that the planets above, the moon, and even our dull earth kept tune with the changing modes of men, especially the rich ones; for when a Zamindar of N——died in A.D. 1785, the Poet Laureate of his kingdom, inspired of course by the never faltering muse, has stated that the sun fled away with grief, that all nature wept, and the moon herself kept out of her heavenly court in mourning. It is not however stated, unfortunately, for how many days the sun kept out of sight, and whether the moon so sympathetic was due that night or not. However that be, the skies wore no mourning for Krishna's death, and life at Dindigul fell into its old rut not very long after the sad event of the place. Even our Annammal and poor Krishna's mother exchanged their grief for a mutual quarrel between them ; the latter gently hinting that her son's death was due to a fault in "the wicked" Lakshmi's horoscope, and the former loudly replying that her dear daughter was widowed because she had been married to the "sinful", "ungrateful", "short-lived" Krishna. A double passion now stirred up the volcano-heart of Annammal, and it required all the philosophy of her husband to prevent an untimely eruption.

Lakshmi, poor Lakshmi, was simply inconsolable. She often seriously meditated suicide ; but she did not dare make an attempt, as she was day and night surrounded by a number of visitors and relatives. Many an eye was bent towards her with deep but ineffectual pity ; and on the tenth day, there was a little row among the elders of the house when she refused to decorate herself, as the custom is, with all her ornaments, and submit to be the cynosure of a crowd of Job's comforters. Annammal insisted on her doing it, with the desire to see her in the height of her beauty before she changed once for all the wife's dress for the widow's. It was really a most melancholy scene when Lakshmi, one of the fairest of her sex, and adorned with costliest jewels from head to foot, sat bursting out in recurrent paroxysms of inconsolable *but useless* grief, amidst a crowd of men and women, most of whom perhaps came out of curiosity, but were all drowned in tears at the sight of her unfortunate angel-like beauty, which, in the course of a few hours, would melt away in the ghastliness of widowhood. There was a roar of weeping all around, and its melancholy noise brought tears into the eyes of the most cruel men. Annammal violently beat her breast, and was simply wild with grief. Even her husband could not bear the heart-rending scene.

VI

SUBBI AND THE "WILD-CAT"

WHILE such wild wailing, terrible beating of breast and
tearing of hair were going on in Krishna's house, a dark
sulky-faced man was sitting at the pial of a house not
far off, absorbed in a day-dream, which, judging from
the changing expressions and contortions on his face,
apparently forebode no good. A boy, naked and dirty,
was at that time playing in the street just before him,
and made some wild shouts, excited probably by his
play. The sulky-faced man aforesaid suddenly started
up from his reverie, and running up to the boy, who was
evidently his son, took him up in his arms, pressed him
again and again to his bosom, and kissed him all over
the body with unspeakable joy. The boy, who was a
perfect stranger to such caresses from his generally
cold and morose father, surnamed the Wild-cat, was
eager to rush out from the hands which held him.
Nayanna Sastri, for that was the name of the man, would
not let him go. "My child, my dear child, my prince,
my joy," he cried; and in reply the child screamed,
"leave me, let me go, or I will tell mother"; and briskly
kicked him. The father's caresses, however, did not
so soon come to an end. He again and again squeezed
his boy, addressed him in a strange farrago of terms of
endearment; but, all the same, the boy kicked him
with his restive legs, and abused him in exchange. The
father, however, did not get offended, but laughed outright, to the impatience and disgust of the child, who

could not make out the meaning of his father's sudden
affection for him. The one laughed and danced, and
the other kicked and screamed.

While this was going on, there came near them a
woman, and wanted water to wash her legs with. She
was the wife of Nayanna Sastri, and was just then
coming from the polluted house of Krishna, and so
asked for water. At the sight of her, the boy aimed a
violent kick at his father's teeth, and, very nearly breaking one of them jumped out to his mother, screaming,
"Wild-cat, Wild-cat!" This amiable surname, "Wild-cat,"
was first conferred upon Nayanna by his beloved wife.
Beginning from the kitchen, it went all round the town ;
and the boys, especially, knew him only by that name.
However much he might have endured it as an expression
of love from his wife, he was not willing to be called by
that name by the street boys, and got angry whenever
he was so addressed. The shrewd boys soon found this
out, and grew more and more eager to provoke him.
So they would always shout behind him, "Wild-cat,
Wild-cat" ; and he muttering to himself, "These rascally
boys !—all are not wives," would rush after them, pouring
forth a torrent of abuses.

It was a regular hunt once a day, whenever he appeared out. His wife alone enjoyed the privilege of
calling him "Wild-cat" with impunity.

Now, as soon as the boy rushed forth to her, invoking
her aid against the said Wild-cat, she directed her
husband into the house, and solemnly proceeded to
institute an inquiry. "What do you mean, you wild-
cat, by standing in the street laughing, while the whole
town pretends to weep ? and what again is the meaning

of your ill-treating my dear child?" The wild-cat could only laugh in reply, his nearly-broken tooth notwithstanding. The wife gently chid him saying, "Have you gone mad?" and employing a few words of abuse by way of endearment, succeeded in eliciting from him the following reply : "I have carefully calculated, and we have grown suddenly rich." The curious wife said : "If by calculating merely, you can make us rich, go on calculating without even taking your food, but why thus trouble my child?" He replied : "It is all through him we have got rich, it is all through him, you know." "What! has he found out any treasure for you, my dear wild-cat?" impatiently asked Subbi, for that was the lady's name. "Not so, not so!" ejaculated Nayanna, "That fellow Krishna is gone ; and so our child will be the heir, you understand."

At this stage, this edifying conversation was unfortunately broken by the sudden appearance of a third person.

———

VII

A TIMELY EXPEDIENT

THE third person who interrupted the edifying conversation between Mr. and Mrs. Wild-Cat was a neighbour of theirs, a pretty remarkable man in his own way. Our world is full of wonders if one has only the eye for them. The little story we are concerned with being a chip of the great world-block, has its own share of these wonders; and Sundarayya, for that was the name of the stranger, was undoubtedly one of these. For he had in him a genius for mischief-making which endowed him with the glorious surname of Narada, the celebrated bard of the Indian Olympus. Sundarayya, while returning from the polluted house of the late Krishna had noticed the sulky-face of Nayanna lit up with an unusual moonlight. To go home, to wear a dry cloth, and reach Nayanna's house were all the work of a few minutes and the self-elected member of God's detective police was busy eaves-dropping when the "Wild-Cats" were gloating over their calculations. When the great secret "that fellow Krishna is gone and so our child will be the heir" with a significant "you understand" added to it, was uttered, our friend Sundarayya was there unobserved. He would have continued where he was, till the whole of the conspiracy was unfolded, had he not feared that his presence had begun to be suspected. To mend matters, therefore, he boldly advanced into the interior of the house and asked Nayanna for snuff. This little powder, it may here be mentioned, has all along played an important part in social politics and has often brought together in close hand-to-hand relation the Brahmin and the Sudra, the Zamindar and his dog-keeper, the Dewan and his cook. This wonderful leveller of privileges as well as prejudices was now invoked by the intruder as an excuse for his intrusion. Nayanna's wife, as soon as Sundarayya entered, withdrew according to custom and the latter sat down saying, "Sankara, how tired I am?" Nayanna also sat down and asked, "Why! what is the matter, why are you so tired?" Sundarayya replied, "I had a very hot quarrel with a beggar fellow from Madura."

Nayanna : "Who was he? and why a quarrel?"

S. : "That fellow, it seems, is a relation of that cursed widow Lakshmi and claims that all Krishna's property must go to her and her devilish father. I said 'there are men who will take care not to let a single pie go to her,' got exceedingly angry and abused him outright. 'These Madura men are wicked. What do you say?'"

N. : "What right have any of these Madura fellows to the property?"

S. : "Surely there are claimants enough here."

"Claimants!" roared out Nayanna, "Claimants! there is only one and he will get it."

S. : Yes, you are right, there is only one and that, of course, is your relation Seetharama.'

Nayanna's face and eyes became red with rage. "I have calculated, I have calculated," he thundered out, "Let Seetharama or any other devil approach it. I will cut his throat. It is mine. I am its master." "You! how!" interrupted Sundarayya. "Yes, I mean, not me but—."

At this stage there was heard a loud scream from the kitchen side, and Nayanna finding that it was the voice of his dear dirty boy, ran in to see what the matter was. Subbi was busy thumping the little imp in the kitchen. Nayanna exclaimed "My dear! my dear! why do you beat him so?" but the thumping only increased in reply and the boy screamed louder and louder. Nayanna again remonstrated and Subbi gave him the following sweet reply loudly enough, "What do you care what I do with him or how the family goes? You have time only to talk about your plans and schemes to every fellow that passes in the street. You have got so much work to do here; the calves are dying with thirst; leaves and vegetables have to be brought from the garden, so many clothes have to be washed; but you keep talking and talking, idle that you are; and this little fellow worries me for food; how to feed him without leaves? You care not about these things but keep talking to all the men in the street," and repeated the thumping operation upon the child's back. Sundarayya heard these words which were spoken loud enough to reach at least two houses and shrewd as he was, found that he was outwitted and that he must wait for another opportunity to draw forth from Nayanna all his schemes. The fact was, as our readers would have guessed, Subbi was hearing from the kitchen all that passed between her husband and his friend, and seeing that the former was foolishly on the brink of divulging what he described as his calculation and what we might call his speculation, resorted to the thumping expedient to draw away her husband and avert the danger. Sundarayya knowing full well the meaning of the device, thought it

42

best to withdraw, saying, for formality's sake, "Nayanna, I go, I have got some business," and vowing within himself to make what he can of Nayanna's plans. Subbi loudly bolted the door on his back and treated her husband to a' severe curtain lecture on the foolishness of divulging one's plans about property to men in the street, especially to Sundarayya. After this lecture he was placed under a sort of quarantine indoors, lest he might be too communicative.

————

VIII

VERY ANGRY WITH NATURE

LET us leave for a while the Wild-Cats (Mr. and Mrs.) and the good people to Dindigul of themselves and run to Madura to see a friend of ours in whom we are greatly interested. That it is late in the night, and that there is just now no train running from the one place to the other, are no considerations with us, nor is there any fear of our sleep getting disturbed, for in a novel which is a dream within the long dream of this world, being *Pratibasika Satta* as the learned *Vedantins* would put it, we all see and act with our *Sukshma sarira*, the subtle body, and though without hands or feet we are the swiftest of approach, though without eyes or ears we see and hear everything, *"though ourselves uncomprehended, we comprehend everything knowable."*

The means of transit and other things thus cheaply settled, we reach an upstair-house at Madura which we readily recognise as that of M. R. Ry. Narayana Iyer Avergal, Dewan Bahadur, C.I.E. The Deputy Collector is fast asleep enjoying perhaps in the astral plane his titles and his gubernatorial interview. Let us pass by, slowly for fear of disturbing him and his family, for our business just now is not with the sleeping. We reach the open space in the upstairs, and there to our surprise find a young man seated in an armless chair, all alone in that dark midnight staring at vacancy, self-absorbed; his young and beautiful cheeks are wetted with tears gently flowing from two dark big eyes, his lips are firmly knit to each other ; one arm listlessly hangs over the chair and the other supports his bright but drooping face, itself resting on his thigh. His dark curly hair spreads uncared over his shoulders like a black cloud and he sat cross-legged, the very picture of melancholy. All nature was still *as if* it respected grief. The sky was perfectly silent with its silent conclave of stars. Below there was not a mouse stirring and the silence of the midnight was enhanced by the darkness of the hour which made it almost dreadful. As if still more to heighten the effect, some dark monster clouds were careering in the heavens and by turns swallowing one another like mountain-snakes. The temple towers stood enveloped in darkness like colossal *Jata munies* and one of them in particular—an incomplete tower with the old old tradition about it of being presided over by a demon-god reputed to have delivered up to Death many an unfortunate man returning by midnight from the arms of clandestine love—was in its unfinished state, enough to have frightened cowards into demoniac possession. But a few years ago, it was the popular belief that the tutelary demon of this tower would never suffer it to be completed, that it was left unfinished because the cock crew before the spirits which were engaged in its building could complete it, and that repeated human endeavours to complete it had proved futile. The great tower has now been completed but still there is the belief in its terrible guardianship : on Tuesdays and Fridays it is garlanded from top to bottom, and people with the Hindu conscience in them would not dare pass that way or ever see it in midnight hours.

But in Sreenivasan's heart, for that is the name of our young friend, there was no fear. In his heart of hearts he defied death. He would be thankful if death would remove him from a world of injustice and wickedness, where, as he thought, all the enjoyment went to the wicked and all the suffering to the good and the god-fearing. "Could there be a god," he argued, "who would suffer harlots to thrive and drive angel-like Lakshmi to widowhood and lifelong misery?" Is such a world worth living in where an innocent and virtuous, god-like Krishna is snatched away in the prime of life? Ah! Krishna, my sweet and only friend who was solacing me in my grief, whose one aim was to woo me out of my melancholy and familiarize me with the bright side of life, to lose you and survive! and ah! Lakshmi, the sweetest wife that ever man had, how often has Krishna spoken to me in secret, of your inestimable virtues, of your sweetness, your love, your kindness to all that lives, the beauty of your family relationship, the poetry of your life, the angelic philosophy you inherited from your father to which, though we did not fully comprehend it, you tuned the least of your actions! Yourself and Krishna to be parted once and for ever, you, never to see each other more! Is this life? Who had the right to send us into this and torture us this-wise? Are we such born-slaves to fate? Where is the sanction for such tyranny? To say that God's pleasure was so and so—! where is that devil who gloats in such human misery, such torturing of helpless creatures? The world is the worst jobbery, nature, the worst swindler, it cheats us, fools that we are, at every turn, now beating us with worn shoes, now patting our heads and patronising us—

a rascàlish Vivien, a siren coaxing us and making pigs of us. These suns, moons and stars, dead worthless masses of matter all rolling forward into sight because their great great grand-mother, yarrow-crooning Nature bade them so, and rolling backward out of sight once again because Nature would have it so, these are the great luminaries where gods reside! And these men innumerable all sleeping and snoring because the old devil bade them, and rushing out into life next morning saying 'I slept, and I woke, I can do this, I can do that, I have done that and so on.' This meaningless 'I' with which every man starts up like a shameless jackdaw is nature's mischief. Nobody ever does anything him= self, whether man or woman or animal. It is all Nature, Nature, Nature. This Nature hurled this me into this life—drove away that Krishna out of it and has broken Lakshmi's innocent and faultless heart. I do not want to live. If people say I must be born again, why should I? I shall put an end to myself and then let me see where this power is that can again start me up into the mad course which foolish men call *life* and the wise should call *death*. Let Nature dare approach mé." He un= consciously roared out these last words and violently stamped his foot on the ground.

Just then there came rushing up to him, as if frightened, a young girl of about 18 years of age, her hair all dishevelled and her dress in wild disorder, and clasped him in her arms crying "My dear, My dear." "Stand off, there is no 'dear' here, anywhere under the sun or above it, stand off," cried out Sreenivasan and pushed her away. "I have got frightened, my dear, don't treat me so, my dear," cried the girl and again embraced him and wept, her tears rolling down on his broad breast. "I am very much alarmed; I am very much alarmed, clasp me in thy arms and comfort me my dear," added the girl almost sobbing. We seem to know the girl; have we not seen her in Vasudeva Sastry's house once with her mother just before the terrible Annammal's arrival from Dindigul? Yes, she is Rukmani, Dewan Bahadur Narayana Iyer's daughter. Sreenivasan, just now so angry with Nature and her ways, is then the Deputy Collector's son-in-law. When Rukmani took refuge in his breast, and he felt her heart beat wildly with fear, he reluctantly but gently laid his arms round her and ground his teeth with rage saying "It is Nature driving me mad; why do you thus come and trouble me? I shall have nothing to do with anybody. You are all Nature's slaves but I will be none." "My Lord, when I am frightened, is this how you would treat me, to whom shall I go for refuge if not to you? Where is your wonted kindness gone? Soothe my fear, my dear, I shall tell you all. First let us go in, I am afraid to be here in this dark midnight." Sreenivasan had to suspend for a moment his rage against nature and had to go in. A woman in distress melts the stoniest heart. They went into the hall, the door was closed; a lamp was lit, and Rukmani, comforted and assured that all was safe, looking up at her husband, said: "My dear, is this how you will leave me alone? I don't know how long you had been sitting in the dark alone before I found you. I dreamt a dreadful dream which found strange confirmation in your conduct." "You girls are the silliest things in the world," muttered Sreenivasan; "was it only, only a dream that frightened you so, what was the dream?" "I dreamt," began Rukmani, "ah, horrible! that you had deserted me and leaving me alone in the bed as Nala did poor Damayanti, fled away into the solitudes of the forest, and there, got up a precipice overhanging a dark fathomless abyss and was about to fall down into it with a view to put an end to your life. I seemed somehow to find you. Just then I even heard you say, 'I will now kill myself and let me see which devil can bring me back to life.' Just at this critical moment I heard some one roaring and stamping on the ground which cut off my terrible dream. I woke and when in your place I saw the empty bed and unpressed pillow; I got awfully afraid and ran out screaming and found you where you were. Ah! what a bad night!" "A very curious dream certainly," interrupted Sreenivasan. "I really did want to get rid of this wicked and tyrannical Nature which has enslaved us, and I did say, 'I will put an end to myself and then let me see where the power is which could start me up into this life again.' Nature is a humbug and I want to get rid of her at any cost." "Will you leave me miserable, my dear?" replied Rukmani weeping, "is this the way to escape *Maya*? Even great sages like Vasishta lived with their wives. I should like to know how they both lived in the world and escaped the devil *Maya*." "It is all nonsense." "I do not know it well, my dear, but uncle Vasudeva Sastry says: 'By the conquest of mind alone is the conquest of Nature attained.' Nature or *Maya* is simply one's mind, he says; and when one subdues the mind he becomes immortal. Only a few days before sister Lakshmi became so miserable, he uttered to me some verses in which a sage says of himself:

'I am always immortal, I am all knowledge, I am all bliss, I am beyond nature. I am not the body—how could I be born? I am not *Ahankara* (false egoism)—how could I be subject to hunger and thirst? I am not the mind, so how could I be subject to passions and grief? I am not an agent, so how could there be slavery and freedom for me?'" Sreenivasan replied: "I too have read such things, but it is all talk, talk; where is the man who has actually gone beyond nature and rent the veil of *Maya* and who cares not what happens, who thinks himself immortal even if the body dies?" Rukmani said: "I have heard uncle say there are men who care not whether the sun is hot or cool, whether fire burns upwards or downwards, whether they are praised and worshipped or abused and beaten or even whether they die the next moment or hundreds of years after—but compose yourself, my dear, and sleep, for you have had no sleep and we have to get up early. Only assure me, my lord, that you will not desert me, that you will not once again expose yourself in the dark midnight." A sort of consent was slowly wrung out from Sreenivasan who desired to be left alone, after which his wife began to sleep. "To subdue the mind! the mind is already too subdued and slavish," he remarked to himself, and once again fell into a fit of meditation which fortunately terminated in sleep. But even his sleep was philosophical, for it was a long dream in which he met a great *Yogin* who spoke philosophy to him and graciously undertook to initiate him into the mysteries of *Yoga*. He was about to become the great *Yogi's* disciple when suddenly he as roused to witness a strange occurrence.

IX

A MYSTERIOUS FIGURE

IT was six o'clock in the morning when a servant woman was engaged in sweeping the entrance to Mr. Narayana Iyer's house, and while so engaged she was also rebuking her young daughter, who was a few steps away from her inside, for her carelessness. "Why do you stare that way," she exclaimed, addressing the little girl who really seemed staring at something tongue-tied with fear, "why do you stare that way, I ask, at passersby in the street, you silly girl. Mind your work or I will beat you with this broom" and so saying she actually raised aloft the weapon in her hand as if to show that she was determined to keep her word. As she erected herself up a little in this menacing attitude, she suddenly caught sight of a terrible figure which was standing just a foot behind her. It was that of a *Yogi* in a yellow robe hanging loosely over him from neck to foot and with a black cobra over his shoulders. His hair was matted and folded round above round over his head like the coils of a serpent ; his beard was long ; he wore a large quantity of sacred ashes on his fore-head and his eye-libs, with a big circle of red powder in the middle and held in his hand a *yoga-danda*. He was of a fair complexion and more than six feet in height with a body as stout as tall and at the same time strong and well-developed. There was a peculiar brightness in his face and his eyes had the power of assuming at will a piercing and terrible look and he had a peculiar manner of rolling them which easily struck terror into the hearts

666

of children and women. When the sweeper woman saw him, he was standing quite stiff and erect like a big statue, just a foot behind her terribly rolling his eyes and darting a piercing look at her. The moment she caught sight of the strange figure with the serpent, standing so near her, she let slip her broom, screamed in terror, ran inside, while her little daughter who stood already terror-stricken now screamed louder than she did and ran with her inside crying "mother, mother." A male servant who was within the house at once ran up to them asking what the matter was. They could not, however, so soon find words and crying and trembling they pointed their hands towards the door. The servant came out and beholding quite unexpectedly the strange figure in *Yogic* pomp standing as stiff as a statue, started back with fear and before he could find words, the *Yogi* said in thundering tones : "Go, tell thy master that his master is come. Go at once and bid him come."

The servant at once ran upstairs in search of his master, but that gentleman was snoring over his soft pillows as if no *Yogi* had come to his house. The servant was now in a dilemma ; between the sleeping Deputy Collector and the terrible *Yogiswara* he was at a loss what to do. The question was, however, solved for him by others. The screams of the servant woman and her daughter had caused a regular commotion in the whole house and Seethalakshmi and Rukmani were themselves puzzled as to the whether and the how of receiving the terrible stranger. The result was Rukmani ran up to her Sreenivasan and Seethalakshmi to the Dewan Bahadur. Rukmani woke up her husband saying: "Come, come, a great, mysterious, *Yogi-Rishi*. Get up at once and run down "

No sooner did Sreenivasan hear the word *Yogi* than he ran down and looking up at the face of the stranger fell at his feet saying : "O Lord, how kind, how true, Thou art the lord of serpents, Iswara of *Kailas*. I was dreaming of thee. What a wonder, come in Swami, my lord, my *Guru*, honour this house by coming in. Peon, bring a seat......" Narayana Iyer, however was not so easily disturbed as his son-in-law from his sleep or rather dream, for he was just then dreaming that he was talking over some important matters with his Collector who was very kindly disposed towards him. From the dream state to the waking is not always an easy transition and the Deputy Collector had to be shaken once, twice and thrice before he would exchange the one for the other and when his servant faithfully—for fear of being cursed—repeated to him the words of the mysterious stranger, he shouted for his tassa-silk, long coat and lace turban, fancying that "his master" meant the Collector and began preparing a little address of welcome for the great *Saheb* in his mind. He was, however immediately undeceived by his wife and ran down to welcome the stranger and ask him what he wanted.

In the meanwhile the stranger himself came up, being led by Sreenivasan and followed by the whole household. He was seated on a chair, the serpent still playing over his shoulders, and Sreenivasan again fell at his feet calling him "*Guru*", "*Swami*" and so on, when the great Mr. Narayana Iyer came. The stranger laughed aloud for reasons best known only to himself as soon as his host saluted him in the orthodox fashion, and said : "A guest comes to you and waits for half an hour to be admitted ! No matter ; good news come to you to-day." Then he took a pinch of sacred ashes in his hand from a purse in his possession and put it in the mouth of a girl who was standing by. At once the girl began to laugh and dance saying : "I see Indra ; there is Indrani ; there is Urvasi ; that is Ramba ; how happy. I am coming to you" and so on, but all that ceased as soon as the mysterious stranger put his hand on her head. A second pinch of sacred ashes burst a boil on the hand of another. As the mysterious stranger was thus giving proofs of his wonderful powers, a Brahmin residing a few houses off rushed in and fell at his feet three times exclaiming : "Thou art verily a *Siddhapurusha.* [1] I beheld this glorious form with the serpent now before me, which for the first time these happy eyes of mine saw at Trichinopoly coming out from the image of Thayumanaswami, flying last night across the sky among a host of radiant forms all of them perhaps *Siddhas* ; and just now I heard that thy sacred feet had lighted here and blessed the house of our master." "My friend," said that stranger, "say not all this in public ; this is nothing." "Certainly nothing," replied the Brahmin, "for a *Siddha* like you." Then the stranger desired to be left alone for an hour in a separate room. A room was accordingly provided and as he was about to enter into it, the Brahmin said, "Swami, even stone walls were not able to keep you in at Madras. Therefore assure us that you will not suddenly leave us" and the *Yogi* condescendingly said, "I shall stay all this day here" and shut the door behind him.

As soon as he went in, the Brahmin approached

---

[1] *Siddhas* are men possessed with the *siddhis,* wonderful powers like flying in the air, etc.

Mr. Narayana Iyer and congratulated him on his extraordinary privilege of having as his guest no less a man
than a *Siddhapurusha*. He related eloquently and with
wonderful vividness how, when once he had gone to
Trichy and was worshipping the god Thayumanavar
along with many others, the glorious guest of the Deputy
Collector came out from the head of the image in the
presence of all the people there, and how, after staying
there for a few minutes to bless the worshippers, he flew
into the air in open day light; how once when he made
his appearance in Madras holding in his hands wine
bottles—for the holy ones can drink and do many other
things with impunity—for which he had not obtained
license, he was shut up by the then Police Commissioner
in his own room and how half an hour after, he was
walking along the beach with the same wine bottles,
though the Commissioner had himself locked up in the
room and kept the key in his own possession, and how
thereafter the police were ordered not to arrest him on
any account whatever; how only the last night he was
seen flying above with a host of *Siddhas*; and many
other equally wonderful incidents of the great *Yogi's*
past life. Narayana Iyer felt it difficult to believe all
of them at the same time, though the wonderful efficacy
of the sacred ashes which the stranger had, had to be
admitted. Sreenivasan, however, thought that they
should be true, all of them, and related his strange dream
and the stranger coincidence that followed. "Otherwise," he argued, "how could I have dreamt that
wonderful dream? He should have been flitting in the
skies at that time and descended here directly. What
a most wonderful coincidence!" It was agreed on all

hands that the stranger was a mysterious being, probably superhuman, possessing wonderful powers. Narayana Iyer was in doubt whether he, being the great and responsible officer he was, might endorse all that was said and thereby lend the weight of his position to it; but just then there happened an event which assured him that not merely all that was said but much more that was not known must be true.

————

X

MORE WONDERS

THE news spread in the street that a great *Siddhapurusha* had descended direct from heaven in broad day-light and entering Deputy Collector Narayana Iyer's house, had performed great miracles and was just then staying as a guest of the great Dewan Bahadur. In a few moments a large and eager crowd gathered of its own accord opposite to Mr. Narayana Iyer's house and all the air was filled with stories of *Siddhas*, *Mahatmas*, *Yogis*, *Rishis*, and so on. Within the house, an informal council of which the Dewan Bahadur was the self-chosen President, was seriously discussing, about the possibility or otherwise of miracles and several were the opinions submitted, which, considering their real worth, I very much regret, I am obliged to withhold for want of space. The most important of them all, was that of the Deputy Collector which for the enlightenment of my readers I shall quote, "Miracles are by the very nature of things impossible, but there is no denying the fact that some men do perform miracles, though in the case of the *Mahatman* upstairs, he was not very sure if he was also a miracle-worker as certainly he must be, considering all the circumstances. Even among Englishmen, some say that miracles are possible, others, that they are not, though, for his own part he would think (as in the many disputes he had settled in the course of his long and much approved service as a high revenue official), that *the truth lies just between the two sides*." After this able,

672

thoughtful and impartial summing up, he looked round
for applause never so well-earned ; his audience understanding his *wishes*, though not his *speech*, gave him
what he wanted, with many deafening cries of : "True,
first class, that is it, that is it," and so on ; but their
blank faces gave the lie to their words and showed that
they were not quite able to understand the golden meaning
between possible and impossible. Their impertinent
brains said to them "Miracles should either be possible
or impossible, how could they be both possible and impossible at the same time ?" and one of the councillor,
evidently not advanced in the arts of the courtier actually
put the question at which there burst forth in the assembly a number of loud and angry hisses like those of
serpents when provoked and the President himself encouraged by these hisses scornfully said : "Do you
think I do not know so much ?" though greatly confounded within himself as to how such a union of
contraries could be possible. Just then, fortunately for
him, a *pundit* who was by came to his rescue. He coolly
said : "Such a thing has been said in our very *Srutis*.
It may be both possible and impossible ; in that case
it is called *anirvachaniyam*" and quoted a text in support
of his statement. What exactly this learned *pundit*
meant, I have not been able to make out, but it seems
to me he was right if he meant that just as the world is
and is not, in other words, only appears to be so, miracles
also are and are not, possible, *i.e.*, they only appear to be
possible, in other words, *are clever frauds*. Whatever
he might have meant, the discussion came to an end
because the postman who came in just at the right
moment handed over a long cover to the Deputy Col-

43

lector after duly "*salaaming*" him. Narayana Iyer opening it found that he had been promoted one grade. Just then there came to his mind the words of his mysterious guest "Good news comes to you to-day" and he shouted for the very joy and said 'Did I not say miracles are certainly possible. So indeed they are. As the great *Siddhapurusha* said, I have been all of a sudden promoted. Mighty are his doings.' At once the whole audience became eloquent over this miracle and a person was despatched upstairs to see if the *Yogi* had come out and he was strictly commanded not to make the slightest noise when going up or any way disturb the *Mahatman*. The man went up, but just then the serpent of the *Yogi* was crawling outside the room occupied by him. Seeing it, the poor man who was mortally afraid of serpents, ran downstairs precipitately; but being ashamed to tell the truth he coined a tale for the eager audience below. He informed them, his heart beating loud enough to be heard by the whole assembly, that the room in which the *Siddhapurusha* was, was filled with a strange celestial light and that as he peeped through the key-hole he found the *Yogi's* body floating in the air three feet above the ground and that all his limbs lay separate from one another, head one side, hands another, feet another, and so on like the several parts of a machine disjointed for purposes of cleaning. The wonder of the audience knew no bounds. As they thus stood wondering, they heard the noise of a bell loudly ringing and as it came from the upstairs they all proceeded there in a body. The room of the *Yogi* stood open; he himself was standing ringing a silver bell in his hand in the act of making *puja* to a golden image four feet high, which was decorated with bracelets, necklaces, ear-rings and so forth, all of gold, diamond and rubies and dazzling to behold. It stood in a flower shed very ornamental and surrounded with lights of various colours. The *puja* vessels were all of silver and there were kept in huge silver baskets flowers and fruits of various kinds. As Narayana Iyer and others went up they were confounded with wonder. The mysterious *Yogi* commanded Narayana Iyer to call in all and accordingly he went down and asked all the people who stood outside in the road to come up. At once a huge crowd rushed up, and though the hall upstairs was very spacious, there was hardly standing room for all. The *Yogi* then solemnly worshipped the goddess, with *Dhupa* and *Dipa* and ordered the fruits and flowers to be distributed among all the people. Then, the room was closed and the crowd was ordered to disperse. Narayana Iyer took leave from office that day. A grand entertainment was given to the *Yogi* and in the evening he came down and took his seat outside on the pial with his serpent playing over his shoulders. Immediately the whole of the Madura population began to assemble in front of Narayana Iyer's house.

XI

SASTRY AND HIS DAUGHTER

WHILE such grand things were going on here, a scene far different occurred at Dindigul. "Dear father," said Lakshmi, addressing Vasudeva Sastry who was trying to console her : "Why did you prevent me from committing suicide. I cannot endure this life. All the philosophy you have taught me from my childhood does not sustain me now. When you advise me, I get consoled ; but the next moment my grief returns with added force like water rushing out from a breach in a big tank." Vasudeva Sastry with a very kind look said : "Child, compose yourself, do not give way to grief," but she continued : "Were they not great heroes, father, who killed themselves either by leaping into the funeral pyre of their husbands or by some other means, unwilling to live after their husband's death ? Have you not taught me, father, that for a virtuous woman her husband is the real God, and did I not look upon my dear, poor—?" and burst out into tears. Her whole body shook with grief and tears rolled down from her eyes in torrents. Her father bending over her with affection wiped her tears with his cloth and spoke very kind words, urging her to compose herself. Interrupting him, she continued : "I am surely a great sinner, father ; though trained by you from my childhood to live up to the ideal of chastity, to be like Savitri and Sita, I did not do so : otherwise this great calamity would not have befallen me. Did not Savitri rescue her husband from the very hands of Yama ? I am a sinner." "Dear child," said Vasudeva Sastry, "I was watching you most carefully in your happy married life and though *Purana* might not record your fame, I can assure you, you even outdid Savitri in your devotion to your husband. He himself told me how much he learnt from you and your worship of him elevated both of you. You need not fear my child. You have performed a sacrifice the equal of which there is none on earth and you have now begun another which is still more difficult and still more meritorious. Your heart naturally inclines to virtue and delights more in virtue than in anything else. I saw that, even when you were a child and I knew that you would be a great woman though none might sing your praise." "Father, father," cried Lakshmi, "you are too generous in your estimate of me. I am a sinner ; far from virtuous : otherwise, God would not have visited me with such a punishment." "Grieve not, my child," said Vasudeva Sastry, "grieve not, for past sins we suffer, it is true ; but God is kind even when he is cruel : our very punishments are blessings in disguise. If you endure this calamity with calm resignation you will have achieved a feat the like of which there is not in all the worlds."

"Ah, how difficult it is, father, how very difficult to endure, how could I for one moment bear the grief."

"You can endure. You have the power, my girl, you are not like other women. From your infancy, to endure was your delight. My darling, I remember how it was one of your favourite exercises while you were but a girl of 5 years to set a number of children to provoke you and vow not to get angry, do whatever they might.

They would worry you in all possible ways and do all sorts of mischief, but you would never get angry. The power to suffer is your chief merit and it is for that you are so dear to me. I am sorry I am obliged to leave you for a few days, but I shall soon return."

"Father, stay not away for more than four or five days, at the most not more than a week. I sadly want you now. Settle all your business and come away soon."

"Fear not, my girl; I shall soon return. Forget not that God is everywhere and he always hears you. This is my advice to you : *Endure, endure, and when you are not able to endure, remember this truth. Thousand times better than an ordinary man is a Rishi ; thousand times better than a Rishi is a woman who worships her husband during his life-time as God ; and thousand times better than such a woman is she who worships her husband as God even after his death.*"

Hardly had Vasudeva Sastry concluded, when Annammal rushed in and pouncing upon her daughter like an eagle on its prey, took her in her arms and pressing her to her bosom, set up a tremendous wailing. After a few minutes she set her down and beat her breasts in her sight and said : "We are going and if you cannot check your grief go and fall into a well. I would rather wish you were burnt to ashes than see you, with my motherly eyes, in this wretched state." So saying, she bade her husband take his bag and start to the train. He accordingly took his bag and addressing Lakshmi said : "Remember my words." Then both of them left the house for the train, which they reached just in time. A few hours more and they were at Madura.

XII

THE PLOT THICKENS

WHEN Seethalakshmi heard that Vasudeva Sastry and Annammal had returned from Dindigul, herself and Rukmani went to them to condole with them for the untimely death of their son-in-law. Annammal, the moment she saw them, began an eloquent tirade on the *Vedanta*, which more than anything else was the cause, in her opinion, of her bereavement. With this preface she commenced weeping in stentorian strains to the great dread not merely of neighbours but also of people furlongs off. Everywhere in the neighbouring streets men and women rushed out of the houses to know what the cause of such a sudden outburst could be. It is said that on that occasion even the temple elephants shook with surprise, but of this I am not quite sure. Whether it was true or not, this much is certain that Annammal's performance was very much admired by the women whom Nature, being herself a female and therefore partial to her sex, has specially favoured with big throats and shrill voices.

When the Niagara-falls' roar, which they had occasioned, was going on, Seethalakshmi and her daughter turned to Vasudeva Sastry to condole with him. That gentleman was all the while looking at Annammal with eyes expressive of wonder, for that day's performance of hers was novel even to him as he had never before seen anything like it. The first thing he said to Seethalakshmi was: "Surely this wife of mine is an

Avatar (incarnation) for Krishna has said, 'Wherever there is power or glory in an extraordinary degree, know that I am there."

After the usual enquiries were over, he described in some detail the circumstances of Krishna's death and the state of his daughter's mind and wound up with saying : "Everything happens for good and this calamity would not have happened to Lakshmi had it been unnecessary. It is by trials that we attain to perfection and this great trial might perhaps take Lakshmi a step nearer God. But who knows? *Everything in the world has its own law.*" Then Rukmani began the topic of the *Siddhapurusha* and the miracles he had worked and asked him if he believed that he was a true *Siddha*. Vasudeva meditated for about a quarter of an hour and then said : "In a day or two you will yourself find your questions answered. In the meanwhile please your husband in all possible ways and see that you do not leave him alone after ten in the night. Always keep pretty near him."

Seethalakshmi was about to ask him why, when there rushed into the house no less a person than Narayana Iyer, Dewan Bahadur, shouting : "Vasudeva, Vasudeva." As he came in, the whole company rose to do him honour and seeing his wife and daughter there he said : "O you are here, talking *Vedanta* I suppose ! Vasudeva, what a great *Siddhapurusha* has blessed our house with his presence ! By the way, you have lost your son-in-law, a good fellow he was. Don't you come to see the *Mahatma* in my house ? It is a fortunate thing that you have come. He wanted to go yesterday ; but I begged him to stay here for a week or ten days more and he has consented. What wisdom he speaks! You might learn much from him, more than we can, for you know something already. Come, come, we shall go." Vasudeva Sastry did not care to go, but Narayana Iyer dragged him by the arm without allowing him to say a word, and so he went.

In the meanwhile Sreenivasan, who, having at the very first appearance of the mysterious stranger mentally appointed him as his *Guru*, waited for an opportunity to see him alone was, by the grace of God, as he thought it, himself called by the latter into the room where he had performed his last miracle. The room was now empty, there were there neither silver vessels nor golden images now. The *Yogi* took his seat on a chair, and Sreenivasan as soon as he entered the room fell at his feet three times and said with tears in his eyes : "O Lord, I have been waiting for an opportunity to see you alone. You know by your *Yogic* power all my thoughts, free me, Lord, from the ills of *Samsara* and give me wisdom. I want nothing else, O Lord : not even *Siddhis* attract me." The *Yogi* replied : "Though young how ripe you are for divine wisdom! That is why I called you in, my child. By a touch of my hand numberless men have acquired wonderful power and wisdom. But are you sure you want wisdom and nothing else?" "Yes, my lord, I want nothing else. Nothing else pleases me." "Do you dare to be a disciple of mine? Will you leave father, mother, wife and relations, and follow me? Remember these will not save you from death nor follow you beyond the grave, but the wisdom I shall teach you will make you immortal." "Truly my master," said Sreenivasan, "I will follow you wherever you go, cross mountains and forests with you and go even beyond the seas." "That is good, that is what is wanted," ejaculated the *Yogi*.

Then the self-elected *Guru* and the would-be *Chela* both came out of the room, and, as wherever Rama was, was Ayodhya, a large gathering assembled in a few minutes' time in the presence of the supposed *Siddha*. And now another miracle happened which was even more wonderful than the preceding ones.

The mysterious *Yogi* suddenly called over Sreenivasan to him, and, in the presence of a large gathering, besmeared his face with sacred ashes and put a small quantity of the same in his mouth, when lo ! Sreenivasan cried at the top of his voice : "I am *Akhanda Satchidananda* (boundless Existence, Knowledge, Bliss), an ocean of bliss. I am the omnipresent God himself. I am *Param Jyotis* (the Supreme Light), I am *Iswara*, I am *Brahma*, I am *Vishnu*, I am the great *Para Brahman*," and laughed so convulsively that the people around were filled with wonder, and feared for the safety of his ribs ; for more than fifteen minutes, the fit of laughter lasted, and it would have continued longer, had not the mysterious *Yogi* shifted him, by gently touching him on his shoulder, from the plane of *Para Brahman* to that of an ordinary mortal. Sreenivasan hardly recovered his every day consciousness, when he began to praise his *Guru Maharaj* in no measured language. All the verses in our books in praise of the *Guru* were instantly on his lips and the great miracle-worker himself, not only heartily enjoyed the garland of praises which Sreenivasan was honouring him with, but was jubilant over the conquest he had made of the young man's heart, and the wonder and awe which he had created in the mind of all around him. Indeed his joy was so great that he could not contain himself, and he cried out : "Ye ignorant men, do ye now see what a *Siddha* is capable of?" And the ready response on all side was : "O Lord *Siddhapurusha*, what is there that is impossible for you who fly in the heavens and subsist on air." At this reply, he looked around majestically and smiled an approving smile.

Just at that very moment, there entered Narayana Iyer dragging Vasudeva Sastry along with him and, making so low an obeisance as if he were before a despotic Sultan in whose hands his life lay. Such courtier-like obeisance was however lost upon the miracle-working *Yogi*, for the latter, the moment he saw Vasudeva Sastry, started with fear, coloured very perceptibly and got too much beside himself to notice the deference which the Dewan Bahadur honoured him with. Indeed it took him one or two minutes to regain his self-possession, and when he came to himself, he was filled with shame and sorrow at having betrayed his emotion. The result was, he hung down his head, was moody and did not dare even to talk to Narayana Iyer in reply to his salutation. Such a sudden change in his manner, was noticed by nearly all present, including Narayana Iyer himself, and every one began to form his own conjecture as to what might be the relation between the mysterious *Yogi*, and the *Vedantin* Vasudeva Sastry. Narayana Iyer could not come at a happy guess, and not having the patience to form one, he bluntly asked his guest if he knew the Sastry at which perfectly unexpected question, he started and with great confusion replied : "Yes, no, not exactly. I have seen him, I remember. Rather he looks very much like an intimate friend of mine in my *Purva Asrama* (former state), *i.e.*, before I became a *Siddha*." All this he uttered in a thoroughly un-*Siddha*-like fashion, but, to cover up the awkwardness of the reply, he at once began to play with his serpent, exciting it and thrusting his fingers into its mouth to the terror of the spectators. This served to divert the attention of the company from Vasudeva Sastry, and the stranger noticing the advantage he had gained, began to tell the audience how the serpent he had was no natural serpent, but a great *Rishi* whom he himself changed to a serpent for having spoken ill of him and how, though unable to speak, it could understand all that was said in its presence in Sanskrit which was the language the *Rishi* knew. To prove the truth of his assertion, he said to it in Sanskrit, "Go up to my shoulder." At once it went up to his shoulder, and when he said : "Come down," it descended. Then he said : "Bite me" which accordingly it did, but he did not to the great astonishment of all feel the slightest injury and seemed to be poison-proof. Then he said : "Leave me and play," which it at once did. By these wonderful performances, he regained the respect and awe of the multitude and his *Siddha*-ship was reestablished on a secure footing.

The night had by this time far advanced, and the *Siddhapurusha* saying, "You may all go home now and come again to-morrow morning," retired into his apartment after duly receiving the farewell salutations of all except Vasudeva Sastry, who left rather abruptly, taking leave only of Narayana Iyer. All the company broke up, and Narayana Iyer himself went to sleep, but Sreenivasan alone stayed after all had gone. Seeing him thus waiting, the *Siddhapurusha* beckoned to him and said : "Be hasty and yet not hasty. Run away and yet be sleeping. Leave all and follow me." Words which he could hardly make out. But before he ventured to ask of their meaning his *Guru* had retired into the room and shut the door.

At about three o'clock in the morning Narayana Iyer was disturbed by a bad dream in which he saw his home pillaged, and woke up. He did not feel easy in mind, and wanted to see if everything was right in his house. He first went to see if his cash-chest was safe downstairs, but what was his surprise when he found the door of his gate left ajar ! He at once flew to see if the chest was safe in its place, but that was not to be found. At once something induced him to go and look for the supposed *Siddha* in his room, which he did, but he was thunder-struck to find it empty.

———————

XIII

SIDDHA'S EARLY HISTORY

Poor Narayana Iyer was so horror-stricken at the state
of things that he could hardly shout aloud. After three
or four desperate attempts, the words "Thief, thief,
ho, ho," which had on account of his fear stuck to his
throat for so long a time, at last came out. The shout
was much louder than what a conscious effort could
have produced, and the result was a general commotion
in the house, which rapidly extended outside. First
the peons rose, then the inmates of the house, then the
neighbours, then an adjacent police station. In the
midst of the general confusion, Rukmani, with her hair
dishevelled and her face expressive of fright, ran
towards her father crying : "He, He, your son-in-law.
Your son-in-law," and Narayana Iyer considerably
terrified shouted in return, "Son-in-law, what about
him, what is the matter, murdered by the thief, what
is the matter, what about him?" Rukmani sobbed out,
"He has left me and fled away." "What!" yelled out
the poor father, "I am undone. I am undone. I am
undone, let me die" and fell down. People raised him up
in their arms, but he freed himself and ran hither and
thither shouting, "thieves, thieves, my son-in-law, my
cash-chest, my cash-chest, my son-in-law," and again
fell down, this time nearly, senseless. People ran upstairs, and downstairs, but neither Sreenivasan nor the
Siddha nor the cash-box could be found. A few moments
elapsed and some coolness came over the party.

Narayana Iyer also regained his consciousness and rose a little calmer. The police were deliberating as to their plan of campaign, and all the men assembled, poured a volley of abuses on the supposed *Siddha* and agreed in thinking that he was a rogue, a rascal, a blackguard, a thief and several other things of the same type. One man said : "I knew from the very beginning that he was a humbug." Another said that he was some vagabond. A third said : "Did you see how he started at the sight of Vasudeva Sastry. Perhaps the latter knows all about him." A fourth said : "We should not talk ill of great men. The theft might have been committed by Sreenivasan." "Both are joint thieves," said another. While the people were thus busily engaged, it occurred to Narayana Iyer's mind that the treacherous *Siddha* might have fled on account of Vasudeva Sastry, whom he seemed to fear. It appeared probable to him that the latter might be in possession of some secret concerning him ; "but why did not the rascal tell me that or at any rate warn me ?" muttered he himself and ordered a peon to bring the Sastry to him at once "by the hair".

When the peon came to Vasudeva Sastry's house, Annammal was snoring over her dirty pillow, while the Sastry was sitting cross-legged on a small plank in the narrow courtyard which formed a part of his narrow house, evidently in an attitude of meditation. His *Rishi*-like face was, as usual in his hours of meditation, lit up with a singular brightness and looked fresh like a lotus just blown. The world had completely ceased to exist for him, and in the Divine Light in which he had lost himself there were no thieves, no sons-in-law, no cash-chests and no *Siddhas*. It was all *peace, peace, peace*. A waveless ocean of indescribable bliss, vaster than all the seas on earth, vaster than the infinite expanse of the sky above, vaster than all the visible universe of stars, moons and suns, and yet neither vast nor small, for space there was not—this was what Vasudeva Sastry was, when Narayana Iyer's peon knocked with vehemence at the door of his house. In him *thought* had expired in the *enjoyment* and the enjoyment expired in the *becoming* and the becoming passed into *being*, so that there was there neither the thinker nor the enjoyer, neither thought nor enjoyment. Another knock at the gate, but no response ; for both the inmates were busy. A third knock yet louder, and Annammal rose with a shout which startled the peon at the gate and made him lose his footing. She was dreaming that she had lost her way in a mountain pass filled with wolves and tigers, and climbed up a steep side of a rock where a false step hurled her down just against the mouth of a hungry tigress. The knock at the gate corresponded exactly with the jump of the furious tigress upon her and she woke up from her dream with a fearful yell which, more than the knock at the gate, disturbed her husband's *Samadhi*. Annammal was considerably relieved to find that no tiger had taken hold of her, but, the moment she saw her husband sitting in the courtyard, she began to scold him saying : "*Vedanta* (*i.e.*, her husband) is sitting all night ; he does not even open the door and see who it is that knocks at this hour." So saying she opened the door and when the peon asked for her husband who had woke from the reality of his Self into the dream of the world but had not yet risen, she ran up to him and, shaking him by the shoulders as if he were a bag of brinjals shouted in his ear to the risk of his tympanum : "*Vedantam*, *Vedantam*, rise up, sitting like a corpse, rise up." Sastry said nothing, rose up, and in a few minutes was in Narayana Iyer's house.

The Deputy Collector, who was eagerly waiting for him, no sooner saw him than he began to scold him roundly for not having previously informed him of what happened. "Why did you not tell me all this before?" asked the enraged Dewan Bahadur and added, "You know what has happened, my cash-box, my son-in-law and the scoundrel of a *Siddhapurusha*. Shame that I went and prostrated myself at his feet, shame ; but why did you not tell me all this before?"

V. : I am very sorry—

N. : Sorry or glad I don't care, but why didn't you tell me?

V. : I did not know.

N. : But you ought to have known, why didn't you know?

Sastry found it was no easy question to answer : so he smiled and kept quiet.

N. : You know that devil of a Sreenivasan has fled away leaving this wretched girl here. Why didn't you tell me all that beforehand? Now tell us all you know about that scoundrel of a *Siddha*. Vasu, I did not know that you would thus betray me. Oh! my son-in-law, my money-chest. Had you told me all last night, 1 would have handed over that rascal to the police and set an example.

V. : It did not occur to me that he would rob you

44

of your money or that Sreenivasan would so easily desert
Rukmani. Are all the women in the house safe? My
friend the *Siddha* is more fond of carrying away women
than men, but the present case seems to be different.

Just then the police head constable reported to the
Dewan Bahadur that he had despatched several parties
of constables in various directions in search of the thief.

Narayana Iyer said : "Very well, see that he is
brought to me before to-morrow" and asked Sastry whether he knew the *Siddha* and what he knew about him
and what made the latter start suddenly on his arrival
the previous night. "On my way to Benares," said
Vasudeva Sastry, "I halted at Gazipore, where I became
acquainted with a rich merchant, a native of our district.
He was very kind to me and very attentive to my wants
and his hospitality induced me to prolong my stay in the
place. Two or three days after I went there, a *Yogi*
came there, dressed in *Garua* cloth with matted hair and a
serpent in his hand ; he had a considerable following
of *Yogis*, who all worshipped him as a *Siddhapurusha*
and ascribed extraordinary powers to him, such as flying
in the air, walking on the sea, and so forth. He was
received and entertained with all his following by a
merchant who was my friend's friend. I warned him,
but he did not heed me and provided lodgings to the supposed *Siddha* in his own house. One day, myself and
my friend went to see him, and, when questioned about
his previous history, he told us that he was in his *Purva
Asrama* (former state) a Sanskrit *pundit* in the Madura
College, that once when he went to the famous Saduragiri
hills in the Tinnevelly District, he met a *Siddha* and
paid his respects to him and the *Siddha*, pleased with his

behaviour, took him over to the *Siddhasrama* in the interior, and, in the course of a few years made him personally acquainted with *Parvati* and *Parameswara* and finally transformed him into a *Siddha*. The serpent, he said, was an emblem of the highest order of *Siddhas*, and, he claimed equality with *Agastya*. He further claimed that by a mere touch of his garment, many persons had acquired wonderful powers. Every day he surprised his host and the people around him with sundry feats of jugglery and mesmerism which, had they been performed by a poor juggler, would have been regarded as mere tricks, but, having been worked by him, were considered miracles. My friend asked me privately if his Sanskrit *pundit*-ship was a fact. I assured him that it was a mere lie, as I knew all the *pundits* of that institution from its very commencement. The sensation he created in the city was however immense, and many were the entertainments given to him and his retinue. Every day he threatened to fly away (for he was a *Siddha* and therefore could fly as he said), but every day he was detained by the foolish merchants of the place. At last however he actually flew away, not in the air however, nor with his old following, but with a very beautiful girl of sixteen who belonged to one of the most influential families in the city. Hardly had he left the place, when an urgent warrant came for arresting him, for he had been convicted of forgery and kept in custody at Madras, from which he somehow contrived to escape. Many and desperate were the attempts made both by the police and by the merchants of the place to trace him out, but all in vain, for, he was nowhere to be seen. Some said he was dead, others that he fled away to the Himalayas. He knew me very well, though he was not aware that I belong to Madura, otherwise he would not have come here. Seeing that I suspected him he had taken from me a promise not to say anything of him to the Gazipore people. I seriously advised him to leave off his wicked ways, though he told me only a little of them, but that was to no purpose. My concern for him curiously enough resulted in his taking an oath from me not to appear to know him, not speak ill of him to any one in any place during his stay there—a curious oath to be sure : but I did not grudge to give it to him, as it is contrary to my nature to betray or speak ill of any man however bad he may be, and I sincerely wished he would improve. *Everything in the world is God and how could I despise even the murderer* ?

"I was very much surprised to find him here in your own house, but I could say nothing on account of that oath, and it was for fear of breaking it that I left you rather abruptly last night. I had no fear of his being able to work any mischief in your house, especially as it is well guarded by peons, and so I went home with an easy mind and now I am glad that it is only your cash-chest that you have lost and that it is only Sreenivasan that has been enticed away."

On hearing this story, Narayana Iyer laughed in spite of his anger and grief and said : "Your philosophy has simply made a fool of you. Annammal is after all right ; *Vedanta* makes dunces of men. To give such an oath to a scoundrel and keep quiet. You should have refused to give it, man."

Vasudeva Sastry : "Yes, but he begged and pressed me so much and I saw no harm in it. Perhaps I might not have given him such an oath had he asked me for it after his elopement with that girl : but even then I am not sure. *For we sould never speak ill of others though we are not bound by an oath not to do so.* I have not told you a hundredth part of what I know of him, and even this I told you to show that comparatively you have not suffered much. Perhaps he has now improved a little."

N.: "Yes he has improved : you too have improved into an idiot. Look at this, this girl (pointing to Rukmani), is weeping tears of blood and you goose, you say I have not suffered."

XIV

SASTRY ON DUTY

To make a long story short, Vasudeva Sastry was entrusted with the commission of finding out Sreenivasan and bringing him back to his senses and his wife, as it was thought none else was competent to do it. He determined to start on his expedition that very day but, before doing so, he took Rukmani aside and asked her to tell him all that had happened between herself and her husband the previous night.

Rukmani told Vasudeva Sastry : "He (her husband) did not come to me for a long time after all in the house had returned to bed, but kept waiting outside the wicked *Siddha's* room. I went to him twice or thrice and entreated him with tears in my eyes to go to bed ; but for all that I was rewarded only with abuse ; and when I persisted in my entreaties, he kicked me and sent me away to my room weeping. Immediately I heard the *Siddha's* room open, and a few minutes after, my husband came to me with a small bottle in hand which he held concealed. He came to me only because he was afraid I might go down and cause a commotion in the house. Seating himself by my side he looked at me sternly for some time and then poured on me a volley of abuses.

"I said, 'I seem to stand in your way. You look upon me as your mortal enemy. O God, I do not know when you will be pleased to recall me from this world !' He replied : 'Yes. You are my real enemy. But for you—.' Then he stopped. I added, 'You would have run away with this wicked, so-called *Siddha*.' He kicked me once again saying : 'Why do you abuse my *Guru*? you wretch, you rogue. I am really going to run away. Who is there who can prevent me? Better to run to the forests and die there unknown than to continue in this world of woe and with a wicked ass like you.' I could say nothing. I was choked with grief and fear. Then he coaxed me a little saying that he did not mean what he said. More than an hour passed in mutual explanations and peace-making, and a sufficiently good understanding had been established between us when suddenly he raised the glass in his hand swallowed a few drops from it, saying that it was a good sleeping draught which he drank as it was very late in the night and wanted to have a sound sleep, and gave me also to drink of the same which I did. Hardly had a few seconds elapsed since I took it when I felt a strange sense of stupor creeping over me and drowning me in sleep. I saw nothing more and woke only on account of the disturbance in the house and to find that he was gone. I am a ruined girl. Nothing remains for me but to die. If he does not come in four or five days I shall put an end to my life. That is all."

Vasudeva Sastry said that in a fortnight's time he was sure to bring him back and comforted her and started on his expedition by the very next train towards the north ; for he saw that Sreenivasan should have gone only northward as the only train that left Madura between twelve and three in the night went in that direction.

XV

A WIDOW CONSOLED

MEANWHILE great things were going on in Dindigul.
My readers will be pleased to recall to their minds our
sulky-faced friend Mr. Nayanna Sastry surnamed the
"wild-cat". We also remember that he was calculating
to become suddenly rich through his child whose name
I forgot to mention before was Kannu. The result of
his calculation was that Krishna's mother who was a
cousin of his and very affectionate towards him should
be made to adopt the dirty child Kannu on the authority
of a will by her late husband, which was not in existence
but to be forged and which should be made to say that
all the estates of the family were the personal acquisition
and therefore the private property of her husband. It
was to state explicitly that, as Krishna was very sickly
from his infancy, the estates should go to him only if he
survived his mother and that otherwise they should go
to her and through her to any one whom she might
choose to adopt. The plan was in due course revealed
to Krishna's mother and with the help of an expert forger
a will was drawn upon a sufficiently old-looking paper
with the signatures of a number of persons who were
bribed into the deed. The adoption too would have
been completed, but fortunately or unfortunately it had
to be postponed for three months, as that interim period
was not auspicious according to custom for the ceremony.
Lakshmi smelt the affair, and was very much pained at
heart not for the chance of losing the property which

696

should, as a matter of justice, go to her, but for the wickedness of the deed and the meanness of the persons concerned in it. She however never said a word of it to anybody, but consumed herself with her grief.

One night she was in her room weeping. The affair of the will came to her mind and she said to herself sobbing "Ah, what a wicked world. My dear, my lord, you did very well in leaving it so early. Happy it was for you that you did not see much of the wickedness and misfortune in the short span of your existence here. And I would not, not on any account, wish for your return here. Not all my suffering loneliness and helplessness should induce me to wish for that. Even if God Yama were to come and promise to restore you to me here as he restored Satyavan to Savitri I would say, 'Not so, let us not meet here any longer. If you so please deign to take me to him.' If he should refuse that high boon I would say to him, 'Promote him to higher and higher regions of bliss on my account as much on account of his innumerable virtues. If my suffering and penance here would avail him anything, I will undergo a thousandfold more torture than I do now. All I wish is his happiness, the happiness of him who was sweeter to me than my own life, my own joy, my prince, my god of love.' Ah! sweet Krishna! How I rejoiced to hear thy sweet name from anybody's lips; and how my heart leaped with joy and pride when I heard it uttered with praise and satisfaction everywhere. To look at you was bliss, to talk to you was heaven and to hear your talk—that sweet voice, that divine love which flowed from every little syllable you uttered—to hear you talk was more than heaven. It would seem to me that the dust of earth which felt your soft tread in the day mounted to heaven and became stars. It would seem to me that the very air you breathed around was sacred and to repose on your mountain-like bosom ! Aye, Parvati is not more happy in the Kailas. How well you deserved the name Krishna, yes, you were my Krishna and I was your Rukmani, Satyabhama and the *gopis* all put together. Vain words ? I am a hypocrite. I speak hollow words. Knowing that you were on your death bed, should I not have died before you did ? There was one opportunity for doing justice to my love, to you and I have lost it, lost it for ever. At least I might have leapt on the funeral pyre which was burning your body, that temple of my love, that which sheltered your mighty soul and whose beauty I enjoyed for many a day, that body burnt to ashes just in my presence. Fool not to have died. A hypocritical wretch still living—to see what—all this wickedness in the world ? O father, why do you not permit me to die, O cruel father !"

Just as she was saying these last words cruel father, she heard a gentle knock at the door and on opening it she found—her own father. Vasudeva Sastry saw her bathe in tears and at once tears rushed forth in his eyes also. He was not able to restrain them. Then controlling himself by degrees he comforted her also with gentle words which he only knew how to speak. At last she asked : "O father, why do you not permit me to die." He replied : "Child, be not hasty, God has sent you into this world and He knows when to take you out of it. Child, you are not fit enough for death."

"Father, you always speak wisdom. Where is the like of you in all the three worlds? But it is we that suffer most," Lakshmi said sobbing. He said : "Don't grieve, my child, grief is *selfish*. There is neither suffering nor grief where there is no selfishness. Joy and sorrow are only in our minds." "Father," asked Lakshmi, "If I am not fit to die, then who else is?" Sastry replied : "Lakshmi, *my dear child, he alone is fit to die who is dead even in life, who is above grief and selfishness*. Believe me, my child, you are born for very great things, and in a short time the world will unfold its secret to you."

In reply Lakshmi remarked what a wicked world it was and related to him in detail the conspiracy that was going on in the house against her. He said : "Fear not, my child, whatever happens, happens for our good. We shall neither want anything that does not come to us nor reject anything that comes to us. Let things take their own course, for they happen under the direction of God. Besides, what if they enjoy the estates or we, it is all the same to us who are not selfish. Their enjoying is as good as our enjoying. Then why grieve?" Lakshmi murmured : "Father, you are too generous. The world is a wicked world." "My child," said he, "Believe me, there will come a time when you yourself will say that the world is not bad, but it is God. It is all a difference of standpoints ; you will know it all in due time." Then he related to her what happened at Madura and she expressed great sympathy for Rukmani and wept a little on her behalf. Then he told her of the commission with which he had been entrusted and took leave of her after a few hours stay there, bidding her take heart, and remember him when she was tempted to put an end to her life. He touchingly added : "Live at least for me, do not desert your poor father and make me helpless." And he left Dindigul in the very next train that went northward.

————

XVI

IN SEARCH OF A GURU

IT was noon time at Trichinopoly and the sun was exceedingly hot when a young man was climbing up the rock and going with great eagerness towards the Temple of Ganesh at its summit. The bare steep rock on which he walked scorched his feet like fire, and he appeared greatly fatigued owing perhaps to want of sleep during the previous night, but still he pushed on. There was an expression of eagerness and hope in his face, and as he walked he recited several stanzas in Tamil, particularly from *Thayumanavar*, expressive of the glory of the *Guru*, perhaps to forget the toil of the ascent but more probably to keep up his religious fervour. He sang :

> My Lord is the Lord of the universe
> My *Guru* is the *Guru* of the universe ;

and pushed on until at last he reached the summit and entered the temple. He went in but did not even see the Image of the God ; the object of his search seemed to be something else, which evidently he did not find there. Then he ran about in all directions shouting forth : "My Lord, my *Gurunath*," and so on but only the echoes gave a reply. He shouted louder still and oftener when a surly voice replied : "What fool is this that shouts in this fashion, 'my lord, my lord.' Is he mad ?"

My readers would easily have guessed who the young man was who was thus shouting at such an hour. Sreenivasan quickly ran towards the voice he heard in response to his shouts, but what was his disappointment when instead of the *Siddha*, his self-elected *Guru*, whom he so eagerly sought, he found an old black *pandaram* wearing a dirty *garua* cloth and resting under a shade waiting for a ball of rice from the food that would be offered to the Deity. Poor Sreenivasan turned away more quickly than he went and flew into the temple, while the *pandaram* who saw him thus run away growled a little and kept quiet without caring to rise and see what the matter was.

Sreenivasan's feelings at the juncture could be more easily imagined than described. He had left his home with the expectation of meeting the *Siddha* at this place, for so he had promised, and the poor youth had taken the train to Trichy fondly believing that his mysterious friend with miraculous powers would do the distance by flying. He had foolishly swallowed up every big lie that had been said of the *Siddha*—such was his anxiety and eagerness to obtain a teacher—and had really fancied that his "*Guru*" was no less than God in human form. He himself did not want the so-called *Siddhis*, flying in the air and the like, but only that freedom from the bondage of *Samsara* which true wisdom brings ; but the *Siddha* had told him that the latter was impossible without the former and that the *Siddhis* were the only signs by which the *gnani* could be discovered. It now clearly struck him that he had been deceived, though he did not know that the *Siddha* had left his father-in-law's house immediately after his own departure and with the gentleman's cash chest. He was sorely troubled in heart and knew not what to do or where to go. He was not willing to return to his father-in-law's house, and he had no house of his own to go to, for he was a poor orphan. He fondly believed for a while that his *Guru* might after all be no cheat, that something might have detained him on the way and that he might yet make his appearance. He did not know that the *Siddha* came to Madura not for the purpose of finding a suitable disciple in his person, but for several others not the least of which was the abduction of his wife and that he was fortunately frustrated in his object by the timely appearance of Vasudeva Sastry and that to make the best of a bad bargain he fled away only with the cash chest.

Sreenivasan stayed the whole day on the rock fasting and every moment expecting the *Siddha*, but the latter did not turn up ; then in the evening he piteously complained of his lot to God Ganesha saying : "Is this the reward for having sought Thee ? Is this the way in which Thou sufferest innocent seekers like me to be deluded ? Great men have said : "Just think of Him only one moment with sincerity and with all your soul ; then He is sure to be at your service. Pronounce His name only once ; and He is yours for ever.' Are they also liars ?" The Image of course made no reply. He then thought that his *Bhakti* was not sincere enough, that he did not love God with his whole soul and he resolved to make penance for obtaining God. The story of Dhruva the infant *Bhakta* came to his mind and he said to himself : "While even that child obtained God by penance, how much more easily should I. Really no one on earth thinks of God. As Sankara has said, 'children are addicted to play, young men to young women and old men to care, but no one desires God.' Yes, I shall from this

moment think of Him and Him alone, think till tears roll
down from my eyes, as many a great sage did of old. I
shall weep in torrents and never rest till I find Him or
at least find a *Guru* who will lead me to him."

He spent the whole night on the rock without sleeping a wink. His body sadly wanted sleep, but he would
not close his eyes and sat muttering. "Siva, Siva, Siva,"
and whenever he felt sleep overtaking him, he hit his leg
with a stone which he held in his hand for the purpose.
In spite of these strong and repeated efforts to keep off
sleep, he slept away unconsciously for over two hours
in the middle of the night and then he suddenly started
up and, finding that he had fallen asleep, he heartily
cursed himself and hit his hands, feet and head with the
stone. Then he resumed his muttering and wept that
he did not love God enough. He was anxious to find
God or at least the *Guru* that will show Him, before the
break of day, so he redoubled his penance saying :
"Gajendra Alwar called God only once when he was
seized by the crocodile and God at once came to his
rescue. But I have called Him more than thousand
times 'Siva, Siva, Siva, but He has not made his appearance, which shows I have not even a ten thousandth
part of the elephant's *Bhakti*. No this won't do." The
day broke but God had not come. But Sreenivasan
did not despair, he increased his austerity, wept and
wept till all his clothes got wetted and fasted the whole
of that day also, expecting every moment that God
would come personally or send one of his messengers ;
but nothing of the kind happened. Then he began to
abuse Him as cruel, unmerciful and so on, but He remained insensible to even abuses.

XVII

VERY ANGRY WITH GOD

AFTER half-past six o'clock in the evening, he felt exceedingly hungry and was unable to endure the torturing sensation. "God is dumb, deaf and blind," he said, "I do not care for Him. Instead of praying to Him I might as well pray to the rock on which I sit." So saying he threw away the stone which he held in his hand to chastise himself with for his want of seriousness and got down slowly with a view to take some supper in some hotel.

In the meanwhile Vasudeva Sastry had come to Trichy and had spent all the day in searching for him in the various hotels and other public places. He had wandered from one end of the town to the other and left no corner, not even small lanes, unsearched. He found nobody who could give him any information about the object of his search and in the evening after sunset he climbed up the rock to see if he may not be found there. He was ascending and Sreenivasan was descending just at the same time. A few seconds more and they would have met, but just then there appeared before him a dark-looking middle-aged man with a strange wild look in his face and beckoning him in a mysterious manner took him away to a retired corner close by.

When Sreenivasan saw the dark-looking man beckoning him in a mysterious manner, his disgust with God abated a little and all his former hopes of finding a *Guru*

705

45

revived in him and he approached the stranger with a
heart wildly beating. The latter looked him straight
in the face for a few minutes and took him farther away
from the common road up the hill and asked him to
direct his attention to a piece of rock that was impend-
ing over their heads. Sreenivasan accordingly looked
at it but found nothing remarkable. "Do you not see,"
the stranger asked, "that the rock has the face of a horse?
well then, know that this is the Kalki Avatar (horse-
incarnation) which is going to appear in the world of
men and work wonders. Keep your eyes steadily fixed
at it for some quarter of an hour and then you will see
certain strange phenomena." Sreenivasan saw not the
slightest resemblance between that rock and a horse,
but yet kept his eyes fixed on it wondering in his heart
if any man could be so foolish as to believe that a rock
would become a man and that an *Avatar*. In the meanwhile his companion kept uttering some strange *Mantras*
accompanied with stranger gestures and occasionally
threw ashes over several parts of Sreenivasan's body
and when he found that he was pretty steadily engaged
with the rock, took a firm hold of his neck by one hand
and with the other began to search his cloth. Sreenivasan
was shocked at such a sudden attempt at robbery and
by giving severe blows on the head and the face of the
stranger, forced him, with some difficulty, to loosen his
grip and then kicked him down saying "Aye, this is
Kalki Avatar. You rogue, you thief, I shall blow your
brains out." But before he could do anything, the
would-be-robber had fled. At once Sreenivasan said to
himself, "What is the use of pursuing that fellow? It
is not his doing; not an atom in the universe moves,

they the so-called sages say, except at God's bidding. So it is really the wicked rogue above the sky, that cruel sneseless despot whom so many pray to, only for breaking their hearts, it is that fellow that is to blame. All this is my fault that I should have left home, wife and happiness only to be made a fool of by this monster! It is all unbearable nonsense. I shall no more think of him and weep to him like a beggar. Ah! that cursed *Siddha*, that rogue. If I should see him, I would send him at once to the netherworld. No more then of God, *Siddha* and such foolish things. Come pleasure, come midnight revels, come dancing girls, come fruits, flowers and sweetmeats. Aye, I am very near Srirangam the dancing girls of which place are famous all over the world. I shall take my supper in a hotel and repair at once to that place and make the best use of this moonlight night. So saying to himself he went to a public hotel and then after a very refreshing supper hired a carriage and left for Srirangam which is only a short distance from Trichinopoly.

XVIII

SASTRY IN SAMADHI

THE temple upon the rock at Trichinopoly though comparatively small, is one of the neatest temples in Southern India. When one enters into it one leaves far below the bustle and noise of the town along with its dirt which is so great a feature of its streets and finds it possible to be alone with God at least for a few seconds. Apart from its *puranic* sanctity and very agreeable appearance, there is one inspiring circumstance connected with it which at least to my mind is of greater value than all its other associations and that is that the great sage of the Tamil land *Thayumanavar*, named after the God of that temple practised *Samadhi* and attained the bliss of realisation there within its sacred walls. Into this sacred and inspiring temple Vasudeva Sastry went hoping to find Sreenivasan there, but when he entered into it he forgot himself in that ineffable ecstasy of Self-realisation which Thayumanavar and others enjoyed, and instead of Sreenivasan the son-in-law of Narayana Iyer, he found the real Sreenivasan (*Para Brahman*), the prototype of the former and indeed of everything else in the universe. After a long time he came to his earthly self and looked about for the object of his search, but not finding him there, descended into the town and by chance went to the same hotel which Sreenivasan had just left. A casual talk after supper with another guest in that messing house brought to light that a young man of the description

of Sreenivasan had just left from that place for Srirangam
apparently on a pleasure trip. Vasudeva Sastry could
not believe that the person of whom his acquaintance
spoke could be Sreenivasan who was not given to such
habits of revel, though the description tallied in every
particular with that young man's form and appearance.
He however desired to try and find out the thing for
himself and so took a carriage and went to Srirangam.

It was a beautiful moonlight night and the grand
tower of Srirangam temple which is one of the biggest
and most ancient temples in Southern India and the
most sacred place of pilgrimage for the *Vaishnavites* of
the south was visible in all its glory at a long distance.
In the clear moonlight it looked like an angel standing
from earth to heaven and proclaiming to the pious world :
"Here, here is the Great God Ranganatha sleeping and,
yet ruling all the universe with its starry abundance
and countless lives of all kinds numbering infinity to
the power of two." Sreenivasan when he passed by
that tower was struck with its grandeur and sanctity
but being angry with God, he made up his mind not to
be impressed by it, and poured forth a volley of abuses
on the innocent God within, who enjoying a dreamless
sleep did not, perhaps, hear them. Only half an hour
after our young friend passed through it honouring it
with a crown of thorns in the shape of abuses, Vasudeva
Sastry also came to that spot and gently requesting the
jatka-driver to stop, alighted out of the carriage, and
looking up at the huge tower which stood rooted on
earth and aspiring to heaven (like himself) and proclaimed the glory of the sacred *Sesha Sayana*[1] within,

[1] For the meaning of Sesha Sayana see Part IV, "Ranganatha".

which is one of the grandest symbolic representations of the indescribable Father of us all. "O God," he exclaimed, "Who art sleeping for the ignorant and misguided but art wakeful for devotees and sages, Who by Thy mere breath controllest even the stars in heaven, sleeping, ruleth all this universe, whose only temple and only home is the milky ocean of which the sages drink but never get satiated, O God, Thou art the Inner Ruler within me, nay, my own self." Thus addressing a few words which welled up from a heart too full for words, he stood rooted to the ground like the tower before him, but in a moment passed far beyond the tower and even the planets that rolled in heaven, and himself slept for a while like the sleeping God before him in the Milky Sea and upon the thousand headed *Adisesha* without having even so slight a difference between himself and God as to say : "I am Thou and Thou art I." After a few minutes of such *silent worship*, he again got up in the carriage and drove along the broad streets. He did not know where exactly to go, but he saw at a short distance a magnificent marriage pandal and heard sweet strains of music. At once he got down, and sending away the carriage, went on foot to the pandal where he thought that Sreenivasan might perhaps be found.

XIX

MOONLIGHT REVELS

THE gathering was very large, and in the middle of a wrapt audience there sat singing a young girl of twenty, one of the fairest of her sex. The proportions of her frame were exquisite, and her bosom swelled voluptuously. Her face was bright like the moon and even more enchanting; her beetle-black hair which had been artistically entwined and folded up, was, as it were, the mystic home of that mysterious and *mischievous* God of Love. The silk dress which she wore and the way in which she wore it set out her beauty and surprisingly heightened the charms of her person. Her eyes were at once sweet like honey and poisonous like, and even more dangerous than, the deadliest venom, for they had the power to kill by their very sight. Her magnificently rounded arms bespoke the bloom of health and youth, and the voice which passed through her coral lips was most charming. It was so rich, so sweet, so gentle and at the same time so powerful. It was natural music and would shame the flute and the *Vina*, and with this music of a voice every syllable of which was a song, she sang so exquisitely, so nectar-like that the whole audience sat wrapt in admiration and worship as if bound by the *Mohanastra*.

Outside the pandal, the moonlight—the only privilege which our poor India continues to enjoy from ancient times—was splendid and it looked as if the whole world had been renewed and illuminated by celestial machinery

for the nuptials of the God of Love himself. It was so
delightful and enchanting, that the universe forgetting
its petty toils and turmoils of the day, seemed filled with
self-conscious rapture and the few stars that were visible—
others had drowned themselves in the flood of light—
appeared like so many "gems of purest ray serene", the
treasures of the Gods above. That day Heaven came down
to the earth and clasped it in one rapturous embrace.
Everywhere there was rejoicing, and the young fairy-
like girl in the marriage pandal, sat scattering heaven
around her, by pouring forth silvery strains of music
to match the magic moon above. The concert had just
begun, when Sreenivasan came to Srirangam and when he
saw the marriage pandal and heard the singing, he blessed
his stars and rejoicing, entered into the assembly. But
who can describe his feelings, when he saw the singer
herself, who, taking him for an influential gentleman,
rose on his approach and "pouring the magic of her gaze"
upon his admiring eyes, saluted him. He took his seat
near her and said to himself, "Here is Heaven and nowhere else ! Ah, how foolishly men torture their bodies
and minds to perceive a dim light within their hearts—
which after all, is but a creation of their own hypnotised
fancy, while there is such an angelic light in the world !
What idiots they should be, who close their eyes and
ears to hear a dull and monotonous sound—which after
all, is but the result of hunger and nervous debility—
while there is such celestial music available here ! What
fools to fly away into lonely forests, when there are such
queens of love living in our midst ! Perhaps those poor
creatures only shun what they cannot get, like the jackal
which despised the grapes as sour, because they were

beyond its reach, or more probably they do penance to obtain such fairies, at least in a future life. Who can describe her beautiful form, how divinely exquisite her song? I dare say the poet had a similar angel in his mind when he sang:

> As the moon's soft splendour
> O'er the faint cold starlight of heaven
> Is thrown,
> So thy voice most tender
> To the strings without soul has given
> Its own.
> Though the sound overpowers,
> Sing again, with thy sweet voice revealing
> A tone
> Of some world far from ours,
> Where music and moonlight and feeling
> Are one.

When Sreenivasan was in this ecstatic condition, Vasudeva Sastry came to the pandal, and the first person that naturally met his eyes was Janaki, that was the name of the dancing girl, but on seeing her, his mind was filled with pity for that poor girl. "So beautiful and accomplished, only to be so immoral and dangerous," he said to himself, "if only she could sing of God with one tenth of this sweetness and inspire her hearers with one hundredth of the love and admiration with which they regard her person! O Lord, this is thy *Maya*. Let it go on. Thou art Thyself the dancing girl, the audience, the marriage party and myself and yet we appear not to know Thee and feel as if we are something different from Thee." These thoughts led him inward into the sacred shrine of his Self, the music serving as a sweet lullaby for him while he slept in the cradle of *Brahmananda*. The silent music of the Self, and the moonlight that ever shines within, all unaffected by the clouds of grief and joy, these were sweeter and more enchanting to him than the songs of Janaki or her beautiful charming face, and he woke only when the company was about to break up. He had slept so long, though he was surprised when the party ended, that it did so soon. He then looked about for Sreenivasan in all directions and even thought that he saw him, but the crowd was so great and broke up so rapidly, people going out by several ways, that he was not able to pursue him. Sreenivasan himself actually caught a sight of Vasudeva Sastry and startled darted out of the pandal after the dancing girl, decidedly preferring her and her love to the *Vedantin* and the wisdom he could impart. But just then, *under the inspiration of the fallen archangel,* a strange idea possessed his mind, which was that he should, that very night, secure the services of Janaki and bribe her somehow to allure the Sastry into the net of her love and cast to the winds his *Vedanta* and *Jnana.* Here was the best opportunity, he thought, to prove the hollowness and insufficiency of the *Vedanta.* "*Vedanta* is well and good," he exultingly said to himself, "when a man is poor and miserable and cruelly treated by a quarrelsome wife, but who can think of God, heaven and all that nonsense when there is Janaki ready to spring into his arms. Even great men like Visvamitra, Parasara and others have been brought back to carnality and lust, by the nameless power of woman and it will be a good joke if I can catch hold of the Sastri and expose his *Vedanta* when he is pillowed on Janaki's bosom. The idea is excellent, I shall at once put it into execution."

Thus thinking, he retraced his steps and stealthily followed the saintly Sastry, who, it having got late in the night, had to put off his search for the morning and laid himself down for sleep on the bare pial of a house in the Brahmin Street. Seeing him take bed and marking the house, Sreenivasan fled up to Janaki's residence even before she reached it, and there made an engagement for a night's stay with her, paying a considerable sum of money to her old grandmother with whom the contract was made.

Janaki returned home in very high spirits, a result of the encomiums which had been unstintingly showered upon her by her entertainers and the presents with which she had been loaded. On her way home, she heard everybody talk only of her beauty and music, and all the streets rang with praises of herself. Even the trees and houses seemed to her to sing her praises. She was all in a flutter, and, as she walked, her feet were barely on the ground and the head seemed to her to touch the very stars. As soon as she came home, her toothless, eyeless, hump-backed old grandmother who had once been a mischievous beauty and now an extinct volcano, took her in her arms, and covering her over with kisses, told her of an engagement she had made for her, adding the "Brahmin boy is a very rich fellow and looks like a prince and has given an enormous sum of money." To assure her of the truth of what she said, she clinked the coins which produced a jingling sound so delightful to the ears of dancing girls.

In the meanwhile, Sreenivasan had been conducted by a handsome maid into a spacious bed-chamber, which was decorated with objectionable pictures of all sorts, large mirrors, massive lustre lights and furnished with ebony chairs, ornamental sofas, stately spring cots, silken mattresses and cushions and things of the kind. The incense of sandal sticks and the offering of milk, fruits, cakes and flowers, were all kept ready for *Manmathapuja*, the propitiation of the God of Love. Sreenivasan looked at himself in the mirror and was delighted with his personal appearance. Though a young man, he had a very stately and dignified look about him, which inspired those that came near him with respect and sometimes even with awe. He had never before gone into a dancing girl's house, so his heart beat violently, and in spite of the Epicurean philosophy which he had taught himself, after his vain search for God, he was not able to lull it into approving submission. There was, however, the other idea that he was doing, nothing for himself, but ony endeavoured to betray the hollowness of another man's professions, which gave him some comfort. He was turning within his mind the *pros* and *cons* of his action and considering the ethics of his position, when all of a sudden the door opened, and with tinkling feet and singing a gentle tune, there sprang into the room Janaki, a thousand times fairer than she had looked in the pandal, in a robe of muslin, which more revealed her limbs than hid them ; and then, as if surprised by the presence of a stranger in her room, she stood aside, her face wearing an expression of infinite modesty and shyness. Sreenivasan was transported with joy at her entrance and stood speechless with admiration and nervously shaking from head to foot.

———

XX

SASTRY STANDS THE TEST

ABOUT an hour after, an Iyengar Brahmin was gently
rousing Vasudeva Sastry from his sleep ; the Sastry
woke and was told that the house on whose pial he slept
being a prostitute's, it was not good for him to sleep
there. Besides, the weather was very chill and he lay
on the bare ground. On these pleas the Brahmin
offered to take him to his house and provide him with
bed, pillows and shawl. Sastry at first declined the
offer, but so polite and pressing was the solicitation
that he accepted it and followed the Brahmin to what
he supposed his house. But what was his surprise,
when all of a sudden, he found himself in a brilliantly
decorated bed-room, which evidently appeared to be a
dancing girl's and the door was fastened behind him.
"A very strange ruse," he cried, and repeatedly knocked
at the door but no one seemed to hear him. A dead
silence seemed to prevail in the house. He was, as it
were, in an enchanted chamber in which he hardly knew
what to do and from which he found no possibility of
getting out. More than half an hour elapsed in this
manner, and he thinking no more of his situation and
resigning himself to God, laid himself down on the *floor*
and began to sleep. When lo, all of a sudden sweet
strains of music are heard in praise of Ganesa, Siva and
Vishnu and expressive of the loftiest conceivable sentiments. He hears the music, but cannot see whence
it proceeds. He looks above, below and on all sides,

but to no purpose, and then turns inward to meditate on the sense of the songs. All of a sudden he hears something like a curtain move. He eagerly looks up, then silence for about five minutes. Then the same sound is repeated. He looks up and again sees nothing. The music gets brisker, sweet odours fill the air, the tinkling of anklets and bracelets is heard and all of a sudden up rises a curtain and lo, there gently dances a fairy-like damsel, clad like Goddess Saraswati, in a snow-white gown and garlanded with a lotus wreath, with a diamond necklace trembling on her breast and profusely and yet very cunningly decorated from head to foot with pearls, diamonds, rubies and gold, a transcendental vision whose beauty is heightened by the moon-like light of lamps fed with magnesium. The music and dancing get brisker, and the mysterious fairy-form dancing, comes nearer and nearer the surprised Sastry. Now she has come very near, there is only a foot's distance netween the bewildered *Vedantin* and the angelic vision. *He gets up to leave the room but finds not the way.* "What is this? I have been treacherously brought into a dancing girl's house, and the girl before me seems to be the same who sang in that marriage pandal. By whose contrivance have I been brought here?" he asks himself, but answer finds none In the meanwhile, the beautiful Janaki, for that was the girl, gently took hold of his hand and impressed upon it a warm kiss.

"I accept your kiss," said Vasudeva Sastry with a peculiarly tender look in his eyes and gently withdrawing his hand, "as that of a daughter, and I have as much love to you as any father has to his daughter, but at the same time feel extremely sorry that such beauty and such accomplishments should be put to auction every day and placed at the disposal of the highest bidder. Certainly you cannot be a bad girl, for your features indicate a good heart and the music you sang this night in the marriage pandal can certainly not belong to an inherently wicked nature. Such music can never come out except from an excellent heart and such beauty can never mask real wickedness. In spite of your present behaviour, there is a gentle modesty in your face which belies your profession and clearly proves that whatever immortality you have been guilty of, must have been the result of circumstances, and very much against your nature and disposition. Besides, the songs which you just now sang seemed inspired, so, they could not have proceeded wholly from thy lips. My daughter, I really wish to know if you sincerely like the profession in which you are engaged. Speak the truth, for, with me, you need have no fear." Poor Janaki was thunderstruck. She had never heard words like these in all her life, so full of love and sincerity and meant so much for her own good. She felt the delicacy with which the reproof was made and was surprised to find that her real heart had been found out under the mask she wore ; her first impulse was to fall at the Sastry's feet and make a clean confession in true filial style, but on further consideration she thought it necessary under the circumstances to proceed with her temptation and this she did with added interest, for she herself became curious to know if the Sastry was really so far above passion as to be unmindful of the unrivalled charms of her person which as far as she knew overpowered and enslaved in an instant all that saw her.

"Alone with me and at this time of the night and seriously advise me to give up my profession!" she said to herself and began her attack more vigorously than before. She pressed his face warmly to hers and smothered him with kisses making his cheeks red and pale by turns with a never failing variety, "ten kisses long as one and one long as twenty." Sastry, however, was utterly frosty in desires and sat still like a statue. Janaki, however, did not despair. She gently entwined herself round him as a jasmine creeper does a margosa tree, played all sorts of *petty* tricks with him and said a thousand *soft nothings*. Still the Sastry remained unmoved. Even then Janaki did not desist. Her wonder at the strange conduct of the Sastry increased and this gave fresh zest to her attack. She rellied, caressed, jested, smiled, frowned, embraced and kissed, but all in vain. One full hour had elapsed in this manner, but not the slightest impression had been made upon Vasudeva Sastry, who sat all the while motionless like a marble figure : and then when all her arts were exhausted and she began to tire, he said : "Do you see, Janaki, for that is the name by which people were talking of you in the streets. I seriously mean what I say and really look upon you as a daughter of mine. All your conjuring arts were to me like the sports of children and all the while I was only laughing within myself at your *powerless* tricks. Whose base coin is it that has bought you to play such tricks on me ? *Women's charms have no more power over the true lovers of God than the sparks of a furnace have over the cold sea.* And in your case, especially, I am filled with pity and really grieve that such beauty and accomplishments should suffer such a fate. I know enough of the world to see that your heart is much greater than your conduct and that your whole appearance is an unwilling lie to yourself."

All this while, Janaki was standing mute with astonishment, grief and fear, astonishment at the supreme indifference of the man to her temptation, grief at her own poor and despicable lot, and fear that the man before her might be a great *Yogi* and think of cursing her for her impudence. "Dear Janaki, daughter," continued Vasudeva Sastry, "can you not abandon this low profession, and marrying some suitable husband, settle in life in a way which would better suit your character and virtues; your broad and elevated forehead indicates a lofty intellect and the space between the two arches of your eyebrows tells of innate spirituality. Your clear countenance is like that of an innocent child, so sweet and blissful. Your lustrous black eyes indicate thought, penetration and quick apprehension. Besides, there is a coolness in your sight, worthy of a sage who holds communion with God. Your voice itself has a rich hymnal ring about it and whatever you sing seems to come from a world much better than ours. Your whole beauty is angelic and instead of exciting lust, creates love, and a strange sympathetic regard for you which borders on veneration. You are certainly meant for much higher things than playing a prostitute's part and unless you are addicted to that profession which I feel certain you are not, I would advise you as a father does a daughter to look up and travel into a walk of life where more of happiness and peace will fall to your

46

lot; where your innumerable accomplishments will
shine to better advantage." Janaki could no longer
restrain her feeling and she burst out with pathetic
sincerity, "You are my father, since I do not know mine
own, nor even my mother, for I was not really born to
this wretched profession, but I believe was kidnapped
while very young and forced into this life—both father
and mother you are to me, none but a real parent would
have spoken like this. This night will mark a turning
point in my life and from this moment, believe me, I
am no more a dancing girl but a daughter of the man
who sits before me and to whose goodness and holiness
I am indebted more than to any other man or woman
in the world. Though in simple plain clothes, you seem
to me to be a *Rishi*. I have read in books that Suka
passed along a tank where the damsels of Heaven were
bathing naked, without even caring to cast a look at
them and with a mind all undisturbed, but I thought
it was a story. To my great joy and astonishment I
see an ordinary looking middle aged man, robust and
muscular, who can afford to be indifferent to the charms
of one of the fairest of her sex and sitting unmoved like
a marble statue in spite of all my kisses and embraces
and numberless other temptations." "I request your
holiness," she continued, falling at his feet and bathing
them with tears, "to forgive my impudence though
unpardonable. You had it in your power to withstand
my follies. You may, if you will, turn me into a black
stone by a single word, but I entreat you, beg you, to
be merciful to a poor creature whose birth and parentage
are unsolved riddles to herself, who is a poor forlorn
creature forced into a wretched life by the intrigues of

wicked women. Dear father, I beg you again and again to forget all the silly things I did to-night and treat me in every respect your own daughter, and if there is any that already stands to you in that blessed relation, let me be her sister. Before morning I shall leave this abode of iniquity and follow you like a spaniel even beyond the seas. You are my teacher, my deliverer, my father, my God, and I look up to you alone for help and guidance. I can see that you are no ordinary man, and by your side I look like a worm that crawls on earth, a glowworm compared with a star. Save me, O Save me, Lord." Janaki spoke these words with such vehemence, sincerity and eloquence that Vasudeva Sastry was moved to tears. Such was the pathos of the occasion that even the stone walls there, *had they only heard her*, would have melted away in grief. Our Sastry wiped away his tears and looking at Janaki whose face bathed in tears was like the moon reflected in a deep flood, said : "Dear girl, you are a thousand times dearer to me now than when I first saw you. I never thought that such a gay hall would contain so repentant a heart."

Just then there rushed out a figure from behind the curtain crying out: "O, it contains another one equally repentant though not possessing one-tenth, one hundredth of the nobility of this angel's heart. Forget and forgive, my lord, one who should have known better and who is filled with shame at his own conduct. I am a wretch, a villain, and a fool and crave your mighty mercy. Save me, O Lord, from this moment, you are my master. So, save me."

*   *   *

IX

MISCELLANEOUS STORIES

I

THE BEACH

THE cuckoo on the Margosa tree just by my room sweetly announced to sleep, the softest and the most soothing nurse of all living beings, that her Mistress, Night, is to take her departure very soon, as she has to visit other parched-up and hot places that want her cooling presence very much and that it was time for her also to be ready to follow in her train. At this warning she gradually and imperceptibly left me in my bed, who finding myself thus left alone rolled hither and thither upon it, for a while, in search of her but found her not and so unwillingly rose up from it at last. By this time other busy bodies such as cocks, crows, rooks and some sweet-singing birds too with various sounds served to shake off my drowsiness, and immediately after, I too caught their freshness, hilarity and joy. Anon I jumped out of my bed, and after washing my hands and face dressed myself to take a walk on the beach.

The beach of Madras! What a splendid place it is! The abode of cool and refreshing sea-breeze, commanding a prospect of vast illimitable ocean on the one side and the best and the most picturesque row of buildings which Madras can boast of on the other side, together with as picturesque a part called Marina, the beach serves at once to fill a man with ecstasy who is fortunate enough to take a walk in the morning over it. For a time the mind forgets all worldly concernments and

727

the thoughtlessness of childhood is again there with buoyancy of spirit. Man feels for a time that the world is a place of enjoyment, and almost disbelieves those sages who decry all sorts of the pleasures of the world.

I was in such a mood of mind when suddenly I saw before me one of my Iyengar friends, accompanied by another of his own class whom I did not know. We there joined together and my friend introduced me to his companion. We began to talk at random. In course of our conversation the new friend gave out his opinion that he could not believe all what men say about God. "For my part," he said, "God is unknown and unknowable. So we should give up the matter altogether. What is the use of troubling ourselves about what we can know nothing of?" Then turning to me he said, "Sir, do you believe in God?"

"Why? Yes," was my reply. "Then what is God?" asked he.

"*God is what resists your desire and leads you as well as the whole universe, without being resisted.*"

"A very curious definition indeed!"

"May be. If there was nothing to resist you in any way, I would have called you God. God is free to do anything. There is nothing to resist God, and so we call that Power Almighty. But since that is not the case with you, since at every step you get resistance from all sides, you are fully under the control of all things other than yourself, *i.e.*, your environments; and the combination of all those other things we call God." At this he said:

"Now suppose I am blind and have a strong desire to go to Mylapore to see a certain dear friend of mine, and I am poor and helpless. Here blindness, poverty, helplessness resist my desire and prevent its fulfilment. Therefore according to you the combination of blindness, poverty and helplessness is God." To this I replied:

"If I say x is equal to $a+b+c+d+e+etc.$, *ad infinitum*, would it be proper for me to say x is equal to a or b or c taken separately? It reminds me of the story of the blind men and the elephant. Some blind men wanted to see an elephant. So one after another they were admitted into the place where the elephant was. The first man touched the trunk of the elephant, and feeling it all through, was satisfied with his knowledge of the elephant, by concluding it to be like a thick club. The second touched similarly the ear of the elephant and feeling it all through, concluded that the animal was like a big winnowing basket. The third touched the belly and concluded it to be like a big basin of water. The fourth touched one of the legs and concluded it to be like a pillar. Now as each one was imparting his knowledge of the elephant to the other three, a quarrel ensued amongst them, for they could not agree with one another, till a man came in, who was not blind and convinced them of their error. It is as absurd to describe God as the combination of blindness, poverty and helplessness as it is absurd to describe an elephant as a thick club. Because your parents and superiors resist your desire in many instances, they are therefore not the whole of God, because society and Government resist you similarly, therefore they are not God in themselves, because another man more powerful, more intelligent, more learned resists you, he is not God on that account. *God is the whole resisting power taken in its entirety."*

"But," rejoined the other, "when we look at an elephant we do not always look upon the whole of its body. We sometimes look at its trunk, sometimes look at its ears and compare them with other things of a similar nature; do we not? Similarly we have full right to look at the different phases of this God of yours and pass our judgments on those phases. This being granted, when we see a widow is deprived of her only child and cast helplessly into the world to perish in the extreme agony of bereavement, is that not very cruel of that power which you call God? And should we serve such a cruel Master?"

"Will or nil you are bound to serve inasmuch as you are completely under Its control, for you cannot deny the resistance which you get from all sides. But this Power appears to you to be cruel when you look upon only one side of It forgetting Its other sides of which this side is a connecting link. As when you simply look upon a portion of the ear of the elephant, it appears to be very ugly, but seen with the whole body, there is no such ugliness. Parents sometimes whip their children. Whipping itself is very ugly, but when we consider the motive of the parents we cannot but praise it. Government hangs a culprit. Now hanging is very nasty and cruel. But the fellow hanged has lately butchered his wife and children. When you know this, does his hanging appear to you to be nasty and cruel at all? So you see what appears to be apparently cruel, may really be not so if you dive deep into the matter."

"But in the cases you have cited," answered my

friend, "the children are wicked and the man is a culprit. As for the widow I am speaking of, she is generally reputed to be a very pious woman. Is the sorrow for the loss of her child the fruit of her piety?"

"No, certainly not. *That is the fruit of her ignorance, and want of piety.* If her devotion and love towards her God were greater than that towards her child then she could not feel the bereavement at all, but on the contrary she would be rather grateful to her Lord for removing her bondage and impediment. But as that Almighty Power does not like that the pious woman should be in darkness of ignorance, It has taken away the child which virtually belongs to It, for through Its influence alone the child came into existence, to its own sire. It is through mistake we call our own what really is not our own. So in order to dispel that mistake It has taken away the child from the widow. She may weep for a few days, but after that period she will find consolation in herself, knowing it for certain that the child was not hers but God's, and that there is nothing else permanent save God, and so if she places her love in God there is no fear of further bereavement, whereas if it be placed in things other than God, there is every chance of separation."

At this the other cried out: "What! children are impediments in the path of virtue! Those sweet innocent cherubs that make this otherwise miserable world an abode of happiness and joy to all men—are they to be considered as barriers on our way? They rather serve to give us joy and vigour in our tedious journeys through the world."

"No, no, they are not barriers, *so long as they do not*

occupy that place in our heart which we should allot to the Power we call God, that Eternal and Great Being—the greatest of all existing things, for by definition everything is under the control of God. As the maid servant of a wealthy man nurses the children of her master, and acts as a second mother to them, chastising them if they do anything wrong, coaxing and caressing them to sleep, and doing sundry other motherly services to them, but all the while knowing that the children are not hers but her master's; so if a man or woman look upon his or her children as the children of God and that he or she is simply a servant employed by God for their sake, then there will be no bondage. All things will go on smoothly." This was my reply.

The other asked : "But then why should your God, create pain, sorrow, anguish, folly, ignorance and all such things at all. As you say that your God is Almighty, He could easily do away with all those nasty things and make this world a place of incessant bliss. There is no necessity of teaching through the process of flogging."

To this I replied : "You may hate pain, sorrow, anguish, folly, ignorance, etc., but, of course, you love pleasure, jollity, enjoyment, knowledge and all such good things. Don't you ?"

"There is no doubt about it," was the quick reply.

"Well, my dear sir," said I, "there can be no pleasure without pain, no knowledge without ignorance."

"Strange ! How can that be ?" questioned he.

To which I replied : "Just imagine one incessant course of uniform pleasure without any break ; since by the hypothesis there is no break in the uniform course, you won't be able to compare your present state of happiness with any intermediate state, and in that case you will not be able to know whether that state is a happy state or not, for we think ourselves happy when we compare our state of happiness with a previous state of inferior happiness, *i.e.*, happiness .mingled with a little bit of pain, and the greater the pain you feel, the greater the enjoyment of happiness you will get in return, for by comparison alone you will come to know how miserable you were and how happy now you are. A hungry man relishes his food much more than one who has not so much hunger. Similar is the case with knowledge and ignorance. You can only know that you are more learned when you compare notes with your past school career. So you see that if you want to enjoy bliss, the pleasure of knowledge and all such good things, you will have to take pain, ignorance, etc., along with them, too. Pleasure and pain are the two sides of the same thing. You cannot take pleasure without pain, nor pain without pleasure. Therefore your idea of a world where there is perpetual, intense and uniform happiness, falls to the ground."

"But do they not tell of a place called Heaven where Indra reigns? and is that not full of bliss perennial? How can you account for that? Do you believe that your Scriptures simply imagine some false impossibilities?" inquired he.

"Why—no. Those who share in the bliss of Heaven, remember their past miseries in the world, and because they have the previous experiences of great miseries they can supremely enjoy the pleasures of Heaven by comparing them with their past miserable lives on the

Earth." Such was my reply, at which he turned the course of our talk by saying: "Very well. Let us return to our old question. You said God is the combination of all that resists our desire and by so doing leads us. It is a sort of antipower as regards ourselves, which is ever free and therefore almighty and always resisting without being resisted. Has that Power any intelligence? Can it feel as we do?" To this my answer was, "Look into the workings of that Energy. Are they not orderly and regular? Can order and regularity come out of non-intelligence? Look at the flowers. How tastefully they are made! Look at the beauties of Nature. How sweetly they are spread before you for your enjoyment! Can they proceed from a Being that has neither feeling nor taste? Look at your own Self. You are nothing but as the Power is making you. It is gradually lifting you up from the lowly basement of ignorance to the exalted pinnacle of knowledge. It is making you more and more unselfish, more and more noble, more and more intelligent, more and more pious, as you grow more and more old. If you dive deep into the workings of this Power, you will gradually see that It is really bringing you up with a thousand times more care and love than what your parents can command."

At this he asked: "How can that be, since this Power resists my desires, whereas my parents love me and readily give me whatever I ask of them?" At this I questioned him in return, "Do your parents not resist you too, when your desires tend towards evil? The senses are the causes of our desire. Unless those desires be checked, we shall be led hither and thither by the senses, which are always misleading, for they confirm us in our error of seeing as permanent, things which are impermanent. So you see that by checking desires, errors are checked. Is that not a great benefit? By timely resistance from this Power we are brought to a proper sense of our real position."

"But," replied he, "the Scriptures attribute to the Power we are speaking of, which you call God, many beautiful male and female forms. How can you account for that? As far as I have understood you, that Power can have no such form, or, if It has any, it is the whole universe. The whole universe is the body of that infinite Power. It cannot be called either male or female, but males and females and all things proceed from It."

"Well, I see you have hit upon the universal Form of the Lord," I replied, "but did I not tell you that that Power is a thousand times more loving than your parents and is the repository of all sorts of powers and that there is none to resist It? This being the case, and it being the more natural the more easy and more attractive for us to know It as our own dearest, most beautiful, most loving and nearest of all friends and relatives in the universe, we naturally look upon It as such and It becomes the most loving He or She, at least for our sake, for, what is impossible for an Almighty All-merciful and All-loving Power? So you see He (henceforth we should not call Him It) cannot be altogether unknown and unknowable. His very loving and kind nature disproves this. When those spotless pure children of Nature, the Sages and *Rishis* of yore, ardently desired to see their unseen Father, their unseen Mother that was supplying them with all their little wants, was keeping them from all unforeseen dangers, was decorating their Sylvan abodes with exquisitely beautiful and divinely fragrant flowers, was entertaining them daily with the melodies poured forth from the throats of Nature's sweet choristers, the gaudily-dressed and clear-voiced merry denizens of the air, that Father or that Mother could not conceal Himself or Herself longer and appeared before them as Brahma, Vishnu or Siva, as Saraswati, Lakshmi or Durga. So you see our Scriptures are nothing but a record of Divine grace poured forth at different times on different fortunate and pure-hearted individuals. These men are the authors of our Scriptures. They knew *something* of God, and what they knew they recorded for the benefit of posterity."

The friend replied : "Well, it may be, if your God is really loving and kind. In that case I cannot deny that, although I have much doubt about His loving kindness. But to return : you just now said that desires lead men to error. So according to you, therefore, the giving up of desire is the best means to escape from the grip of error." To this I answered : "Yes. Moreover if you have no desire you will not experience any resistance from the hand of God. A permanent peace will be established between God and yourself, *i.e.*, your interest will be blended with the interest of God. Your ideas will be His ideas and *vice versa*, *i.e.*, you will lose your own self in His self, as a river loses itself in the ocean."

By this time the Sun had lifted himself up a considerable way above the horizon and was sending over us some of his lusty rays through the branches of the trees to remind us that we should go home and take upon ourselves the shares of our daily duties. Thus we departed.

———

II

MONISM QUALIFIED AND PURE

A CERTAIN philosopher belonging to the School of Qualified Monism, or, what is called the Realistic School of the *Vedanta*, went to a great sage worshipped by the people as a *Brahmagnani*, one who had realised the Self, and challenged him to a philosophical discussion. The sage coolly replied : "Your trouble is unnecessary. I am ready to give you what you want." And so saying he took a bit of paper wrote down on it with his own hand that he was defeated by such and such a philosopher and handed it over to the latter, who was overjoyed at the ready admission of his superior abilities. He at once placed the valuable document securely in his bag and proceeded to bid goodbye to the sage.

Just then the latter asked him : "What use are you going to make of the paper ?"

He replied : "I am going to show it to all the *adwaitins* in the land, and they, seeing that you yourself have admitted my superiority will, I am sure, do the same themselves."

Sage : "It is true I have confessed myself defeated, but I would very much like to know if you derived your knowledge of *adwaita* from *adwaitic* works or from the criticisms of it contained in *visishtadwaitic* works."

Philosopher : "From the latter, for they give all the necessary information."

Sage : "Your knowledge of *adwaita* may be sound I admit, but will it not be better for you to study it

738

from the original works? For there may be some *adwaitins* who may not yield to you so readily as I have done, and may puzzle you with arguments from the original works on their philosophy which you have not studied. But if you study a little from those works I am sure no one can oppose you."

The realistic philosopher admitted the truth of what the sage said and applied himself with zeal to a study of the important *adwaitic* works. He had not proceeded far, when, to his great surprise, he found that what the qualified monists criticised in the *adwaita* had been criticised by the *adwaitins* themselves at a certain stage. The similes of the serpent in the rope, etc., were, he saw, admitted in *adwaita* to illustrate some particular point, and that done, they had been rejected, whereas the qualified monists noticing this fact had criticised it. He became more and more interested in the study and was devouring books after books of *adwaita* philosophy. Nearly two years elapsed in this way and he did not start on his discussion tour. Seeing this the sage asked him why he had not gone out to discuss, and he replied : *"I see that there is no room for quarrel."*

The object of this story is only to illustrate the insufficiency of second-hand information, and not to set up the superiority of one system of philosophy over the other, for both, if sincerely followed lead to the same goal.

III

THE WILDERNESS OF LIFE

AFTER the great battle of Kurukshetra, in which the blind king Dritarashtra lost all his sons, Vidura approached him and did his utmost to console him. In the course of his discourse, he gave out the following remarkable allegory. A certain Brahmin travelling in a wilderness, found himself in the course of his wanderings in a large and inaccessible forest which was filled with beasts of prey. It abounded on every side with lions, tigers and wild elephants and snakes terribly long and ugly. Wherever he turned, he saw nothing but these terrible creatures, all of which began to run towards him the moment they saw him. The poor man was overwhelmed with fear, his hairs stood on end, and he fled hither and thither in fright, but wherever he went, he found that he was disturbing more and more of the denizens of the forest and thus adding to the number of his ugly foes. Seeing that he was encompassed on all sides and hurt by the thorns and wild plants on the ground, which tore his clothes and skin, he ran with desperate haste when he found that the wild forest was girt by a complicated net and that a terrible woman stood at a short distance before him stretching out her arms and eager to devour him like a *Rakshasi*. Around him were terrible five-headed snakes of dreadful size, which though unable easily to move, yet shot forth terror and defiance from their eyes.

While running to and fro in this terrible forest, the

740

poor and terrified Brahmin suddenly fell into a deep pit, whose mouth was covered with many hard and unwieldy creepers and wild plants. At once he got entangled in those clusters of creepers which were thickly interwoven with one another; and like a large fruit of a jack tree hanging by its stalk, he hung down feet upwards and head downwards. While in this position, he beheld a huge and mighty serpent within the pit, and above near its mouth a gigantic elephant, dark in complexion and six-faced and twelve-footed, gradually approaching the pit. At the mouth of the pit there was a tree, about the branch of which roved many bees of frightful forms employed in drinking the honey of a comb which they had built. As soon as they saw the man in the pit they swarmed round him and began to sting him. At the same time a black and a white rat, were gnawing away the roots of the shrubs on which he hung. While he was in this distressful situation, there fell down from the comb above owing to the disturbance of the bees, a few drops of honey fortunately against his mouth. The man tasting them cried: "Ah! how sweet, how sweet," and eagerly longed for more of it. There was a fear from the beasts of prey, from that fierce woman in the outskirts of that forest, from the snake at the bottom of the pit, from the elephant near its top, from the certainty of the shrubs giving way owing to the action of the rats, and there was the trouble of the bees flying about his face and stinging him. He knew all this, but, instead of trying to get out of the forest, he only longed for more and more of the honey, and every time a drop fell down from the comb, he exclaimed: "Ah, how sweet is life!" and continued to remain in that plight without taking any steps to change it.

At this stage Dritarashtra broke out in surprise. "What! is such foolishness conceivable? Who was that man? Where is the terrible wilderness in which he lost himself? Does he still live, and is there none to rescue him? Is it possible for me to do anything for him? I am greatly moved by your description of the poor man's situation. Is there no hope for him?"

Vidura said: "Those who are conversant with *Moksha Dharma*, the Path of Salvation, cite this as a simile. Understanding this properly, a person may attain to bliss. The Brahmin is not some one different from us and represents ourselves. That which is described as the great wilderness is the world, the deep forest within it is the limited sphere of one's life, the snakes, thorns, tigers, lions and other wild beasts represent the innumerable hardships of transmigratory existence and the diseases to which we are subject. The woman of gigantic proportions residing in the forest is identified by the wise with decrepitude, which destroys complexion, beauty, health and intellect. That which has been spoken of as the pit is the body or the physical frame of embodied creatures. The huge snake at its bottom is Death, the destroyer. The cluster of creepers and plants from which the man hung down stands for the desires which bind man to the body. Brahmin hanging head downwards implies that man, though by virtue of the potentiality in him is the Lord of Creation, yet through his low desires suffers as a victim. The six-faced elephant proceeding towards the tree and standing at the mouth of the pit, represents the year.

Its six faces are the seasons and its twelve feet are the twelve months. The rats black and white that are cutting off the tree, are said to be days and nights which are continually lessening the period of life. The bees denote the incessant worry of life, the vexatious trifles which make us miserable and the drops of honey which now and then fell into the man's mouth, are our little pleasures coming to us in the midst of considerable trouble, but to which we are fatally attached. The wise know life's course to be even such and through that knowledge they succeed in tearing off its bonds."

—From the Mahabharata.

IV

THE SECRET OF DEATH

In the days of Ananthaguna Pandya who ruled over
the Madura kingdom with singular justice, a Brahmin
was going with his wife and child from Tiruppatur to
Madura. Owing to the fatigue of the journey, the
wife felt thirsty and the Brahmin had to leave her in the
cool shade of a tree and himself proceed in search of
water. Just then it so happened that an arrow which
had sometime back got stuck among the leaves of the
tree fell down upon the woman and ended her life.
The Brahmin soon brought water, but finding his wife
pierced with an arrow and dead, set up a loud wailing
and vowed vengeance on the murderer. Looking round
him for finding out the culprit, he saw, within a few
yards of him, a hunter holding a bow in his hand and
with a quiver on his back. At once he ran up to him
and seizing him by the arm charged him with murder.
But the hunter denied that he was the cause of murder
and said that he did not throw any dart either on the
tree or on the woman.

The Brahmin of course, did not believe him, abused
him right and left and wanted him to go with him at
once to the Pandyan Court.

The innocent hunter readily consented and the
Brahmin taking the dead wife on his back and his
weeping child in his arms, set out with the hunter to
Madura. On reaching the palace gate, he laid down the
corpse and set up a tremendous wailing which brought

the king himself out of the palace. "O king," said the Brahmin, "had you been just how could my poor wife have been killed in broad day-light by this villainous hunter, who having doubtless committed the murder refuses even to admit his guilt? Is this justice? Is this how you rule the country? The Pandyan kingdom so long famous—all over the world—has approached its end through your injustice. The Pandyan fame is tarnished once for ever." The king appeased the Brahmin's anger saying (kings were different in those days from what they are now), "O best of Brahmins, grieve not; I shall enquire into the case and with Sundareswara's grace find out the truth and do the needful. My injustice is self-proved, for such a horrible deed has been done in broad day-light and so near my capital; I do not deserve to sit on the throne until I fully enquire into the case and get at the truth." Then he addressed the hunter and said: "If you have committed this act, admit it and it will be good for all of us." The hunter said: "My Lord, I am more surprised than your Majesty that such an occurrence should have transpired in so justly governed a country as thy Majesty's. Your Majesty is unto us as God Sundareswara himself, and in His presence and yours, I swear I know nothing of the cause of this death." Thereupon the king held a formal enquiry into the circumstance of the case, but he could not come at the truth. He then adjourned the enquiry for a subsequent day, placing the hunter in safe custody, and directed the Brahmin to burn the corpse and perform the necessary funeral ceremonies.

In the evening he went to the temple and mentally laid the whole case before the God of gods, Sundareswara. On returning home, he declined supper and lay on the bare ground expecting a vision. His penance had the desired effect, for, towards the morning, God appeared to him in his dream and said : "Go this night with the Brahmin to the Chetty's street outside the town. There you will find a house in which marriage will be going on ; entering the house in disguise, remain there in a corner and then you will know the truth about the Brahminis death." The king rose from his bed satisfied and in the night taking the Brahmin along with him went out disguised as a Chetty, and finding out the marriage house, they both entered into it and sat un-observed in a corner.

Shortly after, they heard voices in the air and looking up found—for they were endued for the occasion by the grace of Sundareswara with celestial vision—that a number of messengers of the God of death had come there and were consulting with one another as to how the life of the bridegroom may be taken away to the abode of Yama. One of them said : "He has no disease, what shall we do?" Another said : "We must try for some contrivance as we did yesterday, by making the arrow, which had long stuck up among the leaves of the tree under which the Brahmin woman was lying, fall upon her and do away with her life." Another said : "We shall likewise contrive to-day to let loose the cow in the yard, make it fall upon the bridegroom and put an end to his life." "A very nice contrivance," said a fourth, "for it is very natural that the cow should get excited with the noise of the drums and other musical instruments which are now playing on the pial." "This is even more clever," said another, "than the contrivance of yesterday's by which we made away with the life of the Brahmin woman." The king looked at the Brahmin who was hearing all this and said : "How innocent is the hunter whom we have brought for trial." The Brahmin said : "Yes even so he is. It was all the work of fate but we shall watch how these messengers of Yama manage their present work."

Hardly had he finished, when a cow rushed into the house and furiously dashed the bridegroom to the ground and ran away. The poor bridegroom was fatally hurt by the fall and immediately became a corpse. The marriage changed into a funeral and the house was filled with mourners. The Brahmin applauded the king for his justice and the divine grace which through his *Punya* he had secured, and humbly begged his pardon for his rash accusation and the trouble he had caused him. It is needless to add that the hunter was set free and liberally compensated for the trouble he underwent. The Brahmin also was given by the generous king a large sum of money for marrying again. The details of the case and the divine manner by which the truth was revealed to the king, were proclaimed throughout the kingdom and a public festival celebrated in honour of God Sundareswara.

The above story is an illustration of the truth that behind the apparent causes with which we satisfy our inquisitiveness, there remains a mystery which it is impossible for us to unravel. We may ascribe things to Time, to Fate, or to *Karma* ; but all that does not slove the problem, but only wards off the inquiry. They are not causes, but only apologies for causes. In the question of death, as much as in that of life, there is an authoritative "Thus far shalt thou go and no farther". How true the saying

> Veil after veil will lift—but there must be
> Veil upon veil behind.

After all, however, life and death are only relatively real, and, as the *Gita* says : "He who thinks that one slays another and he that says that one is slain by another, both of them do not know the truth" (II, 19). So also the *Sruti* : "If the slayer thinks I slay, if the slain thinks I am slain, then both of them do not know well" (*Kath.-Up.*, I, ii, 19). "The wise do not grieve either for the living or for the dead" (*Gita* II, 11).

V

A FOWLER AND A SERPENT

THERE was an old lady of the name of Gautami who was remarkable for her patience and tranquillity of mind. One day she found her son dead in consequence of having been bitten by a serpent. A fowler, by name Arjunaka, bound the serpent with a string, brought it before Gautami and said : "This wicked serpent has been the cause of thy son's death. O blessed lady, tell me quickly how this wretch is to be destroyed! Shall I throw it into the fire or shall I hack it into pieces? This infamous killer of a child does not deserve to live longer."

Gautami replied : "Do thou, O Arjunaka! release this serpent. It doth not deserve death at thy hands. By killing it, this my boy will not be restored to life and by letting it live, no harm will be caused to thee. Who would go to the interminable regions of death by slaying this living creature? Those that make themselves light by the practice of virtue, manage to cross the sea of life, even as a ship crosses the ocean. But those that make themselves heavy with sin, sink into the bottom, even as an arrow thrown into the water."

The fowler :—"I know, O thou lady that knoweth the difference between right and wrong, that the great are afflicted at the afflictions of all creatures. Those who value peace of mind assign everything to the course of Time, but practical men soon assuage their grief by revenge. Therefore, O lady, assuage thy grief by having the serpent destroyed by me."

Gautami :—"People like us are never afflicted by such misfortune. Good men are always intent on virtue, the death of the body was predestined : therefore I am unable to approve of the destruction of this serpent. Brahmins do not harbour resentment, because resentment leads to pain. Do thou, O good man, forgive and release the serpent out of compassion."

The fowler :—"Let us earn great and inexhaustible merit hereafter, by killing this creature, even as a man acquires great merit and confers it on his victim as well, by sacrifice upon the altar. Merit is acquired by killing an enemy; by killing this despicable creature, thou shalt acquire great and true merit hereafter."

Gautami :—"What good is there in tormenting and killing an enemy, and what good is won by not releasing an enemy in our power ? Therefore, O thou of benign countenance, why should we not forgive this serpent and earn merit by releasing it."

The fowler :—"A great number of creatures ought to be protected from the wickedness of this one. Virtuous men abandon the vicious to their doom. Let me therefore kill this wicked creature."

Gautami :—"By killing this serpent, my son, O fowler, will not be restored to life, nor do I see that any other end will be attained by its death ; therefore, do thou, O fowler, release that living creature. It came not into life by our order, nor does it live through our sufferance, we have no right to kill it."

The fowler said :—"Nor had it any right to kill thy child, O sacred mother !"

Gautami :—"The death of my child was a predestined affair, it was the will of God and the serpent was only the instrument. And even granting that it was the real and only cause of my child's death, *its committing a sin will not justify our doing the same.* It fell into error through ignorance and our killing it will be much more than an error : it will be a sin committed with knowledge and therefore wilfully."

The fowler : "By killing Vitra, Indra secured the best portion of sacrificial offering and so also did Mahadeva by destroying a wicked sacrifice : do thou, therefore, destroy this serpent immediately without any misgivings in thy mind."

Although thus repeatedly urged by the fowler for the destruction of the serpent, the high-souled Gautami did not bend her mind to that sinful act. The serpent painfully bound with the cord, sighing a little and maintaining its composure with great difficulty, then uttered these words slowly in human voice.

"O foolish Arjunaka, what fault is there of mine ? I have no will of my own and am not independent ! Mrityu (the God of Death) sent me on this errand ! By his direction have I bitten this child and not out of any anger or choice on my part ; therefore, if there be any sin in this, O fowler, the sin is his."

The fowler said :—"If thou hast done this evil led thereto by another, the sin is thine also, as thou art an instrument in the act. As in the making of an earthen vessel, the potter's wheel and rod and other things are all regarded as causes, so art thou O serpent, a cause in the matter."

The serpent said :—"As the potter's wheel, rod and other things are not independent causes, even so I am not an independent cause ! Therefore this is no fault of mine, nor am I guilty of any sin! Or if thou thinkest that there is sin, it lies in the aggregate of causes."

The fowler said :—"Not deserving of life, O foolish one, why dost thou bandy so many words, O wretch, of a serpent? Thou deservest death at my hands."

The serpent replied :—"O fowler, as the officiating priests at a sacrifice do not acquire the merit of the act, even so should I be regarded with respect to the result in this connection."

The serpent directed by Mrityu, having said this, Mrityu himself appeared there and, addressing the serpent, spoke thus :

"Guided by *Kala* (Time), I, O serpent, sent thee on this errand and neither thou nor I am the cause of this child's death. Even as the clouds are tossed hither and thither by the wind, I am, O serpent, directed by *Kala*. All influences appertaining to *Satwa* or *Rajas* or *Tamas* have *Kala* for their soul, as they operate in all creatures. The whole universe, O serpent, is imbued with this same influence of *Kala*. Sun, moon, water, wind, fire, sky, earth, rivers and oceans and all existent and non-existent objects are created and destroyed by *Kala*. Knowing this, why dost thou, O serpent accuse me? If any fault attached to me in this, thou also wouldst be to blame."

The serpent replied :—"I do not, O Mrityu, blame thee. I only aver that I was influenced and directed by thee. Whether any blame attaches to *Kala* or not, it is not for me to say."

Then addressing the fowler, it said :—"Thou hast listened to what Mrityu has said ; therefore it is not proper for thee to torment me who am guiltless, by tying me with this cord!"

The fowler replied :—"I have listened to thee as well as to Mrityu and both of you are the cause of the child's death. Accursed be the wicked and vengeful Mrityu that causes affliction to the good! Thee, I shall kill, that art sinful and engaged in sinful acts!"

Mrityu said :—"We both are not free agents, but are dependent on *Kala* and ordained to do our appointed work. Thou shouldst not find fault with us, *if thou dost consider the matter thoroughly.*"

Hardly had he said this, when *Kala*, himself appeared on the scene and spoke thus to the party assembled together.

"Neither Mrityu nor the serpent nor I, am guilty of the death of any creature. We are merely the immediate causes. The true cause is the past *Karma* (action) of that creature. The child here, died by the result of its own *Karma* in the past. As men make, from a lump of clay, whatever they wish to make, even so do men attain to various results determined by *Karma*. As light and shadow are related to each other, so are men related to *Karma* through their own actions. Therefore none here caused the child's death, he himself was the cause."

Gautami said :—"Neither *Kala*, nor *Mrityu*, nor the serpent is the cause in this matter. This child has met with death as the result of its own *Karma*. I too have so acted in the past, that my son should now die. Let now *Kala* and *Mrityu* retire from this place and do thou Arjunaka release this serpent."

Then *Kala* and *Mrityu* and the serpent and the fowler went back to their respective places, but Gautami who knew the truth smiled and said to herself :—"What

48

a drama all this is! *Karma is itself a conventional word.*
The truth is, not an atom moves but by the bidding of
the Lord, nay not an atom is outside Him and what and
where then are life and death?"

—*From the Mahabharata.*

VI

TIME HOW FAR REAL

ONCE upon a time, there ruled over the country of Uttara-Pandava, a king called Lavana, one of the descendants of the famous Harischandra. He was renowned all over India for his immense wealth and unrivalled prowess in war. One day while he was holding Court in his Durbar hall seated on a high throne bedecked with the most precious gems, there appeared before him a man who was well versed in magic and legerdemain and after duly paying his respects to him announced his profession and entreated him to witness his feats. So saying and without waiting for the king's permission, he waved a big bunch of peacock's feathers to and fro, which the king no sooner saw than lo! before his mental vision he saw the following events enacted. A messenger despatched by the king of Sindhu entered upon the scene leading a high-mettled charger and offered it to him as a present from his master. Whereupon the *Siddha* asked the king to mount upon that horse. In obedience to the words of this great personage, the king stared like a statue intently in the direction of the horse and lay entranced for 4 or 5 hours to the immense surprise and fear of his courtiers like a *Yogi* in *Samadhi*. Then suddenly the king's body relaxed its rigidity and began to fall down from the throne when those hard by propped it up.

Then the king gradually recovered consciousness and the obedient ministers asked him what the matter was with him. "Thank God," replied the king, "I am king Lavana and not a poor *Pariah*. Ah! what a terrible dream! I hope this is my court, you are all my ministers, this country is Uttara-Pandava and I am king Lavana. Is it not so my ministers? Am I not right?" The ministers repeatedly assured him that everything was as he had said and requested to know the cause of his doubt. The king replied: "When this wonderful *Siddha* before us waved his peacock feathers, I got giddy and noticed a horse which I mounted and journeyed a long distance for purposes of hunting. After travelling some time, I entered a desolate waste where the heat scorched all things and even the senses. It was a boundless waste which, as my horse and myself were extremely fatigued, we were not able to traverse before night-fall. With great difficulty, however, I crossed the waste soon after sunset and reached a delicious forest teeming with many kinds of trees. While I was riding through it, a creeper high upon a tree tightly twined round my neck and immediately the speedy horse bolted out of my sight like sins from a bather in the Ganges, leaving me dangling to and fro aloft in the air, with the creeper encircling my neck. Soon it became pitch-dark, chill winds blew over my body which consequently got stiffened and my mind became paralysed. I was at the mercy of the winds all night and my teeth kept chattering on account of the extreme cold.

"After a long and miserable night, the day broke and I managed with great difficulty to cut off the creeper round my neck, and coming down looked about for some living person, but in vain. After an hour and a half had elapsed, I met with a *Pariah* girl who had some

eatables in her hand. Though she was black like darkness and ugly like a toad I entreated her on account of
my hunger, saying : 'O swan-like one ! O thou of deer's
eyes ! please give me what thou hast, for I am dying
with hunger.' The lot of a beggar however is never
enviable and it was specially so in my case for the girl
instead of vouchsafing to give it took to her heels without
even deigning to say a word in reply to my request. I
did not however leave her but hunted her throughout
the forest and at last got at her and piteously complained
of my extreme hunger to her. The dark-skinned girl
replied : "I am an outcaste and it is not meet that thou
shouldst taste the food I have, but if you deignest to do
so, thou must first promise to wed me in my own place
before my parents and live with me there. If so I will
give thee this very instant what I have in my hand.'
A very nice bargain that ! but such was the cruelty of
my hunger that I had to consent and no sooner did I do
so, than she handed to me all that she had. I ate them
and my hunger was appeased. Then she took hold of
my hand, saying I was a jolly young fellow and all sorts
of fine things and making love to me without restraint
led me on to her parents like the subtle body of a person
conducted to hell.

"To make a long story short, our marriage was celebrated with great pomp in the *Pariah* hamlet bespattered
with blood and bones ; numberless horses, monkeys,
fowls, crows and pigs were killed in honour of the occasion.
The old hunchbacked grandmother of the house surveyed
through her large fleshy eyes her son-in-law and was
greatly pleased with the choice. Drums were mercilessly
beaten, and toddy and meat were freely distributed on

the occasion, a galaxy of *Pariah* girls crept about me making all sorts of fantastic jokes, and the marriage lasted seven days.

"Within eight months of my marriage, my lady brought forth a child of the colour of burnt bran. Another three years more and she bore me a son blacker still. Then another child was born. With wife and children in the *Pariah* hamlet I had to work all day to earn my bread, my body became old and emaciated on account of poverty and family cares. And when I was thus enfeebled by dotage, there came a severe famine, the whole air was filled with volumes of dust, raised through heat, then my new relatives began to perish one by one and a few that were alive fled to foreign dominions. In order to escape death by hunger I and my wife left the country, myself bearing two of my children on my shoulders and a third on my head.

"Having crossed their country in the scorching heat I saw a big palmyra tree under the shade of which I dismounted my children and rested myself along with my wife for some time. To my great misfortune, my wife suddenly expired in the very embrace of her children owing to the fatigue of a long travel under a tropical sun. One of my younger children mounted on my lap and weeping incessantly demanded of me flesh to eat as he was unable to endure hunger. I could find no means to appease the hunger of the poor child. My heart broke with grief and I was afraid he and the other children would soon die like their mother; therefore I resolved to put an end to my life and for this purpose rearing a great forest fire, I approached the flames and rose up to fall into it, when I tumbled down from the throne here

and woke up to see you courtiers uplifting me and pronouncing the words, *Jaya* (victory to thee), *Jaya*.
Thus fortunately have I woke to find myself a king and
not a *Pariah*."

In introducing the story, Vasishta says the expansion
of the mind's thoughts is bondage while the abandoning
of the same is emancipation. Through the play of the
mind in an object, proximity appears a great distance
and *vice versa*. Through the course of the mind a *Kalpa*
is reckoned by it as a moment and *vice versa*. What was
only four or five hours to the courtiers was to the king a
large number of years.

Kant rightly says in his *Critique of Pure Reason* :
"I maintain that the properties of space and time in
conformity to which I set both, as the condition of their
existence, *abide in my mode of intuition and not in the
objects in themselves*." Space and time are, according
to him, mere forms of thought. Rosalind in "As You
Like It" speaks real philosophy when she jokes with
her lover saying : "Time travels in diverse paces with
diverse persons, I'll tell you who Time ambles withal,
who Time trots withal, who Time gallops withal, and
who he stands still withal............Marry, he trots
hard with a young maid, between the contract of her
marriage and the day it is solemnised : if the interim be
but a se'n night, Time's pace is so hard that it seems the
length of seven years, etc........."

—*From Yogavasishta*.

VII

THE GLORY OF DEVOTION

ONCE upon a time, while the Pandavas were in exile, the sage Durvasa came to king Duryodhana's court. The king courteously welcomed him and gave him a sumptuous feast : and so greatly pleased was the sage with the welcome and the dinner, that he offered to grant his royal host any boon he might ask. The wicked king Duryodhana's one main desire at all times was to do all the mischief in his power to the Pandavas. He had contrived to drive them away into the forest in exile, and yet was not satisfied, as he learnt that they were leading a very happy life, even in the forest, doing great deeds and conversing with great *Rishis*. All this very much roused his envy, and now, that a new opportunity presented itself for doing them harm, he addressed his guest and said : "O great sage, the great king Yudhishtira is the eldest and the best of our race ; he is now living in the forest with his brothers. Do thou therefore, once become the guest of that illustrious one, even as thou hast been mine. Do thou go unto them with all thy disciples and that, at a time when that beautiful and excellent lady, the celebrated princess of Panchala, after having regaled with food the Brahmins, her husband and herself, may lie down to rest." In asking for this boon, Duryodhana's motive was, that Durvasa and his numerous disciples will be too heavy a burden on the Pandavas, especially if they go at a late hour and being unable to feed them, the latter will be

cursed by the wrathful *Rishi*. The boon was granted
and accordingly the *Rishi* and his ten thousand disciples
repaired to the forest and presented themselves before
the Pandavas at a late hour. Yudhishtira, suspecting
nothing, advanced with his brothers towards the sage,
gave him and his disciples a fit and hearty welcome and
said : "Return quick, O adorable sage, after performing
thy daily ablutions and observances." And that sage,
not knowing how the king would be able to provide a
feast for him and his disciples, proceeded with the latter
to a neighbouring river, to perform their ablutions.
Meanwhile, the excellent princess Draupadi, devoted to
her husbands, was in great anxiety about the food to be
provided for the *Rishis*. And, when after much anxious
thought, she came to the conclusion, that means there
were none for providing a dinner, she inwardly
prayed to Krishna, the protector of the humble.
"Krishna," she said, "O, Krishna of mighty arms, O
son of Devaki, whose power is inexhaustible, O Vasudeva,
O Lord of the universe, who drivest away the difficulties
of those that bow down to Thee, Thou art the soul, the
creator, and the destroyer of the universe ! Thou, O
Lord, art inexhaustible and the saviour of the afflicted !
Thou art the preserver of the universe and of all created
beings. Thou art the highest of the high, and the spring
of all our mental perceptions. O supreme and infinite
Being, O giver of all good, be thou the refuge of the
helpless ! I seek Thy protection ! O God, Thou art ever
kindly disposed towards those that take refuge in Thee !
Do thou cherish me with Thy kindness. Thou art the
supreme light and essence of the Universe. They call
thee the Supreme germ and the depositary of all treasures !

Under Thy protection, O lord of gods, all evils lose their terror. Thou didst protect me before, on several occasions, do thou extricate me now from this difficulty !''

The great and sovereign God and Lord of the earth, of mysterious movements, the Lord Kesava, thus adored by Draupadi, and perceiving her difficulty, instantly appeared before her. Beholding Vasudeva, Draupadi bowed down to him in great joy and informed him of the untimely arrival of the *Rishis*. But Krishna said unto her "I am very much afflicted with hunger, do thou give me some food without delay from the *Akshya-patra*[1] given by the Sun and then we may talk of those things. Hearing this Draupadi got greatly perplexed, for she had no food to give him and said : "That vessel remains full, till I finish my meals, but as I have already taken my meal to-day there is no food in it now ? Then the lotus-eyed and adorable Krishna said unto Draupadi, "This is no time for jest, go thou quickly, bring the vessel and show it to me. I am very much distressed with hunger." "There is nothing in the vessel, Krishna," said Draupadi, "I shall cook a meal for thee in no time. Do thou wait a few seconds, I am very sorry that—." "I cannot wait," interrupted Krishna, "I am extremely hungry. Bring thou that vessel, let me see if there is nothing in it." "I assure thee the vessel is empty : there is nothing in it," said Draupadi, bringing the vessel which Krishna quickly snatched from her hand and looking into it he said : "Do thou look here ! there is a particle of rice and vegetable ; thou wantedest to deceive me !" "Certainly not," exclaimed Draupadi. "It is I that

[1] A vessel which never gets empty and can feed any number of people.

cleaned the vessels and kept it in the usual place. I cannot really say how that little bit of rice came there." "No matter if thou canst not say," said Krishna, "my hunger will be satisfied all the same. This little bit of rice from this vessel is more than enough for me. May this please God Hari, the soul of the Universe and may that God, who partaketh at sacrifices, be satiated with this!" and so saying he swallowed that little bit. "I suspect that thou art at some new trick," said Draupadi. "Thy hunger must have been very wonderful one to be appeased by half a grain of rice." "*This is how you all mistake me*," replied Krishna. "No matter if thou dost not believe me; thou wert talking to me of some *Rishis* come for dinner. Where are they?" "They are at the river performing their ablutions. I do not know how to provide for them," said Draupadi.

Krishna—"Let them come. Send for them."

Draupadi :—"And if they come, what shall we do? I have nothing to feed them with."

Krishna :—"We shall chide them for having come at an untimely hour, tell them to wait till to-morrow and teach them to be more careful about their dinners and suppers in future."

"That is hospitality itself," remarked Draupadi.

"Learning is more valuable than eating," said Krishna, "and so let them, at least by fasting to-day, learn to be more careful in future, as for teaching them that lesson, leave that to me" so saying he called Bhimasena, and said : "Do thou go and speedily invite the *Rishis* to dinner."

Meanwhile, those *Rishis* while bathing and performing their ablutions, suddenly felt their stomachs becoming full. Indeed they became so full, as to render even breathing difficult. The surprise of the *Rishis* knew no bounds, and they stared at one another being hardly able to speak, and turning towards their common *Guru* Durvasa, with great effort said : "Having bade the king to have our meals ready, we have come here for bathing. But how, O holy sage, can we eat anything now, for our stomachs seem full to the throat— we do not know how. The repast has been uselessly prepared for us. What is the best thing to be done now?" Durvasa replied : "Never before in my life was my belly so full ; I do not know by what strange cause this has happened. If Yudhishtira comes and invites us, as he certainly will, in a short time what shall we do? By wasting his repast, we will be doing a great harm to that royal sage. The Pandavas may get angry with us ; I know the royal sage Yudhishtira to be possessed of great ascetic power. Ye Brahmins, I am afraid of men that are devoted to Hari! The high souled Pandavas are all religious men, learned, warlike, diligent in ascetic austerities and religious observances, devoted to Vasudeva, and always observant of rules of good conduct. If provoked, they can consume us with their wrath, as fire doth a bale of cotton. Therefore, ye disciples, shall we all run away quickly without seeing them?"

"O adorable sage," they replied, "we can hardly rise up : how then could we run? We find it difficult even to talk, nay even to breathe. We are 'full to the neck' ; save us, O master, from this misery." Durvasa did not know what to do, he regretted that he foolishly gave power to Duryodhana to use him for his own wicked purpose ; he feared, that his punishment had already begun and was frightened, that further harm might come. While he was in this miserable plight, there appeared Bhimasena and said unto him : "Come, O sage, with all thy disciples, for my brothers, Draupadi and Krishna are waiting to receive thee." At the very mention of Krishna's name poor Durvasa trembled from head to foot ; his fears gathered new strength and he inwardly felt greatly ashamed to face the Pandavas, but there was no helping it. So, he addressed his disciples and said : "Raise ye forth, exert all your might and let us walk on to the abode of the Pandavas, for in sooth, there is no helping it." It was rather a comic sight to see these 'pot-bellied' Brahmins 'swollen up to the neck' (as the Indian saying goes) toiling onward with feet too weak to bear the weight on them, breathing like mountain snakes and sweating in revulets all over the body. Bhimasena looked at their condition and learnt from them what the matter was. With no small difficulty, they reached the abode of the Pandavas and were duly welcomed by Yudhishtira and the rest Krishna showed special attention to Durvasa, which only made him more miserable than before. The face of the poor *Rishi* was covered with shame, he bowed to Krishna and with his head hung down or rather, his eyes hung down, as he could not bend his head, said : "Lord, thou shouldst forgive me for my foolishness. I hastily placed myself under the power of a wicked man but my only consolation was, that no harm could ever come to the Pandavas, who have always been piously devoted to thee" ; and then he related in detail the whole story, and how he and his disciples had already been punished. "I see, O cunning Krishna, artful, farseeing, mysterious and omnipotent Krishna," exclaimed Draupadi, "I now see why thou wert so hungry for half a grain of rice. By your taking in that little bit of rice, all these *Rishis* have got satisfied. What example there could be, more plain than this, to show, that *thou art the soul of the universe, the Paramatman, in whom all men and things live, move and have their being, that thou art in all the world as oil in the sesameseed, as brightness in the diamond, as smell in the flower.* All praise and glory to t ee, that art our refuge, our master, our friend, our relative, our guide and our teacher. No fear can ever come to the followers of Hari, no danger to the worshippers of the lotus-eyed Krishna."

Needless to add that the *Rishis* were forgiven and all rejoiced at the event and sang the glory of Krishna.

—From the Mahabharata.

VIII

THE GLORY OF MENTAL WORSHIP

ARJUNA was fond of making long and ostentatious *puja* (worship) to God. He would every day throw cartloads of flowers at the feet of Siva's image, and conduct worship with great ceremony in a spacious hall reserved for the purpose and lit up with numberless lights. He would use nothing but gold and silver vessels in the course of his *puja* and would spend hours in the external forms of worship. Bhima, on the other hand, never sat for making *puja* and did not appear even to go to the temple. All that he did was to close his eyes, as if for meditation, for a few minutes before dinner. Arjuna began, on account of this difference between them, to look down on his brother and think highly of his own piety and worship. Krishna, whose observation nothing escaped, noticed this, and, with a view to bring Arjuna to his senses, proposed to him in a cousinly fashion a trip to Mount Kailas, the abode of Siva. Arjuna suspecting nothing gladly consented and the cousins were soon on their way up to the Himalayas.

They had not gone far, when they met a man who was dragging a cart loaded to the full with flowers of various kinds. Arjuna asked the man where he was taking the flowers, but the man was so absorbed in his work that he did not even reply. "Let us follow the man and find out the thing for ourselves," said Krishna; and accordingly they followed him, but what was their surprise when they saw him empty the cart by the side of a huge heap of flowers, all half-faded as those in the cart, which was as big as a hill. They had not stood long observing the stranger, when they saw several hundreds of similar carts all loaded with flowers approach the same spot and empty their contents there. Arjuna's curiosity could no longer be controlled, and so he asked the men where those carts came from. None of them however deigned to reply, but, after repeated questioning, one man said : "Sir, pray do not disturb us, we have brought only five hundred carts of flowers and more than five hundred yet remain in the temple. They are the flowers with which one Bhima, a son of Pandu, worshipped our Lord yesterday, and now it is hardly two hours more for his to-day's *puja*, and we must remove all of them within that time, pray do not disturb us."

Arjuna's surprise knew no bounds, and to reassure himself he asked : "Is it Bhima or Arjuna that you speak of ? My friend, I am afraid you make a mistake." The stranger replied : "Pooh, Arjuna ! not at all. It is Bhima that makes such glorious *puja* and not his brother Arjuna who merely makes a display of his worship." Just then there came there another man bearing a small basket of flowers, and Krishna addressing him asked : "Whence my friend these flowers ? Whose offerings are they ?" The man replied : "Oh they were offered yesterday by an ostentatious man who lives on earth, known as Arjuna." Arjuna hung down his head with shame and addressing Krishna said : "O, cunning man, why did you bring me here ? Let us leave this place. You might have warned me of my self-conceit and ostentation at home and saved me all this labour and mortification. I confess I thought highly of my *puja* and regarded Bhima with a sort of foolish contempt : I now see that his short meditation before dinner is more valuable than all my showy worship." Krishna smiled and said nothing.

IX

THE MANNER OF GIVING

KING ASHTAKA of Visvamitra's race once performed a
great Horse sacrifice (*Asvamedha*), and there came to
that sacrifice among others, the three brothers also of
that king, Pratardana, Vasumanas and Shivi the son
of Usinara. After the sacrifice was completed, Ashtaka
was proceeding on his car along with his brothers, when,
they all beheld Narada coming that way. At once they
saluted the celestial *Rishi* and said unto him : "Do us
the favour to ride on the car with us" ; and saying, "So
be it," Narada mounted on the car. While they were
all thus going, one of the kings addressing Narada, said :
"Oh ! Holy one, I desire to ask thee something," and
the *Rishi* said, "Ask." Thus permitted, the king said :
"We all four are blessed with long lives and have indeed every virtue. We shall therefore be permitted to
go to a certain Heaven and dwell there for a long period.
Who amongst us, however, oh sage, shall fall down first."
Thus questioned, Narada replied : "This Ashtaka shall
first come down." Thereupon the inquirer asked for
the cause, and the *Rishi* answered : "I lived for a few
days in the abode of Ashtaka. One day he carried me
on his car out of the town and there I beheld thousands
of kine of various colours and seeing them I asked
Ashtaka whose they were and he answered me saying,
'*These are gifts made by me*'. By this answer he gave
expression to his own praise. It is for this answer of
his that he will have to come down from Heaven." After

Narada had said so, one of the kings again enquired, "Of the other three of us who then will stay in Heaven, who shall fall down first?" The *Rishi* answered : "Pratardana" and on being asked for the cause, he continued, 'Pratardana was one day taking me with him on his car drawn by four horses, when a Brahmin begged him for a horse.' Pratardana replied : 'After returning home I will give thee one.' Thereupon the Brahmin said : 'Pray let it be given to me soon' ; at once the king gave unto him the steed that had been yoked on the right-hand wheel of the car. Then, there came unto him another Brahmin asking for a steed ; the king unyoked and gave the one that was attached to the left wheel of his car and proceeded on his journey. Then, there came another Brahmin desirous of obtaining a horse ; the king at once gave him the horse on the left front of his car and proceeded on his journey with only one horse. A short while after, there came unto him another Brahmin begging for a horse ; the king said unto him : 'On returning home I will give thee a horse' ; but the Brahmin said : 'Pray let the horse be given to me soon,' and the king gave him the only horse he had and seizing the yoke of the car himself, began to draw it ; and as he did so, he said, "*There is now nothing for the Brahmins to ask.*' The king had given away, it is true, but he had done so not quite willingly and with pleasure and for that remark of his he shall have to fall down from Heaven." After the *Rishi* had said so, one of the two kings that remained asked : "Who of us two shall first fall down?" The *Rishi* answered : "Vasumanas." The enquirer asked for the reason and Narada said : "In the course of my wanderings, I arrived at the abode of Vasumanas; at that time the Brahmins were performing a ceremony for the sake of procuring for the king a flowery car from the Gods. I approached the king's presence, and when the Brahmins completed the ceremony and the flowery car became visible, I praised that car and thereupon the king said of his own accord, 'Holy one? By thee hath this car been praised. Let this car therefore be thine,' but he did not give it away to me. I said nothing at that time. But sometime after, when I was in need of a car, I went to Vasumanas and praised the flowery car, and the king said: 'it is thine,' but did not give it to me even then. I went to him a third time and admired the car again; the king exhibiting the flowery car to the Brahmins, cast his eye on me and said merely: *'Oh holy one! thou hast praised the flowery car sufficiently,' without making me a gift of that car*; and for this, he will fall down from Heaven.'' One of the kings then said: ''Of the two, the one who is to go with thee, and yourself who will fall down, thou, or he?'' Narada answered: ''Shivi will go, but I will fall down.'' ''For what reason,'' asked the enquirer, and Narada said: ''I am not the equal of Shivi. For one day a Brahmin came unto Shivi and asked him for food and Shivi replied: 'I am thy servant, let me have thy orders.' The Brahmin answered: 'This, thy son known by the name of Brihathgarbha should be killed, O king, and cooked for my food.' Hearing this, I waited to see what would follow. Shivi then killed his son and cooking him duly and placing that food in a vessel, went out in search of the Brahmin. While he was thus searching for the Brahmin, someone said to him, 'The Brahmin thou seekest, having entered the city, is setting fire to thy abode, thy treasury, thy arsenal, the apartments of the ladies, and thy stables for horses and elephants.' Shivi heard all this with great composure, returned home and said to the Brahmin whom he found there, 'O holy one! the food has been cooked.' But he spoke not a word; and Shivi, with a view to gratify him, said: 'Oh holy one, eat thou the food.' The Brahmin, looking at Shivi for a moment, said: 'Eat it thyself.' Thereupon Shivi said: 'Let it be so, and cheerfully proceeded to eat it.' At once the Brahmin caught hold of his hand and addressing him, said: 'Thou hast conquered wrath. There is none equal to thee,' and saying this, he adored Shivi, and when Shivi cast his eyes before him, he beheld his son, standing as a child of the gods decked in ornaments and emitting fragrance from his body. And the Brahmin having accomplished all this, suddenly vanished from sight. It was Vidhathru himself who had come in the guise of a Brahmin to try the Royal sage. After Vidhathru had disappeared, the councillors said to the king: 'Thou knowest everything, for what didst thou do all this?' And Shivi answered: 'It was not for fame, nor for acquiring objects of enjoyments, that I did all this. *This course is virtuous; it is for this, that I did all that; the path which is trodden by the virtuous is laudable; my heart always inclineth towards such a course.*' This high instance of Shivi's blessedness I know and that is why I say he will continue in heaven longer than I."

The above story is a beautiful instance of what our ancients thought about giving. A begger is *Vidhathru* the God himself. Swami Vivekananda beautifully says: "Do not stand on a high chair and take five cent bits and say 'here, my poor man' but kneel down and say, 'Lord, allow me to help, so that I may be blessed by helping you.' *It is not the receiver that is blessed but the giver.* Give praise to the Lord that you are allowed to exercise your power of benevolence and mercy, and all these things in the world, and thus become pure and perfect........All the work you do is subjective—for your own benefit. God has not fallen into a ditch for you and me to help out by building hospitals or something of that sort. He allows you to work, he allows you to exercise in this great gymnasium, not to help Him but to help yourself. Do you think that even an ant will die for want of your help? most arrant blasphemy! Do you think that you can help the least thing in the universe? You cannot. When you give a bit of food to the dog, you worship the dog as a god. God is in that dog. He is the dog. This should be your idea. He is all and in all. We are allowed to worship. Stand in that reverent attitude to the whole universe and then will come perfect non-attachment."

—*From the Mahabharata.*

X

THE END OF DESIRE

A POOR illiterate Brahmin was once walking in the royal street of Tanjore, when, as chance would have it, he beheld the daughter of the king, who was a paragon of beauty, playing with her mates on the uppermost story of the palace. No sooner did his eyes catch a glimpse of that miracle of loveliness than his heart became laden with love, and he stood rooted to the spot from which he saw her. That love makes men blind is a trite saying, but his passion was of an exceptional nature. For it made him totally blind to everything else but his object of love and he failed even to see that to stand with uplifted eyes in the public street and that before the royal mansion might lead to unpleasant consequences. It so happened unfortunately that while he was thus standing dumb and absorbed, the king himself noticed him in the audacious act of looking at his own daughter, and the order at once passed forth for the fool's being arrested and brought to the royal presence, which, it goes without saying, was immediately executed. The enraged king asked him who he was and how he happened to be so audacious as to look at the princess, to which the Brahmin replied : "Beauty is not for those who possess it, but for those who enjoy it." No sooner did these daring words pass his lips than he was ordered to be branded on his face and expelled from the city. Accordingly he was seized and branded not only over his face, but all over the body and driven out of the city seated on an ass's back with his face turned towards its tail.

It was late in the night when he crossed beyond the last limit of the king's dominions and consequently he did not know where to direct his steps. When at a few yard's distance from him, he espied a small temple of Kali which he unhesitatingly entered and seeing that the Goddess had at that time gone out on her nocturnal visits to the neighbouring villages, he closed the door and fastened the bolt inside to prevent her coming in. He could not however close his eyes for his heart was filled with the vision of the Princess of Tanjore and he busily contrived schemes for obtaining her. After hours of deliberation he felt that no amount of plotting could remove the princess out of her royal mansion, and even if she could be so brought to him, it was totally improbable that she could ever love him who was so illiterate and ugly. While he was thus turing over the pros and cons in his restless imagination, he heard a furious knock at the door and it at once struck him that by refusing to open the door he could extort any boon from the goddess Kali. Accordingly he kept quiet for a number of knocks, and at last said : "What will you give me if I open the door," to which she replied : "Anything you ask ; for I am very much tired ; ask for three boons and they shall be given." The Brahmin thanked his stars and said : "Goddess, if you be the real Kali, grant first that I shall become the king of Tanjore before day• break and secondly that the princess become my wife before to-morrow evening, and thirdly that I shall have three other boons whenever I so desire." The Goddess at once said "granted", and the lucky Brahmin opened

the door and came out. Kali instantly entered her
temple and closing the door began to sleep and snore.

Just at the same time, the king of Tanjore suddenly
died and the state-elephant[1] despatched from the palace
before daybreak to choose a king ran out of the city to
the temple of Kali and garlanding the Brahmin who was
sitting outside, took him upon its back and returned
to the palace and at once he was proclaimed king of
Tanjore. Shortly after, he thought of the three boons
yet left to him and he wished first that the scars on his
face should disappear and he should become very beautiful and secondly that he should become the most learned
man of the time and thirdly that he should have three
other boons whenever he may so desire. At once he
became as beautiful and learned as he could desire, and
the princess no sooner saw him than fell in love with
him and offered him her hand of her own accord. He
lived very happily for a time but he soon got dissatisfied
and longed for *new* happiness. So he again thought of
his boons and wished first that he should become the
ruler of the whole earth, secondly that he should have a
thousand wives even more beautiful than the princess,
and lastly that he should have three other boons whenever he may so desire. All these he attained, but he
was not yet happy. So he again wished that he should
learn all about the universe from the tiniest insect to the
remotest star, that he should be able to work all *Siddhis*
(miracles) and lastly that he should have three other
boons whenever he may want them. He obtained all

---

1 In those days the choice of a king fell upon the state-elephant
which was sent out for the purpose, with a garland in its trunk and
whosoever was garlanded by it became king.

that he wanted and became known throughout the world as a supernatural being, an *avatar* (incarnation) of God Himself, but yet in his heart of hearts he was not satisfied.

Domestic calamities, family troubles, civil wars and the care and worry, incidental to his position, all these disturbed his peace of mind and he was cheerful, depressed, miserable, angry and joyful by turns. His mind was like a thin reed in the midst of a river which trembled at every gentle gale. Life did not please him. He crossed the seas and flew in the air and yet he was not happy, for these gifts soon lost the charm of novelty and for one thing that pleased him, there were ten which displeased him and disturbed his peace of mind. He read the thoughts of all men came to him, but the selfishness, the vanity and the wickedness of mortals which now he saw as clearly as if they were his own, made him much more miserable than he was ever before he got his boons. He was very unhappy and did not want to prolong his life which through the assured favour of Kali he could easily have done for any length of time. *He long thought of the best means of obtaining happiness* and even contemplated suicide, but refrained from it only for fear of being obliged to reincarnate in this world of woe. There was no peace for him in the heaven, in the waters, on the land or up in the mid air. He longed for peace of mind, for happiness, but *he could not find it anywhere in the world*. At last it struck him that *the seat of bliss was within and the giving up of all desire was the real means to peace*. But to give up desires how? Is it by burying myself in endless sleep free even from dreams? Is this the end of it all? Is there nothing to aspire to, yearn for and obtain, nothing by obtaining which I would have obtained all? he said to himself. He could not easily think of anything which he had not yet obtained and felt uneasy on that account, but suddenly it struck him that he had not yet known the most essential of all things—the author of all this wonderful creation. Who or what is He? What is he like? To find out this now became his ambition and gave fresh spirit to his ennui-filled mind. Accordingly he once again had recourse to the precious gift of the goddess and wished first that he should get peace of mind, secondly that he should personally know the creator, and thirdly that he should get three other boons whenever he may ask for them. At once, such was the power and glory of Kali, *Chit Sakti*, he was filled with a new and inconceivable kind of happiness and realised that the great and mighty creator of the most wonderful panorama of the universe was within himself or rather his own Self and when he realised this, all his former knowledge, his wonderful *siddhis*, his extensive dominions, his beautiful wives, the stars among which he travelled, and his hopes, desires, joys, griefs, suffering and discontent, all disappeared out of sight. He found that he had only been dreaming, that all that he had seen and known, together with himself as enjoyer and sufferer was mere illusion and that his own self was the creator or rather that there was neither creation nor destruction and danced with joy crying "I am blissful, I am blissful, I am God. There is nothing higher than me."

A long time after, the Goddess Kali appeared before him and asked him why he had not so long thought of the third boon yet remaining, and he replied : "I have gained that beyond the gaining of which there remains nothing to be gained, beyond the bliss of which there remains no possibility of bliss, beyond becoming which there remains nothing to be known. I have realised the highest end and the best riches, the supremest world, the greatest joy, and so I have no more to ask for. *My only desire is that I should constantly remain in this blissful state in which I am free from all desires."* The Goddess blessed him saying "so be it" and disappeared.

XI

RADHA AND KRISHNA

Or

THE CONFESSIONS OF AN HONEST GOD

RADHA felt a little conceited with the idea that she had conquered the heart of Krishna and made him her slave as it were. The Lord, whose observation nothing could escape, understood this and wanted to make fun of her. One day while they were alone together, the cunning Krishna with a view to draw her out fully, suddenly laughed little and then kept quiet. Radha observing it, asked him what the matter was. Krishna replied: "Nothing, O Radha of coral lips, nothing very particular. Only I laughed to see how all this world is under my control, with all its inhabitants and how great I am." A few seconds passed and then Radha abruptly laughed and kept quiet. Krishna asked in his turn what the matter was and she said: "Nothing, O Krishna, only you are the ruler of the whole world and I am your ruler. The thought of this caused me to laugh." "Who will not become *your* slave?" replied the gallant God, "To grudge to pay homage to *your* divine beauty! A passing glance from that lotus eye would enslave all the three worlds" and so saying he clasped her in his arms, and after a general conversation for some time left her.

A few days after, she sent word to her lover to meet her alone on the silver sands of the Jumna at evening time. All the day was spent by her in decorating herself and otherwise preparing for the joyful meeting. She wavered for a long time between this dress and that and at last chose one which she thought would best please Krishna. She who was already "all grace summed up", put on her best ear-rings, her best necklaces, and bangles all of gold, and with exquisite taste made a splendid nosegay of sweet-smelling flowers just blown, with a beautiful blue one in the middle and lily-white one by its side, to represent Krishna and herself surrounded by a galaxy of admiring damsels. She combed her dark flowing soft hair and wore it in a peculiarly charming fashion saying : "This is a worthy net for so beautiful a prey." Having thus decorated herself, and holding the sweet nosegay in her hand, she, the wonder of her kind, presented herself before a mirror which, inanimate as it was, *seemed* to feel pride in reflecting the form of so fair a person. Radha sweet, amorous, fairy like Radha "a daughter of the gods divinely tall and most divinely fair" drew to her full height her stately form and looked at herself in the glass; "Beautiful," she cried, "like a peacock. Krishna is surely mine. I shall look at him this way, no, not this, that way, and I shall walk like a swan, sing like a nightingale and lisp to him like parrot. I shall hold this nosegay just against his face by one hand and by another raise both his arms to my lips. Aye he is mine, and not any other's. I have conquered him. I have conquered him. Who is there like me?"

When the sun was about to set, she quietly stole out of her house, a perfect miracle of beauty, with flowers, fruits and cakes in her hand, leaving her domestic duties to take care of themselves, and by a secret path arrived at a lovely retreat on the Jumna bank, where herself and her lover had spent many a memorable evening. The mighty river, the beautiful sands, the dark grove behind the white rock on which they used to sit, the stately trees that gave shelter to them, the peacock, the deer and the nightingale which seemed to enjoy their presence, the wild flowers, the music-making bamboo trees, the reed bushes, the irregular rocks close by and the rills like girls playing, flowing from them and adding to the watery wealth of the Jumna, all these were there, lending a strange charm to the place, but not Krishna who was more wonderful and more charming than all of them. He was not there and Radha, who was but a moment ago "so light of spirit and so light of foot" was filled with surprise, but she consoled herself with the thought that he would soon come; five, ten, fifteen minutes and half an hour had passed and Krishna had not come. She fancied she heard a rustling among the plants, thought that he was there, perhaps wantonly hiding himself, and called him in tones which the amorous air drank in eagerly, "Govinda, Gopala, Murari, Mukunda, Krishna, Radharamana," but her words were as a voice in the wilderness. The sun was setting but Krishna had not come. The sky assumed a deeper blue, but he who was bluer still and worth a thousand skies, he was not yet come. The birds had returned to their nests, cows had entered their sheds and even workmen had gone back to their homes and wives, but the truant Murari was yet far away from his home in her soft, balmy bosom.

It was a "beauteous evening calm and free" and everything around her was in a state of perfect peacefulness and repose. The majestic Jumna flowed in a slow noiseless pace, the birds had stopped singing, even the trees were silent. The sky overhead was a waveless ocean of undisturbed blue, and all nature was in a state of *Mauna* (silence) like a sage in *Samadhi*. But the calmness in the outer world tended by contrast only to increase the agitation in poor Radha's heart. "Will he not come? No, no, he will not fail to come when *I* have asked him to come. He will come with the moon," she thought. But soon came the beautiful moon, but instead of bringing the silk-clad, dancing Krishna, it only spread its silvery rays around and rejoiced over Radha's anguish. She looked up at the heartless moon and got incensed "against the truant lover". "I will never forgive this insult—ah, this moonlight! it burns me—I will have nothing more to do with him and when he comes I will scold him and turn away. He has left me to perish under these chilling rays of this cold moon and pierced by Cupid's darts, while he is happy elsewhere. I will show him that I too can be cruel. He will come and beg my favour, then I will spurn him and turn him away," she said to herself. But all this anger was ineffectual as Krishna did not make his appearance. Often she thought of returning home, but had not the heart to do so. A something which she would not confess detained her. It was not the love for Krishna, she said, for she had ceased to love him. But then why did she stay? Gradually her anger gave way to grief and looking at herself and at the nosegay in her hand which had begun to fade *as if* it reflected her grief, she exclaimed: "I am really unworthy of him. What am I to him who is like the god of love to woman? To have thought that I had him under my control and to have said so to him! yes I now see my folly; like the elephant which throws mud over its own head, I am myself the author of my misfortune." She felt exceedingly humiliated and began to weep.

True humility and repentance had taken hold of her and she sat on a rock praying to the gods for Krishna's arrival, her face expressing the divinest grief, and wistfully looking at the direction from which he would be coming, when all of a sudden she felt the lotus hand of her Krishna on her braided hair and heard the soft music of his divine flute behind her back very close to her ear. At once she turned with lightning swiftness and the voice and the hand also seemed to turn with her and as quickly. She turned and turned, but they were always behind her and she could not get at the hand. Her hair was pulled with jerks, pulled now tightly, now gently, and she stretched back her hand to capture the criminal with whom she pretended to be very angry; but every time he receded, bending her body backwards. Then she made a sudden turn behind, when lo! her lover seemed to fly up in the air and looking up, she saw him surrounded by a galaxy of *Gopis*. At once a crowd of feelings rushed into her heart and for a moment she remained confused. The vision endured for a short time and then she saw Krishna alone wherever she turned. He was behind, before, on the right side, on the left, above, below, everywhere. Charming was it; but she was not able to endure it and piteously implored her lover like Arjuna in the *Gita* to disillusion her. "O Krishna, O Govinda, O Murari, I beg of you, O Radharamana, cease this deceiving sport. Tell me where thou

50

really art and assure me of thy love. I am frightened, comfort me O lord, show me thy form. O thou art much too great a match for me—a silly little girl. I had fancied I had completely won you and enslaved you. O Gopala, pardon thou all my past foolishness and show me thy loving face and comfort me," she cried. At once she heard the gentle reassuring sound of the flute and she felt a strange sense creeping over her, that she had somehow become Krishna. It was blissful, immeasurably blissful. She was not Radha, she had got transformed, metamorphosed into Krishna. She was Krishna and Krishna was herself. A new world of un-alloyed bliss had been revealed to her and she stood speechless with joy. She had forgotten herself, she had forgotten her household duties, her little joys and sorrows and with them the vast outer world. All these had ceased to exist for her, for she was one with her lover. How long she stayed in this blissful state, she did not know for she was dead to time, but when she awoke she saw that it was morning.

Krishna pretended to be sleeping by her side with a face on which the most prominent expression was that of perfect innocence and simplicity. She woke him up without scruple, for she knew that he was not really sleeping and he rose from the couch rubbing his eyes and asking if the day had come so soon. Radha took hold of his hands and energetically pressing them between hers said : "Thou canst no longer afford to deceive me. I have brought thee to book" and added :

"Confess that thou art a hypocrite. Thou dost pretend to sleep, while thou art really awake. Thou art beyond both night and day, all wakeful, absolute

Satchidananda as now I saw, yet pretendest to sleep and snore. Art thou not then a hypocrite?"

Krishna replied : "Yes, I am a hypocrite, but not to those who know that I am so. To them I am all simplicity and plainness."

Radha : "Art thou not a liar, thou who hast created this lie of the world?"

Krishna : "I confess I am a liar; but not wholly, for in this confession I speak the truth. Besides I do not lie to those that seek me; and when they see the liar the lie of the world vanishes."

Radha : "Confess thou art a deceiver because thou deceivest us with the idea that we are separate from thee."

Krishna : "I confess I am a deceiver! but I deceive only those who, thinking themselves separate, have already deceived themselves and are eager to be deceived still more."

Radha : "Confess that thou art a thief, for thou stealest away the bliss of Self-realisation from men, blinding their vision by *Maya*."

Krishna : "I am not *a* thief but the prince of thieves, *Taskaranampati* as the *Vedas* say. But I rob only those that are careless of their Self."

Radha : "Confess that thou art cruel, for thou seemest to delight in the suffering of all creatures : What is sport to thee is death to them."

Krishna : "I am cruel to all who are cruel to me, to the worldly-minded who kill me, the Self, in them (*Atmahanah*). But I am kind even when I am cruel, for there is happiness even in grief. Besides I take all to me in the due course and leave none to perish uncared for."

Radha : "Confess that thou art immoral and un-chaste, for thou hast as many favourites as there are sands on the sea shore."

Krishna : "I confess I am very very unchaste. All things in the world are my illegitimate children and every soul is a secret favourite of mine, with whom I indulge in all sorts of play and whom I flatter, tease and coax by turns until they forget their passion for personal ornament and love me for my own sake, as thou dost me, when I absorb them all in me."

Radha was delighted with these honest confessions and exclaimed : "O God, I rejoice that thou art a hypocrite, a liar, a deceiver, a thief and art cruel, immoral and unchaste and Thou art I and I am Thou."

Reader ! try to understand the above story before you criticise it. Radha had not won Krishna when she vainly thought that she had, but when she repented for her vanity and became humble she obtained Krishna, nay she *became* Krishna. To put it in the language of the *Upanishad, Brahman,* is known by him who thinks that He is not known : he who thinks that *Brahman* is known does not know Him. *Brahman* is unknown to those who think they know Him and known to those who do not think they know Him" (*Ken. Up.,* II, 3, see Sankara's Commentary on this).

Ah ! How fond are we in India of the hypocritical, lying, deceiving, thievish, cruel and immoral Krishna— *Jara Chora Sikhamani* !

XII

AN IDLER AND A TEMPLE TRUSTEE

A CERTAIN sage was living in the temple of M—. He occupied a corner in the temple and used to be sitting there all day long and till mid-night with closed eyes; he would never stir from the place except for attending to the calls of nature. Nothing could draw him away from his corner, not even the festivals of the temple, nor the crowds of men and women that were coming and going. The trustee of the temple thinking that he was a sage ordered a ball of rice to be supplied to him from the temple kitchen every day, and in the evenings before going home, would scrupulously pay his respects to him. A few years after, this pious trustee died and was succeeded by his son. New brooms sweep clean; so the new trustee, who like most other young men thought his father a fool, began to reform the temple according to his own wise notions and one of the reforms was that the "idle fellow in the corner," as the sage was respectfully styled by the trustee, was deprived of the ball of rice regularly supplied to him for a number of years. The "idle fellow", however, did not leave the corner on that account, nor seemed to be affected by the reform in any other way except that he went out for a few minutes in the noon to beg for his bread. This done, he returned to his corner and closed his eyes as ever, as if no new trustee had been appointed. To the young man who was anxious that his reform should be appreciated, and the "idle fellow" should be taught to be more busy, it seemed doubtful if the latter even knew that the temple supply had been stopped and that he lived by begging—he seemed to take to the change so coolly and never troubled himself about the cause for that change. This, to be sure, was not sufficiently flattering to the young man who was bowed to and honoured at every turn in the temple as if he were a monarch; and he was determined to bring the "idle fellow" to his senses.

With this object he went to him one day and without the least ceremony asked him why he was idling away all his precious life-time. The sage welcomed him kindly and requested him to take his seat. The trustee accordingly sat down and the sage also sat as motionless as ever and spoke not a word. Thus five minutes passed. The trustee got no reply to his question nor did there seem any prospect of his getting one. He naturally got tired of the interview which was in truth the dullest he had had in his life-time. He was unable to sit composed, a thousand things distracted his attention; he grew restless and so rose up to depart. Just then, the sage looked up and requested him to sit for a few minutes more and the young man had to comply. But he had already exceeded the maximum amount of time he could sit in that fashion and so grew exceedingly restless and uneasy, while to his immense surprise the "idle fellow" was as composed and silent as ever. On his making a second attempt to retreat, the sage entreated him again to sit for a few minutes more; the young man exclaimed "Impossible, I cannot sit for one second more; *sitting quiet is the most difficult thing I have known.* I will do anything rather than sit as you do" and fled away. And the first thing he did after leaving the sage was to order two balls of rice to be supplied to him every day from that time at the rate, as he put it, of,

> One ball to him that runs and jumps and fights,
> And two to him that sits both days and nights.

This funny little story illustrates the difficulty of calm and constant meditation. As Rama said to Hanuman : "One can more easily cross all the oceans, 'drink off' all the air, and play with mountains as balls, than control the wandering mind." In the same way Thayumanavar says : "One may with less difficulty control a mad elephant, bind the mouths of bears and tigers, ride on the back of a lion, play with the cobra, melt and alchemise all the five metals and live by it, roam in the world unseen, command the gods, live in eternal youth; enter other bodies, walk on water, live in fire, and acquire wonderful powers, than subdue the mind and be quiet."

XIII

THE MISSING TENTH

OR

RECKONING WITHOUT THE HOST

Ten men, disciples of a *Guru*, whose name was Avi-vekapurna (*i.e.*, one who was perfect in his ignorance) crossed a river hand-in-hand and when they reached the other shore, they began to count their number, to know if they had all of them crossed safely. One man counted and said with alarm that they were only nine. Another counted and said the same. A third counted and he also said the same. Now the whole party got excited and began to beat their breasts and tear their hair, though the fact was that they were ten and that each man who counted, did so leaving himself. Then seeing a man seated calmly at a distance, they went to him and, complaining of their fate, requested him to help them in discovering the missing member who, they knew not, was dead or alive. The calm man seeing their distress and the foolish mistake which originated it, said to them out of great pity : "You are really ten. The mistake was in your counting, for each one counted all others, but himself. Then he asked every one to utter his name and separated him from the rest and counting one, two, three and lastly ten. They were very anxious till nine ended, and then when the number ten came, they danced with joy and thanking their saviour went their way."

The story is a beautiful allegory of the lot of man. The Avivekapurna *Guru* is Avidya, ignorance. The river represents *Moha* (passion) on crossing which and not before, does man begin to think of himself, to see if he is safe, if everything is right with him. He finds that there are only nine elements in him—seer, seeing and the thing seen, doer, doing and the deed and enjoyer, enjoyment and the thing enjoyed and trembles to find that he is not whole. He distinctly remembers that there was another but is unable to find out whether he is or is not (the same question as was put by Nachiketas to Yama : "Some say that after death the Self exists, others that It does not. Clear my doubt concerning this"). "He weeps at his loss and then approaching the *Guru* the calm man at a distance in the story, requests him with tears in his eyes to help him in discovering the lost tenth. The *Guru* does not create anything new, but only points out what had been forgotten and left uncounted by naming and separating the nine by *neti*, *neti* (not this, not this), till at last the tenth which remains finds itself. Just as in the story the tenth man finds himself, after the nine are separated from him, so the *Atman* finds itself as soon as the *Chetana* and *Achetana prakritis* which together constitute the nine-fold *samsara* above-mentioned, as seer, seeing, thing seen, etc., and with which it was confounded are distinguished from it. When man thus knows himself he thanks and extols the *Guru* and dances with joy exclaiming : "I am not any of the nine, nor am I the aggregate of the nine. One to nine all begin from me and end in me, for it is I that counted them. By their side I am the counter, the witness and considered along with them I am the tenth and the last (*Lingam*), but in myself I am neither one nor two and stand on ever separate."

XIV

HOW RAMDĀS SAW GOD

THERE was in recent times a great *Vaishnavite Bhakta* by name Ramdas. He was very anxious to obtain a vision of God. It so happened that, while he was sitting one evening with a number of devotees in a grove, where he had made a feast that day to a large number of Brahmins, he heard the soft melodies of a *Bhakta* who was singing the praises of the Lord. He at once proceeded in the direction of the voice, and finding that it was no less a personage than the celebrated Kabirdas, who was so singing, at once fell at his feet. After the usual salutations and enquiries were over, Ramdas requested Kabir to initiate him into the mysteries of *Yoga*. Kabir gladly complied with the request and for some days he stayed in the grove as a guest of Ramdas.

Shortly after, Ramdas again approached Kabir and requested to be favoured with a vision of God. Kabir promised a daylight one and asked his disciple to arrange for a grand feast for Brahmins as a preparation for the appearance of the Lord. The feast was accordingly arranged, grand preparations were made on every side and the whole town of Bhadrachalam, where Ramdas lived, decorated for the reception of God. Numberless Brahmins had assembled and the dinner which in sumptuousness outdid even their expectations was ready awaiting the arrival of God. Twelve o'clock was the hour arranged for the vision, but one o'clock and two o'clock and even three o'clock passed away, but the

Lord did not appear. Ramdas began to doubt the sincerity of Kabir and the Brahmins impatient, as a rule, of hunger, and now very angry with the Lord who stood between them and their dinner, complained in no murmurs.

While thus suspense was growing into disappointment, a wild buffalo, all dirty and covered over with mire, rushed into the grove and began to roll its nice person over the heap of food that had been stored up in tempting abundance. It upset the pots containing ghee, milk, soup and other things and made a thorough bear-garden of the whole dinner. All the food became spoiled and the angry Brahmins and the mortified Ramdas, seeing the mess which the dirty creature was making, surrounded it on all sides and beat it till the blood came, branded it on several parts of the body and then drove it away. All the feast being thus spoiled, fresh rice was brought and cooked and the Brahmins fed, but, of course, not in the grand style originally designed. For this disappointment they were very severe on poor Ramdas, cursed him with all their heart and went home in no pleasant mood. Ramdas himself was filled with shame at having been thus duped by a *Fakir*. In the meanwhile, the buffalo went to Kabir who seeing the scars on its body and the blood which was still oozing from its wounds was filled with grief and exclaiming : "O God, is this the treatment you received !" began to apply medicine to its wounds, but the buffalo said—it was God Himself who went to Ramdas in the form of a buffalo—"This is the treatment which Ramdas, to whom I went at your request, gave me. You need not grieve, however, as it is nothing by the wounds with which my body was covered in the battle with Ravana" and took leave of him. In the evening, Ramdas came to Kabir with an angry face; but his anger gave way to grief when he learned how God had come and gone and with what sort of treatment. Sage Kabir then told Ramdas how everything in the universe was really God and how the *Bhakta* should recognise God not only in the temple but in everything he sees, for there is nothing outside the Lord. So says the *Yajnavalkya-Upanishad*. "One should know that God is in everything and worship the horse, the *Chandala*, the cow, the ass and every other thing, falling on the ground before them like a log."

XV

GOODNESS IS HAPPINESS

A HUNTER once caught hold of a skylark while it was seated on a twig and singing most sweetly:

> Like a high born maiden
> In a palace tower
> Soothing her love-laden
> Soul in the secret hour
> With the music sweet as love
> Which overflows her bower.

The hunter was about to kill it, when it looked up to the cruel man and begged him to let him go. The hunter was moved by the piteous appeal of the poor bird and at the same time felt that he was doing a very cruel deed in putting to death an innocent bird which was so merry just a minute ago. He looked at the bird intently for a minute and struck with the contrast between himself who was usually sullen and careworn and the ever happy little creature, he said to it: "I will let you go, on one condition, however, namely, that you tell me truly why you larks are always so happy. I am always melancholy: but I see you singing, singing as if you have nothing else to do all your life." The lark said: "Let me go first and then I will tell you, but now I am afraid of you."

The man let him go and the bird flying up said: "You are melancholy and miserable because you are bad. Wickedness consumes your hearts. But we are happy because we are good and do harm to none."

The hunter no sooner heard the words of the "pilgrim of the skies" than was struck with their truth and from that day forward gave up all his wicked deeds.

————

THE STORY OF BALI

THE king Maha Bali, feeling very much the same grief as that of Alexander the Great, at having no more kingdoms to conquer, asked his minister to find out some new occupation for him. The minister replied: "True it is that you have conquered all the world, but there is a kingdom which is larger and more wealthy than those you have conquered. Until you conquer that, you can hardly regard yourself as a hero." The king to whom the map of the world was very familiar asked in surprise where that kingdom lay and who is its king and said that he would start immediately to subdue it. The wise minister replied: "The sovereign of the empire is a very mild and inoffensive person easy to be captured, but his minister is a very cunning, intriguing diplomatist and it is impossible to kill him by any means and unless he be subdued, no one can even approach the kingdom." The king said: "Is it so? I should be all the more eager to capture that kingdom. My name is not Mahabali if I do not conquer it. Tell me at once where it is and prepare yourself at once to start with me." The minister coolly replied: "That kingdom is within yourself." The king was struck dumb with surprise, and at last said: "You speak the truth. The *Atman*, the inner ruler immortal could not even be approached unless his minister—mind—is subdued. But ah! the difficulty of it. Still what is the good of gaining the whole world and losing one's soul! "From that day forward, the story adds, the king devoted himself to *Brahmanishtha*.

THE EXTENT OF MY DOMINION

ONCE upon a time, a certain Brahmin in the kingdom of Videha was accused of a serious offence and brought for trial before king Janaka. The Emperor found him guilty and ordered him to quit his dominions at once. The Brahmin asked in reply : "Pray, tell me, O King, what the limits are of the territories subject to you. I wish to repair to the dominion of some other king. I am ready to obey your command this moment, but I am at a loss to know what portion of the earth belongs to you and to you exclusively." Janaka was startled at the reply. He was about to say "Do you not know, Sir, which is my kingdom and which is not?" but just then a thrill passed through his body, and hanging down his head with shame, he heaved repeated and hot sighs, and said not a word in reply to the Brahmin's question, but sat plunged in thought. When that sense of shame passed away and he became comforted, he replied to the Brahmin as follows :

"Although a large inhabited tract is subject to me within this ancestral kingdom of mine, yet I fail to find my dominion, though I search the whole earth. There were several persons who called this dominion theirs, but they are all gone, and this remains. If it really belonged to anybody, it should have ceased to exist when he died. The goddess Earth once truly said, 'Kings after kings came and claimed me each to be his and fought with one another. They are all gone, but I remain, for I do not really belong to any one.' What a fool was I to have forgotten this simple thing! This country is mine only in my imagination. Not knowing this, I searched for my dominion. First I thought that the whole earth was mine; this appeared unreasonable; then I sought for my dominion in Mithila, and this too appeared foolish, for every part of Mithila has its owner, then I sought for my dominion among my children, and that too appeared foolish, for in the first place I am not master over my body, and in the second place it belongs more properly to the corpuscles, worms and parasites in it while living, and after death to the dogs, kites and jackals and worms, that will feed on it after death. Failing thus to find my dominion anywhere, I became filled with shame at having so rashly ordered you to quit my dominion. Just then there flashed upon me the idea that *I have no dominion and that everything is my dominion*. Do you, therefore, dwell here as long as thy choice leads you and do you enjoy this country as long as you please."

The Brahmin said : "When there is a large ancestral kingdom belonging to you, tell me, have you say that you have no kingdom; your ancestral dominion has its bounds, and yet you say that everything is your dominion. Tell me how you came to such a strange conclusion."

The king replied : "I examined who I was, whether I was the body, the mind, the senses, or the intellect, and found that I was none of these, and thus realised my infinite nature. I found nothing outside me, and so I have no dominion. Whatever I see, whatever seems to exist is only Myself. I am the sun, I am the moon,

I am the stars, I am the waters, I am man, I am woman, indeed I am everything, and there exists nothing outside Me, and thus I have no dominion. And yet all is my dominion, for I do not desire for my own self, even those smells that are in my nose. Therefore the earth subjugated by me is always subject to me. I do not desire for my own self, those tastes, that exist in contact with even my tongue. Therefore, water subjugated by me is always subject to me. In the same way, all other objects of sensation are subject to me, for I have mastered my senses, and am free from desire. The whole world is only a collection of objects of sensation, and I having transcended these sensations, the whole universe is subject to me. Besides, and in a much higher sense, I am the inner ruler of all that exists, for sage Yajnavalkya has taught us:

"He, who, dwelling in the earth, is within the earth whom the earth does not know, whose body is the earth. who from within, rules the earth, is thy soul, the Inner Ruler immortal.

"He, who, dwelling in all the elements, is within the elements, whom the elements do not know, whose body is the elements, who from within, rules the elements, is thy Soul, the Inner Ruler immortal.

"He, who, dwelling in the mind, is within the mind, whom the mind does not know, whose body is the mind, who from within, rules the mind is thy Soul, the Inner Ruler immortal."

XVIII

SEEING GOD?

PARVATI once wanted to see her Lord. She was always with Him, yet she thought she had not fully seen Him. Learning that by penance (*tapas*) alone the real *swarupa* of God could be known, she retired to a lonely place (*ekanta*) and there made severe and steady penance. After some time Siva, her lord, appeared before her, riding on a snow-white bull and followed by his usual retinue (*Bhuta gana*); and said, "Uma, I admire your penance and here have I come that you might see Me." Parvati opened her eyes and seeing the Lord on the bull, said : "I that see you am greater than Thou that art seen. Besides, whatever is seen, is liable to change. I want the Unchangeable One." Presently the vision disappeared.

A short time after, there appeared in her mind the form of a bright figure with a radiant face, saying : "Behold, I am God." Parvati dismissed the vision with the remark, "Thou canst not be God, for Thou being a conception, art lesser than my mind which conceives Thee." The vision disappeared at once and was soon followed by a boundless expanse of space and light which seemed almost infinite and undefinable. "May this be God" thought Parvati for a while. "But then," she added within herself, "there are here two things, first the undefinable expanse before me, and secondly, my mind which perceives it. The former cannot therefore be the Infinite and Omnipresent God." Several other visions and conceptions floated in her mind now and then, all of which, however, she dismissed in a similar way. At last her mind ceased to go out. It attained a state of perfect halcyon repose without a single idea rising to disturb its peace. It stood concentrated as it were, without any distraction, without any dispersion—like a vast ocean without the slightest ripple. It knew nothing but itself. The limitations of time and space were not there. It was free from pain of any kind, it was bliss itself. All that could be said of it was that it was, that it knew itself and that it was bliss itself. It was, in other words, *Satchidananda*. Parvati had lost all sense of her body, her mind and the world around her. After a long time (of which however she had no idea) her mind slowly began to stir; slowly she woke up to a sense of the world; but she retained a vivid recollection of the bliss she had been in. When she woke up, the first thing she said was: "I am God, I am God. Not knowing my nature, I thought I was a goddess ruling over the world. My body, mind, and the world are all but the broken reflections of the Light within me. They are like the circle of light which appears when a torch is swung round and round. Just as, when the motion of the torch ceases, the circle of light which appeared to be real disappears, so, when my mind, ceases to wander, the illusion of the world vanishes. I am the Blessed One, the Eternal, the Infinite, the Ancient whom the *Vedas* seek without rest, I am He whom the sages praise, whom the Gods adore. I am all forms and yet formless, the Lord of the Universe and yet one without a second. I am the only one that is, the only one that is."

(Adapted)

XIX

AN UNCONSCIOUS PROPHECY

ONCE upon a time, there lived at Benares a great sage by name Nirgunananda Saraswati. Like a beautiful jasmine flower that knows not the perfume it breathes around, he was the unconscious source of a most beautiful and elevating influence which purified all that came in contact with him. The inner calmness of such sages, the beatitude that overflows their hearts and shows itself out in all their thoughts, words and deeds, nay, in every line of their faces, their universal benevolence, their extreme humility, their boundless love for humanity, their readiness to sacrifice themselves for the sake of those that seek their help, are among some of the divine qualities which mark them out from the rest of mankind. Swami Nirgunananda was really one of the most eminent of the sages that are, even in our holy land, only few and far between. He was one of those who bring down Heaven to earth and themselves become God even in this mortal coil. He was very learned in Sanskrit, chiefly in sacred literature; and it was a privilege to hear him talk with all the eloquence of sincerity, all the devotion of a pure heart, and all the sweetness of his divine realisation. He had only one topic—God; and like the true lover that he was, he delighted to view that only object in all manner of ways. Never would he descend even for the space of a second from the high plane of thought in which Suka, Janaka, Jada Bharata, and other sages rejoiced to dwell. His easy accessibility, combined with his other qualities, gathered around him a pretty large number of disciples, some of whom were very earnest in seeking that Lord of Thieves (*Taskaranam Pati*) as he has been styled—because He hides Himself from all—the *Paramatman* or God.

Among those that were attached to the great master, was a certain Brahmin of the South, named Narayana Sastri. After great trials and sufferings in life, he had learnt to seek refuge in God; and having sought in vain for a long time for a *Guru* who would lead him along the narrow way of divine realisation, he at last went to Swami Nirgunananda. No sooner did he see the divinity that clearly shone in the face of the great sage, than he fell down at his feet, crying: "Here at last I take my shelter, Oh God, Oh my *Guru*, thou alone must protect me, and I the poorest of men now seek thy most potent help. The poor ship of my life has been tossed over on the stormy ocean of *Samsara* (wordly existence) and has now at last reached a safe harbour, where it must find its rest or perish." Nirgunananda kindly took him up in his arms; and wiping away his tears with his orange-coloured cloth, asked him what exactly he wanted, adding that he would most willingly do anything for him that lay in his power. The poor Brahmin was rejoiced at the soft words of the great sage, and humbly besought to be saved from the misery of wordly existence and led on towards God. The Swami replied: "To those that sincerely seek Him, God is never far off. He, the infinite Ocean of mercy, is the humblest servant of His lovers; and nothing perhaps pleases Him more than to be commanded. Just call Him by loving names and He is yours at once. If you want Him to be your father he is your father at this very moment. If you desire to have Him as your friend, He is so at once. Or think of Him as mother or as a dear lover even, He is at once at your service. Oh! who could be kinder than he from whom all kindness flows, or who could be sweeter than He who is sweetness itself? Blessed indeed are they that seek Him. Only, my son, you should seek Him sincerely. From the heart that is true He conceals nothing; but the divinity of his presence, the sweetness of His love is far away from those that are not sincere. As for me, I am yours at this very moment, ready to do anything for you that would comfort you." The gentle words of the Swami were like nectar to the grieving heart of poor Narayana; and he, again falling at his feet and bathing them with his tears, exclaimed: "My Lord, my only friend, my master, from this moment I am thy child, and I resign myself entirely to thy divine care." Nirgunananda consoled him; and greatly pleased with the sincerity of his young visitor's devotion, promised to do for him all that lay in his humble means.

A few days passed on, and Narayana was listening with rapt attention to every word that fell from his master's lips. Like the Chataka bird, fabled or real, that ever keeps open its mouth for the rain drop that might fall from heaven, he longed to have now and then a word from his Swami, if only one; and as soon as he had it, like a miser pouring intently over his treasures in a lonely place, he would retire to some calm retreat close by, to muse over his master's teachings. Nirgunananda found in him a very worthy *Chela*, already possessed of the four great qualifications for discipleship (*Sadhana*

Chatushtaya, i.e., (1) the discrimination between the real and unreal, (2) utter indifference to the fruits of one's action, (3) patience, calmness, etc., (4) a strong desire for Salvation).

One day as our young friend was sitting under a large Banyan tree closed by the *asrama*, the Swami observed him rapt in serene contemplation; and, pleased with the calm expression of his face and the intelligence of his features, thought within himself: "This young man is the youngest of my disciples, and apparently the worthiest. I should like to know if he is married, or whether he has yet to experience the stormy passions of the married state. Renunciation after experience is the safest, for, otherwise, the poor man might tumble down during his ascent." A few minutes later, Narayana rose from his meditation and entered the *asrama*. His master asked him to sit by his side; and after a brief conversation on the subject of the morning's instruction questioned him if he was married or a bachelor. He replied that he was married, but had lost his wife. The Swami immediately observed: "Our world is full of wonders; there are some persons who, on account of some domestic bereavement or calamity, fly to philosophy for refuge; in most of these cases they do not understand themselves rightly, and fall back. This of course may not be the case with you—," but Narayana, almost interrupting him, said, "My lord, I had an earnest desire for philosophy long before I was married; and even my marriage was against my will; and my seeking shelter under your feet is due to no domestic calamity, but to my intense thirst for salvation."

Day after day, Narayana's store of knowledge increased and he was in due course initiated into the mysteries of practical realisation, which a *Guru* alone can reveal. A few years passed, and Swami Nirgunananda leaving Narayana and other disciples in the *Mutt*,[1] proceeded, to what is called the *Sanchara*[2] *Samadhi*, towards the south visiting the different holy places. The object of such a travel is that persons having qualifications for discipleship but not yet possessed of a *Guru*, might, if so ordained be benefited by it. In the course of his travels, the Swami came to a small village on the banks of the Tambraparni, a river in the Tinnevelly District. It is one of those places we very often meet with, especially in the south, where nature is profuse and where the contemplative man finds an undisturbed calmness in the outer world, which singularly harmonises with that of his own inner soul. Naturally, Nirgunananda chose a retired corner in a grove on the river-side, and was enjoying that ineffable peace and blessedness which sages alone can obtain. A young woman returning home from the river, happened to see the saintly figure of our Swami sitting under a tree in the attitude of contemplation, and led by the holy impulse of reverence, a quality which still lingers in our women, noiselessly approached him and stood at a respectful distance till he awoke from his meditation; and on his waking, she prostrated herself at his feet. The Swami blessed her saying, "God grant you long life, worthy children, and a happy home."

---

1 The place where a *Guru* and his disciples live.

2 Travel made for the benefit of qualified men seeking for a teacher—so called because the meditation of the travelling sage should be unaffected by change of place and surroundings. It is a practice specially described by sages for themselves and their disciples.

No sooner did the blessing cross the lips of the sage than the young woman burst into tears, and weeping, said : "O lord, your blessing can be of no avail for I never once saw my husband after marriage ; and it is now nearly fifteen years since he went away. God knows where." But the sage calmly replied : "My child, *Ramodwir nabibhashate, i.e.,* Rama (*Atman* or God) will never tell a lie ; the words came to me of their own accord and they are His." The Brahminee quietly bowed to him and went her way. She had a vague hope in her mind that the words of the sage might, in some mysterious manner come to pass. The next morning, she again paid her respects to him, and to visit him and sweep and clean the place which he occupied thenceforth became a part of her daily routine.

By this time, the disciples, not having heard of the whereabouts of their *Guru* for a long time past, went in search of him ; and after long wanderings, came to the place where he was, just when the Brahmin woman was paying her daily respects to him. Narayana saw her and started back ; the woman saw him and at once burst out with tears of joy and said, pointing to Narayana, "This is my husband, this is my husband, my lord." The Swami was surprised at the exclamation of the woman, and looking at Narayana, who was trembling with fear from head to foot, asked him what the matter was. The poor man at once fell down at his feet, and, weeping, said, "My master, I have deceived you, I have told a lie to yourself. Such was my fear. So kindly excuse me, oh lord. A fool that I was, I was afraid to tell you that my wife was alive lest you might not initiate me. I told you I was a widower, my lord ;

I confess my sin and beg your gracious pardon. Any punishment you may choose for me—nothing can be too severe for such a sinner—I am quite ready to undergo, my lord. Punish me as severely as you can, only take me back into your favour."

Nirgunananda rejoiced within himself at the drama that had been enacted in his presence; and, addressing the woman exclaimed, "*Ramodwir nabibhashate.*—His words do not fail. How inscrutable are his ways!" Meanwhile, Narayana waxed louder in his exclamations of repentance; and to him the sage coolly observed, "Be not afraid, my son, there is no harm done; you were afraid when there was no occasion for it. In your ignorance you thought that to be freed from the married life was a necessary condition for obtaining wisdom. Marriage may not be a necessity in some cases, but, as a rule, renunciation after sufficient experience of the married state is the safest. Woman is difficult to conquer; and great men like Viswamitra, Parasara, Tondaradipodi Alwar and others have been led astray in the very midst of their severe penances. Renunciation proceeding from sufficient experience or satiety is certainly much more firm than that which proceeds from occasional disgust, family accidents and the like. Your fear was absolutely unnecessary; and for this sin of lying there is a *prayaschitta* (purification), and that is to do as I tell you. Join your wife, live with her, make yourself and her happy; and this is the only remedy." Narayana Sastri exclaimed, "Oh master, save me from this punishment. Even death would be more welcome than again to bind myself with the very chains which I have been trying so long to break asunder, save me oh lord" ; and so saying he fell at his master's feet. Nirgunananda raised him from the ground and said, "My child, you have not yet understood what true renunciation is. Attachment and freedom belong to the mind ; and so long as that is unattached, there can be no fear. The true warrior does not shrink from battle, but boldly faces it and wins it ; and similarly, he is the true sage who does not take fright and fly away from the strife of the world, but keeping himself in it, lives totally unattached to it. Fear is weakness, and shows that perfection is yet far off. Arjuna was advised not to shrink from war with fear, but to fight it on bravely and unattached." [1]

Narayana felt the truth of his *Guru's* teaching, joined his wife and lived with her, contributing to her happiness without, at the same time, entangling "his unbounded spirit into bonds again".

In the above story, we have a prophecy fulfilled in a remarkable way. There is a power in the pure heart which often works wonders. Prophecies, strange cures, remarkable intuitive flashes, sudden inspiration, and several other phenomena apparently miraculous, are among the ordinary privileges of the pure mind. The way in which genuine sages—gods on earth—get on in life just like "the fowls of the air" and "the lilies of the field" without any thought for the morrow, and the mysterious manner in which their wants are divined

---

[1] Compare Nirgunananda's advice with the following passage of the *Chandogya Upanishad* : Having studied the *Veda* in the house of a tutor and having paid to the *Guru* what is his due, one should *dwell with his family* in a healthy country, reading the *Vedas*, bringing up virtuous sons and pupils, devoting himself with all his senses to the universal Soul and injuring no created being....(VIII, XV).

and provided for, to all appearance, by an unknown
power, would readily strike all that care to observe.
But the miracles cease the moment the mind gets impure.
Let the prophet get conscious of his prophecy and think
highly of his powers, the oracle becomes at once dumb,
for the mind has become impure. The prophet strives
to continue a prophet, but that is impossible, and the
power that came to him of its own accord now eludes
his grasp. He loses his power, but tries at least to preserve his fame; and imposture and humbug, so very
often met with, are the result. Wise men care not for
the powers that might come to them or the noise they
might make. They never take the credit of such powers
to themselves; they feel it is not theirs and say they
are Rama's, Krishna's, or God's. They are not the least
anxious whether the words coming from their lips are
fulfilled or not. Look at Nirgunananda's cool reply to
the woman when she exclaimed that his blessing was
impossible of fulfilment. *The power of prophecy or even
the power to raise the dead cannot drag down to the plane
of the lower self (ahankara) the sage's mind concentrated
all upon the Absolute Brahman.*

XX

JNANA—THE HIGHEST SACRIFICE

The very highest of sacrifices is Jnana-Yagna or Wisdom-Sacrifice.—Satyayani Upanishad.

KRISHNA had a bow on which were hung a number of little bells. They had the power of ringing by themselves whenever any offering was made to Krishna; and the number of the bells ringing, the loudness of their sound and its duration were in proportion to the piety, wisdom and pure-mindedness with which the offering was made. When Yudhishthira, the eldest of the Pandavas, otherwise called Dharmaputra, performed his celebrated *Rajasuya Yagam* (a kind of sacrifice), feeding numberless brahmins and distributing a fabulous amount of money in charities, only one of the bells rang and that not very loudly. Dharmaputra was however gratified at even that recognition, for he had never before heard any of them make more than a slight tinkle, and felt proud within himself at the sacrifice he had celebrated. Pride is one of the most dangerous weaknesses to which man is liable and *however justifiable it may seem*, should never be suffered to enter into our hearts; for in proportion as we think highly of ourselves we hinder our further growth. *Pride, moreover, argues an inability to look into the infinity which surrounds us everywhere, in the midst of which we are nothing.* Yudhishthira was generally a cautious man; but the mind of man being always on the alert to deceive him, once in his life even he felt a little proud.

815

Not long after, however, when Krishna and Dharma-putra were together, all the bells on the former's bow began to ring at the same time and kept up their loud and continued music for more than half an hour. Poor Yudhishthira was struck dumb with surprise, and on recovering from the shock, humbly asked his divine companion the cause of the strange phenomenon. "Nothing very particular, my royal friend," said Krishna, "a *Brahmajnani* (one that has realised God) who lives close by the cremation ground at Muttra cooked dog's flesh, which was all he could get for his dinner to-day, and is now eating it having first offered it to me. Nothing extraordinary O Samrat." Dharma-putra at once rose and falling down at the feet of the all-knowing Krishna confessed to him the sin of pride he had carelessly committed and said, "*Better far than a thousand sacrifices is the true knowledge of thee, O Lord.*"

Brahmajnanam is the highest kind of sacrifice, for it means the total annihilation, the complete sacrifice of the lower self in man—which is a necessary condition for the realisation of the Supreme Self, *Atman* or God.

Wealth, friendship, love may all be sacrificed but the sacrifice of these things is not enough, for it leaves behind, as in the case of Dharmaputra, a residue, *i.e.*, the self which is the most difficult thing to surrender. Therefore it is that Lord Krishna says : "Better than the sacrifice with objects is Wisdom, the highest sacrifice, O Parantapa. All actions in their entirety, O Partha, are fulfilled in Wisdom" (*Gita*, IV, 33).

All actions are contained in Wisdom, for Wisdom, *i.e.*, the realisation of God, is our highest duty, and in the performance of that duty is involved the discharge of all other duties. "Know Thyself, it is the only thing for which thou art born," is the precept of the *Vedas* ; and all acts done by him who has known himself, are done with the knowledge that the Supreme Self being beginningless, without qualities and imperishable though seated in the body, worketh not nor is soiled (*Gita,* XIII, 31).

The idea of *Jnana-Yajna* (wisdom-sacrifice) is beautifully elaborated in the *Taittiriya Upanishad*. In every sacrifice there should be a performer, and he should be a *Grihastha, i.e.,* one living with his wife. A particular ground should be selected, cleaned and decorated ; and the sacrificial fire should be reared and fed with the fuel of the *Aswatthah* (the sacred Peepul) tree and ghee. The animal for sacrifice should be tied to a pole called *Yupa Stambha* and made to die, not by slaughter but by the force of *Mantra*. There should be three brahmins or parties of brahmins reciting the *Rik, Sama* and *Yajur Vedas* and another brahmin representing the Prajapati or *Brahma*. The performer should wear *diksha* (should not get his head shaved)[1] till the close of the sacrifice, drink soma juice and distribute offerings (*Dakshina*). In *Jnana-Yajna* the performer is *Atman* in the sense of pure Jiva and *Sraddha, i.e.,* faith in the teachings of the *Guru* and the *Sastras,* is the wife. The breast is the sacrificial ground and *tapas,* the destroying of even the germs of desire in the light of the knowledge that the *Brahman* alone is real and the world an illusion—is the fire fed by the ghee of attachment (*abhilasha*). The body is the sacred fuel for the fire, for without it *Jnana*

1 It is a customary vow among Hindus not to get one's head shaved till a particular undertaking is finished.

52

is impossible. "Body is the boat by which we have to cross the ocean of existence," says the Mahabharata. *Krodha* or anger is the animal to be sacrificed, and it is to die by the force of *Mantra* (that which is beyond *manana* or meditation—*nididhyasana*). The pole to which that animal is to be tied is the firm heart. The mouth is the *Ritwik* (the brahmin reciting the *Rig Veda*), *Prana*—the life, the *Udgata* (the brahmin reciting the *Sama Veda*) and the eyes the *Adhvaryu* (the brahmin reciting the *Yajur Veda*) : the mind is the Prajapati or *Brahma* because of its creative power. The sacrifice and its *diksha* last till the *prana* lasts, all that is eaten and drunk by the performer of the wisdom-sacrifice has the virtue of the *Soma* juice and the offering made (*dakshina*) is *Sama*—the wisdom that all that exists is God.

This *Jnana-Yajna*, a further elaboration of which may be found in *Taittiriya Upanishad*, is the highest and truest sacrifice ; other sacrifices have their uses in cleansing the mind or conferring temporal and spiritual benefits, but this is the most glorious and the most laudable. No wealth, no extraordinary learning and no favour from except ourselves and our *Guru* are needed for this glorious *Yajna* : and seeing that it is so cheap and so precious may we all do it !

APPENDIX

APPENDIX

SOME QUESTIONS AND ANSWERS

1. How and why is there *desire* for *action*? *action* not of the external organ only but of the internal organ also?

2. Is such desire for action *innate*?

3. Or, is it created by impact with the external world or the world of sense?

4. Is it a mere *Upadhi* or *Guna*?

5. If the desire for action is created by external impact, why should there be difference in the *kind* and *degree* of such desire in mankind?

To go to the root of the matter. It is the "sense of separateness," the sense of finiteness that is primarily responsible for the desire for action. As was observed in one of our recent articles, "Where there arises the slightest differentiation in the shape of a *Jiva*, the footing being lost, the natural result is rolling down and down and the creation of an infinitely variegated universe."[1] It will be seen from these remarks that the primary sense of separateness brings with it by its innate restlessness (*chalana*) or desire for action, the variety of non-self, and the finite soul is attracted and repelled by the latter, in other words that desire increases. So says the *Sruti*. "Where there is duality, as it were, another sees another thing, another hears another thing, etc." (*Bri.,Up., IV*, 5, 15). The desire for action is thus innate and at the same time increases in proportion to the degree of impact with the external world. It is not *created* by such impact, for, as we have seen, the external world itself is a projection so to speak of the

[1] Is the world real or false, II.

Jiva. However, the world and the *Jiva,* or practically, the mind, act and react upon each other. To take an example, we see a wooden chair. The chair is only wood all through, the idea of a chair being only in our mind. For name and form are not outside the mind. Though thus the chair is only a projection of the mind, it appears to have an independent existence outside and in its turn reacts upon the mind, suggesting the ideas of its being good, wanting repair and so on.

Just as, in this example, the mind by its *chalana,* created the chair and the chair in its turn, reacted upon the mind and increased its restlessness, so also the world sprang out of the *chalana* of *Jiva,* its desire for action and in its turn reacting on it, induces greater restlessness. It did not originally create the desire for action, for it itself was the result of such a desire, but it increases it. With reference to question IV this desire is a *Guna.* It represents a tendency and is thus more a *Guna (Gita,* Chapter XIV). With reference to the question, "Why should there be difference in the kind and degree of such desire in mankind?" the reply is, because the individual souls are different among themselves, though not in their essence, at least in their tendencies and in the respective part they are intended to play in the world of manifestation. There are certain difficult points in connection with this last question, but as we cannot discuss them here, we refer the reader to *Vedanta Sutras,* II, 1, 32—36, and Sankara's Commentary thereon. If it be asked how this desire for action can be overcome, the reply is, proper inquiry into the nature of the Self and practice under the instructions of a proper teacher. This is a question we have often discussed.

HOW TO KILL OUT ANGER

THE renowned philosopher, Sree Vidyaranya Swami gives in his *Jivanmukti "Prakarna"* the following advice to the *Mumukshu* (aspirant for salvation) as to how anger may gradually be overcome :

When you are tempted to get angry with others, you should address your mind and say : "Oh, mind ! if you would get angry with those who do mischief to you, then why do you not get angry with anger itself ? For it does the greatest mischief ; it prevents a man from attaining the four great ends of life—Duty, wealth, happiness and salvation and throws him into hell (even before his death) : therefore there is no enemy worse than anger." The meaning of this truth should be repeatedly thought upon, and you should get angry with anger. By doing this you will attain peace and salvation. When anger grows so far as to give birth to abuse and blows, it at once destroys all charity and fame : when it does not develop to this full extent it scorches the mind at least. Therefore how could anger, which gives rise to so much mischief here and hereafter ever spring in the minds of the sages ? To think as above is the best means of killing out anger. When others get angry with you, you should not think, "I have done no wrong. Why do these people get angry with me who am innocent," and get angry with them in return. You are not really innocent, for is it not a great wrong that you have not yet crossed beyond the three bodies (*Sthula, Sukshma* and *Karana*) and attained the bliss of wisdom ? The attainment of *jnana* is the true innocence ; and until you have attained that, how could you think that you are innocent?

There is yet another means by which we may avoid being provoked by others' anger towards us; and that is that we should regard those that get angry with us as our benefactors and feel thankful to them for their anger; for by getting angry with us, they reveal to us our faults and strengthen our *Vairagya* (non-attachment). To do us this service, they sacrifice their own peace of mind and therefore we should feel all the more thankful to them. Thinking in this way is a great help to us.

THE STORY OF JADA BHARATA

Asathananuchintanam bandhanaya Bharatavat, Sankhya Karika, Book IV, Aphorism 8—"That which is not a means of liberation is not to be thought of ; it becomes a cause of bondage, as in the case of Bharata."

THIS Bharata was a great king, who once ruled over our country, and whose memory has been perpetuated in the Sanskrit name for India, "*Bharata Varsha*" or land of Bharata. He was the son of the great Royal Sage Rishabha. Rishabha carefully instructed his son while young, in all the kindly duties and the sublime philosophy of the *Vedanta*, and in everything else that was necessary to make him a worthy successor of himself. When Bharata attained his age, his father, who was then in the plenitude of power, abdicated the throne in his favour, and betook himself to the forest to meditate undisturbed on the lotus-feet of the Lord.

This would seem strange in these days. But ancient India was essentially a land of religious realisation. It is no matter for wonder, therefore, that kings, who were foremost in the land in point of wealth, power, and position, were also great philosophers and saints. Rama was taught the solution for the problem of life, when quite young. It was on account of this priceless possession that he interpreted struggles and sufferings, and was able to endure them, in a manner essentially different from that of a Hamlet or a Prometheus. The secret of it was that, in the midst of all agitation, Rama had his eye fixed on that "Star above the storm", the luminous Self within. Janaka's cheerful equanimity at the destruction of the city which was the object of his tender solicitude, is too well known to need more than a passing reference here. Thus it was generally the aim of men in those days to live and move and have their being in God, the material things being held merely subservient to this end.

To return to the subject. Soon after he ascended the throne, Bharata entered the holy *grahasthasrama* and took for his wife, Panchajani, the daughter of Viswarupa. He had five sons, who were as great and powerful as himself. He was a model king and a centre of moral and spiritual force, protecting the people from foreign aggressions, and providing for their material and spiritual needs with more than paternal solicitude. During several years of just and beneficent reign, he never once forgot that this vast and wonderful universe was but the "shadow of beauty unbeheld," the reflection of a glorious and eternal light seen through a perverse medium—our mind, which is a poly-sided mirror distorting to many a shape of error that which is really One without a second. Through his mind, purified by the *nishkamakarma* (action without caring for reward) which he incessantly performed, he became able to see, like Narada and other chosen devotees, the divinity which shines formless within the lotus chamber of his heart, with us much vividness and reality as if the God were there in as embodied form adorned with conch, mace and disc. The more he saw Him, the more his love grew in intensity and force.

Bharata now saw that he had fairly worked out his *Karma* which had determined his position in life as king ; and he accordingly transferred his sacred trust to his

son, and himself went to the hermitage known as
Pulahasrama. It was a place of

> ......more pellucid streams,
> An ampler either, a divine air,
> And fields invested with purpureal gleams.

The *asrama* was sanctified by the waters of the
Gandaki which flowed round it, and it was the general
resort of great and noble souls who wanted to realise
God. The peace and tranquillity that reigned there
was highly expressive of the God sought therein ; and
of it, it might well be said, "one impulse from that vernal
wood will teach you more of God and Man than all your
sciences can." In this beautiful hermitage, at a solitary
place, and with his senses at rest, Bharata would daily
worship God with flowers and tender leaves, and drink
with avidity the sweet nectar which silently welled up
at the time from within his calm and tranquilled spirit.
Often with his senses completely ravished, his hair
standing erect, and with eyes swimming with tears, he
would totally lose himself in the flood of divine rapture
which overflowed even the fathomless depths of his
heart and made him forget even that he was worshipping.
Indeed, in moments of such divine ecstasy, he did not
worship, but himself became God. Early in the morning,
he would bathe in the river, clothe himself in deerskin,
and with his face to the east, would thus sing the glory
of the Lord symbolised in the rising sun, "May we
attain that Supreme effulgence which shines through
the sun, that pure *Sat* which manifests itself as Iswara
and creates through *Maya* all this universe."

We now come to a different chapter in Bharata's

life. He was not to remain long in this blissful condition. One day, after bathing in the waters of the *Mahanadi* (holy river), Bharata seated himself on its banks, and was meditating on the sacred *Gayatri*. Ere long, he was roused by the terrible roar of a lion close by. A female deer which was just then quenching her thirst in the river got terrified at the sound; and, with her delicate frame trembling with fear, violently jumped on to the bank, while the young one in her womb, slipped out of it into the river. The shock was too much for that naturally timid creature; and, before proceeding a few steps, it dropped down dead by the side of a cavern. Bharata, who was observing all this, took pity on the young fawn, which was being carried away helplessly by the floods; and ran to its rescue. He took it into his *asrama*, and was kindly attending to its wants. He made it a part of his worship to look after the young one, and spared nothing on his part to make it live. He would divine its wants with more than maternal instinct, and would procure them with a like zeal, and solicitude. The young one was regularly fed with cow's milk and tender grass, and was lodged in a comfortable place in the *asrama*. Gradually, however, it engaged Bharata's attention more and more; and he came to look upon it as something like his property— because he had rescued it from the floods—and to think that *he* had a claim to look after it, more than any one else. No sooner did he cherish such an idea, than he became personally and passionately attached to it. Worship and meditation gradually slipped away, while he was constantly engaged in nursing, protecting, pleasing and fondling it by turns. Often he would say to himself, "This poor little thing which has been thrown helpless on the world, has come to *me* for protection, and is so much attached to me that it never thinks of its parents or relatives. Therefore I should not hesitate to devote myself to its service. To neglect one's helpless dependents would be sinful. Therefore it is, that noble-minded men set aside their own superior spiritual interests, and devote themselves to the protection of those who need their care and kindness."

Fortified with such an argument, he allowed the fawn to be his companion at all times and places. It was with him while bathing, meditating and sleeping. He would take it with him when he went out to fetch fruits, leaves, kusagrass, etc. On the way, under an impulse of warm affection, he would sometimes take it, and bear it on his shoulders. It will be extremely interesting to follow the development of Bharata's relations with the fawn. Often he would pine for its company on account of the pleasure it gave him. Even during worship, he would mount it on his laps, dally with it, and shower on it his choicest blessings.

While thus having a pleasant time of it with the fawn, he one day missed it all of a sudden. He searched for it hard and for a long time, but in vain. At last, he lost all hope of finding it, and feeling miserable like a miser robbed of his wealth, he broke out into most cowardly ejaculations, "O unfortunate wretch that I am, how cruel have I been to that helpless young! Else why should it run away from me? Will it, in its nobility, overlook my failings, and confide in me again? Can I see it again safe, grazing on the outskirts of the forest? Will not some kind gods take care of it? Or has it al-

ready been devoured by wolves and tigers abounding
in the forest? Even the sun is set, still my darling has
not turned up. Will it return and comfort me, a poor
wretch, with its graceful and charming presence? Will
it be given to me to lose myself once more with eyelids
closed, while the little thing frisks and gambols with all
the divine charms of a summer landscape melting under
the mellow moon? Shall it again approach me with
affectionate familiarity, and rouse me from that pleasant
slumber by suddenly throwing itself into my lap? Or
shall I live to enjoy again its pleasant interference with
my *puja*, and its sensible withdrawal at a glance from
me?" So prating, he worked himself up into a state of
infatuation; and walking a few steps again in search
of the fawn, he discovered its foot-prints, which elicited
a fresh outburst, "This *asrama* must be blessed indeed
to bear these tender, graceful and sacred foot-prints
which give me life and hope. I can now find out my
lost treasure." With these words, he walked up a few
steps, when he saw the moon with its deer-like speck
peeping down through the thick-set leaves of the *asrama*
trees, and struck into a still more frantic strain, "Lo,
this great Lord of the stars shelters in his bosom a
beautiful fawn; while mine, which was even more
beautiful, and which I tended so fondly, sheltering it
more securely than this moon does hers, has strayed
from me, leaving me thus wretched" and began to
weep.

The poor king, who had cheerfully renounced his
wife and children and his extensive dominions, had no
strength in him to reconcile himself to the separation
from the young deer to which he latterly became at-

tached ; for, having previously renounced everything else, now he focused on a single object all the love which his lower self was capable of. Thus an attachment formed at an advanced stage of renunciation, is specially disastrous in its consequences. Bharata's one idea was to recover his lost treasure, which was, however, not to be. His frame, already wasted by an abstemious life in the forest was soon eaten away by a mortal anguish ; and the unhappy king one day breathed his last, with his head full of his dear fawn. The result was that, in his next incarnation, he was born as a deer, forfeiting for the time the merits he had acquired as a *Bhakta* in the earlier years of his previous existence. Thus the ill-fated attachment he contracted for his fawn, utterly blasted the immediate purpose of a life begun so well.

The above story might be easily misunderstood. To the careless reader, it might mean that Jada Bharata was made a beast, because he showed great compassion for the deer ; and that, by the laws of Heaven, kindness and pity merit only punishment. The laws of Heaven are, however, incapable of such an absurdity.

On the other hand, *the story of Jada Bharata is a standing example, to illustrate the sufficiency of our narrow and personal love*—narrow, because we love a man or a woman in preference to the rest, and for one that we love we hate ten ; and personal, because, through it, we emphasise our personality, and joy and grieve by turns. *The course of such love never runs smooth*. In most cases, it is a brief emotion, "the perfume and suppliance of a minute" fading away like a floweret.

> Love hath forlorn me,
> Living in thrall ;

> Heart is bleeding,
> All help needing,
> O cruel speeding !

is the usual cry of all lovers ; and even while it lasts, it may be said of it, "Of love and death, I know not which is sweeter, no, not I." True love is not this narrow, personal, selfish, and, often, miserable love. *It is love in God* ; *loving*, not because this particular thing, or that, is pleasing to me, in preference to others ; but *because it is the manifestation of God, of the God within me, my own Self.* "I am myself the cow, the dog, the leper and the richman," says the *Vedantin*, and whom could he hate ? He sees himself in all things and loves because love is the essence of his soul, because he cannot but love, because Love is Light and Light is Love. There is in such love no pandering the lower self ; for that narrow individuality is long since dead, and *true love is the flower upon its grave.* Infinite is the sphere of this love, for God is everywhere ; and incapable of death or misery, for God is immortal and blissful. The sage, healing a leper, takes no pride in it, any more than we for scratching our bodies during sleep, for he sees himself in the leper. His love is instinctive and spontaneous, like the light of the moon ; and in it there is no exclusion, no preference of one to another, and no selfishness. The true *Yogi* is the embodiment of this highest love, which, to be highest, cannot exclude anything from its scope. Like a cloud, he pours out his love and kindness to all ; and, in the act, he wears out and dissolves his own personality (his lower self). Dwelling in that Sun of suns, the eternal Self within, as he looks below from that lofty height, the little differences which separate man from man are no longer real to him, and he loves all men equally. He is like a fragrant flower, which is full of cheer and tenderness in all surroundings, and unconsciously emits its sweet odour for the benefit of both the good and the bad. In short, he sees the God in all things, and loves them for Him; and hence his love is impersonal, and, therefore, the highest. It was this highest love which inspired Buddha, Jesus and Sankara to help struggling humanity as they did.

But until the mind is turned permanently inward, and rests with the Higher Self, which alone can feed that infinite and impersonal love, the little self will persist and externalise the mind. The more the *Yogi* is away from the earth, the greater and subtler the force with which it drags him down. Rambha and Urvasi, and hosts of other heavenly damsels are specially fond of people going Heavenward. Even artificial summers and untimely moons are called into existence to entrap the poor *Yogis*; and it required an effort, even on the part of Iswara, to burn away the seducing *Manmatha*. So, from the time he leaves the earth behind, till he reaches the Himalayan summit of Self-realisation, the earnest seeker after God should avoid all things which feed his little self, which drags him down; and renounce all *personal* attachment to things. Love to his wife, and even love to his country, are not good for a *Yogi*, if he loves them because they are his. In so far as he bestows a thought upon others beyond his immediate little self, it is true love, it is self-sacrifice. But in so far as he does so, *with the idea that they are his*, it is selfishness; the result is therefore not perfect love. A

53

passionate love to one's kindred and countrymen is good for one who is not aware of any love at all. In the case of Silas Marner his devotion to the charming little child Eppie, alchemised his sterile existence, and called forth all his latent humanity. But in the case of Bharata, whose love had outgrown his family and his country, and was already becoming impersonal, a reversion to a limited attachment would be as unwise as the attempt of a man who has half climbed a steep rock to snatch at something that attracts him in the lower regions. That Bharata conceived a *personal* attachment for the fawn was natural, as his evolution was not yet complete, and as he was still within the sway of the earth. But instead of brushing aside such an idea when it arose, and steadily looking upward, he hopelessly flagged, and allowed his lingering egoism to develop and assert itself, and it completely dragged him down from the spiritual eminence he had attained. For the human mind never rests halfway, if Godward, it must reach God, if earthward, it must reach earth.

—Adapted from the Bhagavata.

THE LIVING ARE FEW

BUT

THE DEAD ARE MANY

KRISHNA GAUTAMI had an only son, and he died. In her grief she carried the dead child to all her neighbours, asking them for medicine, and the people said : "She has lost her senses. The boy is dead."

At length Krishna Gautami met a man, who replied to her request : "I cannot give you medicine for your child, but know a physician who can."

And the girl said : "Pray tell me, Sir ; Who is it ?" And the man replied : "Go to Sakhyamuni, the Buddha."

Krishna Gautami repaired to Buddha and cried : "Lord and Master, give me the medicine that will cure my boy."

Buddha answered : "I want a handful of mustard seed." And when the girl in her joy promised to procure it, Buddha added : "The mustard seed must be taken from a house, where no one has lost a child, husband, parent or friend."

Poor Krishna Gautami now went from house to house, and the people pitied her and said : "Here is mustard seed ; take it !" But when she asked : "Did a son or daughter, a father or mother, die in your family ?" They answered her : "Alas ! *the living are few, but the dead are many.* Do not remind us of our deepest grief." And there was no house but some beloved one had died in it.

Krishna Gautami became weary and hopeless, and sat down at the way side, watching the lights of the city, as they flickered up and were extinguished again. At last the darkness of the night reigned everywhere. And she considered the fate of men, that their lives flicker up and are extinguished. And she thought to herself : "How selfish am I in my grief ! Death is common to all ; yet in this valley of desolation, there is a path that leads him, who has surrendered all selfishness, to immortality."

Putting away the selfishness of her affection for her child, Krishna Gautami had the dead body buried in the forest. Returning to Buddha, she took refuge in him and found comfort in the *dharma*, which is the balm that will soothe all the pains of our troubled hearts.

Buddha said :

The life of mortals in this world is troubled and brief and combined with pain. For, there is not any means by which, those that have been born can avoid dying ; after reaching old age there is death ; of such a nature are living beings.

As ripe fruits are early in danger of falling, so mortals when born are always in danger of death.

As all earthen vessels made by the potter end in being broken, so is the life of mortals.

Both the young and adult, both those who are foolish and those who are wise, all fall into the power of death ; all are subject to death.

Of those, who, overcome by death, depart from life, a father cannot save his son, nor relatives their relations.

Mark ! while relatives are looking on, lamenting

deeply, one by one the mortals are carried off, like an ox that is led to the slaughter.

So the world is afflicted with death and decay, therefore, the wise do not grieve, knowing the terms of the world.

Not from weeping nor from grieving will anyone obtain peace of mind; on the contrary his pain will be the greater and his body will suffer. He will make himself sick and pale, yet the dead are not saved by his lamentation.

He who seeks peace, should draw out the arrow of lamentation, and complaint and grief.

He who has drawn out the arrow and has become composed, will obtain peace of mind; he who has overcome all sorrow will become free from sorrow, and be blessed.

—*From "The Gospel of Buddha".*

THERE was a Brahmin, a religious man, fond in his affections but without deep wisdom. He had a very promising son, of great intellect, who, when seven years old, was struck with a fatal disease and died. The unfortunate father, unable to control himself, threw himself upon the corpse and lay there as one dead. The relatives came and buried the child, and when the father came to himself, he was immoderate in his grief, and behaved like an insane person. He no longer gave way to tears, though he wandered about asking for the residence of *Yama Raja*, the King of Death, to beg of him humbly that his child to be allowed to return to life.

Having arrived at a great Brahmin temple, the sad father went through certain religious rites, and fell asleep. While wandering on in his dream, he came to a deep mountain-pass, where he met a number of *Shramanas* (*ascetics*) who had acquired supreme wisdom. "Kind sirs," he said, "can you not tell me where the residence of *Yama Raja* is?" And they asked him, "Good friend, why do you want to know it?" Whereupon he told them his sad story, and explained his intentions. Pitying his self-delusion, the *Shramanas* said: "No mortal man can reach the place where *Yama* reigns. But some four hundred miles westward, lies a great city in which many good spirits live. Every eighth day of the month *Yama* visits the place, and there you may see him and ask him for a boon." The Brahmin, rejoicing at the news, went to the city, and found it as the *Shramanas* had told him. And he was admitted to the great presence of *Yama*, who, on hearing his request, said, "Your son lives now in yonder *Brahmaloka*. Go there and ask him to follow you." Said the happy father, "How does it happen that my son, without having performed one good work, is now living in Paradise?" *Yama Raja* replied : "He has attained celestial happiness not by performing good deeds, but because he died in faith and love to the Lord and Master. He was a born wise man. 'The heart of love and wisdom spreads, as it were, a beneficent shade from the world of men to the world of gods,' so says Buddha. This glorious utterance is like the stamp of a king's seal upon a royal edict." The happy father hastened to the place, and saw his beloved child all transfigured by the peace and blessedness of heavenly life. He ran up to his boy, and cried, with tears running down his cheeks, "My son, my son, do you not remember me, your father who watched over you with loving care and tended you in your sickness? Return home with me to the world of men." But the boy cast on him a look of pity and replied : "In my present state, I know no such words as father and son, for I am free from delusion. *True love knows not limitation*, and spreads alike to all, heedless of restricting relations like those of father, mother, son, and brother. I am love itself; and if you also become that, getting free from delusion, and learn to look upon all the world alike, you will also come here and we can have a happy life together." On this the Brahmin departed, and, when he woke from his dream, he bethought himself of the sweet words of his blessed son, and resolved to acquire that heavenly wisdom which alone can give comfort to an afflicted heart, and, freeing him from delusion, make him love all the world alike.

The above story, which is adapted from a Buddhistic parable, illustrates some splendid truths. Says the *Brihadaranyaka-Upanishad*, 3rd Brahmana, 4th Chapter, 21 and 22, "As in the embrace of a beloved wife one is unconscious of aught from without or within, so, embraced by the All-knowing soul, this *purusha* (he who has attained his highest place) is unconscious of all without or within. This is the true nature when all desires are satisfied, where the only desire is for the soul, where there is no desire, where there is no grief. Then the father is no father, the mother no mother, the worlds no worlds, the gods no gods, the *Vedas* no *Vedas*, then the thief is no thief, the murderer of a Brahmin no murderer of a Brahmin, the Chandala no Chandala, the Paulkasa no Paulkasa (chuckler), the Shramana no Shramana, the ascetic no ascetic." All that is *satyam-jnanam anantam anandam sarva sariropadhivinirmuktam*, that which is eternal, all knowing and blissful and free from the limitations of any kind of body or form (*Sarvasaropanishad*). Knowing these truths the sage loves all the world alike, irrespective of distinctions of father, mother, and so on. Says the *Isavasyopanishad*, "Whoever beholds all beings in the soul (his *Atman*) alone and the soul in all despises naught. When a man knows that all beings are even his *Atman*, when all beings have become to him himself, then there is no delusion, no grief" (6 and 7). "He who loves all alike and looks upon other's griefs and joys as his own, he is the highest *Yogin*," says Krishna (*Gita*, VI, 32). "They are called wise men who, seeing the same *Atman* in all regard with equal love the cultured and respectful Brahmin, the cow, the elephant, the dog and he who eats dogs" (*Gita*, V, 18).

The real *Brahmaloka* is the pure mind free from *rajas* and *tamas*, and of unmixed *Satwic* disposition. "O emperor, here (in this world) and nowhere else is the true *Brahmaloka*," said Yajnavalkya to Janaka—*Esha Brahmaloke Samrat iti hovacha* (*Brihadaranyaka Upanishad*).

—*Adapted from "The Gospel of Buddha"*.

HARIH, OM

THE SKANDOPANISHAD

The Peace Chant

OM! May He protect us[1] both; may he be pleased with us. May we develop strength; illumined may our studies be. May there be no dispute.

Om! Peace, Peace, Peace! Harih, Om.

Om! O Mahadeva! Through a small fraction of Thy (boundless) grace, I am immortal; I am *Vijnana-ghana* (all-wisdom, the Universal consciousness, boundless and pure); I am blissful. What is there higher than this!

Truth shone not as truth, because the mind was not pure. By the death of the (impure) mind, Hari is all wisdom. As my nature also is àll-wisdom, I am birthless. What is there higher than this!

All non-Atmic, non-real things (*jada*) vanish like dream. He who sees the real and the non-real, that

---

1 The *Guru* and the disciple. The *Upanishads* are more in the nature of *Sravanam*, *i.e.*, that which is heard—a discourse addressed by the teacher to the disciple, than regular treatises on philosophy. The knowledge of the identity of the *Jiva* and the *Brahman* is according to Sankara called *Upanishad* because it completely annihilates the world together with its cause ignorance (*Shad* means to destroy, *Upa* near, and in certainty). An exposition of that knowledge is also called *Upanishad*. The word also means "the knowledge of That which ever shines nearest to us—the *Atman*".

842

immortal One (Achyuta) is by nature all-wisdom. He, verily is the Great God (*Mahadev*). He, verily is the Great Hari. He, verily is the Light of all lights. He, verily is the Great Lord (*Parameswara*). He, verily is the *Brahman*. I am that *Brahman*. There is no doubt (about this).

Verily the *Jiva* (the individual soul) is Siva. Verily Siva is the *Jiva*. That *Jiva* is verily none but Siva. What when bound by husk is paddy, becomes rice when freed from the husk. In the self-same way, the *Jiva* bound by the effect of past actions is, when freed from it, always Siva. The *Jiva* is *Jiva* so long as it is fettered by desire. When freed from desire, it is Siva.

Prostration to Siva who is of the nature of Vishnu, and prostration to Vishnu who is of the nature of Siva! Verily Siva's heart is Vishnu and Vishnu's heart is Siva. In what measure I see no difference between them both, just in the same measure may life and happiness be granted unto me! No difference is there between Siva and Vishnu.

Verily is the body said to be the temple. The *Jiva* within is surely the bright, ever blissful One. After removing the faded flower of ignorance, worship should be done with the thought "I am He that Siva".

To view all things alike as *Brahman* is *jnana* (wisdom). The non-attachment of the mind to sense-objects is *dhyana* (contemplation). The control of the senses is *Saucha* (cleaning). The nectar of *Brahmic* bliss should be drunk. This is the real drink (*pana*). The body should be kept up by means of begging. One should dwell alone in a solitary place without a second, *i.e.*, rapt up in the contemplation of the non-dualistic

Brahman. His whole mind should be absorbed in the secondless *Brahman*. The wise man who behaves this way attains salvation.

Prostration to *Srimat Param Jyotis*—The Great Blissful Light! May bliss and immortality be granted unto us! O Narasimha! O God of Gods! By thy grace do men know the real nature of *Brahman* who is of *Virinchi Narayana Sankara Swarupa*, who is beyond thought, unmanifest, infinite, free from pain, and who is the Divine Soul.

The wise always behold the glorious state of Vishnu as easily and freely as the naked eye beholds the vast expanse of heaven. The Brahmins (the knowers of the *Brahman*) whose eyes of wisdom are ever awake, praise the glorious state of Vishnu in diverse ways and make it widely known.

Thus commands the *Veda* regarding salvation. This is the *Upanishad*. *Om Tat Sat*.

SADHANAS OR PREPARATION

FIRST among the qualifications required of the aspirant for *Gnana* or wisdom come *Sama* and *Dama*, which may be taken together. They mean the keeping of the organs in their own centres without allowing them to stray out. I shall explain to you first what the word organ means. Here are the eyes : the eyes are not the organs of vision but only the instruments. Unless the organs also are present, I cannot see even if I have eyes. But given both the organs and the instruments—the organs being in what are called the nerve-centres in the brain—the moment the mind attaches itself to these two, vision takes place. So, in each act of perception, three things are necessary—first the external instruments, then the internal organs, and lastly the mind. If any one of them be absent, then there will be no perception. This mind then acts through two agencies— one external, and the other internal. When I see things, my mind goes out, becomes externalised ; but suppose I close my eyes and begin to think, the mind does not go out, it is internally active. But, in either case, there is activity of the organs ; when I look at you and speak to you, both the organs and the instruments are active. When I close my eyes and begin to think, the organs are active, but not the instruments. Without the activity of these organs, there will be no thought. You will find that none of you can think without some symbol. In the case of the blind man, he has also to think through some figure. When, for example, he thinks through figures of touch, as heat and cold, hardness and softness, these will act on the mind, and so his organs of touch will be active at the time he is thinking. The organs of sight and hearing are generally very active; you must bear in mind that by the word "organ" is meant the nerve-centre in the brain. The eyes and ears are only the *instruments* of seeing and hearing, and the organs are inside. If the organs are destroyed by any means, even if the eyes or the ears be there, we would not see or hear. So in order to control the mind, we must first be able to control these organs. To restrain the mind from wandering outward or inward, and *keep the organs close to their centres* is what is meant by the word *sama* and *dama*. *Sama* consists in not allowing the mind to externalise; and *dama* in checking its internal activity.

Then comes the next preparation, (it is a hard task to be a philosopher)! *Titiksha*, the most difficult of all; it is nothing less than the ideal forbearance—"resist not evil". It requires a little explanation. We may not resist an evil, but at the same time we may feel very miserable. A man may say very harsh things to me, and I may not outwardly hate him for it, may not strike him back, and may restrain myself from getting apparently angry, but anger and hatred may be in my mind, and I may feel very badly towards that man. That is not non-resistance. I should be without any feeling of hatred or anger, without any thought of resistance; my mind must be the same as if the man had blessed me : and only when I have got to that state, have I attained to non-resistance, and not before. Similarly with regard to the "*Dvandvas*", the duality of nature, heat and cold, pain and pleasure, one should bear them all; forbearance of all misery, without even a thought of resisting or driving it out, without even any painful feeling in the mind, or any remorse—this is *titiksha*. Suppose I do not resist something, and some great evil comes thereby, if I have *titiksha*, I would not feel any remorse for not having resisted. When the mind has attained to that state, it has become established in *titiksha*. People in India do extraordinary things in order to practise this *titiksha*. They bear tremendous heat and cold without caring; they do not even care for snow; they go on just as they are, because they take no thought of the body; it is left to itself, as if it were foreign.

The third preparation is *Uparati*, which consists in not thinking of things of the senses; most of our time is spent in thinking about sense-objects, things which we have seen, or we have heard, which we will see or will hear, things which we have eaten, or are eating, or will eat, places where we have lived, and so on. We think of them or talk of them most of our time. One who wishes to be a *Vedantin* must give up this habit.

The next qualification required is *Sraddha*, faith. One must have tremendous faith in religion and God; until he has that, he cannot aspire to be a *Jnani*. A great sage once told me that not one in twenty millions in this world believed in God. I asked him why, and he told me, "Suppose there is a thief in this room, and somehow he gets to know that there is a mass of gold in the next room, and only a very thin partition between the two rooms, what will be the condition of that thief?" I answered: "He will not be able to sleep at all; his brain will be actively thinking of some means of getting at the gold, and he will think of nothing else." Then he replied : "Do you believe that a man believes in God and does not go mad. If a man sincerely believes that there is that immense, infinite mine of bliss, that there is a Being reaching Whom ought to be the one end and aim of life, and that He can be reached, would not that man go mad in his struggles to reach him." Strong faith in God and the consequent eagerness to reach Him constitute *Sraddha*.

Then comes *Samadhana* or constant practice ; nothing is done in a day. Religion, like anything else, cannot be swallowed in the form of a pill ; it requires hard and constant practice ; the mind can be conquered only by slow and sure practice.

Next is *Mumukshutvam*, the intense desire to be free. Those of you who have read Edwin Arnold's *Light of Asia* remember his translation of the first sermon of Buddha, where Buddha says :

> Ye suffer from yourselves. None else compels,
> None other holds you that ye live and die.
> And whirl upon the wheel, and hug and kiss
> Its spokes of agony,
> Its tire of tears, its nave of nothingness.

All the misery we have is our own choosing ; such is our nature. The old Chinaman, who having been kept in prison for 60 years was released on the coronation of a new emperor, exclaimed when he came out that he could not live ; he must go back to his horrible dungeon among the rats and mice ; he could not bear the light. So he asked them to kill him or send him back to the prison, and he was sent back. Exactly similar is the condition of all men ; we run after all sorts of misery wantonly, so to speak, and are unwilling to be freed from it. Every day we run after pleasure, and before we reach it, we find it is gone, it has slipped through our fingers ; still we do not cease our mad pursuit, but on and on and on we go, blinded fools that we are.

In some oil mills in India, there is a bullock that goes round to grind the oil, and there is a yoke on the bullock's neck. The Indian people are very kind to animals ; they do not like to beat them. But the bullock would stop working if they did not beat it. So they have a device to take the place of beating. They have a piece of wood fixed on to the yoke, and on that is a wisp of straw. The bullock is blinded in such a way that it can only look forward, and so it stretches its neck forward to get at this straw ; and when it does so, it pushes the piece of wood out a little further ; and it makes another attempt with the same result, and yet another, and so on. It never catches the straw, but goes round and round in search of it and, in doing so, grinds out the oil. In the same way you and I who are born slaves to nature, and money and wealth, and wives and children, are always chasing a wisp of straw, mere chimeras ; and going through an innumerable round of lives without obtaining what we seek. The great dream is love ; we are all going to love and be loved ; we are all going to be happy and never meet with misery, but the more we go towards happiness the more it goes away from us. Thus the world is going on, society goes on, and we blinded slaves have to pay for it without knowing. Study your own lives, and find how little of happiness there is in them, and how little in truth you have gained in the course of this wild chase of goose of the world.

Do you remember the story of Solon and Croesus? The king said to the great sage that Asia Minor was a very happy place. And the sage asked him : "Who is the happiest man ; I have not seen any one very happy ?" "Nonsense," said Croesus, "I am the happiest man in the world." "Wait, sir, till the end of your life ; don't be in a hurry," replied the sage and went away. In course of time that king was conquered by the Persians, and they ordered him to be burnt alive ; the funeral pyre was prepared and when poor Croesus saw it, he cried aloud "Solon ! Solon !" On being asked to whom he referred, he told his story, and the Persian Emperor was kind enough to forgive him.

Such is the life story of each one of us ; such is the tremendous power of nature over us. It repeatedly kicks us away, but still we pursue it with feverish excitement. We are always hoping against hope ; this hope, this chimera maddens us ; we are always hoping for happiness.

There was a great king in ancient India who was once asked four questions, of which one was "What is the most wonderful thing in the world ?" "Hope" was the answer ; this is the most wonderful thing. Day and night we see people around us dropping down dead, and yet we think we shall not die ; we never think that we shall die, or that we shall suffer. Each one of us thinks that success will be his, hoping against hope, against all odds, against all mathematical reasoning. Nobody is ever really happy here. If a man be wealthy and have plenty to eat, his stomach is out of order, and he cannot eat. If a man's stomach be good, as hard as iron, and he have the digestive power of a cormorant, he has nothing to put into his stomach. If he be rich, he has no children. If he be hungry and poor, he has a whole regiment of children, and does not know what to do with them. Why is it so? Because happiness and misery the obverse and reverse of the same coin; he who takes happiness must take misery also. We all have this foolish idea that we can have happiness without misery and it has got such possession of us, that we have not control over the senses.

When I was in Boston, a young man came up to me and gave me a little piece of paper on which was written Mr. so-and-so, and Number so-and-so house, and it went to say "All the wealth and all the happiness of the world are yours, if you only know how to get it. If you come to me I will teach you how to get it. Charge $5." He gave me this and said : "What do you think of this?" I said "young man, why don't you get the money to print this; you have not even enough money to get this printed."

He did not understand this; he was infatuated with the idea, that he could get the wealth and happiness of the world in masses without its pains. These are the two extremes into which men are running; one is extreme optimism when everything is rosy and nice and good! the other, extreme pessimism, when everything seems, to be against them. The majority of men, have more or less undeveloped brains. One in a million, we see with a well developed brain; the rest either have peculiar idiosyncracies, or are monomaniacs, or maniacs or something else.

Naturally we are running into extremes. When we are healthy and young we think that all the wealth of the world will be ours, and when later we get kicked about by society like footballs, and get older, we sit in a corner and croak, and throw a bucketful of cold water on others. Few men know that with pleasure there is pain and with pain, pleasure; and as pain is disgusting so is pleasure as it is the twin brother of pain. It is derogatory to the glory of man that he should be going after pain and equally derogatory that he should be going after pleasure, so both should be turned aside by men whose reason is balanced, and who have not a screw loose; we should look down upon them as fit only for children. Why will not men seek liberty from being played upon? This moment we are whipped, and when we begin to weep, nature gives us a dollar; again we are whipped and when we weep, nature gives us a piece of gingerbread and we begin to laugh again.

The sage wants liberty; he finds that sense objects are all vain, that there is no end to pleasures and pains. How many rich people in the world want to find fresh pleasures, all pleasures are old, and they want new ones. Do you not see how many foolish things they are inventing every day, just to titillate the nerves for a moment, and that done, there will come a reaction. We are just like a stream of sheep. If the leading sheep fall into a ditch, all the rest follow and break their necks. In the same way what one does all the others do, without thinking about what they are doing. When a man begins to see the vanity of worldly things, he will feel he ought not to be played upon or borne along this way by nature and that it is slavery he is in. If a man has a few kind words said to him, he begins to smile, and stretch his mouth from ear to ear, and when he hears a few harsh words he begins to weep. He will see that he is a slave to a bit of bread, to a breath of air, a slave to dress, a slave to patriotism, to country, to name and to fame. He is thus in the midst of slavery and the real man has become buried within through this bondage. This slave is what you call man. When one realises all this slavery, then comes the desire to be free, an intense desire comes. If a piece of burning charcoal be placed on a man's head, see how he struggles to throw it down; similar will be the wise man's struggles to become free.

We have now seen what *Mumuksutwam*, or the desire to be free, is. The next discipline is also a very difficult one. *Nityanityaviveka*—discriminating between that which is true and that which is untrue, between the eternal and the transitory. God alone is eternal, everything else is transitory. Everyone dies; the angels die, men die, animals die, earths die, sun, moon and stars, all die! everything undergoes constant change. The mountains of to-day were the oceans of yesterday and will be oceans to-morrow. Everything is in a state of flux! sun, moon, stars, the human body are all constantly changing; the whole universe is a mass of change. But there is one who never changes, and that is God; and the nearer we get to Him, the less will be the change for us; the less will nature be able to work on us; and when we reach Him, and stand with Him, we will conquer nature, we will be masters of these phenomena of nature, and they will have no effect on us. Then will the bullock's blind fall and he will know his own way.

You see, if we really have the above disciplines, we really do not require anything else in this world ; all knowledge is within us, all perfection is there already in the soul. But this perfection has been covered up by nature ; layer after layer of nature is covering this purity of the soul. What have we to do ? Really we do not develop our souls at all ; what can develop the eternal ? We simply take the evil off ; so by these disciplines, the veil will come away, and the soul will manifest itself in its pristine purity, its natural, innate freedom.

Now begins the inquiry, why is this discipline so necessary ? Because religion is not to be understood through the ears, or through the eyes, nor yet through the brain. No scriptures can make us religious, we may study all the books that are in the world, yet we shall not understand a word of religion or of God. We may talk all our lives and yet shall not be better for it ; we may be the most intellectual people the world ever saw, and yet we shall not come to God at all. On the other hand have you not seen what diabolical men have been produced out of the most intellectual training ? It is one of the evils of your western civilisation that you are after intellectual education alone, and there is no safeguard with it. Here is one mistake made ; you give the education, but you take no care of the heart. It only makes men ten times more selfish, and that will be your destruction. It is intellect every time. When there is conflict between the heart and the brain, let the heart be followed, because intellect has only one state, reason and within that intellect works, and cannot get

beyond it. Intellect is most wonderful and strong.
The heart is a lower plane; it generally makes mistakes
but it is soft and gentle. It is the heart alone which
takes one to the highest plane, which intellect can never
reach; it goes beyond intellect, reaches to what is called
inspiration. Intellect can never become inspired, only
the heart when it is enlightened. Never do you see a
dried up old intellectual man become an inspired man.
It is every time the heart that speaks in the man of love,
the soft man, it discovers a greater instrument than
intellect can give you, the instrument of inspiration.
Just as the intellect is the instrument of knowledge, so
is the heart the instrument of *inspiration*. In a lower
state it is a much weaker instrument than intellect.
An ignorant man knows nothing, but he is a little emotional by nature; compare with him a great professor,
what wonderful power the latter possesses! But the
professor is bound by his intellect and he can be a devil
and an intellectual man at the same time; but the man
of the heart can never be a devil; no man with emotion
was ever a devil. Properly cultivated the heart can
be changed and will go beyond intellect; it will be
changed into inspiration and man will have to go
beyond intellect in the end. Men of heart have attained to "butter" and the "butter milk" is left for
these intellectual fools. The knowledge of man, his
powers of perception, of reasoning and intellect and
heart, all are busy churning this milk of the world; out
of long churning comes butter and this butter is God.
The man of the heart gets that, and the fools who are
churning all their lives with only intellect, never reach
true understanding.

These are all preparations for the heart, for that love, for that intense sympathy appertaining to the heart. It is not at all necessary to be educated or learned to get to God. A sage once told me, "To commit suicide a pen-knife is sufficient, but to kill others swords and guns and bucklers are necessary, so, if you want to teach others, knowledge is necessary, but for your own salvation, not at all." Are you pure? If you are pure you will reach God. "Bl ssed are the pure in heart, for they shall see God." If you are not pure, and you know all the sciences, in the universe, that will not help you at all; you may be buried in all the books you read, but that will not help you. It is the heart that reaches the goal, follow the heart. A pure heart sees beyond the intellect; it gets inspired; it knows things that reason can never know, and whenever there is conflict between the pure heart and the intellect always side with the pure heart, even if you think what your heart is doing is unreasonable. Reasoning will come later on. Even though it may be every instant desiring to do good to the poor, and your brain may tell you that it is not politic to help these poor men, yet follow your heart, and you will find that you make less error than by following your intellect. The pure heart is the best mirror for the reflection of truth, so all these disciplines are purifying the heart, and as soon as it is pure all truths flash upon it in a minute; all truths in the universe will be there in your heart if you are sufficiently pure.

These great truths about the atoms, and the finer elements, and the fine perceptions of men, have been discovered ages ago by men who never saw a telescope, or a microscope, or a laboratory. How did they know all these things? It was through the heart; they purified the heart. It is open to us to do the same to-day; it is the culture of the heart, really, that will lessen the misery of the world and not that of the intellect.

Intellect has been cultured: result—hundreds of sciences have been discovered, and their effect has been that the few have made slaves of the many—that is all the good that has been done. Artificial wants have been created; and every poor man, whether he has money or not, desires to have those wants satisfied, and when he cannot, he struggles and dies in the struggle. This is the result. Through the intellect is not the way to solve the problem of misery, but through the heart. If all this vast amount of effort had been spent in making men purer, gentler, more forbearing, this world would have a thousandfold more happiness than it has to-day. Always cultivate the heart; through the heart the Lord speaks, and through intellect you yourself speak.

You remember in the Old Testament where Moses was told "Take off thy shoes from off thy feet, for the place whereon thou treadest is holy ground." We must always approach the study of religion with that reverent attitude; he who comes with a pure heart and a reverent attitude, his heart will be opened; the doors will open for him and he will see the truth.

If you come with a crude sort of intellect you can have a little intellectual gymnastics, and when I have time enough I will be very glad to give a little exercise in that line. You can have intellectual theories but not truth. Truth has such a face that any one who sees that face becomes convinced. The sun does not

require any torch to show it ; the sun is self-effulgent.
If truth requires that evidence, who will evidence that
evidence ? If something also is witness for truth, where
is the witness for that witness ? We must approach with
reverence and with love, and our heart will stand up
and say this is truth, and this is untruth.

The field of religion is beyond our senses, beyond
even our consciousness. We cannot *"sense"* God.
Nobody has seen God with his eyes or ever will see ;
nobody has God in his consciousness. I am not conscious of God, nor you nor anybody. Where is God ?
Where is the field of religion ? It is beyond the senses,
beyond consciousness. Consciousness is only one of the
many planes in which we work, and you will have to
transcend the field of consciousness to go beyond the
senses, approach nearer and nearer to your own centre
and as you do that, you will approach nearer and nearer
to God. What is the proof of God ? Direct perception,
pratyaksham, just as there is proof of this wall. I perceive it. God has been perceived that way by thousands
before, and will be perceived by all who want to perceive
Him. But this perception is no sense perception at all ;
it is supersensuous, super-conscious, and all this training
is needed to take us off from the senses. This body as
it were, by means of all sorts of past works and bondages
is being dragged downwards ; these preparations and
purity will make it pure and light. Bondages will fall
off by themselves, and we will be buoyed up beyond
this plane of sense perception to which we are tied down,
and then we will see, and hear, and feel things which
men in three ordinary states neither feel, nor see, nor
hear. Then we will speak the language, as it were, of

madmen, and the world will not understand us, because they do not know anything but the senses. This religion is entirely transcendental. Every being that is in the universe has the potentiality of transcending the senses, even the little worm will one day transcend the senses, and reach unto God. No life will be a failure; there is no such thing as failure in the universe. A hundred times man will hurt his foot, a thousand times he will tumble, but in the end he will realise that he is God. We know there is no progress in a straight line; you throw a stone into the air, and if you could stand long enough, it will come back exactly to your hand. Every soul is in a circle, and will have to complete it, and no soul can go so low but that there will come a time when it will have to go upwards. It may start straight down, but it must also have to take the upward curve, in order to complete the circuit. No one will be lost. We are all projected from one common circle which is God. We are like little bits of stone projected from a common centre; some go a little lower or higher, but each one will have to complete the circuit, and come back to the centre from which it started. The highest intelligence, and the lowest intelligence God ever projected, will come back to the Father of all lives, "From whom all beings are projected, in whom all live, and unto whom they all return; that is God."

MANANAMALA

OR

THE MEDITATIONS OF A MAUNI

[Here we publish "Meditations of a Mauni", to which we request the special attention of *Mumukshus*, though they have lost in translation three-fourths of the charm with which they were originally uttered by the great sage. *Mauni* does not mean one who is dumb, but a *Brahmagnani*, a *Muni*. As for the meaning of *Mauna* please see verses 107 and 108 of Sankara's *Aparokshanubhuti*.]

1. All things are in God and the Lord taught Arjuna to behold them not by themselves, but as in Him. This is the meaning of the glorious *Visvarupa* (Universal Form) scene.

2. He is the greatest teacher in whose mind the distinction between the teacher and the taught has no place. For in the plane of absolute truth the teacher and the taught are both one and the same.

3. Though milk is a good thing and the milk-vendor cries "milk, milk" in the streets, it is only those that want it that buy ; in the same way, though the excellent *Vedanta* be preached from house-tops and temple towers it is only those who thirst for the truth contained in it that seek its help.

4. Birds and reptiles approach not a burning volcano ; in the same way pleasure and pain do not affect a sage who is radiant with the fire of wisdom.

5. What an amount of wisdom there is even in common proverbs ! For instance "Winnow while the wind blows" means to the philosopher "strip off (in

mind) the sheaths (*Kosa*) which hide the Self—as husk does the rice-grain—while thy breath endures ; in other words realise the Self before you die."

6. The conception of sin varies with various stages and in the highest, to be deluded by name and form and forget the God within, is itself a sin.

7. The *Atman* is a vast ocean and hands, feet, etc., are icebergs floating on it ; when the sun of wisdom comes they too get dissolved in the ocean of Self and lose their names and forms.

8. The best offering a disciple can give to his *Guru* (spiritual teacher) is a mind purified by the four *Sadhanas* (preparation)—discrimination between Self and Not-Self, etc.

9. The greatest benefit which a *Guru* does to his disciple is to show that Truth alone is true. So did Sri Krishna say to Arjuna : "There is no existence of the unreal, of the real there is no cessation of existence. The truth regarding these two is seen by the seers of the Real."

10. Clean a diamond and the brightness comes of itself ; in the same way one has only to purify the mind ; then the *Atman* will shine there of His own accord. For He is already there ; only He has been forgotten through ignorance.

11. A blind man trembles with fear even when he treads on straw on his way ; so do the ignorant become filled with fear at every petty occurrence. (Ignorance here means *avidya*, *i.e.*, ignorance about the real nature of the Self, which is the worst sort of blindness). The wise man—*Jnani*—on the other hand cares not what comes or what goes, for he knows that in this God-world

what is ordained to happen will never fail to happen and what is not so ordained will never come however much we may desire it, that *Prarabdha* (past *Karma*) is only for the *Sthula*, the body, and that he is really only the witness of all that comes and goes.

12. There are two kinds of relationship—*Marjala* and *Markata*. The former is that which subsists between a cat and its kitten which is, without any endeavour on its part, taken care of by the mother and carried by it in its mouth wherever it goes. The latter kind of relationship is that which exists between a monkey and its young. In this case, it is the young one that has to be careful in not losing hold of its mother's body which it tightly entwines by its arms. The relation between a priest and a member of his flock is the *Marjala* one, while that between the disciple and his *Guru* is the *Markata* one, for the disciple has to take care that he does not lack in faith and zeal and he should steadily and firmly cling to the Teacher and then just as the infant monkey is not hurt or frightened when its mother to which it firmly clings leaps over rivers and jumps from one tall tree to another, so the disciple will not get confounded, or despondent when the Teacher carries him to the dizzy heights of truth and jumps from one grand position to another.

13. One has to bind oneself firmly to the holy lotus feet of his *Guru* and Sri Sankara did a very wise thing when, as he says, he married to the holy Lord the maiden which was his mind.

14. The scriptures are the boat which those great souls who crossed to the other shore by means of it have

sent back out of love and grace repaired and strengthened
for those who may desire to follow.

15. This child (pointing to one in the house) is my
Guru, for when I offered him a bit of sweetmeat he refused it saying : "I do not want it, for I do not know
what it is like, you first put it in your mouth and show
that it is good." What the child wanted me to do is
exactly what a *Guru* does, for he does not merely offer
Brahmajnana—Self-realisation—to the disciple who may
not .by the mere offering take it, but himself enjoys it
and shows through his own example that it is good,
and then the student longs for it. Because the child
reminded me of this great truth, he is one of my
teachers.

16. What is meant by saying that *Brahman* is
beyond the reach of words and thought ? The answer
is that just as the sweetness of sugar is not expressible
in words nor conceivable by the mind and has to be
understood only by actually tasting it, so can *Brahman*
be known only by realisation and no amount of talking
or imagining can tell us what He is like. This is a very
simple instance, but is worthy of being meditated upon.

17. What is the mind ? It is not a substance in
itself but only that *standpoint* viewed from which
Brahman appears diversified in the shape of the world.

18. There are two kinds of giving : One is pure and
the other impure. The first is to give without any
concern about the result and without taking any credit
for it and immediately forgetting it—this is giving in
the name of God as Thayumanavar gave away the shawl
presented to him by the king, to a poor *Pariah* woman.
When asked by the king who felt insulted by this, where

the valuable present he made was, he replied he gave it to *Akhilandeswari*—the Mother of the universe.

19. *Satsanga* means not merely good company, for men however good may not wholly agree with one another; and then they are liable to separation by various accidents, disease, etc. The real *Satsanga* is companionship with the only *Sat*, Existence Absolute, the *Atman*; this is a changeless companionship when once rightly formed; it is above all accidents and is inseparable. The best of friends is the *Atman*.

20. The attempt to kill the mind is like digging a pit and trying to bury one's shadow in it. However deep one may dig and however carefully he may close the pit, the shadow will always be above it. So whatever means one may take for killing the mind it cannot be killed, for with what is it to be killed? The only way in which it could be subdued is by bribing it into subjection through gentle means, by lulling it into sleep with the help of such internal objects as it could rest on with ease and thus making it realise its true nature which is unchangeable *Pragna* the Self.

21. The world is the shadow of the soul.

22. A fruit can ripen only in the natural course and no amount of beating it with a stick will make it ripe. But its ripening will be accelerated by placing it in the midst of fruits already ripe. In the same way every man has to learn and realise the truth of his own accord and cannot do so merely through others' efforts, however sincerely they may work for him. But the company of wise men who have already attained to truth hastens his progress.